DOUGLAS HAIG

*

The Educated Soldier

JOHN TERRAINE
DOUGLAS HAIG

*

The Educated Soldier

CASSELL & CO.

Cassell & Co
Wellington House, 125 Strand
London WC2R 0BB

First published in Great Britain by Hutchinson 1963
This edition published 2000

A CIP catalogue record for this book is available from the British Library

ISBN 0-304-35319-1

Printed and bound in Great Britain by
MPG Books, Bodmin, Cornwall

*This book is dedicated
to those who helped.*

Contents

Illustrations

The King with his Army commanders

Sir John French, Lord Kitchener, Sir William Robertson, Sir Henry Wilson

John and Sir Hubert Gough, Brigadier-General Charteris, Sir Herbert Lawrence, Sir Lancelot Kiggell

Sir John Monash with Mr. Hughes, King Albert with Sir Hubert Gough, Sir Edmund Allenby with Spanish generals

Lord Haldane, Mr. Asquith, Lloyd George with Thomas, Haig and Joffre

Major Winston Churchill with General Fayolle, Lord Curzon with Lord Milner, Lord Derby

Joffre, Haig and Foch, General Nivelle, Pétain and Allied commanders

Lord Balfour with Haig, Briand with Joffre, Clemenceau with Haig

Prince Rupprecht, the Kaiser, von Below, von Falkenhayn, Ludendorff

General Pershing and General Currie

Somme mud, German prisoners

Haig's diary, July 20th, 1915

Maps

Acknowledgements

To LIST all the sources on which this book is based would be to catalogue a quarter of a century's reading. Some of them, however, imperatively call for tribute.

Through the great kindness of Earl Haig, I have been privileged to have access to his father's wartime Diary and associated papers. It is difficult to express the full value of these documents. Mr. Robert Blake, who published an edited version of them in 1952, representing, he told us, 'about one-fifth of the total', has also said that 'the diary alone consists of at least three-quarters of a million words'. The typescript is contained in thirty-eight solid foolscap volumes; associated with it is a mass of papers, ranging from scribbled Intelligence appreciations, Minutes of Army Commanders' Meetings and General Staff Instructions, to comprehensive letters from the Commander-in-Chief of the French Army or the Generalissimo, from formal congratulations to searching analyses of the War situation by, say, Sir Winston Churchill. The scope of this collection is remarkable; an indication of its compiler's methodical thoroughness. It has formed the basis of Cabinet Papers, when other records failed; it has prompted the Official Historian. There is hardly any aspect of the War that is not touched by it. Lord Haig has permitted me to use it without any restriction whatever, and I am greatly indebted to him.

It is right to link with this great original two published works: Duff Cooper's *Haig* (Faber & Faber, 1935), to which I refer in the Preface, and Robert Blake's *The Private Papers of Douglas Haig 1914–1918* (Eyre & Spottiswoode, 1952), mentioned above. Duff Cooper's book contains a great deal of direct quotation from the Diary; Robert Blake's, of course, is all quotation, apart from an Introduction which includes the best very brief account of the First World War that I know. Both of these books have been enormously helpful to me.

Also in the category of 'Haig material', and also of great help, are the biography *Field-Marshal Earl Haig* by Brigadier-General John Charteris, C.M.G., D.S.O., and Charteris's own diary notes and letters published under the title *At G.H.Q.* Since General Charteris served on Haig's intimate Staff from before the War until almost the end of it, the value of these two statements will not need to be stressed.

Sir Douglas Haig's Despatches, edited by Lieut.-Colonel J. H. Boraston, O.B.E. (Dent, 1919), give Haig's own account of his tenure of Command-in-Chief.

Other publications and private conversations or letters have supplied more information on the subject, but these are the main sources which concern Haig himself.

No one can study or write about that War without reference to the compendious Official Histories, compiled under the direction of Brigadier-General Sir James Edmonds. With their maps and Appendices, they constitute a mountain of knowledge without access to which it is hard to know how one could proceed.

It is my pleasant duty to thank individuals and publishers who have given me permission to quote copyright material in this book. Some of the sources I have already mentioned; there are others, the memoirs and reflections of great protagonists, which have been rich mines of information.

Two letters, one written by H.M. King George V and the other written on his behalf, are quoted by gracious permission of Her Majesty The Queen. (The second of these was previously published in *King George V* by Harold Nicolson.)

Thanks are due to Cassell & Co. Ltd., publishers of *Field-Marshal Earl Haig* (1929) and *At G.H.Q.* (1931) by Brigadier-General John Charteris, *Field-Marshal Sir Henry Wilson, Bart., G.C.B., D.S.O., His Life and Diaries* (1927) by Major-General Sir C. E. Callwell, K.C.B., and *Soldiers and Statesmen 1914–1918* (1926) by Field-Marshal Sir William Robertson, Bart., G.C.B., G.C.M.G., K.C.V.O., D.S.O.; to the Controller of H.M. Stationery Office, publishers of the official *History of the First World War 1914–1918*; to Lord Beaverbrook for the *War Memoirs of David Lloyd George*, published by Odhams Press Ltd. (1938); to Odhams Press Ltd., publishers of *The World Crisis* 1911–1918 (1938) and *Great Contemporaries* (1938) by Winston S. Churchill, and to Eyre & Spottiswoode (Publishers) Ltd., publishers of the other book of Sir Winston's referred to, *The River War* (1933); to George Allen & Unwin Ltd., publishers of the invaluable *The Supreme Command 1914–1918* (1961) by Lord Hankey; to T. Rowland Slingluff for *The Memoirs of Marshal Foch* translated by Lieut.-Colonel T. Bentley Mott, published by William Heinemann Ltd. (1931); to Hutchinson & Co. (Publishers) Ltd., publishers of *General Headquarters and its Critical Decisions* (1919) by General Erich von Falkenhayn and *My War Memories* (1919) by General Ludendorff; to Hodder & Stoughton Ltd., publishers of *Haldane: An Autobiography* (1929); to Angus & Robertson Ltd., publishers of *The Australian Victories in France* 1918 (1936) by General Sir John Monash; to Jonathan Cape Ltd., publishers of *Prelude to Victory* (1939) by Major-General Sir Edward Spears, who possessed an extraordinary knack of being present at great occasions; to Constable & Co. Ltd., publishers of *The First World War 1914–1918* (1920) by Colonel Repington, an onlooker who saw a very great deal of the game; and to Major-General J. F. C. Fuller, C.B., C.B.E., D.S.O., and the editors of the *Spectator* and the *R.U.S.I. Journal* for extracts from two of General Fuller's letters which appeared in those periodicals.

Three more works which have been valuable to me are *The Memoirs of Marshal Joffre* (Bles, 1932), *Eyewitness* by Major-General Sir Ernest D. Swinton, K.B.E., C.B., D.S.O., 'Ole Luk-Oie', (Hodder & Stoughton, 1932), and another book by Sir Edward Spears, *Liaison 1914* (Heinemann, 1930).

I am grateful to Mr. D. W. King, O.B.E., F.L.A., War Office Librarian, for pointing out to me a series of articles by Lieut.-General Sir Gerald Ellison, K.C.B., K.C.M.G., which appeared in *The Lancashire Lad*, the journal of the Loyal Regiment (North Lancashire) between October 1931 and August 1939, under the title 'Reminiscences'.

Mr. John Connell and Mr. John Danvers both read this book in manuscript, and made a number of valuable suggestions, for which I owe them thanks.

I must also acknowledge a debt to the British Broadcasting Corporation, which granted me permission to undertake this work while serving as a full-time member of its staff.

JOHN TERRAINE
August 1962

'Haig undoubtedly lacked those highest qualities which were essential in a great Commander in the greatest war the world has ever seen. . . . It was far beyond his mental equipment.'

David Lloyd George

*

' "Brilliant to the top of his army boots," father said.'

Richard Lloyd George

*

'There are, upon the side of the Allies, only two Fighters: you and Lloyd George. I apologize for the bracket, but it is a hard basic fact.'

Lord Esher to Haig

*

'He might be, he surely was, unequal to the prodigious scale of events; but no one else was discerned as his equal or his better.'

Winston Churchill

*

'Douglas Haig was not born into the world with a silver spoon in his mouth; but possibly with a silver pencil in his hand ready to start his calculations.'

General Sir Ian Hamilton

*

'Haig had a first-rate General Staff mind.'

Lord Haldane

Modern professional soldiers, of high rank and experience, use the adjective 'educated' with a definite but subtle meaning of its own: it means an officer who takes his work seriously, who studies it from all aspects, who (above all) has the mind, as well as the aspiration, to think an issue through for himself, from first to last; the reading, the battlefield experience, the staff courses and other qualifications are taken for granted. 'Educated' means a man who has learned and will put into practice *all* those lessons and many more.

Preface

THIS BOOK is not meant to be a biography of Field-Marshal Earl Haig; it is an attempt at a study of him as a soldier, and in particular, as a Commander-in-Chief. It is my belief that such a study can only have meaning through careful attention to the context in which the subject's career was made. Much published criticism of Haig seems to me to lack value because of insufficient understanding or neglect of this context, and of the sheer pressure of successive events.

Those who wish for more biographical material should turn to the three existing 'Lives', by Duff Cooper (Lord Norwich), Brigadier-General John Charteris, and Sir George Arthur. All three have their special merits. I must here admit to the increasing respect with which, throughout my work on this book, I turned to Duff Cooper's great double volume, written amid all the cares of an Office of State. It is a fine achievement, from which proper recognition has been withheld.

But a word of warning: neither Haig's career nor his personality lent themselves to gossip-mongering or petty anecdote. His private life was private indeed; all that need concern us is that it contained no disturbances likely to affect his handling of public affairs. In this respect he affords a remarkable instance of concentration and single-minded devotion. In some ways this makes his story easier to tell; but, as the discerning may perceive, in others, not.

Introduction

THE LAST GUN fell silent; the clatter of small arms died away; the Great War was over; the Army's task was done. At the moment when Germany's acceptance of defeat became effective on the Western Front, at 11 a.m. on November 11th, 1918, the strength of the British Army on that front stood at just under 2,000,000 officers and men. This was the largest array of British soldiers ever to be deployed in one theatre of operations in any war, before or since. The whole force was divided into five armies; it comprised 61 divisions of infantry and 3 of cavalry; it included 5 Australian divisions, 4 Canadian and 1 from New Zealand, while among the smaller formations was represented every part of what was still then known as the British Empire. Together these troops had endured the severest trials in the annals of the British Army, sustained its highest casualties in any war, suffered one of its worst defeats, and won one of its most decisive victories in the field. At the head of them all, in their hour of triumph, stood Field-Marshal Sir Douglas Haig.

It is not a conspicuous habit among British commanders, in the moment of danger or success, to strike flamboyant poses or make memorable statements for posterity. Haig was the last man to do either. His own personal record of the last day of the War in which he had served from beginning to end, and had been Commander-in-Chief of the British Armies on the Western Front for thirty-five consecutive months, was flat, factual and practical. The nearest that he permitted himself to come to self-revelation was when he contemplated the collapse of the German Empire, which he had himself done so much to bring about: riots and revolution in Germany herself, the German Army reduced to semi-mutiny, the Kaiser in flight. It put him in mind of a remark of John Bunyan's, on seeing a man going to be hanged: 'But for the grace of God, John Bunyan would have been in that man's place!' Without rancour against the defeated enemy, with pride in what he and his soldiers had done together, but without presumption, with relief but without sentimentality, he recorded the conclusion of his toil.

There is no place in modern war for the Te Deum on the field of victory.

Nor would Haig have wished it; he never sought for personal glorification. He did not have the height and commanding presence of Lord Kitchener; he did not radiate dynamic energy from relatively few inches like Lord Roberts or Viscount Montgomery; he did not even have one marked ugly attribute on which to focus attention, like Wellington's nose. Slightly bowed, by November, 1918, by the great burden which he had borne, the impression which he imparted was yet mainly one of solidity and strength. This was not so much a matter of his prominent, jutting jaw; few more persevering generals have ever existed than Wolfe, who had no chin at all. It was to do with squareness of stance, and firmness of carriage. Closer inspection, as Orpen's portrait particularly reveals, showed behind his regular and handsome features the thoughtful and considerate nature of the man. Above all, thoughtful; Douglas Haig was, during his period of high command, the Army's most 'educated soldier'.

PART I

'... after surveying the whole Army, I took it upon myself to ask Lord Haig, who was then in India, to come over to this country and to think for us. From all I could discover even then, he seemed to be the most highly equipped thinker in the British Army.'

Lord Haldane

1

Military Education

T HE HAIGS have always been a military line. One look at Bemer-
syde is sufficient to tell their story; for the house on the hill-top by
the Tweed, guarded to this day by a captured German 5·9, despite all
its unassuming charm, is no more than an excrescence tacked on piecemeal
to one of the square Border keeps which, as late as the sixteenth century,
were regarded as essential to the national security of Scotland. The Haigs
came over among the first waves of Norman invasion, and as early as the
first part of the twelfth century had established themselves amid the baronage
of North Britain; it is not known when they transferred their allegiance from
the English to the Scottish Crown, but certainly they were present on the
Scottish side at Stirling Bridge, Halidon Hill, Otterburn and Flodden.
Strictly speaking, it made little difference, for until the middle of the
eighteenth century Border life followed much the same pattern, whichever
side one lived on; it was a life of sudden alarms, scares in the night, violence
and danger. One learned to be wary, cautious and distrustful; one learned to
take thought; not to be rash.

The family, of course, divided. Douglas Haig did not spring from the
landed Marcher side, although its characteristics were a part of him, and in
the end he returned as owner to the ancestral home, to fulfil the prophecy of
the thirteenth-century Border poet, Thomas of Ercildoune – Thomas the
Rhymer:

> 'Tide what may, whate'er betide,
> Haig shall be Haig of Bemersyde.'

That branch of the family which was to give Scotland one of her greatest
sons was also the branch which had contributed, and still does, to one of her
greatest pleasures. Douglas Haig's father was a distinguished whisky distiller,
a calling which requires no apology, and no elaboration of its advantages.
Scotland's emblem may be the thistle; her international renown stems from

3

other plants. As was customary in the nineteenth century, John Haig begot
a large family, eleven, of whom nine survived; Douglas, born on the
nineteenth of June, 1861, was the youngest son. He was born in Edinburgh,
at No. 24 Charlotte Square, only a few doors away from the house where,
five years earlier, another great Scotsman, with whom he was to be much
associated, had come into the world – Richard Burdon Haldane.

The young Nelson was seen to tackle a Polar bear, thus indicating the
stuff that was in him; the young Napoleon is said to have marshalled his
fellow pupils at Brienne in a snow-fight; the young Wellington was regarded
as the blockhead of the family; the young Churchill was the dunce of Harrow;
such are the varied auspices under which great war leaders have made their
early mark. The young Haig played with a drum, which bore the inscription:
'Douglas Haig – *sometimes* a good boy.' In childhood, his mother's upright,
religious influence was very strong, as was his father's industrious example.
He went to a day school in Edinburgh, where he absorbed the rudiments of
that Scottish education which, once experienced, is never forgotten; he spent
four years at Clifton College, where he proposed the motion, at the School
Debating Society, that 'The Army had done the country more service than
the Navy'. What he made of that somewhat thankless brief is not recorded.
On leaving school, he visited America, in company with one of his elder
brothers. On his return, he went up to Brasenose College, Oxford, and was
greeted by the Principal with the injunction: 'Ride, sir, ride – I like to see the
gentlemen of Brasenose in top boots.' Haig rode.

It is all too easy to pick upon particular incidents in the youth of men
who subsequently become famous or notorious, and to treat these as
symptomatic. The truth is that it is almost impossible to see any distinct
pattern in the life of Douglas Haig until he entered the Army; after that, the
pattern is absolutely clear. At Oxford, he played a part in the life of the
fashionable clubs; he took up riding, and became the admirable horseman
that he remained throughout his life; he also tasted the pleasures of polo. It
has been recorded that he worked hard; but in the end, through sickness, he
did not take his Schools, and this fact seems not to have disturbed him in the
least. One of his contemporaries has recorded that on the evening of his
arrival at Brasenose, Haig announced that he intended to go into the Army.
One of his biographers has said: '. . . in his veins there ran the blood of the
Covenanters, and in his heart there remained the teachings of the Presbyterian religion which he had learnt at his mother's knee. And Oxford, which
gave him a sense of his own importance, filled him also with the determination to do himself justice, and to succeed in the career that he had decided to
adopt.'[1] On the other hand, another biographer, who came to know him

1. Duff Cooper: *Haig*.

very well indeed, has said: 'He spent three years at Oxford, but the atmosphere was not congenial. Life still held no object for him. He did not shirk his studies, but they failed to interest him.'[1] Whichever of these views is the more correct, one thing is not in dispute: from the moment when, in February, 1884, he entered the Royal Military College, his interest was fully occupied, and from that time onwards he became a dedicated man.

The intake at Sandhurst from the universities was not large in those days; cadets who entered the College in that manner would find themselves somewhat apart from their fellows, on grounds both of age and of general knowledge. Probably for this reason, Haig at the age of nearly twenty-three, a fish out of water among his much younger fellows, made eminence a goal. He certainly achieved it, but in doing so undoubtedly learned to appreciate – and accept – its cost. There was, first of all, an unalterable minimum of sheer work to be done, and to this he applied himself with all the doggedness and perseverance that were later so remarked in him in other contexts. The habit of planning out his day in a set pattern was now formed. Leisure became an early casualty; even his off-duty hours were allocated to pursuits that fitted the plan. Partly because of this, and partly because it was an irrelevance, popularity was also at a discount. He became an Under-Officer, and exacted strict discipline from the cadets under him. If they did not much care for this, it is not to be wondered at; if they regarded his aloofness as arrogance, his taciturnity as something other than shyness, that is not surprising either. They could not fail to admire his evident merit, but it was, on the whole, admiration without warmth, and it had an unfortunate effect. For all through his life Haig was to be cursed with a painful inability to communicate. There can be no doubt that, under other circumstances, Sandhurst might have done much to prevent this, but it was not to be. There were, however, other compensations; in less than a year Haig passed out first in order of merit, winning the Anson Memorial Sword as Senior Under-Officer, and with athletic distinction. One of the instructors, asked who was the most promising cadet, replied: 'A Scottish lad, Douglas Haig, is top in almost everything – books, drill, riding and sports; he is to go into the cavalry, and, before he is finished, he will be top of the Army.'

*　　*　　*　　*

Haig joined the 7th (Queen's Own) Hussars in February, 1885. The Army which he was entering was passing through one of its bad periods. There have been three outstandingly poor spells in the British Army's history, up to the present: the last part of the eighteenth century, including the War of American Independence and the early campaigns against Revolutionary

1. Charteris: *Field Marshal Earl Haig.*

France; the period between Waterloo and the Crimea; and the final decades
of the nineteenth century, culminating in the South African War. During
this last period, despite the great progress made through the Cardwell
Reforms, the Army suffered from many grave defects. At the root of them
all lay a circumstance which, so far from having been altered by Cardwell,
lay at the root of his system: it was not, in the Continental sense, an army at
all; it was a reservoir of Imperial garrisons. All the faults of organization and
training stemmed from this. It meant that there was no Expeditionary Force;
there was no General Staff; there was no central body of doctrine to bind the
parts together; there was little organizational unity. On the other hand, for
regimental officers and soldiers alike, there was unlimited boredom and
stultifying routine. Presiding over the whole, in the office of Commander-
in-Chief which he held for thirty-nine years, from 1856 to 1895, was Queen
Victoria's cousin, the Duke of Cambridge. Although he was popular with
the Army, the Duke's influence was almost wholly negative, and against its
best interests. He was the very epitome of military conservatism, and almost
broke the hearts of many fine officers who were perfectly ready to tackle the
vast labour of modernization which was palpably overdue. Field-Marshal Sir
William Robertson, who in 1885 was a Warrant Officer in the 16th Lancers,
has given us a picture of the Duke of Cambridge presiding in the chair at an
Aldershot lecture on foreign cavalry; the Duke introduced the lecturer with
the following remarks: 'Why should we want to know anything about
foreign cavalry? We have better cavalry of our own. I fear, gentlemen, that
the Army is in danger of becoming a mere debating society.'

Yet working against the Duke's influence, at first largely by stealth, but
as the years went by more openly, there were a number of men who deserve
to be better remembered than they are. Chief among them were Lord
Wolseley and Sir Evelyn Wood; upon these two fell the burden of the fray
in Whitehall. In India, Lord Roberts was keeping the Army's nose to the
grindstone of practical experience, teaching the field virtues, and raising a
school of thoughtful and intelligent fighters, of whom the most outstanding
was Sir Ian Hamilton. It was a sad misfortune, far from the wishes of either
of the great leaders concerned, that the Army should fall into faction, the
Wolseley School against the Roberts School. Such divisions are almost invariably the work of juniors, the smaller fry. Nevertheless, they can be
dreadfully damaging; matters came to a pass where no 'Wolseley' officer
could expect advancement in India, in the ordinary course of events, and no
'Roberts' man could expect to do much in England, or, worse still, in Egypt,
where it was known that big things were brewing. These were difficult considerations for young officers at the beginning of their careers. If their
regiments were in India, as Haig's shortly was, it became very much a

question whether to seek promotion in that sub-continent, where small wars
were always afoot with their opportunities of distinction, and risk becoming
identified with a faction, or to trust to luck and the end of the tour of duty to
get one out of the dilemma.

Characteristically, Haig appears to have kept clear of the trap of partisan-
ship. His very entry into the Cavalry arm was evidence of a detachment that
was always one of his notable attributes. It was not a very Scottish thing to
do. Sir Colin Campbell, Sir Hector Macdonald and Sir Ian Hamilton are
examples of distinguished Scottish soldiers whose reputations are linked with
Scotland's own regiments. Haig did not even select the Scots Greys; his
choice of the 7th Hussars is part and parcel of his indifference to purely local
loyalties and causes. Not even the Cavalry itself could be said to have commanded his full allegiance; it was the arm which he had joined, and he made
himself proficient in it. But to call him a 'Cavalry General', placing him in a
category of which such disparate examples exist as Oliver Cromwell, Lord
Cardigan, and Sir John French, or, abroad, Genghiz Khan, Marshal Murat
and General J. E. B. Stuart, is to miss a main truth.

The first nine years of Haig's army life were spent, without particular
distinction and without unusual episodes, as a regimental officer. The
Regiment was, in those days, the very core of the Army. Most officers would
remain with regiments all through their careers, and the apparent stultifica-
tion of such a life was made bearable by the tremendous loyalty that each
unit attracted to itself, the *esprit de corps* that made membership of it a
privilege and service to it both a duty and a fulfilment. Generally speaking,
the impression of his first regiment on a young officer, if he stayed with it for
any length of time, remained with him for ever. Yet Haig seems never to
have developed any special feeling for the 7th Hussars, although the Regiment
enjoys a long and splendid fighting tradition. The year after he joined them,
the 7th went to India. Just before their departure, Haig was selected to play
polo for England against America; the English team won both the games
played by substantial margins. On its arrival in India, the regimental team
quickly made its mark against the stern competition of that station, and no
doubt Haig's prowess in this sport – almost obligatory for a cavalry officer,
and highly regarded in other arms – helped to win him a degree of popularity
that had been missing at Sandhurst. But he had not joined the Army to play
games, and within three years he had become Adjutant of the Regiment.
From that time onwards military studies and training occupied his mind
more and more.

If Haig stood out among his fellows at this time, it was for the seriousness
with which he took his profession. Small rewards accrued from this, and
showed that his hard and careful work was not passing unnoticed; in 1891 he

was selected to act as Brigade Major at a cavalry camp, and in the following year he was briefly attached to the Headquarters Staff of the Bombay Army. In both these years he took no European leave, but travelled instead on the North-West Frontier of India (the graveyard of so many young British officers and of the reputations of so many older ones), in Ceylon and to Australia. But neither his work in the Regiment, nor brief attachments outside it, nor travel to strange and exciting lands gave him real satisfaction. None of these could provide him with the opportunity to do himself justice as he intended to do. He fixed his eye upon the Staff College. Without the magic letters 'p.s.c.', he realized that he would get nowhere. Accordingly, in 1893 he said goodbye to the 7th Hussars, and set off for England to present himself for the Staff College examination. Since his Oxford days he had been an intermittent diarist, and so we have his own description of his departure from Bombay:

'Find Regimental Sergeant-Major Humphries waiting at launch for me. We all go on board *Peninsular* – quite melancholy parting. Humphries wrung my hand and said I was "the best sort he had ever had to do with". They go down the ladder into a small boat, the tide running very strong towards the lighthouse. I watched them with my glasses till they were quite a small speck, and were out near Colaba point. It was about 6 p.m., and getting dark. I feel quite sorry at leaving them all.'

'Quite sorry at leaving them all': making every allowance for the habit of military brevity, for Haig's own chronic difficulties of utterance and for his deep shyness of any emotional expression, there remains something undeniably tepid about this observation. For, no matter how shy one might feel of saying so, this *was* one of the outstandingly emotional moments of a soldier's career – parting with the regiment that had been his first 'home'. It is hard to resist the conclusion that, for Haig, the 7th Hussars had been simply a stepping-stone (as any other regiment would have been), and that his mind was already elsewhere, beyond the narrow horizons of the Mess and the parade-ground. Ironically, however, this parting was not to be a final one. His first attempt to enter the Staff College failed; not only did he not score enough marks in the compulsory subject of arithmetic, but, to his amazement, it proved that he was colour-blind. The defect was not grave, but it was undoubtedly there, and the shock of discovering it must have been considerable. There is nothing in the least degree shameful, or, indeed, notable, about colour-blindness; but for the rest of his life this was a sore subject with Haig, one which he tried to conceal, and discouraged jokes about. For the time being it was an obstacle to his progress, and he immediately set about finding a means of circumventing the medical test which had tripped him so unexpectedly. Until that could be done, however, he had to return to the Regiment. In what spirit he resumed his duties with it, in spite of the lack of sentiment which we have already noticed, and in spite of the severe disappointment which he must have felt, can be judged from the letter which he received from his Colonel the following year, when he left the 7th Hussars for the second and last time:

'My dear Douglas,
    'I cannot let you go without saying how I have appreciated what you have done for the Regiment. You came back to a position that a great many people would have disliked extremely, second fiddle in a squadron. Instead of making a grievance of it all, I know what a lot of pains you have taken and how much improvement in that squadron has been owing to you; and up to the last moment when you knew you were off, you have taken just as much interest in the preliminary musketry in the squadron as if you would be here to see the results. I cannot say how much you will be missed by all of us, officers, N.C.O.s and men. Your example in the regiment has been worth everything to the boys. You know I wish you every luck. You are, I think, bound to succeed because you mean to. I hate saying "Goodbye" as I am sadly afraid I shall never soldier with you again, but only hope I may.
                            'Yours very sincerely,
                                    Hamish Reid.'

    Taking this second leave of the 7th Hussars in 1894, Haig reached, without knowing it, the first turning-point in his military life. For this time there was no return, his connection was severed with the normal avenue of progress up the Army hierarchy, from squadron to regiment, from regiment to brigade, and so on, up the ladder of command. Haig's advance would be by a different road.

*   *   *   *

    The two years that elapsed between Haig's departure from his Regiment and his entry into the Staff College were well spent; indeed, but for the good use to which he put them, it is possible that he might never have arrived at Camberley. His first appointment was as A.D.C. to the Inspector-General of Cavalry in England during the autumn manoeuvres of 1894. A stirring was beginning to be felt in all the limbs and sinews of the Army, as the Duke of Cambridge's tenure as Commander-in-Chief drew to an end; but the task that lay before the 'progressive' school of officers was gigantic, and the time available for its completion was shorter than they knew. Haig's particular contribution during these two years lay not in what he performed directly with British Cavalry, but in the critical appreciations which he supplied of what was going on in France and Germany. In 1893, during his European leave, and again in 1894, he observed and reported on French progress. He wrote a very full account of the French manoeuvres of 1893, rectifying the commonly held view that the French were in all respects inferior to the Germans, and containing a comment which was to become, if anything, more characteristic rather than less in later years: 'Napoleon has written that "a cavalry force, to be of any use, must be composed of young generals and old captains". Now the fault of the French Cavalry is that they have too many old officers in both ranks.'

In 1895 he followed this up with a long visit to Germany, during which he received full facilities for watching the German Army at work, and also met the Kaiser. The German Emperor was not at that time in the bellicose mood which, a dozen years later, made the visits of British officers such an ordeal, and caused so many of them to return home with the direst misgivings about Germany's policy. Haig met with politeness and friendship on all sides, but nevertheless noted the special sensitivity of his hosts over all military matters, and their exaggerated anxiety, in British eyes, about anything that could remotely concern security. He was summoned back from Germany in June to attend one of Sir Evelyn Wood's[1] 'staff rides'; his function was to act as Staff Officer to Colonel French, who was 'commanding' the Cavalry on one side. Both of these associations were to affect him profoundly. With French, his association was to be long and varied, but in its early stages entirely successful and rewarding to Haig personally. On Wood he made a great impression, enhanced later in the year, when he drew up a full report on the German Army for Sir Evelyn's information. Years later, when the First World War had already broken out, Wood still remembered this paper, and wrote in his recollections: 'Haig knows more about the German Army than any officer in England.' At the time, this report, and his conversations with that eminent general, probably had a decisive influence in his progress towards the Staff College. For only a special dispensation could open those doors to him, after the findings of the previous medical board. The hurdle was, however, surmounted, in the last year of the Duke of Cambridge's command, most likely through his direct intervention on Wood's prompting. The kind of autocracy which the old Duke wielded was not entirely devoid of compensations.

At Camberley, it was a vintage year. Among the instructors was Colonel G. F. R. Henderson, whose biography of General 'Stonewall' Jackson remains standard to this day. Henderson's studies of the American Civil War supplied an enlargement of the mental horizons of British officers which was not matched on the Continent, where the American example was dis-

1. Then Quartermaster-General.

regarded, on the broad grounds that it was no more than a vast scuffle of amateurs, without interest to professional soldiers. Nothing could have been more wrong than this view. The pity is that British officers did not profit more than they did from Henderson's enlightened teachings, but if he was not able to save the generals from disastrous mistakes at the outbreak of the South African War, such flexibility as the Army later developed in that theatre was probably due to him as much as to anyone, while his direct influence on the strategy of Roberts, when the veteran Field Marshal took command, is widely acknowledged. A longer-distance result of his teachings may be seen in the sympathy with which Haig, almost alone among senior Regular officers, approached the problems of the Citizen Army. The essence of Civil War studies is the creation of a mass army from a tiny standing force; this was to become the essence of Britain's problem too, when she was drawn into the conflict of the Continental giants.

Among the Camberley students who were contemporary with Haig were many later distinguished figures: Allenby, of Palestine fame; Sir Thomson Capper, who became one of the outstanding trainers of troops in the Army, and who would certainly have risen to great eminence, had he not been mortally wounded at Loos; Sir George Macdonogh, who despite the handicap of extreme diffidence, rose to undisputed standing as Head of Intelligence during the World War; Sir J. E. Edmonds, who became the Official Historian of the War; and Sir Richard Haking, a Corps commander during it. Among the examiners was Plumer, then a Lieutenant-Colonel, and later to make his mark as the most methodical and reliable of the 1914–1918 Army Commanders. Three Field-Marshals from one batch is not bad going.

The Staff College had been Haig's goal for many years; when he reached it, he wasted no time. The capacity for hard work, already well developed in him, stood him in good stead. The intercourse of equals and seniors was profitable and salutary. Again, as at Sandhurst, wide popularity eluded him; at thirty-five habits and manners were becoming fixed, and it was not easy to break through the reserve of a lifetime. Nevertheless, he made friends at the College who remained with him all his life. In his studies, again probably because of the age factor, he was impatient of all that was purely academic, and distinguished in his approach to what was practical. Edmonds tells us that he never 'made the slightest attempt to "play up to" the instructors. If a scheme interested him he took tremendous pains with it; if he thought there was no profit in working it out, he sent in a perfunctory minimum. I remember a road reconnaissance sketch on which most of us had lavished extreme care, marking all the letter-boxes, pumps, gateways into fields and such-like. Haig handed in a sheet with a single brown chalk-line down the centre, the cross roads shown and the endorsement "twenty miles long, good surface, wide enough for two columns with orderlies both ways".' At his final examination, conducted by Plumer, Haig worked with Edmonds and another officer. He gave a general outline of the solution, and then told Edmonds that he could 'provide the *jargon* which the examiners expected'. In short, the full man was beginning to appear: severely practical, impatient of empty forms, and concerned above all else with the elucidation of general principles on which alone right action rested. This was the Scotsman coming out; it is a frame of mind which worries the English, but by contrast their empiricism and opportunism looks frivolous from north of the Tweed.

Haig spent just under two years at Camberley, years of great profit to him. As well as the value that he extracted from the instruction, his own somewhat tart observation revealed to him defects in the Army system itself. He did not often exercise gifts of humour – indeed, they were not marked in him at any time – but the Staff College provided him with some anecdotes which he would afterwards dryly retail. One of them concerned an exalted inspecting officer, who was said to have addressed three students in the following terms:

'Your commandant tells me that you all three show independence of judgment, intelligence, willingness to accept responsibility, and self-reliance: all of these drawbacks you will in time learn to correct.'

The story illuminates a dire fault in all hierarchical systems, none more so than the Army of the period; no doubt that is why it stuck in Haig's mind. In his own case, the verdict on him was somewhat different. Colonel Henderson said to one of Haig's brother students: 'There is a fellow in your batch who one of these days will be Commander-in-Chief.' Many years later, when Haig became C.-in-C. at Aldershot, Edmonds reminded him of this prophecy. Pointing out that the Aldershot command was not at all the same thing as the Command-in-Chief, Haig replied: 'I think that dear old Henderson must have been talking very much through his hat when he said that he thought I would ever be Commander-in-Chief of the British Army. I only wish to be of some use somewhere.' But Henderson was not a bad judge of military intellect, and he had observed that quality in Haig which is best summed up in the words of Charteris: 'From the Staff College he carried away with him a belief in the "educated soldier", which never afterwards faltered.'

2

Boot and Saddle

THIRTY-SIX YEARS old, and still a captain: it could hardly have been said, as he emerged from the Staff College, that Fortune had recklessly lavished her attentions on Douglas Haig. His career had been steady, purposeful, but devoid of brilliance; the qualities that had brought such distinction as had come his way were known only in a restricted circle; there had been no limelight. What he now needed above all was active service – the only limelight that is worth anything to a member of the fighting Services, but a dangerous one, not merely to life but to reputation. How many excellent peace-time soldiers have come to abrupt and bitter ends when the guns began to fire? The next few years were to add to their number with a painful bounty, but for Haig the hard test that was coming was, in truth, Fortune's first major exertion on his behalf. Out of many officers whose strongest wish was to go to Egypt to take part in the final stages of the long campaign which Kitchener had been waging against the Dervishes of the Sudan – a campaign dating back to the death of Gordon in 1885 – Haig was one of the few chosen. The immediate agent of the choice was Sir Evelyn Wood, so if it was Fortune that provided a campaign for Haig to go on at this critical juncture, it was equally his own past efforts that won him the right to do so.

For the greater part of the next five years, Haig was in the field. The Sudan Campaign, followed after less than a year's interval by the South African War, marked the beginning of a period of tremendous shock and change for the British Army. This was inevitable, after decades during which the only major military efforts of the Empire had been in India, and therefore largely the business of the Indian Army. The effect of these two wars, miniature though they look in mid-twentieth-century perspective, has been astonishingly far-reaching, for the whole reshaping of the Army's organization and of its thinking in the years leading up to the outbreak of the World

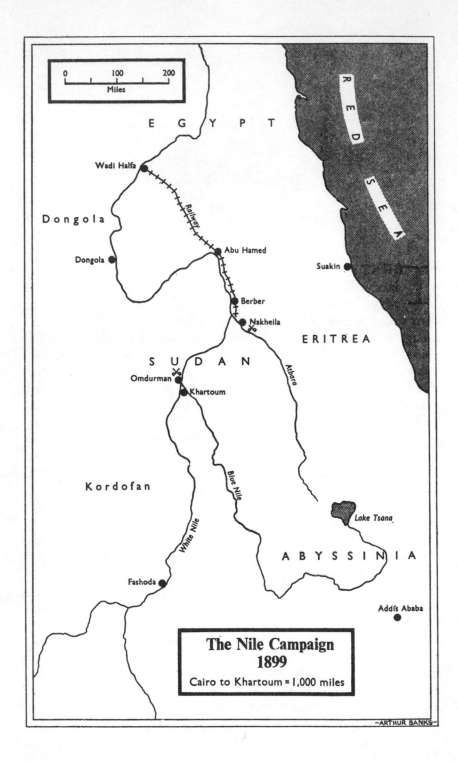

The Nile Campaign
1899

Cairo to Khartoum = 1,000 miles

War was decided by them. Many of the faults of British military thought between 1914 and 1918 stem from lessons correctly learned in the Sudan and South Africa. This has been sneeringly described as 'preparing for the last war' by critics who have apparently failed to observe that other lessons, also correctly learned, proved to be of huge value, while our Continental allies and enemies distinctly suffered from the lack of practical experience that British commanders possessed. The essence of both the wars in which Haig was now to take part was mobility, and it is to miss a whole historical truth if one does not understand what the basis of mobility was at that time. In the Sudan it was a railway and a river; in South Africa it was railways and horses. Indeed, right up to 1918, *strategic* mobility still depended on these two last factors, although to restore *tactical* mobility new weapons had had to be invented. There has been much cheap amusement at the expense of 'stick-in-the-mud' generals who were preoccupied with horseflesh. What they were really preoccupied with was the mobile element of war.

For Haig, in 1898, the first preoccupation was not a new weapon, but a new army – the reconstructed Egyptian Army that Kitchener had been building up on the slenderest budget for many years, and that was now to be put to the test. With our after-knowledge of his inexorable progress up the Nile, and of the holocaust of Omdurman, it is hard to recapture the doubts and trepidations which then existed. But there were many who said that the Egyptian soldiers would never stand in battle against the wild Dervishes, flushed with their innumerable victories. Only a large contingent of British troops, some believed, would be able to finish the job properly; and these, it was understood, were not likely to be forthcoming. Kitchener was more optimistic, and prepared to gamble; but lacking British troops, he needed a considerable number of British officers to put the final touches on the preparations of his Egyptian regiments and their Sudanese brothers-in-arms, who were recruited not only from the enemy's country, but largely also from the enemy's ranks. Of all the parts of the new Egyptian Army, that which commanded the least confidence was the Cavalry; few believed that it could possess any useful amount of that special morale which the mounted soldier must have. Haig's first duty was to take one of the Egyptian squadrons and train it. He recorded with pleasure that, as each squadron was an independent unit, the commanders had a free hand, which was not the case with their equivalents in the Infantry. Whether for this reason, or because Kitchener was quite ruthless in rejecting any officer who seemed unfit for the work, the Cavalry came on splendidly, and very soon confounded the critics.

The detailed story of the River War does not concern us; but for Haig it was a particularly important experience, because now, for the first time, he was under fire – a circumstance which possibly 'concentrates a man's mind wonderfully', but can equally reduce it to jelly, and dispel in an instant all the carefully learned lessons of classroom and parade-ground. Fighting against the Dervishes frequently tended to produce the latter effect; they were masters of the surprise attack; their sudden onslaughts materialized in the most alarming manner out of empty desert, or out of the grey half-light of dawn. In a few moments their battles were won or lost. If things went against them, they vanished into the emptiness from which they had sprung: a cloud of dust, and they were gone. Haig's first encounter with them was very much on these lines. It occurred on the banks of the Atbara, during a cavalry reconnaissance towards the end of March, 1898; Haig sent a long account of it to Sir Evelyn Wood. The vividness with which he tells the story is evidence of the sharp impression that the occasion made on him – and evidence too that somewhere along the line – from his tutor, Walter Peter, perhaps? – he had learned how to set his thoughts down on paper:

'. . . When just north of the thick scrub near Mutrus we saw a single Dervish scout, but only for a second, as he vanished at once. We went after him a short way, but as we had already proceeded farther than ordered, we returned through the scrub and the deserted villages along the river bank. We got back to Abadar about 1.45 p.m. I had watered my horse and was still in the river bed, when I heard the order to turn out as the Dervishes were on us. Briefly what had happened was this: The single scout had collected some hundred or more mounted men and followed Le Gallais and myself back to the halting place. They were met by a patrol from the outposts, which they raced back and reached the picket simultaneously. The picket was dismounted; several men composing it were shot or speared; and the leaders of the Dervishes were then close to the main body . . .'

In other words: a typical Dervish rush. On this occasion they were beaten off after a confused fight, in which the Egyptians suffered heavier loss than they were able to inflict. Haig had a number of comments to make on the event:

'1. The outpost service, tho' *theoretically* right, was carelessly done. When I passed the picket in question, many were lying down apparently asleep.

'2. The eyesight of the Egyptian vedette can't be relied on. For the Dervishes passed the front line of vedettes!

'3. The pluck of the Egyptian Cavalryman is right enough in my opinion.

'4. The Horse Artillery against enemy of this sort and in scrubs is no use. We felt the want of machine guns when working along outside the scrub for searching some of the tracks.'

It is worth noting that in Haig's very first fight he 'felt the want of machine guns'. Sixteen years later he would be feeling the same want again, and the results would be vastly more dire.

Haig's first action was little more than a disorderly scuffle; his second was a much more serious affair. The whole of the Egyptian Cavalry, under Colonel Broadwood, were acting as escort to Generals Hunter and Maxwell, on a reconnaissance of the main Dervish position on the Atbara. Haig was now acting as Staff Officer to Broadwood, his first appearance in a role that was to become habitual, and a pointer even further into his future. As the force completed its task and prepared to withdraw, it was suddenly attacked from several directions by Dervish infantry and cavalry, the latter trying to cut across the rear of the Egyptians and making a bid to capture their Horse Artillery. 'The situation was a difficult one,' Haig wrote, 'and to add to it a strongish north wind prevented our seeing clearly the moment a squadron moved.' The next half-hour passed in a wild tangle, with Haig dashing from one part of the field to another, through the whirling clouds of dust, trying to keep some cohesion in the force. Colonel Broadwood was out in front, with his leading squadrons, and there can be no doubt that but for Haig's activities a grave setback might have occurred. His first duty was to see to the safety of the guns; as he brought them out, he came upon Captain Mahon, with the main body of the Cavalry:

'He could not see anything for dust. . . . Mahon is a sound fellow, and said, "I can't see what has happened, what do you suggest?" I at once said, "Place one squadron on flank . . . of guns and support Le Gallais with your other two on *his* left. I will then bring Baring and remaining three squadrons on your left rear as a third line." Mahon advanced. I gave Baring his orders, putting all three squadrons under him. I then galloped on to find Broadwood (who I knew must be with Le Gallais' squadrons) in order to know his wishes as to the action of the guns. On my way I found the 2 squadrons coming back at full gallop. We were able to stop them (the horses were pretty well beat), and they advanced a little way. I thought there was no time to lose to ask for orders, so I went direct to the maxims and told them they must come into action against the most threatening of the enemy (which I indicated) as soon as the cavalry cleared their field of fire. I then went off to Broadwood . . .'

A flank charge, led by Broadwood in person, saved the day. The casualties (about thirty) were not so severe as they might have been. When they all got their breath back, the Egyptian Cavalry felt decidedly pleased with themselves; nor were they alone in this sentiment: 'This I hear is the *first time* the Gyppe Cavalry has ever had anything in the way of fighting to do. This accounts for the delight at Headquarters at discovering that they don't run away.' This time Haig had only one criticism to make – of Broadwood himself: 'He . . . was wrong to charge as he did with the first line, for the whole Brigade then passed from his control. But he is a very sound fellow, and is excellent at running this show.' His fellow-captain, Mahon, as we have seen, was also 'a sound fellow'; General Hunter, he concluded, on brief acquaintance, was a 'first-rate fellow'. Broadwood's opinion of Haig was expressed in a recommendation to Kitchener, which resulted in a brevet majority.

The two battles (deserving of the name) of the River War were the Atbara and Omdurman. The Atbara was fought on April 8th, 1898; it was a straightforward assault by the Anglo-Egyptian Army on the Dervishes' fortified camp. It resulted in complete success, the almost total destruction of the Dervish army under Mahmud, and the somewhat inglorious capture of Mahmud himself. The Cavalry had little to do in the affair, once the enemy's outposts had been driven in; the brunt fell upon the Infantry. Sir Winston Churchill has given us a description of the scene:

'At twenty minutes to eight the Sirdar ordered his bugles to sound the general advance. The call was repeated by all the brigades, and the clear notes rang out above the noise of the artillery. The superior officers . . . dismounted and placed themselves at the head of their commands. The whole mass of the infantry, numbering nearly eleven thousand men, immediately began to move forward upon the *zeriba*. The scene as this great force crested the ridge and advanced down the slope was magnificent and tremendous. Large solid columns of men, preceded by a long double line, with the sunlight flashing on their bayonets and displaying their ensigns, marched to the assault in regular and precise array. The pipes of the Highlanders, the bands of the Soudanese, and the drums and fifes of the English regiments added a wild and thrilling accompaniment.'

It was the last essay in war in this familiar style. Against the outnumbered Dervishes, lacking both modern weapons and modern science, it succeeded well enough. But Haig, from his vantage point outside the main engagement, had certain questions in his mind about it all. To begin with, there was the British public's reaction to the news of the victory: 'We have just received the London papers of 9th April with accounts of the Battle of the Atbara. What rubbish the British public delights to read. The exaggeration of some of the reports almost makes a good day's work appear ridiculous. The headings of the *D.T.* are so overdrawn that instinctively one says "Waterloo Eclipsed".'

The full truth, as Haig well knew, was not quite so glamorous. He proceeded to put forward (all this in a letter to Sir Evelyn Wood, three weeks after the battle) certain pertinent queries: 'For instance, Why was the attack frontal? It seemed to me, from the very first day that we reconnoitred the place, that an attack on the enemy's right offered great advantages. . . . Next, what about the use made of the artillery? Distant fire was not required; in fact, the 1st and only range was some 700 yards. Our side says the guns did tremendous damage. Mahmud and over 300 [enemy] questioned by Fitton (who is a sort of intelligence officer here) say, "We did not mind the guns, they only hurt camels and donkeys. The infantry fire was what destroyed us" . . . Another point is the formation of the force for the attack. Each brigade attacked on a front of about 300 to 400 yards. (For a straight line of 1,000 yards would more than reach from the enemy's right to his left.) So looking on, it struck me that our formation was extraordinarily deep. This may have accounted for our severe losses . . .'

But it was not, Haig realized, enough merely to criticize. He rounded off his observations to Wood by putting forward a battle-plan of his own, based on subduing the enemy by fire power, including enfilade of their main trench by machine guns, and then cutting across their line of retreat. But with becoming modesty he was prepared to admit that his idea might not have proved so clever as it sounded: 'The weak point in my plan is that I calculated as if I had troops that can shoot and manoeuvre. It would be un-wise to rely upon the Blacks doing either *well*. So all the more credit is due to the Sirdar for limiting himself to a moderate victory instead of going for annihilating Mahmud's army.' It can be presumed that Haig was learning for himself the old truth that in war nothing is quite so easy as it looks. There are always unseen factors that make nonsense of paper calculations. Within twenty years, there would be many criticizing him in much the same terms as he had criticized Kitchener at the Atbara – and few with the same afterthought of humility.

The final battle of the campaign was Omdurman, fought on September 2nd. It was a strange affair. Kitchener, an Engineer officer, never regarded himself as a tactician; at the Atbara, having brought the Army to the enemy's camp, he considered that it was the job of the other generals to win the battle for him. At Omdurman, having taken the precaution of securing one flank by resting on the River Nile, with its gunboat flotilla, and for the rest contenting himself with drawing up his army in three sides of a hollow square, he seemed quite satisfied to let events take their course. The Dervishes, superbly brave, but utterly incompetent, played into his hands. They hurled themselves in successive masses at the British and Egyptian lines; smitten by shrapnel, by machine-gun fire, and by rifle fire which the Grenadier Guards opened at 2,700 yards, the extreme range of the Lee-Metford rifle, they fell in thousands. Even at that distance, aimed at such a dense throng, the Guards' volleys could scarcely miss. The Cavalry played an important part in dis-tracting the attention of a large division of the Dervish Army – at some peril to themselves. Kitchener's orders to the Cavalry to withdraw were carried by his A.D.C., Henry Rawlinson, later to become one of Haig's most distinguished Army commanders in France. Shortly after the battle,

Rawlinson wrote down his impression of what he saw as he approached the Cavalry:

'At length we could see our contact squadrons under Douglas Haig gradually withdrawing as the Dervishes advanced. . . . I rode out to him over the ground which an hour later was heaped with dead and wounded Dervishes. When I reached him he was within about six hundred yards of the enemy's long line, and I noticed that his confident bearing seemed to have inspired his fellaheen, who were watching the Dervish advance quite calmly.'

The Egyptian Cavalry drew off, having completed their mission. (The charge of the British 21st Lancers, in which Sir Winston Churchill took part, occurred in a different part of the field, later in the day, and was quite un-connected with the manoeuvres of the Egyptian squadrons.) The battle, or rather, massacre, drew to its conclusion, not without moments of peril to the Anglo-Egyptian force, despite its great superiority in weapons and fire power. But the final outcome could scarcely be doubted. The Khalifa himself escaped in the confusion at the end of the day, in spite of all the efforts of the by now exhausted Cavalry to catch him; but his army was destroyed; his empire was smashed. Upwards of 20,000 Dervishes lay dead and wounded; the British and Egyptians had lost less than 500 men and officers. The death of Gordon was avenged. Nevertheless, satisfactory as the outcome had been, to some who were present the battle did not wear the glorious aspect with which, once again, the British Press and public invested it. To many who took part, it seemed to have been a very muddled business, the honours for which were due far more to mechanical than to mental superiority.

Haig, writing again to Wood, considered that Kitchener had been very lucky in that the enemy had abandoned the key of the position to him before the battle began, through no effort of his. 'Then,' he continued, 'on morning of 2nd when the enemy had divided his forces, the Sirdar's left should have been thrown forward to this hill, and gradually drawing in his right and extending his left south-westwards, he might have cut the enemy off from Omdurman and really *annihilated* the thousands and thousands of Dervishes. In place of this, altho' in possession of full information, and able to see with his own eyes the whole field, he spreads out his force, thereby risking the destruction of a Brigade. He seems to have had no plan, or tactical idea, for beating the enemy beyond allowing the latter to attack the camp. . . . Having 6 Brigades, is it tactics to fight a very superior enemy with one of them and to keep the others beyond supporting distance? To me it seems truly fortu-nate that the *flower* of the Dervish army exhausted itself first in an attack and pursuit of the cavalry. Indeed the prisoners say, "You would never have defeated us had you not *deceived* us." '

Omdurman now seems a very long way back in time, a battle belonging to a vanished era, to a century of wars against savage peoples. It was fortunate for the future of the Army that the River War was immediately followed by South Africa, with its succession of shocks to dispel the complacency that would otherwise have attended Kitchener's victorious march up the Nile. Many Sudan reputations were seen to be decidedly fragile on the veldt. But for a brief time all those who had shared in Kitchener's triumph enjoyed a fraction of his fame. Certainly the campaign had had a powerful developing effect on Haig. Above all, he had found his *métier*: he had moved very quickly to a Staff position, and had instantly distinguished himself in it. The contrast between him and his immediate chief, Broadwood, illustrates the error of regarding Haig as a 'cavalry general' in the accepted British tradition. It was not a tradition to be altogether proud of; after Cromwell, the British Cavalry had fallen into bad habits which had greatly reduced its effectiveness.

The Duke of Wellington summed up one of the worst defects, after a typically bungled affair in the Peninsula: 'Our officers of cavalry have acquired a trick of galloping at everything.' In 1826 the Duke wrote: 'I considered our cavalry so inferior to the French from want of order, that although I considered one of our squadrons a match for two French, yet I did not care to see four British opposed to four French, and still more so as numbers increased, and order (of course) became more necessary. They could gallop, but could not preserve their order.' It was a fault which was never eradicated, and it is interesting to see, seventy years later, in the Sudan, how the galloping instinct, bred in the hunting field, was still the enemy of good order. Even Broadwood, as we have seen, would abandon control to lead a charge; Haig, who did not greatly care for hunting, preferred to spend his energies in preserving order. This is the mark of the Staff man. There was very little 'Tally-ho!' about Douglas Haig.

Two other attributes had become noticeable in him, by the time Khartoum was reached. First, he had shown clearly that he was not afraid of responsibility; he did not hesitate to grip a situation without reference to orders from higher up. This was probably due in great part to the fact that he was still, at this stage, a few years older than most officers of his rank. Secondly, he revealed powers or criticism, and a disposition to use them, that were rare in Army officers of his day. As the years went by, this inclination did not depart from him, and as he moved closer to the centre of affairs, some of his comments on men and methods became tart; but they never excluded remarks of a different kind – approval and appreciation of the deserving. The military lessons of the campaign were not numerous, but included two which had significance for the future. Never was there an expedition in which logistics were so decisive; every new hundred yards of

Kitchener's railway represented a small defeat for the Dervishes without a battle. It was, in a sense, a triumph of organization – but not of organizational method. Rawlinson put his finger on Kitchener's weakness when he wrote: 'He is a long-headed, clear-minded man of business, with a wonderful memory. His apparent hardness of nature is a good deal put on, and is, I think, due to a sort of shyness. . . . The one serious criticism that I have is that this is too much of a one-man show.' Modern war was fast moving out of the realm of the one-man show – indeed, the British Army was already seriously behind the times, with its lack of a proper General Staff organization. Haig, whose personal leanings had now been revealed, would find both his immediate avenues of progress and much of his future fulfilment in remedying this want.

*   *   *   *

Haig returned to England shortly after Omdurman, and after a brief interval of leave and regimental duty he found himself once more in a Staff appointment, as Brigade Major of the 1st Cavalry Brigade at Aldershot. That his work in this capacity gave satisfaction was evident, five months later, when he was ordered out to South Africa with General French, who was to command the Cavalry in Natal in the event of war with the Boer Republics. This duly came in October, 1899, and within a matter of days French and Haig were engaged with the enemy outside Ladysmith. Their first experience of battle against the Boers was a happy one, the minor victory of Elandslaagte, which enabled Sir George White to concentrate the some-what scattered British forces in Northern Natal at Ladysmith. But Elands-laagte was the last gleam of success that was to fall on British arms for some time. Just over a week later the first disaster of the war occurred at Nichol-son's Nek, where two battalions, Gloucesters and Royal Irish Fusiliers, with a mountain battery, were cut off and captured. The swelling Boer commandos gathered round Ladysmith, and it was only in the nick of time that a message arrived from the new Commander-in-Chief, Sir Redvers Buller, ordering French and Haig to leave the now practically encircled town to take charge of the Cavalry Division that was on its way out from England. They left Ladysmith in the last train to get away; with French's two A.D.C.s, they were the only passengers, and all four officers had to spend the greater part of the journey lying on the seats or squatting on the floor in order to keep out of sight. Nevertheless, the train came under sharp fire, and it was afterwards found that a shell had passed through one of the trucks and damaged Haig's luggage. 'It is odd,' remarks Duff Cooper, 'in the light of subsequent events, to picture the two Commanders-in-Chief of the British Expeditionary Force crouching on the floor of the little railway carriage in positions which could

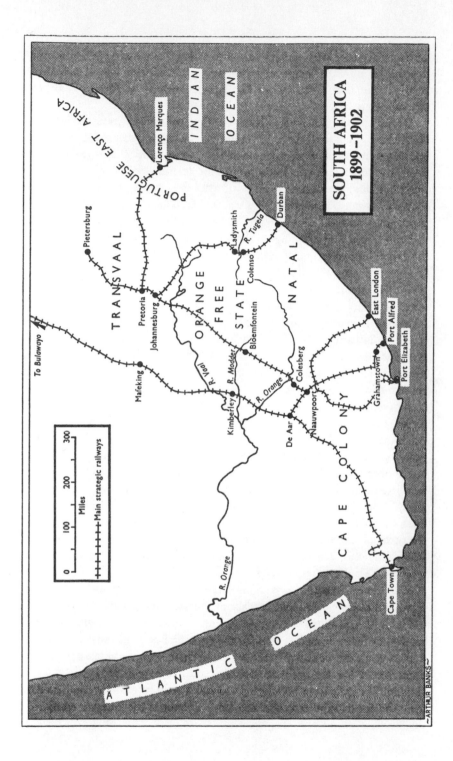

SOUTH AFRICA
1899–1902

INDIAN OCEAN

PORTUGUESE EAST AFRICA

Lorenço Marques

Durban

Ladysmith

R. Tugela

Colenso

NATAL

Pietersburg

TRANSVAAL

ORANGE FREE STATE

Pretoria

Johannesburg

Bloemfontein

East London

Port Alfred

To Bulawayo

Mafeking

R. Vaal

R. Modder

R. Orange

Colesberg

Grahamstown

Port Elizabeth

Kimberley

De Aar

Naauwpoort

CAPE COLONY

R. Orange

Cape Town

ATLANTIC OCEAN

300

200

100

Miles

Main strategic railways

0

—ARTHUR BANKS—

hardly be assumed with dignity and wondering . . . whether at any moment they might not find themselves at the mercy of their enemy and condemned to spend the rest of the war in inglorious captivity at Pretoria.' It was a narrow escape.

Odder things, however, than the discomforts of two future Field-Marshals, were shortly seen in South Africa. Few wars have caught the British Army so ill-prepared in thinking, organization and training; few governments have shown less capacity for war leadership in adversity than Lord Salisbury's administration. Nor was the mood of the country itself calculated to produce good results; as *The Times* historian has said: 'Its Imperialism was still tainted with that self-satisfied irresponsibility, that contemptuous ignoring of things as they are, that belief in the power of wealth and large figures in general, and that disbelief in the power of scientific thought and earnest will concentrated upon national objects which the word "jingoism" most nearly expresses.' By mid-December, 1899, the birds had come home to roost. In 'Black Week' three successive disasters fell upon the Army and the nation: Stormberg, Magersfontein and Colenso. Three British garrisons, in Ladysmith, Kimberley and Mafeking, remained surrounded and in evident danger. All over the world a howl of glee arose at the humiliation of the British Empire by a few thousand untrained farmers; all over the Empire the shock was felt.

It is extremely difficult for us now, in the light of the twentieth century's altered scale of values, to grasp just how severe this shock was. The three lost battles cost, between them, approximately 3,000 casualties – about as many as one brigade might lose on a bad day in the 1914–1918 War. But to a country which, for almost half a century had experienced nothing more serious than frontier skirmishes and expeditions against savages, this revelation of what a resolute white enemy might do with modern weapons had a fearful impact. The Government was entirely at a loss; so far from giving direction to the national upsurge that occurred when the news of 'Black Week' came in, it seemed rather to wish to damp the fires down. One concession was made to the sense of crisis, however: Field-Marshal Lord Roberts of Kandahar, sixty-seven years old, but still full of fire and vigour, was appointed to take command in place of the incompetent and hesitant Buller, and with him, as Chief of Staff, he would have Kitchener of Khartoum. This augury, at least, promised well for the future; but until these two eminent soldiers could arrive and grip the situation, there would evidently be difficult times ahead for the separate British columns covering Natal and Cape Colony. Some delicate holding operations would have to be conducted. Of these the most important was that which covered the railway complex of the North-eastern Cape, where the lines from Cape Town and Port Elizabeth converged on their way north to Kimberley, Bloemfontein and Pretoria. The vital locality was around the railway junction of Naauwpoort and the little Dutch township of Colesberg. It was to this point that French and Haig were now ordered, to take charge of a small mixed force and 'maintain an active defence not running any risk'. The Colesberg operations which ensued became a minor military classic which marked both men for later high command.

While he was in Cape Town, awaiting orders, Haig turned his short respite from action to good account; with characteristic method, he drew up a memorandum of Tactical Notes, embodying the lessons of the fighting in which he had taken part. 'These operations', he noted, 'have shown clearly the greatly increased power of action possessed by Cavalry, now that it is armed with a good carbine.' He instanced four occasions when the Cavalry, acting *dismounted*, both offensively and defensively, had made an important contribution to success, and he concluded this section of his paper: 'Again, the use made by the Boers . . . of their ponies to carry them to a position . . . from which to deliver a flanking fire upon attacking troops should not pass unnoticed by us, and might sometimes be imitated by our Cavalry with good results . . .' Characteristically again, his next section dealt with matters requiring attention 'in order to improve our Cavalry in dismounted action'. His first point was: 'Pay more attention to this class of work in time of peace. Musketry training and field firing to be made more practical. Tactical schemes for Cavalry in *all* kinds of country; and check Cavalry Officers when in broken ground they sit still and complain that "they can do nothing in this damned country!" (2) It is a question whether the Dragoon-lancer is not a mistake! His lance hampers him . . .'

Haig then turned to the Infantry: '. . . for offensive warfare in Natal the offensive power of Infantry is limited. Infantry is essential for the assault on positions which the Boers hold as pivots, but about half of the attacking force should consist of mounted troops in order to secure the flanks of the attacking Infantry column, and to outmanoeuvre the Boers.' On the Artillery (which had been a great disappointment against the enemy's Krupp armament) he had more to say: 'The effect of Artillery fire is chiefly moral! The teachings of peace manoeuvres and text-books require to be considerably modified. Briefly, in our Army many have over-estimated the power of shrapnel fire. . . . At Lombard's Kop, though we had almost 50 guns on the battlefield, not a gun of the enemy was *permanently* silenced. They withdrew their gunners and then, when our guns were turned upon another target, they recommenced firing. The Boers on the defensive divided their guns with telling effect: for they managed to bring an occasional gun or two up as a surprise, and enfiladed our lines of guns when our gunners seemed least to expect it.' His last points were a criticism of the traditional dense formation of British troops both in defence and attack: 'Sufficient attention is not, as a rule, paid in our Army in peace time to *concealing troops* holding a position. Frequently, too, troops seem to be posted too thickly upon a defensive position. . . . Ian Hamilton's attacking lines at Elandslaagte seemed, judging by results, well arranged. They were thinner than the normal formation. A Battalion . . . with men extended at intervals of 3 or 4 paces, and the distance of some 50 yards from company to company, seems a very difficult formation to hit.'

Haig's paper, written when the war was still barely a month old, is remarkable because it embodied all the major tactical lessons which the British Army learned and re-learned at much cost throughout its course, and continued to debate long after it. When the World War came, it was seen that some of them had still not sunk in: the Artillery was still depending on shrapnel; Infantry formations, once the Regular Army was expended, were once again too dense, and a steady refrain in Haig's Diary from 1914 to 1918 is his reiterated plea to subordinate commanders to thin their troops out on the ground. In November, 1899, the paper revealed him as an outstandingly equipped Staff Officer; though still only a substantive Major of Cavalry (acting Lieutenant-Colonel in South Africa), he had clearly already studied the work and methods of other Arms. In consequence, he proved an invaluable right-hand man to French in the Colesberg operations. Too trivial in themselves to deserve detailed notice now, these were vital at the time. Not only did they frustrate the projected Boer invasion of Cape Colony, but they served also to cover Roberts's concentration for his great flank march to Bloemfontein, and at the same time went far to restore the tottering morale of the Army, by showing that the Boers could be beaten at their own game – by mobility and bluff. French had, for this work, the support of a number of subsequently prominent soldiers: Allenby and Horne, future Army Commanders, de Lisle and Hunter-Weston, future Corps Commanders, were all present in junior posts. But as *The Times* historian said: 'In Major Douglas Haig he possessed an invaluable staff officer, one of the few in the whole Army capable of doing real general staff work. The intelligence, under Captain Lawrence, was admirably conducted . . .'

This is the first linking of Haig and Herbert Lawrence, who were to come together again, after a less agreeable conjunction, with great effect in 1918. The influence of Haig was, however, the most significant at Colesberg. As Charteris says: 'The orders, which it fell to his lot as Chief Staff Officer to issue on behalf of his Commander, were almost all written in his own hand. His precise and accurate mind enabled him to indite them with hardly a correction. They are models of lucidity.' French himself, when he made his report, said: 'Major D. Haig, Acting Assistant Adjutant General and Chief

Staff Officer, has shown throughout the same zeal, untiring energy, and consummate ability as have characterized his conduct and bearing since the very commencement of the campaign [in Natal] during the whole of which time he has acted in this capacity. I.have had occasion to speak of him in a similar sense in former despatches.'

Despite this high praise, the next stage of Haig's career contained disappointment. Perhaps because he lacked the patronage which still counted for much in the Army of those days, possibly because some of his outspoken criticisms had done him a mischief (the Prince of Wales, with whom he was acquainted through his sister Henrietta, rebuked him for this, saying that his 'criticisms may be correct, but it does not do'), Haig now learned that, when Roberts's march began, he would be replaced as French's Chief of Staff by Lord Erroll, a full Colonel who had just arrived from England. French protested vigorously to Roberts, but the Field-Marshal was not to be shifted; it was therefore in a less important capacity that Haig accompanied the Cavalry Division on its famous dash to Kimberley in February, 1900. At the end of that month his personal fortunes looked up again: he was promoted to substantive Lieutenant-Colonel and offered command of a brigade, but before this could become effective Erroll was removed to another post, and Haig resumed his position as French's Chief Staff Officer. He commented: 'This will suit me very well.'

Later in the year Sir Evelyn Wood, who as the doyen of the British Cavalry was very much disturbed at its poor performances everywhere except under French, proposed that Haig should take a regiment, in order to begin training a new generation of Cavalry leaders. In a letter to Henrietta, Haig recounted: 'French is replying that I had once been appointed to a Brigade, and that I might now be in command of one were it not to the interests of the service that I should remain on in my present billet. My present appointment of Chief Staff Officer of a Cavalry Division of 4 Cavalry Brigades is superior to any regimental appointment. . . . Personally I don't care much what happens to me in the way of reward, for I despise those who only work when they hope to get something in return! Many thanks for the shaving soap. It arrived at the right time. I always shave and I was getting a bit short. I hear our Staff is considered well dressed and clean; this has a good effect on all ranks.'

One month later, prompted no doubt by affectionate sisterly enquiries from Henrietta, who had always stood to some extent in the place of the mother who died when he was eighteen, he returned to this question of rewards: 'Don't make a fuss about my being now in the same position as I started in. Recollect also many have gone lower down. And as to rewards, if you only knew what duffers will get and do get H.M.'s decorations and are promoted, you would realize how little I value them. Everything comes in time, and decorations come in abundance with declining years and imbecility. No one yet on this Staff, fortunately, has got a decoration of any kind, otherwise we might have achieved disaster like the other décorés.' The acid note in this passage suggests that French's hard-worked division may have come to regard themselves as something of a 'forgotten army'. Mounted Infantry were all the rage at this juncture, and the Cavalry itself at a discount. Glittering commands (until the Boers wore the shine off) were being distributed to men whom Roberts knew and trusted. Was the old faction still working, this time against the 'Wolseley school'?

Lord Roberts carried the flag from Bloemfontein to Pretoria, dispersing the Boer field armies wherever he met them. The war appeared to be won, and the old Field-Marshal returned home loaded with honour. He is one of the most attractive figures in British military history, a soldier by thought, and a leader by instinct, with a wonderful ability to inspire all who fought under him, all the martial races of India as well as the British Army.

> There's a little red-faced man,
>   Which is Bobs,
> Rides the tallest 'orse 'e can –
>   *Our* Bobs.
> If it bucks or kicks or rears,
> 'E can sit for twenty years,
> With a smile round both 'is ears –
>   Can't yer, Bobs?

The country had not seen the last of Bobs by a long chalk. Unfortunately, it had not seen the last of the Boers, either. Unaccountably, despite the occupation of the two capitals and the overrunning of both the Free State and the Transvaal by British forces, despite the evident impossibility of defeating the invaders decisively in the open field, the farmers continued to fight on. Lord Kitchener had been given the task of 'mopping up'; it took him the best part of three years to do it, and the enemy were still in the field at the end. The later stages of the War declined into the boredom and frustration and incidental brutality of guerilla warfare – one of the most vexatious experiences that any Regular Army can endure. In South Africa it was made the more difficult for Kitchener and his subordinates by a tendency on the part of the Government and the War Office to act as though there were no war on at all. This led to the withdrawal and disbandment of many units, just as they had become acclimatized, and their constant replacement by raw formations and drafts. Guerillas eat raw soldiers for breakfast.

Kitchener's method was based upon the splitting of the Army into mobile columns, which then conducted 'drives'. These met with varying success, according to the luck or flair of the column commander, the condition of his troops, and the skill of the enemy. But it was wretched, back-breaking work. In 1901 Haig was given command of a group of columns in the Cape, a mainly defensive role, whose object was to prevent the Boer commandos from the Free State and the Transvaal from raising a rebellion in the Colony – a long-standing nightmare of the British command. The chief difficulty, as he wrote at the time, was that 'all the farmers are secretly their friends, and the Government [of the Cape] almost seem to assist the invader . . .' There was little opportunity for distinction in this (though less chance of disaster than with the more offensive columns in the north); one of Haig's opponents was Smuts, whose reputation for 'slimness' was already established. Haig was no more capable of catching him than anyone else was; this was not his style of war. The ideal column commander had to be almost a bushman, an instinctive fighter, who could 'smell' the enemy out; General Staff methods hardly helped at all. It is worth reflecting, as one ponders the problems and performances of the British generals against the Boer bands, that there is hardly a case in history of Regular forces subduing determined guerillas, except with the active help of the population. Napoleon's calamities in Spain, and the achievements of Marshal Tito's Partisans even against the modern armament of Hitler's Wehrmacht, illustrate the case.

More satisfying than chasing elusive Boers round the Cape was Haig's appointment at this time to a regimental command (in addition to his column) as Sir Evelyn Wood had suggested. The regiment in question was the 17th Lancers, whose skull-and-crossbones badge is one of the most famous in the Army. The appointment brought Haig into rivalry with Herbert Lawrence, himself a 17th Lancer, and who was generally thought to have earned the command of his own regiment rather than an outsider. Lawrence himself was disappointed at being passed over; he 'sent in his papers' and the Army lost his services for several years. Nor was this a good auspice for the incoming Colonel. Possibly because of the extra effort that he had to make to win over his somewhat angry and apprehensive officers (for Haig had a reputation for being a strict disciplinarian), the 17th Lancers thenceforward occupied a special and hitherto unfilled place in his affections. But the more likely reason is that this was his first experience of what Field-Marshal Slim has called 'one of the four best commands in the Service – a platoon, a battalion,[1] a division, and an army. A platoon, because it is your first command, because you are young, and because, if you are any good, you know the men in it better than their mothers do and love them as much.

1. Read 'regiment' for Cavalry.

A battalion, because it is a unit with a life of its own; whether it is good or bad depends on you alone; you have at last a real command.' Certainly Haig's attachment to his new regiment began at once. When one of his squadrons suffered a disaster at Smuts's hands, his grief and his pride were both stirred in a new way: 'Our men held the position to the last, and not a man surrendered. Out of 130 men, 29 were killed and 41 wounded. The other men were still fighting when the next squadron came up to their support and the enemy made off. All the officers were either killed or wounded. Such nice fellows too.'

This sympathetic touch is indicative of a rounding out that had taken place within him, as a consequence of almost five years of continuous active service. It is best expressed in a letter which he wrote, towards the end of the war, to a young nephew: 'I am anxious not only that you should realize your duty to your family, your country and to Scotland, but also to the whole Empire – "Aim High" as the Book says, "perchance ye may attain". . . . Don't let the lives of mediocrities about you deflect you from your determination to belong to the few who can command or guide or benefit our great Empire. Believe me, the reservoir of such men is not boundless. As our Empire grows, so there is a greater demand for them, and it behoves everyone to do his little and try and qualify for as high a position as possible. It is not ambition. This is *duty*.'

This was Haig's creed.

3

Perchance Ye May Attain

HAIG RETURNED from South Africa in September, 1902, after a
brief spell in command of one of the military sub-districts of Cape
Colony. Both for him and for the Army, the twelve years that
separated the Peace of Vereeniging from the outbreak of the World War
were years of accomplishment and fruition. The honours that had earlier
been withheld from him and his colleagues in the Cavalry Division were now
showered upon them in the euphoria of peace. Sir John French became a
national hero. Haig became a brevet colonel; he received a C.B.; he was
appointed A.D.C. to King Edward VII; he was mentioned four times in
despatches and bore every medal and every clasp of the two campaigns
through which he had fought. Moreover, he was looked to as one of those
who would play a vital part in the re-shaping of the Army which even
slothful Unionists and pacific Liberals could now recognize as an urgent need.

For a short interval, however – just over a year – Haig was permitted to
enjoy what was virtually a rest after his long exertions. Two eminent soldiers
were competing for his services: Sir John French, now Commander-in-Chief
at Aldershot, wanted him to command the Cavalry Brigade there; Lord
Kitchener, newly appointed Commander-in-Chief in India, wanted him as
Inspector-General of Cavalry in that country. Haig was sceptical of the politicians' intentions towards the Army. One of the most disfiguring features of
the next era would be the steadily mounting mistrust and misunderstanding
between the civil and military arms of the State. The rise of the Liberal Party,
with its strong pacifist tradition, certainly helped to aggravate the process,
particularly when Liberal social policies collided with the interests of the class
from which most Army officers were drawn. Yet the antagonism was only
to a certain extent due to Party feelings; at the turn of the century Haig had
written from South Africa: 'I would disband the politicians for ten years.

We would all be the better without them.' At that time the Liberal Party's prospects did not seem to be worth a straw. And now, in 1902, with the Unionists still in power, he wrote: 'I fancy these politicians will let everything slide as they did before the war.' This conclusion decided him against the Aldershot command, and in favour of accepting Kitchener's offer when the post became vacant. In the meantime, there was his new regiment.

On their return home, the 17th Lancers were quartered in Edinburgh, Haig's birthplace; this was not altogether a matter of satisfaction to him. 'Edinburgh is a bad place for cavalry,' he wrote to his sister, 'no drill ground and half the regiment on detachment – so I wired General French and asked him to try and get the station altered to York or Aldershot. Indeed, any place is better as a cavalry station than Edinburgh.' However, Edinburgh it had to be, and there he settled down for a time. Although he was near relations and among friends, he did not go much into society; neither dancing nor cards held much appeal for him. On the other hand, he was able to resume an old pastime and develop a new one. He took up polo again, and had the great satisfaction in 1903 of leading the regimental team to victory in the Inter-Regimental Tournament, beating the Blues by five goals to one. Those who recalled the team's celebration at the Savoy on the night of the match remembered Haig in a rare mood of relaxation and joviality. He also took up golf, particularly on Sundays. Because of Scottish Sabbatarianism, this involved a four-mile walk to and from the links, carrying his clubs, as well as the two rounds which he normally played: not a bad day's exercise for a man of forty-one. In both of these sports he mixed freely and easily with the officers of the Regiment, but at other times he still tended to remain aloof – partly out of consideration, believing that young officers prefer not to have too much of the inhibiting presence of their Colonel in the Mess. This was a happy interlude during which he formed individual friendships and a collective attachment to the 17th Lancers that remained with him always.

*   *   *   *

Kitchener's summons came in October, 1903, and Haig's departure to India, which closed his career as a regimental officer, at the same time thrust him into the stir of change and reform which was beginning to sweep right through the armed forces of the Empire. India was probably the most intractable area of all in which reform had to operate. Writing to Kitchener before his appointment as Commander-in-Chief, the Viceroy, Lord Curzon, had said: '. . . I look forward with much confidence to the benefit of your vast energy and great experience. I see absurd and uncontrolled expenditure; I observe a lack of method and system; I detect slackness and jobbery; and in some respects I lament a want of fibre and tone.' Whatever one may think of

Lord Curzon's elevated prose, this summary was about right. Kitchener's attack upon the Augean stables constituted one of the most sustained bursts of peacetime activity that India has ever seen; indeed, taken in conjunction with the array of civil reforms initiated under Lord Curzon, it must be seen as an essential part of the building of modern India. The core of Kitchener's purpose was to make the large but ramshackle military establishment of India fit to take its part in twentieth-century war. His first step, wrote one of his Staff Officers, Lord Birdwood, 'was to abolish the term "Indian Staff Corps" and substitute that of "Indian Army". . . . K's next great scheme had as its object the welding of the Army in India into a powerful, modern striking force. . . . Till K. took over, there was not even one single war brigade, organized as such. . . .' When war came, great blemishes were soon revealed even in the reformed system in India, and brought with them their inevitable train of disasters; but the fact that India was able to participate in the War at all effectively, let alone immediately, as she did, was the fruit of Kitchener's work.

Haig's part in all this was necessarily a minor one, in relation to the whole task – he was a Colonel still – but important. His duty was to modernize the war training of the Cavalry arm, an exercise which instantly plunged him into one of the most ferocious controversies of the day. As we have seen, the reputation of the Cavalry had not come well out of the South African War. Apart from some spectacular exploits under French, the Regular British regiments, officered mainly by the young lions of Society, and tending to believe that their chief function in war was 'to give tone to what would otherwise be a mere vulgar brawl', had found their traditions and training poor equipment against the Boer mounted riflemen. Since all the Boers were mounted, since they had given such a convincing demonstration of the potentiality of mobility combined with modern fire-power, and since every large army in Europe was known to have a formidable cavalry, the question of reforming the mounted arm assumed obvious priority. The knowledge that horsed cavalry was shortly to become obsolete should not blind us to the reality of the problem at that time. Some of the best civil and military brains in the country were rightly absorbed in it. Unfortunately, this being England, many of these excellent brains sought their solution in expedients and compromises which diverted attention from inner truths. One favourite theory was based on the 'Mounted Infantry' doctrine. Mounted Infantry units, drawn from existing infantry battalions, or raised as such, had been formed in numbers as the South African War progressed. Contingents from the Dominions, who generally proved to be a good match for the Boers, particularly favoured this title. In fact, of course, it is nonsense; by definition, an infantryman is a foot-soldier; the man with the horse is a cavalryman; he has a horse because it makes him more mobile, *and for no other reason*. In fact, the horse does not really matter: what does matter is the horse-*power*. The failure to understand this, stemming in large part at least from emotions about man's 'four-legged friends', did much to bedevil the progress of the tank. Even much later, during the 1939–1945 War and afterwards, the loud echo of 'Mounted Infantry' thinking may be discerned in the proliferation of special formations on which Field-Marshal Slim has sharply commented: 'The rush to form special forces arose from confused thinking on what were, or were not, normal operations of war. In one sense every operation of war is a special one . . . each has its particular requirements. Yet all are and have always been familiar operations of war; any standard unit should expect that, at some time or other, it may be called upon to engage in any of them. . . . This cult of special forces is as sensible as to form a Royal Corps of Tree Climbers and say that no soldier, who does not wear its green hat with a bunch of oak leaves stuck in it, should be expected to climb a tree.'

Haig, certainly, opposed the 'Mounted Infantry' school. The question, as he saw it, was one of training, of instilling true professional aptitude in the existing mounted arm – the Cavalry. We have seen how, in South Africa, he particularly noted what properly handled cavalry could do *dismounted*, both in attack and defence. Linked with their further capacity for shock action, and above all with their ability to exploit success by swift manoeuvre, this convinced him that well trained cavalry could be a decisive factor in war. What he aimed at was proficiency in *all* the functions of the arm, not just some of them: mounted riflemen, incapable of shock action or of pursuit, did not appeal to him, any more than '*arme blanche*' fanatics who were stuck to their saddles and could not shoot. It is at least possible that he may have had in his mind yet another lesson implanted by Colonel Henderson, with his Civil War studies at Camberley: the image of General Philip Sheridan's United States Cavalry, who could drive infantry off a position by fire-power, and disintegrate their fleeing remnants, sabre in hand. What is beyond doubt is that when war came in 1914, the British Cavalry was the only cavalry that *could* shoot, and that was prepared to get off its horses in order to do so. One of the first portents of this was when Cavalry regiments began winning musketry competitions in India.

Being trained by Haig was no joke. Charteris has described his method of inspection: 'It was a ruthless testing out of every phase of the life of the unit. . . . When the outdoor work was over there followed a most searching examination into the minutiae of administration. Nothing escaped his notice; no failure or shortcoming was allowed to pass without comment. Praise was scanty and very rare. The utmost that could be hoped for was that the Inspector-General should appear not dissatisfied.' But Haig was now forming definite ideas, not only about military training and professional matters, but about politics, and what the Army might be called upon to do as a result of them. 'The Cavalry of India will play a great part in warfare far beyond the frontiers of India', he would say. Old methods and old standards, in other words, would no longer suffice; above all, old men were a trouble to him. 'The subaltern and junior captain of the Indian Cavalry', he said, 'are the best of their rank in the Army. There is a sad falling off in the rank of Major, and the Commanding Officers are almost all past their work.'

Partly because of this weakness at the regimental level, and partly also because he was himself a fully trained Staff officer by now, Haig saw that a system based solely on inspection and on the necessarily spasmodic exercises that were permitted to the Army in peacetime would not do. He supplemented these activities by Staff Rides, or what would later be called 'Tewts' – Tactical Exercises without Troops. These were a novelty in India at that time, and one of which Haig made the fullest use. The proceedings and lessons of five of his Rides were published subsequently as a book called *Cavalry Studies*; if a great deal of the detail is now of purely academic interest, some of his general conclusions are enlightening. In the introduction he wrote: 'Certainly a knowledge of military history is all-important to an officer. In studying it we see the great masters at work. We learn from their experience and become acquainted with the difficulties to be encountered in applying principles. But such work contributes little to developing our powers of decision. On the other hand "War Games" and "Staff Rides" should be framed chiefly with the latter object.' This strikes the practical note which was the key to his method. Among other general observations of that kind by Haig, we find the following:

'Napoleon's constant preoccupation, as must be that of every commander in the field, was how to reduce the number of troops employed on matters of secondary importance, in order to increase the numbers available for the decisive battle.' In the form of the problem of the 'tail', this preoccupation reached vast proportions, both in the First and Second World Wars and in Korea.

'Military history teaches us that the whole question of cooperation with an ally is fraught with difficulties and danger. When the theatre of operation lies in the country of the ally, these difficulties increase, for war can rarely benefit the inhabitants on the spot, and ill feeling is certain to arise.' This prophetic statement was not arrived at by gazing into a crystal ball, but by hard thinking about strategy and politics ten years before the Great War began.

'. . . we must not forget that we are dealing with men of flesh and blood and nerves.' Haig never did forget; his tragedy was that he could so rarely say what he felt.

Two particular achievements, over and above what was accomplished at inspections or on Staff Rides, distinguished this tour of Haig's duty in India. The first of these, an extension of the Rides, was the formation of a permanent Cavalry School, at which officers could be constantly brought up to date with current trends. It is recalled that, at his first inspection of this establishment, Haig was astonished to see that a road in it was called 'Childers Road'. Erskine Childers's book, *War and the Arme Blanche*, had made him a champion of the 'Mounted Infantry' party. The Commandant of the Cavalry School explained the matter: 'Ah, sir, that road is a cul-de-sac, and leads to the cemetery.' Besides this work for the Cavalry, Haig was also concerned in the long-overdue creation of an Indian Staff College, one of the most valuable of Kitchener's acts. Approval for the College at Quetta had been given, and studies had commenced in a temporary building before Haig left India in 1906. A year earlier, planning his leave in Europe, he revealed in a light-hearted letter to his sister how his strategic ideas were developing: 'I see that you are still excusing yourself for assisting the enemy by travelling on German subsidized mail boats, alias commerce destroyers. I am going to travel home by the Messageries Maritimes steamer. . . . I shall be much better off in the French boat besides encouraging "l'entente cordiale".'

But the journey had for Haig a quite different significance, altogether apart from the Entente Cordiale and the growing German menace.

*   *   *   *

Haig's appointment as A.D.C. to the King during his period with the 17th Lancers had ripened his acquaintance with Edward VII into a friendship; they now corresponded regularly. Apart from its own satisfaction, this friendship had not so far brought Haig any notable benefit; he became a Major-General in 1904, having already been doing a General officer's work for a year. (There was no rank between Colonel and Major-General at that time; Major-Generals commanded brigades and Lieutenant-Generals had divisions in South Africa.) Apart from that and a C.V.O. he had gained nothing. Now, however, the King's favour brought an unlooked-for reward. Haig was invited to Windsor Castle for Ascot. Arriving on the Monday, he met at golf on the Thursday one of Queen Alexandra's Maids of Honour, Miss Dorothy Vivian. They played golf again together the next day, and on the Saturday, when the guests were due to leave, Haig suggested another game. As soon as they met on the course, Haig dismissed the caddies and proposed to Miss Vivian. She accepted, and they were married within a month, in the private chapel at Buckingham Palace. The briskness of these proceedings was naturally commented upon, but Haig's reply was: 'Why not? I have often made up my mind on more important problems than that of my own marriage in much less time.'

Yet it was far from being an unimportant matter. He had made a good choice. 'Lady Haig', says Charteris, 'fulfilled to perfection the difficult role that falls to the lot of the wife of a great man. She never interfered in official business, yet she was always there to help her husband. Her tact and intuition never failed. She was a discreet and sympathetic confidante and she strengthened his faith in his own power to overcome difficulties. She devoted every moment of her married life to her husband; and in the midst of all the heavy responsibilities which he was called upon to face she was never absent from his mind. . . . Marriage brought to Haig completeness.' It cannot be doubted that this is true; indeed, the very success of his marriage worked to some extent against him. As it continued, and children came (the first in 1907), it became more and more the exclusive focus of his emotional life. It mellowed him, certainly, but also offered to an inherently withdrawing nature a new private refuge and delight. This largely accounts for the absence of legends about Haig, and the accusations of aloofness. Always tidy-minded, he now tended to departmentalize his whole life, keeping quite private that part of it which was sentimental, and reserving for public view the outward aspect of a public man. It was not that he lacked emotions; it was that he formed the habit of keeping them to himself and the family circle – even emotions about the great public events on which he became engaged.

*   *   *   *

The next phase of Haig's life was decisive: it was a period during which he was drawn right to the centre of a ferment of change which possessed the whole nation, and the Army not least of its parts. The Parliament which resulted from the Liberal landslide of 1906 was the most eminent and intellectually formidable of this century. The uproars that accompanied the implementation of the Liberal platform overshadow all subsequent disputes; not since Peterloo and the militant days of Chartism has the threat of Civil War been so real as it became in the later part of the Liberal régime. In their early period, it was as though a great wind were sweeping through the land, blowing down all before it that was shaky and decayed of the Victorian legacy and the Edwardian dream. It is one of the great ironies that these statesmen, with all their profound ideas of social progress, and with all the brilliance and energy that they applied to carrying them out, should have been the ones to lead the country in the greatest disaster that has ever befallen it.

Of all the remarkable figures who came to the fore in the Liberal revival, one of the most considerable was Richard Burdon Haldane. Although he was already fifty years old in 1906, he was, and remained, as truly a twentieth-century person as any of the century's politicians. His work in Philosophy, with particular attention to linking it with Science; in Law, attempting to bring order into that vast and confused study; in Higher Education, playing a leading part in the foundation of London University and the Redbrick network; and in Army reform, was everywhere of lasting value for the growth of the body politic in modern times. Oddly enough, it was his work for the Army that was to bring him his most lasting fame; yet that was the very field for which his background and accomplishments seemed to fit him least.

Haldane has recorded how, when the Offices of State were being distributed, he said to Sir Henry Campbell-Bannerman: ' "What about the War Office?" "Nobody", answered Campbell-Bannerman, "will touch it with a pole." "Then give it to me. . . ." ' It sounds a strangely fortuitous beginning, but there could not have been a better choice. Beatrice Webb noted in her diary; '. . . the great coup is to get Haldane to take the War Office – the courtly lawyer with a great capacity for dealing with men and affairs, and a real understanding of the function of an expert, and skill in using him.' This was the heart of the matter: Haldane had the humility to learn from his advisers, and the strength of deep reason in interpreting what they told him.

The Office of Secretary of State for War in 1906 was without doubt one of the most taxing that could have been taken on by any man. It had this special feature, that while reform in it was as urgent as in any field of government, given the broadly pacific nature of the Liberal Party, such reform would benefit less from their crusading zeal than any other, and might, indeed, find it an obstruction. 'Army Estimates as in 1899!' was a popular Liberal slogan at that time. Equally, within the Army itself, there was an understandable degree of doubt and alarm at the prospect of another reformer at large. Mr. Arnold-Foster, Secretary of State in the Balfour Administration, had already fluttered the dovecots. He was a man who had thought and written much on military affairs; he had taken office with a number of fixed ideas, which he tried to put into practice. In 1903 he had launched the famous Esher Committee into an investigation of the War Office itself, with a view to beginning upon the organization of a General Staff, the lack of which had been one of the outstanding lessons of the South African War.

This committee of three, namely Lord Esher himself, Admiral Sir John Fisher and Sir George Clarke, had gone about their work in a manner so hasty and abrupt as almost to deserve the epithet 'hysterical'. Sir Henry Wilson wrote: 'Our days pass like nightmares. The Triumvirate are carrying on like madmen. This morning I was in Nick's[1] room talking things over with him, and his opinion is that all these sudden changes lead straight to chaos, when in walked Jimmy Grierson[2] and said *Esher* had ordered him up from Salisbury to take over Nick's office. Nick himself had not been informed, nor had he been told to hand over, and he called me to witness that he gave over the keys of secret boxes etc. to Grierson simply on the latter's word. This is most scandalous work. Gerald Ellison lunched with me and I impressed on him with all my power that this bull-headed way of proceeding will absolutely ruin the scheme, which in itself has some excellent points.'

Sir Gerald Ellison[3] was Secretary to the Esher Committee. It is evident that their methods made an unfavourable impression on him, for he relates that when Lord Esher asked him, at the end of 1905, whether he was willing to be Haldane's Principal Private Secretary, 'I asked at once whether Mr. Haldane had any cut and dried plan of his own for the Army, and Lord Esher assured me that the new Secretary of State's mind was destitute of any preconceived notions at all about military affairs. This being so I said I would gladly do what I could to help him. . . .' The soldiers on the Army Council were equally quickly reassured; at their first meeting with him, says Haldane, they said 'that they all felt that, without going into details, they would like to have some general idea of the reforms which I thought of proposing in Parliament. My reply was that I was as a young and blushing virgin just united to a bronzed warrior, and that it was not expected by the public that any result of the union should appear until at least nine months has passed.'

If Haldane revealed in this reply the quality of tact which lay at the root of all his achievement, he was, nevertheless, being somewhat less than frank. Ellison, who was to be his chief assistant, met him on December 11th, 1905. 'Before the end of 1905', he wrote, 'I accompanied the Secretary of State to Scotland where he spent the next three or four weeks on electioneering business. During the daytime he was engaged in canvassing and it was not till after dinner that we got busy with military affairs and then we were often at it till one or two a.m. Hour after hour we would walk backwards and forwards in a big billiard room, Mr. Haldane on one side of the table, smoking the best cigars procurable, I on the other. . . . Before we left Scotland the conception of an Expeditionary Force and of a Territorial Army organized and administered by the County Associations had been embodied in a memorandum addressed to the Army Council. As Mr. Haldane's ideas gradually expanded during 1906 other memoranda followed, but throughout

1. Field-Marshal Sir William Nicholson, who became the first Chief of Imperial General Staff in 1908.
2. Lieutenant-General Sir James Grierson.
3. Then Lieutenant-Colonel; later Lieutenant-General.

there was no departure from the original conception evolved during the month of January.' This was an astonishing feat; the two main heads of the now historic Haldane Reforms gripped and outlined within a month – the long-overdue Expeditionary Force which alone could enable Britain to take effective part in a major modern war, and the second-line Army which alone could enable her to maintain that part. Together with the rounding-off of the General Staff system, these measures absorbed the whole of Haldane's tour of office, but at the end of it Britain had a modern Army for the first time. This was not, indeed, what the Liberal Party had intended; in 1906 their main wish was to reduce the Army Estimates below the current figure of £28,000,000. But, remarks Ellison dryly, 'It was entirely due to Mr. Haldane's plans having matured so rapidly that his Bill became the main plank in the Government's programme in 1907. Radical members were waiting impatiently for far-reaching measures of social reform, and pretty disgusted they were to be fobbed off with a military problem in which they took very little interest. The other Departments of State had been too slow in getting off the mark.'

It was one thing to outline great measures of reform and modernization in a billiard-room in Scotland; it was another matter to work out all the details and push the scheme through. For this Haldane would need the help of the right kind of men. He has told us who they were: 'The men who co-operated in advising me were Ellison, Harris,[1] Haig, Ewart,[2] and Nicholson.' Haig was back in India when he received Haldane's summons in April, 1906. 'It is a very great honour', he wrote, 'to be sent for at this critical time to help to decide the future organization of the Empire's forces. So I ought to be thought very lucky.' The luck was on both sides. 'Haig', says Haldane, 'had a first-rate General Staff mind. When he arrived in London he grasped the situation completely and gave invaluable guidance in the fashioning of both the Regular first line and the Territorial second line.' The post which Haig entered was called Director of Military Training, but the term was inter-preted in no narrow sense; it involved the application of General Staff methods to a wide field of the Army's activities. Finance, for example, was a subject with which Haig was much concerned during his early War Office days.

A note which Haig wrote to Ellison in October, 1906, reveals the basic preoccupations which guided his work throughout: 'Our object in my opinion should be to start a system of finance suited to the "supposed situa-

1. Sir Charles Harris, Permanent Head of the Financial Department of the War Office.
2. Lieutenant-General Spencer Ewart, who became Director of Military Operations under Haldane.

tion", i.e. a great war requiring the whole resources of the nation to bring it to a successful end. Even if the proposed system costs more in peace, it should be inaugurated provided that it is more practical in war. The Swiss system seems to me to be exactly what is wanted "to root the army in the people".... The Germans seem to be going ahead in every direction with the utmost self-assurance and energy, so that the crisis is sure of coming before many years are over.'

'The whole resources of the nation'; ' "to root the army in the people" ': these concepts have been made familiar to modern readers by two World Wars, but in 1906 they were revolutionary. Haig, of course, was not the only man to see the needs of the future, but he was one of the first, and one of the most practical. Bitter controversy surrounded the whole question of Army expansion in time of war. South Africa had shown how necessary it was to have a thought-out system – but what? All the formidable prestige of Lord Roberts, backed by an able group of writers and thinkers, was thrown behind the idea of Compulsory Service on the Continental model; it was hard to see how else Britain could hope to operate on the same battlefields as Continental powers. In the end, as we know, it had to come; but in 1906 the short, practical answer to the Conscriptionists was, as Ellison has said, that: 'The mention of compulsory service would have spelt political suicide to any Minister who proposed it.' Haldane, a politician to his fingertips, definitely set his mind against it. The question was, to hit upon a realistic alternative, and carry it through: that alternative was the rationalization of what were broadly called the Reserve forces, the Militia, the Yeomanry, the Volunteers, into one complete organization, cast in the image of the Regular Army, and able, after a short interval, both to replace it in garrison or Home Defence work and to supplement it in the field. The working out of the details of this tremendous innovation was Haig's first and perhaps greatest duty at the War Office.

The original Territorial scheme adopted by Haldane was for a second line Army of no less than twenty-eight divisions with a corresponding number of Yeomanry Cavalry brigades, the whole to be fully equipped with Artillery, Engineers and all ancillary services. Mainly for financial reasons, this concept had to be cut in half; Haig opposed the cut, and, as we are aware, even the full number of Territorial divisions proposed would not, in the event, have been enough. They would, however, have gone a long way towards re-dressing the fatal British military weakness in the early part of the World War. But despite his misgivings, Haig threw himself vigorously into the building of the cut-down Territorial force prescribed. His essentially practical nature disposed him to make all that could be made with the tools and materials provided, rather than howl to the moon for what could not be.

Here he was in distinct opposition to some other Regular soldiers who, from the first, affected to despise Haldane's new Army, and even went to the lengths of trying to reduce its effectiveness. Ellison tells us that Haig 'at once tackled the organization of the Territorial Force in detail, laying stress on its being an Army complete in every respect. Certain senior officers had taken exception to mobile artillery being included in the Territorial Force on the ground that citizen soldiers could never master the mysteries of the gunners' art. This argument left Haig quite cold. After full consideration of the matter and consultation with the younger school of Royal Artillery officers, he wrote to Mr. Haldane as follows: "I deprecate any change in the policy of creating a second line Army complete in *all* arms and services." '

The opposition was stiff; Lord Roberts, himself an artilleryman, asserted that the Territorial Artillery would be a danger to the country. Vested interests in the Militia and the Volunteers opposed the transformation of their units, some of which had origins clothed in all the tradition that is so dear to the British mind. But Haldane and Haig stood firm, and their will prevailed. Haig was the chairman of the organizing committee that did the work; Ellison, a member of it, wrote: 'On this committee and on the work of his own Department the gradual evolution of the Territorial Force as we know it today mainly depended. In saying this I in no way wish to detract from the part Mr. Haldane himself played in the enormously important changes effected during his administration at the War Office, but this I do say unhesitatingly that, without Haig, Mr. Haldane would have been hard put to it to elaborate a practical scheme of reorganization in the first instance, or to drive the scheme through to its logical conclusion.'

At first, the Territorial Army question was largely one of organization; later, when the Force was on its feet, it became one of training also. In this field, for Territorials and Regulars alike, Haig's work was of tremendous importance. South Africa had exposed the want of a general doctrine of war in the British Army, a system of thought and organization, laid down by a General Staff, to which every officer would automatically conform, and *would be known* to be conforming. In large-scale modern armies, this is an essential prerequisite; so far from stifling initiative it actually promotes that quality, as the Germans had revealed in 1870, by freeing commanders at all levels from doubts about their colleagues. General De Pree, who was on Haig's staff at this time, has left an account of Haig's policy in action, in the teeth of reactionary opposition to such an un-British concept. 'The fight was finally won', says De Pree, 'over the question of *Field Service Regulations Part II*. This was a manual of the system of War Administration and Organization, for which there was nothing laid down up to this time . . . the Q.M.G., or someone, had always baulked its coming out. Haig determined to push it through, and put it down for discussion at the General Staff Conference at the Staff College in January (1907). After much discussion one of the Members of the Army Council got up and in a most amusing speech poured ridicule on the whole thing. The assembly was greatly amused till Haig rose with a face of intense anger and, in a cutting voice, said "If General X—— will tell us what we ought to do instead of pulling everything to pieces, we shall get on much better. Let us have some system to start with, and if it is not perfect we can improve it." General X—— despite his seniority and high position made no rejoinder. . . . After this there was very little opposition to the reforms of the General Staff, and the Army which fought the Great War was administered and organized on the lines laid down in this book. . . .'

The final value of this achievement, when it came to the entirely novel problem of raising an army of millions, need hardly be stated; coupled with the similar approach to Operations in *Field Service Regulations Part I*, it constitutes a major, but almost entirely forgotten contribution to later victory. A revealing interchange on this subject took place between Haig and Henry Wilson, then C.I.G.S., in 1918, when Haig was on the full tide of triumph.

Sept. 19th, 1918.

'My General,
'Well done! You must be a famous General!

Henry.'

Sept. 20th 1918.

'My dear Henry,
'Very many thanks for your kind little note of yesterday. No, certainly not! I am not nor am I likely to be a "famous general". For that must we not have pandered to Repington and the Gutter Press? But we have a surprisingly large number of *very capable* generals. Thanks to these gentlemen and to their "sound military knowledge built up by study and practice until it has become an instinct" and to a steady adherence to the principles of our Field Service Regulations Part I are our successes to be chiefly attributed.'

With the Expeditionary Force organized, the Territorial Army in being, and General Staff principles being applied to both, there remained one further field in which a burst of Haldane's cerebral energy was urgently required – the welding together of all the Armed Forces of the Empire into a coherent whole. The Minister turned to Haig and Nicholson to work out proposals whereby this might be achieved; he tells us: 'When this scheme was completed, there was held in London in 1909 a Dominion Conference on military affairs. The last Conference had failed so far as these matters were concerned because of the desire of the old War Office to centralize authority. But we were now able to say that the Dominions and India could remain completely autonomous. All we asked of them was that they should organize on our pattern local sections of their own of the General Staff, and should appoint to them officers who had a General Staff training at headquarters and in the Staff College. . . . Haig worked out the details of the plan, and Nicholson embodied them in admirable drafts for the assistance of the Colonial and India Offices. I could not have had finer help than I got from these two.' Haldane himself contributed at the Conference a speech in his most winning vein, with the result that the proposals were found entirely acceptable by the Dominion delegates – most of whom, it has to be added, were enthusiastic about setting their military houses in order. Haig noted in his diary: 'Mr. Haldane's speech was very well received. . . . His motion was also agreed to. The latter practically creates the Imperial General Staff and so puts 50% on to the value of the General Staff.'

And so three notable years of accomplishment drew to an end. Haig had made his mark once and for all in the group of what Haldane called 'young and modern officers'. Shortly after taking office, Haldane had told the House of Commons:

'The men one comes across, the new school of young officers, entitled to the appellation of men of science just as much as engineers or chemists, were to me a revelation; and the whole question of the organization of the Army is fraught with an interest which, I think, is not behind that of the study of any other scientific problem. A new school of officers has arisen since the South African War, a thinking school of officers who desire to see the full efficiency which comes from new organization and no surplus energy running to waste.'

The essence of all these reforms was a looking forward, not backward. In his perception of the nature of the future enemy; in his grasp of the need for a citizen army; in his appreciation of the potential role of overseas forces; in his application of considered General Staff principles to the whole; and not least in the patient and untiring toil which he freely gave, Haig had been one of Haldane's most useful assistants. This was not without cost to himself. Haldane's methods of work were not unlike those of Sir Winston Churchill in the Second World War, and the strain upon his military advisers was similar to that suffered at times by Lord Alanbrooke. Haldane, too, was a great man for after-dinner work, which might go on into the small hours, on a well-filled stomach. Duff Cooper remarks: 'To Haldane such work was the breath of life, such hours were habitual and the discussion of difficult problems to the accompaniment of continual cigars was the pleasantest way of passing the time. But Haig did not talk easily and did not smoke at all. He was accustomed to early hours, fresh air and much exercise. It is not surprising, therefore, that after a year and a half of such strenuous labour his health gave way and during April and May 1908 he was seriously ill.' This was one of the few grave illnesses of his life; but the effort was not without its reward. Replying to a memorandum which Haig sent him after leaving the War Office, Haldane said: 'It gives me the sense of comfort which comes from seeing that there are in our Army those who are thinking out military science with a closeness which is not surpassed in the great military schools of thought on the Continent. You have cause to look back on three memorable years' work with satisfaction, and to say to yourself "*quorum pars magna fui*".'

4

The End of Peace

HAIG LEFT the War Office at the end of 1909. In both his next appointments, as Chief of Staff in India until 1912, and thereafter as Commander-in-Chief at Aldershot, his main preoccupation was to prepare the troops and officers under him for the conflict which he knew to be in store. The practical task that faced him (and the small group of cognizant, forward-looking senior officers like French, Wilson and Grierson) was to instil the spirit of the Haldane reforms into the body of the Army itself; to effect upon the limbs and sinews something of the cure that had already been performed upon the brain. This is, of course, a process that takes time, and in the event it proved that there was not time enough. The pre-1914 British Army, although transformed out of all recognition from South African War standards, was still stubborn material, and five years was a very short space indeed in which to change old traditional habits and develop the new class of officer that was needed if Haldane's work was to reach full fruition.

Nowhere was resistance to change more stubborn than in India. Even Kitchener's driving energy, although it had brought about the resignation of a Viceroy, had not succeeded in reducing the military administration in that country to sanity. He had obtained a fusion of the roles of Commander-in-Chief and Military Member of the Viceroy's Council which, while it was an improvement on previous discords, and workable by a man as forceful and ruthless as himself, nevertheless produced anomalies of its own. Not only did the Commander-in-Chief have a dual function, but so did his principal Staff officers, who were Heads of divisions in the Army Department. Charteris aptly describes the working of the system: 'As principal staff officers they had direct access to the Commander-in-Chief and could act in his name; as heads of divisions in the Army Department they could only approach the Army Member through the Secretary, and receive the Army Member's orders through him. As the Commander-in-Chief and the Army Member were one and the same person, and as the Army Secretary was secretary to the Government of India, with direct access to the Viceroy, it is easy to realize the confusion and friction that inevitably resulted. . . . Cases were not unknown of the Commander-in-Chief disagreeing with himself as Army Member.' Haig described the whole thing as the 'canonization of duality'; by any name, it was a discouraging context in which to prepare for modern war. Haig attacked the system vigorously, as others had done before, and as yet others were to do later; but so solidly entrenched was the disorder that only at the fringes could he make any real impression. His real work lay elsewhere, in guiding the minds of officers in India towards the problems of fighting a European enemy.

For Haig himself, as well as for the officers whom he was seeking to instruct, the next two years were filled by the most intense study of war. Once again he used the Staff Tour as his chief instrument of instruction, even going so far as to send out his first scheme for a Tour in India before he had left London. Each of these Tours, says Charteris, 'as carried out under Haig's directions, was very far from being a formal exercise: it required an immense amount of preliminary work. He himself sketched an outline of the particular lessons in military teaching which he wished to enforce. Every detail of the actual operations of the army, which the Staff Tour officers were assumed to be directing in the field, was most carefully prepared prior to the Tour. All the minutiae of administration during the period of mobilization and concentration were worked out with the same completeness and fullness as had been devoted to the preparation of the plans for the Expeditionary Force during Haig's time at the War Office.' One of his main objects, as Haig himself stated, was to free the minds of Staff officers, a batch at a time, from the preoccupations of routine which could so easily supplant in hard-worked professionals the steady contemplation of fundamental problems. But above all what he was concerned with was the concentration of their minds upon the future enemy. It was for that reason that he took the somewhat extraordinary step, for a general serving in India, of instituting a close study of German Army organization, comparing it with that of Britain and India, and comparing German and French strategic doctrines.

'Each of the Staff Tours', says Charteris, 'was devoted to a definite phase of fighting against a European enemy. . . .' Haig's own ideas on war were now reaching maturity, and these exercises gave him the opportunity of bringing them to precision. His belief in the inevitable phasing of operations never left him, and was to guide all his strategy in the struggle ahead. Following the teaching of great masters before him, he pronounced that there would be four definite phases to pass through, before victory could be expected:

1. The manoeuvre for position.
2. The first clash of battle.
3. The wearing-out fight of varying duration.
4. The eventual decisive blow.

He was not to know just how long that third phase, which consumed the strength and man-power of the Allies for some three and a half years, would be; but he never doubted that it *would* be long, and he never doubted that it would be hard. As we have seen,[1] as early as 1906, he was writing to Ellison that 'the whole resources of the nation' would be required to bring the future war to a successful end. As regards the second phase, his prescience was even more exact, for one whole Tour was given up to the problem of a small force facing an overwhelming enemy, and to the questions whether it should attempt to give battle or should disengage itself. This was useful training, but we shall see that it had its dangers.[2]

As prescient was Haig's final Tour in 1911, in which he directed attention to the problem of sending a contingent from India to Europe. Unfortunately, this was also rank heresy. The assumption then was that the Indian Army would never be required to serve beyond its frontiers, and so touchy was the Indian Government on this subject that the Viceroy even informed the Commander-in-Chief that, in his opinion, the very study of foreign military organizations was unnecessary and dangerous. This applied even to the ever-present possibility of war with Afghanistan, and when Haig ordered a study of that problem, maps had to be made giving Egyptian names to Afghan localities. It may be imagined, when it became known through a leakage in London that Haig had also ordered a study of an Indian Expeditionary Force to Europe, what the consternation was. The information rapidly came to the ears of the Secretary of State for India, Lord Morley. Morley, in whom pacifism was a deeply ingrained principle, and who, despite his great intellect, could never fully understand the need for military preparations in peacetime, was much incensed. He telegraphed to the Viceroy, who immediately ordered not only that work should stop at once on Haig's scheme, but that work already done should be destroyed. The officer chiefly concerned was Hamilton Gordon, later a Corps Commander of distinction. Haig passed the Viceroy's orders to him, but, Hamilton Gordon said later, 'There was a look in Haig's eye which made me realize that he would not regard any deviation from rigid adherence . . . with undue severity.' In fact, copies of the plans were preserved, with the result that an Indian Army Corps was able to appear in France before the end of 1914. The experiment did not turn out to

1. See p. 41.
2. See p. 88.

be a great success – in the end. But there were precious few other reinforcements available at that time, and the roll-call on the Menin Gate at Ypres testifies to the service that the Indians did in many critical hours. Similar work was also done, under Haig's orders, on the preparation of expeditions to the Persian Gulf and to East Africa. The disasters and setbacks that occurred in both these theatres were a direct result of ignoring this preparatory work, and failing to follow it through. Modern war can be merciless to improvisation.

All these efforts (besides his attempts to streamline Staff procedure) bore directly upon future events. Yet more important, in the light of Haig's own future, was the crystallization of his philosophy of war. This was far advanced by the end of his last Staff Tour, and the essence of it was flexibility, a refusal to become committed to any of the appealing doctrines which swept like crusades through the General Staffs of Europe. In his summary of the 1911 Tour, Haig wrote: 'No plan of operations can with any safety include more than the first collision with the enemy's force. . . . Plans aiming far beyond the strategical deployment and first collision have been submitted. Such speculations may become harmful if they are allowed to hamper the judgment as the campaign progresses, and to impede initiative. Commanders in war have been known to become so imbued with an idea as never to think of any other contingency; and what we wish for we like to hope and believe. . . .'

Turning to a deeper question, Haig added: 'Certain critics of the British General Staff and of our regulations have recently argued that a doctrine is lacking. While the German General Staff preaches the doctrine of envelopment, and the French General Staff advocates a large general reserve with a view to a concentrated blow at a decisive point of the enemy's battle order, the critics urge that the British General Staff hesitates to publish and to teach a clear line of action. The reasoning seems to be that unless some such definite doctrine is decided and inculcated in peace, action in war will be hesitating and mistakes will be made. The critics seem to lose sight of the true nature of war, and of the varied conditions under which the British Army may have to take the field. It is neither necessary nor desirable that we should go further than what is so clearly laid down in our regulations. If we go further, we run the risk of tying ourselves by a doctrine that may not always be applicable, and we gain nothing in return. An army trained to march long distances, to manoeuvre quickly, and to fight with the utmost determination will be a suitable instrument in the hands of a competent commander, whether the situation is to be solved by "envelopment" or "penetration." ' This tactical flexibility (not to be confused with strategic opportunism) became Haig's settled view. When war broke out, he had not departed from it by one jot. India was, in truth, the finishing school of his military education.

Service in India which, in common with so many British officers, had by
now taken up a considerable part of Haig's career, ended for him in February,
1912. A few months earlier, a specially decoded telegram had been brought
to him late one evening. It was from Lord Haldane, and it read: 'Would it be
agreeable to you to be appointed to the Aldershot Command?' Haig's immediate and characteristic comment was: 'That could have waited until the
morning.' Nevertheless, his acceptance was prompt, and his pleasure was real
and understandable, for as Charteris says: 'He was still in his fiftieth year, with
barely twenty-seven years' service to his credit. At a time when most of his
contemporaries were still awaiting the command of their battalions or
regiments, he was taking over the greatest active command that Great
Britain had to offer, and had been selected in preference to many distinguished
soldiers senior to himself, including Sir Herbert Plumer, Sir James Grierson
and Sir J. Wolfe-Murray.' A captain at thirty-six; a lieutenant-general at
fifty: the start had been slow, and at times, no doubt, disappointing and
frustrating, but now he had made up for it with a vengeance. At each stage,
merit had been the decisive factor: his impression on Sir Evelyn Wood had
brought his attachment to the Omdurman Expedition; his good work in the
Sudan had brought a valuable appointment in South Africa; his work in
South Africa had brought him into a wider regard, and ultimately into
Haldane's notice; his performance with Haldane at the War Office now
brought him the Aldershot Command and the certainty of a leading role in
the Expeditionary Force. Its sailing, he knew, would not be long delayed;
before he left India, he told his personal staff that war in Europe was very
probable 'within three or four years'.

The Aldershot Command, the 1st and 2nd Infantry Divisions and the 1st
Cavalry Brigade, was the only formed Army Corps in the British Empire in
peace time. In war it would immediately become 'I Corps' of the Expeditionary Force; there was thus no distraction for Haig, as there might have been
in some garrison appointment (e.g. Ireland), from the intensive preparation
for European war that he had so solidly begun in India. The whole of his time
at Aldershot was spent in perfecting the Army Corps for its future role. There
were obvious advantages in having his mass of Regular troops of all arms
under his hand; this was, in fact, the one and only post which gave a British
officer the chance of handling troops in mass, and it was an important experience for Haig, one that he had so far lacked. On the other hand, it was more
difficult to use his favourite method of the Staff Tour for instruction, if only
because there were fewer Staff officers now available to him than in India,
and because they were all consequently much more tied to their daily duties.

At first, too, he encountered some resistance, if not hostility; this was
partly due to the accident of following an extremely popular and able officer,

General Smith-Dorrien (the British normally react against newcomers), and partly to the resentment caused by his importation of a small personal staff from India. These were his Assistant Military Secretary, Captain John Charteris, whose influence upon his life was to become somewhat *grise*, and who later wrote his biography, and his A.D.C., Captain H. D. Baird. He and they together were at first known as the 'Hindu Invasion'. Haig undoubtedly suffered too, at first, from sheer lack of acquaintance with many of the officers in the Command, through having spent all his recent years either overseas or in the close confines of the War Office. He overcame this difficulty, by degrees, through the expedient of small dinner parties at Government House. These permitted him a more personal and intimate touch than the larger entertainments which Smith-Dorrien had favoured. 'There were not many of those who served under Haig', says Charteris, 'who did not at one time or another have an opportunity of making themselves known to the "Chief" within his own home.' Within two years – all that remained of peace – he undoubtedly imbued the Army Corps with a formidable corporate spirit, and his officers with a particular loyalty to himself that lasted throughout the War.

What was the foundation of that loyalty? What was the nature of the man, poised now on the very brink of the great business which, more than anything else, has determined the course of the twentieth century? A quality which emerges with special emphasis from this period of his life is repose. This had both its professional and personal aspects. Professionally, he knew what he was about, and where he was going; he was not distracted; he knew he was going to war, and against whom. This lent to his ideas and his actions a focus and a composure that was bound to come across to all his associates. Furthermore, he had nothing to eat his heart out about; his swift rise in the past ten years had brought him to one of the Army's most coveted assignments. Also, as it turned out, it enabled him to achieve a brief but important spell of personal rest and happiness before the storm.

Charteris, a member of his household, wrote: 'For the first time in his married life he was settled in a real home. Government House, if not palatial, was spacious, and in those pre-war days it stood in country surroundings. Happy in the reunion with his family, Haig set himself to the just admixture of the life of a serving officer and a country gentleman. His private means, though not great, were sufficient to enable him to meet the demands on his income. He entertained frequently, but not extravagantly. . . . Golf replaced polo as his chief means of physical exercise. His attack on the citadel of golf was characteristic. He spared no pains to conquer its difficulties. He was determined to succeed. He took lessons from a professional. He practised assiduously. Each stroke was treated as a separate and all-important problem. He was not content until he felt that he had acquired the utmost proficiency within his scope. His ball never left the fairway. His play was as consistent as that of Colonel Bogey himself. If his official handicap was never very low, he was a most difficult opponent to beat. . . . The days passed evenly. The early hours of the morning he spent on horseback, supervising the training of the units of his command: when the inspection was over, he would indulge in a sharp gallop across country and took a mischievous pleasure in evading the staff officer and escort who accompanied him. . . . At eleven o'clock he reached his office at Army Headquarters and worked there until lunch-time. From lunch to tea was play-time – either golf, or tennis, as the days grew warmer – or sometimes he preferred the role of onlooker and watched the games of some section of the Command. After tea two hours were devoted to reading, and this brought his day's work to a close. The hours after dinner were spent with his household, which comprised, in addition to his family, his immediate personal staff, his military secretary and his A.D.C.s. There were the usual number of official dinners to officers in his Command – generally two each week.'

Charteris writes as one who developed an immense admiration and affection for his 'Chief', but not as one who was blind to faults in him. Naturally, these existed. With regard to Haig's tremendous future responsibilities, two deserve to be mentioned. First, there is the question of mental texture. Armies are not, on the whole, and certainly were not at that time, institutions calculated to broaden and enliven the mind. Haig's War Office experience and his high position in India made him more fortunate than many in this respect; at least he had felt the stimulus of contact with large events, and large men. But his own bent of mind was towards order, method, precision, all valuable qualities, tending towards depth of thought, itself also a valuable quality (and rare), but tending away from breadth. Haig's military studies were deep and voracious, not only in English, but also in French and German, both of which languages were a labour to him, though he did not shrink from them on that account. These military studies were not counterbalanced by others of anything approaching equivalent depth. His absolute lack of interest in politics, while it freed him from the partisan prejudices that disfigured some officers (and well-nigh wrecked the career of Henry Wilson, for example), cannot be considered as other than a serious defect. Bound, as he was, and as he intended, to play a significant part in affairs of state, he owed those affairs something more than the perfunctory attention that he paid them. 'He listened to the conversation of politicians with momentary interest,' says Charteris, 'but it was the same interest that he would take in an article on ancient history; he had no concern as to the outcome of their actions and activities.' It was the same with other subjects. 'Haig's reading was varied but not deep. He had strangely little learning; his military work absorbed him, and he only glanced at other subjects, never studied them. His favourite reading was the monthly reviews; he read few books and never a single novel. . . . He had not a critical mind. An article in a review was accepted by him as a final standard. His mental attitude in his miscellaneous reading was much the same as that of a theatregoer on a first night: he would be interested, his attention for the time being would be engaged, and he would store extracts in his memory, but no profound impression was made, and he was never impelled to delve deeper into the subject.' Looking into what the future held for him, it is clear enough that this single-minded concentration on his profession, which set him apart all through the War, and was the source of so much of his strength, also worked against him. He may, in a way, be compared to a scientist, engrossed in his laboratory; the outside world becomes a shadow-play; one day the scientist cries 'Eureka!'; but what a job it is to make people listen and understand.

Haig's second large defect, which we have already noted, and which un-doubtedly fed upon this single-mindedness, was in this very matter of causing people to listen and understand. Communication did not become easier to him as be became older. There are many anecdotes which illustrate this. There was the occasion of the prize-giving at the inter-regimental cross-country race, for example. Haig addressed the winning team with these words: 'I congratulate you on your running. You have run very well. I hope you will run as well in the presence of the enemy.' This was comic, but did not matter very much; and on another occasion the same inability to express himself actually worked to the advantage of the cause that he was upholding. A more eloquent general, at a Staff conference, had made a witty, polished, but distinctly unhelpful speech. Haig was enraged; he rose to reply, but all he could find to say was: 'You old destructor!' His evident passion and sincerity served him well; as he sat down abruptly, he won a burst of applause.

At other times his inarticulateness could be damaging. The manoeuvres of 1912 were not a shining hour for Haig. His opponent was General Grierson, an officer of great talent, generally regarded as Haig's most notable rival for advancement. Largely through his intelligent use of the still infant Air Service, Grierson succeeded in outmanoeuvring Haig. Consequently the latter's speech at the final conference in Trinity College, Cambridge, to be delivered before the King as well as the Army's most senior officers and the University's dignitaries, was a matter of some delicacy. Haig, as usual, had thought the whole thing out, and prepared it carefully. But for some un-fathomable reason, on an impulse, he abandoned his carefully prepared reasoning, and attempted to extemporize. The result was utter disaster. Charteris writes: 'In the effort he became totally unintelligible and unbearably dull. The University dignitaries soon fell fast asleep. Haig's friends became more and more uncomfortable; only he himself seemed totally unconscious of his failure. A listener, without other and deeper knowledge of the ability and personality of the Aldershot Commander-in-Chief, could not but have left the conference with the impression that Haig had neither ability nor military learning. Fortunately the men in responsible positions knew better. Those who were present at Cambridge had little difficulty in later years in realizing why it was that politicians, who are apt to judge men more by their gifts of speech than by their deeds, found it difficult to appreciate Haig's real worth.'

This is a matter so central to Haig's story that it may be as well to anticipate events again. Haig, of course, was not the only inarticulate general in our history. In his own generation there were many, two notable examples being Field-Marshals Allenby and Robertson; an example from later times was Field-Marshal Wavell. But Charteris is right in pointing out the serious effect that this blemish can have, particularly when dealing with politicians. Lloyd George, for example, wrote in his *War Memoirs*, referring to Haig: 'Fluency is not a proof – nor a disproof – of ability, but lucidity of speech is unquestionably one of the surest tests of mental precision. . . . Lucidity of mind ensures lucidity of expression. Power and light go together and are generated by the same machine. . . . In my experience a confused talker is never a clear thinker.'

Lloyd George was both a lawyer and a House of Commons man, as well as being one of the outstanding orators in the history of our tongue; it was not unnatural that he should think in this way. But, as Charteris says, 'men in responsible positions knew better'. Haldane, for example, was also a fine speaker, a House of Commons man, and before that an advocate of the very highest distinction; he was also a man with an extraordinarily well-organized intellect. J. A. Spender has given us this picture of Haldane dealing with the problem of un-speech: 'I have a memory of Haldane in respectful talk with a tongue-tied, verbally incoherent, but extremely able soldier. How patiently he worked at him, how skilfully he brought up the buried treasure, without breaking any of it, with what goodwill they parted, and what mutual desire to meet again! Haldane was in all these respects an extraordinarily modest man, and entirely free from that worst vice of politicians of putting the dialectically unaccomplished in the wrong when they are essentially in the right. He knew the value of the able inarticulate and could never be imposed on by voluble superficiality.'

There is one final matter to be considered about Haig, a defect and a quality too, linked with what has been said. Partly because of his professional concentration, partly because of his inability to communicate widely, he tended to lean very much upon his intimates. These, naturally, were generally his staff or his immediate subordinates. Neither category would feel themselves in a strong position to argue with him, and having no dialectical proficiency, he felt no inclination to seek debate. One detects in him a certain gaucheness in relations with those who were his superiors or equals in rank – though this did not preclude real friendships. Grierson, for example, was counted as a friend; Sir John French, now C.I.G.S., was conscious of a loan from Haig of £2,000, dating as far back as 1899. But, in general, Haig's personal relations, outside his family, were only developed warmly with men who were constantly around him, his juniors. To them he was unfailingly loyal, and they, without exception, to him. These men, who truly understood him, and what he was after, who could 'interpret' him, admired him deeply; the troops admired him too, detecting in him, instinctively, the essential quality of strength of character – but their admiration was necessarily at a remove. In the space of two years I Corps had become a very remarkable military organization. It would not be too much to call it a 'band of brothers'. It is a major attribute of leadership to imbue a large body of men with this spirit. As the war came nearer, month by month, the confidence of I Corps in 'the Chief' continued to grow; some of them, indeed, had begun to think of the appellation as having wider meaning than simply 'the Chief at Aldershot'. He, for his part, developed an unstinting admiration and affection for his Command. Concerning himself, he had no doubts.

* * * *

The year in which Haldane summoned Haig back from India marked the last significant milestone on the road to total war: it was the year of the Agadir crisis. Just as Munich gave Britain a short breathing space – time for one last flurried review of her defences – before the Second World War, the Agadir incident in 1911 concentrated attention on war as an immediate prospect, with the difference that the longer interval gave more time for final preparation. It also drew attention to certain grave omissions in the preparations already made. These had, nevertheless, been strikingly wide in their scope, and very far-sighted. It is a remarkable historical irony that the Liberal Administration, despite the deep veins of Radicalism and pacifism that ran through the party, the absolute aversion to militarism in all forms that possessed so many of its members, should have been the one to have prepared for war more logically and more thoroughly than any other at any time.

'Our policy', Lord Hankey says, 'may have been good or bad; there may be room for argument on this. But there are two criticisms to which Asquith's Government is not open – that it had no policy or that its policy was not arrived at after the most thorough investigation.' The terms of reference of all the investigations carried out by Asquith's Government were laid down before its time, in the first Report of the Esher Committee, issued in 1904. 'The British Empire', stated the Report, 'is pre-eminently a great Naval, Indian and Colonial Power. There are, nevertheless, no means of co-ordinating defence problems, for dealing with them as a whole, for defining the proper functions of the various elements, and for ensuring that, on the one hand, peace preparations are carried out upon a consistent plan, and, on the other hand, that, in times of emergency, a definite war policy, based upon solid data, can be formulated.'

To meet the need stated in the Esher Report, the Committee of Imperial Defence was set up by Mr. (later Lord) Balfour; for this act, and the con-tinuous personal interest which he took in the Committee's work (Lord Hankey tells us that 'In his last two years of office he did not miss one of the sixty meetings') if for nothing else, Lord Balfour deserves the most respectful remembrance. Asquith followed in his footsteps, and under him Enquiry followed Enquiry until, as he himself wrote: 'It would not be an unjust claim to say that the Government had by [1909] investigated the whole ground covered by a possible war with Germany – the naval position; the possibilities of a blockade; the invasion problem; the continental problem; the Egyptian problem.'

The key Enquiry of them all concerned the question of Invasion, prompted by Lord Roberts's vehement campaign for National Service, and his warnings of imminent peril. This Enquiry took place in 1908, and reached a number of conclusions, of which the essential was the first: 'That so long as our naval supremacy is assured against any reasonably probable combination of Powers, invasion is impracticable.' This was the triumph of the 'Blue Water' school over the 'Blue Funk' school. But the value of the Enquiry went much further than this simple (though profound) statement; as Lord Hankey says, it 'focused the attention of our statesmen and the naval and military authorities, on one of the most important problems which they would have to face in the event of war with Germany. It defined the respec-tive responsibilities of the Admiralty and War Office, and laid down the broad lines of policy on which their plans would have to be based. It gave a clear indication of the role to be fulfilled by the Territorial Force, and pro-vided a basis for its mobilization plans for Home Defence, which was at once adopted by the War Office. It brought our statesmen and our leading sailors and soldiers into intimate personal contact, to their mutual advantage. The whole subject was lifted out of the sphere of party politics by Asquith's decision to send the whole of the evidence to Balfour, the Leader of the Opposition, and to hear his views before adopting the report. Finally it revealed many weaknesses, and a number of problems, great and small, requiring exploration.' We shall revert to these shortly; meanwhile it will be as well to descend from the 'stratosphere' in which these debates were being conducted, and to see what was going on 'on the ground'.

The bass accompaniment to the work of the Committee of Imperial Defence was played in the Admiralty and in the War Office. Haldane's reforms constituted one part of it – a part of vital importance, since unless the Army was effective all the plans that concerned it would be worthless. A somewhat similar labour was taking place in the Navy, which also was completing a phase of fundamental reform – but with one great difference. The essence of Haldane's army reforms was reorganization, to be implemented by reinvigorated training under men like Haig; the essence of the naval reforms, under the aegis of Admiral Fisher, was re-equipment. Fisher's great contribution was his perception of the complete reorientation of naval thought that was implied in the prospect of war with Germany. Hankey says: 'The basic cause of Fisher's reforms between 1904 and 1910 was the growth of the German Fleet. His predecessors had diagnosed the disease, but it was left to Fisher's logical, ruthless and iconoclastic mind to forestall the danger. The principle he applied was the sound one of concentrating strength at the decisive point.'

'*Strength* at the decisive point', says Lord Hankey; it was not sufficient to regroup the units of the Navy, stripping down distant squadrons, which Fisher did; it was not sufficient to overhaul the whole question of naval man-power and recruitment, which Fisher did; it was not sufficient to begin the construction of new bases, which he did; nor to lay the foundations of a Naval War College, which he did. The main point was that, ship by ship, the Royal Navy should be the equal or superior of the Imperial German Navy, *and outnumber it as well*. This meant a huge programme of rebuilding, particularly after the launching of H.M.S. *Dreadnought* in 1906, which rendered all earlier types of battleship obsolete, and therefore, to a large extent, placed all ship-building nations on equal terms. Battleships had to be constructed; Fisher's pet battle-cruisers had to be designed and constructed; gunnery and torpedo work had to be fundamentally revised. Into all these channels Fisher poured his enormous energy, and galvanized the Navy. If, in other respects, he omitted to deal appropriately with vital subjects, it is scarcely surprising; but it was unfortunate that the fiery Admiral's force of character was such that nobody else could make an advance unless it had his blessing. His weakness, the defect that underlay all his achievement, was his stubborn opposition to anything that resembled a true Naval Staff. His theory was that the element in which the Navy performed was totally different from that of the Army; that Nature compelled the sailor to be an instant realist, and that it would be a weakness to trammel him in any way. The result was, says Hankey, that 'Fisher was hatching his naval plans in complete isolation from the General Staff of the War Office', while in the meantime 'events were taking place which were destined to exercise a considerable influence on our eventual military policy, plans and preparations'. Before we examine the baleful effect of this self-imposed isolation, we must examine those 'events'.

Before Haldane was even in the saddle at the War Office, indeed, during the period of interregnum that attended the General Election of 1905/1906, the first step had been taken in the military implementation of the Entente Cordiale which led Great Britain inexorably towards Mons, the Somme, to Passchendaele, and the sombre glories of 1918. France, deeply uneasy over the Moroccan crisis of 1905 and Germany's brutally threatening posture, was naturally eager to know how Britain proposed to act in the event of war. So imprecise was the Entente that no answer to that question existed, nor had it been deeply considered. The assurance of the Liberal Foreign Secretary-designate, Sir Edward Grey, that he intended to stand by the Entente, did not carry this particular question forward very far. To arrive at some precision, Lord Esher and Sir George Clarke (Secretary of the Committee of Imperial Defence) used the irregular (though not irresponsible) medium of the Military Correspondent of *The Times*, Colonel Repington, to sound out the French Government on its views of Anglo-French military co-operation. Repington addressed eleven questions to the French Government, and the answers were drawn up by the French Prime Minister and the Minister of War. The details need not concern us;[1] the gist of the matter was that the French were fully agreeable to leave the whole question of naval strategy to Britain, and they wanted the British contribution on land to 'be joined to that of the French Army, that is to say, be placed under the same direction, whether the two armies act in the same theatre of operations, or in different theatres. . . .' It was on this basis that Staff talks were begun between the two Powers in 1906.

As more peaceful conditions returned, and as the new British Liberal Government embarked upon its formidable programme of social reform in addition to its other Defence preoccupations, these talks languished. They did not receive any sharp impetus again until 1910, when Sir Henry Wilson became Director of Military Operations at the War Office. In the meantime, however, it was generally assumed that there would be a British contingent fighting beside the French Army, if France should be invaded by Germany. *Certainly no British counter-proposal was put forward.* The Liberal Government took the view that the Staff talks, while necessary, were in no way binding

---

1. The whole correspondence is set out by Repington in his book, *The First World War* – prescient title – Chapter I. See also an article by the present author in *History Today*, July, 1960, entitled 'The Genesis of the Western Front'.

upon the two Governments. A great deal of secrecy surrounded them; Hankey tells us: '. . . the authority of the Cabinet was not sought, and only the Prime Minister (Campbell-Bannerman), the Leader of the Government in the House of Lords (Ripon), Haldane and the Chancellor of the Exchequer (Asquith) were informed. . . . No reports of them were made either to the Cabinet or the Committee of Imperial Defence.' This is an omission that one might not have guessed at from Asquith's claim quoted above.[1] But it had the most serious consequences, for when it came to Wilson's turn to plan military policy in detail he elected, under the influence of Foch (who was then Commandant at the Ecole de Guerre) and his own Francophile inclinations, to interpret the understanding with the French Staff in the narrowest possible sense. His whole thinking was addressed to the concept of placing the entire British Expeditionary Force on the left flank of the French Army; the French reference in 1906 to the possibility of the two Armies operating 'in different theatres' was completely ignored; there was no other plan whatsoever. And the one authority which might have provided, and insisted on, an alternative plan was in that respect practically defunct. This was revealed when the next crisis arose, in 1911, over Agadir.

The story of what happened then has not been better told than by Lord Haldane. Here is his account of it: 'At a meeting of the Defence Committee . . . the Prime Minister . . . was enquiring into our joint war plans. Sir Arthur Wilson [First Sea Lord] unexpectedly said that the plan of the Admiralty for the event of a war with Germany was quite different from ours. They wanted to take detachments of the Expeditionary Force and to land them seriatim at points on the Baltic coast, on the northern shores of Prussia. We of the War Office at once said that such a plan was from a military point of view hopeless, because the railway system which the Great General Staff of Germany had evolved was such that any division we landed, even if the Admiralty could have got it to a point suitable for debarkation, would be promptly surrounded by five to ten times the number of enemy troops. Sir John Fisher appeared to have derived the idea from the analogy of the Seven Years' War, more than 150 years previously, and Sir Arthur Wilson, his successor, had apparently adopted it. The First Lord (McKenna) backed him up. I said at once that the mode of employing troops and their numbers and places of operation were questions for the War Office General Staff and that we had worked them out with the French. The results had been periodically approved in the Committee of Defence itself. Sir William Nicholson [C.I.G.S.] asked Sir Arthur whether they had at the Admiralty a map of the German strategic railways. Sir Arthur replied that it was not their business to

1. See p. 56.

have such maps. "I beg your pardon," said Sir William, "if you meddle with military problems you are bound not only to have them, but to have studied them." The discussion became sharp; I, of course, agreeing *ex animo* with the utterances of the C.I.G.S. He had a rather too sharp tongue, and I remember that on a previous occasion Sir John Fisher had said to me that he wished I would enjoin "Old Nick" not always to stamp his hoof on his (Sir John's) toes.

'The Prime Minister was clear that the arrangements made must be carried out in accordance with the plan of the General Staff. But the Admiralty were evidently not convinced when the meeting came to an end. The difficulty had its origins in the fact that the Navy then possessed nothing like a General Staff. Sir John Fisher had always objected to having one. . . . He did not realize that in the 20th Century it is impossible to conduct military operations successfully either at sea or on land, without close preliminary study on an intensive scale.'

Haldane's reference to the 'periodical approval' of the General Staff's plans requires some qualification. Certainly, in 1908, as a by-product of the Invasion Enquiry, the Committee of Imperial Defence had recorded that 'the plan to which preference is given by the General Staff is a valuable one, and the General Staff should accordingly work out all the necessary details'. This Wilson had done with gusto, going beyond the 1908 decision that only four infantry divisions and one cavalry division should be sent to France; he planned for the despatch of the entire available British strength – six divisions as well as the cavalry. It is by no means clear that this extension of the brief had been grasped by the Defence Committee. Lord Hankey writes of Wilson's exposition of the General Staff scheme, at the meeting that Haldane described, as though this was the first time he (or the Committee as a whole) had heard the details: '. . . when the Committee adjourned for lunch', he says, 'there was no doubt that Henry Wilson had made a profound impression, which I am the more ready to admit because he had entirely failed to carry conviction in my own mind.' It was most unfortunate that the man who would have been the first and most active to challenge Wilson's hypothesis – Morley – was not present. It was equally unfortunate that the Admiralty made asses of themselves. The result was the acceptance of the (Henry) Wilson plan, *without any full discussion or realization of its implications.* That this is what occurred is shown by the facts that, when war broke out, and those implications came closer into view, it transpired that neither the recent C.I.G.S. (French), nor the C.-in-C. of I Corps (Haig) were fully aware of what had been decided; two Cabinet Ministers (Morley and Burns) resigned as soon as they understood; and a number of other Ministers (chief among them Churchill and Lloyd George) were never able to bring themselves to accept those implications, with which they should have been familiar for years. And the debate about the consequences has not yet ended.

This is not to say that the spur of the Agadir crisis did not produce a useful effect; it did. Much was done during the interval between Agadir and the outbreak of war; Winston Churchill took over the Admiralty, and began the formation of a Naval Staff; the Navy's eccentric schemes were abandoned; the reinforcement of the Fleet continued at an even greater pace; an Air Service was belatedly created; the War Book was composed. Lord Hankey was the man most intimately concerned in this last invaluable act, and with the general acceleration of British war preparations; let him sum them up:

'... The naval plans were fully elaborated, and the Admiralty had ready alternative plans to meet developments in the situation. . . . The fleet rendezvous was decided on. Subject to some important exceptions the bases were equipped and defended. Forces were allocated for coastal defence. The arrangements for coal and oil fuel were complete. Merchant vessels had been earmarked as auxiliary cruisers. . . . Details had been worked out for taking up colliers. . . . Rapid mobilization was ensured. . . . Every detail had been worked out for the mobilization of the Regular Army and its transport to a place of concentration in France prearranged with the French General Staff, as well as for its protection by the Navy. The railway and shipping and embarkation arrangements were complete. . . . Plans had been worked out for home defence. . . . The maximum of secrecy both of naval and military movements had been provided for. . . . The risks of espionage and sabotage had been reduced to a minimum. The smooth working of our cable and telegraphic communications . . . had been arranged for. Provision had been made for cutting the enemy's cables. World-wide systems of naval and military intelligence had been preconcerted. Preparations had been made for warning our merchant shipping. . . . A complete scheme for effecting war insurance on ships and cargoes was in existence. In all parts of the British Empire plans had been worked out for seizing and detaining enemy ships. . . . A commercial policy . . . had been decided on. . . . Our dependence on the possible enemy countries for supplies and markets and the possibilities of alternative sources of supply had been explored. The general lines of our policy on all these questions were known to the Governments of the Dominions, and corresponding arrangements had been made throughout the British Empire. Every detail had been thought out and every possible safeguard provided for ensuring that, once decided on, these arrangements should be put into operation rapidly and without a hitch. . . . From the King to the printer, everyone knew what he had to do.'

This is a very formidable statement, and an astounding record for a primarily peace-loving Liberal Administration. Unfortunately, it contains two most grave omissions. First, and we shall be returning to this at intervals, there was no provision for any modification in the structure of Government itself in a time of acute national emergency. Secondly, and this is our immediate concern, there was the failure to grasp the nature of the war that was to be embarked upon when the enemy struck, and the implications of the agreements entered into, the strategy accepted. Sir William Robertson, with his uncanny knack – on paper – of putting his finger exactly where the hurt was, later summed it all up; the whole thing came back to those Anglo-French conversations, and the gloss put upon them by the Operations Branch of the British General Staff: 'Not only was the Cabinet unaware of the conversations, but even the Foreign Secretary, who gave permission for them, knew nothing about their results. Writing to the Prime Minister on the subject in 1911 he said: "What (the General Staff) settled I never knew – the position being that the Government was quite free, but the military people knew what to do, if the word was given." It was, however, of little use for the "military people" to "know what to do" unless adequate means were available for doing it, and this there could not be if the Cabinet knew nothing about what was taking place. On the principle that half a loaf is better than no bread the conversations were useful, but a more unsatisfactory method of ensuring co-operative action can hardly be imagined than that of leaving the two General Staffs to patch together a plan which the British Government, as such, declined to endorse with its formal approval. . . . Moreover, since there was no such undertaking the French authorities were forced to frame their plan of campaign not knowing whether they would or would not receive British assistance, *while we, on our side, were not able to insist upon our right to examine the French plan in return for our co-operation.*[1] When the crisis arose there was no time to examine it, and consequently our military policy was for long wholly subordinate to the French policy, of which we knew very little.'

In other words (Lord Hankey's): 'The creation of an army on the continental scale was completely out of the picture until the outbreak of war.' And yet, in effect, Britain had been committed to continental war since 1906.

The effect of this extraordinary hiatus of thought was inexorable; it meant, as Robertson says, that Britain went to war on a French plan, not a British one; and as the French forthwith lost the initiative to the Germans, the British effort was, in fact, dictated by the enemy. And once in, there was no going back: the German initiative saw to that. Haig's Army Corps at Aldershot, tens of thousands of other British soldiers, hundreds of thousands of

1. Author's italics.

men from all over the Empire, who had never dreamed of becoming soldiers, were the victims of this particular blindness on the part of the Liberal Government, a blindness which one cannot quite believe was entirely involuntary. Haig, like everyone else, was swept along on this dark secret tide.

*   *   *   *

We have reached the point when war was very near. In Europe, a super-ficial calm reigned during the first months of 1914; in the United Kingdom, on the other hand, the scene was anything but calm. Of all the problems that had beset the Liberal Government since it came to power, of all the violent controversies in which it had been involved – Lloyd George's Budget, em-bittered industrial relations, the rise of Labour, the House of Lords issue, Women's Suffrage – the most intractable was Irish Home Rule. It was an ill chance that brought this most suggestive of party quarrels to a head in the year that took the world to war. The details of the proceedings which carried Great Britain to the edge of civil war in March, 1914, need not concern us now; the essential point for us is the effect on the Army of the Government's stated intention of implementing Irish Home Rule, despite the furious opposition of Ulster. This is the issue which triggered off the Curragh incident, through the ineptitude of the General Officer Commanding in Ireland, who put to the officers of the 3rd Cavalry Brigade, serving on that station, the hypothetical question, whether they were prepared to march against Ulster, if so ordered. The question, of course, should never have been put; the answer was frightful in its implications. Brigadier-General Hubert Gough, commanding the Brigade, and fifty-seven out of the seventy officers under him, declared that they would prefer to send in their papers, if ordered north. It could safely be assumed that the remainder of the Army would react in much the same way, and probably a large portion of the Navy, too. There had not been such a collision between the Armed Forces and the Government since the seventeenth century. Internally and abroad, the effect was deplorable.

It is difficult now to recapture the extreme passion of those times, but the effort has to be made. In Ulster, Volunteers were drilling, arms were being smuggled in, military depots and magazines were in danger; in Southern Ireland the Sinn Fein movement was gathering impetus; there was turmoil throughout England; the House of Commons was in a ferment. Professor Gilbert Murray has given a vivid description of the scene there: 'The sight of the House rather shocked me. The opposition seemed wild with delight. There was a mutiny: There was to be a rebellion: The Government would fall and the Conservatives get office: All the questions, all the speeches had a ring of triumph. A powerful counter note was struck by a Labour Member, Colonel Ward, but it was a note almost equally dangerous. In ringing tones he warned the Tories that, if they wanted Civil War they could have it. If there was to be a mutiny in the Army, it would not be a Tory mutiny but a mutiny of the working-class. The debate was exciting, but deplorable.'

In the Army, consternation and disorder reigned. A large number of senior officers were Ulstermen, and the dilemma for them was tragic; they solved it – or failed to solve it – in different ways. Lord Roberts gave active support to the Ulster Volunteers and cut the C.I.G.S., Sir John French, dead in the street for not opposing the Government of which he was a prominent servant; French himself was like a man caught in a storm, flung first one way and then another, and then wrecked; Henry Wilson, the Director of Military Operations, was a leading figure in anti-Government circles, and thought nothing of giving away Government secrets to the Opposition in this cause, or of intriguing with the agitated officers; Hubert Gough and his fellows had obeyed their consciences, but had no idea where this would lead them; Brigadier-General John Gough, Hubert's brother, was Haig's Chief of Staff at Aldershot, and the first Haig (who was on holiday) knew of the crisis was a message from John Gough, submitting his resignation.

Haig acted promptly; he refused to forward Gough's resignation, and rushed to London to see Haldane, who was now Lord Chancellor. The two Scotsmen were able to stand somewhat apart from the rage of events; above all, they were able to perceive the terrible prospect of the Army which they had done so much to build together being suddenly shattered. Haig himself strongly disapproved of Army officers intervening in politics under any circumstances; but things had now gone far, and he recognized that the Army was seriously disaffected. He urged on Haldane the immediate need for a clear and unequivocal statement by the Government. Two days later, Haldane concluded a speech in the House of Lords with the words: 'No orders were issued, no orders are likely to be issued, and no orders will be issued for the coercion of Ulster.' Meanwhile the Secretary of State for War, Seely, and the C.I.G.S. had given Hubert Gough a signed statement to similar effect. This, unfortunately, appeared in the Press, and the impression instantly arose that the Government had given way to Army pressure. As a result, Asquith had to repudiate, in some measure, Haldane's affirmation. The crisis deepened, with Henry Wilson playing a sinister part in it. He knew well enough what was at stake; on the day after the Curragh incident, he told Seely 'the same story as I had told French – no officers on the General Staff at the War Office, the regiments depleted of officers, a hostile Europe, our friends leaving us because we have failed them and our enemies realizing that we had lost our army'. Yet this did not prevent him from pursuing his intrigues: 'I wired Hubert at midnight to stand like a rock. This is vital. Any false move now on our part would be fatal. So long as we hold the paper we got on Monday, we can afford to sit tight.' And the next day: 'It seems to me Johnny French must resign, but the rest of us must stand fast unless the Government take action against Hubert. Wired him again to keep absolutely quiet.' By contrast with this dangerous activity, Haig's influence was all on the side of steadiness, keeping the larger issues well in view. In the end, the fever burned itself out. Seely resigned, and with him French and the Adjutant-General, Spencer Ewart; but there was no mass exodus from the Army, there was no open, armed conflict between Government forces and the Ulster Volunteers.

It had been a near thing. The Irish problem itself remained unsettled and continued to engross the attention of British statesmen well into July, long after the assassins at Sarajevo had done their deed. The Army remained gravely weakened by the whole affair. On the day Seely resigned, Haig wrote in his diary: 'At 12 o'clock held meeting of G.O.C.s of Divisions and Brigades. I pointed out the danger of disruption in Army and Empire and begged them to induce regimental officers to give up dabbling in politics. We were all united to do anything short of coercing our fellow citizens who have done no wrong.'

The contradiction in this passage, even for a man with as strong a sense of duty as Haig, is revealing; as Robert Blake has said: 'There is, in fact, no easy escape from the conflict of loyalties which must arise when a lawfully elected government passes measures genuinely repugnant to the consciences of those who have to enforce them; and no one need blame Haig for failing to solve a problem to which no one else has ever offered a satisfactory answer.' He adds: 'The [Curragh] incident created a rift between the Army and the Liberal Party, which was to have serious consequences when war broke out. The history of the First World War is full of the difficulties created by the mistrust and suspicion which befogged the relations of the soldiers and the politicians. There were many reasons for this, but the Curragh incident was at least partly responsible.' It was an ominous overture.

PART II

'We cannot hope to win until we have defeated the German Army.'

Haig

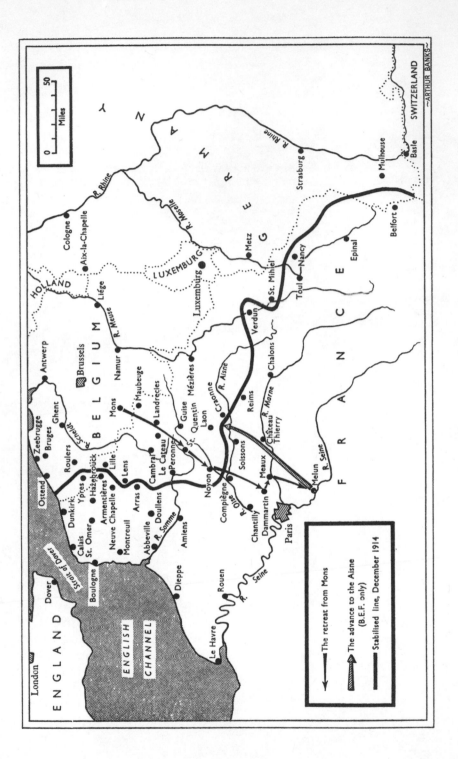

5

The Clash of Battle

THE Archduke Franz Ferdinand was assassinated on June 28th, 1914. Sir Edward Grey referred to the outrage in the House of Commons on July 10th, expressing horror, and sympathy with the victims and with the Austrian Empire. Not until July 21st did the consequences of the Sarajevo plot rate the main news page of *The Times*, and not until July 27th were they referred to again in the House of Commons. On that day also the European situation became the first news story in *The Times*, under the heading: 'PEACE IN THE BALANCE'. The intricacies of the diplomatic proceedings during the intervening weeks and thereafter do not fall within the scope of this book, but this delayed awareness in Britain of what was happening is a matter of moment. It meant, in effect, that the Government and the country had just one week in which to adjust themselves to the catastrophe that had fallen upon them. Deliberations were therefore conducted in an atmosphere of perturbation and alarm that could only have an ill result. In particular, it meant that the synchronization of British and French preparations, which was a basic assumption of the plans of both Staffs, went by the board. France mobilized on the same day as Germany, August 1st; British mobilization was not ordered until late on August 3rd, which meant that it was not effective until August 4th, the official date of the declaration of war on the Central Powers. This delay, which reflected the doubts and hesitations and qualms of conscience of the British Government, had, needless to say, a bad effect in France; the question whether Albion would prove to be perfidious once more was raised in the sharpest terms. The French Ambassador in London made no bones about his country's anxiety. It became a factor in its own right, weighing upon the thoughts of the British Government and its advisers.

At Aldershot, the orders for the 'Precautionary Period' to be put into force were received on July 29th. But for the soldiers on that station this was not the first awakening to the portents. Haig's profound conviction of the imminence of European war had made him deeply conscious of danger from the Balkans; in 1912 he had despatched officers from Aldershot to observe and report on the Balkan Wars. As soon as he heard of the assassination of the Archduke, he ordered his staff to prepare an appreciation of its probable consequences on East European politics. They concluded that nothing worse was likely than war between Austria and Serbia. 'Haig', says Charteris, 'was not convinced. With deep and concentrated attention he followed the meagre news as it appeared from day to day in the Press. To his immediate friends he frequently referred to the prospect of a great continental war originating from the Balkan trouble.'

When the precautionary period became operative, it found Aldershot fully prepared. 'All our arrangements were ready,' Haig wrote in his diary, 'even to the extent of having the telegrams written out. These merely had to be dated and despatched.' As a result, when the order to mobilize followed six days later, Haig was completely free from considerations of routine or detail; 'I had thus all my time free to make arrangements for my own departure for the front, to visit Field-Marshal French's G.H.Q. now established at the Hotel Metropole in London, and to ponder over the terribly critical military situation as it gradually developed day by day.' In view of the theories subsequently attributed to him, it is valuable that we should know exactly what course his ponderings were taking at this stage. They are revealed in a letter which he wrote to Lord Haldane from Aldershot on August 4th:

'My dear Lord Haldane,

'What an anxious time you must be having, but what a satisfaction it must be to you to see that this country is *able* to draw on her vast resources at the moment of crisis as a result of the thought and labour you spent on the problem when you were Secretary of State.

'So I make so bold as to write and express the hope that you will, even at great personal inconvenience, return to the War Office for as long as war lasts and preparations are necessary. No one knows the details of the problem of organization as you do! This war will last many months, possibly years, so I venture to hope that our only bolt (and that not a very big one) may not suddenly be shot on a project of which the success seems to be quite doubtful – I mean the checking of the German advance into France. Would it not be better to begin at once to enlarge our Expeditionary Force by amalgamating less regular forces with it? In three months' time we should have quite a considerable army, so that when we do take the field we can act decisively and dictate terms which will ensure a lasting peace.

'I presume, of course, that France can hold out even though her forces have to fall back from the frontier for the necessary time for us to create an army of 300,000.

'Forgive me bothering you with a letter, but I do see the great advantages for the Empire of having you at the War Office at this time, and with every good wish,

'I am, yours very truly,
(Sgd.) Douglas Haig.

'P.S. I have dashed off this letter on reading the leader in today's *Times* on Lord K.

'What I feel is that we have such a mass of undeveloped power which no one knows better than yourself how to organize and control. This will be impossible if the bulk of our highly trained regular officers are at once carted off to France and a Secretary of State is appointed who is new to the existing system. I do hope you will set to work at once to complete the organization you started in 1906.

(Sgd.) D. Haig.'

This letter makes several things clear: first, that unlike both the Cabinet and the War Office,[1] Haig expected a long war; secondly, that he was opposed to the idea of plunging into it and 'shooting our bolt' too soon; thirdly, that, *from the very first*, he had little faith in French military planning, although he did not doubt that France could hold her own; fourthly, he was opposed to the idea of using up all Britain's trained man-power in the Expeditionary Force. This last was to become a matter of great import; in January, 1915, Churchill wrote a trenchant memorandum to the Prime Minister, advocating exactly what Haig was now saying – with the difference that Haig was thinking of the Territorial Army, whereas Kitchener opted for the New Armies, and Churchill was referring to them. Haig's idea of not intervening until Britain could put 300,000 men in the field was, of course, already out of the question for psychological reasons, as he soon came to realize, but it underlines the sense of Robertson's comment quoted above;[2] if France had been assured of such a contribution, she could not have refused British participation in the planning stage which would decide how such a force would be used. It would not then have transpired, as now immediately happened, that *no one* on the British side really knew both what the French were about to attempt, and how well they were likely to be able to bring it off. Wilson had a fair knowledge of their plans, but was so dazzled by France's military reputation and by Foch's personality that he never subjected

1. See Hankey, *The Supreme Command 1914–1918*, Vol. I, pp. 162 and 179.
2. See p. 62.

them to hard penetrative criticism. It is astonishing that a man in Haig's position was never drawn into such a study of French intentions, and should be allowed to remain substantially in the dark about them, except for what he could learn from French publications; it is not less astonishing that the ex-C.I.G.S. was in the same boat. This amazing lapse was now swiftly revealed.

At four o'clock in the afternoon of August 5th Mr. Asquith assembled a Council of War at 10 Downing Street. Both the summons itself and the array of personalities to whom it went out were indicative of Asquith's approach to war problems – and indicative also that, despite the huge achievements of the Committee of Imperial Defence and the Service Ministries, all was not well with the development of British war policy at the highest level. This Council of War – strictly an *ad hoc* gathering, let it be understood – was remarkably constituted; the Prime Minister was in the chair; from the Cabinet he called the Foreign Secretary (Grey), the First Lord of the Admiralty (Churchill), and Haldane, who was briefly holding the seals again at the War Office; the First Sea Lord (Prince Louis of Battenberg) was also present; so was the C.I.G.S., Sir Charles Douglas. So far, so good; all of these men were vitally concerned with the immediate conduct of the War. The same might be said of Field-Marshal Sir John French, who had just been appointed Commander-in-Chief of the Expeditionary Force. But in addition to French there were also present on the Army side the following officers: Sir Archibald Murray, French's Chief of Staff; Henry Wilson, his sub-Chief of Staff; Haig, commanding I Corps; Grierson, commanding II Corps; Sir John Cowans, the Quartermaster-General; Sir H. Sclater, the Adjutant-General; Sir Stanley von Donop, the Master-General of Ordnance; Sir Ian Hamilton, the Inspector-General of Overseas Forces. Finally, in addition to this long list, there were Lord Kitchener, whose qualifications for the post of Secretary of State for War had been canvassed in *The Times* the day before, and the redoubtable figure of Field-Marshal Lord Roberts of Kandahar, eighty-two years old, but with his faculties unimpaired and his energy still phenomenal. *What were they all wanted for?*

The answer is: to decide what to do. In other words, in spite of all the labours of the Committee of Imperial Defence, in spite of Agadir, in spite of the War Book, in spite of the fact that the only military strength of the nation was already on the move for France in accordance with a prearranged plan, the British Government had not grasped what the nature of its commitment was, and *neither had its chief professional advisers.* The haplessness and the misfortunes of so much of British (and Allied) strategy in after years can only be fully understood if this is held in mind. The truth of the matter is that the binding force of this commitment only now became apparent, and when the distinguished gathering delved into it, they found that the only area of initiative left to the United Kingdom was the decision whether the Expeditionary Force should concentrate at Maubeuge or Amiens. It is indicative of the degree of misunderstanding which existed that French, upon whom it fell to expound the Army plan, so failed to grasp its implications that he threw out an entirely different idea which occupied the discussion for some time – of going to Antwerp instead, to co-operate with the Belgian Army, and possibly also the Dutch, under the impression that Holland's neutrality had been infringed.

Wilson was in agony when he listened to this 'ridiculous proposal'; Haig remarked in his diary: 'Personally, I trembled at the reckless way Sir J. French spoke about "the advantages" of the B.E.F. operating from Antwerp against the powerful and still intact German Army!' The matter was settled when Churchill said that the Navy could not guarantee a safe passage across the wider part of the North Sea, and by the reminder that the approaches to Antwerp lay through Dutch waters, and Holland was not, in fact, likely to depart from neutrality.

That disposed of Antwerp; but the proposal gave Haig an opportunity, *alone in the gathering*, of putting forward some fundamental questions concerning the War. His first queries arose specifically out of the Antwerp proposal: ' "Have we enough troops with the Belgians, to carry on a campaign independently of the French or do we run excessive risk if we act separately, of defeat in detail?" and "What does our General Staff know of the fighting value of the Belgian Army?" '

These enquiries were pertinent: the Belgians were stubborn in defence (but not always: the resistance of Liége has overshadowed the disappointingly swift fall of Namur) but their Field Army was certainly not able to compete with the Germans: the small B.E.F. would have risked a more disastrous Dunkirk by detaching itself from the French. Haig then continued with his deeper questions, which, said Wilson, 'led to our discussing strategy like idiots'. But Wilson had his reasons for not wanting grand strategy to be discussed; what he wanted was a rubber-stamp approval of his own plans. Haig was looking further ahead:

'I also made these points: 1st. That Great Britain and Germany would be fighting for their existence. Therefore the war was bound to be a long war, and neither would acknowledge defeat after a short struggle. I knew that German writers had stated in their books that a modern war in Europe would not last more than a few months. In my opinion that was what they hoped for and what they were planning to make it. I held that we must organize our resources *for a war of several years*.

'2nd. Great Britain must at once take in hand the creating of an Army. I mentioned one million as the number to aim at immediately, remarking that that was the strength originally proposed for the Territorial Force by Lord Haldane. Above all we ought to aim at having a strong and effective force when we came to discuss peace at a Conference of Great Powers.

'3rd. We only had a small number of trained officers and N.C.O.s. These must be economized. The need for efficient instructors would become at once apparent. I urged that a considerable proportion of officers and N.C.O.s should be withdrawn forthwith from the Expeditionary Force. . . . *Lastly*, my advice was to send as strong an Expeditionary Force as possible, and as soon as possible, to join the French Forces and to arrange to increase that force as rapidly as possible.'

It will be noted that, in the space of one day, Haig's ideas had moved substantially beyond what he had written to Haldane, though the tenor of them was the same, except in one important respect. He now appreciated that it was quite unrealistic to think of standing aside while the French bore the whole brunt of the German onslaught. In conversation and cogitation he had come to the conclusion, says Charteris, that 'with an army and nation of moral so sensitive as the French, the Alliance itself might be endangered by alterations involving delay, and that therefore the Expeditionary Force must move in its greatest possible strength at the earliest possible moment, and *conform to the plans of the French Command*[1] in the initial stages of the war'. Already inexorable realities were imposing themselves, and the most inexorable of all was this subjection to French strategic control. The British Empire was firmly caught in the net of Henry Wilson's agreements and time-tables (which went so far as to include a halt at Amiens of '*dix minutes pour une tasse de café*'). There was no going back: despite Lord Kitchener's misgivings, it was decided that all six British Regular divisions and the Cavalry should go, as planned, to Maubeuge. Kitchener, who was appointed Secretary of State for War on this day, was able to modify that decision, and hold back two divisions, amid Wilson's loud lamentations. Kitchener continued to press for a less exposed point of concentration, and urged his argument for Amiens during the whole of the following week. But Wilson, with the aid of French Staff Officers, overbore him. Haig was, and remained, entirely of Kitchener's opinion, as we shall see; meanwhile he, as much as Kitchener, was beginning to feel the pressure of the French connection: it was to be a main preoccupation throughout his period of Command: the basic difference

1. Author's italics.

between him and others who grieved at Britain's strategic plight was his deeper understanding of this factor.

* * * *

In war, large errors are quickly exposed, and their penalties are promptly exacted. In 1914, no Great Power was free from serious error (any more than in 1939), and the miseries and sufferings of the world are traceable to this fact. The worst mistake of all was Germany's; it cost her the victory. Basically, it was a failure to appreciate the degree to which sea-power can be applied to land warfare; in other words, the fatal consequences of incurring Britain's enmity, as well as that of France and Russia. But France, through a lapse of the reason for which she is famed, came near to throwing away her considerable advantages. Britain, through her long naval tradition, which had not been brought up to date with twentieth-century conditions, also failed to grasp the heart of the matter, and to do herself full justice. Russia, through the incompetence of an expiring tyranny, never put forward her full strength. Austria, accepting a secondary status from the beginning, was barely able to live up even to that.

To understand the War, it is necessary to shift our viewpoint. It is only intelligible when seen from the German position. For her the dilemma was manifest, once France and Russia had come to a military understanding: the whole aim of Bismarck's policy had been to prevent such an alliance: as soon as it came about, Germany was faced with the prospect of war on two fronts. The only solution to this was to destroy one enemy at a time; that involved two factors: a calculated risk on one front, lightning speed on the other. This was the essence of the Schlieffen Plan, whose outline was composed in 1905; it was modified, over the years, but the basic idea remained unchanged. The intention was to destroy the French Army completely in forty days, before the ponderous Russian mobilization was complete. For this purpose, 62 divisions were to be concentrated in the West, leaving only 10 to assist the Austrians in holding the Russians at bay. Because of the impossibility of rapidly forcing the French system of frontier fortresses, Belgian neutrality would have to be violated; 54 out of the 62 divisions would pass north of Metz, through the Ardennes, through Brussels, round by the *west* of Paris, to pin the French against the *back* of their fortress system, and there destroy them. It would be a Cannae all over again, a remorseless encirclement, of which the essence was weight and speed. 'The German plan', Sir Frederick Maurice has written, 'was in conception bold, simple, and based on a careful abstract study of war. It was at the same time utterly ruthless and immoral in its cold-blooded contempt of international pledges and of the rights of the weak, and was fundamentally defective in its disregard of the psychology both of potential enemies and of possible allies. It was, in fact a *chef-d'oeuvre* of Prussian militarism naked and unashamed, and like all plans which defy the laws of morality, it contained the germs of weakness which were to bring it to failure.' Just so; but this weakness was very nearly eliminated by the strange illusions of Germany's first enemy.

The French plan was also simple; it led directly to the edge of the cliff. It was founded, not upon reason, but upon emotion. Since 1870, the French nation and its General Staff had been obsessed with the idea of *'revanche'*, and their thoughts were drawn magnetically towards the lost provinces, Alsace and Lorraine. The memories and fears of 1870 drew the French persistently towards fallible strategic and tactical doctrines: the rediscovery of the Napoleonic offensive seemed to point the way to prevent the enemy from imposing his will; it also contributed to the revival of national and Army morale which was a first essential. Stage by stage, despite the warnings of more sober officers, under the influence of Foch at the *Ecole Supérieure de Guerre*, and later of his more ultra pupils headed by Colonel de Grandmaison, French thought and planning moved towards the concept of a headlong, all-out offensive by the whole mass of the Field Army across the German frontier. In this, it was believed, the French soldier would recapture his natural *élan* and warlike instinct; he would demonstrate a personal superiority over the German; and German plans, whatever they might be, would be disrupted and thrown into confusion by the vigour of the French attack. By 1914, this crude theory had crystallized into the notorious Plan XVII, whose preamble stated:

'From a careful study of information obtained it is probable that a great part of the German forces will be concentrated on the common frontier. . . .

'Whatever the circumstances, it is the C.-in-C.'s intention to advance, all forces united, to the attack of the German armies. . . .'

'*Whatever the circumstances* . . .'; the final subtlety of the Schlieffen Plan, completely missed by the French, was that this very advance by them would assist towards their undoing, for while they thrust their heads into the trap in this manner, the door of it would be slammed behind them. The further they advanced, the more desperate their ultimate plight would be; as Captain Liddell Hart has said, the Schlieffen Plan was designed to act 'like a revolving door – if a man pressed heavily on one side, the other would swing round and hit him in the back'. Fortunately for France and her Allies, von Schlieffen's successor, the younger von Moltke, lacked his nerve, and abandoned this section of the plan in favour of stopping the French offensive in its tracks. But for this accident of personality, it is hard to see how the French could have survived the disaster which they were bringing upon themselves.

It was into this ill-considered adventure that the British Army was committed to plunge with uncritical enthusiasm, as a small appendix to the French left wing. Only one man in authority in England had the temerity to question the assumptions of the French General Staff: Lord Kitchener. This was the meaning of his repeated advocacy of a concentration at Amiens instead of at Maubeuge. His fears were dictated by instinct, the almost female instinct which so often guided him in the secret workings of his mind towards large decisions. Unfortunately, his introduction to the war plans came too late; he was unable to check the momentum of the schedules and timetables. He continued to try until August 12th, on which day Colonel Repington published in *The Times* a very complete map of the German deployment which exposed their plan of envelopment through Belgium. Kitchener sent for French, Murray and Wilson, with the representatives of the French Staff in London, that afternoon; Wilson relates: '. . . we wrangled with K. for 3 hours. K. wanted to go to Amiens, and he was incapable of understanding the delays and difficulties of making such a change, nor the cowardice of it, nor the fact that either in French victory or defeat we would be equally useless. He still thinks the Germans are coming north of the Meuse in great force, and will swamp us before we concentrate.' The combined weight of the two groups of Staff Officers was too much even for Kitchener; he had to give way.

The next day Sir John French told Haig where the Army was going. Where Kitchener, who had been out of Europe far too long, worked by instinct, Haig worked by reason and study. The result was the same: 'We are to detrain . . . some 60 or 70 miles to the east of Amiens! In view of ignorance still existing regarding the enemy's movements, the rate of his advance into Belgium, and his intentions, it seems to some of us somewhat risky to begin our concentration so close to the enemy. . . . I have an uneasy feeling lest we may be thoughtlessly committed to some great general action before we have had time to absorb our reservists. Any precipitate engagement of our little force may lose us the inestimable value which our highly trained divisions do possess not only as a unit in battle, but also as a leaven for raising the moral of the great National Army which the Govt. is now proceeding to organize.'

The idea of the National Army was very close to Haig's heart, as it was to Kitchener's. We have seen that Haig had already urged, in the highest councils, the need to hold back Regular officers and N.C.O.s to train the force. This notion, too, met with fierce opposition from French and Wilson, who were persuaded that the decisive battles would take place at once ('All over by Christmas' was a popular theory) and that it would therefore be criminal to weaken the Expeditionary Force in any way. Kitchener was able to insist on some retention of key personnel, though nothing like enough, as soon became apparent; nevertheless, Churchill has said: 'I consider that this prudent withholding from the army in the field, in the face of every appeal and demand, the key-men who alone could make new armies, was the greatest of the services which Lord Kitchener rendered to the nation at this time, and it was a service which no one of less authority than he could have performed.'

Kitchener's same authority, however, acted sometimes less helpfully. To the sorrow of Haig, and all those who understood the matter, Lord Kitchener determined to set aside the Territorial apparatus. 'He insisted on raising', wrote Lord Haldane, 'not Territorial line after Territorial line, each of which would have stepped into the place of the one in front as it moved away, but new "Kitchener" Armies through the medium of the Adjutant-General's Department of the War Office. The result was the confusion which arises from the sudden departure from settled principles.' It can hardly be doubted that another result was delay in the strengthening of the Expeditionary Force which alone could have saved it from continued subjection to French strategic control. This will always be a vexed question. The fairest summary comes from Lord Esher: 'Since it was conceded that the War should be fought under a system of voluntary enlistment and unequal sacrifice – a concession for which England was destined to pay, and is still paying a heavy price – it is more than doubtful whether armies could have been raised by any method other than the one he chose . . . the pride and glee with which men of all classes flocked to "Kitchener's Army" amazed the nations of the world. It was impossible to speak with him on the subject and not realize that he was stirred by the response to his call. Perhaps this quickening of the pulse made it easier for him to follow his colleagues in their resistance to the fairer way of collecting the youth of the country for the holocaust of battle – resistance fatal to the sober ordering of the nation for the desperate work of provision and supply which lay behind the trenches.'

It will be seen that, before a shot had been fired by British troops, through a defect going far back in the country's preparations for war, and through a chance of personality at the very outbreak, two grave hazards were implanted in the British effort: first, the subjection to French control from which it would be necessary, sooner or later, to be freed; secondly, a failure to grip satisfactorily the question of manpower which alone could sustain and enlarge the national effort to the point of freedom. It fell on Haig to bear the brunt of these mischances and grapple with their distant consequences.

*   *   *   *

Haig marched to war with deep misgiving. Doubting the strategy, regretting the relegation of the Territorials, he also questioned the quality of the men under whom he would serve. On August 11th, the King inspected the Aldershot Command. He expressed delight that Sir John French was to command the Expeditionary Force, and asked Haig's opinion. 'I told him at once, as I felt it my duty to do so, that from my experience with Sir John in the South African War, he was certain to do his utmost loyally to carry out any orders which the Government might give him. I had grave doubts however, whether either his temper was sufficiently even or his military knowledge sufficiently thorough to enable him to discharge properly the very different duties which will devolve upon him during the coming operations with Allies on the Continent. In my own heart, I know that French is quite unfit for this great command at a time of crisis in our Nation's history. But I thought it sufficient to tell the King that I had "doubts" about the selection.'

These fears weighed on Haig's mind. They had nothing to do with envy; he found his own position most gratifying: '. . . in all my dreams I have never been so bold as to imagine that when . . . war did break out, I should hold one of the most important commands in the British Army. I feel very pleased at receiving command of the First Army [Corps] and I also feel the greatest confidence that we will give a good account of ourselves, *if only* our Higher Command give us a reasonable chance! I have a first-rate Staff and my troops are throughout well commanded. . . .' This was on the 13th; the doubts that he had expressed to the King two days before were increased by what he now learned of the strategic plan, and built up into a distinct uneasiness: 'This uneasy feeling which disturbs me springs, I think, in great measure from my knowledge of the personalities of which our "High Command" is composed. . . . Sir John French's . . . military ideas often shocked me when I was his Chief of Staff during the South African War. . . .' Nor did French's new Chief of Staff, Sir Archibald Murray, inspire him with confidence:

'In some respects he seemed . . . an "old woman". For example, in his dealings with Sir John. When his own better judgment told him that something which the latter wished to put in orders was quite unsound, instead of frankly acknowledging his disagreement, he would weakly acquiesce, in order to avoid an outbreak of temper and a scene. With all this knowledge of the Chief and his C.G.S. behind me, I have grave reason for being anxious about what happens to us in the great adventure upon which we are now to start this very night. However, I am determined to behave as I did in the South African War, namely to be thoroughly loyal and do my duty as a subordinate should, trying all the time to see Sir John's good qualities and not his weak ones. For most certainly both French and Murray have much to commend them although neither, in my opinion, are at all fitted for the appointments which they now hold at this moment of crisis in our country's history.'

The echo of all this will not escape the modern reader: Lord Alanbrooke's Diary recorded almost identical sentiments whenever he (also a Corps Commander) came into contact with the atmosphere of G.H.Q. in 1939–1940. To be almost alone in estimating the magnitude and the potential of events; to know how far leading figures fall below them; but to be a subordinate; and to be a soldier – that is, a member of an organization which cannot function without loyalty: all this poses a terrible dilemma. Haig did not find reassurance as he neared the battle-front. He sailed from Southampton on the night of the 15th, taking with him, as a farewell gift from Lady Haig, a well-stocked luncheon basket; that basket was to become a highly valued possession throughout the War. He and Grierson had cabins, and their crossing was comfortable; their Staff Officers, bedding down on deck, had a less pleasant time, particularly when rain fell in the early hours of the morning. It is not recorded whether Haig and Grierson discussed the situation together; it is likely that they did.

In any event we know that, the next day, Haig was still full of trepidations; Charteris wrote in his diary: 'D.H. unburdened himself today. He is greatly concerned about the composition of British G.H.Q. He thinks French quite unfit for high command in time of crisis. . . . He gives him credit for good tactical powers, great courage and determination. He does not think Murray will dare to do anything but agree with everything French suggests. In any case he thinks French would not listen to Murray but will rely on Wilson, which is far worse. D.H. thinks Wilson is a politician, and not a soldier, and "politician" with Douglas Haig is synonymous with crooked dealing and wrong sense of values. Personally I do not think this matters much, as French will be subordinate to Joffre, and D.H. and Grierson can be relied on to pull their Corps through. What does matter is Joffre. All we know about him is good, but as far as our Corps H.Q. is concerned we know very little.'

*   *   *   *

General Joseph Jacques Césaire Joffre was sixty-two years old, a tall, burly man who ate well and said little. He was an Engineer, who had risen, via Colonial appointments, by unremarkable stages to the top of the French Army. In 1911 he became Chief of the General Staff, and *ipso facto* Commander-in-Chief designate in time of war. The historian Mermeix tells us: 'In all the posts that he had held he had distinguished himself by his exactitude in the performance of duty. His superiors had always taken approving note of this calm, thoughtful Engineer, who was so poised in mind and body, and whose optimism was so robust. He was so cool . . . that he gave the appearance of insensibility. Nothing excited him. Silent, ruminative, more given to reflection than to imagination, his mental qualities were solid rather than brilliant. No one expected from him those swift improvisations by which bold captains, wanting to settle the issue, win – or lose – the game at a single throw. Because of his balance and his discretion, Joffre seemed to be the man who would take the fewest risks (*l'homme du moindre risque*).'

This pre-war impression was utterly mistaken. Behind his sober front, Joffre (the nominee of the offensive school) was putting the finishing touches on strategy and tactics so remote from reality that the word 'risk' is almost inapplicable; it was not risk, it was downright peril. But when the moment came to avert the danger, his stolid, patient, optimistic placidity stood him in good stead, and he was able to find the nerve to improvise on the grand scale.

Both the French and the German war plans were considerably modified in execution. The German Chief of Staff, von Moltke, lacked Joffre's nerve; steadily he had whittled down the Schlieffen Plan until, when war came, in the vital matter of the proportion of the German right wing to the left he had reduced it from 6 : 1 to 2 : 1. This still left a formidable mass of 60 divisions to carry out the great envelopment of the French. By August 16th, the date on which Haig landed in France, the advance of this huge mass had already made considerable progress. The last of the Liége forts capitulated that morning under the crushing fire of the German siege artillery. The French had launched their cherished offensive in Lorraine and Alsace, but elsewhere the signs and omens were becoming more and more difficult to read, and when read, less and less pleasing. The French armies, far from concentrating their mass for the offensive *à outrance*, were forced to take ground steadily towards their left, to the north, where vague but perceptible threats were increasing hourly. As their flank Army, the 5th, edged up to the Meuse, and towards contact with the British Expeditionary Force, their Reserve Army was drawn into the line of battle. Nevertheless, Joffre determined to carry on with his grand plan; on the 18th, deluded by some easy successes against German covering forces, General de Castelnau, commanding the French 2nd Army in Lorraine, ordered a pursuit 'with the utmost vigour and rapidity'.

There was vigour enough, but little rapidity; the French now began to come up against the main body of the German left, under Prince Rupprecht of Bavaria. In a moment of weakness, marking his virtual abandonment of the essence of the Schlieffen Plan, von Moltke had agreed to allow the Prince to undertake an offensive of his own, which would have the effect of substituting a double encirclement of the French for the single long sweep that von Schlieffen had prepared. On the 29th, the French 1st and 2nd Armies ran into this German advance; the result was complete French defeat at Morhange and Sarrebourg, with very high casualties and great ensuing confusion. The next day, the French Armies of the centre, the 3rd and 4th, advancing in the Ardennes, came into contact with the enemy, while the 5th Army, bent round along the Meuse to Charleroi, began to feel the German pressure. The Royal Flying Corps reported the presence of long columns of German troops (von Kluck's *I Army*) marching southward from Brussels, *outside* the left wing of the French. On the 22nd, at the battles of Virton and the Semoy, the events of Alsace-Lorraine repeated themselves in the Ardennes. The French were defeated again with heavy losses. On the front of the 5th Army, the Battle of Charleroi was growing in intensity, and the weakness of training and equipment which had already done so much damage to the French cause at other parts of the line were seen again, with the extra factor of moral failures under the uninspiring leadership of General Lanrezac. This was the eve of the Battle of Mons.

Haig was now proved right. Henry Wilson had, indeed, supplanted Murray as French's chief adviser, and was busy pumping into the Field-Marshal all his own Francophile optimism. From Joffre's headquarters ominous rumblings reached G.H.Q., but the information coming in from British sources, the Royal Flying Corps and the Cavalry Division, was con-clusive enough. Wilson disregarded it all, and the British Army remained in the posture of advance. On the 21st, he wrote in a letter: 'Today we start our forward march . . . I am full of confidence, but nothing is certain in war. . . .'

The outcome could hardly have been more certain, to one who could read the signs – as Haig was doing. On the 19th, Haig noted: 'I gather that . . . the Germans are crossing the Meuse in considerable strength (at least four Corps) about Huy and Liége and marching with all speed westwards on Brussels and Namur. . . . This looks as if a great effort is to be made to turn the French left. . . .' The next day he met French, and learned: 'The intention is for the British to advance beyond Maubeuge and prolong the French left. Are we strong enough?' And on the 21st, the day when Wilson was 'full of confidence': 'I and my Staff were rather anxious about our position. We are advancing against a difficult position (Charleroi to Mons); a boggy valley, many coalpits and greatly intersected country. . . . Briefly a country in which enemy could hold us with a few troops; meantime his great masses are marching as fast as possible round our left flank, and as far as we know *are unopposed!*'

Even as late as the afternoon of the Battle of Mons, Henry Wilson was able to persuade himself that 'we only had one corps and one cavalry division (possibly two corps) opposite to us. I persuaded Murray and Sir John that this was so, with result that I was allowed to draft orders for an attack tomorrow. . . .' Yet Haig, in conversation with Colonel Macdonogh, the Head of G.H.Q. Intelligence, had learned that 'all the roads running west from Brussels to Ath and Tournai were thickly covered with masses of German troops of all arms marching very rapidly westwards. This was indeed an alarming situation. Yet our C.-in-C. ordered my Corps to press on! Wilson had news that the French would re-establish the situation by a break-through in the Ardennes or Alsace! De Castelnau was about to deliver an enormous attack which must succeed! Macdonogh seemed quite alive to the danger of our position.' But French and Wilson preferred not to listen to Macdonogh; it was not 'one' or 'possibly two' corps that faced the British, but three, with another close behind; the French were not preparing any counter-stroke, but were everywhere in retreat. At the last moment the danger that the B.E.F. would be overwhelmed in a rash attempt to advance on the following day was averted – but not by paying heed to British Intelligence; it was a belated and only half-correct message from Joffre that started the British Army on the Retreat from Mons.

The Battle of Mons itself scarcely touched the I Corps; its casualties for the whole day amounted to forty. The forward units saw plenty of German troops in the distance, and there was some shelling, but the regimental history of a Guards battalion which was in reserve states that they 'knew practically nothing about the battle going on far away on their left. The battalion diary passes it unnoticed, and an officer's private diary describes it as "a day of rest" after the last two days of heavy and trying marching in very hot weather.' Mons was a II Corps battle, ably conducted by General Sir Horace Smith-Dorrien, who had come out in great haste to replace General Grierson, when the latter died suddenly on the 17th. The battle was not in any way decisive; it was fought in a mist of misapprehensions by both sides. But Mons proved one thing: that the British Regular was a first-rate soldier, more than a match for the Germans in shooting and manoeuvring ability. It indicated to the thoughtful that great care should consequently be taken over how he was used, since there were not many of him. This thought was very much in Haig's mind, and much else besides; whatever pleasure there may have been in being so dramatically proved correct in his fears and prognostications was obliterated by the extreme danger in which the Army now stood. But one thing is clear: this demonstration of ineptitude on the part of the leading figures at G.H.Q. made a lasting mark on him. Grave as his doubts of their capacity had been, they were no graver than the outcome. His confidence in French stood little chance of reviving after these setbacks; and he now also had good reason to mistrust his Allies, too.

*   *   *   *

The Retreat from Mons was a searing experience for all ranks and arms of the British Expeditionary Force. It was hardest of all for Smith-Dorrien's II Corps, on the left, where the threat of von Kluck's encirclement was always more acute. After the Battle of Mons, the Corps had to fight sharp disengaging actions, which added to its casualties and fatigue; on August 26th it was brought to bay at Le Cateau. Haig's Corps, lying between Smith-Dorrien and the by now considerably demoralized French 5th Army, was never in such danger, but endured very trying marches in great heat, often entangled with retreating French Reserve Divisions whose appearance added to the growing prejudice of the British against their seemingly fickle Allies. At G.H.Q., when realization dawned of the catastrophe which had befallen French plans, and which had so nearly involved the B.E.F. in utter destruction, a violent reaction set in. Sir John French's volatile temperament was not constituted to stand such buffets as these; he and Murray swung into a pessimism and gloom as vehement and almost as irrational as their earlier optimism. Not even Henry Wilson's ebullience could shake them out of it, though now, facts having so rudely asserted themselves, his brave spirit and good cheer became an asset instead of the liability that they had been before. It was symptomatic of the crack in G.H.Q. morale that the actual planning of the Retreat – one of the most difficult operations in war is to slip away under the nose of a superior and alerted enemy – was left entirely to the two Corps Commanders to arrange. Haig had reason to congratulate himself on having the services of John Gough as Chief of Staff; much of the detail fell upon him. Haig's rearguard was ably handled by Brigadier-General H. S. Horne, his C.R.A.

The eve of Le Cateau was a fateful day in the history of the War; it was also the occasion of a particularly trying experience for Haig. It was on August 25th that Joffre at last emerged from the cloud of illusion that had hitherto possessed the French headquarters (G.Q.G.). At first completely baffled by the repulse of his Armies, he had later come to the conclusion that their misfortunes stemmed from internal faults – bad training and bad handling; these were, indeed, a factor in the French defeat, but it took G.Q.G. a long time to understand that the main cause was the sheer weight and scope of the German movement. On the 25th Joffre grasped this, and took the momentous decision, against the advice of his Staff, to form a new French Army *on the left of the B.E.F.* His reasoning was entirely sound: he knew now that the supreme danger was the encirclement of his left flank; yet that was precisely the point where he could exercise the least influence, because stationed there was an Allied army to which he could not issue direct orders, only requests. He had to have an army on the left which he could command. From this decision, in the fullness of time, flowed the

Battle of the Marne and all its consequences. Rightly, Joffre kept most of his thoughts to himself; for a long time they were, after all, only thoughts, which it would take many days to translate into facts. Meanwhile, who could tell how the fight would go? Neither Joffre nor anyone else could foresee the precise course of events that would lead to the Allied counter-stroke; it was enough that he appreciated the point of decision, and took the measures that would reverse the spin of fortune's wheel. For the time being, however, none of this was any comfort to the harried B.E.F.

On this second day of the Retreat, the lines of march of the two British Army Corps were divided by what was believed to be an impassable natural feature, the Forest of Mormal. There were east-west tracks through the forest, but it was not known that there was a north-south path. The Corps divided, and this separation was to continue, causing still more anxiety at G.H.Q., almost to the end of the Retreat. As the exhausted II Corps staggered into Le Cateau that night, covered by the newly arrived and incomplete 4th Division, Haig's Corps was arriving by separate brigades at its billets and bivouacs in the villages along the banks of the Sambre. Haig himself was a sick man that day. He had contracted a gastric ailment on the 24th, but for some time had stubbornly refused treatment. Charteris forced him to see the Corps Medical Officer, Colonel Ryan, that night: 'D.H. was at his worst, very rude but eventually did see Ryan, who dosed him with what must have been something designed for elephants, for the result was immediate and volcanic! But it was effective, for D.H. ultimately got some sleep, and in the morning was better though very chewed up, and ghastly to look at. He wanted to ride as usual, but Ryan insisted on his going in a car that day.'

The day's march was taxing, says Charteris: 'Always there was the sound of guns – now distant, now seeming much closer. The Battalion Commanders knew what we were in for, and made the men lie down at every halt. At first the men resented this, but as the hours slowly passed they dropped as if hit immediately the halt was ordered, and were asleep almost before their bodies reached the ground. At first there was some whistling and singing, but that soon stopped and by early afternoon there was no noise to be heard save gruff orders enforcing march discipline. But the men were amazing. Practically none fell out. They stuck to it. Here and there you could see a man carrying another's rifle for a spell to ease the burden for even a few minutes. All the side roads were filled with refugees; a curious sight, men women and children struggling along, every known form of conveyance pressed into service to carry the most treasured of the household gods – fear on every face.'

The Corps Staff arrived at Landrecies, the halting-place of the 4th (Guards) Brigade, about four o'clock that afternoon. Almost immediately there was a panic among the refugees, who poured into the little town proclaiming that the Uhlans were at their heels. Haig ordered Charteris to investigate, but the latter could find no sign of the enemy; he returned to Landrecies, reported, and went back to sleep: 'I think I was asleep, although it cannot have been more than ten minutes later, when I was aroused by a sharp rifle-fire and some shelling. Almost immediately after reports came in that Landrecies was surrounded. There was a good deal of confusion, and some amusing incidents. D.H. ordered the whole town to be organized for defence, barricades to meet across the roads with furniture and anything else handy, all secret papers, etc., to be destroyed. . . . For once he was quite jolted out of his usual placidity. He said, "If we are caught, by God, we'll sell our lives dearly." '

It was not customary for Haig to use such dramatic language. This was one of the rare moments during the War when he was caught 'off balance', and the reason for it may quickly be discerned in his shaky physical condition. As it turned out, the situation was very much less desperate than it appeared to be in the first confusion. The sang-froid of the Coldstream Guards, despite their fatigue, rose to the occasion, and after a protracted scuffle in the dark they drove the Germans off. Inflated stories about this action circulated, and found their way into history books; they should be dismissed; losses on each side were about 120; the Germans were as surprised (and as tired) as the British, and made off when British artillery came into action.

Nevertheless, Landrecies has its significance. It made a sharp impression on Haig. As soon as the first flurry had died down, the necessity of extracting the Corps Staff from this warm corner became pressing. Charteris was ordered to guide the driver of Haig's car: 'I asked for five minutes to study the map. Then off we started. It was rather eerie work, quite dark, and of course no lights on the car. There was a little mist, which was helpful in one way, but made it more difficult to find the road. There was still a good deal of firing, and it looked rather a forlorn hope to try to get through. But anyhow it was better than staying in Landrecies and having sooner or later to surrender, which seemed the alternative. . . . Owing to the ground mist, we could not see anything other than the roadsides. . . . Once I came to a dead halt; the road I was on was at right angles to another road and did not cross it. I had no recollection of this being marked on the map, and had no idea whether to turn right or left. I took the left – pure luck – but it turned out to be correct, and a little afterwards we ran into some of our own men of the 1st Division. . . . All the same it was a close shave; it might have ended in us all – including D.H. – being prisoners !'

This scramble (recalling his escape from Ladysmith) confirmed in Haig's mind the sense of the unsuitability of senior officers being too closely involved in front-line fighting. Before the year was over, he would have reason to be reinforced in this view. Meanwhile, there is no denying that he was 'rattled'. He left Landrecies, it must be remembered, before the fighting ended; he was firmly convinced that the 4th Brigade was in serious danger, and his first preoccupation was the need to extract them from it. He issued orders to the 1st Division to set in hand a rescue operation. Next he reported to G.H.Q. that the position of I Corps was 'very critical'; a couple of hours later he asked that II Corps, eight miles away across the Sambre at Le Cateau, should come to his assistance. These reports had a dire effect on Sir John French, despondent as he already was; they also reacted badly upon General Smith-Dorrien, who had reluctantly come to his decision to fight at Le Cateau. This conclusion was dictated by his Divisional commanders, who were at one in asserting that the troops were incapable of another march unless the enemy were knocked away from their heels; but Smith-Dorrien was firmly expecting I Corps to appear to prolong his right. He left that flank open for them to fill – but it was the Germans who arrived to fill it.

This was in part Haig's fault. There is no doubt that his alarming reports had badly shaken G.H.Q. At 6 a.m. on the 26th French ordered Haig to retreat either to St. Quentin (i.e. across the rear of II Corps) or *south-east* into the area of the French 5th Army. General Lanrezac was warned to expect the arrival of the British, and philosophically (if cynically) prepared to give them protection. Lieutenant Spears,[1] the British liaison officer at Lanrezac's head-quarters, who had seen the Belgians fleeing from Namur, prepared himself for a similar spectacle; when he saw the units of I Corps he was amazed and delighted at their proud, confident and orderly bearing. Even the 4th Brigade had come away in good order, leaving only some wounded in Landrecies. The Corps as a whole marched south that day, not into the French sector; one sharp rearguard action took place, in which the Connaught Rangers were cut off; otherwise they were unmolested. But they were no help to Smith-Dorrien, engaged against six German divisions and a Cavalry Corps. Making every allowance for the effect of Haig's message in the early hours, it is astounding that G.H.Q., knowing that Smith-Dorrien was standing at Le Cateau and awaiting I Corps, not only did not order Haig to make every effort to join him, but actually ordered him to retreat in directions *away* from II Corps. Nor did Haig receive any response to his offer, later in the day, to try to help Smith-Dorrien. It was a bad business all round; fortunately II Corps summoned up, on this day, the very best qualities of the British soldier, managing what should have been virtually impossible – to fight, defeat and elude a greatly superior enemy in broad daylight. Le Cateau is, indeed, one of the great unremembered glories of British arms.

1. Now Major-General Sir Edward Spears.

Haig never forgot Landrecies. Apart from the alarums and excursions, he had a Scottish reason for remembering; he lost a wrist-watch there, leaving it with a watchmaker to have a new glass put in. On the day before the Armistice in 1918, Haig was back in Landrecies, and saw the watchmaker again: '. . . he remembered the whole incident but said he gave the watch to one of my "suite" – that I very much doubt.' From the alarums themselves he soon recovered. Early on the 26th Charteris found him at the headquarters of a brigade which was having a sharp skirmish with the enemy – '. . . a good deal of shelling, but not many casualties. Shell-fire is rather nerve-racking at first, but it is extraordinary how many miss. The Brigade Commander was very rattled and nervous, and D.H. was walking him up and down, holding his elbow and soothing him, just like a nurse with a nervous child. It was an interesting study in psychology. D.H. was showing no signs of his customary curtness with anybody who fell short of requirements. He was adopting the attitude that "bogy men" did not exist, that everything was quite normal, the Germans much more tired than we were, and so on. All this after a night without sleep, and heavy with great anxiety. But when we left the Brigade he was very incisive in his criticism, and I fancy the Brigade Commander will be sent home very soon.' Such is the difference that can come over a man in the space of a few hours; such, indeed, is the effect of a simple stomach ache.

For the rest of the War, Haig's health was astonishingly good, and there is no record of him ever again being under such a physical strain at a moment of crisis. That he was conscious of having fallen below his own standards on this occasion is suggested by his steady refusal afterwards to admit that Le Cateau was anything but a mistake. For months ahead, he was quick to notice lapses of morale in II Corps which he attributed to the hammering they had taken on that battlefield. We have seen[1] that he had long ago (in India) formed definite conclusions about the role of a small force in the face of a superior enemy. These conclusions made his verdict somewhat arbitrary, and he did not take into account the special circumstances of Smith-Dorrien's action.

Only one further incident in the Retreat from Mons requires our present notice. Two days after Le Cateau – so masterly was Smith-Dorrien's withdrawal – General von Kluck entirely lost the B.E.F. He turned the whole of his Army south-westwards, swinging out as far as Amiens, with his centre headed towards Montdidier. This produced two effects: first, it created a gap between the *I Army* and its neighbour, von Bülow's *II Army*; secondly, it caused columns of the *I Army* to march across the front of Haig's Corps. This was reported to him by the ever-present and invaluable R.F.C. The lesson of air reconnaissance at the 1912 manoeuvres was well-digested. Haig was now right back on form. He was seen that day by one of General Lanrezac's

1. See p. 48.

Staff Officers, Captain Helbronner. Joffre had been trying to screw Lanrezac up to the pitch of giving battle, and was rapidly reaching the conclusion that the latter would never fight. Helbronner writes: 'A British airman was reporting to Sir Douglas, who was very animated and conveyed to me the news he had just received. . . . This was that important German columns had been observed advancing south-west of St. Quentin. General Haig was good enough to mark these himself in pencil on my map. His words to me were "Go quickly to your General and give him this information. Let him take advantage of it without delay. The enemy is exposing his left flank as he advances. Let him act. I am anxious to co-operate with him in his attack." '

Lanrezac accepted Haig's offer, and sent Helbronner back to complete arrangements and tell Haig his plan: 'Sir Douglas expressed himself as satisfied, only making reservations concerning the hour at which his infantry was to attack. . . . He asked me to note that he had several heavy batteries at his disposal. He added that it would be necessary that, before participating in the attack, he should obtain Sir John French's sanction to the agreement he had come to with General Lanrezac.'

Haig sent his formal request to French at 7 p.m. on the 28th. The atmosphere at G.H.Q. had deteriorated even beyond the low level of the 26th. It was on this day that Sir Archibald Murray fainted at his desk through strain and overwork; on this day, too, Wilson sent orders to II Corps to abandon all their impedimenta and 'hustle along'. (Smith-Dorrien countermanded this, as soon as he knew of it; John Gough tore up a similar order to I Corps.) The French liaison officer at G.H.Q. was reporting to Joffre that I Corps 'still presents some aspects of cohesion', but that 'Conditions are such that for the moment the British Army no longer exists. . . .' It is not surprising, given these delusions, that Haig received the following prompt reply to his message:

'Commander-in-Chief does not approve of any active operations on the part of our First Corps tomorrow and has already ordered a halt for one day's rest.'

Haig accordingly then suggested that he should support the French with artillery only; G.H.Q. replied: 'The Commander-in-Chief repeats the order that no active operations of any arms except of a defensive nature will be undertaken tomorrow.' Thus it came about that the British took no part in the Battle of Guise, the first counter-stroke by the French that achieved any success worth noting, and an action which played a major part in creating the necessary conditions for the Battle of the Marne.

There was a sequel. Early on the 29th Haig was aroused to read this message from G.H.Q.: 'Please be good enough to inform C.-in-C. how it was that any confidential promise of support by First Corps was made to

General Lanrezac or why any official exchange of ideas was initiated without authority from Headquarters.' To this sharp and infuriating query Haig replied:

'I do not understand what you mean. I have initiated no "official exchange if ideas".

'G.H.Q. not having secured from the French roads for the retirement of my Corps, I had for my own safety to enter into relations with the nearest French force on my right. As far as it was possible I have maintained touch with the left of these French troops – and due to the presence of this Corps their left has been protected ever since we left Maubeuge.

'My Corps in its present position still protects their left, and if the enemy advances from St. Quentin southwards, I shall have for my own safety to deploy guns etc., without asking for the authority of G.H.Q. to do so.

'The extrication of this Corps from the false position in which it was placed still demands the greatest exertion from us all, and my sole objective is to secure its retreat with honour to our arms. I therefore beg you will not give credit to such allegations as the one under reference without first ascertaining whether it is true or not.'

This correspondence marked a further stage in the decline of Haig's relations with French. The immediate quarrel was patched over, but the memory of these tart words remained on both sides.

*   *   *   *

Joffre's hour struck on September 6th. On the previous day, taking advantage of the inward wheel of von Kluck's *I Army* across the northern front of the Paris defences, General Maunoury's 6th Army, which Joffre had so farsightedly begun to form thirteen days earlier, struck the Germans on their outer flank. This effectively checked their manoeuvre, with the result that a growing gap between von Kluck and von Bülow remained unfilled. On the 6th, Joffre ordered his whole line of battle, from the extreme left to Verdun, to pass to the counter-offensive. This included the 6th Army, the B.E.F., the 5th Army (now under Franchet d'Esperey in place of Lanrezac), Foch's 9th Army, de Langle de Cary's 4th Army, and part of Sarrail's 3rd Army; it was a manoeuvre on the grand scale – the Battle of the Marne. This was one of the decisive battles of the War, and, indeed, of history, for one reason: it marked the final failure of the German war plan. The plan had achieved striking results: huge losses had been inflicted on the French; most of Belgium and a large part of northern (industrial) France had been overrun; the Germans had come within sight of Paris; above all, they had obtained a strategic initiative which they never relinquished until 1918: but the French Army remained in being; the true object of the plan had not been gained.

Their retreat from the Marne signalized, for the Germans, the entry into a period of strategic uncertainty and improvisation which ultimately proved fatal to their cause.

This statement once accepted, the other side of the picture has to be regarded. The German retreat was largely self-imposed. Gigantic as its consequences were, the Battle of the Marne was, from the Allied point of view, little more than a chain of confused scuffles, with swaying fortunes in different parts of the field; both Maunoury and Foch, at different times, although in theory attacking, found themselves hard put to it to hold their positions; the discipline and courage of the German Army are habitually seen at their best in defeat, and the Marne proved no exception to this. It has to be remembered that their forces were intact; there was no question of their having been pulverized in battle, as they were in 1918, or in the Falaise Gap, or in their retreat after Stalingrad. Their retirement was orderly and deliberate, to positions which they lost no time in preparing along the banks of the River Aisne, and where they remained for the next four years.

The B.E.F. began its advance behind the French: its mere presence was disconcerting to the enemy, who had permitted themselves to believe that the British, at least, had been destroyed. But in terms of actual fighting, of effective intervention in the battle, it has to be stated that the B.E.F. did not perform much. The transition from continuous, exhausting and frequently hazardous retreat to bold attack was too much for all the Allied armies. It was also too much for G.H.Q., where distrust of French intentions and promises had now become deep-rooted; Sir John French was determined never to find himself again, if he could help it, 'out on a limb' with his flanks exposed, and the French failing to support him on either side. His present doubts were reinforced by the wide gap that existed between his right (I Corps) and the 5th Army. What were the French doing, beyond the horizon? Were they *really* advancing this time? Or was this just another of their empty gestures? As it turned out, the 5th Army had taken a new lease of life under its energetic, resolute and aggressive commander Franchet d'Esperey; but it was some time before this became apparent to the once-bitten British.

Haig shared some of French's doubts; when Charteris reported to him the new spirit in the 5th Army, and added that he thought the French would fight well in the counter-attack that was about to begin, Haig replied: 'That's all very well, but there are two IFs and big IFs: *if* the French advance and *if* the Germans do not attack them before their own attack is organized.' When the advance began, however, Haig was quick to see the need to press it forward, and was correspondingly disappointed at the slow progress that was made. He wrote on the 7th: 'I thought our movements very slow today, in view of the fact that the enemy was on the run! I motored and saw both Monro and Lomax[1] and impressed on them the necessity for quick and immediate action. . . . I thought [the Cavalry] were not doing much, in fact our Infantry was in front of their right flank!'

Charteris, who thought the whole movement was going 'absurdly slowly', commented: 'The cavalry were the worst of all, for they were right behind the infantry. This was gall and wormwood to [Haig], for he had always been first and foremost a cavalry officer. Personally, I could not help feeling a little unholy joy, for I have never thought cavalry, or indeed any form of horseflesh, would be of much use in war.' It is interesting to note that such views of Haig's own arm were held on his Staff, and by one of his most trusted officers. Charteris is incorrect in saying that Haig was 'first and foremost a cavalry officer'; his close connection with the arm had been in abeyance for many years; what he believed in, and he said this repeatedly, was the value of a balanced force of all arms; guided by this belief, he could not disguise his criticism of the Cavalry's performance. Two days later he wrote:

'. . . I met the 5th Cavalry Brigade (Chetwode) moving at a walk and delaying the advance of our Infantry. I trotted on and saw Chetwode. At my suggestion he at once trotted on. I explained to him that a little effort now might mean the conclusion of the War! The enemy was running back. It was the duty of each one of us to strain every effort to keep him on the run.'

The next day he noted: 'Our Cavalry Division . . . does not seem to have taken advantage of its opportunities today.' The Cavalry Division, under General Allenby, had performed prodigies during the Retreat; it was no doubt suffering now from those exertions. But the German rearguards, Jägers, cyclists and picked detachments, well equipped with machine guns, were the main factor in holding up the British advance.

Each day the Army gained more ground, skirmishing rather than fighting, and never in contact with the enemy's main forces. On the 11th, Joffre ordered a change of direction; the B.E.F. swung north-eastwards, pivoting on Haig's Corps, which consequently made little movement. 'Personally,' he wrote, 'I think it is a mistake to have changed direction now, because the enemy on our front were close to us last night and was much exhausted. Had we advanced today on Soissons, with cavalry on both flanks, large captures seemed likely.' The opportunity was missed, and two days later the B.E.F., with its French Allies, was brought up against the prepared German entrench-ments along the Aisne. Haig was quickly aware of the new 'feel' of the situation; on the night of the 12th he wrote: 'Reports . . . showed that

1. Commanding 2nd and 1st Divisions respectively.

opposition to our advance on the Aisne might be serious, and that possibly the enemy, instead of retreating, has decided to stand and fight on the line of the Aisne.'

This was precisely what they had decided upon, and it was fortunate that Haig anticipated the change, modifying his tactics accordingly. G.H.Q. had veered back by now into an ill-considered optimism closely resembling that with which it began the campaign. On the 13th, Haig received these orders: 'The Army will continue the pursuit tomorrow at 6 a.m. and will act vigorously against the retreating enemy . . . the heads of Corps will reach the line Laon-Suzy-Fresne. . . .' These objectives were twelve miles north of their actual position. Henry Wilson was talking to Joffre's Assistant Chief of Staff: 'Berthelot asked me when I thought we should cross into Germany, and I replied that unless we made some serious blunder we ought to be at Elsenborn in four weeks. He thought three weeks.'

Realities were more evident nearer to the line. This is commonly the case, and it later became an argument against Haig, in his turn, that orders issued from his headquarters were inapplicable on the ground. On this particular occasion, it needs to be remembered that Sir John French was commanding a force of six divisions; when Haig became Commander-in-Chief, each one of the three Armies under him was considerably larger than that. Furthermore, the principle which he adopted as C.-in-C., and from which he very rarely deviated, was, after laying down the broad outlines of strategy, to leave all levels of execution to his subordinate generals, and to be largely guided by them. It is a more valid criticism of him that he did not overrule them more often, or replace them. It could even be said that an exaggerated respect for 'the man on the spot' was born in him during these months under French, submitting to orders and interventions which he knew to be unsound.

The Battle of the Aisne was the first major engagement of I Corps; it was also the Army's introduction to Trench Warfare. There was still to be a phase of movement before the long lines of trenches settled into their almost immutable pattern from Switzerland to the sea. But indications of what the future would be like became very clear on the Aisne. Haig's Corps fought one more offensive action, on September 14th, and won a foothold along the ridge on the north bank of the river; casualties in the two divisions amounted to 160 officers and 3,500 other ranks on that day; Haig called these 'severe'. This was the last advance; from then onwards the whole Army passed to the defensive in the positions where it had been stopped. It was now that deficiencies, disguised during the war of movement, became apparent. The British Regulars, thoroughly disciplined, in good physical condition despite the large number of Reservists in their ranks, able to shoot faster and more accurately than any European army, possessing a good rifle and a good field gun, brilliantly served by fully trained gunners, with a Cavalry that surpassed any other in dismounted work over and above its ability to fight in the saddle, and with all these elements backed by well-organized administrative services, had so far given an excellent account of themselves. The South African War had taught them the value of marksmanship and of open formation; their trained Regimental officers and N.C.O.s gave them a flexibility and initiative that doubled their worth. Now, however, they were to encounter conditions which largely offset their advantages.

There can be no doubt that the Germans were more fully prepared than any of the Allies for a war of trenches. This was a natural consequence of their bold envelopment tactics; while one portion of their army – overwhelmingly the larger – would be required to cultivate all possible speed of manoeuvre, the smaller portion, probably greatly inferior to the enemy in its front, would have to hold its positions against all attacks. To do this, it would require every possible form of assistance from weapons and special equipment. In South Africa and Manchuria the value of trenches and barbed wire had been noted; German inventiveness quickly appreciated what the conjunction of machine guns with these would be likely to produce. They equipped with machine guns on a lavish scale – and with much else besides. Sir James Edmonds, who became the British Official Historian, attended the German Manoeuvres in 1908; there, he has related privately, he saw 'hand-grenades, light-ball pistols, camouflage suits for wire-cutting at night. Haig who was Director of Military Training tried to get similar things. . . . They were turned down by the Finance Branch.' With machine guns themselves, one of the dominant weapons of the War, it was a similar story: the School of Musketry had urged, in 1909, that battalions should have six machine guns each instead of two. The suggestion was turned down on financial grounds, and subsequent cuts in the Army Estimates rubbed the point home. The Chancellor of the Exchequer at the time was Mr. Lloyd George; when he became Minister of Munitions he very properly put in hand a vast machine-gun programme, for which he was not backward in claiming credit. Meanwhile the Army had had to make do; the rapid rifle-fire training was instituted by the School of Musketry because machine guns were not forthcoming.

All these wants were now felt. In addition to their plentiful trench equipment, the Germans obtained a most damaging Artillery superiority. The mobility of their 5·9 howitzer (as well as other large calibres) came as a surprise to all. In retrospect, this would seem to have been the most outstanding gun of the War, exceeding in effect even the famous French '75', and gaining a reputation akin to that of the '88' in the Second World War. The French had pinned their faith to the 75s, which were light and easy to handle, and had a prodigious rate of fire, but which were hopelessly outranged and out-calibred by the 5·9s. The British were at first in a slightly better position; South Africa had taught them not to neglect the role of heavy artillery in the field, and they had with them, in consequence, a small number of excellent 60-pounders. But there were nothing like enough of these, and their ammunition was inadequate both in quantity and quality. On September 16th Haig wrote: 'Our own high explosive is of little use compared with the German, so the enemy's big guns possess a real moral superiority for some of our gunners. In fact, our gunners cannot "take-on" the enemy's heavy batteries.'

This material inferiority was to continue until 1917. In what was to become primarily an artillery war, it was a terrible deficiency. Haig noted others; on September 24th he encountered one of his senior officers looking particularly despondent. The reason for this was that an entire platoon of the Grenadier Guards had just been wiped out by one huge German bomb which had been projected into their trench. Haig commented: 'This form of attack is novel and seems difficult to deal with. . . . Such large bombs are terribly demoralizing. The bomb makes a crater in the ground like a 'Black Maria'[1] and destroys trenches and men within a radius of 60–100 yards. . . . Our troops are certainly fighting at a great disadvantage in not having

(a) large bomb-throwers (*Minen Werfer*)
(b) small effective hand bombs with mechanical safety catch arrangements.'

It is a complete distortion, which has been sedulously fostered, that Haig was uninterested in the material side of the War. He understood better than most the value of equipment, and while he certainly did not have a technical mind in the sense that might apply to an Engineer Officer, he took great interest in all the inventions and new weapons that came to his notice. His diary contains numbers of descriptions of these, always with a detailed account of the working mechanism of the instrument, and generally with an accompanying sketch.[2] Trench mortars, liquid fire, gas and smoke appliances, wireless communication, dug-outs, camouflage, mines, light automatic weapons, balloons, aeroplanes, armoured cars, surgery, dentistry, bridging devices, light railways, tanks – above all tanks – each in turn received his enthusiastic attention. Indeed, so far from being resistant to new devices, it could be said of him that his enthusiasm for them was sometimes naïve and over-optimistic, though few would call this a fault.

His general attitude is summed up in a letter written in late 1915, after a meeting at Chantilly where Ministers and Generals had been discussing

1. 8-inch howitzer shell.
2. Plate facing p. 367.

new weapons: 'I thought that the meeting was good for the Generals as well as for the Government. Generals after a certain time of life, especially French, are apt to be narrow-minded and disinclined to take advantage of modern scientific discoveries. The civilian Minister can do good by pressing the possibility of some modern discovery.' Meanwhile, at the close of 1914, civilian Ministers still had all to learn themselves. Memories of shortages of transport, of dive-bombers, anti-tank guns and tanks capable of meeting the enemy's, of assault craft, jungle equipment, even rifles (let us not forget that the Home Guard was issued with pikes) in the Second World War indicate that a later generation was not that much wiser than its fathers.

At the Aisne the Allies reached an impasse; the solution to it was obvious and occurred to both sides simultaneously: to turn the enemy's line by attacking his exposed flank. Since it has been asserted that First World War generals had an unnatural predilection for frontal assaults, it may not be out of place to point out that, *while there was a flank*, generals on both sides went at it as hard as they could. When there was *not* one, of course, the matter became slightly more complicated. But von Kluck had carried his Army from Aachen to the outskirts of Paris in thirty days by a flank march; a flank attack had brought the Allies back from the Marne to the Aisne; and now the so-called 'race to the sea' was to be undertaken on the same principle. It had nothing to do with 'racing to the sea'; Germans and Allies both largely ignored the littoral during the opening weeks of the War. What brought them to it at last was the frustration, stage by stage, of their mutual attempts to outflank each other.

The B.E.F. did not at first take part in this manoeuvre. It was not until September 30th that French told Haig that he had asked Joffre to move the whole Force round to the French left again, so that it could be based on the Channel Ports. 'A very good proposal,' Haig commented, 'but difficult to carry out at present; as we are in such close touch with the enemy, it would be difficult to withdraw.' The next day he warmed even more to the idea, as he took stock of his situation: 'In front of this Corps, and for many miles on either side, affairs have reached a deadlock, and no decision seems possible in this area.' Joffre duly assented to the move, but I Corps was the last to go from the Aisne front, its rear units not leaving until October 16th, when the Battle of Ypres was already in full swing.

Before we turn our attention to that famous battle-ground, it will be well to review one further aspect of Haig's development – his relations with the French. During the Retreat, the impression that he had formed of the French Army had not been encouraging. His neighbours then (and later) were the XVIII Army Corps, at first under the command of General de Mas Latrie, a man who was not only incapable but also hysterical, and who was shortly removed. He was succeeded by General de Maud'huy, an officer of the old aristocratic school, as brave as a lion, dedicated to his profession, a hard fighter, but not, perhaps, over-endowed with brains. He formed a deep respect for Haig, who in turn recognized his qualities. His Corps contained a number of Colonial troops, Moroccans, whose losses in officers in the early fighting had greatly reduced their effectiveness, while their light uniforms, suitable for North Africa, made them chilled and depressed as the European autumn wore on. At one stage Haig learned that they were also short of food, and promptly sent them, on his own initiative, 10,000 rations of British Bully Beef. The response of these hungry soldiers to this confection might have amazed some of their British comrades, who were already beginning to know it only too well. De Maud'huy wrote to Haig: 'Nothing could touch me more deeply than your kindness towards my half-starved soldiers, and those 10,000 rations are a gift which I shall always remember.'

At a higher level, despite the poor performance of General Lanrezac, then commanding the 5th Army,[1] Haig had not hesitated to offer him full co-operation at Guise. Lanrezac's successor, d'Esperey, he quickly saw was a very different type of man: 'He seemed an active, determined little man, and gave me a feeling of greater confidence than the majority of French officers with whom I have had dealings had done. . . .'

Haig already realized that, whatever their shortcomings, co-operation with the French was an absolute prerequisite for all British policy and strategy, whether it was a matter of gifts of food, or of plans of operations. When you are in an Alliance, you are in it up to the neck; Sir John French had already provoked a major crisis by his failure to understand this. Haig may not have liked it, but he did understand. Second World War students will not be unfamiliar with the dilemma that is posed for the junior partner.

1. See p. 89.

6

First Ypres

YPRES IS the outlying fortification of Dunkirk. Throughout the Middle Ages its strategic significance was apparent; attacked, besieged, pillaged, impoverished, revived, the town's story was interwoven with the violent history of the Flanders Wars. Fortified again by Vauban, as the left tip of his defence system of Northern France, it ceased to be a *place d'armes* in 1855, but Vauban's ramparts and their encircling moat remained as a memorial of the stormy past. By 1914 Ypres had become a backwater; its 16,000-odd inhabitants lived quiet and reasonably prosperous lives, manufacturing ribbons, lace and cottons, and serving as the market centre of the rich surrounding agricultural district. Partly mediaeval, mainly seventeenth century, the town was one of the architectural jewels of Western Europe, dominated by the tall towers of its Cloth Hall and St. Martin's Cathedral, from the tops of which, on clear days, one can see the sea. Outside Ypres, at distances of from six to three miles, in a semi-circle from north-east to south-west run the gentle slopes of the Flanders 'ridges', whose actual heights – 70 to 150 feet – give no indication of the degree to which they dominate the town. They form the rim of a saucer, with Ypres in the middle; in 1914 it was a green saucer, thickly sprinkled with spinneys, parks and woods, cut up by hedges bordering the fields, 'with little white islands marking the positions of the rich villages, with their fine churches and graceful steeples'.[1] It was what soldiers call 'blind country'. Not that this was a matter of concern to the unwitting bourgeois of Ypres. The badge of their town is a black cat, honoured annually to this day with a lavish carnival; but in 1914 the luck of Ypres was right out.

The B.E.F. began to arrive in the Flanders region on October 8th, to play its part in the great outflanking manoeuvre on the left of the French 10th

1. Foch.

Army, commanded by General de Maud'huy, Haig's neighbour on the Aisne. The progress of the Allied left, in its attempt to turn the enemy's flank, has been aptly described by General Galliéni as 'always twenty-four hours and an army corps behind the enemy'. The first British troops to arrive were II Corps, and they entered the battle immediately; to the north of them was the Cavalry, consolidated into a Corps under General Allenby the next day. II Corps gained ground, but not much of it, as the Germans thickened in front; its casualties averaged from 1,000 to 2,000 a day, a steady drain. It was soon clear that only the success of a further 'left hook' could carry the Allied left forward. III Corps entered the battle on the 13th, the Cavalry side-stepping to the north where, on the following day they linked with IV Corps, coming down from Belgium, where it had been covering the retirement of the Belgian Army from Antwerp. IV Corps was an incomplete formation, consisting of only one Infantry Division (7th, under Major-General Thomson Capper, a doughty fighter) and the 3rd Cavalry Division. Despite the assistance of these troops, III Corps was not able to advance its line far beyond Armentières. The dream of liberating Lille quickly faded in the face of the resistance of the German *VI Army*.

Once again the German High Command was pursuing its classic strategy: powerful envelopment of a flank, combined with a stern defensive elsewhere. To carry out their plan, the Germans were in process of forming a new *IV Army*, consisting partly of troops set free by the Fall of Antwerp, partly of new Reserve formations recruited, contrary to the German system, of volunteers, many of them students; this was the cream of the youth of Germany, fired with an ardent patriotism, impatient to serve before its time. Six army corps were formed of these devoted young men; four of them marched on Ypres. The decision to use them there was not taken without deliberation; General von Falkenhayn, who had replaced the timorous von Moltke after the failure of the opening offensive, has defined the German objective:

'The prize . . . was worth the stake. . . . There was no doubt about the resolute offensive intentions of the English and French. Not only had the danger that the Germans would be finally cut off from the Belgian coast again become acute, but also the danger of an effective encirclement of the right wing. They both had to be removed unconditionally. If this, at least, was not done, then the drastic action against England and her sea traffic with submarines, aeroplanes and airships, which was being prepared as a reply to England's war of starvation, was impossible in their present stage of development. It was also questionable in certain circumstances whether the occupied territory in Northern France and Western Belgium was to be held; the loss of it would necessarily have led to evil results. If, on the other hand, the German Army succeeded in throwing the enemy back across the Yser sector and in following him, it could expect to force a favourable change in the whole situation on the Western Front....'

The German offensive, then, had two targets: there was not only the project of rolling up the Allied line of battle; it was also aimed directly at England.

On the Allied side, the game was also being played for big stakes. General Foch had been appointed by Joffre to command the northern group of French Armies (G.A.N.): Castelnau's 2nd Army, de Maud'huy's 10th Army and a Flanders detachment. He had no powers of actual command over the B.E.F. or the Belgians, but it was well understood that he must exercise co-ordinating powers over these forces, if their efforts were to be effective. Foch has stated his aims: 'The question was: would we have the time, and did we possess the means of effecting a break-through before the enemy could complete defensive measures against which we would be more or less impotent? This was the effort we were about to make; *it was an attempt to exploit the last vestige of our victory on the Marne.*[1] The idea dominating our tactics was that, in view of our feeble armament, notably in artillery and machine guns, we were powerless to break through the front of an enemy who had had time to organize the ground, construct trenches and protect them with wire entanglements. Our plan, therefore, was to forestall him, assail him while he was in full manoeuvre, assault him with troops full of dash before he could organize his defence and bring his powerful armament into play.' One has to make allowance for Foch's habitual fiery and imaginative speech; but he makes his meaning clear. What he was aiming at was an open battle of movement. What happened was a head-on encounter, and deadlock.

Haig arrived at Sir John French's headquarters at St. Omer on October 16th, the day on which his last units were leaving the Aisne front. He found French in a buoyant mood. Both Foch and Wilson were pleased to be closely associated with each other in battle, and no doubt the pair of them had been working on French. 'He seemed quite satisfied with the situation and said that enemy was falling back and that we "would soon be in a position to round them up".'[2] It would be a few days before I Corps would be able to take part in the action; Haig was anxious that they should have at least a brief rest after their trying time in the Aisne trenches. Meanwhile, he occupied himself with reconnaissance of the area, and meeting the commanders with whom he would be associated. He noted here, as in France, the pathetic refugee problem; there was not much he, or anyone else, could do about these people. He talked to them, and did what he could: 'They had walked all the way from Ostend with a basket on the arm or a pack of clothes on

1. Author's italics.
2. Haig.

their backs. All that was left to the poor things of their property. I thought the women seemed to bear up much better than the men of the party. I gave them 2 doz. "Oxo" soup squares for which they seemed most grateful.'

He met Sir Henry Rawlinson, commanding IV Corps, who was to be his neighbour. Rawlinson, a close friend of Wilson, was a 'card'. 'Rawly is a fox', his contemporaries would say. Haig was amused at the meeting. Rawlinson, says Charteris, 'was flying an enormous Union Jack on his car, and D.H.'s first remark was rather caustic – "I thought only the King and the C.-in-C. are permitted to fly the Union Jack." Rawlinson's reply was that it helped to encourage the inhabitants. I shall be interested to see whether he is still flying it when we see him again !' Haig also remarked on the curiously 'amateur' look of IV Corps Staff, and commented: 'I should prefer for serious business to have on my Staff more trained officers of the Regular Army.' But his general impression was a good one; Rawlinson 'seemed most cheery and anxious to get on . . . his bright joviality is of great value to an army when on active service and things are not going too well'. The last phrase strikes a note which suggests that Haig was not altogether convinced by the optimism that he had found at G.H.Q., any more than he had been on the way to Mons.

Inspired by this optimism, French ordered a general advance by the B.E.F. on October 18th, with the exception of I Corps, which was still assembling. Haig received his marching orders from French personally the next day: 'Sir John stated that he "estimated the enemy's strength on the front Ostend and Menin, at about one Corps, not more". I was ordered to march via Thourout and capture Bruges. "Defeat enemy and drive him on Ghent." My right "would pass through Ypres". After passing that place, I was free to decide whether to go for enemy on the north of me, or that part of him which was towards Courtrai.' There is a familiar ring about the grandiosity of these orders; they were not in keeping with the progress of events during the day, summed up in the Official History: 'The attempt at an Allied offensive, undertaken in the face of very superior numbers, had not prospered.' From information from neighbouring formations, as well as from his own Corps Intelligence, the impression grew on Haig that a stern fight lay ahead.

During the Battle of the Aisne, Haig had become so dissatisfied with the Intelligence that was passed on to him by G.H.Q. (as opposed to what it received itself) that he had set up a I Corps Intelligence Section and had appointed Charteris to be in charge of it. The idea was sound, the appointment questionable. Haig was very fond of Charteris (who had accompanied him from India), and defended him against all comers, even Lady Haig. Charteris was quick-witted, observant, humorous, methodical and, in turn, devoted to Haig. On the other hand, he was intellectually arrogant, which annoyed many people (later he became known as 'the principal boy'), at times opinionated, and in awe of Haig to an extent that made him chary of passing on distasteful information. This was to be a grave weakness; but since much blame has been attached to both Haig and Charteris on these grounds, it may now be well to look forward a few months and examine the system on which they worked. On February 11th, 1915, Charteris wrote:

'Intelligence work teaches scepticism, if... nothing else. Nothing can be accepted until it is confirmed from at least two other independent sources, and if it appears inherently improbable, it requires confirmation from at least one other source. The Head Intelligence Officer at G.H.Q. has this scepticism developed to the highest point. His strongest affirmation is that "Something or other appears not improbable", that means it is practically certain. D.H. demands more than this. Everything that goes to him has to be sharply divided into Fact, Probability, Possibility, Improbability but reported, and he holds me responsible that everything is in its proper category. I think he is right. "Not Improbable" is rather like the miss in balk, playing for safety. But French, at the beginning anyhow, did not trust the Intelligence, and that "Not Improbable" was an obvious and necessary measure of precaution. The fault lies with the C.-in-C., not with the Intelligence.'

This revealing passage shows that Haig, having laid down a system – an admirable system – *and believing that this would always be applied*, gave great trust to his Intelligence Branch, unlike French, who frequently ignored his. The tragedy is that Macdonogh, whom French ignored, was a first-rate Intelligence officer, whose only defect was diffidence; while Charteris did permit himself to twist facts. Haig never resented unpalatable facts; what infuriated him was unreasoning pessimism; proved facts he would always accept; Charteris should have known him better.

On October 19th, 1914, however, Charteris served him well. He had been ferreting about for information, and had gleaned much from the Belgians as well as from Macdonogh's department. He learned that there was at least a distinct possibility of two more German Corps being present, as well as the one which French had spoken of to Haig. 'I mentioned it to D.H. and he seems rather impressed and cross-examined me closely.... So we are going to move forward cautiously....' During the day G.H.Q. Intelligence identified three and a half German Army Corps; actually there were five and a half already present on the northern sector. Haig's doubts about his orders grew as the day wore on; at the close of it he wrote: 'My objective is to advance via Thourout and capture Bruges! But considerable opposition must be overcome before I can reach Thourout.' This may read like the understatement of the War. It meant, however, that Haig was considerably closer to reality than French, who still clung to the idea that only one German Corps was present.

Yet before we condemn French's optimism entirely, we may note that error was not all on one side. The German writer Rudolph Binding was on reconnaissance with his squadron of Dragoons. One of his men reported the presence of British troops in numbers ahead: 'I rode with him to Divisional Headquarters. "Scattered troops from Antwerp", opined the G.S.O.1 casually, while fighting is already beginning up in front. If the volunteer's report is right, and I don't doubt that it is, if they don't find that the scattered troops from Antwerp that they expect are in front of us, we may have a rough passage. We are very upset over the casual way in which this report has been received.'

The encounter battle began on October 20th. The brunt of it fell on III Corps, the Cavalry, and Rawlinson's incomplete IV Corps. While Haig's men began their deployment between Rawlinson and the French northern group, now known as 'Le Détachement d'Armée de Belgique' under General d'Urbal, the formations to the south had hard fighting. The German attacks by the IV Army advancing south-westwards, and by the VI Army advancing west- and north-westwards, both converging on Ypres, forced in the British line on both its flanks. The notable feature of the day was the achievement of Allenby's Cavalry Corps, fighting *dismounted*, and defending a line between Messines and Hollebeke. Armed with the Infantry rifle, which they well understood how to use, the British Cavalry were far better adapted to this work than either the Germans or the unfortunate French horse. The latter, in the north, mostly Cuirassiers, complete with breastplates and helmets, and having for a firearm what the British Official History calls a 'toy carbine', were far less able to hold ground, as they showed next day. All the signs of the 20th were that the Germans were making a determined attack, but, says the Official History, 'the British commander was still under the impression that there was only a force of indifferent troops collecting on his front'. The presence of the Reserve Corps of 'young soldiers' had been recognized, but their quality was underestimated by both British and French Headquarters.

Checked along his centre and right, and forced back there on the defensive, but still believing that he had found the end of the German line of battle, French persevered with his plan; I Corps was his last large intact formation; it was now thrown into the fight. Fortunately, both Haig and Rawlinson (whose 7th Division sustained very heavy attacks that day) were disposed to act with great caution. Haig's Corps advanced with the 2nd Division forward and on the right, between Zonnebeke and Langemarck, the 1st in rear and to the left of it. General de Mitry's French Cavalry Corps covered Haig's left, watching the exits of the Forêt d'Houthoulst, north of

Langemarck. The start was late, owing to congestion on the roads, but at first the going was easy enough, despite the close nature of the country. By 2 p.m. the 2nd Division was almost in line with the hard-pressed 7th Division; the advance had not been without loss – the 2/Oxford and Bucks Light Infantry, for instance, had 220 casualties, mainly from enemy flanking fire. On the other hand, British batteries had excellent targets against Germans in mass formation.

At this stage, the 1st Division was coming up on the left, and all seemed to be reasonably well; Haig writes: 'The enemy by this period appeared to be withdrawing through and from Poelcappelle and all indications pointed to a successful advance, when, about 2 o'clock in the afternoon, without any warning whatsoever, the French Cavalry Corps on our left received orders to retire west of the canal. The reason for this withdrawal was stated to be that the enemy was advancing in strength of about a division from the direction of Clercken. The G.O.C. of the French Cavalry Division on the immediate left of our 1st Division fully realized the effect of his withdrawal, and declined absolutely to obey this order until it was repeated. He refused to uncover our flank without "*une ordre formelle*". It was certainly a strange proceeding to withdraw troops supporting an ally's flank during a battle.'

Throughout the Battle of Ypres there were incidents like this. Whenever two allies are fighting side by side, and both are hard-pressed, there is always a tendency for one to feel 'let down' by the other over some tactical incident. Only a firm joint command can prevent divergence of plans. But all in all, the distinguishing feature of the battle was the high level of co-operation between the British and French, who became greatly intermingled.

The abrupt withdrawal of the French created a serious threat to Haig's left from the direction of the Forêt d'Houthoulst. The 1st Division now had to form a defensive flank, facing due north. Under these circumstances, further advance was evidently impossible; Haig halted the 2nd Division, which was already meeting with stiffening resistance, and ordered all troops to dig in where they stood. This line was short of the first objective of the day, Poelcappelle and Passchendaele. (The famous place-names of the Ypres Salient were already making their impact on the annals of the British Army.) The day had not been entirely unsuccessful; the Official History sums up: 'In spite of the numerical superiority, 5 divisions against 2, and the exposed left flank of the I Corps, the Germans had done little more than bring the British advance to a halt, and that at exceedingly heavy cost.'

Although somewhat disappointed by these results, Sir John French concurred with Haig's decisions: 'He explained that he would soon be taking the offensive and approved of the position I had taken up. The advance was to be discontinued for the present.' It is difficult to know exactly how French's mind was working at this juncture; volatile at the best of times, he would seem to have fallen prey again to conflicting thoughts. Wilson records that Joffre visited French on this day: 'All went satisfactorily until Sir John asked for facilities to make a great entrenched camp at Boulogne to take the whole E.F. Joffre's face instantly became quite square and he replied that such a thing could not be allowed for a moment. . . . So that nightmare is over. . . .' It certainly seems an odd idea to have in one's mind in the middle of an offensive designed to 'round up' the enemy. Reporting the day's events to Kitchener, French said: 'In my opinion the enemy are vigorously playing their last card, and I am confident that they will fail.'

It was not their last card that the Germans were playing, but their first. During the next three days this phase of the battle worked itself out. Powerful attacks were launched against the whole Allied front from La Bassée to Bixschoote. But the chief threat was from the north, where all the time the Allied High Command was trying to press its own advance. Foch, the pre-war prophet of the offensive, was the inspiration behind this; he has stated that among his reasons were the nature of the ground, in this region where sub-surface water rapidly filled any excavation, and lack of entrenching tools, which together made it impossible to organize a continuous line of defence. Yet the Salient was to be held by such a line for the next four years. A truer reason follows: 'Finally, a merely passive resistance on our part would indicate to the enemy that we were abandoning the fight, and would be an acknowledgement of weakness that could only stimulate him to redouble his efforts. Our only recourse, therefore, was to maintain an offensive attitude and to defend ourselves by attacking.' In accordance with this concept, whenever any new troops came to his hand, Foch made it an unvarying principle never, if he could help it, to use them for the relief of exhausted units, or to thicken the line, but always to try to push them forward in a renewed advance. Whatever may be said in favour of this policy (and it had an undoubted psychological effect on the enemy) it certainly placed a heavy burden on the fighting troops.

This chapter cannot attempt to give a detailed account of the First Battle of Ypres. The fighting of II Corps and III Corps forms part of the same operation, so that the front really ran from La Bassée to the sea at Nieuport. In their insular manner, the British have always regarded this as *their* battle; it has to be remembered that both the French and the Belgians were actively and critically engaged as well. Foch, obviously somewhat irritated by the tone of British histories, wrote in his Memoirs (speaking of the central sector): 'On October 31st the French held about fifteen miles of the front, the British twelve. On November 5th, the French held eighteen miles and the British nine. It can be seen that the French troops, both as to length of front occupied and numbers engaged, had to sustain the major part of the battle. It would therefore be contrary to the truth to speak of the battle and victory of Ypres as exclusively British.' Even allowing for the extension of the British front to the south which Foch excludes from this analysis, it is clear that he had a point.

Nevertheless the First Battle of Ypres was a momentous and terrible experience for the British Army; never before had nearly a quarter of a million British soldiers been assembled on one battlefield; never before had fighting of such ferocity been sustained for so long. The nature of the War exposed itself to the British Army at Ypres, in a manner far transcending anything known before, or guessed at. One short impression of the whole scene must suffice to cover many glorious deeds, some recorded and remembered, others not: 'To give a true picture of the long hours of patient and stubborn resistance there should be some mention on almost every page of bursting shells, blown-in trenches, hunger, fatigue and death and wounds . . . it must be remembered that the fighting was almost continuous, hardly interrupted at night, and that the troops had no rest . . . [they] must be imagined as fighting in small groups scattered along the front in shallow trenches, often separated by gaps amounting to two, three or even four hundred yards. . . . It was only at night that supplies could be got up to the troops and the wounded removed, and as soon as it was dusk the streets of Ypres and the roads radiating from Ypres were crowded with vehicles passing backwards and forwards.'[1]

This narrative will now confine itself largely to that part of the battle which concerned Haig. As on the Aisne, he was quick to sense the changing 'feel' of the situation. On the 22nd he ordered his Corps to strengthen its positions 'and to prepare for the attacks which there could be little doubt would be made upon us . . . from yesterday's operations I had come to the conclusion that the enemy was in considerably greater strength than had originally been anticipated by Sir John French when he gave me my instructions at St. Omer. Further, it seemed certain now that enemy's action was going to take the form of a determined offensive and not, as had been anticipated, that of a rearguard action.' He was right; the 1st Division, opposed by three German divisions coming from the north, had severe fighting all day and maintained itself with difficulty. The French IX Corps, under General Dubois, was now arriving, and Foch, true to form, promptly ordered them to take the offensive on the 23rd; he wrote to French: 'It is greatly to be desired that the whole British Army should support the French attack by acting offensively along its whole front, the left moving on Courtrai.'

1. Official History.

There was not much the British could do; the arrival of the French, in fact, created difficulties, for they entered the battle on the front of the 2nd Division, which had to side-step to the right to make room for them, causing the 7th Division to perform a similar manoeuvre. In view of this division's losses the contraction of its front was timely. But Haig's Corps was now split by the insertion of the French, and on the 24th, to rectify this, the withdrawal of the 1st Division began. It was no easy matter to carry out these movements in the middle of a battle. All along the front German attacks were continuing, sometimes stopped in their tracks by rifle fire, or by artillery (though a shortage of ammunition was already being felt), sometimes by counter-attacks. Haig remarked with admiration upon the bravery of the young German soldiers; fortunately for the Allies, the lack of training of the Reserve formations told against them: 'Time after time during the battles of Ypres the same phenomenon will be observed: the Germans having come on in overwhelming numbers and succeeded in penetrating our line, sat or stood about helplessly and without precaution. Either they were content to rest after reaching the objective they had been given, or they did not know what to do next.'[1] In 1915, when the British New Armies were taking the field, their enemies noted the same fault in them, particular examples of it being Suvla Bay and Loos. It is one thing to raise men; it is quite another to turn them into trained soldiers. The dreadful losses of the German volunteers at Ypres underline the moral.

Some advance was made on the 23rd, and for once the Allies had some large units in reserve; the Germans passed temporarily to the defensive: 'For the time being, any further thought of a break-through was out of the question. . . .'

But the Germans, even if no longer attacking, were not to be shifted easily; neither French nor British were able to make any notable progress. Sir John French, indeed, was forced to warn Kitchener that, unless he received large quantities of ammunition very soon, his troops would be forced to fight without artillery support. He was told to economize.

The main encounter battle was now over. For the next four days the Germans were quiescent on the greater part of the front, only continuing with their spoiling attacks and counter-attacks on the sectors of the French IX and British I Corps, where Foch was still seeking his offensive victory. Haig had set up his advanced H.Q. at Hooge Château on the eastern side of Ypres, his main Corps Staff being far back at Poperinghe. Charteris was with him, working hard on Intelligence and noting how out of touch with the realities of the battle G.H.Q. seemed to be: 'Indeed, we actually know more about what is happening on our own front than G.H.Q. does . . . there is an

1. Official History.

admirable Belgian officer who comes daily and gives us all the information that Belgian H.Q. has, and they seem very well informed. There is also an accommodating German Corps Commander who sends out constant messages and orders to his units by wireless, without coding them. I suppose he thinks we do not know any German! . . . God bless him! I'll give him a drink if ever I see him when the war is over.'

The line scarcely moved at all; on the 26th the weakened 7th Division (by that evening it had lost 43·6 per cent of its officers and 37·2 per cent of its other ranks) was driven from the hamlet of Kruiseecke, south of the Menin Road. This was very close to Haig's Advanced H.Q.: 'I rode out about 3 p.m. to see what was going on, and was astounded at the terror-stricken men coming back. . . . It was sad to see fine troops like the 7th Division reduced to inefficiency through the ignorance of their leaders in having placed them in trenches on the *forward* slopes where enemy could see and so effectively shell them.' The next day French placed the 7th Division under Haig's command, Rawlinson going home to supervise the formation of the 8th Division which would complete his Corps. French was undismayed by all setbacks and seemed oblivious of the fact that the front, in so far as it had moved at all, had moved backwards. On the 24th he told Kitchener that the battle was 'practically won'; on the 25th he reported that the situation was growing more favourable every hour; on the 26th he was convinced that the Germans were 'quite incapable of making any strong and sustained attack'; on the 27th he 'expressed himself as confident and very hopeful; he considered that it was only necessary to press the enemy hard in order to ensure complete success and victory';[1] on the 28th he ordered that the offensive should be continued. Haig's information, however, led him to somewhat different conclusions.

The third phase of the Battle of Ypres, which contained its first great crisis, is the most familiar to modern readers. It was marked by the intervention of an entirely new German Army under General von Fabeck, consisting of six divisions whose arrival gave the Germans twofold superiority over the Allies at the point of attack. Nor was this all: on the front of Haig's Corps and Allenby's Cavalry, where the blow fell, the British had only 26 heavy guns, including those with the divisions, and all short of ammunition; von Fabeck had over 250. The Germans were determined to make an end; their Order of the Day, issued on October 29th, read: 'The break-through will be of decisive importance. We must and will conquer; settle for ever with the centuries-long struggle, end the war, and strike the decisive blow against our most detested enemy. We will finish with the British, Indians, Canadians,[2]

1. Official History.
2. The Indian Corps was beginning to arrive; no Canadians were present.

Moroccans and other trash, feeble adversaries, who surrender in great numbers if they are attacked with vigour.'

Inspired by these thoughts, and encouraged by their own force, von Fabeck's advance guards crashed forward through the dense mists of early morning along the Ypres-Menin Road, at the junction of the 1st and 7th Divisions. Some British units were taken by surprise; there was trouble with badly fitting rifle ammunition at many points along the line; two Guards battalions were annihilated; the cross-roads east of Gheluvelt were lost, as was ground to the south of the Menin Road. Counter-attacks in the afternoon regained most of this, but not the cross-roads. It had been, says the Official History, 'an unlucky day. . . . It was a bad preparation for the desperate struggle that was to follow.' Haig, recognizing that the main stress of battle would fall on his Divisional Commanders, took steps to facilitate their close co-operation: 'I move the "Reporting Centre" back to White Château near level crossing on Menin Road to enable Lomax to make himself comfortable in Hooge Château. I found him living with his Divisional Staff in small cottage of two rooms, so I sent him into Hooge Château.' Lomax and Monro were now able to share the Château; Haig's new headquarters were at 'Hellfire Corner'. Sir John French, apparently over-impressed by the I Corps counter-attack in the afternoon, reported to Kitchener:'. . . if the success can be followed up, it will lead to a decisive result.' A more helpful contribution by him, however, was the relief of II Corps by the Indian Corps in the south; tired and weakened as it was, II Corps would yet play an invaluable role.

It was on the 30th that the main body of Fabeck's force entered the battle; five divisions were brought into line without any suspicion on the part of the Allies. Foch and French saw no reason to change their orders for an offensive; Haig was more cautious; he ordered his troops to entrench and reorganize, adding: '. . . orders as to the resumption of the offensive will be issued . . . when the situation is clearer than it is at present.' This was a wise interpretation, for the enemy's attack scored important successes and imposed the greatest strain on Haig's command on this day. The weight of the attack fell on the much-reduced units of the 7th Division, and on the Cavalry at Zandvoorde and Hollebeke; the Germans on this sector had an advantage of six to one. The first attack fell on the Cavalry, forcing them out of Zandvoorde, and thereby gravely compromising the 7th Division immediately to the north of that place.

Since so much has been said about Cavalry, and Cavalry-minded British generals during the First World War, a brief digression may be appropriate here. We have noted that the firearm of the British Cavalry gave it an advantage over that of any European Army; during the days that followed, this was to be amply proved. It is more than doubtful whether any cavalry in the world could have put up the performance of the British Cavalry at Ypres. They acted, in fact, as Mounted Infantry, as they were to do throughout the War, demonstrating that it would have been folly to raise a special arm of such troops. They had the advantage of mobility, which enabled them to be switched quickly from one point to another; General Byng's 3rd Cavalry Division acted from now on as a mobile reserve. On the other hand, like Marines, or Commandos and Paratroops in the Second World War, their lack of heavy equipment was a disadvantage in any prolonged defensive fight on fixed positions; the whole artillery of Allenby's Corps consisted of only 7 R.H.A. Batteries. Their numbers, too, put them at a disadvantage.

From some accounts, one might suppose that France was flooded with British Cavalry during the War; for the benefit of generations to whom Cavalry organization will be wholly unfamiliar, it may as well be stated now. Allenby's three divisions comprised 7 brigades (3 in the 2nd Cavalry Division); each brigade contained 3 regiments, and each regiment 3 squadrons. On taking the field, each regiment would number about 500 men; adding in Horse Artillery, Signal Troops, Royal Engineers, etc., a normal division of 3 brigades would have a strength of about 5,500. In a dismounted fight, allowing for horse-holders and men on special duties (Cavalry were always being called on for special duties as orderlies, escorts and so on), more than one-third of the strength of each regiment would need to be deducted to show its actual rifle strength. At its highest, the Cavalry component of the original B.E.F. was about 12 per cent; at Ypres, if the Cavalry had been intact, it would have amounted to just over 6 per cent, but it was not intact; in 1916, when the B.E.F. numbered 1½ million, and there were five cavalry divisions, they added up to under 2 per cent; in 1918, to 1 per cent. This is the truth behind the allegations of 'masses of Cavalry' and 'Cavalry-minded strategy'. The point is, quite simply, that Cavalry always *look* a mass; a few of them fill up a lot of space. Allenby's Corps at Ypres had a lot of space to fill – nine miles; even with the support of two Indian battalions, it could only average about 1,000 rifles per mile, but they were rifles in good hands.

The break-in on his right flank warned Haig of what was afoot: 'The position at this period was serious. . . . It was now evident that the Germans were in great force, and accordingly orders were issued at 12.30 p.m. for the line Gheluvelt to the corner of the canal to be held at all costs.' As conditions stabilized, Haig also began to organize a counter-attack to retake the lost ground; at the same time, I Corps being fully extended, he asked his neighbour on the left, General Dubois, for help. 'With soldierly regard for the situation as a whole,' says the British Official History, 'General Dubois at once abandoned his own plans and set in motion his corps reserve. . . .' Charteris comments: 'We had a splendid French general working alongside

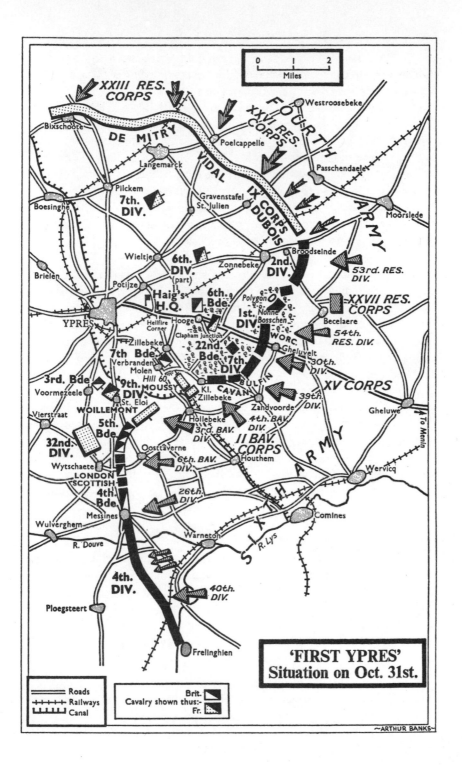

~ARTHUR BANKS~

'FIRST YPRES'
Situation on Oct. 31st.

Roads
Railways
Canal

Brit.
Cavalry shown thus:-
Fr.

0   1   2
Miles

XXIII RES. CORPS
DE MITRY
Bixschoote
Langemarck
Boesinghe
Pilckem
Brielen
Potijze
YPRES
Haig's H.Q.
Zillebeke
7th Bde.
Verbranden Molen
3rd. Bde
Voormezeele
9th. DIV.
St. Eloi
Vierstraat
WOILLEMONT
5th. Bde.
32nd. DIV.
Wytschaete
LONDON SCOTTISH
4th. Bde.
Messines
Wulverghem
R. Douve
Ploegsteert
4th. DIV.
Frelinghien
Warneton
Comines
R. Lys
SIXTH ARMY
Wervicq
Gheluwe
To Menin
XV CORPS
Houthem
II BAV. CORPS
6th. BAV. DIV.
26th. DIV.
40th. DIV.
Oosttaverne
3rd. BAV. DIV.
4th. BAV. DIV.
Zandvoorde
Hollebeke
KL. CAVAN.
Zillebeke
BULFIN
39th. DIV.
Gheluvelt
30th. DIV.
WORC.
Becelaere
54th. RES. DIV.
XXVII RES. CORPS
53rd. RES. DIV.
Moorslede
Passchendaele
Westroosebeke
FOURTH ARMY
XXVI RES. CORPS
Poelcappelle
IX CORPS DUBOIS
VIDAL
Broodseinde
2nd. DIV.
Zonnebeke
Gravenstafel
St. Julien
7th. DIV.
Wieltje
6th. DIV. (part)
6th. Bde.
Polygon
Nonne Bosschen
1st. DIV.
WORC.
Hooge
Hellfire Corner
Clapham Junction
22nd. Bde.
17th. DIV.
Hill 60
MOUSSY
Hollebeke

of us – Dubois – who never fails; a great soldier and most loyal ally.[1] He sent help at once, the gap was filled, and that crisis was safely past. By night-fall we began to hope that the worst was over. It was only beginning.'

That night Haig wrote: 'The situation at nightfall had to a certain extent been restored, but was still full of anxiety for the following day.' He ordered every effort to be made to secure the line; plans for offensive action would have to wait until that precaution had been completed. G.H.Q., taken aback by the turn of events, issued no orders, but authorized Haig to send orders to the Cavalry Corps, so that he was now in effective command of half of Sir John French's army. It had been his practice to return to Ypres at night to sleep, but on this night: 'I dined in Ypres, but returned to White Château near the level crossing to sleep, in order to be closer to the troops.'

October 31st marked the climax of the German attack; the Kaiser arrived at *IV Army* headquarters to inspire his troops; they had already gained important advantages, including the annihilation of four priceless Regular battalions, which they now prepared to exploit. Certain weaknesses, however, were already being shown on the German side; the bravery of their troops, mostly raw, was astounding, but divisional commanders were already pro-testing at the high casualties (one platoon of Gordon Highlanders counted 240 dead Germans in front of it on the 29th); these protests were overruled. There were also other hesitations; the close, wooded nature of the country-side prevented the Germans from seeing what they had achieved, and how thin the British line was. Their leaders, it seems, 'were paralysed by the thought that fresh British forces might appear at any moment from the shelter of the woods and surprise them, just as the original B.E.F. had suddenly stood in their way at Mons.'[2] It was not fresh forces, however, that stood between the Germans and Ypres – just courage. The Official Historian writes:

'The line that stood between the British Empire and ruin was com-posed of tired, haggard and unshaven men, unwashed, plastered with mud, many in little more than rags. But they had their guns, rifles and bayonets, and, at any rate, plenty of rifle ammunition, whilst the artillerymen always managed to have rounds available at the right place at critical moments.'

It was a warm, fine day, with early mist which cleared by 10 a.m. The first blow fell again on the Cavalry, between Messines and Wytschaete; at Messines, twelve weak squadrons were attacked by twelve battalions; to the north of them, General Hubert Gough's 2nd Cavalry Division could only

1. 'I have some first-rate French officers to deal with now – very different from some of the old fooslers we had to deal with near Mons at the beginning.' Haig to Lady Haig, November 3rd.
   2. Official History.

muster 1,350 rifles in all. Messines fell, and though part of it was retaken later in a counter-attack, in which featured the London Scottish, the first Territorial Infantry battalion to enter the fighting, for a long critical stretch of time the salient won by the Germans created a grave threat to the centre of Haig's line across the Menin Road. Reports soon reached him that the 'situation in the trenches south and south-east of Gheluvelt was serious.'

'Reports reached him'; all through the battle – and the remainder of the War – the whole question of reporting was to prove a terrible stumbling block. Time after time, at Ypres, one learns of every runner being 'killed almost immediately after leaving the headquarters trench', 'none of the messengers reached brigade headquarters', etc. Vision was restricted, telephone lines were continuously cut; it is almost impossible, in this age of highly developed communications, to imagine what the 'fog of war' was like at that time. Every *known* device was tried to overcome this problem, at one time or another during the War; devices which required another twenty or thirty years to be invented and produced could not, of course, be used. And the answer to the often repeated question, 'Why didn't General X do this or General Y do that?' is all too often, 'Because he had no information; he simply did not *know* what was happening'. Nor was this a matter of 'going up and having a look'; very often the men in front saw least of all.

Nevertheless, when the second German blow fell, on the village of Gheluvelt, this was precisely what Haig felt impelled to do. The defence of Gheluvelt, in which the 1/Queens was annihilated after a magnificent fight,[1] should rank as an epic equally with its recapture later; at the time it was a disaster, all the signs of which were clearly visible in the retirement of British artillery, the streams of wounded and unwounded men coming back down the Menin Road, and the ominously lengthening range of the German guns. A Staff Officer brought Haig the news of the loss of Gheluvelt, but stated that the 1st Division's line was still holding; shortly afterwards, however, another report came in, saying that the 1st Division had broken. Haig decided to see for himself, and set off up the Menin Road, 'his appearance,' says the Official History, 'moving up the road at a slow trot with part of his staff behind him as at an inspection, doing much to restore confidence'. He could see the confusion for himself; he could not see much else. As a gesture, this ride had its value; as a source of information, it only underlines what has been said

1. It was of this defence that the German Official Account, *Ypres 1914* (*Die Schlacht an der Yser und bei Ypern im Herbst 1914. Herausgegeben im Auftrage des Generalstabes des Feldheeres*) wrote: '. . . over every bush, hedge and fragment of wall floated a film of smoke, betraying a machine gun rattling out bullets.' It betrayed no such thing; machine guns were very sparse at this stage; it was British musketry, sixteen aimed rounds per minute, which some experts could work up to thirty in what was called the 'mad minute'. Nothing like it was ever seen again.

above. Haig did not learn any more hard facts until he returned to his Advanced H.Q., where John Gough told him that the 1st Division's line had, indeed, gone. Almost immediately afterwards, there was worse news: four big shells had fallen on Hooge Château, where Generals Lomax and Monro were conferring with their staffs. General Lomax was mortally wounded, Monro was stunned; seven of the Staff Officers of the two divisions were killed. It was a shocking calamity, all the worse for Haig, because he had put them there.

Almost simultaneously with the news from Hooge, Sir John French arrived at I Corps H.Q. Haig told him what had occurred: 'Sir John was full of sympathy and expressed his gratitude for what the Corps, as well as I myself, had done since we landed in France. No one could have been nicer at such a time of crisis. But he had no reinforcements to send me, and viewed the situation with the utmost gravity. After a few sharp words of criticism about the lack of "French help", he left me to go to his motor and visit Foch. I then mounted my horse.' Haig was about to go up once more to the front, when, Charteris relates: '. . . Rice[1] came galloping back, as red as a turkey-cock and sweating like a pig, with the news that Gheluvelt had been retaken and the line re-established. Can you imagine what that meant? It was just as if we had all been under sentence of death and most suddenly received a free pardon. It had all seemed so hopelessly bad, defeat staring us in the face and then this news that meant, at least, a good fighting chance. I remember shaking Rice's hand, as if he himself had retaken Gheluvelt. Everyone else was just as excited as I was, except D.H. who pulled at his moustache and then said he "hoped it was not another false report". Rice was certain his information was correct, but I don't think D.H. was quite convinced, although he sent an A.D.C. after the C.-in-C. to tell him. Then he went off up to the front to see for himself.'

The news was true: three companies of the 2/Worcestershire, seven officers and 350 men, under Major E. B. Hankey, had retaken the village. It is difficult to call to mind another occasion, during the rest of this war of masses and large formations, when such a small unit produced such an effect.

Although French had received the news of Gheluvelt, he was still in a very shaken condition by the time he met Foch: 'The Field Marshal painted a particularly black picture of the state of the I Corps. The troops were in full retreat towards Ypres. . . . It was the beginning of a defeat. With troops as exhausted as these men were, and who could not be collected and reformed, the British line was definitely broken. If they were asked to continue the battle, Sir John French said, there was nothing left for him to do but go up

1. Brigadier-General S. R. Rice, C.R.E. of I Corps, whom Haig had sent out to collect information.

and get killed with the British I Corps.'[1] Foch's immediate reaction was to think of relieving the British by an attack elsewhere. This, of course, would require time; what of the interval? He scribbled his views down on a piece of paper and handed it to French:

' "It is absolutely essential *not to retreat*; therefore the men must dig in wherever they find themselves and hold on to the ground they now occupy. . . .

' "But any movement to the rear carried out by a considerable body of troops would lead to an assault on the part of the enemy and bring certain confusion among the troops. Such an idea must be utterly rejected. . . ."

'The Field-Marshal had the good sense and straightforwardness to take the paper I handed him. He added on the back in his own hand a few words to the effect that he concurred entirely in my views. He then sent it . . . to General Haig for execution.'

Foch's qualities and drawbacks were all of a piece. If he was largely responsible (with Wilson's help) for French's earlier unreasoning optimism, his influence now was entirely healthy. His attitude, however, could be maddening to men who were closer to the battle. Charteris had been sent by Haig to procure help from the French; he met Foch in a sour mood. 'Foch treated me to some play-acting. When I was shown into his H.Q. he was gazing moodily towards the north, and took no notice for some time. It was probably only a few minutes, but it exhausted my patience. After trying a cough to attract his attention without any result, I butted straight in and spoke to him. He shook himself with a start, as if awakening from a day-dream, and said, "Ah, pardon, I was thinking what we should do on the Meuse." Utter nonsense. He was doing no such thing, but was, I suppose, trying to hearten me, and through me D.H., by pretending that the fighting at Ypres was relatively unimportant, and that we must win anyhow. But once he did apply himself to the problem he was excellent.'

Haig, at the front with his Brigadiers, appreciated the truth: 'The opinion on all sides is that the troops are very exhausted . . . Landon and Fitzclarence assure me that if the enemy makes a push at any point, they doubt our men being able to hold on. Fighting by day and digging by night to strengthen their trenches has thoroughly tired them out.' Fortunately, the Germans did not push. On the right of the 1st Division, a counter-attack under General Bulfin, supported by eighty – just eighty – Gordon Highlanders, regained half a mile of lost ground and demoralized the Germans. British and French Cavalry were coming up into the line and also drove the Germans back.

1. Foch: *Memoirs*.

Haig observed the entry of the dismounted French troopers into the battle: 'I watched the smart dapper little fellows march off. Several had "jemima boots", most unsuited for war and mud such as we soon encountered in Flanders. They went off in great spirits to take on the German infantry, though the little carbine with which they were armed was not much better than an ordinary rook rifle.'

The day's fighting came to an end; but for the morrow, says the Official History, 'it was a question whether the line of battered and ever-diminishing British battalions and squadrons, patched in places by French reinforcements, could continue to hold on. . . . With infantry brigades reduced below the establishment of battalions, and cavalry regiments below that of squadrons, with only some thirty medium heavy guns – some of which were obsolete – and with the imminent danger of lack of gun ammunition, the future looked gloomy and doubtful. The sin of unpreparedness for war of the British nation was indeed being visited on its children, the men and officers of the British Expeditionary Force.'

For five days there was a lull in the fighting, in the sense that neither side was making an all-out effort against the other. For the fighting troops and their immediate commanders, however, it was a lull only in name. The German artillery was at work all the time; the bombardment of Ypres itself now began in earnest, multiplying the difficulties of communication for the British. Shells descended continuously on all parts of the British position; Charteris writes: 'D.H. himself had rather a narrow escape. . . . He was looking at a map opened on a table under a great glass candelabrum. A shell hit the house and down came the candelabrum on the map, very narrowly missing his head. A couple of signallers were killed at H.Q. at the same time. He was quite unperturbed – but we prevailed on him to change his H.Q., as once the German artillery had got the range of his château it was certain to be struck again.'

That incident was on the 2nd; two days later the Corps Reporting Centre was hit again, and two Staff Officers were killed. Rumours of German spies began to circulate, and added to the nervous strain. Meanwhile, apart from their artillery, the Germans remained active at different parts of the front. The British Cavalry were withdrawn, and replaced by a new French Army Corps (XVI); Haig's Corps was now sandwiched between two French formations. He had little doubt that shortly he would be attacked again, and set in hand a precaution which was to be of great significance: he ordered General Rice to superintend the construction of 'keeps', or all-round defence positions which could hold even if the enemy got in behind them, or penetrated past a flank. Labour and tools for this work were few, but Rice managed to complete a small number of these posts, in a rudimentary manner.

It was an idea of Haig's which paid dividends all through the War, but one which met with constant resistance from below which would be unaccountable, were it not for the British soldier's habitual dislike of spade-work and his eternal fatigue. Not until 1918 did labour battalions appear in anything like sufficient numbers, and one of the worst tortures of the War was the endless round of digging, wiring, roadmaking and other toil inflicted on men who were supposed to be resting from battle.

The condition of his troops was by now a serious preoccupation for the Commander of I Corps. On November 4th he urged on French the need to relieve the 1st and 7th Division immediately, pointing out that the former was now reduced to 3,491 men and 92 officers – less than the normal strength of one brigade. On that day he sent one-third of his artillery to the rear, since there was not enough ammunition to feed the guns. The next day, when three 'brigades' of II Corps joined him in place of the 7th Division, he noted that eleven battalions between them mustered only 3,500 rifles. The 7th Division itself was stronger than that, though utterly exhausted – 'a mere wreck of the fine force which had landed in Belgium almost exactly a month before'.[1] Foch himself was aware of the critical condition of I Corps, and sent an officer to Haig on the 3rd to tell him that 'it was most necessary to hold on for two more days, because by that time large reinforcements to the French troops would arrive and be ready to advance. It was General Foch's intention not to use this force until it was all concentrated ready to strike a united blow'.

Foch's optimism had once again infected French; he telegraphed to Kitchener that he and Foch were now convinced that the Germans were removing troops to the Eastern front, where Hindenburg's armies had sustained a sharp defeat. If there were any more attacks at Ypres, French said, they would merely be to cover this move, and could not succeed in doing much damage. When Haig attended a Corps Commanders' conference at G.H.Q. on the 5th, 'I was very astonished to find that the point which attracted most interest was "Winter Leave" for the Army. Personally, my one thought was how soon I could get my battle-worn troops relieved, and given a few days' rest out of the trenches and shell-fire.' Charteris called the attitude of G.H.Q. 'sublime detachment'; once again it was quite unrelated to information supplied by the Intelligence Branch, which very accurately discerned significant changes in the German Order of Battle. No less than six new divisions were being assembled against Ypres, including two which had been set free by the Belgian inundations along the Yser, as well as the famous Prussian Guard.

November 6th was a day of thick fog, which hampered the operations of

1. Official History.

both sides; it may, all the same, have been the saving of the Allies. The German attack now fell on the French on the right of I Corps. One of those unpredictable panics to which the French Army has always been liable occurred at St. Eloi, where two battalions suddenly retreated about a mile. This brought the Germans within two miles of Ypres, and thrust a dangerous wedge into the junction of the French and British forces. There was nothing that Haig could do about this, except to patch the gap on his own sector, and urge General d'Urbal to retake the lost ground with a counter-attack. Both d'Urbal and Foch were free with promises to act, but little came of them; Haig's relations with the French on his right were in sharp contrast to those with General Dubois, and led inevitably to bitterness. The danger of I Corps being encircled was terribly real; on the next day: 'I wire to G.H.Q. that French must be urged to attack and reoccupy their old line, and I sent cypher message "If by this afternoon French are not on their old line, I recommend my force to be withdrawn on a N. and S. line through Ypres." We all feel that the French are not doing their fair share in attacking the enemy. . . .'

Haig continues: 'The ignorance of the French Commander 16th Corps of the positions of his own troops about Klein Zillebeke is also alarming. Few French Generals or Staff Officers ever seem to go forward to visit their troops in advanced positions. They rely too much on telegrams and written reports from regiments.' It is a fact that the French were carrying out many 'paper attacks' at this stage; Foch himself was obliged to repeat orders and make them 'definite' in order to procure action. At the same time, Haig noted signs of cracks in British morale. While he was visiting the 3rd Division (from II Corps), 'Several shirkers pass Divisional Headquarters. . . . I order all men to be tried by Court Martial who have funked in this way, and the abandoned trenches to be re-occupied at once.' He attributed the 'want of fighting spirit in the 3rd Division' to the effect of Le Cateau; this was unfair; II Corps had been through a great deal since Le Cateau which accounted perfectly well for any breakdown; it had been fighting in Flanders continuously since October 8th. This was one of Haig's blind spots.

The next day Haig went to meet Foch and French at Cassel. 'There was', says Charteris, who was present, 'a good deal of straight talk. D.H. was very emphatic that the French custom of very high-placed officers issuing energetic orders and leaving it at that, without themselves taking active steps to see that they were carried out, was useless. . . . He urged that they must go forward and take a personal grip of things. Our own G.H.Q. is not very much better. Sir J. French himself goes round Divisional Headquarters, but very few of the Staff Officers ever seem to come as far forward even as Corps H.Q. D.H. himself errs, I think, in the other extreme. He is constantly in extreme danger of being hit; he goes everywhere on horseback. I do not know what would happen if he were knocked out.'

The question of command in battle remained vexed until the end of the War. The instinct of every Regular officer was to go forward, to be with his men; Sir Thompson Capper (7th Division) told Charteris at Ypres: 'No good officer has a right to be alive during a fight like this.' Capper lived up to this dictum – and died of it at Loos. Haig, as we have seen, went up to the front constantly; as a Corps Commander, on a narrow front which was still fairly fluid, this had value. As the War went on, however, the advantages of 'being with the men' (which 'men' – those between one trench traverse and the next?) became smaller and smaller. The position was even arrived at when *Battalion Commanders were forbidden* to accompany their leading waves in attacks. The supreme irony was, perhaps, the spectacle of Sir Ian Hamilton, the most gallant of personal leaders, conducting his battles from a ship off-shore, while his soldiers struggled forward at Gallipoli. A glimpse of the alternative comes from the other side of the line. Binding writes of a German brigadier who, 'when his troops were having the hottest time, when they were in the most dire need of calm, clear orders, when everything depended on his doing something decisive . . . cried to his Brigade Major in a state of terrific excitement, "The horses, my dear L.! Come, let us fling ourselves into the battle!" ' No doubt, remarks Binding, he thought he was doing the right thing.

On November 7th, winter made itself felt; from then onwards mud and weather became a factor in the battle. The sufferings of the British troops were great, although for a few days the main fighting was on the French fronts – first to the south, then on the north, where their resistance was much firmer. The German policy was 'to attack somewhere every day', and a costly error this proved to be. 'We are still stuck here for perfectly good reasons;' wrote Binding on the 8th, 'one might as well say for perfectly bad reasons.' But now at last the Battle of Ypres was nearing its end. The last stroke of the German High Command – the last shot in its locker – was delivered on November 11th, a portentous date. It was a foggy morning again, until noon, when rain came, turning into a downpour later in the day. The German bombardment, greatly reinforced, was the most severe that the British troops had yet experienced. 'For the infantry in the front line and the fighting staffs', says the Official History, 'there was nothing to do but lie at the bottom of the trenches and in the holes in the ground, which, when they had a few planks, a door, or some branches, and a few inches of earth over them, were in those days called "dug-outs". The British battalions had now been fighting continuously for three weeks, practically without relief or rest, under all the hardships of wet and cold in the open, and to many of the infantry it seemed that the end was now at hand. Without losing heart or faith in the final victory, they had ceased to feel that their lives were any longer their own.'

The first crisis came, once more, on the right of I Corps, when the French lost Hill 60; and once again an appeal from Haig to Dubois for help was not unanswered. That general had only one light cavalry regiment to offer; he sent it. With its aid, and the courage and skill of Lord Cavan, commanding in that sector, the position was restored. On the left, the remains of the 2nd Division swiftly defeated the Germans who came against them, inflicting frightening losses. The danger was in the centre, along the Menin Road again. Here the Prussian Guard launched its attack, part of which fell upon the British 1st Guards Brigade under General FitzClarence. This circumstance has given rise to a certain amount of legend, British Guards against Prussians, etc. But in fact FitzClarence's brigade was a Scottish one, 1/Cameron Highlanders, 1/Black Watch, with about 200 men of the 1/Scots Guards, about 800 rifles in all. Behind their line were five of the strong points which Haig had ordered to be constructed,[1] and these, according to a Staff Officer who was present, 'were the saving of the day'. When the German attack came, on both sides of the Menin Road, it consisted of 25 battalions of the most famous regiments in the Prussian Army, 17,500 infantry, against 19 battalions and 3 cavalry regiments, whose sum total, including all their reserves, was no more than 7,850.[2]

Both south and north of the road, the Prussian Guard was able to make some progress at first. To the south, however, where II Corps units were holding the line, this was quickly brought to a standstill; the 1/Royal Scots Fusiliers put in a brave counter-attack; the 2/Duke of Wellington's practically exterminated the *Fusilier* battalion of the *2nd Guard Grenadier Regiment*. To the north, the *1st* and *3rd Foot Guard Regiments* fell upon FitzClarence's exiguous command, and overwhelmed the forward line by sheer weight of numbers. The British units were driven back to their strong points, and there they held on; the Germans, taken by surprise when they came to these positions, and already greatly disorganized by the rifle- and gun-fire of the defenders, were not able to deal with these obstacles. Nevertheless, they had created a dangerous gap in the British line. The war diary of the 1/King's (2nd Division) tersely remarks that the regiment found itself 'supported on the right by the Prussian Guard'; it did not, however, feel disposed to shift on that account, and its flanking fire played a large part in breaking up the German attack.

Yet it was precisely here that the Germans, emerging from the wood known as Nonne Bosschen, came in sight of the line of guns of the 2nd

1. See p. 116.
2. Official History.

Divisional Artillery; with point-blank gun-fire, and the rifle-fire of gunners, cooks, brigade headquarters men and other details, the Germans were driven back into the wood. A wounded German officer who was captured asked a battery commander, 'Where are your reserves?' 'The answer was to point to the line of the guns. Obviously disbelieving, the German then said "What is there behind?" and on getting the reply "Divisional headquarters", he exclaimed from the depths of his heart, in German, "God Almighty!" '[1]

This was the final crisis, and it was out of the hands of the Higher Command. 'We at Corps H.Q. had not much to do', says Charteris, 'for it was fought out by the troops on the spot, and we had no reserves to put in.' General FitzClarence was the soul of the defence, and set about organizing counter-attacks immediately with whatever came to hand. The 2/Oxford and Bucks from 2nd Division cleared the Nonne Bosschen, 'driving the Prussian Guards, big men, some in helmets and some in caps, pell-mell before them, and killing or capturing all who resisted.'[2] Later in the evening, trying to push his success even further, General FitzClarence was killed, a tragic loss; with his death the fighting died down on a cold, pitch-black, rain-soaked night, 'one of the most miserable ever experienced by the troops in Flanders'.[3] And with the fighting of the 11th, the First Battle of Ypres itself drew to an end. The last of the great German attacks had utterly failed. 'At the beginning of November', says Falkenhayn, 'G.H.Q. could not conceal from itself that a further thorough-going success was no longer to be obtained. . . .' Captain Binding noted: 'This business may last for a long time.'

Why, then, had the Germans, with their enormously superior resources, come to grief? Falkenhayn says: 'The young army corps . . . fought with incomparable enthusiasm and unexcelled heroism. The disadvantages of their urgent and hasty formation and training, and the fact that they were led by older and for the most part retired officers, as others were not to be had, naturally made themselves felt.[4] In particular there were deficiencies in the new field-artillery formations, a fact that was emphasized all the more strongly by the shortage of ammunition. Nor was the leadership entirely satisfactory.' A German critic has underlined this point; the generals, he says,

1. Official History.
2. Official History.
3. Official History.
4. He might be speaking of the British New Armies. Germany was fortunate in that her existing system permitted her to wage the war without further recourse to haphazard methods of recruitment. The British Army, however, continued to suffer from these defects, once the Regulars were expended, certainly until 1917, and to some extent right through to the end. That is why subsequent British experiences so often so closely resembled those of the young German corps at Ypres.

did not 'help' the troops, 'but thought that the art of leadership was exhausted when they had urged their troops forward. "The attack mania was a
weak point in the German peace training", and offensive spirit and offensive
tactics were often confused.'[1] The British Official Historian sums up: 'Apart
from the first and all-important factor, the determination of the Allies not to
let them pass and the dogged resistance of the rank and file, the decisive
features would appear to be the superior shooting by the French 75s, and by
the British both with gun and rifle; the skill in the use of ground; the employment of cavalry as a mobile reserve; and the bold and skilful use in counter-
attack of small reserves drawn, as a rule, from parts of the line that General
Haig and other leaders judged might be thinned for the benefit of more vital
sectors. . . . Whilst on the Allied side the generalship and staff work largely
contributed to the victory, on the enemy side it was generalship and staff
work that failed.'

The cost had been terribly high; 'The old British Army was gone past
recall, leaving but a remnant to carry on the training of the New Armies.'[2]
Whole battalions had vanished; of those that remained, their trained drafts
already absorbed and used up, many were reduced to less than a company
strength. And it was not as though these handfuls of invaluable men could
now be taken out of the line and sent home to do the work that they should
have done – the stiffening of the new battalions that would take their place.
Partly because of Kitchener's deliberate decision to turn away from the
Territorial Army, but mainly because of the lack of all kinds of equipment
and facilities for training, the survivors of the Expeditionary Force had to
stay in the field. The relief of I Corps did not begin until November 17th, a
whole fortnight after Foch had asked Haig to hold on for two more days.
'We cannot go on for ever,' Charteris had written on the 9th, 'we must have
men. . . . We are suffering, as England always suffers, for the peace parsimony
of the politicians. We pay now in blood for the pennies they saved. I wish
those who are responsible were here to take their share of it all.' The strain
had taken its toll; on the 13th Haig noted: 'Landon seemed to have a long
face. . . . Wing (3rd Division) seemed inclined to make difficulties. [Byng
said] . . . some of his officers were beginning to talk of their troubles in the
trenches; this was a sign of nerves. . . .'

Haig was not insensitive to these matters. On the 13th, too, he had
evidence that all was not well with men who had had far less time at the
front. We have noted the entry of the London Scottish, first of the Territorials,
into the battle.[3] Their Colonel wrote to Haig that day:

1. Official History.
2. Official History.
3. See p. 113.

'Dear General,

'It is with regret that I have to report that my Battalion at the present moment is not in a fit state to take the field. After the last 5 days and nights in the trenches without sleep as the whole Battalion was in the firing line, the men are thoroughly broken. It is not that the men are not brave because I think they have proved their steadiness under fire, but being highly educated they are more highly strung and at the same time lack the advantage of the training of the regular soldiers. . . . What is urgently required for the Battalion is a period of rest *behind* the guns. . . . I feel that without the required rest it might be disastrous for the Battalion.'

Haig noted: 'It struck me that the Colonel . . . wanted rest more than his men. So I told Landon[1] to see the battalion and make them as comfortable as possible in "dug-outs" in reserve.' Landon moved the London Scottish back into reserve, and reported next day: 'I think the situation has shown them that they are required and all are prepared to do their best. . . .' A fortnight later Haig, who, like all great commanders, paid meticulous attention to detail, remarked that the battalion 'seem to have greatly benefited from their rest, and they are quick and lively now'. Their casualties had been about 60 per cent. The episode is revealing. The performance of the London Scottish and other Territorials showed that they could, with proper encouragement, have played a larger part in the battle, and taken some of the strain off the Regulars; on the other hand, criticism of Kitchener must be tempered by this revelation of the difference between citizen and regular soldiers. Many British generals, in the future, would find it hard to understand that their men, wearing the badges of famous regiments, were nevertheless quite different in character from those who had first borne those badges in the field. Haig, critical of the Commanding Officer, was considerate of the men.

On November 20th, Haig was promoted to full General, in recognition of his services with I Corps, of which formation Sir John French generously wrote: 'It is doubtful if the annals of the British Army contain any finer record. . . .' On the 22nd he took five days' leave in England, which was uneventful, apart from an interview with Kitchener, at which they particularly discussed 'the equipment and armament of the Force in France', and with the King, who told him that more Territorials could not be spared because they were wanted for Home Defence. 'I remarked that the surest way to prevent the enemy from attempting to invade Great Britain was to engage and press him hard on the Continent.'

The First Battle of Ypres was a powerfully formative experience for all British commanders who took part in it. The sense of the nearness to

1. Commanding 1st Division.

catastrophe, of the thinness of the line, of the enemy's weight, of the closeness of the sea, of the finality of a decision in this sector, never left them. It played its part in the whole strategy of 'Westernism', a part that should be recognized as existing for the solid reason of this experience. It led promptly, as the Expeditionary Force was piece by piece destroyed, to the endless demand for reinforcements – drafts for the shattered formations in the field, new formations to support them, to take over more line as the French constantly requested, and more drafts for the new formations when their turn came to be devoured; ammunition, guns and equipment of all kinds for them all. It was never-ending; in the condition of British war-readiness, it made nonsense of all otherwise intelligent thinking about the higher strategy of the use of the New Armies. This was another fruit of the seizure of initiative by the Germans; it drew the might of Britain inevitably to France.

There was also an emotional factor, equally real; when so much suffering is endured, and so much blood is spilt on a stretch of ground, it goes bitterly against the British grain to give it up, no matter how compelling the logical reasons for doing so may be. The anguish at the loss of Tobruk after the epic of its earlier defence, although to defend it again could only have been a handicap, shows that this sentiment did not diminish between the two World Wars. There were solid reasons for holding on to Ypres – the defence of the Channel Ports, the need to preserve every possible inch of Belgian soil from German occupation – but it was probably this emotional reaction which prevented rationalization of the actual line until Plumer took over during the Second Battle. Only the dustiest historian can neglect emotion. The Ypres Salient had become a battle-ground of imperishable renown; the Western Front had gripped the British Army.

7

High Command

'THE YEAR 1915', wrote Sir Winston Churchill, 'was disastrous to the cause of the Allies and to the whole world. By the mistakes of this year the opportunity was lost of confining the conflagration within limits which though enormous were not uncontrolled. Thereafter the fire roared on till it burnt itself out. Thereafter events passed very largely outside the scope of conscious choice.'

There speaks a statesman for whom this year was to be a crisis in his destiny. The statement itself is only half correct. 1915 was, indeed, a disastrous year; but did an opportunity truly exist of averting the disaster? The answer is: only if the Allies could regain the initiative lost in 1914. How was this to be done? Two factors dominate the attempt to find a solution to this question: first, France was already the prisoner of German strategy; secondly, Britain, despite her overwhelming sea-power, was as yet incapable of a major land effort. It is easy enough to be critical of the French; in the rarefied air of government councils; amid the salty breeze which one expects to blow through the Admiralty; in the silence and calm of the critic's study, there is no difficulty in condemning the strategy which France adopted in 1915, or in attributing to its failures the subsequent miseries of the world. But history is composed of feeling as well as thought; indeed, the first is more often a mainspring of action than the second.

There can be no understanding the War, unless the French dilemma is grasped. It consisted, first, of a terrible shock to the pride of a sensitive nation; secondly, of fear. France's last experience of war with Germany had been the humiliating débâcle of 1870; the national revival after the initial catastrophe of that war had not succeeded in preventing defeat. The determination to reverse the decision of 1870 was a steady current flowing through all French political and military thinking up to 1914. It took the form of frank acceptance that France could not, herself, begin a war against Germany;

but in the event of her being engaged in one, a primary objective would be to turn the tables, and the expression of this would be the liberation of the 'lost provinces', Alsace and Lorraine. Now what had happened? Immediately, at the very opening of the campaign, France had suffered a series of defeats all too reminiscent of those of 1870. If, through the nerve and address of Joffre, there had been no Sedan, no Metz, there had, nevertheless, been terrible losses. According to the French Official History, these amounted to 4,478 officers (10 per cent of the entire Officer Corps) and 206,515 other ranks, *for the month of August alone*. And this is, if anything, an understatement. There followed the Marne, the Aisne, First Ypres, and smaller, but always costly operations elsewhere, men fighting and dying somewhere every day until the end of the year. The final figure of France's losses in 1914 has never been, and will never be, computed. In addition to this human calamity, there was the loss of territory. So far from liberating Alsace and Lorraine, France now saw all her north-eastern provinces in the grip of the enemy, including some of her most highly developed industrial regions. Industries, natural resources, fortresses, famous and historic cities, all lay in the invader's power. The threat to Paris had been turned aside, but not before the French Government had had to withdraw to Bordeaux; nor was this threat so far removed; the Germans remained as close to Paris as Canterbury or Huntingdon are to London. For the whole French nation the awful question posed itself: was it to be 1870 all over again?

It is only against the psychology created by these circumstances that French strategy can be understood and judged. It is legitimate to criticize French planning before the War broke out, and to criticize Britain's failure to modify that planning while there was yet time, but by that very token, by the grave errors that one perceives there, it must be admitted that the Germans had been enabled to win important advantages, and that what followed was the fruit of their success. The effect upon France was natural: two preoccupations obsessed her High Command (political and military) from then onwards. These were, first, security in the West, i.e. preventing Germany from gaining more advantages on French soil, and secondly, throwing the Germans off that soil. The larger visions of a naval power were pipe-dreams to a nation which felt the hands of the invader at its throat.

On November 1st, 1914, during the crisis of the Battle of Ypres, Foch had a significant interchange with Kitchener, who had come over to meet the French leaders. 'Lord Kitchener . . . accosted me with the words: "Well, so we are beaten!" I answered that we were not, and that I greatly hoped that we would not be. I then related in detail the events of the last three days, which had brought such heavy losses to the Allied Armies. In finishing I asked him to send us reinforcements as soon as possible. On that first day of

November, 1914, when each day seemed as long as a month, Lord Kitchener replied as follows:

' "On July 1st, 1915, you will have one million trained English soldiers in France. Before that date you will get none, or practically none."

' "We do not ask so many, but we would like to have them sooner – indeed at once", we all cried as if in preconcerted union.'

Great armies in the future, far-flung manoeuvres across the globe, both alike were unreal to the French; both were jarring discords to their passionate, overwhelming desire to smash the invader. Great Britain's own fears of an invasion *which never was likely to materialize*, but which held large numbers of trained troops at home throughout the War, rob her of the right to condemn the French. And the historian who does not consider the emotional effect of enemy occupation of national territory misses a major factor in the decision of events.

British thinking, however, could not be expected to be entirely in step with the French, in a situation which was revolutionary for all who had to deal with it. This, incidentally, is the key to differences between the First and Second World Wars: that the 1914 situation marked a revolution which transformed the world, whereas the 1939 position was a continuation of what had gone before, and was not unfamiliar. But by the end of 1914, the novelty, as much as the unheard-of scope of events, had given rise to deep misgivings in Britain. Many powerful brains addressed themselves to the problems that now disclosed themselves. Of these, the most disconcerting was the tactical impasse that had been reached on the battlefields. Kitchener, swinging away from his promise to Foch, wrote to Sir John French on January 2nd, 1915: 'I suppose we must now recognize that the French Army cannot make a sufficient break through the German lines to bring about the retreat of the German forces from Northern Belgium. If that is so, then the German lines in France may be looked on as a fortress that cannot be carried by assault and also that cannot be completely invested, with the result that the lines may be held by an investing force, whilst operations proceed elsewhere.'

There was a familiar prophetic quality in this utterance of Kitchener's which has obscured its failure to grasp the large truth about the nature of the French alliance and French pressure; Kitchener was propounding an ideal; but in France's circumstances the suggestion of operations proceeding 'elsewhere' was heresy. In any case, there was the matter of defining this 'elsewhere'. The Official History says: 'Various views were tentatively put forward, all having the exploitation of British sea-power as a factor. The First Sea Lord, Admiral Lord Fisher, favoured the Baltic. The Secretary of the Committee of Imperial Defence [Lord Hankey], in a paper that he drew

up at the request of the Prime Minister, considered that . . . Germany could
be most easily affected through Turkey. . . . Mr. Lloyd George went further,
and in a paper suggested that, leaving a large reserve near the coast in case of
emergency, the whole of the rest of the B.E.F. might be taken from France
and despatched to a new theatre.'

Lloyd George's preference – it would recur frequently – was for an
attack on Austria through the Balkans, with the assistance of Roumania and
Greece (neither of whom were actually at war), or an attack on Turkey from
Syria. In addition, Winston Churchill was advocating an advance up the
Belgian coast, to free Ostend and Zeebrugge before the Germans could turn
them into dangerous submarine bases (this was the first seed of the Passchendaele campaign in 1917); the Government of India had already launched an
expedition to Mesopotamia; the Colonial Office was engaged in campaigns
against the German colonies in Africa; the defence of Egypt and the Suez
Canal was a major preoccupation; and Imperial garrisons had to be maintained. All in all, the diversity of counsel and the multiplicity of endeavours
seem to deserve the stricture later passed by Sir William Robertson: 'A more
deplorable state of affairs can surely never have existed in the conduct of any
war.'

These discussions, and the actions that followed from them, are echoes
of the wasteful dispersion of the British effort against Napoleon I, until the
Peninsula became the main theatre of war, or of the scattered and ineffective
operations of the United States, until Grant took command and gave reality
to Lincoln's ideas of unified, concentric manoeuvres.

All this was terribly academic to the commanders in France. Sir John
French was an enthusiastic supporter of the idea of freeing the Belgian
coast; there was this to be said in favour of it, that the Navy would be able
to co-operate in a large-scale action by the Army. On the other hand, there
was the weakness of the B.E.F. (despite the arrival of a V Corps, comprising
practically the very last of the Regular Army, the 27th and 28th Divisions,
under General Plumer); there was the rapid fortification of the coastal area
by the Germans; there was the chronic shortage of munitions and equipment;
above all, there was Joffre's veto. To him, such an attack was purely eccentric,
a diversion of strength from the main axis of any Allied advance towards
Germany. It may as well also be added now that it was a settled policy of the
French Government throughout the War, to avoid having the British occupy
a zone next to the sea, and to prevent too close liaison between the British
and the Belgians. This was a political undercurrent which even the gravest
perils and the most loyal joint endeavours did not divert. Frenchmen of all
descriptions, many of whom should have known better, shared the traditional
suspicion of England's motives. Repington has given an illuminating account

of a conversation with Foch in 1914: '. . . he took me into his sanctum, and having shut the door, said, in a most impressive way, that there was one subject upon which he seriously desired my opinion, for he said that he could not ask anyone else, and he knew that I would not misinform him. I wondered what it could be. He took up a map of northern Europe, spread it out, and asked me solemnly how much European territory we should expect for ourselves at the end of the war.'

These thoughts, that Britain was fighting the War 'on the cheap', while France paid a dreadful price, and that Britain would aggrandize herself, while France might become too exhausted to protect her interests, affected Anglo-French co-operation from beginning to end, and awareness of them deeply influenced both British Commanders-in-Chief in turn in their responses to French demands.

Politics apart, Joffre had other plans in mind, which precluded a British offensive in Flanders. The close of the Battle of Ypres had coincided with German and Austro-Hungarian defeats on the Eastern Front, which together posed a serious problem to the German High Command. It is indicative of the falling off from the bold thinking of the elder von Moltke and von Schlieffen that the solution arrived at was a compromise, with all the faults implied in that. It is, however, also indicative of the different scale of values applied by the German High Command to the fighting on the two fronts. Advances or retreats of seventy or a hundred or more miles in the East were mere incidents; in the West, they would be decisive. Even with their great gains of enemy territory acting as a buffer, the Germans were sensitive about any retirement in the West. Their decision was to send to the East as much as they could spare to retrieve the position there, but to retain the main body of their Army on the Western Front. To secure their line on that front, they now departed from a cardinal German principle of war, that only one line of defence should be constructed; they embarked upon that complex and successive system of fortifications which was to become an altar of sacrifice for the manhood of the Allied nations. For the manhood of Germany, too: Falkenhayn tells us: 'In spite of this innovation the second German principle that the line apportioned to troops for defence was to be maintained at all costs, and if lost to be retaken, was rigidly preserved.' In short, a determined defence in the West, and an offensive against Russia, although the High Command knew that this could not be decisive, was the German plan.

It was quickly realized that the Germans were thinning opposite the French and British; Joffre determined to take advantage of this fact. He owed it to his Russian Allies, whose premature offensives had served France well in 1914, to try to support them in this way; all the dictates of strategy demanded this of him. But above all it was the weakening of the main German Army on French soil that drew him on: 'This situation made it clear to every Frenchman that our task consisted in defeating the enemy, and driving him out of our country.' An abortive thrust by Foch at the end of 1914, in which the British co-operated against the Messines-Wytschaete Ridge, led to nothing but further loss. It became clear to Joffre that no major step forward could be made until he had a reserve under his hand capable of sustaining a large operation. Where was he to get it? The French Army had made an astonishing recovery from its early disasters; reorganized, and re-equipped with heavy artillery drawn from the fortresses of France, backed by a prodigious expansion of munitions production, it was now a much more formidable force than it had been in August, 1914, for it had shed many of its illusions and become far more practical. It was not strong enough, though, stretched out on the long front from the sea to Switzerland, to build up a mass of manoeuvre by itself, despite the thinning of the trench garrisons which Joffre set in hand.[1] Something more was needed, and it had to come from the British.

Recognizing the weakness of the B.E.F., Joffre's first request was simply that the British should take over more of the line, to release French troops for the offensive. On this basis, he was able to gather men for an attack in Champagne. No great results stemmed from this, and those that did were illusory: 'The success was in itself small and incomplete, but it seemed to me to mark the first stage on the road to victory.'[2]

Even in early 1915, the French had shown that it was possible to break into a well-defended trench system; it would take commanders on both sides a long time to understand that there was a world of difference between 'breaking in' and 'breaking through'. Meanwhile, inspired by the ardour of Foch, Joffre began to plan a more grandiose operation for the late spring; the British contribution to this would have to be more than defensive; this time they would have to take part in the attack. Nor was this greatly against the inclination of British G.H.Q. 'Appreciated from the British point of view', says the Official History, 'the situation seemed to demand something more than patient waiting until the British Expeditionary Force was completely ready to strike. It had for several months been constantly hammered by the enemy; the depression of some of the troops during the winter of 1914-'15 was evident. It was of the utmost importance as regards morale that our men should see that the enemy could be paid back in kind and was not going to

1. Like Haig later, he encountered much resistance to this process from forward commanders; he says: 'The idea seemed to prevail that trenches could only be defended by cramming them full of men.'

2. Joffre: *Memoirs*.

have things all his own way. These various motives for offensive action tended to induce Sir John French to concur in General Joffre's plans, although *theoretically*[1] it might have been wiser to have waited until the New Armies were trained, and guns and munitions provided.'

Above all, Sir John French was conscious of the need to reassure the French that the British were actually doing something. The performance of the 'something' fell to Haig.

*   *   *   *

On Christmas Day, 1914, Sir John French reorganized the B.E.F. into two 'Armies', the First, under Haig, comprising I Corps (Monro), IV Corps (Rawlinson) and the Indian Corps (Willcocks); the Second Army (II, III, V Corps) was placed under General Smith-Dorrien, although by now relations between him and French were rapidly deteriorating. The new organization, an unfamiliar one to the British Army, which had never been designed to fight on such a scale, brought added responsibilities and problems; Charteris, who now became Army Intelligence Officer, wrote: 'It is interesting work getting a new headquarters into being. We stand intermediate between the Corps Headquarters and General Headquarters. All orders and all information to and from G.H.Q. pass through our offices. The risk is that Army Head-quarters becomes solely a bureau, and out of touch with things that are happening in the front-line trenches, as G.H.Q. had become. But D.H. is quite determined to prevent this.'

General Butler, who shortly became Haig's Chief of Staff, described the methods adopted by Haig as Army Commander: 'D.H. always visited some corps, division or brigade H.Q. *every day* whether a battle was in progress or not . . . as regards the First Army Staff it was our rule that

(a) every Staff Officer had to go out once every day (or night) and visit some unit,

(b) every portion of the front held by the Army had to be visited at least once every day.'[2]

'So far', wrote Charteris on January 8th, 1915, 'all the efforts of the First Army Staff have been devoted to trying to keep the trenches habitable. . . . A great deal of my time is taken up studying statistics of rainfall and floods, and trying to foresee the vagaries of water let loose from overgrown rivers and flooded ditches.' Water, indeed, was the enemy at this stage, far more than the Germans (who were similarly afflicted). Almost every trench was to some degree or other flooded; there was nothing to choose between the

1. Author's italics.
2. Letter to Sir James Edmonds after the War.

Second Army front to the north, and the First Army's position in the low ground near La Bassée. Concrete dug-outs were still unknown to the British; pumping equipment was terribly scarce; duck-boards had only just appeared; even sand-bags were in ludicrously short supply. Under these conditions the hardships of the troops were most severe, and the astonishing thing is that their health did not suffer more than it did. It was, nevertheless, a constant pre-occupation of Haig's. 'It is contrary to my orders', he wrote on January 12th, 'to keep men in water for any length of time.' He was disgusted to find that some Cavalry with I Corps had been up to their hips in water-logged trenches for twenty-four hours; meeting the Divisional and Corps Commanders con-cerned, 'I gave them both a good talking to. . . .' The same Corps Commander (Monro) was in trouble again a few days later, when Haig discovered that I Corps men in reserve were not being allowed to remove their boots: 'Very strict discipline is necessary, but unnecessary fussiness and over-anxiety should be discouraged . . . I telegraphed to Monro. . . .' Sanitation was always a problem: 'Corps Commanders . . . are personally to go into the matter.' Some of their troubles the troops brought on themselves: 'Men should rest during the day when they know they will be on sentry duty at night. Instead of rest-ing they run about and play football.' The British devotion to sport can have its disadvantages; but the organization of relaxations for the men out of the line was still in its infancy, and football helped them to forget the War for a few brief moments.

Besides the abominable condition of the trenches themselves, the whole Army was at a disadvantage through its lack of equipment for the new type of warfare. Until production in the United Kingdom could be geared to meet-ing this necessity, improvisation had to be the order of the day. While he was still a Corps Commander, Haig set in hand experiments with new weapons and devices. On December 12th, 1914, when the B.E.F. was trying to retake the Messines Ridge, 'I offered my new extemporized trench guns, and four are to be sent to the 2nd Corps and four to the 3rd Corps. Neither corps had apparently yet started to make any. They seemed to me rather slovenly in their methods of carrying on war.' These 'trench guns' (mortars) were the outstanding production of the First Army Engineer Workshops;[1] the Indian Corps, in particular, played an important part in devising them. At first the patterns produced were very rough and ready, and as dangerous to their users

---

1. There were other productions, notably hand-grenades of various types, some practical, others not. The 'jam-pot' variety was very rough, but filled a need. Some were downright dangerous, such as one which, on being demonstrated to an exalted gathering, disintegrated in mid-air. All the spectators threw themselves flat, but nothing happened. When the charge was finally discovered, it was underneath a recumbent general.

Periscopes were also produced by First Army Workshops.

as to the enemy. Later, however, the famous Stokes mortar, which had been turned down by the War Office, was saved by the intervention of one of the Indian Divisional Commanders, and demonstrated to Haig. He was immediately impressed, and urged the War Office to reconsider their verdict. As a result, Lloyd George tells us: 'Out of 19,000 trench mortars and trench howitzers issued during the War to our troops, 11,500 were Stokes guns. Throughout 1917 and 1918 the 3-in. Stokes gun was the only form of light trench mortar manufactured. . . .'

In June, the year of shortages, when Mr. Lloyd George had become Minister of Munitions, he sent out one of his assistants to discuss needs with the generals on the spot; Haig relates: 'I said large numbers of *heavy* guns and howitzers because enemy's defences have become so strong. . . . I suggested a small calibre gun for counter-battery work, like Naval 12-pdr., to save the large heavy shells. We have 14 types of hand-bombs; only two types should be provided. Develop the bomb mortars so as to supplement the heavy artillery. Produce a trench mortar to throw a 100-lb. shell of H.E. up to 500 yards. A *lighter* machine-gun, with tripod and gun in one part is a necessity. Mobility is most important. Captive balloons are required. . . .' Throughout the year his diary reveals Haig as restlessly forward-looking in the search for weapons that would give his troops a reasonable chance in battle against their well-advanced enemies.

It was not only weapons that he was thinking about. At the end of the passage quoted above he wrote: 'But even if ample guns and ammunition etc. be provided, progress will be disappointing unless young capable commanders are brought to the front.' This was a fixed idea with him, dating from before the War. At the end of November, 1914, he wrote: 'There are many capable young fellows both in the ranks and as N.C.O.s who are quite fit for promotion to be Company Officers. The time has come when all who are fit to become leaders must be sought out and promoted.' On his brief leave at that time he urged the War Office to 'Send out young Oxford and Cambridge men as officers; they understand the crisis in which the British Empire is involved.'

When the Prime Minister visited him in July, 1915, they talked about various needs; machine guns were one of them, but another was: 'Necessity for promoting young officers to high command. To make room some of the old ones must be removed. We went through the lists of Major Generals etc. in the Army List. I said it was important to go down low on the list and get young, capable officers. He agreed.' In the same month he told French of 'the importance of making the command of a company an "appointment", in order to bring young officers to the front who show ability as leaders. He agreed, and decided to appoint them local Captains and Majors as required.'

Throughout the War, however, Haig met with official resistance to this concept. When he became Commander-in-Chief, his own G.H.Q. was criticized on the grounds that many of his officers were too young for their high positions. He did his best, but it was an uphill struggle against a prejudice so deeply entrenched that it had defeated even Wellington.

Haig's relations with Sir John French improved distinctly after Ypres; that ordeal had revived their comradeship. As regards French's military capacity, however, nothing had happened to change Haig's views – rather the contrary. During the December operations in 1914 he noted: 'The general instructions given seemed to me rather vague.' He still gravely doubted the quality of some of the officers at G.H.Q., and when Murray's health finally broke down at the end of the year, Haig was much alarmed lest Wilson should replace him. He told French: 'Wilson was an intriguer, and had up-to-date subordinated the interests of the British Army to those of the French. I knew the Army had every confidence in Robertson.' Lieutenant-General Sir W. R. Robertson was at that time Quartermaster-General. He was a cavalry trooper who had risen from the ranks to high estate by sheer hard work and application. Crusty, stubborn, inarticulate, Robertson was also brave, loyal and clear-headed; on paper he was extremely lucid; in official documents and memoranda while in office, and in his book *Soldiers and Statesmen* later, the methodical functioning of his mind is constantly revealed. He was to become one of the large figures of the War; in January, 1915, he began his progress by becoming Chief of Staff of the B.E.F. Wilson's activities during the Curragh affair were remembered against him. He became, however, French's Liaison Officer at Joffre's Headquarters, an appointment which was not distasteful to him. Haig commented:

'Wilson may still "intrigue" and will certainly cause trouble to G.H.Q. and Robertson in that appointment. General Murray writes to me that he "goes home on Saturday". Murray was a kindly fellow but not a practical man in the field. Most of us commanders felt that French had done right to remove him, though we did not like the way it was done. We have confidence in Robertson's judgment as a Staff Officer.'

In certain vital matters, Haig and French were fully agreed. At the beginning of 1915 the New Armies began to pose a double question: how they were to be used, and where. It was Kitchener's wish to bring them into action complete as large formations, with their own Divisional, Corps and Army organization. To Haig and other senior officers of the B.E.F., this was a dangerous intention: 'We all think these new formations, with rather elderly Commanders and inexperienced Staff Officers, a great mistake. . . . Much better to send (the New Army) out by Battalions or even by Brigades, for incorporation in our existing Divisions and Corps.' They had a supporter in

Churchill, who wrote to Asquith on January 6th: 'I can quite understand the misgivings of a Commander-in-Chief who contemplates one portion of his forces consisting entirely of new troops and inexperienced staffs, while the other consists entirely of tried and seasoned units. . . . The sound and accepted principle of military organization is undoubtedly that young troops should be brigaded with seasoned troops. . . .' But Kitchener was a hard man to persuade, and clung to the unity of the New Armies; events proved him to be mistaken: Suvla Bay exposed the dangers of his idea at the Corps level; at the Divisional level, it would take years to iron out the weaknesses, and the cost was terribly high for the gallant souls who filled the New Army's ranks.

As regards grand strategy, Haig and French were equally at one. French read out to his senior officers 'a letter from K. in which the latter hinted that the New Army might be used better elsewhere than on the French frontier. . . . I said that we ought not to divide our Military Force, but *concentrate on the decisive point* which is on this frontier against the German main Army.' This was now to become a rooted conviction in Haig's mind. A few days later, replying to Colonel Repington, who 'much doubted whether we would ever get a General sufficiently fearless of public opinion to incur the losses which must be suffered in any attempt to pierce the enemy's fortified front', Haig replied that 'as soon as we were supplied with ample artillery ammunition of high explosive, I thought we could walk through the German lines at several places'. This delusion, which was widely shared in all armies, exacted a frightful penalty.

The commonest trap for later students has always been the confusion of strategy with tactics: because the fighting on the Western front was so costly and so apparently barren for so many years, the strategy of 'Westernism' has been discredited. Contemporary statesmen fell into the same trap. The strategic issue, as Haig saw it, was this: the diversion of large forces to another theatre 'seems a violation of a sound strategical principle which in my opinion is to concentrate at the decisive point, namely against Germany's main army. *We cannot hope to win until we have defeated the German Army.*[1] The easiest place to do this is in France, because our lines of communication are the shortest to this theatre of war.' The key to the whole matter was communications. If it had been possible to win swift and overwhelming victories on other fronts by sudden blows, that would have been a different matter. But it was not.

1. Author's italics. This passage, from Haig's Diary of March 28th, 1915, is one of the tersest and earliest statements of a position which he restated time after time in official papers for the benefit of successive Governments and Ministers. He never departed from the thought contained in the sentence italicized; it guided him equally in defeat and in victory. It would be repetitious to continue to quote him on this subject; but it must never be forgotten that his central aim was 'to defeat the German Army'. It is only by this that his battles can be judged.

The whole story of the War in the secondary theatres is a story of astonishing German success with minuscule resources. Everywhere, at Gallipoli, in Mesopotamia, Palestine, Italy, against Salonika or Roumania, even on the Russian front against a major foe, Germany was able to sustain campaigns through her allies which tied down large Allied forces at the cost of small diversions of German strength – a handful of officers, experts, specialized units, or a small group of divisions. Roumania occupied an Army Group – but not for long. All in all, the British Empire used 3,500,000 men in the secondary theatres, as against 5,400,000 in France. The most spectacular example of this feat on Germany's part was East Africa, where a force that never numbered more than 15,500 men engaged, from first to last, the attention of 372,950 British, and surrendered twelve days *after* the Armistice. Everywhere, the Allies met the same obstacles as they met in France: the same barbed wire, the same machine guns, the same artillery, with a wider array of diseases thrown in. The strain upon the Navy of supporting these expeditions grew to perilous proportions as the submarine campaign developed. And whenever the Allies were able to make a move that seemed in the least degree dangerous, the Germans were able to profit by their interior lines of communication to parry it with a smaller force before they could press its advantage home. Field-Marshal Wavell encountered the same phenomenon in 1940, when he was studying the possibilities of a campaign in Greece; he wrote: 'As in the last war, Germany is on interior lines, and can move more quickly to attack Greece or Turkey than we can support them.' This state of affairs continued as long as the German Army remained in being and was able to sustain its allies. There could be no complete victory without the defeat of the German Army; owing to diversions of strength this was not fully achieved until 1945. And then it was the Russians who marched to Berlin and Vienna, the only true conclusion of a war against the Central Powers.

To this belief that victory could only be gained by beating the main body of the German Army, Haig added another sobering reflection. In February, 1915, Charteris wrote: 'D.H. does not think there can be any end until the autumn of 1916 at earliest. He is still very insistent on careful analysis of the manpower problem. His view is that France has now put into the field every man she can. Her yearly quota is much smaller than Germany's, and will not suffice to meet her casualties. As time goes on, therefore, the French Army will decrease.' The same idea, doubtless, was in the minds of the French Staff and Government, and was one of the reasons why they gambled with such heavy stakes on a decision in 1915. As it wore on, and French losses mounted without any promise of early justification, Haig became more anxious than ever. By June this question had assumed a major interest for him, which it never lost.

On the 14th of that month, as his diary records, one of Joffre's A.D.C.s made a 'serious statement' to Haig: 'This was to the effect that "the French people are getting tired of the war".' On the 23rd, commenting on the latest of France's habitual political crises, Haig wrote: 'The important point seems to me to be to prevent the peace party in France from gaining the upper hand otherwise they will make peace in the autumn.' A few days later, pondering on the Dardanelles campaign, he reverted to this fear: 'By going on in the way in which the Cabinet is now acting great risk is run of the French making peace by the winter....' Haig underestimated the determination of a generation of French leaders who, whatever their faults, were possessed of a fortitude in glaring contrast to the trepidations of 1940 or 1958; he underestimated also the endurance of a people still largely peasant; he did not foresee – no one did, even in France – the shifts and contrivances by which the French Army would be kept in being, the ruthless tapping of colonial manpower by which it held its divisions in the field. But he was not far wrong. The break did come – in 1917; he, at least, was prepared for it.

The immediate question was, how could the small B.E.F. give more help to France? A plan was evolved for a joint attack on the German lines by the British and their right-hand neighbours, de Maud'huy's 10th Army. This would synchronize with, and lend support to, Joffre's main offensive in Champagne. But it was a condition of the 10th Army's participation that the British would relieve the French IX Corps north of Ypres. This seemed just feasible; the last of the Regular divisions, the 29th, was due to join the B.E.F. in February, as well as the 1st Canadian Division; French agreed to do as Joffre wished. But the 29th Division did not arrive; it was withheld by Lord Kitchener as the doubts and perplexities of the Dardanelles Campaign grew upon him.

Kitchener did not firmly allocate the 29th Division to the Middle East, but he did not send it to France. Sir Winston Churchill has graphically recorded the ill-effect on Dardanelles planning that this uncertainty produced. It was now to find itself in somewhat the same position as d'Erlon's Corps, marching all day between the battlefields of Ligny and Quatre Bras, but taking part in neither engagement. The effect of the Division's absence from either theatre was serious, but in France the more so, since it meant the abstention from battle of a whole French Army. For Joffre was adamant, and when Haig met de Maud'huy on February 28th, he had to report that 'The net result . . . is that our proposed offensive action must be considered an entirely independent operation'. It is a remarkable reflection that the British Empire's plans in two theatres of war should have been so compromised by the presence or otherwise of one single division; all examination of grand strategic enterprises for 1915 should be tempered by the memory of this.

Joffre confirmed Haig's report to French on March 7th, only three days

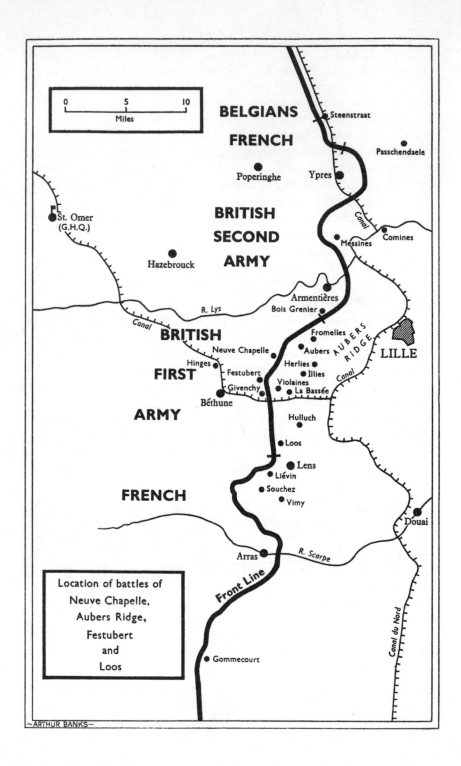

BELGIANS
FRENCH

Steenstraat
Passchendaele
Poperinghe
Ypres

BRITISH
SECOND
ARMY

St. Omer
(G.H.Q.)

Canal
Comines
Messines

Hazebrouck

R. Lys
Canal
Armentières
Bois Grenier

BRITISH

Fromelles
AUBERS RIDGE
Neuve Chapelle
Aubers
LILLE
Hinges
Herlies
Illies
Festubert
Violaines
Givenchy
La Bassée
Canal
Béthune

FIRST

ARMY

Hulluch

Loos

FRENCH

Lens
Liévin
Souchez
Vimy

Douai

Arras
R. Scarpe

Front Line

Canal du Nord

Location of battles of
Neuve Chapelle,
Aubers Ridge,
Festubert
and
Loos

Gommecourt

0   5   10
Miles

~ARTHUR BANKS~

before the British attack was due to take place. French was certain that he could not both extend his front and simultaneously launch an attack; he had now to decide which it should be. The determining factors, says the Official History, were these: 'Sir John French desired to co-operate as effectively as possible with the French. He also particularly wished to foster an offensive spirit in the Expeditionary Force after its trying and enervating experiences of a severe winter in the trenches.' Neither the French nor the Germans took the British Army very seriously at this period; it was a practical necessity to show both of them that they were wrong. It was equally a necessity to revive in the largely raw Expeditionary Force a sense of its own capacity; pride is a factor in war; without it armies sink into rabbles. French decided to attack – alone.

*   *   *   *

The British attack was entrusted to Haig's First Army; the objective selected was the so-called 'Aubers Ridge', an almost indistinguishable feature of the flat land north of La Bassée, described in the Official History as 'dismal country to work over and depressing to dwell in'. Hearts sank at the mere sight of this level, waterlogged, industrial landscape. Within it, however, lay an important prize – Lille. It was quite out of possibility that the British by themselves could liberate that great city, but by establishing themselves on the Aubers Ridge they could interrupt communications between Lille and La Bassée, which would help towards a more valuable advance later. The actual point of impact of Haig's attack was the German salient around the ruined village of Neuve Chapelle.

The Battle of Neuve Chapelle was the first significant British offensive effort of the War. The methods and tactics evolved became the standard pattern for almost every British attack up to the end of 1916, and exercised considerable influence on French and German operations too. The essence of Haig's procedure was methodical preparation and surprise. Sometimes the two conflicted with each other, chiefly through executive faults; Neuve Chapelle demonstrated that they need not do so. Haig's ideas were already forming at the beginning of February; on the 10th he '. . . saw General Freddy Mercer, C.R.A. First Army, regarding the action of the artillery against Neuve Chapelle. He proposed bombarding it "by compartments" and to take four days over it. In my opinion, such a slow action would lose much of the effect of the heavy shells. It would, I think, be of more effect to compress the fire into a terrific outburst for three hours . . . and follow it by a sudden rush of our infantry. This will take advantage of the element of surprise!' Three days later he issued his orders to General Rawlinson, whose IV Corps would actually make the assault: '. . . I propose to bombard and then storm the village – you will be in command of the attack, so begin at once to go thoroughly into every detail, because success depends upon methodical preparation.'

At once the command weaknesses of the British Army were revealed. Rawlinson – a Rifleman – was one of the most intelligent and versatile British generals of the War, as his later record amply proves. But despite his keen wits and professional training, the mounting of a modern attack in 1915 was at first beyond him; on February 19th, Haig recorded: 'I sent General Rawlinson a note regarding the two papers he gave me yesterday re the attack of Neuve Chapelle. "They deal with the general principles on which an attack on any defended locality should be conducted" – and I added "As the fine weather will soon be upon us, please put forward a scheme *for this particular operation*[1]" – "I hope to discuss your scheme at the Conference . . . on Monday 22nd inst., so please get to work on it at once." I ended by giving him a number of questions to answer. . . .'

This was to be Haig's method throughout the remainder of the War: it was one which enforced itself on the senior commanders of all armies. Whenever one speaks of 'Haig's attack', 'Joffre's attack', or 'Ludendorff's attack,' one has to remember that the *details* in each case would have been worked out by subordinate commanders closer to the front; if their plans were unsatisfactory, they would have to make new ones; the approval of the senior commander implied his acceptance of full responsibility for what his subordinates had devised. This system was adopted in both World Wars; it did not always guarantee success, but a major departure from it – Nivelle's plan in 1917, which he *imposed* upon his subordinates – brought disastrous failure.

The problem was to define where responsibility lay. Haig did not greatly care for Rawlinson's plan when it was submitted on the 22nd; it envisaged the capture of Neuve Chapelle 'by "halves"': one half one day, followed by the other half next day . . . there would be no element of surprise on the second day, but enemy would be ready for us.' Rawlinson was told to think again, and the next day Haig asked the Chief of Staff of IV Corps 'what action had been taken as the result of my conference yesterday. He replied that . . . the problem . . . had been given to the G.O.C. 7th as well as the G.O.C. 8th Division to work out. I said that the time for setting schemes had passed. . . . In my opinion, it was necessary to give full responsibility for the plan to whoever would have the task of attacking. . . . If any commander did not do what was required, he would be dismissed. If each problem is to be given to two commanders, where are we to stop? Why not give the Brigadier's scheme to two brigadiers, and so on? The idea is ridiculous.' Two days later Rawlinson reported that General Davies, commanding the 8th Division, had been entrusted with the planning of the capture of Neuve Chapelle: 'The

1. Author's italics.

operation was now to be carried out as I wished in a simple common sense way.' Haig impressed on Davies 'that every man must know exactly what his duty was', and preparations went forward accordingly. But subsequent mis-fortunes are traceable to this initial confusion of thought. The British Army had everything to learn.

It is astonishing, nevertheless, how much was accomplished in a short time. The assaulting infantry were rehearsed in their task; their officers familiarized themselves with the ground; 'forming-up trenches' were dug, and dummies elsewhere, so as not to give the game away; advanced depots (dumps) were created; roads were improved, and a light railway laid down; heavy artillery was concentrated, and for the first time an artillery time-table was issued, showing the targets of each battery at successive stages of the action; plat-forms were devised to stabilize the guns in the soft, muddy ground; also for the first time, aerial photographs of the whole area were used to build up a photographic map showing the German trench network; secrecy was closely guarded. All this was a triumph of Staff work in an army suffering from a con-stant shortage of trained Staff officers. It was made all the more difficult for Haig by the death, on February 22nd, of his Chief of Staff, John Gough, mortally wounded by a stray bullet while visiting his old regiment. Gough was a great friend whose loss was a severe blow; as the years went by, his absence was not less felt. Yet Gough himself would often say to Haig 'that we were wasted together as I did not need the help of a staff officer such as he, while he could well be doing more necessary work by keeping some feeble general straight!' Charteris noted at the time: 'In many ways D.H. is his own Chief of Staff. He knows so much more about fighting than any of the Staff, and he goes around the divisions and brigades so constantly that his Chief of Staff has little to do, except to see that things go smoothly.' Gough was suc-ceeded by Brigadier-General R. H. K. Butler, from the 3rd Infantry Brigade.

Preparations were completed by March 9th. The omens were not inauspi-cious; a major victory was, of course, out of the question, but there seemed to be a good chance of breaking into the German position, rolling up their line on a considerable frontage, and gaining the Aubers Ridge. Only two German divisions faced the First Army (six divisions); the Intelligence Branch calcu-lated that the Germans could only receive 4,000 reinforcements during the first twelve hours, and another 16,000 by the evening of the second day. This proved to be an accurate forecast; it implied that much would depend on maintaining the impetus of the first assault. This, in turn, would depend greatly on surprise, as Haig had insisted throughout; partly to assist the sur-prise (but partly also to conserve ammunition), the opening bombardment had been reduced to a thirty-five-minute 'hurricane'. The unprecedented number of sixty-six heavy guns (more than the whole B.E.F. possessed at

Ypres) was assembled for this purpose. The only uncertainty was the weather; rain and light snow fell on the eve of battle; not until one hour before the bombardment was due to start did Haig, fortified by an Air weather reconnaissance, feel justified in allowing the battle to proceed.

At 7.30 a.m. on March 10th, the most striking British artillery action of the War to date took place; at 8.05 the infantry of the IV and Indian Corps left their trenches and went into the attack, on a front of nearly 9,000 yards. Neuve Chapelle itself was not directly assaulted; the points of impact were on either side of it. The bombardment, except at one point allocated to a battery which had only arrived the previous afternoon, had done its work. The German front trenches (largely breastworks because of the sub-surface water) were swept away in many places, and their defenders wiped out or demoralized. Forty-five minutes after zero hour Neuve Chapelle was captured; the first objective was gained along the whole centre of the attack, though setbacks had occurred on each flank. It was a most promising opening; but then, wrote Charteris on the 12th, 'for some reason not yet explained, the whole machine clogged and stopped. It was maddening.' The rest of the battle can be summed up in two sentences: 'The initial success was speedily held up, every subsequent attempt at exploitation gained less or no ground at the cost of progressively increasing losses. Practically all the ground won in the three-days' battle was won in the first three hours.'[1] On the 13th, recognizing that the advance had come to a full stop, and that ammunition was running low, Haig brought the battle to an end. The First Army had lost 583 officers and 12,309 other ranks, the Germans about as many, including 30 officers and 1,657 other ranks taken prisoner. The British had gained no more than their first objective, a penetration of some 1,200 yards on a front of 4,000 yards.

This result naturally came as a shock to Haig and his Staff, after all their forethought and careful planning. It was not difficult to see that the breakdown stemmed from the delays on the first morning and afternoon, which had given the weakened defenders at least five invaluable hours in which to reorganize their defence and begin the movement of their reserves. Charteris continued on the 12th:

'... D.H. was determined to find out the cause of the delay and went today to both Corps and Divisional H.Q. to investigate the matter personally. The breakdown was undoubtedly at a Corps H.Q. where D.H.'s orders stuck, and were not transmitted to the division concerned for some hours. Corps H.Q. tried to put the blame on the division, and there was rather an unpleasant incident, which leaves a very nasty taste in one's mouth. It is no good finding scapegoats. The important thing is to find out where the failure took place, and see that any similar failure is impossible in the future. In any case we were

1. C. R. M. F. Cruttwell: *A History of the Great War 1914–1918.*

short of ammunition towards the end of the battle, and could not have pressed home our advantage. . . . One thing has resulted; D.H. in all future battles will have his battle H.Q. still farther up, so that he will be in closer touch with his Corps and Divisional H.Q.'

This was only satisfactory as far as it went. Undoubtedly there had been command failures, in which the residual friction of Rawlinson's earlier mis-understanding of the role of his own subordinates played a part. He now tried to lay the blame for the failures of IV Corps on General Davies of the 8th Division; on the strength of this, Haig considered sending Davies home. The next day, however, he examined that officer's own evidence: 'This at once showed that Rawlinson felt himself to blame for the delay and not Davies.'

The matter was referred to G.H.Q., where Robertson opined that it was Rawlinson who should be sent home. Haig defended the IV Corps Com-mander: 'I am afraid Rawlinson is unsatisfactory in this respect, loyalty to his subordinates. But he has many other valuable qualities for a commander on active service.' Haig did not believe in witch-hunts. Rawlinson himself com-mented: 'I feel quite sure that I shall get justice at D.H.'s hands.' That was pre-cisely what he did get; he was warned never to do it again. It was, indeed, a disagreeable incident, but the end of it contrasted well with French methods, for example, of which Charteris wrote a few weeks later: '. . . the French do indulge in a system of slaughter of those who for any reason do not succeed, the general principle being that to save your own skin you must get someone under you sacked first – a sort of band of fratricides, the modern equivalent of Nelson's band of brothers. Fowke (our witty Chief Engineer at G.H.Q.) says that after every reverse the tumbrils go round French G.Q.G. with the cry "Bring out your dead." ' The French were not noticeably more successful for this rigour.

The Rawlinson-Davies episode had an unfortunate effect: it helped to divert attention from the deeper reasons for the failure at Neuve Chapelle. These were rooted in the unfamiliar character of trench warfare itself; the Neuve Chapelle pattern would be repeated all too often during the following years. The problem was always this: once the set-piece (usually successful) was over, as the Official History says, 'there came unforeseen delays. Command of the operations became slow and difficult, and the assistance of the infantry by the artillery was hampered by the breakdown of the telephone system. The vulnerability of our means of communication and methods of inter-communi-cation in the face of modern artillery, and the difficulty, under conditions of siege warfare, of getting reinforcements to the required positions at the proper time, up trenches already congested, exceeded all expectation and calculations. The enemy gained time to bring up reinforcements, and construct a retrenchment, to use the old word of siege warfare, behind the threatened breach. Thus equilibrium was very quickly re-established, mere repetition of the first effort only brought repetition of failure,and, for the moment, all hope of further progress vanished, except after renewed preparations and an entirely fresh attack. Given that the new front of attack was wide enough to make it impossible for the small local reserves of the defence to deal with the situation, success was shown to be a time problem, a question of whether a break-in – which, with adequate artillery preparation, was always possible – could be converted into a break-through before the enemy could be certain of the point of attack and rush reinforcements to it.'

The Official Historian, Brigadier-General Edmonds, was himself a Royal Engineer. He traced much of the continued tactical failure of the Allies on the Western Front to an unwillingness to recognize that the problem was actually the classic one of siege warfare, for which a whole technique existed. The very nomenclature of 'trench warfare', he says, added to the confusion: 'Instead of using the old-fashioned word "breach", the higher commands called upon troops to make a "gap"; a "retrenchment" became a "switch"; a "sap" was not made by sapping; "mining" was renamed "tunnelling"; "subsidiary" attacks, mere demonstrations that could not possibly be developed into a "break-through", took the place not only of "false" attacks, but also of the minor attacks of old days; and the new words were misleading.'

This theory is wrong in one very important respect. The essence of a siege is that *the enemy cannot get away*. Whether he is assaulted, invested or sapped, he must stand his ground. This did not apply to the Germans in France between 1914 and 1918; it was always open to them, when the Allies attacked them by siege methods, to make a small withdrawal, nullifying the whole advantage gained, and forcing the whole process to be endlessly repeated, while they themselves, probably, played the same game somewhere else. This was the weakness of the system of what were later called 'step-by-step' advances; they were usually successful, but their repetition involved immense labour. Always the Germans succeeded in extracting their artillery intact, and that meant, unless their forces were much worn down, that a full-scale set-piece had to be mounted for each successive phase. Important results were sometimes achieved by 'step-by-step' methods, as we shall see, but it is hard to believe that the War could have been ended by them in 1918. One is left with an uneasy feeling that it might have continued up to this moment of writing. The truth is that it was not wrong to attempt to break through; but what was needed was the weapon for the job, which only appeared in 1918 – the Mark V Tank, with the 'Whippet' for exploitation. Until then the *only* weapon of exploitation was Cavalry; that was why Haig clung to his small number of horsemen – 'We cannot hope to reap the fruits of victory without a large force of mounted troops' he wrote in April, 1915 – but modern conditions were reducing the value of Cavalry in this role to almost nil.

When all this is said, and the failure at Neuve Chapelle accepted, it has to be remembered that *at the time*, to an Army which had been incapable of *any* offensive effort, the action wore many of the aspects of success. On April 4th, Charteris wrote: 'Neuve Chapelle has had unexpected results. It has made the French think highly of our Army. Joffre is sending his Corps Commanders to see D.H. and learn how we succeeded in attacking and ousting the Germans from an entrenched position.' He added: 'That is sufficient answer to the complaints in the Press about our losses. I am afraid England will have to accustom herself to far greater losses than those of Neuve Chapelle before we finally crush the German Army.'

Meanwhile, Field-Marshal Sir John French, sensitive to the new tune that was being played, was disposed to take credit to himself for the success, such as it was, of the battle. By his orders Haig's report was amended to read as though G.H.Q. had been responsible for the whole planning of the affair, whereas in fact this had been completed before G.H.Q.'s orders were received by the First Army. Haig's Staff were naturally furious; his own reaction was more philosophical: 'The whole thing is so childish, that I could hardly have credited the truth of the story had I not seen the paper. The main thing, however, is to beat the Germans *soon*, and leave to the British public the task of awarding credit for work done after peace has been made.' Less than a week later, however, there were fresh signs of a relapse in the relations between the Commander-in-Chief and the First Army's Commander: 'I received back a letter which I had sent to the C.G.S. stating what I proposed to do in the way of exploding mines and harassing the enemy during the next few weeks. The C. in C. approved my proposals but, with reference to the last para. of the letter, in which I "requested that the 2nd Army might be directed to make similar arrangements to mislead the enemy . . ." he wrote a long story to the effect that the G.O.C. 1st Army was not to give orders to other parts of the Force: that he (Sir John) would direct what they should do, and that the G.O.C. 1st Army was to carry out the orders given him by the C. in C., etc. In reply, I merely noted on the letter that the "C. in C. seemed to have overlooked the point to which the para. in question referred". I infer that something must have upset Sir John's balance of mind. Some think Lord K. has found him out, as he has gone out of his way *to assert his position*.' However, the only thing that one ought to consider is how best to act so as to end the war.'

* * * *

April was a cruel month. On the 22nd, the Germans launched the Second Battle of Ypres, which introduced poison gas into the War. The psychological effect of the new weapon was tremendous: 'In the face of gas, without protection, individuality was annihilated; the soldier in the trench became a mere passive recipient of torture and death. A final stage seemed to be reached in the whole tendency of modern scientific warfare to depress and make of no effect individual bravery, enterprise, and skill.'[1] Strategically and tactically, however, it is clear that the Germans made a grave mistake in introducing this new element in what was never intended to be more than a minor operation. Gas became a precision weapon later in the War, freely used by both sides; the Germans therefore lost an advantage.

Three days after the opening of Second Ypres, which drew in the whole strength of the British Second Army, and effectively stopped all operations on the remainder of the front of the B.E.F., the landings at Gallipoli took place. A long-standing tendency to regard the events of the First World War in isolation has obscured the fact that the Gallipoli Campaign was launched simultaneously with an acute crisis at the most sensitive part of the Western Front.

The story of Gallipoli is as absorbing as all great tragedy; it cannot be retold in detail here. This was by far the most promising of all the'side-shows'. 'The advantages to be derived from forcing the Straits were perfectly obvious', wrote Sir William Robertson. 'Such a success would, as the advocates of the project said, serve to secure Egypt, to induce Italy and the Balkan States to come in on our side, and, if followed by the forcing of the Bosphorus, would enable Russia to draw munitions from America and Western Europe, and to export her accumulated supplies of wheat. There is seldom any lack of attractive-looking schemes in war. The difficulty is to give effect to them, and one of the difficulties in the Dardanelles scheme was that nothing really useful could be achieved without the assistance, sooner or later, of troops, and, according to the War Minister, no troops were available.' The hesitations and alterations in the original planning of the Gallipoli Campaign were its downfall; it became a classic example of 'too little and too late'. 'Many reasons', says the Official Historian, 'combined to frustrate an enterprise the success of which in 1915 would have altered the course of the war. But every reason will be found to spring from one fundamental cause – an utter lack of preparation before the campaign began.'

Haig's view of the Gallipoli Campaign was expressed in a letter which he wrote at the end of July to Major Clive Wigram, Assistant Private Secretary to the King: 'In spite of what you write me and the decision of the Cabinet, I still think it is fatal to pour more troops and ammunition down the Dardanelles sink. The whole British Expeditionary Force here if added to the Force now there cannot clear the two sides of the Dardanelles so as to make the

1. Cruttwell.

Straits passage safe for ships and ensure the fall of Constantinople. . . . To the onlooker here there seems no supreme control exercised over the war as a whole. I attribute this to the failure to make use of the General Staff in London. You allow our policy to be directed by whoever is the ablest speaker. Fundamental principles of strategy seem daily to be ignored. This is the decisive point: bring all the strength of the Empire to this point and beat the enemy. Then all else will be ours for the picking up.'

And with that we shall have to turn away from the gallant, forlorn adventure at Gallipoli, but remembering that, from the first to last, it employed the efforts of 410,000 British and 79,000 French soldiers in 1915, of whom, through death or wounds or sickness, 205,000 British and 47,000 French became casualties. Winning the War was never conspicuously easier on a secondary front.

*   *   *   *

Overhanging all British operations in 1915, whether at Gallipoli or in France, was the shadow of the munitions shortage. No one had envisaged the consumption of artillery ammunition which modern conditions would call for; both the French and the Germans were to a certain extent similarly afflicted, while the Russians rapidly reached a point of disaster in this respect. In Britain the crisis was overcome, but not before it had helped to bring about the fall of the Liberal Government. There is no understanding the year's fighting, unless the ammunition situation is kept in mind. According to Lloyd George it amounted to this: Sir John French informed the War Office in December 1914 what his requirements of shells would be, taking into account both defence and special attacks.

'For the principal artillery of his forces – the 18-pounders, the 4.5-inch howitzers and the 4.7-inch field guns – he laid down his requirements as:

50 rounds per gun per day for the 18-pdrs.
40   ,,   ,,   ,,   4·5-in.
25   ,,   ,,   ,,   4.7-in.

The number of rounds per gun per day actually supplied to him for these weapons, month by month, were:

	Month	18–pdr.	4·5-in.	4·7-in.
1914	Nov.	9·9	6·8	10·8
	Dec.	6·0	4·6	7·6
1915	Jan.	4·9	4·2	7·6
	Feb.	5·3	6·5	5·3
	Mar.	8·6	6·5	5·3
	Apr.	10·6	8·2	4·2
	May	11·0	6·1	4·3

These figures . . . speak for themselves.'

They do indeed. They show the utter impossibility of maintaining any successful large-scale operation over and above the Western front; they show also how difficult it was to conduct action on that front itself.

In May two more attempts were made by Haig's Army to complete the work begun at Neuve Chapelle; both enjoyed the advantage, previously lacking, of large-scale French co-operation – Foch's offensive in Artois; both were abortive, expensive failures. The 'Battle' of Aubers Ridge on May 9th was stopped in its tracks in one day, with a loss in the three attacking divisions of 145 officers and 9,400 men. The failure, says the Official History, was due to three causes: 'first, the strength of the German defences and the clever concealment of machine guns in them; secondly, the lack on the British side of sufficient shells of large calibre to deal with such defences; and thirdly, the inferior quality of much of the ammunition supplied and the difficulties of ranging, so that the British gunners were unable to hit their targets and the German counter-batteries and machine guns were not silenced. . . . According to British aeroplane reports the registration before the battle was useless. . . . As a general result, the brief 40-minutes bombardment, though it raised a curtain of dust and smoke immediately above the enemy's front line, did no appreciable damage, and merely gave the enemy warning to stand-to to meet an assault which he had been expecting.' Pondering this poor result, Haig reached two conclusions:

'1. the defences in our front are so carefully and so strongly made, and the mutual support with machine guns is so complete, that in order to demolish them a *long methodical bombardment* will be necessary by heavy artillery . . . before Infantry are sent forward to attack.

'2. To destroy the enemy's material 60-pdr. *guns* will be tried, as well as the 15-in., 9·2 and 6-in. hows. Accurate observations of *each shot* will be arranged so as to make sure of flattening out the enemy's "strong points" of support, before the Infantry is launched.'

Haig was less taken aback than some by the Aubers failure, because he had told French that 'in my opinion we had not enough troops and guns to sustain our forward movement, and reap decisive results. . . . Sir John . . . wished me to attack and do the best I could with the troops available.' Now that the fight was over, he reviewed his tactics. It was not the case that Haig clung obstinately to particular methods, irrespective of their suitability. At Neuve Chapelle he had banked largely on surprise, and whatever useful result was obtained there was obtained through that. He tried the same swift rush at Aubers; against the much improved German defences, it came to nothing. Now he reshaped his views, taking into account the new quality of German defence. He explained to French on May 10th that 'it was necessary now to proceed methodically and to break down the enemy's strong points and entrenchments. Yesterday's attacks showed that we are confronted by a carefully prepared position, which is held by a most determined enemy, with numerous machine guns. An accurate and so fairly long artillery bombardment will be necessary. . . . Sir J. French said he could not see what I could do better.' The long bombardments and careful preparations of later setpieces, with the inevitable loss of surprise, are thus seen to be a direct result of altered conditions which first revealed themselves at Aubers. Haig, like every good general, preferred surprise, and when he possessed a weapon which enabled him to achieve it – the tank – he reverted again to the short bombardment and the rush. Meanwhile, it was still 1915, with all that that meant in terms of shortages and inexperience. The troops themselves paid the highest price for these disadvantages; the Aubers losses, commented Haig, were 'probably 25% too high'.

Six days later, the First Army made another attempt to get forward; again this was dictated by the need to lend support to the French, who had gained some success in the opening stages of their attack towards the Vimy Ridge, but were now engaged in hard, stubborn fighting against stiffening resistance. In less than a week there was no time to perfect the new methods which Haig had settled upon; nevertheless the fighting (the Battle of Festubert) revealed that the British were learning fast. In ten days (May 15th–25th) they did, this time, make a small amount of progress at a cost of 710 officers and 15,938 men – only some 60 per cent more than the Aubers losses on *one* day for no result at all.[1] 'The British leaders', says the Official History, 'felt that they were on the right lines, and that with more gun support they might have reached the Aubers Ridge. . . . Another similar effort might break through the German line, and at any rate compel the enemy to bring up greater reinforcements, which otherwise might be used against the French, who had made good progress.' Higher Allied strategy continued to be determined by the thought that 'the opportunity for an offensive to expel the invaders of France and Belgium, now afforded by the absence of so many German divisions in Russia, might never recur.' It was easy enough later to say that this was all too sanguine; at the time these matters presented themselves not simply as hopes, but as vital needs.

Haig's reputation was certainly enhanced by these operations, for which Sir John French gave him generous credit. The observant Charteris noted a stream of distinguished guests at First Army Headquarters after Neuve Chapelle. The first was Lord Esher, early in April: '. . . . his chief characteristic is that he is always close friends with those that matter. So his visit probably means that D.H's star is in the ascendant.' In June the Prime

1. But note the much higher proportion of officers, indicating that all was not well with morale.

Minister arrived: 'He gave great praise to D.H. and to the First Army.' Haig noted: 'Mr. Asquith was most enthusiastic about all he had seen, and on bidding good-bye, he asked me to write to him whenever I could spare the time.' He added dryly: 'It was interesting to see Mr. Asquith having tea with General Gough as his host after the dealings they had together in the Spring of 1914, after the Curragh incident.' Lord Esher returned, and Charteris recorded: 'Esher says that in "political circles" there is considerable speculation as regards the length of Sir J. French's period of command, and as to his probable successor. "Political circles" with Esher probably means K. of K. himself. There has apparently been much more friction between French and K. than we know; obviously K. must resent French's incursion into the Press on the munition question.'

This refers to the celebrated article, not by French, but by Colonel Repington in *The Times* on May 15th, containing the words 'the want of an unlimited supply of high explosive shells was a fatal bar to our success'. This statement flatly contradicted the Government's public pronouncements; coming in conjunction with the resignation of the First Sea Lord, Lord Fisher, over Dardanelles policy, it brought about the fall of the Liberal Government and the formation of the First Coalition. Repington says: 'These words were my own, and were not suggested by Sir John French.' But French, relating how he had struggled for a more ample supply of munitions (particularly high-explosive shells) by every means – official channels, lobbying public men, Press interviews – adds that after the Aubers fiasco 'I immediately gave instructions that evidence should be furnished to Colonel Repington . . . who happened to be then at Headquarters, that the vital need of high-explosive shells had been a fatal bar to our Army success on that day.'[1]

The ensuing uproar had beneficial results – the setting up of a Ministry of Munitions with Mr. Lloyd George, who had a reputation as a 'hustler', at its head; but it certainly did French no good with the Ministers and officials who were affected by the revelation, among whom Kitchener was the outstanding figure. French's subsequent downfall owes more to this incident than to any other, and it is only fair to say that he was trying to do his best for his Army. To be fair also to Kitchener, it has to be added that he was already engaged in a vast expansion of munitions production which began to make itself felt in September, 1915. The work of the Ministry of Munitions did not become effective until 1916, and then only to a limited extent. Kitchener's irritation with French is understandable. Both were victims of circumstances which had been outside their control at the critical time.

Kitchener himself was the next important visitor at First Army Head-

1. Repington's account of this episode, if not of certifiable accuracy, is full of interest, and may be found in *The First World War*, pp. 35-41.

quarters, on July 8th. Privately to Haig 'He explained how he found it difficult to get Sir John French to comply with any of his suggestions. Whereas in bygone days F. obeyed his smallest suggestion. However, he (K.) was ready to do anything "to black French's boots" if need be, in order to obtain agreement and win the war! He wanted me to assert myself more, and to insist on French proceeding on sound principles. I replied that that was easier said than done – and in any case it was more his affair to control Sir John French than mine. I had really to do as I was ordered by Sir John, and French had much more self-confidence now than when I was with him in South Africa.' Haig could hardly have said more – or less – than this; Kitchener went away dissatisfied.

A week later, at Buckingham Palace the King conferred on Haig the G.C.B. with suitable kind words: 'He referred to the friction between Sir John and Lord K. and hoped I would do all I could to make matters run smoothly. He said he visited the Grand Fleet last week where all the Admirals were on the most friendly terms with one another. In the King's opinion, the Army would be in the same satisfactory state and there would be no back-biting and unfriendly criticism of superiors if the officer at the head of the Army in the Field – a most splendid body of troops – was fit for his position! He (the King) criticizes French's dealing with the Press, *The Times*, Repington and Lord Northcliffe, etc. All most unsoldier-like and he (the King) had lost confidence in Field Marshal French. And he had told Kitchener that he (K.) could depend on his (the King's) support in whatever action he took in dealing with French. The King's one object was efficiency. He would approve of any action to ensure the Army being in as fit a state as possible to end the war. I pointed out that the time to get rid of French was immediately after the retreat. Now the Army was stationary and could practically be controlled from London. The King hoped that I would write to Wigram, and said that no one but he and Wigram would know what I had written.'

That afternoon Haig had an interview with Kitchener, who came specially to meet him: 'He was most affable, and . . . wished me to write to him on any subject affecting the Army and in which I thought he could be of assistance. He would treat my letters as secret, and would not reply, but I would see my proposals given effect to and must profess ignorance when that happened! . . . At both my interviews today, I was urged to write regarding the situation and doings of the Army in Flanders to Lord K. The King quite realized the nature of such conduct on my part, because he told me he had said to Lord K. with reference to it "If anyone acted like that, and told tales out of school, he would at school be called a sneak". K's reply was that we are beyond the schoolboy's age!'

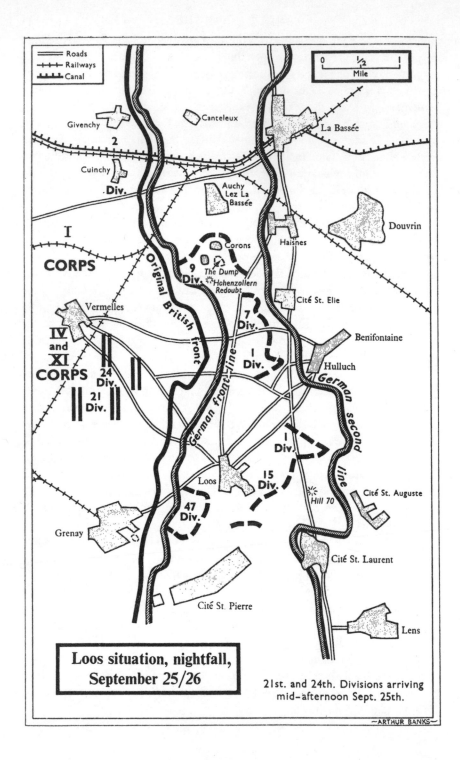

Roads
Railways
Canal

0   ½   1
Mile

Givenchy

Canteleux

La Bassée

2

Cuinchy

Div.

Auchy
Lez La
Bassée

Douvrin

I

Corons

Haisnes

CORPS

9
Div.

The Dump
Hohenzollern
Redoubt

Cité St. Elie

Vermelles

7
Div.

Benifontaine

IV
and
XI
CORPS

24
Div.

1
Div.

Hulluch

21
Div.

German second line

1
Div.

Cité St. Auguste

Loos

15
Div.

Hill 70

47
Div.

Grenay

Cité St. Laurent

Cité St. Pierre

Lens

**Loos situation, nightfall,
September 25/26**

21st. and 24th. Divisions arriving
mid-afternoon Sept. 25th.

~ARTHUR BANKS~

This very frankly narrated episode, first brought fully to light when an edited version of Haig's Diary was published in 1952, has attracted much attention; it requires to be looked at with coolness. The first point to notice is that the initiative for secret communication did not lie with Haig, nor arise out of any statement or complaint on his part. Secondly, he did not press for French's removal, but on the contrary said that the time for it had passed, and that French could be adequately controlled from London. Thirdly, it is evident from the last passage that he did not much care for this secret letter procedure. (In 1918, when Wilson made a similar suggestion, he turned it down flat.) On the other hand, Kitchener was the Secretary of State for War, as well as being the Army's senior serving Field-Marshal. The King was the titular Head of the Army, having a special relationship with it which at that time meant far more to Regular officers than is easy to imagine today, after two experiences of sweeping dilution of the Officer Corps. It is difficult to see how Haig could have refused suggestions coming from such quarters and involving the commonweal. Public school morals did not offer a complete solution to the problems of national survival in a global war. We shall see that Haig did not avail himself of the secret channel now open to him until a matter arose which affected, in his opinion, the very safety of the Army itself.

*   *   *   *

Undaunted by the poor results of his spring offensives, or by the evident German qualities in defence, Joffre decided to make one more attempt to reach a decision before the winter. This time it would be a large double stroke, made possible by the increase of strength of the French artillery; the main attack would be in Champagne, with a heavy secondary blow, which at the least could be expected to tie down German reserves, in Artois. He desired the British to take part in this by co-operating with Foch's Army Group in the area which had already proved so disappointing to British hopes. French would have preferred to switch British offensive efforts to the Ypres region, but, says Joffre: 'At my request, he relinquished this plan and acquiesced in mine. In a spirit of real as opposed to conventional discipline, he subordinated his will to the wishes expressed by me "in my capacity of Commander-in-Chief" . . . I shall often be obliged to refer to the absence of a Supreme Command, which was one of the major causes of our weakness. Consequently, it gives me great pleasure to testify here how greatly the British Commander-in-Chief and, later on, Sir Douglas Haig, by their chivalrous recognition of my authority, lessened the consequences of this serious omission.' Beneath all the discussion that later raged about the need for, and advantages of a Supreme Allied Command, there remains the fact

that, in effect, one existed throughout the War (except for a short period in
1917 and early 1918); it was represented by the French Commander-in-
Chief; when a Generalissimo was finally appointed, he, too, was a French
officer. How could it have been otherwise? The Second World War underlined the dominating role of the senior partner; only equality on land could
have given the British strategic independence.

The lack of anything approaching strategic independence in 1915 brought
about the Battle of Loos. At every stage in the preparation for this battle,
British interests were subordinated to those of the French, with the inevitable consequence that it marks the true beginning of the martyrdom of
the British Army. This fact is concealed in Joffre's approving statement
quoted above, as are the sharp disagreements which arose between him and
French during the planning stages in July and August. These centred around
the precise locality of the British attack. Joffre's wish was for this to take
place *south* of the La Bassée canal, alongside the French 10th Army. He always
favoured side-by-side co-operation between the Allies, not only, as some
critics have suggested, because he had unworthy doubts about the British
'pulling their weight', but because trench warfare experience repeatedly
showed the ineffectiveness of distant support, particularly in counter-battery
work. He remained unrepentant; the next year, on the Somme, he insisted
on the same point. Both French and Haig, however, would have preferred to
make their effort north of the canal again. Ill-starred and unsuitable as the
ground there was, at least it did not contain such an obstacle as the huge
complex of industrial buildings and artisans' dwellings contained within the
triangle Loos-Lens-Liévin; even Foch baulked at this, and planned to by-pass
the area on both flanks. Nevertheless, he and Joffre were determined that the
British should be engaged on its fringe, in close conjunction with their own
troops. Even the revelation, early in July, of a second German defence line
running right through the area selected for attack did not shake them. Sir
John French, on the other hand, was much disturbed.

Haig had reached the conclusion, at the beginning of June, that 'an
attack on Loos is not practical unless the enemy is dislodged from Lens, which
is a mass of ruins organized as defended localities and coal heaps'. He moved
slightly away from this position later in the month, but returned to it even
more emphatically when he learned of the new German defences. He told
Robertson on July 21st 'that the enemy's position on my front is very strong
all the way along and that the conclusion to attack immediately south of the
canal . . . was arrived at because I was told it was necessary to attack as close
as possible to the French flank. Further south on my front the enemy's
position is still less favourable for attack. I still think the capture of the Aubers
Ridge will have the greatest tactical results.' On August 2nd he noted: 'Sir

John apparently accepted my view that the Aubers Ridge would be a better objective, and has written to General Joffre putting forward his views, but saying that the British will do whatever Joffre thinks best. Sir John seems now to have . . . put himself and the British Forces unreservedly in Joffre's hands!'

Haig had a fair inkling of the disciplines of the French Alliance already, but the exclamation mark shows that only by personal experience could the British Commander-in-Chief's dilemma be fully understood.

French himself, grappling with it day by day, was growing more and more uneasy. By every shift that he could think of, he tried to wriggle out of the full implications of his promise to Joffre. His motives were altogether creditable, though the French could hardly be expected to appreciate this; he knew that the British Army was not yet fit for a large undertaking, and that the front selected was a bad one. On August 7th Haig recorded: 'Sir John has decided to comply with General Joffre's wishes even though he disagrees with the plan. I am therefore to work out proposals for giving effect to the decision, *but my attack is to be made chiefly with artillery and I am not to launch a large force of infantry*[1] to the attack of objectives which are so strongly held as to be liable to result only in the sacrifice of many lives. That is to say, I am to assist the "French by neutralizing the enemy's artillery and by holding the hostile infantry on my front".'

Joffre, not surprisingly, flatly refused to accept this compromise; on August 12th he wrote to French: 'you will certainly agree with me that (British) support can only be effective if it takes the form of a large and powerful attack, composed of the maximum force you have available, executed with the hope of success and carried through to the end.' Robertson remarked in a letter to Haig that the 'attack was not a very satisfactory matter from any point of view'. He added – this was as late as August 16th: 'There is just a possibility of the Aubers plan being thought about again.' But it was not to be.

The whole matter was finally resolved by Kitchener, who visited Joffre on the day of Robertson's note. He imparted the conclusions which he reached at G.Q.G. to French in an unmistakable manner, and repeated them to Haig on the 19th at First Army Headquarters: '. . . Lord K. came into my writing room upstairs, saying he had been anxious to have a few minutes' talk with me. The Russians, he said, had been severely handled, and *it was doubtful how much longer their Army could withstand the German blows*. Up to the present, he had favoured a policy of active defence in France until such time as all our forces were ready to strike. The situation which had arisen in Russia had caused him to modify these views. He now felt that the Allies must act vigorously in order to take some of the pressure off Russia, if possible. He

1. Author's italics.

had heard, when with the French, that Sir J. French did not mean to co-operate to the utmost of his power when the French attacked in September. He (Lord K.) had noticed that the French were anxiously watching the British on their left. And he *had decided that we must act with all our energy, and do our utmost to help the French, even though by doing so we suffered very heavy losses indeed.'*

Thus, by stages, the Battle of Loos acquired its major outline. It is an instructive story, showing the minds of all the British leaders concerned in movement, according to the fluctuations of pressures upon them. Only un-imaginative hindsight, the glacial still of after-knowledge, can accuse them of being mentally petrified or insensitive.

All that remained now was the actual fighting of the unwanted battle. This would be a matter of tactics, and these were Haig's responsibility. We have seen how his mind was moving in this matter. In June, discussing the ammunition situation with Hubert Gough and General Birch (the new C.R.A. First Army), he told them: *'I had no intention of ordering any infantry under my command to attack until the hostile position was thoroughly prepared,* so they were not to underestimate merely to please G.H.Q.! If we had not enough ammunition now, we must wait until it accumulated.'

Methodical artillery preparation was the essence of his plan; the infantry advance was to be carried out with the utmost flexibility possible. In December, 1914, he had told one of his brigadiers: 'No advance is ever to be made in mass or in rigid lines when under fire.' The influx of new and relatively untrained troops, however, made flexibility an ideal that became increasingly difficult of attainment. The outstanding lesson of all the year's operations was the need to exploit early success *immediately*. This meant having a fresh Reserve ready at hand in the first stages of the battle. Haig made this point to French on August 17th: 'I discussed the forthcoming attack with Sir John, and said that the front on which we attacked and the distance to which we go will depend on the orders and Reserves which he gives me.' Four days later he learned from Robertson what the Reserve would consist of: General Haking's XI Corps, the 21st and 24th New Army Divisions (not yet in France), with the recently-formed Guards Division. Haig com-mented:

'I question suitability of New Army Divisions for this duty on first landing.'

Worse was to follow: as the day of battle (September 25th) approached, it became clear that a fundamental difference of opinion had arisen between the Commander-in-Chief and the Commander of the attacking Army over the use of the Reserve. On September 18th Haig met French and urged 'the importance of having the General Reserve (which the C.-in-C. retains under

G.H.Q.) with the head of its two divisions at Noeux les Mines and Verquin, respectively, by *the morning* of the 25th. Sir John seemed to think that was too close up.' The next day he received detailed orders from G.H.Q.: 'The Reserves are not to reach the area south of Lillers till 24th. This is too late!'

On the 20th he met Kitchener again, and was perturbed enough to broach the question to him in the course of a conversation which touched upon many large matters. Haig wrote: 'K. did not realize how congested the whole front of attack becomes, and how difficult it is to get fresh troops forward to reinforce or replace those which have been engaged. This was in reference to Sir J. French's decision to hold back the General Reserve in his own hands.' Nothing came of the conversation. It is not difficult to imagine what happened. Haig, inarticulate as ever, was thinking of a particular problem connected with the specific battle that he was about to fight, but not expressing himself well; Kitchener, preoccupied with national problems, did not appreciate the immediacy of what Haig was saying. Haig, had, however, already raised the matter also with Foch, and begged him to discuss it with French. Foch's ideas coincided with Haig's, and it was because of his intervention with Joffre's backing that the latter learned, on the 22nd, that: 'General Haking's XI Corps of three divisions will now, I believe, be close up ready to support . . . Sir J. French . . . said that he would release XI Corps to support me on the earliest possible moment.'

The wish was being father to the thought; when Robertson came to lunch with Haig the next day the position was still far from clear: 'It seems that Sir J. French does not realize the size of the units with which he as C.-in-C. is fighting the forthcoming battle. He still clings to Haking's three divisions with which he, in his own mind, is about to fight the battle when really he is fighting with 3 Armies[1] and 2 Cavalry Corps! However, the 3 divisions will, I hope, be close up in the places where I have arranged to put them, and will go forward as soon as any opportunity offers. General Haking came to see me and quite understands my plans.' If this entry shows that Haig was not trying to make difficulties with French, it also shows that he was too sanguine about the latter's intentions, as events proved. Charteris, on the 24th, the eve of battle, recorded: 'D.H. . . . is satisfied that as far as the Army is concerned everything possible has been done – except the three Reserve divisions. They are too far back. If our first attack gets through we shall want them at once. It is the first real break through between him and Sir John French. Last week D.H. might have asked Kitchener to overrule French, and I am sure K. would have done so. I wish he had. It is so vital. But, after all, it *may* go all right.' The omens were not good. Haig met French and Robertson for a final check on details. He learned what their

1. The Third Army, under General Monro, was formed in July.

movements would be. 'I expressed wonder how the C.-in-C. hoped to control operations twenty-five miles away from his C.G.S. and Staff.' The only certainty was, as Charteris wrote, that:

'Whatever the issue of the battle, the casualty list will be huge. That is the sad part of it.'

*   *   *   *

Haig had not abandoned his quest for surprise; he wrote to Robertson on September 16th: 'In my opinion, under no circumstances should our forthcoming attack be launched without the aid of gas.' He pinned great hopes on this new weapon, the only means at his disposal for counteracting the increased strength of the German defences and the continuing British shortage of artillery and munitions. But gas, as used in 1915, released from cylinders and depending on a favourable wind, was a dubious asset. 'An anxious night,' he wrote on the 25th, 'wondering all the time what the wind would be in the morning! The greatest battle in the world's history begins today. Some 800,000 French and British troops will actually attack today.' It was a heavy responsibility that lay upon the First Army's Commander. As he went to bed on the eve of battle, the wind was actually blowing *from* the German trenches; but Captain Gold, the Meteorological Officer attached to the Royal Flying Corps, predicted either a flat calm or a change in the British favour for the morning.

'I went out at 5 a.m.', wrote Haig in his diary. 'Almost a calm. Alan Fletcher[1] lit a cigarette and the smoke drifted in puffs towards the N.E. Staff Officers of Corps were ordered to stand by in case it were necessary to counter order to attack. At one time, owing to the calm, I feared the gas might simply hang about *our* trenches. However, at 5.15 I said "carry on". I went to the top of our wooden look-out tower. The wind came gently from S.W. and by 5.40 had increased slightly. The leaves of the poplar trees gently rustled. This seemed satisfactory. But what a risk I must run of gas blowing back upon our own dense masses of troops!'

The smoke of Fletcher's cigarette, according to Charteris, 'moved quite perceptibly towards the Germans. But it died away again in a few minutes, and a little later D.H. sent down a message from the tower to 1st Corps to inquire whether the attack could still be held up. Gough replied that it was too late to change. I was with D.H. when the reply was brought in. He was very upset. Actually I think Gough was quite right. There would have been great confusion if any attempt had then been made to postpone the attack.' These are the pressures of command; these are the frightening

1. Haig's A.D.C.

decisions that have to be made; and these are the circumstances that surround them, a world removed from the quiet atmosphere in which they are judged.

The story of the Battle of Loos has often been told; it can only be baldly summarized now. The First Army attacked with everything it had, the main assault being by I and IV Corps, with all their six divisions in line. On one flank Haig's fears were realized; the gas blew back on the 2nd Division; its attack failed completely. On the other flank, progress was slow. But in the centre there was once again a delusive initial success. The Germans only mustered a strength equivalent to one division against the whole British front; as the waves of infantry swept over their front trenches and even penetrated their second line at certain points along a frontage of 8,000 yards, it seemed to the Germans for a time that disaster was certain. Headquarters Staffs and orderlies were turned out to take part in the defence, as their British counterparts had done at Ypres; transport was hooked in for a rapid retreat. Everything depended on the prompt arrival of the British reserves. They did not come. Once again a great opportunity was missed; once again the battle was lost in the first few hours. The Germans held on by the skin of their teeth, and when the British Reserves at last came on the scene, hungry, exhausted by a long and trying march, inexperienced and confused, it was too late. Attempting to carry the advance forward on the 26th, the raw New Army divisions[1] received a terrible baptism of fire. Their dense formations, due partly to misapprehensions about the actual dispositions of the British and German forces on the battlefield, partly to the sheer inexperience of their commanders, were swept by artillery and machine guns. They advanced gallantly at first, but after a time began to waver, and then come back in disorder. Guns were abandoned. Fortunately the Guards Division was at hand to restore the situation, and fortunately, too, the Germans were in no condition to take advantage of the situation. But this spelt the end of all hopes of a substantial victory. Taken in conjunction with the French failure at Vimy and disappointing results in Champagne, coming fast upon heavy Russian and Italian defeats, added to further setbacks at Gallipoli and in Mesopotamia, Loos was a symbol of the shattered Allied hopes of 1915.

At the desire of the French, the Battle of Loos was continued, despite its

1. In the 21st Division, says the Official History, 'Of the four brigadiers, two were Regular officers, and two retired Regulars. All the battalion commanders were ex-Regular officers, mostly retired officers of the Indian Army; besides these there were only 14 Regular and ex-Regular officers in the 13 battalions. Other officers of the infantry were newly commissioned, mostly without special training.'

In the 24th Division, 'No battalion had more than one Regular or ex-Regular officer besides the C.O., who was in all cases except one a retired officer either Regular or Militia. All the brigadiers were retired officers, two of them from the Indian Army.'

miserable opening, until October 16th. By that time the British Army had lost (including subsidiary attacks, one of them by the Second Army) 2,466 officers and 59,247 men. Its gains were meagre, but they did exist. The Official History says: 'There were the definite results that eight thousand yards of German front had been taken, including localities fortified at leisure by all the skill and experience of the German engineers. In places the British troops had advanced over two miles from their front line, the largest advance made by the Allies on the Western front since trench warfare had begun.'

The belief that the German front could be broken, given enough munitions and correct tactics, remained unshaken; above all, the admirable performance of the 9th and 15th New Army Divisions (both Scottish) showed that with proper handling and time to acclimatize itself the British citizen Army would be capable of playing a great part in the War. This was a fact that many had doubted; a year earlier, for example, Henry Wilson had written: 'Under no circumstances can these mobs . . . take the field for two years. Then what is the use of them?' and 'K's . . . ridiculous and preposterous army of 25 corps is the laughing-stock of every soldier in Europe.' We have seen that it was by no means a laughing-stock to Haig. Appreciating the great difficulties under which the 21st and 24th Divisions had striven – 'They should have had experience in the trenches before being sent into a great battle!' he noted on the 28th – he felt quite certain that such soldiers could beat the enemy, if their commanders would permit them to. But would they? This now became the uppermost question in his mind.

*   *   *   *

September 29.

'My dear Lord Kitchener,

'You will doubtless recollect how earnestly I pressed you to ensure an adequate Reserve being close in rear of my attacking divisions, and under my orders. It may interest you to know what happened. No Reserve was placed under me. My attack, as has been reported, was a complete success. The enemy had no troops in his second line, which some of my plucky fellows reached and entered without opposition. Prisoners state the enemy was so hard put to it for troops to stem our advance that the officers' servants, fatigue-men, etc., in Lens were pushed forward. . . .

'The two Reserve Divisions (under C.-in-C's orders) were directed to join me as soon as the success of the First Army was known at G.H.Q. They came on as quick as they could, poor fellows, but only crossed our old trench line with their heads at 6 p.m. We had captured Loos 12 hours previously, and reserves should have been at hand *then*. This, you will remember, I requested should be arranged by G.H.Q. and Robertson quite concurred in my views and wished to put the Reserve Divisions under me, but was not allowed.

'The final result is that the enemy has been allowed time in which to bring up troops and to strengthen his second line, and *probably* to construct a third line. . . .

'I have now been given some fresh Divisions. . . . But the element of surprise has gone, and our task will be a difficult one.

'I think it right that you should know how the lessons which have been learnt in the war at such cost have been neglected. We *were* in a position to make this a turning point in the war, and I still hope we may do so, but naturally, I feel annoyed at the lost opportunity.

'We were all very pleased to receive your kind telegram, and I am

Yours very truly,

D. Haig.'

This letter marked the crystallization of Haig's conviction that, for the sake of its security and the national interest, Sir John French could no longer remain at the head of the Army in France. It is not an objective letter; it is a passionate cry that was wrung out of him by the bitterness of seeing his troops, towards whom his sense of responsibility has been demonstrated, wasted through the Commander-in-Chief's sheer failure to grasp the nature of the War. Charteris noted: 'I do not think that after Loos, D.H. and French can work satisfactorily together. One or other will have to go elsewhere.' Haig had been tolerant of French's failings up to this point; now, however, his attitude changed into contempt. On October 2nd he wrote: 'Sir John French returns to St. Omer today. Robertson tackled him on the question of reserves. His reply was "the second day of the battle was the correct time to put them in and not the first". It seems impossible to discuss military problems with an unreasoning brain of this kind. At any rate, no good result is to be expected from doing so.'

War does not wait while generals settle their disputes; at the imperious bidding of Joffre, the British First Army continued to make attempts to advance. Haig, receiving Joffre's impulse through French, noted on October 5th: 'The fact is Sir John seems incapable of realizing the nature of the fighting which has been going on and the difficulties of getting fresh troops and trench stores forward until adequate communication trenches have been dug.' Three days later, French 'wished me to try and hurry things up so as to attack on the 12th. I said I would do my best.' Meanwhile, in England, as the wounded from Loos arrived and began to tell their stories, uneasiness grew. Kitchener asked French for a full report on the action of the 21st and 24th Divisions, and on October 9th Lord Haldane arrived at First Army H.Q., charged with the mission of discovering the truth from witnesses on the spot:

'I gave him all the facts. The main criticism to my mind is the fact that the Reserves were not at hand when wanted. The causes for this seem to me to be:

1. Neither the C.-in-C. nor his staff fully realized at the beginning (in spite of my letters and remarks) the necessity for reserves being close up before the action began.

2. The two divisions were billeted in depth a long distance from where they would be wanted, and no attempt was made to concentrate them before the battle began.

3. When the course of the fight showed that reserves were wanted at once to exploit the VICTORY, the two divns. were hurried forward without full consideration for their food etc., with the result that the troops arrived worn out at the point of attack and unfit for battle.

4. But the 21st and 24th Divns. having only recently arrived in France, with staffs and commanders inexperienced in war, should not have been detailed for this work. It was courting disaster to employ them at once in fighting of this nature. There were other divisions available as shown by the fact that they arrived three days later upon the battlefield, namely the 28th Divn., the 12th Divn. and the Guards Divn.

'I also felt it my duty to tell Lord Haldane that the arrangements for the supreme command during the battle were not satisfactory. Sir John French was at Philomel (near Lillers) twenty-five miles nearly from his C.G.S. who was at St. Omer with G.H.Q. Many of us felt that if these conditions continued it would be difficult ever to win! Lord Haldane said that he was very glad to have had this talk with me, and seemed much impressed with the serious opinion which I had expressed to him.'

It was a difficult, distasteful and embarrassing position for Haldane, who counted both French and Haig as his personal friends. With his lawyer's tact, and human understanding, he concluded that both men were for the time being inflamed with feelings of disappointment and recrimination, and that the best thing to do would be to try to pour oil on the waters. A note inserted in his diary later by Haig records: 'In spite of the views I expressed, as given above, to Lord Haldane, the latter went back to England and stated that no blame for failure could be attached to Sir John French.' Matters, however, were rapidly passing the stage where soothing syrup might provide a remedy. As the examinations of the German prisoners taken at Loos proceeded, the First Army Staff became even more conscious of a lost opportunity. On October 9th Charteris wrote: 'The really maddening thing about it all is that now we are really getting the German side of the show disentangled by examination of prisoners and captured documents, it becomes clear, without any shadow of doubt, that we had in fact broken the German line as clean as a whistle. For 4 hours there was a glaring gap; then it was gone.'

On the 16th Haig noted: 'Statements from C.O.s of battalions and also captured diaries of prisoners and killed bear out all I said in my report. I am glad that the facts should be elicited now when it is possible to get more or less at the truth.' Disagreements on sheer matters of fact between the Commander-in-Chief and the Commander of the First Army could no longer be concealed.

On October 17th an important meeting took place between Haig and Robertson. Two days earlier, Robertson had returned from a week in London, whither he had been summoned by Kitchener to give guidance to the Cabinet on grand strategy. The Gallipoli Campaign was entering its last phase; the question of evacuation was now being seriously considered. At the same time, under French pressure, there was a movement towards the despatch of a large number of British troops to Salonika, partly to assist the unhappy Serbs who were now being attacked in flank by Bulgaria, partly to 'persuade' Greece to join the Allies. Mr. Lloyd George was an eloquent champion of such manoeuvres in the Balkans. The General Staff in London, however, under the sound if somewhat unsteady guidance of Sir Archibald Murray, continued to advocate the concentration of all resources on the Western Front. Lord Kitchener himself, apprehensive of the effects of evacuation at Gallipoli on the Middle East, was considering sending eight divisions from the West to the Dardanelles, in a last attempt to save that theatre from disaster. There was plenty to talk about, and no shortage of rival views. Robertson was present at several Cabinet meetings. The decision was taken to send an experienced officer out to Gallipoli to report on the situation there, and recommend for or against evacuation. It was suggested that Haig should go, but this immediately raised the question of a possible successor to French, and Sir Charles Monro, commanding the Third Army, was selected instead. At this stage there was no firm determination in the Cabinet to remove French from his command, merely a shifting of opinion in that direction. Robertson told Haig 'that the members of the Cabinet who had up to the present been opposed to removing French had come round to the other opinion. F. does not get on with the French; Joffre seems to have no great opinion of his military views and does not really consult with him. It is most important at the present time to have someone to put the British case and cooperate with the French in aiming at getting decisive results in their plans and operations.'

A surer pointer at the direction in which matters were moving, however, came outside the Cabinet's deliberations. While Robertson was in London,

Lord Stamfordham, the King's private secretary, telephoned him at the King's orders to ask him bluntly whether he did not consider that the time had come for French to go. Robertson did not answer, but the King himself pressed the point at a subsequent meeting. Robertson was in a dilemma. On the one hand, he was French's Chief of Staff, and owed loyalty to him. On the other hand, like Haig, he now firmly believed that Sir John had failed to measure up to the unprecedented burden which had fallen upon him. He gave guarded answers to the King, but now he wanted Haig's advice on how to act in this delicate situation. Haig 'told him at once that up to date I had been more [than?] loyal to French and did my best to stop all criticisms of him or his methods. Now at last, in view of what had happened in the recent battle over the reserves, and in view of the seriousness of the general military situation, I had come to the conclusion that it was not fair to the Empire to retain French in command on this the main battle front. Moreover, none of my officers commanding Corps had a high opinion of Sir J.'s military ability or military views; in fact, *they had no confidence in him*. Robertson quite agreed, and left me saying "he knew now how to act, and would report to Stamfordham".'

So matters rested until October 24th, when the King visited the Army, and invited Haig to dine with him. 'After dinner, the King asked me to come to his room, and asked me about Sir J. French's leadership. I told him that I thought the time to have removed French was after the Retreat, because he had so mismanaged matters, and shown in the handling of the small Expeditionary Force in the Field a great ignorance of the essential principles of war. Since then, during the trench warfare, the Army had grown larger and I thought at first there was no great scope for French to go wrong. I have therefore done my utmost to stop criticisms and make matters run smoothly. But French's handling of the reserves in the last battle, his obstinacy, and conceit, showed his incapacity, and it seemed to me impossible for anyone to prevent him doing the same things again. I therefore thought strongly, that, for the sake of the Empire, French ought to be removed. I, personally, was ready to do my duty in any capacity, and of course would serve under anyone who was chosen for his military skill to be C.-in-C. The King said that he had seen Generals Gough and Haking that afternoon, and that they had told him startling truths of French's unfitness for the command. General Robertson also told him that it was "impossible to deal with French, his mind was never the same for two consecutive minutes".'

An unfortunate accident now occurred. Four days later, when the King was inspecting First Army units, riding a horse lent to him from Haig's stable, a sudden burst of cheering caused the horse to rear and fall. The King was partly pinned under the animal, and suffered injuries which did not immediately reveal themselves. The incident caused a great fuss at the time, for reasons which are understandable. The next day Haig dryly noted: 'The King had a good night and is only bruised. Few bruises have had so much attention.' But in fact George V was considerably shocked and weakened by this incident, and suffered from its results for a long time afterwards. Generously, he hastened to reassure Haig and sent a message 'to say that His Majesty knew very well that the mare had never done such a thing before and that I was not to feel perturbed at what had happened'.

This sequence of events constitutes the basis of the allegation that Haig 'intrigued with the King to supplant Sir John French'. When the edited version of Haig's Diary appeared in 1952, containing the extracts given above, it caused great excitement, and otherwise sober reviewers commented freely on the constitutional propriety and general morality of these proceedings. The more one examines them, the less cause there seems to be for excitement. What does it all amount to? To begin with, the episode has to be seen against the background of the War as a whole: it was a period of great perplexity; nothing was going right for the Allies; Great Britain in particular felt herself drawn into a series of costly impasses such as she had never dreamed of. On all sides, old-fashioned methods and modes of conduct were being found useless and tossed away. Kitchener had scrapped the rules to form New Armies; Lloyd George was doing the same to produce munitions, and would repeat the process in many other spheres; Kitchener and the King had both arrived at the opinion that the Army's problems could not be solved by the codes of the 'old school tie' or 'House spirit'. They needed to know what was going on; they asked Haig; he told them. He did not tell them anything until an actual military disaster had taken place in the field, and driven him to the conclusion that the Commander-in-Chief must go. If this was an intrigue, the word must have hidden meanings.

If Haig only wished to supplant French out of personal motives, he could hardly have found a stupider way to go about it. The proposition that effective power lay in Buckingham Palace has only to be stated for its absurdity to be seen. In truth, of course, the King could wield no influence without the accord of his Ministers. This was the same King, working with the same Prime Minister, who only four years earlier, at the very beginning of his reign, had learned one of the most drastic constitutional lessons in British history, when the House of Lords threw out the Budget, and the monarch found himself faced with the prospect of creating new Peers on a scale large enough to swamp that House. Nobody, after such an experience, could make any mistake about where real power lay; and in fact George V learned the lesson so well that he became the very epitome of the constitutional sovereign. As to Kitchener, his authority had greatly declined, and it was only one week after the King's visit to France that Haig recorded: 'The papers today announce that Lord K. has left the War Office and is replaced by the P.M. Some seem to think K. has left the War Office for good.'

This was, indeed, the consummation which many devoutly wished; but Kitchener, on his way now to the Middle East, was not quite the exhausted force that they supposed. For the time being, however, he was out of action. If Haig had seriously had any intention of 'intriguing' for French's place, it is not to these quarters that he would have turned. He would have addressed himself to the Press, as French did over the munitions shortage; but this he steadfastly refused to do; indeed, throughout the War, his sense of Press relations was very poor. Or he would have addressed himself to politicians; and this also he refused to do. On the day of the King's visit Robertson urged him to write to friends in the Government to protest against the projected operations in the Balkans: 'I said I hated intriguing in such a way . . . I would express my views to the King. . . .' Haig turned to the King (but only at the royal command to do so) for the simple reason, stated earlier, that the monarch was the titular Head of the Army, from whom he held his commission, as well as the Head of the State. It is a misuse of the language to describe the relations between them as any kind of 'intrigue'.

In any case, events were finally decided, not by Haig, nor by Kitchener, nor by the King: they were decided by Sir John French himself. On November 2nd *The Times* published his Loos Despatch; Haig recorded: 'It is full of misstatements of fact. My Staff are comparing the despatch with the orders and telegrams received from G.H.Q. and will make a note on the subject. It is too disgraceful of a C.-in-C. to try and throw dust in the eyes of the British people by distorting facts in his Official Reports.' The controversy centred around the times at which the Reserve divisions actually came under Haig's control at Loos; this was the very core of the matter, and Haig was not now prepared to accept inaccuracies, as he had been after Neuve Chapelle; the documentary evidence was all on his side, and he was determined that the truth should be known. A sharp correspondence ensued between G.H.Q. and First Army H.Q. On November 8th Haig received two letters from the C.G.S. (Robertson, of course), one of them directing that this correspondence should cease, and the second stating on French's instructions that the disputed passages in the despatch were ' "substantially correct" and call for no amendment'. Haig ignored the order that the correspondence should not be continued, and replied that those passages 'convey the impression that at 9.30 a.m. on the 25th Sept. I was able to use the 21st and 24th Divns. in support of the attacking troops, and similarly that I could make use of the Guards Divn. on the *morning* of the 26th. This was not the case, and I beg to request that this fact may be placed on record.' Charteris commented next day:

'The despatch on Loos has put the fat in the fire. . . . As long as the squabble does not get into the Press it will do no harm, but it will make it impossible for D.H. to serve under French. It is ten thousand pities that we should have squabbles like this in the Army – it reduces us to the level of the Cabinet – but I do not see that D.H. could have let the despatch pass without strong objection.'

The Commander-in-Chief also realized that he had gone too far; on November 10th Haig wrote: 'I saw Sir John in his own room regarding the correspondence which I have had on the subject of Reserves, and his recent despatch. He promised to send all my letters on the subject to the War Office, and to let me see his covering letter. . . . I said all I wanted was that the *true facts* of the operations should be placed on record. He was most anxious that I should know that he had nothing to do with an article by Repington in *The Times* of November 2nd.[1] I said that my only thought was how to win the war, and that my duties as G.O.C. 1st Army took up all my time. I gather that no one of importance takes much notice of Sir J. French when he goes to London, and that he feels his loss of position.' This was the beginning of the end for French – in effect, a capitulation.

As fighting died down on the Western Front in the autumn of 1915, Haig's mind began to turn to wider issues. Nothing could be more false or ridiculous than the suggestion that at this time he was engrossed in con- siderations of personal advancement. The opposite was the case; Charteris wrote on October 30th: 'Now that things have settled down for the winter, D.H. has called for notes on the problems in the various other theatres . . . he is urging that Robertson should go to the W.O. as Chief of Staff, to give the Government the strategical advice they need so badly. He and Robertson are the only two men big enough to take this task on. One of them must remain in France and the other go to the W.O.; it does not matter which goes and which stays. K. could work with either.' Certainly, if Haig could in any sense be described as intriguing at this stage, he was doing so on behalf of Robertson. On November 7th, after a meeting with the latter, he noted: 'I hope that Robertson will go home as strategical adviser of the Government with the rank of General, in fact, as Chief of Imperial General Staff. Besides advising Govt. he should frequently meet representatives of the French H.Q. Staff at Calais and settle the whole policy of the Allies of how to win the war.' On November 14th Lord Esher came to lunch, and they agreed 'that he should go to London tomorrow and recommend:

1. An article in which Repington wrote favourably about French's qualities as a commander, with the implied suggestion that he should have had direct control of the battle of Loos instead of Haig. No doubt both men's memories of French's dealing with Repington earlier in the year, over the munitions question, prompted this disavowal.

1. That General Robertson should be appointed C.I.G.S. and to advise the War Committee of the Cabinet direct (not through S. of S. for War).

2. That the D.M.O.[1] and D.S.D.[2] directorates be removed from the War Office and placed in the Horse Guards under General Robertson. This to be the "Imperial General Staff".

3. That the D.M.T.[3] (which deals with Home Defence and Training) be re-organized as a local General Staff and be placed under a C. in C. of the United Kingdom. Sir A. Murray could remain as the Chief of this General Staff.

'The effect of these proposals, it is hoped, will be to strengthen the Imperial General Staff, and keep it free from the administrative details carried out in the War Office. The C.I.G.S. can then devote his whole time to thinking over the war and its problems – will advise the Cabinet, and will be in a position to keep in closer touch with the French.'

These thoughts were still uppermost in Haig's mind when he himself went to London later in the month. On November 23rd he lunched with Asquith at Downing Street. He urged on the Prime Minister the same organizational proposals that he had put forward to Lord Esher: 'The P.M. agreed and added that General Robertson had been of great assistance to him. The matters we discussed were of such vital interest to the Empire that I never alluded to my own affairs, and the differences which I had had with Sir. J. French. . . .' The next day Haig returned to the charge with Bonar Law and Lord Edmund Talbot, the Opposition Chief Whip, adding two further points for immediate attention: the unification of the Army, replacing the three existing categories of Regulars, Territorials and New Armies, with their different methods of recruitment and organization; and the question of manpower, noting that 'My Army alone is 21,000 of all ranks deficient'. Once again there was no time to talk of personal matters. At the same time he was hard at work, at the request of the War Office (though ostensibly on leave), drawing up a paper on the defence of the Suez Canal. The document, when finished, had all the Haig hallmarks – great thoroughness and clarity. When it was completed, he met Kitchener who had returned from his Middle East visit full of anxieties, but reinvigorated by the air of that region in which he had first won fame. They discussed the general situation, Salonika, Gallipoli, Egypt; and then Kitchener came to the point:

'As regards myself, nothing had been definitely settled but today he had written to the Prime Minister recommending that I should be appointed to succeed Sir J. French. If the P.M. did not settle the matter today, he would again press for a settlement tomorrow, but in any case he had taken the matter

1. Director of Military Operations.
2. Director of Staff Duties.
3. Director of Military Training.

in hand and I must not trouble my head over it. As soon as I was in the saddle, he would see me again.'

One more week elapsed before the disagreeable formalities of changing Commanders-in-Chief were concluded. Then, on December 10th, 1915, Haig recorded: 'About 7 p.m. I received a letter from the Prime Minister marked "Secret" and enclosed in *three* envelopes! It was dated 10 Downing Street, Dec. 8, 1915, and ran as follows: "Sir J. French has placed in my hands his resignation of the Office of Commander in Chief of the Forces in France. Subject to the King's approval, I have the pleasure of proposing to you that you should be his successor. I am satisfied that this is the best choice that could be made in the interests of the Army and the Country." Mr. Asquith then went on to ask my views about a Chief of Staff. I wrote at once accepting the appointment and recommended Major-General Butler to be C.G.S.'

It was by now established that Robertson would not be returning to France, though his elevation to the post of C.I.G.S. would not become effective for another fortnight. Haig himself did not take up his new duties for nine days. During that time there were several matters of personal relations to be settled, some pleasant, others less so. There was the question of Murray, whom Robertson would soon displace: 'I raised no objection to giving Archie Murray a Corps, because he is quite fit to command a Corps on a defensive front, and is an educated soldier, though rather lacking in decision and judgment.' Actually, Murray went to command in Egypt; he might have done better with a Corps under Haig. Then there was the question of Haig's own successor: 'I recommended Sir Henry Rawlinson. Though not a sincere man, he has brains and experience. Robertson agreed that he was the best choice.'

A few days later Haig met Rawlinson himself: 'He told me that Lt.-General Henry Wilson was thinking of going on half-pay. As Henry Wilson is a friend of his, I told him on no account was it possible for an officer of his standing to do that. I was willing to help him in every possible way to find a suitable appointment: that this war was so gigantic in its proportions, that there was room for everyone of us. I told him to offer H.W. a Division from me. I did not add that I knew H.W. had been abusing me and other British Generals and that he instigated an article in the *Observer* suggesting that the British Army in France should be placed under the command of General Foch!' Before the War ended, Haig would be the instigator of that very step, and Wilson would be disconcerted by its consequences. No novelist can ever emulate the ironies of history.

Finally, there was a meeting with French: 'Saturday, December 18. I left Hinges about 1.30 and motored to St. Omer where I saw Sir John French at 3 p.m. He did not look very well and seemed short of breath at times. He expressed a wish to help me and the Army in France to the best of his power at home. Then he said that "there was a delicate personal matter" which he wished to speak about. This was that he had wanted to give Winston Churchill an Infantry Brigade. This had been vetoed but he was anxious that Winston should have a Battalion. I replied that I had no objection because Winston had done good work in the trenches, and we were short of Battalion C.O.s. I then said goodbye. Winston Churchill then appeared and I told him what I had said to French. I next saw the Military Secretary and arranged for W. to be posted to the 9th K.R.R. in the 14th Divn.'

Sir John French returned to England to command the Home Forces. Sir Winston Churchill, who was with him all through his last day in France, and accompanied him from headquarters to headquarters as he said his goodbyes, has written: 'His pain in giving up his great command was acute. He would much rather have given up his life.' Brave, devoted, warm-hearted, it was entirely characteristic of French that his last request to Haig should be on Churchill's behalf, although the latter had been critical of the whole Loos campaign, including French's part in it. His defects were a hot temper, and the instability of mind that goes with it, which caused him to swing violently from optimism to pessimism and back again. He lacked the steady thread of intellectual discernment that stems from a deep fund of knowledge. On the other hand, as long as the War retained any human aspect, he brought to it an important asset; as Colonel Repington wrote: 'He possessed the sacred fire of leadership in a rare degree.'

Haig took up the office of Commander-in-Chief on December 19th. Lord Haldane greeted him in it with this letter:

'My Dear Haig,

'It was with mingled feelings that I read the news – sadness about Sir John – whom I like much – and rejoicing over the chance that has come to the brilliant soldier whom I have known and admired for so long.

'I have for months past wished that you had been in London from the beginning – with the supreme direction of the war and the opportunity of playing chess against the Great General Staff of Germany. I know which I should have backed. You have a great strategical mind – a rare gift in this country.

'But now you have a great task and responsibility, a task and responsibility with which you are admirably fitted by gifts and by training to deal.

'My best wishes are with you in this new and higher phase of one of the most brilliant military careers of modern times.

'Believe me, yours very sincerely,

Haldane.'

PART III

'Victory is measured not by a comparison of casualties or losses, not by tactical incidents in the battle, but only by results.'

Lord Hankey

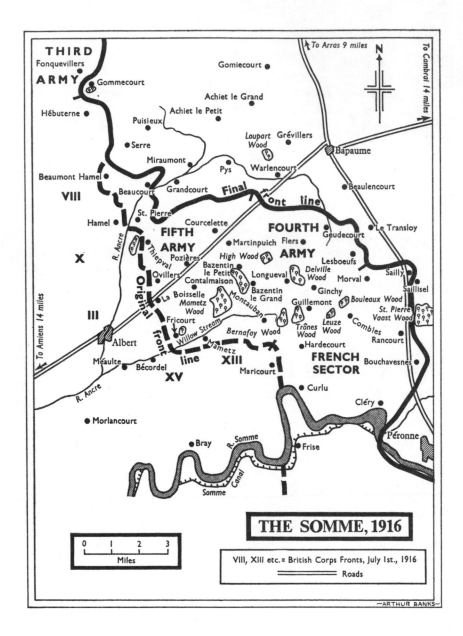

THE SOMME, 1916

VIII, XIII etc. = British Corps Fronts, July 1st., 1916
═══ Roads

THIRD
Fonquevillers
ARMY
Gommecourt
Hébuterne
VIII
Beaumont Hamel
Beaucourt
Grandcourt
St. Pierre
Hamel
X
FIFTH
ARMY
Pozières
Thiepval
Ovillers
La Boisselle
Mametz Wood
Fricourt
III
Willow Stream
Albert
Bécordel
Méaulte
XV
Mametz
XIII
Maricourt
Morlancourt
Bray
Frise
Curlu

Gomiecourt
Achiet le Grand
Achiet le Petit
Puisieux
Serre
Miraumont
Loupart Wood
Grévillers
Pys
Warlencourt
Bapaume
Beaulencourt
Final front line
Courcelette
FOURTH
Geudecourt
Le Transloy
Martinpuich
Flers
High Wood
ARMY
Lesboeufs
Bazentin le Petit
Longueval
Delville Wood
Morval
Sailly
Contalmaison
Bazentin le Grand
Ginchy
Saillisel
Montauban
Guillemont
Bouleaux Wood
St. Pierre Vaast Wood
Trônes Wood
Leuze Wood
Combles
Bernafay Wood
Rancourt
Hardecourt
FRENCH SECTOR
Bouchavesnes
Cléry
Péronne
R. Somme
Somme Canal
Somme

Original front line

To Arras 9 miles
N
To Cambrai 14 miles
To Amiens 14 mimiles
R. Ancre

0 1 2 3
Miles

~ARTHUR BANKS~

8

The Year of the Somme

HAIG ENTERED the office of Commander-in-Chief half-way through his fifty-fifth year. Sure of his own professional qualifications, confident of the capacity of his troops, absolute in his conviction that victory would lie at the end of a long, hard road, if only the British nation was true to itself, he took up his great burden with composure and humility. It is at this stage that an element in him – certainly not new, but hitherto less evident – begins to be marked: a religious faith, planted in him by his mother in his earliest years. On December 27th, 1915, he wrote to his wife: '. . . all seem to expect success as the result of my arrival, and somehow give me the idea that they think I am "meant to win" by some SUPERIOR POWER. As you know, while doing my utmost, I feel one's best can go but a short way without help from ABOVE. . . .' The sense of working under a Divine Providence never left him, no matter what tribulations the days of the War might bring. But it would be altogether wrong to think of him as in any sense a 'Crusader', to link him with Cromwell, or any leader of Religious Wars. Nor, in his Orders and addresses, did he invoke on his side 'the Lord mighty in battle', as Field-Marshal Montgomery was accustomed to do during the Second World War. The clergyman who saw him most often, and came to know him best during his period of command, has written: 'Haig's faith was essentially practical. There is not the slightest evidence that he ever allowed it to pervert or overrule his military judgment. What it did for him was to give him an unshakeable confidence in victory, a resolute will for victory, and a serenity which remained unclouded in the darkest hour.'

The clergyman in question was the Very Reverend Dr. George S. Duncan, of the Church of Scotland. The manner of his first meeting with Haig is instructive; it took place on Sunday, January 2nd, 1916, when Dr. Duncan was a very junior Presbyterian Army chaplain at St. Omer. He was astonished, on that Sunday, to see the new Commander-in-Chief among his congregation, 'one of the first officers of any rank who had ever found his way to it'. The next Sunday, Haig was back again; he noted in his Diary: 'I attended the Scottish Church at 9.30 a.m. The clergyman (George Duncan) is most earnest and impressive. Quite after the old covenanting style. . . . I wrote to the King, also to Wigram to discourage high dignitaries of the Church from coming to France. They only come when the weather gets finer, and then chiefly for a "joy-ride", or for self-advertisement.'

It was this dissatisfaction with the Church of England that caused Haig to turn to and remain with the Scottish Church. Personal faith apart, he recognized that failings on the part of the Established Church (which was no more 'mobilized' for total war at this time than any other part of the nation) could have a serious effect on the morale of an Army that needed every encouragement that it could get. On March 30th he wrote in his Diary: '. . . the clergy of the Church of England are squabbling terribly amongst themselves over High Church and Low Church methods. It seems to me most disgraceful at a time like the present, that the National Church should be divided against itself, instead of giving us a noble example of unity and good fellowship.' When the Archbishop of Canterbuty visited G.H.Q. in May, Haig expressed two wishes to him: '*Firstly:* that the Chaplains should preach to the troops about the objects of Great Britain in carrying on this War. We have no selfish motive, but are fighting for the good of humanity. *Secondly:* The Chaplains of the Church of England must cease quarrelling amongst themselves. In the Field we cannot tolerate any narrow sectarian ideas. We must all be united whether we are clerics or ordinary troops.'

Haig's request was part and parcel of his continuous concern with the feelings of his great Citizen Army, plunged into experiences calculated to shatter the strongest spirit. It was over the Church's function as a nourisher of the spirit that he was anxious now, as he was over everything that could affect the frame of mind of his soldiers. Two years later, in a remarkable con- versation with the King, he said that 'it was very desirable to tell the Army in a few unambiguous sentences, what we are fighting for. The Army is now composed of representatives of all classes in the Nation, and many are most intelligent and think things out. They don't care whether France has Alsace and Italy Trieste; they realize that Britain entered the War to free Belgium and save France. Germany is now ready, we have been told, to give all we want in these respects. So it is essential that some statement should be made which the soldier can understand and approve of. Few of us feel that the "democratizing of Germany" is worth the loss of a single Englishman!'[1]

Before we leave the subject of this powerful influence which hence-

1. Haig Diary, January 2nd, 1918.

forward fortified and comforted the mind of the new Commander-in-Chief, two more glimpses of its working are worth noting. On June 4th, 1916, shortly before the opening of the Battle of the Somme, Haig wrote: 'I attended the Scottish Church at 9.30 a.m. Mr. Duncan took as his text a letter from St. John to the Christians of Smyrna. "Be ye faithful unto the end." "To you shall be given a crown of everlasting life." The contents of the letter might have been addressed to the British Army in France today. We must look forward to still harder times, to the necessity for redoubled efforts, but in the end all will be well. How different are our feelings today, to those with which the British people and men in the Army began the War. Then many people prophesied a race to Berlin, with the Russian steam-roller, etc. Now we are beginning to learn our lesson, and to be sobered by hard experience and to be able to be patient. An excellent sermon.' Almost a year later, on April 29th, 1917, Charteris (himself a son of the kirk) wrote in equally characteristic vein: 'We had a regular Scottish Sunday. D.H. took me to church in a little wooden hut in the village. The sermon was to the effect that we all had to believe that God is working in us for a definite purpose; all very cheering if you are quite certain that the purpose is our victory. But it is difficult to see why a German preacher could not preach just such a sermon to Hindenburg and Ludendorff. All the same, D.H. seems to derive an extra-ordinary amount of moral strength from these sermons. We discussed it after lunch, for all the world as one used to do as a boy in Scotland. Then suddenly D.H. switched off to a paper which he is preparing for the War Cabinet at home, and was back in 1917 and at war.'

*   *   *   *

Haig took up his high office under mixed auspices. Some of its limitations were made clear immediately; neither in the matter of his Chief of Staff nor in that of his successor in command of the First Army were his wishes complied with. In the latter case, on the somewhat pedantic grounds that the commander of the First Army was the heir presumptive of the Commander-in-Chief, in the event of any accident, Kitchener insisted that Monro should be appointed, not Rawlinson, whom Haig had suggested. Monro, of course, was an old Aldershot and First Army colleague, so that this decision of Kitchener's was not to be compared with the forcing of General Smith-Dorrien on Sir John French in 1914. Yet it was indicative: the question of the Staff was even more so. Haig's inclination – understandable, if somewhat dangerous – was to keep around him the men he knew. He would have liked to translate his First Army officers wholesale to G.H.Q., starting with Major-General R. H. K. Butler as Chief of Staff. But Butler was thought to be too junior for this post, and Haig had to make a second choice. It fell upon

Lieutenant-General Sir Launcelot Kiggell, then Director of Home Defence at the War Office. Haig explained his motives for this choice in a letter to Lady Haig: 'I took Gen. Kiggell as my C.G.S. because I wished to get him out to the front. We can't afford to lose an officer like him. After he has been with me 3 or 4 months he will be able to take command of a Corps and Butler will then take his place. Meantime there is ample work for us all, and we are quite a happy family.' In fact, Kiggell remained with Haig as C.G.S. until the large reorganization of G.H.Q. at the beginning of 1918. They worked very well together, but it is hard to resist the conclusion that Kiggell never was, nor aspired to be, more than a mouthpiece for Haig. He was an efficient Staff Officer, and Haig respected his opinions when offered; but in two years Kiggell made little mark on the Army, remaining always a shadowy figure in the background, signing orders, circulating papers, minding the machine. It is not to be supposed for a moment that General Butler, who was even more junior to the Chief, would have done better; in truth, a distinct weakness of Haig's period of command is the lack of a forceful and energetic personality at his side until the last months of the War, when Sir Herbert Lawrence joined him.

Under Kiggell came Butler as Deputy Chief of Staff, and two more First Army men in key positions: Brigadier-General J. H. Davidson at the head of Operations, and Charteris, now also a Brigadier, at the head of Intelligence. 'I hear', Charteris noted, 'there is a good deal of criticism of the new Staff – and especially of my own appointment – on the grounds of youth.' As time went by, this criticism increased in volume, and usually centred round these two officers. Haig paid a considerable price for his belief in bringing young men forward, and for his great loyalty to his associates. Again, on all the evidence, one must conclude that he could have done better with these two appointments, both of them so vital in the running of the War. Neither of these men, though both were talented, had the stature to argue with their C.-in-C. or change his opinions when they privately believed him to be in error. This was a dangerous and costly defect; the 'happy family' was too much in awe of Papa. But it is wrong to assert sweepingly, on these grounds, that Haig was a bad judge of men. On the other side of the picture should be borne in mind his attitude to the host of people who came directly from civilian life to take up specialized appointments at G.H.Q. Of these, the most important was Sir Eric Geddes, who came to him later in the year, and whose talents were such that, apart from the King, he became the only man to hold simultaneously the ranks of General and Admiral. Against much opposition, Haig always defended these appointments with great vigour.

On October 27th, 1916, he wrote revealingly in his Diary: 'There is a good deal of criticism apparently being made at the appointment of a civilian like Geddes to an important post on the Headquarters of an Army in the Field. These critics seem to fail to realize the size of this Army, and the amount of work which the Army requires of a civilian nature. The working of the railways, the upkeep of the roads, even the baking of bread, and a thousand other industries go on in peace as well as war. So with the whole nation at war, our object should be to employ men on the same work in war as they are accustomed to do in peace. Acting on this principle, I have got Geddes at the head of all the railways and transportation, with the best practical civil and military engineers under him. At the head of road directorate is Mr. Maybury, head of the Road Board in England. The docks, canals and inland water transport are being managed in the same way, i.e. by men of practical experience. To put soldiers who have no practical experience of these matters into such positions, merely because they are generals and colonels, must result in utter failure.'

Many years after, when the late Earl Lloyd George, in composing his *War Memoirs*, arraigned 'the supercilious folly miles behind the shell area which stigmatized all civilian aid in the construction or direction of the war machine as unwarranted interference by ignorant amateurs', he would have done well to have made it clear that Haig was excluded from this castigation, and that his own ideas and Haig's in fact coincided exactly in this matter; but such was not his purpose.

Few people, unless the subject is brought particularly to their attention, can realize to what an extent G.H.Q. itself marked a revolution in the art of waging war. The sheer size of the organization itself was something undreamt of; ultimately it comprised about 1,000 people, besides the Staffs of all the subordinate formations. In the end, not without some jealousy and bickering, reflected in Haig's Diary as a recurring annoyance which he had to deal with, soothing ruffled susceptibilities, sorting out complicated truths from the heated outcrys of overworked officers, the whole machine became a remarkable fusion of the best available talent, civilian and military, in the country. Indeed, *in the end*, one can say with assurance that it was a better machine than the more rigidly professional Continental Staffs. But France and Germany enjoyed a long advantage through having a much stronger corps of trained Staff Officers to draw upon in the early years of the War, and a much clearer anticipation of the extraordinary range of functions that a General Headquarters would have to fulfil. Even to the officers engaged in them, these functions were a source of wonderment. Charteris, shortly after Haig removed G.H.Q. from St. Omer to the little walled town of Montreuil, a few miles inland from the seaside resort of Le Touquet, set down an account of the complexities of business which he saw[1] going on around him.

1. Charteris, *At G.H.Q.*, pp. 208–210.

A short extract must suffice for our purposes: 'Here at G.H.Q., in our little town away back from the front-line trenches, although we think of nothing but war and deal only with war, there are few visible signs of war. We might almost be in England. Nearly every one of the ramifications of civil law and life has its counterpart in the administration departments. Food supply, road and rail transport, law and order, engineering, medical work, the Church, education, postal service, even agriculture, and for a population bigger than any single unit of control (except London) in England. Can you imagine what it is to feed, administer, move about, look after the medical and spiritual requirements of a million men, even when they are not engaged in fighting, and not in a foreign country? Add to that, the purely military side of the concern. That we have to concentrate great accumulations of this mass of humanity quickly into some particular restricted area, have to deal with enormous casualties, and have to keep a constant flow of men back and forward for hours. . . . The work goes on continuously; office hours are far longer than of any civilian office in peace-time. There are few, if any, officers who do not do a fourteen-hour day, and who are not to be found at work far into the night.'

And this, Charteris might well have added, was the first time that such a thing had ever been done in the history of England. With everything to learn, the marvel is that the lesson was picked up so quickly.

There was, of course, a danger in this inevitable elaboration, so different from the personal command, exercised through a small entourage, of earlier wars. Charteris continued: 'One of the great difficulties of everyone at G.H.Q. is to get away from their office often and long enough to get in close touch with the front. Few can ever get much farther forward than the H.Q. of the Armies . . . the Divisions are mostly in farmhouses, but well in the fighting line. One can almost always get one's car up to them. But that is about the limit, and visits forward of them consequently take up a good deal of time. We all manage, anyhow, to see something of Divisional Head-quarters, but it is only when there is some particular object, more than simply looking round, that one can give up time to go beyond them. I have not seen even a Brigade Headquarters in the front line for the last month.'

This was a state of affairs which did not improve as the Army expanded, and the work of G.H.Q. expanded with it. At the end of 1917 Colonel Repington noted the opinion of a distinguished Corps Commander (General Pulteney) that G.H.Q. officers did not come round the front often enough, 'but at Cambrai a number turned up, including X, and Putty told him that he must be unwell'. Haig's solution was, in ordinary times, to spend as long as possible inspecting troops either in billets behind the front or at base camps or at camps of instruction, in order to see as many of them at once as he could, and when a great battle was taking place to remove himself from Montreuil to an Advanced Headquarters usually closely adjacent to the H.Q. of the Army that was fighting the battle. It was not a complete solution; one hears endlessly of people who 'never saw the C.-in-C. all the time they were in France'. But in view of the extent of the front and of the extreme difficulty of movement once one entered the labyrinth of trenches, it is hard to see, realistically, what more he could have done personally; it is a valid criticism, however, that he might have used his Staff more fully as 'eyes and ears', through the medium of liaison officers such as the Duke of Wellington or Field-Marshal Montgomery employed. It must be remembered, however, that subordinate commanders generally resent the visitations of these agents of the All-Highest. Neither in the French nor in the German Armies, which both used this system, was it regarded with undiluted pleasure. It was never likely to appeal to Haig, who was, if anything, over-scrupulous about the rights and responsibilities of subordinates; it was practically a sacred principle with him to leave to Army and Corps commanders a free hand, and to interfere as little as possible once a course of action had been decided.

To ensure good understanding between himself and his Army Commanders, as well as between all of them and their various Staffs, he instituted immediately, in January, 1916, weekly Army Commanders' Conferences held at each Army H.Q. in turn, and these took place punctually, with a proper agenda and recorded minutes, except when great battles were on. Whatever could be done by order and method, he did; but he was not unconscious of a degree of shortcoming at other levels. Underlying all his conduct in this connection were two factors: first, his habitual shyness and inability to communicate generally robbed him of the appeal of electrifying addresses and gestures, or of the warm relationship with soldiers enjoyed by Lord Roberts in an earlier generation, Plumer with the Second Army or Birdwood with his Australians among Haig's contemporaries, and some generals of the Second World War in totally different conditions. Secondly, there was the question of the conditions themselves: in a war in which it might take several hours to penetrate from Divisional H.Q. to the front line on a quiet day, and probably a whole day to traverse a Divisional front; in which visibility at the front was reduced to a matter of yards, and contact to adjoining sections of ragged trench or adjacent shell-hole positions, the sense of isolation and impersonality was bound to grow. It was inevitable, though tragic, that it should often extend to a feeling of utter separation between soldiers and Staffs. This was one of the burdens of Haig's command; as Charteris said: 'Perhaps the hardest thing of all is that we cannot share the dangers we send others to endure.' Haig never lost sight of that endurance.

*   *   *   *

Four days after Haig took up the Command-in-Chief, Sir William
Robertson became Chief of the Imperial General Staff. His translation to that
high office had been mooted for some time, and, as we have seen, had been
ardently backed by Haig. What delayed matters was Robertson's insistence
that certain conditions should be guaranteed before he accepted this great
responsibility. Both he and Haig attributed the evident failings in the supreme
direction of the War to the working out of Kitchener's method of personal
rule during his whole preceding tenure as Secretary of State for War. Sir
Ian Hamilton, one of Lord Kitchener's greatest friends and admirers, commenting on the catch-phrase that 'Kitchener was an organizer', wrote:
'history has now revealed to us what is the absolute stark truth; he hated
organizations; he smashed organizations. . . . He was a Master of Expedients.'

To Haig and Robertson it was clear that one of the first casualties in
Kitchener's 'smashing' process had been the General Staff at the War Office,
which should have been running the War. In taking up his new post, says
Lord Esher, 'General Robertson wished to have it clearly understood that the
responsibility for operations on all fronts should be placed on the Chief of
the Imperial General Staff; that the reports from the armies in the field should
be sent direct to him and not to the Army Council; that orders to the Armies
in the field should go out under his signature; and that he should be the sole
adviser of the War Council on operations.'

Field-Marshal Kitchener would thus be reduced to the position which a
civilian Secretary of State would expect to hold. He resisted the change
stubbornly for as long as possible, while never doubting Robertson's absolute
disinterestedness in demanding it. Finally he gave way, saying: 'I hope
Robertson understands that, much as I dislike the plan, now that I have
agreed, I mean to carry it out.' To this Kitchener adhered with absolute
loyalty, while Robertson, on his side, wrote on February 4th, 1916: '. . . it is
no part of a C.I.G.S's duty to intrigue against his Secretary of State. At any
rate, I won't. He has been all that could be desired so far as I am concerned.'
And when Kitchener was drowned in the *Hampshire*, Robertson said:
'Latterly I have found him a most helpful and kind friend. I am more than
sad to lose him. I feel remorseful because of my brutal "bargain". It was
never necessary, and was made only because I was misinformed of the man's
nature. He was a fine character, lovable and straight – really.'

Nevertheless, the situation which Robertson had to tackle on taking office
was a daunting one. '. . . I found things here even in a greater state of muddle
and chaos than I had feared,' he wrote to Haig on December 26th, 1915,
'. . . no one can . . . make even a rough shot at an order of battle. . . . Generally
speaking the Navy seems to be adopting a very helpless attitude. . . .' The
two outstanding questions of the hour were, what strategic course did

Britain propose to follow in 1916? and what resources did she propose to apply to it? It was indicative of the confusion into which the British Empire had fallen that, while 51 divisions (or their equivalents) were distributed in the United Kingdom and in secondary theatres, in France there were only 38, and these were 75,000 men short of the strength they should have had, although it had been agreed at an Inter-Allied Conference early in December that France should be the main theatre of war. France at this period had 95 divisions deployed on the Western Front alone, but, as Joffre says, 'she now began to reach the limit of her resources in men, while the diminution which her effectives would suffer during the course of 1916 already stared her in the face'. The time for Great Britain to begin to shoulder the main burden of the War was evidently at hand, but it found her in no posture to do so.

The strategic issue dominated everything. It posed itself to Haig in relatively simple terms; the key paragraph in the Instructions which he received from Lord Kitchener on December 28th, 1915, read: 'The defeat of the enemy by the combined Allied Armies must always be regarded as the primary object for which British troops were originally sent to France, and to achieve that end, the closest co-operation of French and British as a united Army must be the governing policy. . . .' This was a much stronger wording than that used by Kitchener to Sir John French in 1914, who had only been told that 'every effort must be made to coincide most sympathetically with the plans and wishes of our Ally'; it went far to reduce the sense of the next phrase, couched in terms almost identical with those used to French: '. . . but I wish you distinctly to understand that your command is an independent one, and that you will in no case come under the orders of any Allied General further than the necessary co-operation with our Allies above referred to.' There was, in fact, a contradiction here; if the French and British were to act 'as a united Army', Haig's command could scarcely be 'an independent one' except in the most restricted sense of the word. What it meant was that while he would bear full responsibility for the safety of the British Army, he would have only a lesser say in deciding on the operations to which it would be committed. In other words, the subjection of British military policy to French which had begun with the very opening of the war was un-diminished.

Haig recognized and accepted this situation from the first without repining; he understood very well the reasons for it. On December 21st, 1915, he wrote in a note to Kiggell: 'In the past there has certainly existed on the part of the French a feeling that we were not always willing to take our fair share. No doubt that feeling has existed on our side also. There must be give and take. The present moment (with the change in command) is opportune for creating a good impression and paving the way for smooth negotiations with the French, especially as important matters in regard to combined operations are pending.'

With the same thought on January 13th, 1916, he wrote to Lady Haig: 'It is sad to read of the selfishness of many people at home over the Universal Service Bill. The French have shed their blood lavishly, all married men have been fighting for their country since the very beginning and have suffered very heavily. For instance General d'Urbal has organized as his Guard a company of men who have 5 children or more! – and now in England only the unmarried are to be sent out to fight! How very different the British Public would feel if they had the Germans on their soil, and how anxious they would be to leave nothing undone to secure that the Enemy is driven out!'

As a concrete demonstration of his desire to co-operate fully with his Allies, on January 1st Haig sent for the Head of the French Mission at G.H.Q., General des Vallières: 'I told him that when I am at my H.Q. I see all my head Staff Officers at 9.30 a.m. daily, and I hoped he would attend also. He was much pleased.' Des Vallières – 'a retiring gentlemanly man. Yet he has seen and read much . . .' – suited Haig well, and reciprocated this mark of confidence. It was to des Vallières that Haig now explained his view of the Alliance: 'I showed him the instructions which I have received from the S. of S. for War containing the orders of the Govt. to me. I pointed out that I am *not under* General Joffre's orders, but that would make no difference, as my intention was to do my utmost to carry out General Joffre's wishes on strategical matters, as if they were orders.'

Joffre's strategic wishes were expressed in the unanimous resolutions of the Inter-Allied Military Conference at Chantilly on December 6th–8th, 1915, which he says 'marks a vital date in the history of the conduct of the war'. Fully authorized representatives of France, Russia, Italy, Belgium, Serbia and Great Britain agreed on the following:

'. . . that the decision of the war can only be obtained in the principal theatres, that is to say in those in which the enemy has maintained the greater part of his forces (Russian front, Franco-British front, Italian front).

'The decision should be obtained by co-ordinated offensives on these fronts. All the efforts of the Coalition should therefore be directed to giving these offensives their maximum force from the point of view of both men and material.

'Decisive results will only be obtained if the offensives of the Armies of the Coalition are made simultaneously, or at least at dates so near together that the enemy will not be able to transport reserves from one front to another.

'The general action should be launched as soon as possible. . . .

'The wearing down ("*usure*") of the enemy will henceforward be pursued intensively by means of local and partial offensives, particularly by the Powers which still have abundant reserves of men.

'The Conference are unanimous in recognizing that only the minimum forces should be employed in the secondary theatres, and that the troops now in the Orient seem, as a whole, sufficient to meet requirements. . . .'

This was the substance of the strategic agreement which Haig inherited on taking command. Joffre was right in saying that it marked a turning point: it was the first organized attempt of the Allies to arrive at a unified strategy. What remained to be seen was how the idea of a simultaneous drive against the Central Powers would be carried out. As regards the British Government, Robertson told Haig on December 28th that the War Committee[1] had accepted the following principle of action: France and Flanders were to be the main theatre; every effort would be placed behind a spring offensive in that theatre; a defensive attitude would be adopted in Egypt where the Turks, released by the evacuation of Gallipoli, were advancing upon the Suez Canal. Salonika was to be evacuated; here the British Government ran into the strongest opposition from the French, and this decision had to be amended to an agreement to hold a British contingent in Salonika, but not expand it. Haig now encountered directly the tendency to vacillation and sudden change of policy which bedevilled the proceedings of successive British Governments throughout the War. At first through a multitude of counsellors, later through distrust of its responsible military advisers, the Government found itself forever in the position of reversing or watering down its own decisions. On January 13th the War Committee endorsed the substance of its earlier resolution to undertake a spring offensive in France, but added: '. . . it must not be assumed that such offensive operations are finally decided upon.' It was not until April 7th, after a direct question from Haig, and when the spring was practically over, that Robertson was able to procure a firm statement in favour of a combined Allied offensive in the West. Such were the difficulties under which Joffre laboured in trying

1. The organs through which the British Government conducted the War were as follows: at first, the Cabinet itself; from November 25th, 1914, by a Committee of the Cabinet called the War Council; from June 7th, 1915, this body was renamed the Dardanelles Committee; on November 1st, 1915, its title was again altered to the War Committee. All these bodies were more or less *ad hoc*, of fluctuating, but usually large membership. Not until Lloyd George became Prime Minister in December, 1916, did a small, permanent, 'stream-lined' War Cabinet come into existence, capable of the brisk business which the War demanded. By far the best authority on this subject is Lord Hankey, in his book *The Supreme Command 1914-1918*.

to achieve a unified strategy, and under which Haig laboured in trying to implement it.

Haig himself agreed with the substance of Joffre's plan; indeed, it was hard to do otherwise. Contemplating the vast resources of the Allied Powers, and comparing them with those of their enemies, it was clear that, for the Allies, the problem was simply that of actually bringing their strength to bear. The German advantage of the 'interior lines' was a real one. In practical terms it meant that while Germany could, if pressed, switch 24 divisions (say 500,000 men) from East to West or vice versa in one month, it took the Allies, in 1916, nearly four months to transfer 9 divisions (say 185,000 men) from Egypt to France. Shipping shortages and the presence of enemy submarines in the Mediterranean, forcing an over-extension of naval power, robbed the Allies of the freedom of manoeuvre that supremacy at sea should have given them. On the other hand, by attacking simultaneously on three fronts, all directly menacing the Central Empires, it was evident that they ought to be able to nullify this advantage of the interior lines. Haig had no doubts about the general proposition. However, very quickly after his accession, two some-what conflicting considerations (as is often the way, in face of the facts of life, instead of neat theories) began to weigh with him. There was the question of France herself, about which, as we have seen, he had long been doubtful. On January 14th he noted: 'I think the French man-power situa-tion is serious as they are not likely to stand another winter's war. There is no doubt to my mind *but that the war must be won by the forces of the British Empire.*'[1]

Five days later he wrote to Kitchener: '... I am told that the French are looking to the British and Russians to carry on the preliminary actions or "wearing-out fights" which are designed to attract and exhaust the enemy's Reserves before the main or decisive battles ... are begun. The French Army (except some 6 or 7 divisions) is to be reserved for this last phase. As yet I have heard this indirectly, but I have every reason for thinking that this is the view of the French G.H.Q. No doubt Joffre will tell me the truth tomorrow. The fact is the French "depôts" are so empty of troops that their Army is only capable of one big effort in their opinion.'

Haig was correct; reporting their meeting to Asquith later, he wrote: 'General Joffre told me privately last Thursday that although his companies are quite up to strength he has no longer large reserves behind them. The French Army is thus only capable of undertaking *one* big offensive effort.' Haig, then, took up his command with the anomaly that, while he remained in subjection to his Ally's strategic control, that Ally was already in a state of military decline. It was not encouraging.

1. Author's italics.

Bearing this in mind, Haig was drawn to a somewhat critical appreciation of the details of Joffre's plan. It was easy to see that the French would wish their Allies to take the burden of these 'wearing-out fights' of which Joffre had spoken, and reserve their own strength for the climax. But if that climax was delayed and Great Britain had to shoulder the main role in the West, then it would not be wise to fritter away the strength of the British Army in subsidiary operations. In his letter to Kitchener on January 19th, Haig added:

'My view is that the "wearing-out fight" should be carried on simultaneously (or nearly so) from the right of the Russians in the Baltic right round via Italy to our left on the North Sea. And that not until the enemy's Reserves have been drawn into the struggle should we make the blow which is intended to be decisive. I have already put these views to Joffre, and he agrees with the principle. Tomorrow I shall urge that the French take their share with us in the wearing-out fight, otherwise it is possible that the Allies get worn out in detail.'

Haig already had doubts about these 'wearing-out fights'; in a jotted note on January 14th he wrote: 'The possibilities must be limited by the quantity of munitions we can spare and by the need to assure ourselves that the enemy is likely to suffer at least as heavily as we do.' His conviction that the French, despite their weakness, must also play their part in the preliminary fighting hardened in him; at the same time, his ideas on how the 'wearing-out fight' should be conducted clarified. A letter from Joffre on the subject on January 23rd provoked a note from Haig to Kiggell, saying: 'The above plan is nothing less than a series of disjointed attacks in which our troops will be used up no less, possibly more than those of the enemy. We can do better than that! In my opinion, the various "preparatory attacks to wear out" and exhaust the enemy's Reserves should be continuous, and should immediately precede those general attacks which are intended to be decisive and gain the victory.'

So strongly did Haig feel on this matter that, despite the brevity of his tenure of command, and despite his full recognition of Joffre's authority expressed earlier to des Vallières, he felt that he must make an issue of it. On February 1st he wrote a long and considered letter to Joffre, once again urging the need for simultaneous action at all stages by the Allies, and then going in detail into the question of the 'wearing-out fights'. These he separated into two categories: those immediately preceding the main effort with a view to drawing off the enemy's Reserves, and those not immediately preceding the decisive battle. As regards the first, he felt that ten to fourteen days would be a suitable period before the main offensive for them to begin and force the enemy to commit his Reserves. As regards the second, he wrote: 'The "*batailles d'usure*" which you ask me to undertake in April, and again (in certain circumstances) in May, would not have the same result, as the Germans would have time to replace losses from their depots and to reorganize and refit their Reserves before the commencement of our general offensive two months or more later. For these reasons I feel that we should reap little, if any, advantage from such "*batailles d'usure*" carried out a long time before the commencement of the general offensive. They would undoubtedly entail considerable loss on us with little to show for it; while the results on the morale of the troops, and more especially on public opinion in England, Germany and elsewhere might be unfortunate. The enemy would claim that he had defeated an attempt to "break through", and as our real object would not be generally understood, his claim would probably be widely accepted. We cannot ignore the possible effect of this on public opinion and on the financial credit of the Allies – a serious consideration. For these reasons I submit that it is most desirable that once fighting begins this year on a large scale it should be carried through as quickly as possible to a decisive issue.'

Charteris noted: 'Joffre is coming to discuss this, presumably to try to get D.H. to change his views. He will not succeed.'

The crucial discussion between Haig and Joffre took place at Chantilly on February 14th; Robertson was present, but Haig and Kiggell represented the British Army, and it was Haig who spoke for it. The meeting passed straight to the main issue: 'General Joffre began the discussion by giving way on the question of the wearing-out fight. He admitted (no doubt on Castelnau's advice) that attacks to prepare the way for the decisive attack and to attract the enemy's reserves were necessary, but only some 10 to 15 days before the main battle, certainly not in April for a July attack. This seemed quite a victory for me.' Under the circumstances, it was indeed a victory; how many British lives were saved by it can hardly be computed, but an estimate may be arrived at by comparison with British losses at Arras in just such a subsidiary role in 1917: over 150,000. Joffre, unwilling to give something away for nothing, then pressed Haig to undertake the relief of the French 10th Army, which was sandwiched between the British First and Third Armies:

'I said that the state of the British Army (75,000 below strength in 39 divisions) and all divisions wanting training combined with the difficulty of moving so many divisions made it impossible to carry out the relief of the 10th Army in the near future. General Joffre asked if I would accept the principle of relieving the 10th Army. I said "Certainly" and he asked "When?" I replied "Next Winter". The old man laughed, and I remarked we could not do impossibilities. . . .'

The meeting then discussed the main offensive. Haig wrote: 'Today's was a most important conference. Indeed, the whole position of the British Army in the operations of this year depended on my not giving way on:

1. the nature and moment of carrying out the wearing-out fight and
2. not using up divisions in relieving the 10th Army.

By straightforward dealing, I gained both of these points. But I had an anxious and difficult struggle. . . . I felt at the conference that I had been given some power not always in me.'

The main offensive: it was also decided on February 14th that this should take place on or about July 1st, and that the locale for it should be the Somme, with French forces operating on both sides of the river. As far back as December 25th Joffre had revealed a predilection for this area, writing to Haig: '. . . *l'offensive française serait grandement favorisée par une offensive simultanée des forces britanniques entre la SOMME et ARRAS*.' Haig's own inclinations were quite different; early in February he told Rawlinson that he would be placed in command of a new Fourth Army, and ordered him to study at once the possibilities of action in both the Third Army area (Somme) and at Ypres. A few days later Plumer was told to prepare a plan for the capture of the Messines-Wytschaete Ridge. There was no doubt in Haig's mind that the relative bottle-neck of German communications in Western Flanders presented the most promising target for the British Army's endeavours. The important railway junction of Roulers stood out as a most suitable early objective. It must be remembered that this area had almost nothing, in 1916, of the formidable field defences which sprouted all over it during the next year; in terms of strategic possibilities it had great advantages. Charteris wrote on February 8th: 'I am sure Flanders is the right place to hit. I think D.H. agrees, but the Operations Section (or some of them) are all for the Somme, on account of it being much easier ground to attack over.' After the conference of February 14th, Flanders was reduced to the status of being simply the terrain of the preparatory attack, and there was no further discussion of the pros and cons of the Somme. This was the price of the subordination of British strategy, for, as the Official Historian says:

'The decision of the French Commander-in-Chief to make the main offensive of 1916 astride the Somme seems to have been arrived at solely because the British would be bound to take part in it. . . . The Somme offensive had no strategic object except attrition. Applied close to the apex of the salient, it might, if moderately successful, flatten it out; if highly successful it would make a pocket in the German front, leaving the Allies themselves with a vulnerable salient.'

The Official Historian ignores, in this analysis, the true purpose of the battle:

it was intended to be decisive, to defeat the German Army, in which case there would be no question of the Allies being 'left' in any salient. But what happened, as he well knew, in 1916 – the tragedy of the year – was that circumstances forced the 'decisive offensive' to become in fact, the 'wearing-out fight'.

*   *   *   *

Within a week all the decisions taken at Chantilly on February 14th, as well as the further-reaching plans made in December, were put in hazard; the savage roar of the German barrage at Verdun signalized another transformation of the pattern of the War. Once again Germany was making use of the strategic initiative which she had won in 1914 and which, so far, the Allies had been unable to wrest from her. True, the divisions of opinion among the Central Powers, and, indeed, within the German High Command itself, with their consequent dispersion of effort between the Eastern and Western Fronts (intensified by Italy's entry into the War in May, 1915) had prevented the full reward of that initiative from being reaped. No decision had been achieved. But enough strength remained for another powerful throw, unhindered by the delays which afflicted the Allies. The question was, where should the Germans aim their stroke? Falkenhayn had few doubts; his conclusions were set down in a paper at Christmas, 1915, and two months later he began to implement the most important of them. Such are the advantages of an autocratic military régime in war, compared with the slow, confused processes of democracy.

The most interesting feature of Falkenhayn's Memorandum is his assessment of England's role in the War. The whole purpose of his thinking was to procure the defeat of the English whom, on the analogy of history, he saw as the core, or cement of the Entente, and therefore as Germany's chief enemy. With considerable acumen, he noted that 'for England the campaign on the Continent of Europe with her own troops is at bottom a side-show. Her real weapons here are the French, Russian and Italian Armies. If we put those armies out of the War England is left to face us alone, and it is difficult to believe that in such circumstances her lust for our destruction would not fail her. It is true that there would be no certainty that she would give up, but there is a strong probability. More than that can seldom be asked in war.' It is a curious irony that it was the German Chief of Staff who saw most clearly what was, indeed, the unconscious wish of most British statesmen. Dragged reluctantly into Continental war at the coat tails of two major military Powers, it would have been a matter of deep surprise to most of them to realize that they had supplanted both of those Powers as Germany's main target. Yet, partly because of that very reluctance, and partly because of the historic role of Britain in earlier European wars, Falkenhayn was exact in saying that it was a prime British motive to fight the land war with other people's armies. This is the basis of the argument between 'Easterners' and 'Westerners': it was fundamentally a clash between those who saw that Britain must assume a major part in the land struggle, and those who shied away from the awful cost of doing so. Falkenhayn, correct as his assessment was, underrated the steady perception by the British military leaders of what their task must be, and the courage with which they were prepared to carry it through, in the face of political obstruction and frightful losses.

Developing his theme, Falkenhayn first examined the possibilities of an outright attack on the British forces in France. With some sorrow, he rejected this line of action, mainly because even in the event of complete success, of driving the British out of France altogether, the French Army would still be left, and Britain would not give up the struggle. 'A second operation would have to be undertaken. It is very questionable whether Germany would be able to dispose of the forces required.' Hindsight permits us to question this analysis severely; would France – *could* she, indeed – have gone on with the War, with the whole left flank of her line (for that is what is implied) destroyed? It scarcely seems possible. Nevertheless, the direct blow at the British Army was ruled out. This did not mean that no attempt would be made at all to strike at England directly; Falkenhayn laid great stress on the value of the submarine campaign – '. . . there can be no justification on military grounds for refusing any further to employ what promises to be our most effective weapon.' Allied action in 1916 has to be regarded always in the light of this stepping-up of submarine activity, although Falkenhayn did not possess the powers of command over his naval colleagues to weave their operations into his own as though they were Army commanders. As regards other fronts, Falkenhayn saw no advantages for Germany in the secondary theatres, nor any threat from them, actual or potential, which would warrant making large efforts there.

Dismissing them, Falkenhayn turned to the continental fronts. Italy and Russia, he concluded, were neither of them to be regarded as likely to play a large part in further operations; their internal difficulties would prevent them from doing so; it would be best to leave them alone. The only snag here was the strong adherence of his Austro-Hungarian allies to the contrary view. One way to persuade them would be to make it clear that they should expect no support from Germany for any 'adventures' which they might wish to undertake against the Russians and the Italians. This Falkenhayn did; once again one questions his reasoning in the light of after events. Russia and Italy were yet to play the largest part in destroying the military power of the Hapsburg Empire. In 1916, before that power had entered its final decline, there existed a better chance for the Central Powers of knocking Italy out of the War than any that was ever offered to the Allies of knocking out Austria by an offensive from Italy. However, such was Falkenhayn's conclusion, and it left him with only one course to adopt – a renewed attack upon the French.

It has been pointed out[1] that behind all Falkenhayn's thinking there lay a tendency towards compromise which found almost no echo in other leading German soldiers. Indeed, it has been said that in one particular aspect of this inclination he stood apart from the War leaders of all countries: 'No other of anything approaching his position held the doctrine that "a good peace" rather than decisive and overwhelming victory should be the goal.'[2]

In the planning of his 1916 campaign one can detect the influence of this compromising tendency, for what it boiled down to was an attempt to end the War by what was always conceived as a relatively minor expenditure of effort; this clearly implied the abandonment of all notions of a 'Cannae', an outright victory in the field.

Let us see how the German commander expounded his ideas: 'We can probably do enough for our purposes *with limited resources*.[3] Within our reach behind the French sector of the Western Front there are objectives for the retention of which the French General Staff would be compelled to throw in every man they have. If they do so the forces of France will bleed to death – as there can be no question of a voluntary withdrawal – *whether we reach our goal or not*.[4] If they do not do so, and we reach our objectives, the moral effect on France will be enormous. For an operation limited to a narrow front Germany will not be compelled to spend herself so completely that all other fronts are practically drained. She can face with confidence the relief attacks to be expected on those fronts, and indeed hope to have sufficient troops in hand to reply to them with counter-attacks. For she is perfectly free to accelerate or draw out her offensive, to intensify it or break it off from time to time, as suits her purpose. The objectives of which I am speaking now are Belfort and Verdun.'

Two faults in Falkenhayn's reasoning transpired during the year, and brought about his dismissal. First, it was a fallacy to suppose that, once committed, Germany could limit and regulate her offensive as though it was a barrel with a tap. Secondly, his decision to stand and fight on the Somme, his rejection of 'an exchange of excellent positions for others less good', subjected his own army to that very process of 'bleeding to death' which he had devised for the French.

1. *The First World War* by Cyril Falls.
2. Cyril Falls.
3. Author's italics.
4. Author's italics.

The Verdun offensive opened on February 21st. Within a week it had made important advances, of which the most spectacular was the occupation of Fort Douaumont, practically without firing a shot. French opinion was stunned. Joffre's reputation sustained a blow from which it never recovered, when reports circulated that G.Q.G. had been taken by surprise, and had neglected warnings from the commanders on the spot. This allegation was only partly true; Falkenhayn's preparations had been conducted with great skill, particularly the assembly of the mass of artillery on which he depended, but they had not gone undetected. G.Q.G. tended to take the line, right up to the eve of battle, that whatever might occur at Verdun would only be a feint to cover a larger offensive towards Amiens; nevertheless, prompted by the urgings of the Minister of War, General Galliéni (his last great service to his country), Joffre had sent his Chief Staff Officer, Castelnau, to Verdun early in January. Castelnau's report led to an immediate reinforcement of the sector, entitling him to be called, as one French historian puts it, 'le premier sauveur de Verdun'.[1] Had it not been for this reinforcement, the French would almost certainly have been rushed off their feet by the violence of the German attack, and the result might well have been complete disaster. As it was, the intensity of the fighting was hitherto unequalled, and the strain upon the French Army rapidly rose towards the level which Falkenhayn intended. It never, however, reached the pitch of complete exhaustion. Castelnau, Pétain, Herr, Nivelle and Mangin, in turn and at different strata of command, organized a brilliant defence, counter-attacking at every opportunity. But, by June, no less than sixty-five French divisions had passed through the Verdun battle; by the time it ended over 300,000 Frenchmen had fallen. Falkenhayn bought this result dearly: German casualties were very nearly as high, and in the last stages of the battle almost all their early gains were snatched back from them.

The immediate impact of Verdun on British plans and on Haig's policy was the reversal of his adamant refusal, on February 14th, to relieve the French 10th Army. This relief was completed in three weeks, and at the same time Haig agreed to place a group of divisions behind the extreme left of the French front, as a precautionary measure. Despite the sharp tone of Joffre's letters when the crisis broke upon him, and despite reports that the French had partly brought their difficulties upon themselves by poor tactics in the early stages, Haig's chief thought now was how to support and encourage his Ally. On February 27th he 'telephoned to Gen. Joffre that I had arranged to relieve all his 10th Army, and that I would come to Chantilly tomorrow to shake him by the hand, and to place myself and troops at his disposition.' This friendly gesture had the desired effect of restoring good relations between

1. M. Pierre Dominique, in Miroir de l'Histoire, June, 1961.

the two High Commands, but it could not, of course, alter the pressure of
events. It was inevitable that the French, in their ordeal, should look constantly over their left shoulders at the growing British Army, standing beside
them in apparent idleness. For Haig, the four months between the end of
February and the beginning of July were an exercise in tightrope-walking.

As the Battle of Verdun intensified in violence, it became an almost daily
question whether the British should not make a strong intervention to take
the weight off their Ally. But at the same time, the increasing casualties and
exhaustion of that Ally indicated that whatever large-scale offensive effort the
Entente might carry out in 1916 would have to be a mainly British endeavour,
with the consequent need to husband resources for that. Within this large contradiction, there were others. On the one hand, it was not possible to prepare
Staffs and formations for a vigorous offensive by adopting complete passivity
– even if the enemy were prepared to permit this. Nothing was more cor-
rosive of the human spirit than trench warfare, whose main components were
ever-present danger, fatigue, squalor and inertia. To counteract its effects,
G.H.Q. had, from the end of 1914, adopted the policy of frequent raids
against the German lines. This was part and parcel of the British doctrine of
the 'active front', in sharp contrast to French and German practice. They, on
the contrary, in between large battles, often adopted a policy of 'live and let
live' which permitted the routines of trench life – ration parties, reliefs, wiring,
sentry duty, sanitation, etc. – to take place on both sides of the line unhindered. The British rejected this. Yet the 'active' policy unquestionably
conflicted with other needs of the Army. If it inculcated an attacking spirit,
it also added tremendously to the strain upon the troops; it meant that there
were practically no 'quiet sectors' on the British front where divisions could
actually be in the line but, in effect, resting. This was an important point. In
addition, it is a plain fact that, during the greater part of 1916, the Germans
were still very superior, both in equipment and in training, to the British.
This meant that the cost of small operations often far exceeded their value,
and the opposite effect to that intended was produced on morale, when a high
proportion of the men whom it was hoped to encourage became casualties.
The policy was overdone. In the hands of frustrated junior commanders,
hungry for distinction amid the drab round of the Western Front, it became
at times a positive danger.

Haig was certainly conscious of the limitations of his Army. At the end of
March, Kitchener visited him after a conference in Paris. Kitchener was much
disturbed by the feeling displayed by the French at that meeting; he was firmly
of the opinion that no further large effort could be expected from the French
Army.

Haig recorded: 'They mean to economise men, consequently it is possible that the War will not end this year. Lord K. wished me for that reason to beware of the French, and to husband the strength of the British Army in France. I said that I had never had any intention of attacking with all available troops except in an emergency to save the French from disaster, and Paris from capture. Meantime, I am strengthening the long line which I have taken over and training the troops. *I have not got an Army in France really, but a collection of divisions untrained for the Field. The actual fighting Army will be evolved from them.*'[1]

This passage expressed his guiding thought during the first half of the year, and naturally influenced his attitude towards the minor operations in which his Army became involved. In each of them, his main preoccupation was to limit the cost. At the beginning of March, when one of these operations was in full blast, he told his Army Commanders: '. . . The voluntary abandonment of an unimportant portion of our line, as part of a scheme of defence designed to cause the maximum of loss to the enemy at a minimum cost to ourselves, will often be the wisest course to take. . . . The possession of a few acres of ground of no importance for tactical or other reasons can have no influence on the course of the war, which must be decided by the defeat of the enemy's forces. It is quite a different matter to be driven from a position which it was intended to hold, owing to insufficient preparation of defences.'

Unfortunately, in anything that affected more than a few hundred yards of forward trench, this doctrine, sensible as it was, ran quite counter to the settled intentions of G.Q.G., which had now come to regard any withdrawal whatsoever, particularly if carried out by their Allies, on the sacred soil of France, as a heinous crime. Also, it involved subordinate commanders in very nice calculations of what might or might not be regarded as permissible, in the general context of 'maintaining the offensive spirit'. Thus we find that, while men close to the front line – battalion or brigade commanders – could keenly desire to give up some especially obnoxious and dangerous part of their position, and might well have had the support of the Commander-in-Chief on general principles, the Staffs in between would veto the manoeuvre, in case it was misinterpreted. It is so often out of these minor perplexities that major tragedies are compounded. In the event, between December 19th, 1915, and June 30th, 1916, the British Army lost no less than 5,845 officers and 119,296 other ranks in 'small' operations. But it has to be noted that out of eight such operations which swelled to a size deserving special treatment in the Official British History, six were begun on the initiative of the Germans. Economical strategy, after all, does require the enemy's concurrence.

*   *   *   *

1. Author's italics.

As the hour drew nearer, the omens of the Battle of the Somme did not become more encouraging. It was not until April 14th that Haig, in answer to a blunt question, extracted from Kitchener and Robertson a firm statement that the Government approved his intention to undertake the battle at all. The question of manpower continued to give Haig and Robertson grave anxiety; the Government summoned up all its resolution to avoid the drastic measures which alone could solve this problem. The concept of total war, and total mobilization, did not really emerge in Britain, it may be said, until after Dunkirk; all through the First World War there was stubborn political resistance to it – not all ill-founded, as a study of labour relations shows – which could only have been overcome by the firmest appeal to the nation. The failure of successive Governments to make that appeal was one of the deepest misfortunes of the War. On December 31st, 1915, Robertson told Haig: 'We have heaps of men as it is, but there is no intelligent plan for using them.' On March 22nd he wrote again: 'The present Military Service Act is a farce and a failure. It was a regular political dodge, and of course political dodges will not stand the stress of war with Germany. We want men.' On April 14th, Kitchener told Haig: 'There are now 1,300,000 men under arms in Great Britain.' And yet, on June 19th, just over a week before the opening of the great offensive, the Army in France was 41,521 men below War Establishment.

It was never realized, in Whitehall, what being below Establishment meant to the fighting troops. Quite apart from the effect on morale of empty ranks, there was the sheer physical burden. As early as February, 1916, Haig was asking for Labour Battalions, which he described as 'quite essential'; his request was brushed aside; Robertson was finding it difficult enough to get soldiers for France. Until the very end of the War, this shortage meant that periods of so-called 'rest' were, as often as not, periods of purgatorial exertion for the men in the ranks. Bowed under their huge loads, they stumbled into battle exhausted before they began to fight. And all the time, for reasons which now seem inscrutable, their half-trained, half-equipped comrades in the United Kingdom were standing by in hundreds of thousands; agreed that they were not ready to fight, but they could at least have helped to dig.

For Joffre, this was a sad and anxious time. He saw his plans for a simultaneous onslaught on the enemy collapsing in ruin while his own army was being pulverized at Verdun. Only the Italians were actually attacking, the fifth of their ill-starred offensives on the Isonzo, as fruitless as its predecessors. The Russians, like the British, spoke only of delays. Naturally, relations between British and French Headquarters fluctuated. On April 7th, Haig reluctantly reached the conclusion that 'The old man . . . is really past his work. . . .'

He was nevertheless determined to do all he could to maintain cordiality and co-operation. When Clemenceau, the Chairman of the Military Committee of the French Senate, a long-standing opponent of President Poincaré and a severe critic of Joffre, proposed to visit G.H.Q. at the beginning of May, Haig loyally put him off until he had time to inform Joffre. The latter, in a sunny mood again after an earlier tiff, 'was quite delighted to see me and when I made some ordinary remark about the day clearing up, he said "*Il fait toujours beau temps quand vous venez me voir*." ' Clemenceau's visit took place two days later. As Haig had suspected, it was not unconnected with Joffre: 'His object in coming to see me was to get me to exercise a restraining hand on Gen. Joffre, and prevent any offensive on a large scale from being made until all is ready, and we are at our maximum strength ... the French people are in good heart, but if there was a failure, after a big effort, it is difficult to say what the result on their feelings might be. Quick changes are apt to take place in their modes of thought. .... I assured him I had no intentions of taking part prematurely in a great battle, ...'

Such were the conflicting courses that were urged upon the British C.-in C. by different sections of French opinion. Fortunately, there was a more positive outcome to this encounter. Strange as it seems, an immediate understanding sprang up between the laconic Scottish gentleman and the Radical French politician who had already earned the title of 'The Tiger' for his ferocious attacks upon his opponents. Haig's generalizations about 'the politicians' have to be tempered by reflection upon the number of exceptions which he made. On this occasion he wrote of his guest: 'He is 75 years old, he told me, but is wonderfully active, and spent two hours in the Front trenches today. I found him most interesting and we parted quite friends, for, as the proverb says "Friends are discovered, not made". ' Later in the War, when Clemenceau became Prime Minister of France in a dark hour, this friendship was to prove of particular value to the Allied cause. The Chief of Clemenceau's Military Cabinet recorded '*la grand sympathie, ou plus exactement la grande affection, qui liait les deux hommes, le Maréchal Haig et M. Clemenceau.*' It was more than unfortunate that this spontaneous understanding with the future French Premier was matched only by misunderstanding with the rising star on the British political scene.

Mr. David Lloyd George was Chancellor of the Exchequer when the War broke out; for a time, all his abundant energy was absorbed in bringing under control what might easily have become a most damaging financial crisis. The impact of the vast novelty of modern war on the City of London was as violent as the shock of battle. It is well-nigh impossible to recapture the feelings of the Stock Exchange when the Bank Rate soared to 10 per cent. The Chancellor displayed a cool address in handling the situation, coupled with the capacity to 'think big' which proved to be one of his most valuable assets throughout the War. His instincts were not military; but he found himself drawn more and more strongly towards the contemplation of military problems as such, under the powerful influence of his friend and colleague Winston Churchill. Yet for the first part of the struggle it was in the organizational field that his talents displayed themselves. In May, 1915, he was given the task of creating a Ministry of Munitions whose function was to mobilize the productive force of the nation into the war effort. There can be no doubt that without the formation of this Ministry, and the tremendous drive that Lloyd George imparted to it in its early days, Britain could hardly have continued to wage war, let alone take the leading part which she progressively assumed. Some of the claims made for the Ministry of Munitions (Lloyd George may be pardoned for advancing many of them himself; he was justly proud of his achievement) were exaggerated. Its immediate effect was not as dramatic as some would have it; the expanded flow of war material which made possible the much enlarged British effort during the second part of 1915, in France, Gallipoli and other theatres as well, was the fruit of work already done by the much-maligned Service Ministries. Ammunition shortages persisted all through the Battle of the Somme, while defects through the inexperience of firms newly drawn into munitions work became a positive danger. It was not until 1917 that the British Army was able to count on unlimited supplies of material; the real triumph of the Ministry came in 1918, when it was able to replace, instantly and without perceptible strain, all that had been lost to the enemy in the German Spring Offensive.

On June 4th, 1916, just over three weeks before the great battle was due to begin, a very special tragedy afflicted the British nation: Lord Kitchener was drowned in H.M.S. *Hampshire*, on his way to Russia. Just over a month later, Lloyd George succeeded him as Secretary of State for War, and from that time onwards the state of relations between him and the two most important British soldiers, Haig and Robertson, became of vital significance. As regards Haig, the omens were not good for that relationship; Lloyd George had the very opposite effect on him to that produced by M. Clemenceau. The two men had had little to do with each other until July, 1916, both being deeply engaged in their separate sectors of the national effort. But at the end of January, when Haig had been in supreme Command for some six weeks, Lloyd George had visited him, in company with other Cabinet Ministers. Haig received them with his usual somewhat aloof civility; he did, however, go out of his way to arrange for Lloyd George's two sons, who were 'somewhere in France' to be brought to G.H.Q. to meet their father. Lloyd George was not insensitive to this attention, and wrote to him on February 8th:

'Dear Sir Douglas Haig,

'I want to thank you so much for the great courtesy which you showed me during the interesting visit which I paid to your Headquarters. I was specially touched by the kindness shown to my two boys.

'The visit, if you will permit me to say so, left on my mind a great impression of things being *gripped* in that sphere of operations; and whether we win through or whether we fail, I have a feeling that everything which the assiduity, the care, and the trained thought of a great soldier can accomplish, is being done.

'I hope you will not think it an impertinence on my part to write in this strain: but I felt bound as a Member of the War Council to report as much to the Prime Minister, to Lord Kitchener, and to my other colleagues on the Council: and perhaps you will forgive a mere civilian for presuming in a military matter to communicate these impressions to you.

'There are two or three questions on the artillery document you were good enough to supply me with which I wish to be enlightened upon, but I am sending those questions through Sir William Robertson.

Yours sincerely,

D. Lloyd George.'

If this letter seems strangely at variance with the general trend of Lloyd George's thoughts; if parts of it seem somewhat fulsome; if the 'humble pie' does not seem to be baked all through, it must still be given the credit of good intention. The misfortune was that Lloyd George was an emotional and impressionable man, whose immediate views rarely achieved the stability of his main purpose. Haig, never greatly impressed by smooth speech, penetrated this aspect of Lloyd George's character at once. Admitting that Lloyd George 'was most anxious to be agreeable and pleasant' at their meeting, he nevertheless recorded in his diary: 'Lloyd George seems to be astute and cunning, with much energy and push but I should think shifty and unreliable.' Charteris's account of the occasion is revealing. Lloyd George, he says, 'set himself to fascinate everybody. He certainly was most attractive. D.H. alone seemed quite impervious to his allurements. . . . But whatever else may be said of "the little man", there is no doubt that he has genius. He dominates. One strange physical feature draws one's eye when he is not talking – his curious little knock-kneed legs. When he is talking one would not notice if he had no legs or nor arms, his face is so full of vitality and energy, and after all, it is from the chin upwards that matters. One of the Staff called him "an intriguing little Welshman", but he is much more than that.

'D.H. dislikes him. They have nothing in common. D.H. always refuses to be drawn into any side-issues in conversation, apart from his own work.

Lloyd George seemed to think this meant distrust of him. It is not so much distrust of him personally as of politicians as a class. D.H. hates everything but absolute honesty and frankness and it is only when he knows any politician intimately and long that he can find it possible to give him credit for these characteristics. But can anyone in politics be really frank and honest?'

Charteris was somewhat overstating Haig's point of view, for among those who accompanied Lloyd George was Bonar Law, and Haig's comment on him was: 'Mr. Bonar Law strikes me as being a straightforward and honourable man . . .'; while, as we have seen, in the most unlikely case of Clemenceau, an instant friendship was struck up. The crux of the matter lay in the two brief sentences: 'D.H. dislikes him. They have nothing in common.' The passionate, eloquent, ruthless and indomitable Welsh politician and the thoughtful, methodical, silent and indomitable Scottish soldier were poles apart. In the few words that convey the fundamental antipathy between them one may perceive the cloud no bigger than a man's hand.

The cloud which, on the other hand, covered the sky on the eve of battle, threw the whole nation into mourning. Tersely, refraining from any comment, almost icily, as was his habit in poignant moments, Haig, recording his passage to England on June 6th, 1916, wrote: 'On reaching Dover, Military Landing Officer showed me a telegram from Police stating it was reported that Lord Kitchener and Staff on H.M.S. *Hampshire* had been drowned. Ship struck a mine and sank. Sea very rough.' His private thoughts and grief must have been tempered by the reflection that his own relations with Kitchener had been unfailingly close and cordial from the time of his accession to command, and that he had been able to gratify the great leader also with small attentions. On February 9th he had noted: 'Lord Kitchener arrived soon after 5 p.m. I had a Guard of Honour of Artists Rifles for him. He was much pleased and said they were very smart. He had not before been given a Guard of Honour by Sir John French.' The country's greatest serving soldier was not to visit G.H.Q. again without due respect being paid to him.

As regards Kitchener himself, much has been said for and against him, and much will continue to be said. The essence of the matter would seem to be this: Kitchener was one of the few men whose vision was large enough to embrace the whole War; but the War itself was too large to be dominated by any one man. Vision is one thing, control another; the great unanswerable question is whether, had he lived, Kitchener might have found, in the second half of the War, a means of imparting his vision through a proper machinery of control. There are indications that he might have done, signs that he was moving in that direction; certainly, that was the only thing which could have saved the British Empire from the full price that it had yet to pay.

*   *   *   *

At 7.30 a.m. on July 1st, 1916, eleven British divisions, belonging to five Army Corps, with five French divisions on their right, a total of over 150,000 infantry, rose from their trenches to assault the German positions on the Somme. At the end of the day, taking into account both the main and sub-sidiary attacks, the British Army had lost 57,470 men and officers. Of the officers, 993 were dead, 1,337 were wounded, 108 were missing. Of the soldiers, 18,247 were dead, 34,156 were wounded, and 2,129 were missing. Of these it is established that only 12 officers and 573 soldiers were taken prisoner. This was the first day of battle; the Battles of the Somme continued for 140 more days.

Nothing in the experience of the British Army or nation has ever equalled this sequence of battles, not even 'Passchendaele', certainly nothing in the Second World War. Sir Winston Churchill, in a passage from *The World Crisis* which, if not impeccable in accuracy, is entirely correct in feeling, has described the feat of the British soldiers:

'Struggling forward through the mire and filth of the trenches, across the corpse-strewn crater fields, amid the flaring, crashing, blasting barrages and murderous machine-gun fire, conscious of their race, proud of their cause, they seized the most formidable soldiery in Europe by the throat, slew them, and hurled them unceasingly backward. If two lives or ten lives were re-quired by their commanders to kill one German, no word of complaint ever rose from the fighting troops. No attack however forlorn, however fatal, found them without ardour. No slaughter however desolating prevented them from returning to the charge. No physical conditions however severe deprived their commanders of their obedience and loyalty. Martyrs not less than soldiers, they fulfilled the high purpose of duty with which they were imbued. The battlefields of the Somme were the graveyards of Kitchener's Army.'

The Somme made a lasting impression on Churchill; it affected all his thinking and strategy for the British Army during the Second World War. 'Memories of the Somme and Passchendaele and many lesser frontal attacks upon the Germans were not to be blotted out by time and reflection', he has told us. He hated those battles. And yet it is he, in the passage quoted above, who has most movingly expressed 'with what a strength and majesty the British soldier fights.'[1] No account of the Battle of the Somme approaches the inner truth without that perception.

1. Napier: *Peninsular War*, Book XII, Chap. 6.

The moment of impact, in modern battle, is the moment of anarchy. As the soldiers pass through the fiery curtain of shells and smoke, they pass out of the control of their commanders. This has always been true. 'Again and again, in the regimental histories, we come across the same old story – "the set had conked out, Company B were out of radio touch", and as a result, Battalion H.Q. goes blind, together with the long chain of communications stretching towards the rear from which alone help can come.'[1] This passage does not refer to the First World War, but to the Second; there were no portable radio sets – 'walkie-talkies' – in World War I. One hundred and fifty of them on the Somme might have made all the difference. But they did not exist. The flexibility which good communications alone can provide lay in the future. To counteract this defect, the set-piece battle was developed to a very high degree. The Somme was, *par excellence*, a set-piece battle. What happened on July 1st is incomprehensible unless one takes into account all the preparation which had gone before.

The detailed planning of the Battle of the Somme may be said to have begun on March 1st, 1916, when the Fourth Army was formed under General Sir Henry Rawlinson. Following his usual course, Haig demanded from Rawlinson, who was to be the commander of the actual operation, a battle plan. He received this a month later; on April 5th he wrote in his Diary: 'I studied Sir Henry Rawlinson's proposals for attack. His intention is merely to take the enemy's first and second system of trenches and "kill Germans". He looks upon the gaining of three or four kilometres more or less of ground as immaterial. I think we can do better than this by aiming at getting as large a combined force of French and British as possible across the Somme and fighting the enemy in the open. . . .' A week later, in a long instruction from G.H.Q. to the Fourth Army, Rawlinson was told: '. . . Experience has shown that tactical advantages may be secured with comparative ease during the first few hours of an attack which, if not secured then, are very costly and difficult to capture later. . . . The first advance . . . should be pushed as far as the furthest objectives of tactical value which we can reasonably hope by fore-thought and tactical skill to be able to retain after capturing . . . the C.-in-C. desires that further consideration may be given to the possiblity of pushing our first advance further than is contemplated in your plan. . . .'

It is very easy to understand Haig's mind, if one is disposed to do so. He was acting in the spirit of the resolution made by the Allied Powers at Chantilly in December, 1915, to seek a decision in the following year. The weakened condition of Russia was palpable; Joffre and Poincaré had told him that France had only one more large effort in her; this was confirmed by Clemenceau, and by every other source of information at Haig's disposal;

1. Wynford Vaughan-Thomas: *Anzio*, Longmans, 1961, p. 116.

now he observed the remaining strength of France being sucked remorselessly down the vortex of Verdun. The conclusion was obvious: the British effort must be made with the maximum strength, aiming at the maximum result – the defeat of the German Army in the field. On this reasoning, which had clarified in him by the middle of March, Haig abandoned all thoughts of other major diversions on his front – the 'preparatory attacks' about which he had argued so strenuously earlier with Joffre – and ordered all resources to be concentrated on the Somme; he rejected anything and everything which appeared to tend towards reducing the battle there from the all-out endeavour which he now believed to be essential.

It is hard to see a flaw in this strategic assessment. Indeed, criticism of the Battle of the Somme is rarely made on strategic grounds. What has attracted the dismay and condemnation of successive generations of commentators is the great loss incurred through tactical errors. A distinguished officer who took part in it said, 'The Battle of the Somme was lost by three minutes'. This is a dramatic phrase, highly disputable, but valuable in concentrating attention on the heart of the matter – the fact that time after time Haig's intention was within a very short distance of being fulfilled. The factors which prevented it from being fulfilled require careful analysis; they are not to be dismissed in the crude terms which have all too often been thought appropriate for the discussion of this battle.

The first consideration, in a judgment of Haig's tactical approach to the Somme, is his own experience. As an Army Commander he had already conducted two important British offensives (the *only* offensives by the British Army on the Western Front). In both of them the same phenomenon had occurred: at Neuve Chapelle there was a distinct initial success, and then (we may recall Charteris's phrase) 'the whole machine clogged and stopped. It was maddening'. At Loos, eight thousand yards of the German first position were seized, but the Reserves were not present to exploit this gain, and once more the battle 'clogged and stopped'. The lesson was clear: given sufficient artillery and munitions, the capture of the enemy's front line was not a great problem. What *was* a problem, a highly intractable one, was getting forward from there. The experience of both the French and Germans at Verdun confirmed this. Deploying hitherto undreamed-of masses of guns and howitzers, both sides did frequently obliterate the opposing positions; and yet neither seemed able to make any significant penetration. This could be attributed to the fact that they were, generally speaking, very evenly matched. Given a large preponderance of force, it should be possible to maintain momentum. The whole direction of tactical thinking at Haig's Headquarters was towards this end: maintaining the initial momentum. The event itself, the first day of the battle, with its terrible loss for almost no gains of ground (some divisions were wrecked on their start lines), showed that there was a serious flaw in this argument. It did not take into account three important elements.

First, there was the sheer strength of the German positions on the Somme. Villages had been turned into fortresses. Multi-storied concrete dug-outs had been sunk into the rolling chalk downs. Everything that German ingenuity could conjure up (and the Germans displayed qualities in defensive preparation which were never matched by the Allies during the War, for the simple reason that the German role in the West was mainly defensive, and it behoved them to apply their minds to the matter) was done in the two years that they had occupied this position. G.H.Q. simply did not know what it was up against. This is not a criticism of the Intelligence. Until the German line was captured, and could be studied, it is hard to see how this information could be obtained. The second element was the inadequacy of the British artillery preparation despite the great addition to the numbers of guns available. There were reasons for this, too. In the first place, the actual number of guns, though large, was insufficient. This applies particularly to the all-important heavy calibres; the French had one heavy piece to every twenty-one yards of front on July 1st, the British one to every fifty yards. Secondly, the British ammunition was extremely defective. Approximately one out of every three shells did not explode. Stacks of these British 'duds' may still be seen beside the Somme roadsides to this day, turned up by farmers in the course of ploughing, and waiting to be taken away; highly dangerous they are, still exacting a toll of the life and limb of careless handlers; a reminder of one more serious disadvantage against which the British Army had to contend in 1916. Besides this, the disposition of the British artillery was faulty; even with the weakness stated, it could probably have been more effective if it had been concentrated upon particular sectors, but instead it was spread evenly along the front of attack. For this only G.H.Q. can be blamed; the result was an inflexibility on the day which worked against those parts of the attack which were making progress, without effectively helping those that were stuck. Finally, with all this against them, the British gunners were further handicapped by having to prolong their preparatory barrage by two days at the request of Foch, with consequent dilution of its effect. The third element overlooked by G.H.Q. was an outstanding lesson of Verdun; the amazing resilience of human flesh and blood under heavy fire, the ability of small bodies of survivors to emerge from their shattered trenches and bring their weapons into action, above all their machine guns. It was too easily assumed that complete obliteration of the enemy front could be achieved. For this, also, the blame must lie at the door of British Headquarters, and therefore of Haig, since he was the responsible head of the concern.

With all this in mind, we may now turn to the contemplation of the

British tactical method itself, against which so much criticism has been directed. This was expounded in a Memorandum on 'Training Divisions for Offensive Action' issued by G.H.Q. on May 8th, which became the 'text-book' in the education of all the commanders and formations concerned in the attack. Three central ideas emerge from a study of this document. First, there is the 'all-out' nature of the operation; Paragraph 4 states clearly: 'The attack must aim at continuity and must be driven home without intermission . . . till the endurance of the enemy is broken down.' Paragraph 17 (the final section) says: 'Troops once launched to the attack must push on at all costs till the final objective is reached. . . .' Secondly, there is a frank recognition of the difficulties likely to be encountered: 'All must be prepared for heavy casualties, and must realize that the magnitude of the interests at stake necessitates the greatest self-sacrifice from one and all.' (Para. 9.) Thirdly, and this is the key to almost all that followed, there is G.H.Q.'s assessment of the quality of the Army itself. Much has been said about the character of Kitchener's Armies, about their patriotism, their spirit, their devotion, about the wonderful upsurge of feeling which carried the mental, spiritual and physical *élite* of the nation into the ranks of this great Volunteer Force. It tends to be forgotten that in strictly military terms they were, as Haig told Kitchener, just 'a collection of divisions untrained for the Field'. But this belief ruled all the thinking at G.H.Q.

'. . . It must be remembered', says the Memorandum, 'that officers and troops generally do not now possess that military knowledge arising from a long and high state of training, which enables them to act promptly on sound lines in unexpected situations. They have become accustomed to deliberate action based on precise and detailed orders. . . .'

To regulate an army of five Corps on a front of 25,000 yards by 'precise and detailed orders' delivered in advance is no easy matter. The G.H.Q. Memorandum could do no more than lay down the main headings: consolidation, the formation of protective flanks, communications; and it could direct special attention to particular matters: 'The employment of Brigade Machine Gun Companies and Lewis guns to ensure that full advantage is taken of this great increase in fire-power . . .', the use of bombers, trench mortars, 'the strictest attention must continue to be paid to the cultivation of the power of command in young officers . . .' etc., etc. The rest had to be filled in at a lower level, and this was done on May 17th in a 31-page pamphlet of 'Tactical Notes' issued by Fourth Army itself to officers down to the rank of captain. This document was conceived in the same spirit as the G.H.Q. Memorandum; in the wording of them both may be discerned the dark outlines of the tragedy that was to follow.

The lasting image of July 1st, 1916, has not been better delineated than by

Sir Edward Spears who, not for the only time in his remarkable career, occupied a special point of vantage. In his capacity as Liaison Officer, he stood at the junction of the French and British Armies; he wrote: '. . . my memory was seared with the picture of the French and British attacking together on the Somme . . . the British rigid and slow, advancing as at an Aldershot parade in lines that were torn and ripped by the German guns, while the French tactical formations, quick and elastic, secured their objectives with trifling loss. It had been a terrible spectacle. The German artillery, with targets no gunner could resist, neglected the more dangerous but invisible French groups and concentrated on the British. For long minutes this line or that of the many waves succeeding each other was completely invisible in the smoke of explosions a mile long, and when seen again, though showing gaps of hundreds of yards where there had been men before, was perceived to be slowly advancing at the same even pace. As a display of bravery it was magnificent, as an example of tactics its very memory made one shudder. . . .'

The origins of this great tactical blunder are to be found, first, in the words used by Rawlinson at a Corps Commanders' Conference: '. . . nothing could exist at the conclusion of the bombardment in the areas covered by it'; secondly, in the preoccupation at G.H.Q. with the problem of momentum: '. . . the assaulting columns must go right through above ground to [the] objective in successive waves or lines. . . . From the moment when the first line of assaulting troops leaves our front trenches, a continuous forward flow must be maintained. . . .' The combination of these two concepts, within the context of the belief that the troops were incapable of exercising local initiative through lack of training, proved to be fatal. At bottom, what appeared to be a display of gigantic over-confidence was, in fact, the fruit of exaggerated doubt and caution. The New Armies would soon show that they possessed military qualities and instincts far beyond anything that they had yet revealed, or that G.H.Q., impressed by the sombre memory of the 21st and 24th Divisions at Loos (as well as by defects in the early fighting of 1916), dared to depend on. Denunciation is easy. When one has said that Haig, his Staff and his chief subordinates were all involved together in a vast and tragic mistake, one has said everything.

*　　*　　*　　*

The long, careful preparations for the battle drew to their conclusion; the last arguments with Joffre about which way the Allies should go after they had broken through were settled; Foch and the weather imposed last-minute delays but there was nothing to suggest that the great offensive would be anything but a success. As we have seen, G.H.Q. never supposed that it would be a cheap one. On June 27th, Haig once more told Rawlinson 'to prepare for a rapid advance'; on the 29th and 30th, paying his last eve-of-battle visits to the Corps Commanders, he found no hint of anything to disturb him seriously. In the VIII Corps sector there had been a setback owing to the failure of raiding parties to enter the enemy trenches, but the commander, General Hunter-Weston, 'seemed quite satisfied and confident'. General Morland of X Corps was 'quietly confident of success'; General Pulteney (III Corps) was 'quite satisfied with the artillery bombardment and wire cutting'. At XV Corps H.Q., Haig found General Horne and his Chief of Staff 'very pleased with the situation and in high hopes. Preparations were never so thorough, nor troops better trained. Wire very well cut, and ammunition adequate'. General Congreve and his C.G.S. at XIII Corps 'expressed themselves as full of confidence'. These were the 'men on the spot' on whom the Commander-in-Chief depended for close daily supervision of the fighting units and for accurate reporting on the state of those units. He could only accept what they said to him, in the absence of significant contrary evidence. There was none. His own impression of the troops coincided with that of their immediate commanders: 'The men are in splendid spirits, several have said that they have never before been so instructed and informed of the nature of the operations before them. The wire has never been so well cut, nor the artillery preparations so thorough.'

The gap between reality and the words which were being used in order to convey it is so astounding that it almost defeats comment. Nothing could have reduced the gap except a constant stream of urgently expressed misgivings from the line itself. They did not come. From top to bottom there was a tendency to 'look on the bright side', a valuable British characteristic which can, at times, be perilous; this was such a time. Where reports conflicted, it was the optimistic ones that filtered upwards. In some cases they conflicted sharply; two patrols of the 29th Division, for example, reported the enemy wire 'very much damaged', while two others reported it 'not much damaged'. The conclusion that the German wire on this division's front was 50 per cent intact was not drawn. In the 31st Division (both of these belonged to VIII Corps) two battalions reported that at no point was there a clear gap in the wire opposite them; another battalion reported that the wire was not a serious obstacle, while a fourth mentioned gaps about every twenty yards. General Hunter-Weston's satisfaction was evidently misplaced, and seems incredible. Obviously what was needed was a searching enquiry by the Corps Staff, and a considered statement to the Army Commander of the true situation. The cost of neglecting this was over 5,000 casualties in the 29th Division, 3,600 in the 31st Division, and for the Corps as a whole 'nothing to show for its very heavy losses' (in the words of the Official History). Haig's private observations, on June 29th, that 'Hunter-Weston and the majority of his officers are amateurs in hard fighting and some think that they know much more than they really do of this kind of warfare . . .' would appear to be justified.

Unfortunately, such experiences were not confined to VIII Corps; they occurred all along the line. If it is asked why Haig continued to employ such officers, why he did not part with them, the answer is simple; in the form of a question, it reads: 'What, *all* of them?' Because that is what the matter amounts to: practically re-Staffing the whole Army on the eve of battle or during it. And what with? Everyone, in the British Army of 1916, including Haig, was a learner in the hard business of modern Continental war. Only two of the Corps commanders who took part had commanded as much as a division in peace-time. Only three out of twenty-three divisional commanders had had experience of as much as a brigade. The battlefield, particularly against an organ like the German Army, is not a good place for learning. But, to their credit, it has to be stated that the British generals *did* learn – and quickly. Otherwise it is inconceivable how the battle could have been kept going for 140 days, with mounting intensity, after that terrible opening day. And it is inconceivable, otherwise, how the cost of it could have been brought down from the appalling figure of nearly 60,000 on the first day to a daily average of 2,500. Even the bitterest of critics must see the difference there.

Many accounts of the Battle of the Somme exist; there is not one of them that does not make the most harrowing reading. By far the most detailed, and, because of its cool and factual tone, the most depressing, is the Official History. There can be no attempt here to follow the details of the long-drawn-out encounter; readers who desire to do so must go to other sources. Only the salient points can concern us. The first day was an almost unredeemed disaster. Only on the right, on the short sector facing north from Maricourt to Fricourt, did the British make useful progress at a reasonable cost. And it has to be admitted that even this was in part due to the success of the French on their right, whose very participation in the battle took the Germans by surprise, and who were consequently able to make a large stride forward. The British profited here too from the density of the French artillery, some of which was able to give direct assistance. As a result, the XIII Corps was able to gain and hold the whole of its first objective at a cost of just over 6,000 men in two divisions. The XV Corps failed to take the 'little Gibraltar' of Fricourt, one of the most heavily fortified localities of the whole front; but judicious use of a more highly developed creeping barrage than was normal enabled the Corps to make and hold deep penetrations on either side of Fricourt which brought about the collapse of the defence later. The Corps lost over 8,000 men. The remaining three Corps of the Fourth Army, and the unfortunate VII Corps of Allenby's Third Army, accounted for the rest of the frightful casualty list, and had nothing to show for it. The VII Corps attack at Gommecourt was perhaps the most forlorn endeavour of the whole day, for this was purely a diversionary manoeuvre which was not even intended to succeed; 7,000 men fell at Gommecourt, and it is not clear that a single German was 'diverted'. For the rest, one short passage may be quoted from the Official History, as typical of many heroic, barren exploits:

'Only a few isolated parties of the 31st Division were able to reach the German front trench, where they were in the end either killed or taken prisoner. The extended lines started in excellent order, but gradually melted away. There was no wavering or attempting to come back, the men fell in their ranks, mostly before the first hundred yards of No Man's Land had been crossed.'

What is difficult to grasp, from the vantage point of today, is how a disaster of such proportions could fail to be instantly apparent. Yet such was the case. It is perfectly clear from Haig's Diary that he had no sense whatever, on July 1st, of the catastrophe that had befallen his army. Even as low down the scale as Divisional Commanders, one finds that there was a great unawareness of the actual conditions of the fighting. This, of course, added greatly to the loss when supports and reserves were thrown in behind attacks which had already totally broken down. Two reasons may be discerned to account for what now seems to have been sheer blindness – but sudden, universal blindness of the most unaccountable kind. First there was the 'fog of war'. It was literally impossible to keep track of an attack, once launched, under these conditions. Even at the best of times it was difficult, but on the Somme on July 1st it was just simply impossible. Every device (and there were many – communications were a matter which the G.H.Q. Memorandum called 'of the first importance') broke down. So much has been said about the effect of the German machine guns that it is often forgotten that the German artillery played a great part in breaking the British assault. On the British soldiers and their supports fell a dense curtain of shells; they passed out of the sight of their commanders into a private infernal region of their own; many attempts were made to penetrate this curtain, by runners coming back and by Staff Officers and others going forward, but very few of them led to anything but the quick death of the man concerned. At the rear, ignorance was universal. The second factor which helped to disguise the truth was the sheer courage of the British troops; many soldiers would have run screaming from this shambles. The British soldier 'stuck it'.

At the end of the day, Haig noted in his Diary: 'Hard fighting continued all day on front of Fourth Army. On a sixteen-mile front of attack varying fortunes must be expected.' He was aware that matters had gone badly on the left flank, but he was inclined to believe that this was an VIII Corps disaster, and we have seen what his misgivings were about the commander of that formation. 'The 8th Corps seems to want looking after', he wrote; this was true, and in a sense other than the one he intended. His immediate remedy was to separate off the two left Corps of Rawlinson's army (VIII and X) and form them into a Fifth Army under General Hubert Gough. It was clear that, for a time, at any rate, these units would not be capable of any further large effort. At the end of the next day, on the strength of such returns as the Adjutant-General had been able to compose out of the chaos, Haig still believed that his losses had been 40,000 in two days, instead of nearly 60,000 in one day, and more on the next. But he was beginning to come to a more correct appreciation of the situation; he called July 2nd 'a day of ups and downs'. Characteristically, he thought that 'The enemy has undoubtedly been severely shaken. . . . Our correct course, therefore, is to press him hard with the least possible delay . . . in any case, pressure must be maintained both to relieve Verdun and to assist the French on our right.' He did not enjoy the advantage that we possess of having the facts on both sides of the line available to him; he did, however, have the consciousness of being told by the French President only a month earlier, that Generals Pétain and Nivelle were of the opinion that, without immediate relief from the British, '*Verdun sera prise*'. His decision to continue the attack was therefore unhesitating. A mere repetition of the events of the previous day, however, was not what he had in mind. He urged Rawlinson to concentrate upon his right, and try to exploit the small success that had been gained there 'instead of from Thiepval and the left. He did not seem to favour the scheme.' Haig made it an order. The next day he found that Joffre disagreed with him even more strongly than Rawlinson, who did not possess Joffre's authority.

On July 3rd Joffre and Foch came to see Haig 'to discuss future arrangements'. It was a day of decision for the High Commands on both sides. General von Below, the commander of the German *II Army*, issued an Order of the Day which, as well as showing that the French initial success, coupled with British persistence, were beginning to produce an effect, laid down what was to become the pattern of the fighting from the German point of view. Von Below told his officers and soldiers:

'The decisive issue of the war depends on the victory of the *II Army* on the Somme. We must win this battle in spite of the enemy's temporary superiority in artillery and infantry. *The important ground lost in certain places will be recaptured by our attack after the arrival of reinforcements.*[1] For the present, the important thing is *to hold on to our present positions at any cost and to improve them by local counter-attack.*[2]

'I forbid the voluntary evacuation of trenches. The will to stand firm must

1. Author's italics.
2. Author's italics.

be impressed on every man in the Army. I hold Commanding Officers responsible for this. The enemy should have to carve his way over heaps of corpses. . . .

'I require Commanding Officers to devote their utmost energy to the establishment of order behind the front.'

The tone of this Order, making every allowance for the customary somewhat excitable German manner, indicates clearly that all was not well with the enemy. The insistence on counter-attacks is most significant. Because it was, in broad outline, an Allied offensive, the Battle of the Somme is almost always depicted as a series of costly British (or French) attacks being mown down by German machine guns and artillery. In fact, what gave the battle its peculiarly frightful quality was the stubborn courage with which the Germans counter-attacked after every Allied gain, so that hard-won positions had to be taken and taken again. But this is what wore down the German Army; this is why their casualties became so forbidding that they ceased to publish any details of them in December, but merely listed the names in alphabetical order. This was why the Somme became the crucial 'wearing-out fight' of the War.

If von Below was showing signs of agitation, the meeting between Joffre and Haig was far from placid. Haig's description of it is unusually lively, indicating the impression it made on him: 'Joffre began by pointing out the importance of our getting Thiepval Hill. To this I said that, in view of the progress made on my right near Montauban, and the demoralized nature of the enemy's troops in that area, I was considering the desirability of pressing my attack on Longueval. I was therefore anxious to know whether in that event the French would attack Guillemont. At this, General Joffre exploded in a fit of rage. "*He* could not approve of it." He "*ordered* me to attack Thiepval and Pozières". If I attacked Longueval, I would be beaten, etc., etc. I waited calmly until he had finished. His breast heaved and his face flushed! The truth is the poor man cannot argue, nor can he easily read a map. But today I had a raised model of the ground before us. . . . When Joffre got out of breath, I quietly explained what my position is relatively to him as the "Generalissimo". *I am solely responsible to the British Government for the action of the British Army;* and I had approved the plan, and must modify it to suit the changing situation as the fight progresses. I was most polite. Joffre saw he had made a mistake, and next tried to cajole me. He said that this was the "English Battle" and "France expected great things from me". I thanked him but said that I had only one object, viz., to beat Germany. France and England marched together, and it would give me equal pleasure to see the French troops exploiting victory as my own. After this, there was a more friendly discussion between Foch and me. . . . All present at the interview felt ashamed of Joffre. This is evidently the way he behaved before Gilinsky, the Russian General, who was the first to tell me of Joffre's impatience. Still, Joffre has his merits. I admire the old man's pluck under difficulties and am very fond of him. However, I have gained an advantage through keeping calm.'

This was probably the nearest that Haig and Joffre ever came to falling out; at the end of the scene, Haig was still 'very fond of him'. Their companionship in arms was a real one. The important thing, though, was that Haig had gained his point and all similar points thereafter. Many times he would be pressed by Joffre to take certain courses of action, to attack when he was not ready, to move in a direction which seemed wholly unpromising, and many times he had to stand out; they often disagreed, but they never had another set-to like this. Nor did Joffre, in the end, ever try to order Haig about again. The British Army was coming of age. As to the point at issue, in the light of all our after-knowledge of what had happened on the left flank and the condition of the formations there, Haig's decision appears indisputably correct, although his knowledge of the situation was still incomplete. It led to one of the remarkable feats of the war, an enterprise so unlike the dismal story of July 1st that it seems to belong to another battle, if not another year; and yet it took place only thirteen days after the great failure of the opening. So fast were the Army and its leaders learning their business in this grim school.

The assault on July 14th marked the end of the first phase of the Battle of the Somme; already, three days before, a primary object of the battle was achieved, when Falkenhayn gave orders to suspend all offensive operations at Verdun. He was now to find that large combats, once entered, are not easily broken off. In August, October and November, French counter-attacks forced the Germans out of much of their conquest in fighting of renewed intensity. The initiative passed from them on July 11th; it was on that day also that Rawlinson's plan for his new assault came under Haig's scrutiny. Inevitably, this was a much smaller affair than that of July 1st; Gough's Army could only help with artillery fire; the French were not taking part. That much Haig had not been able to extract from Joffre; the latter and Foch, presumably sceptical of the capacity of their Allies to do anything of note so soon after the setback of the opening day, had turned their attention to the south bank of the River Somme, where the French were preparing a large new operation. Their absence was not an unqualified disadvatage; it was at the insistence of the French that the July 1st attack had been made as late as 7.30 a.m., in full daylight, with all the help which that had given to the defence, instead of at dawn, as many British commanders, including Rawlinson, had desired. He now proposed to revert to that idea; his proposal was to attack at dawn with two Army Corps, the assaulting brigades having been drawn up in No-Man's Land close to the German line, and to herald the advance with no more than a five-minute bombardment instead of the protracted artillery preparation which normally advertised the imminence of an assault This was certainly in very sharp contrast to the methods of July 1st; at first sight Haig thought it was going too far.

Haig's immediate reaction was alarm at the concept of a night assembly of a large mass of relatively untrained troops, in the open, under the enemy's noses; it was, he noted, a manoeuvre 'which one cannot do successfully against flags in time of peace!' He went at once to see Rawlinson, taking Kiggell with him, and no doubt expressed himself very forcibly about Rawlinson's plan:

'I gave him my opinion that it was unsound. He at once, in the most broad-minded way, said he would change it.... Gen. Montgomery[1] was most anxious to adhere to the original plan, but I declined to discuss the matter further.'

With this, Haig left; Rawlinson, however, firmly backed by the Corps and Divisional commanders, as well as by the bulk of the Staff officers concerned, decided to make another attempt to persuade the C.-in-C., this time working through Kiggell: 'About 3 p.m. Rawlinson spoke to C.G.S. on telephone stating he still thought his old plan the best. I considered that the experience of war, as well as the teachings of peace, are against the use of *large masses* in night operations, especially with inexperienced staff officers and young troops. . . .' And there, once more, the matter rested, but not for long. The Fourth Army had taken into account Haig's objections, the force of which was undeniable; they still confidently believed, in the words of the official General Staff record,[2] 'that the original plan could be carried out with excellent prospects of success, very careful arrangements having been made.' It was no joke to prolong an argument with Haig once his mind was made up on a military matter, but Rawlinson felt that it was his duty:

'After dinner Rawlinson rang Kiggell with a further proposition based on my discussions with him this morning. The XIII Corps is constructing supporting points and the divisions will form on them by brigades. I said I would go carefully into the proposals and reply in the morning.'

The whole course of this transaction is illuminating. So far we have seen the Fourth Army making a radical revision of tactical doctrine in the light of palpable facts; we have seen this revision overruled by Haig on the grounds that it involved much too big a risk (the South African War was full of examples of this); and we have seen the Fourth Army, so far from adopting the posture of mute acceptance generally attributed to the subordinate commanders of the First World War, returning twice to the 'attack' upon the

1. Major-General A. A. Montgomery, M.G.G.S., Fourth Army.
2. O.A.D. 60, July 11th, 1916.

C.-in-C.'s convictions. Finally, in contradiction to the inflexibility often attributed to him, we have seen Haig, despite the fact that he had 'declined to discuss the matter further', promising later that he would reconsider it carefully. When morning came, he was still anxious, but prepared to give the Fourth Army a fair hearing: 'I thought carefully over Rawlinson's amended plan and discussed it in detail with Kiggell, Butler and Davidson. General Birch also gave me his opinion of the artillery situation . . . viz. that by advancing certain guns he felt fairly sure that we could dominate the enemy's artillery. I put four questions to the General Staff:

1. Can we take the position in the manner proposed?
2. Can we hold it after capture?
3. What will be the results in case of a failure?
4. What are the advantages, or otherwise, of proceeding methodically . . . ?

They all agreed that Rawlinson's new plan materially altered the chances of success, and there seemed a fair chance now of succeeding. They thought we could both take the position and hold it. In the case of failure – the supporting points must be held, and we can then proceed by deliberate methods. . . . For the above reasons I concurred in Rawlinson's amended plan, and sent General Kiggell to discuss certain details with him, and to emphasize the necessity for constructing *good supporting points* on the front of XIII Corps, and for holding Trônes and Mametz Woods firmly to cover our flanks. . . . A nice letter from Rawlinson reached me saying that whatever my decision might be, "it will be carried out to the very best of our ability".'

The whole episode forms a good example of Haig's methods. In the first stages of planning the tactics of the Battle of the Somme, impressed by German methods at Verdun, Haig had suggested that the British infantry should advance in detachments, rather than waves; the three Army Commanders who were infantrymen themselves were opposed to this, and Haig had accepted their judgement. They had been shown to be seriously wrong; hence his pronouncedly more vigorous interference in the details of their plans, contrary to his normal practice. Nevertheless, his aversion to over-ruling the men on the spot remained strong; with modifications in the direction of security, he accepted their proposals. The Socratic method of question and answer, rather than the assertion of doctrine (favoured by the French), was to become his standard procedure for the future. His questions were searching; if he received satisfactory answers to them, he acted accordingly. One of his main objects was to avoid friction and rancour in these discussions, and this was almost invariably achieved. He knew perfectly well that those who have to carry out plans must feel identified with them. It may be felt that sometimes he allowed this belief to sway him too far; the examples of foreign armies in the same War show the equal dangers of the opposite course.

By dawn on July 14th, 22,000 infantry with their supporting troops, six brigades belonging to four divisions of the XIII and XV Corps, were assembled on their tapes in No-Man's-Land within 500 yards of the German line (some of them much closer) without any confusion, and without raising any alarm in the hostile trenches. It was an amazing feat. Most of the troops belonged to the New Armies; their Staffs were the same men whose in-experience had weighed so heavily in the first planning of the Somme battle. Both now revealed those hidden qualities of adaptability and military instinct which had been stifled in the débâcle only thirteen days before. There was no mistake about this assault. The Official History records:

'Surprised by the shortness of the intensive . . . bombardment, by the deployment of the stormers so near in the dark, and by the creeping barrage of high-explosive, the enemy made by a feeble and spasmodic resistance to the first onslaught. The leading British wave reached the German wire before a shot was fired, and in the hostile trenches the only serious opposition came from men who rushed from dug-outs and shelters after the first waves had passed to engage those which followed. The enemy counter-barrage, when it came down a little later, fell in Caterpillar Valley behind the assaulting troops.'

A very curious conversation was heard on the telephone, when the reports of the sweeping success of the first stage of the attack began to pour in. Captain Serot, the French Liaison Officer at Fourth Army H.Q., rang up General Balfourier, the commander of the crack French XX Corps on the right. His message was as terse as it could be: '*Ils ont osé; ils ont réussi.*' The reply was unexpected: '*Alors, le général Montgomery ne mange pas son chapeau.*' The reason for this odd exchange was this: General Balfourier, when he learned what the Fourth Army plan was, regarded it as sheer madness, and repeatedly implored the British not to attempt it. Finally he sent Captain Spears, the British Liaison Officer, over to point out that the operation was quite impossible for such inexperienced troops. Major-General Montgomery said to Spears, imagining that the latter would rephrase his words in trans-lation: 'Tell General Balfourier, with my compliments, that if we are not on Longueval ridge at eight tomorrow morning I will eat my hat.' As well as being astonished at the British achievement, General Balfourier was no doubt relieved that this gastronomic outrage was now ruled out.

The Fourth Army had solved the problem of the assault; the problem of momentum, in the conditions of 1916, remained. For a few hours the pros-pects were magnificent; cavalry were able to pass up to the front, and a few British and Indian squadrons actually made a charge across the open uplands.

But the Fourth Army was now entering that fatal lozenge-shaped area of ill-renown pointed at three corners by woods whose names were to dominate the whole central period of the Battle of the Somme, and end by becoming amongst the most evil of its memories: Bazentin-le-Petit Wood, High Wood and Delville Wood. These three, laid out in classic defence formation against attack from the south, brought Rawlinson's attack to a long halt. The cost of July 14th itself was 9,000 men – half the rate of loss of July 1st, and with far more to show for it. But the German policy of counter-attacking furiously to regain every scrap of lost ground turned the three woods and the villages clustered around them into bloody battlegrounds. With help on the flanks on the 14th, they might have been seized, and much suffering might have been spared. It was not forthcoming. Gough's Army was still too weak; the French preferred to make their effort elsewhere. If Joffre really believed, as he had said to Haig, that this was the 'English battle', he must be blamed for not giving them more help in it. From now on the Battle of the Somme took on its true character – a long, swaying struggle, flaring into furious intensity, now on the left, now in the centre, now on the right, sometimes in a combination of them, but never silent, never still anywhere. It was, without comparison, the supreme ordeal of the British Army during the War. As the summer wore away, and the weather deteriorated, conditions became indescribable; that neither the Army nor its Chief faltered in this terrible task is hardly less than a miracle. The German Army suffered irreparable harm.

*   *   *   *

In the course of the forbidding central period of the Battle of the Somme, Haig's army received a powerful accession of strength and a potent new weapon. The accession of strength was marked by the entry into the battle of the 1st Australian Division opposite Pozières on July 20th. The 2nd, 4th and 5th Divisions followed.[1] Together they made Pozières a place-name in Australian history; a plaque on the site of the Windmill commemorates to this day the fact that the Australian dead lay thicker on this ground than on any other battlefield of the War.

The Australians began to arrive in France from the Middle East in March, 1916. At the end of that month Haig inspected the 2nd Division; he wrote: 'The men were looking splendid, fine physique, very hard and determined-looking. I spoke to all the Company commanders. I found two or three old acquaintances who had been in South Africa with me. . . . The Australians are mad keen to kill Germans and to start doing it at once! I told the Brigadier

1. The Third Division was still forming in England.

to start quietly, because so many unfortunate occurrences had happened through being in too great a hurry to win this campaign!'

A certain reputation had preceded the Australians; we find Haig noting cautiously: 'So far the Australians are behaving well.' At the beginning of June the Australian Prime Minister, Mr. Hughes, visited Haig, and expressed to him the keen desire of the Australian people to have their own 'Army'. The same feeling existed in Canada, and already it had become a sacred principle that the Canadian Divisions should always fight together as a unified Corps. Haig told Hughes that 'I had no intention of breaking up the Australian Corps, but even if they put six divisions into the field that force was not large enough to admit of "an Australian Army" being formed. He said he had the most thorough confidence in me and would do all he could to help me in my difficult task.' Hughes was as good as his word. It was a severe disappointment to him and to Australia that a homogeneous Australian Corps was not formed until 1918. (Until that date the Australians fought alongside their New Zealand brothers in the I and II Anzac Corps.) But the Australian Government did not allow their very natural desires to influence military exigencies. By the end of the War, five Australian Divisions were fighting in France, as well as the Mounted Division in Palestine; in quantity and in proportion this was the greatest effort by any single Dominion, although the casualties sustained by the superb New Zealand Division show the highest rate of loss in the whole of the British Empire.

Haig had no doubts about the potential capacities of the Australian soldiers; he had some doubts, however, about the training of their senior officers, while the 'Imperial' (English officer who commanded the I Anzac Corps and later the Australian Corps, Lieutenant-General Sir William Birdwood, never found great favour in Haig's eyes. Birdwood later became an Army Commander – another instance in which Haig's wishes were over-ruled in a major matter. With his successor in command of the Australian Corps, Lieutenant-General Monash, Haig's relations were always excellent. His admiration for Monash was noted after every meeting, perhaps the greatest volume of unmitigated approval for any one man in the whole of his Diary. The entry of the Australians into the great battle was watched by Haig with most particular care. On July 20th he wrote: 'The Australians went in last night opposite Pozières. . . . I told Gough to go into all details carefully, as 1st Australian Division had not been engaged in France before, and possibly overlooked the difficulties of this kind of fighting.' His anxiety still persisted on the 22nd: 'I visited General Gough after lunch to make sure that the Australians had only been given a simple task.'

Justifiable qualms: the Battle of Pozières was part of a double-fisted assault in the centre and on the right by the Fifth and Fourth Armies. The latter made little progress, but at first it appeared that Gough's thrust had done very well. The Australians took Pozières itself, but their claim to have reached the Windmill proved untrue; prompt German counter-attacks made their position very delicate. As usual, these facts took some time to emerge; on the 24th Haig was still under the impression that 'The Australians are getting on well. . . .' On the 25th the true picture began to clarify, and Haig was naturally disappointed.

In his diary that day he wrote: 'The situation seems all very new and strange to Australian H.Q. The fighting here and the shell-fire is much more severe than anything experienced at Gallipoli. The German, too, is a very different enemy from the Turk! The hostile shelling has been very severe against Pozières today and owing to clouds our observation was bad and our counter-battery work could not be carried out effectively. I spoke to Birdwood about his C.R.A., Brig.-Gen. Cunliffe Owen . . . I also saw Cunliffe Owen and explained how sorry I was to have to move him, but in the present situation I would be failing in my duty to the country if I ran the risk of the Australians meeting with a check through faulty artillery arrangements.'

The ding-dong fighting around Pozières continued with varying fortunes. The Australians, like their British comrades, were learning the art of war the hard way; they learned amazingly fast. Their morale was terrific. On the 27th Haig wrote: 'The Australians are in great spirits. One regiment began the fight with 900 men and finished up with 1,300. This was due to men joining up from other units which had been ordered to withdraw for a rest.' The next day the Australian 2nd Division was due to take its part in the attack.

Once again Haig had to intervene personally: '. . . . the Australians had at the last moment said that they would attack [the Windmill] without artillery support and that "they did not believe machine-gun fire could do them much harm!" Birch at once saw Gough and arranged that the original artillery programme should be carried out. The Australians are splendid fellows but very ignorant.'

The 2nd Australian Division's first attempt was an expensive failure. 'From several reports', Haig commented, 'I think the cause was due to want of thorough preparation.' He went on to make, in his Diary, a detailed analysis of the Australian methods. During the day he visited I Anzac Corps H.Q., where he met Birdwood and his Chief of Staff, General Brudenell White, who was already revealing himself as another great Australian soldier. 'Some of their Divisional Generals', remarked Haig, 'are so ignorant and (like many Colonials) so conceited, that they cannot be trusted to work out unaided the plans of attack.' (A far cry from 1918, when the Australian battle-plan at Le

Hamel was issued to the whole Army as an example of the perfect battle-plan!) His impression of White was very different: 'the latter seems a very sound capable fellow, and assured me that they had learnt a lesson, and would be more thorough in future. Luckily, their losses had been fairly small. . . .' His final comment on this phase of the operations was: '. . . the capture of Pozières by the Australians will live in history.' It certainly should.

In this account of the Australian entry into the main fighting on the Western Front a number of significant factors will be observed. Haig's habitual concern for his soldiers, this 'collection of divisions' which had yet to become an army, and in particular for the men of the New Armies whose qualities, he perceived, were so different from those of the old Regulars, was enhanced in dealing with the troops of the Overseas Dominions. He was tremendously impressed, as everyone was who saw them, with their bearing and morale, but by July, 1916, he could not fail to be conscious of certain weaknesses. At St. Eloi in April there had been a disagreeable episode with the Canadians in Plumer's Second Army, when they claimed that they were in possession of a group of craters and air photographs showed that the enemy was, in fact, holding these positions strongly. (This is why Haig refers to the 'conceit' of 'Colonial', not just Australian, officers.) There was talk of dis-missing certain senior officers of the Canadian Corps; Haig decided against such a course, on grounds of Imperial diplomacy. It has to be stated and remembered that the young nations of the British Commonwealth, in the process of finding their feet, tended to adopt attitudes towards the Old Country which were full of the blunt criticism and self-assertion which is common in large families. At the root of it often lies an almost invincible affection; the outward symptoms can take the appearance of a perpetual family row. There is no doubt that during the 1914–1918 War, Dominion contingents were far more disposed to adopt the tone of 'We'll show 'em' than they were during the Second World War when their nationhoods had matured. Yet the same phenomenon was not unknown in World War II.

It was awareness of this weakness (the Australians themselves had revealed the same propensities as the Canadians in their first small combats) that made Haig cautious about them, and prompted the special care that he took over their main début. Nevertheless his overriding inclination was to think well of them, to believe in their success; when he made sharp criticisms, it was disappointment, more than anything else, that incited them. As the War continued, his admiration for these notable soldiers grew, though they never ceased to puzzle him, as they did most British officers – and ordinary Tommies too. Behind the lines, the Australians had modes of behaviour which con-flicted totally with the British Army's habits. At the end of February, 1918, we find Haig remarking gloomily in a letter to Lady Haig: 'We have had to separate the Australians into Convalescent Camps of their own, because they were giving so much trouble when along with our men and put such revolutionary ideas into their heads.' A few days later he was considering a chart which showed that while the Canadians, New Zealanders and South Africans had an average of 1·6 per 1,000 men in prison at any given time, the Australians had 9 per 1,000. He was convinced that this was largely due to General Birdwood's relaxed disciplinary methods. The truth is that Birdwood, whatever his failings as a strategist or tactician, was one of the very few senior British officers who possessed the 'touch' to command Australians, the perception necessary to extract their fine qualities. By the end of March, 1918, Haig had returned to a truer estimate of them. In the great crisis of the War he found that it was the Australians who were prepared to scrap their national ambitions and give him freedom to use their divisions one by one, wherever they were needed, while the Canadians, despite their undoubted military virtues, insisted on homogeneity, and took no part in the great defensive battle.

The last word on the Australian soldier's qualities, not unnaturally, was said by their own leader, Sir John Monash: 'Very much and very stupid comment has been made upon the discipline of the Australian soldier. That was because the very conception and purpose of discipline have been misunderstood. It is, after all, only a means to an end, and that end is the power to secure co-ordinated action among a large number of individuals for the achievement of a definite purpose. It does not mean lip service, nor obsequious homage to superiors, nor servile observance of forms and customs, nor a suppression of individuality . . . the Australian Army is a proof that individualism is the best and not the worst foundation upon which to build up collective discipline.'

That Haig's own attitudes were not distantly removed from those of Monash is shown by what he said to the King on January 2nd, 1918, quoted earlier.[1]

*   *   *   *

On September 15th, 1916, the climactic Allied attack of the Battle of the Somme took place; on the British sector, opposite Flers-Courcelette, the advance out of the early morning mist was accompanied by thirty-two tanks. This was the first appearance on the field of battle of the dominant weapon of land warfare of the twentieth century, the weapon which would later incorporate in itself many of the qualities of both Cavalry and Artillery; in the form in which it appeared, it was a British invention whose existence, according to the minutes of the Royal Commission on Awards and Inven-

1. See p. 174.

tions 'was primarily due to the receptivity, courage and driving force of Mr.
Winston Churchill. . . .' Its furthest origins, as a machine, might be traced
back to Leonardo da Vinci; as an idea, to the Roman testudo. As a practi-
cality, the name of Sir Ernest Swinton should always be linked with that of
Churchill, when the 'parentage' of the tank is being discussed. It was born
out of the tactical impasse of 1915, out of the need to find an answer to the
twin problems of machine guns and barbed wire. Many have wondered that
it should have been the Admiralty, under Churchill's direction, and not the
War Office, that gave the first impetus to the development of the tank; but
there is nothing to wonder at: the Navy's own problems were of just such a
kind as to point the way to a solution of those of the Army. In Churchill's
words:

'The strongest fleet was paralysed in its offensive by the menace of the
mine and the torpedo. The strongest army was arrested in its advance by
the machine gun. . . . This was the evil that lay at the root of all our
perplexities. . . . The remedy when stated appeared to be so simple that it was
for months and even years scouted and disregarded by many of the leading
men in both the great fighting professions. Reduced to its rudiments, it
consisted in interposing a thin plate of steel between the side of the ship and
the approaching torpedo, or between the body of a man and the approaching
bullet.'

It is not necessary here to delve into the complex story of the tank's early
life and hard times. What concerns us is how tanks came to take their place
in the Battle of the Somme, and what prompted Haig's decision to use the
very small number of them that were available in what proved to be, not the
decisive thrust that was intended, but just one more spasm in the prolonged
agony of that awful conflict. It was a decision that brought upon him more
particular criticism than perhaps any other.

Winston Churchill wrote: 'This priceless conception, containing if used
in its integrity and on a sufficient scale, the certainty of a great and brilliant
victory, was revealed to the Germans for the mere petty purpose of taking a
few ruined villages.'

Swinton wrote: 'The employment of a small number of tanks during the
Somme Battle was against the advice of those who had given most thought
to the potentialities of the New Arm. So far I have seen nothing to justify it,
and personal inquiries have produced similar negative results.'[1]

Lloyd George wrote: 'So the great secret was sold for the battered ruin
of a little hamlet on the Somme, which was not worth capturing.'

In the latest history of the Royal Tank Corps, Captain B. H. Liddell Hart

1. Swinton: *Eyewitness*, Hodder and Stoughton, 1932.

wrote: 'Haig's decision to throw in the tanks at this moment was a long-odds gamble, like the new attack on which they were staked.'

The Official History concluded: 'To divulge our new methods whilst attacking with insufficient means was to squander possibilities of surprise just as much as the first effect of gas was wasted by the Germans at "Second Ypres", and the first effect of tanks was thrown away at the Somme in September 1916.'

It is a formidable indictment. Is it just?

Churchill's cryptic instruction to begin making tanks ('Proceed as proposed and with all despatch. On account of secrecy this may be taken as sanction') was delivered on March 26th, 1915. It was almost a year later (February 2nd, 1916) when the first trials of the tank prototype, 'Mother', were held at Hatfield Park, before a distinguished gathering including Lord Kitchener, Mr. Lloyd George and Sir William Robertson, with representatives of G.H.Q. Such was the secrecy surrounding the new weapon that Haig's first awareness of its existence was not until Christmas Day, 1915, a week after he became Commander-in-Chief. Among other documents for his scrutiny was Winston Churchill's powerfully argued paper, 'Variants of the Offensive'. Haig pencilled on his copy: 'Is anything known about the Caterpillar referred to in para. 4, page 32?' His interest, as always, was instantly awakened at the suggestion of an important addition to his armoury. The reports of his officers at the Hatfield trials evidently impressed him, for G.H.Q. immediately placed an order for 40 tanks, later increased to 100,[1] and Haig began, *from that moment*, to count them among the resources at his disposal for the great battle. The first reference to tanks in his Diary occurs on April 5th, 1916. Already, three months before the Battle of the Somme opened, and just over five months before the tanks made their début, without having seen them, he was weaving them into his detailed plans. 'As we are on higher ground than the enemy west of Serre', he wrote, 'it seems a suitable point for making use of our new "tanks". These might materially assist in capturing the ridge, and then be placed as "*points d'appui*" to hold it while it is being entrenched. . . .' Two days later (April 7th) he told Hunter-Weston, the sector commander, 'that I hoped to use "tanks" and that we must be fully prepared to take advantage of the surprise and demoralizing effect which seem likely to produce [*sic*] the first time they are used'. These entries dispose completely of two accusations that have been levelled against Haig: that he was unreceptive to new ideas – on the contrary, in this case we shall shortly see him being blamed for over-enthusiasm: and that his use of tanks in September was a 'gamble'. How could it possibly be a gamble, if it was

[1] Swinton, p. 214.

planned five months before, when the battle had not even begun, and *every competent authority knew that this was so?*

On April 14th Haig was in London. At the War Office he held a meeting with Swinton, at which Generals Butler (Deputy Chief of Staff) and Whigham (Deputy C.I.G.S.) were present. Haig's and Swinton's accounts of the proceedings do not tally; the discrepancy is important in one respect, as we shall see. Haig's account is a diary entry, compiled at the end of the day; Swinton's is a narrative in a book published sixteen years later. Haig wrote: 'I next saw Colonel Swinton . . . regarding the "tanks". I was told that 150 would be provided by the 31st July. I said that was too late – 50 were urgently required for 1st June. Swinton is to see what can be done and will also practise and train "tanks" and crews over obstacles and wire similar to the ground over which the forthcoming attack will be made. I gave him a trench map as a guide and impressed on him the necessity for thinking over the system of leadership and control of a group of "tanks" with a view to manoeuvring into a position of readiness and during an action.'

Sir Ernest Swinton's narrative of this self-same meeting reads: 'Half-way through April I saw Sir Douglas Haig in London. He was much interested in what was being done and told me that he had read my memorandum of February [on the tactical use of tanks] with which he entirely agreed. His mind was occupied with the coming offensive on the Somme; and he was anxious, if possible, to get some machines over to France by the 1st June. He asked whether it could be done. My answer was that no Tanks could be sent to France by that date, or even by the 1st July, but that there was just a possibility that some might be shipped by the 1st August, and that, if sufficient were delivered during July, the crews for seventy-five might be trained by August. Towards the end of May I had a talk with . . . General Kiggell, who was also in London. He was as anxious as the Commander-in-Chief to ascertain when they would have Tanks in France, but I could tell him nothing more encouraging than I had told his chief. He, too, informed me that he had read my memorandum and agreed with it. I was much relieved that the two senior officers in France were in accord with my ideas. It implied that they approved the policy of not employing Tanks in driblets, a point which I had emphasized.'

What is absent from Swinton's account is the raising of Haig's hopes by the mention of 150 tanks being ready by the end of July. This was already late for his purposes, and he clearly realized the need for the tanks to be in France for training long before they entered the battle. But the figure stuck in his mind. Swinton's detailed reply probably took longer to arrive at than his narrative suggests. On May 24th G.H.Q. drew up a table showing the resources that would be available for the battle, listing Divisions, Guns,

Ammunition, Trench Mortars, Gas, etc., etc., stage by stage. In the last column, headed 'Heavy Armoured Cars – "Tanks" ', in manuscript (probably Kiggell's), we may read:

'July 1st ⎫
July 15th ⎬ No reliable estimate

Aug. 1st   150 Tanks of which only some may have been delivered in France, and only half the crews trained.'

It is thus clear that G.H.Q.'s intention was to use as many tanks as possible, as early as possible; it is clear that this intention was fully known in London, and formed the basis for production orders; it is also clear that Swinton had made a tentative promise of 75 trained crews with vehicles by August 1st, that G.H.Q. accepted this, *faute de mieux*, and that Swinton himself was not disposed to describe 75 as a 'driblet'. In the event, on September 15th, when the tanks were committed to action, there were only 49 available, of which only 32 reached their starting points, and of these 9 broke down with mechanical troubles, while 5 more became ditched, so that only 18 were effectively in action. But these were accidents; the intention was to use the whole 49 (or more, if possible – G.H.Q.'s maximum estimate was 66): so the difference between 'driblets' and what was authoritatively approved was at most 26 tanks.

From the foregoing it is apparent that the question whether Haig was 'gambling' by throwing in the tanks at Flers–Courcelette on September 15th is not a real one. The real question is whether it was permissible, given the level of development of tank production and crew training, to hold out any hopes to him at all of using the tanks in 1916. Captain Liddell Hart has said: 'Swinton does not seem to have scented a danger in [Haig's] welcoming attitude – for wherever there is a sense of urgency it carries a risk of precipitancy.' This comes near to the truth of the matter. As we have seen, all through the year, Haig had drawn steadily towards the conclusion that the British Army's effort must be decisive in view of the growing weaknesses of his Allies; the action of September 15th was planned as the final Franco-British thrust which would clinch the matter. On August 11th, a few days before the first tanks reached France (such were the production delays) he noted:

'... A letter received from "Munitions" stated that "accessories for tanks" will not be delivered till September 1st. This is disappointing as I have been *looking forward to obtaining decisive results*[1] from the use of these "Tanks" at an early date.'

Granted that Haig was now engaged in what he hoped was a deci-

1. Author's italics.

sive battle, offered what, even without experience of it, he perceived was a decisive weapon, it is absurd to suppose that he could do other than use it. If the weapon was not really ready – after eighteen months of experiment and production – he should have been told that it was not available. If available, he was bound to use it. It is difficult to see how he can be blamed for a 'welcoming attitude' – one can imagine what might be said of the opposite.

It was on the very day that Haig himself referred to the possibility of obtaining 'decisive results' from the use of tanks, that Joffre began to press for another combined Allied assault on the German positions on the scale of July 1st. On August 11th, Joffre wrote to Haig: '*La situation générale exige, qu'en ce moment plus qu'à tout autre, notre offensive de la Somme donne l'impression d'être conduite avec vigeur et continuité. . . .*

'*J'estime donc indispensable de reprendre, sans délai, des actions* d'ensemble. . . .'

Haig agreed in principle with Joffre's ideas, but stated firmly that certain subsidiary operations had to be completed before any further great assault could be launched. On August 25th Joffre renewed his demands, on the grounds that the Russians were in dire need of support, and proposed September 6th as the date for a combined Franco-British attack. On August 27th Haig met Joffre with Foch and the other French Army Group Commanders, as well as the President, Prime Minister and Minister of War of France – a formidable assembly; '*nine in all*', he underlined in his Diary. He took the opportunity of telling Joffre that he could not take part in a large action until September 15th; he had agreed to co-operate with Foch in local attacks on August 30th and the Army would need a fortnight's rest. Joffre 'replied "*C'est trop tard. C'est la mort*". But could give me no reason'. There was some sharp discussion after this, but Haig was adamant. September 15th was agreed, the President insisting that the attack should not be any later, and Haig promising to do his best to keep to that date. Even so, Joffre was not satisfied, and as late as September 9th we find him writing to Haig: '. . . *je vous demande de tout faire en votre pouvoir, pour avancer la date de l'offensive générale de vos IV° et Reserve Armées que vous m'avez annoncée – dans votre dernière lettre – pour la mi-Septembre.*' Haig was not to be persuaded; September 15th was settled.

It was, then, not merely into a big British attack that the tanks were flung, but into a major Allied stroke, the last one on such a scale that would be possible that year, the last chance of reaping a great reward for all the endurance and suffering that had already been displayed. That reward did not seem to be too far distant. Three days before the Battle of the Somme had even opened, Lord Esher had secretly told Haig of German Peace feelers to France; letters from home captured on dead German soldiers or on prisoners indicated that internal difficulties in Germany were increasing. A letter from Dresden, dated May 18th, said: 'I am afraid that it will soon be all over with us; we are on the downward path. There have been riots again in the market. . . .' One from Cologne, dated June 22nd, said: 'England is not so wrong about starving us out. If the war lasts three months more we shall be done. It is a terrible time for Germany; God is punishing us too severely.'

One from Bruchsal, June 26th, said: 'You reproach me with writing so little to you; what can I write? If I told the truth about conditions here I should be locked up. . . .'

There was a great deal more in this gloomy strain; naturally, British Intelligence drew certain conclusions. We know now that those conclusions were too optimistic; with the experience of two wars, our knowledge of German psychology is deeper; we are now aware that the Germans are capable of immense fortitude, even when they are uttering loud cries of pain and despair. All this had yet to be learnt. In other matters, however, British Intelligence erred in the opposite direction; on August 25th it estimated German casualties on the Somme at 200,000, with 43 divisions engaged in the battle. The German Official Account later revealed that at the end of August their true casualties were 243,129 (excluding Corps, Army and other troops) and that 49 divisions had been engaged. The Adjutant-General's return of British casualties at the end of August was 196,277, while the French had lost 70,351. The balance was thus only slightly in Germany's favour (and more than accounted for by the abnormal British losses on the first day); the damage done to her, in addition to Verdun, and the severe mauling of her Austrian allies by Brusilov's brilliant offensive in the East, was already enormous. It was not without reason that British G.H.Q. circulated a document stating that '. . . the C.-in-C. has decided that the attack projected for the middle of September is to be planned as a decisive operation and all preparations made accordingly.'

Once again, as the day of battle approached, there was disagreement between Haig and Rawlinson. On August 29th, Haig noted: 'I studied Rawlinson's proposals for the September attack and for the use of Tanks. In my opinion he is not making enough of the situation with the deterioration and all-round loss of moral of the enemy troops. I think we should make our attack as strong and as violent as possible, and plan to go as far as possible.' Two days later, he desired 'that the "tanks" may be used boldly and success pressed in order to demoralize the enemy and, if possible, to capture his guns'. On September 10th: '. . . I directed the C.G.S. to impress again on Rawlinson the need for bold action . . . in order to derive full value from the element of surprise, which, after all, is fleeting! Moreover the season for fighting is nearly over.'

The next day he repeated these orders to Rawlinson personally, and, under the impression that the latter 'shares my views', saw him off for two days' much-needed rest by the sea before the battle opened. The sad truth, however, was that neither Gough nor Rawlinson shared Haig's enthusiasm for the tanks. Neither of these generals felt disposed to make any large altera- tions to the standard methods of bombardment and assault – and this was understandable, in view of the small numbers of the new weapons. Instead, *because* they were so few, they made the mistake of spreading the tanks out thinly along the fronts of their assaulting divisions. G.H.Q., in a memoran- dum on the tactical employment of tanks on August 16th, had prescribed that: 'Each tank attack will be a definite operation against a limited objective allotted to a selected number of tanks and a selected body of infantry, all under one commander.' As it turned out, it was only in the one place where, owing to the accidents of battle, these conditions were fulfilled, that a resounding success occurred.

What happened in the neighbourhood of the ruined village of Flers on September 15th, 1916, where for a time 13 tanks found themselves engaged in mutually supporting actions, forces one to speculate on what might have happened if all the 49 tanks available had been concentrated on the front of one Corps, and all 32 that got off the mark had been able to act together. At Flers the deepest British advance of the whole battle was made, producing the dramatic signal from a contact aeroplane to XV Corps H.Q.: 'Tank seen in main street Flers going on with large number of British troops following it.' This was freely translated by excited Press correspondents into: 'Tank walking up the High Street of Flers with the British Army cheering behind.'

There is evidence that the 'cheering army' behind the tank was, in fact, nothing more than a small batch of German prisoners who were being formed up, prior to being sent back. As regards the tank, it vanished into the blue towards the next objective, all by itself, and was never seen again. There was no doubt about the success of the break-through, however. An officer of the East Surrey Regiment, possibly the only infantry officer on his feet in Flers at that stage, told this author in a letter that: '. . . some time after the village action I walked alone with more curiosity than discretion far beyond Flers, towards the fourth objective, inspecting a German Defence system in seemingly unoccupied country. The only sign of life was a team of gunners harnessing up a heavy howitzer and hauling it away up, I believe, the Bapaume Road. Unfortunately I had only one precious clip left. Later the vision of Germans advancing in perfect drill-book open order sent me back towards the village of Flers to find my 28 men, a machine gun Subaltern and an orderly-room sergeant.' What should have been the spear-head of a deep penetration was whittled down to two officers and twenty-nine men. Another great opportunity had gone.

What was the balance sheet of the action? Once again, only a partial success had been scored; the decisive victory had eluded the Allies, despite the use of the new weapon. The decision to use it has been explained; the reasons were powerful and compelling. The manner in which it was used is another matter; here again it is hard to resist the conclusion that Haig should have intervened more forcefully to make his Army Commanders devise a tactic more in keeping with the proposals of Swinton's Memorandum, with which he had declared his agreement. Nine days later he was urging Gough to make a new attack 'by surprise with a line of 50 or 60 tanks and no artillery bombardment' – a presage of Cambrai on a smaller scale. Without such direct interference, the innate conservatism of the military organism would never be capable of taking such a revolutionary weapon on trust. When the battle ended, Haig was almost the only senior officer who perceived the full quality of the tanks' achievement. 'Some of the Tanks', he wrote, 'have done marvels. . . .' Swinton, who had done so much to bring the tanks into existence, crossed to France on September 15th, full of anxiety for the fate of the New Arm, and went at once to G.H.Q. 'Here I ran up against a very smooth proposition in the person of one of the Commander-in-Chief's staff, who did his best to convince me that the "Chief" was far too busy and tired to see me.' Swinton insisted that Haig should at least be told that he was there.

'He received me almost at once and very cordially. He thanked me for what I had done, and said that though the Tanks had not achieved all that had been hoped, they had saved many lives and had fully justified themselves; that he wanted five times as many. . . . These were the first words of appreciation given to the Tanks – to my knowledge – since the King saw them at Elveden.'

The following day (September 18th) Haig was talking again to Admiral Bacon, commanding the Dover Flotillas. (Right up to the end of 1917 he and Bacon spent much time trying to organize amphibious diversionary operations along the Belgian coast; such a feint had just been carried out with good results in support of the latest Somme attack.) On this occasion he had a startling proposition for Bacon: 'In view of the successes obtained by the Tanks, I suggested that he should carry out experiments with special flat-bottomed boats for running ashore and landing a line of Tanks on the beach with the object of breaking through wire and capturing the enemy's defences. . . . The Admiral was delighted with the idea, and is to go to the Admiralty with a view to having special boats made. I asked him also to urge the loan of sufficient personnel from Navy for manning a hundred Tanks.'

This conversation by itself, foreshadowing the L.C.T.s and L.S.T.s of World War II, and all the amphibious operations which they made possible, should once and for all dispose of the myth that Haig lacked imagination. As though to emphasize the ludicrousness of that myth, on the next day he sent Butler, the Deputy C.G.S., to the War Office to ask for 1,000 tanks.

He never got them. When, after eleven months of secret trial and experiment, he asked for 100 in February, 1916, he found, six and a half months later, that only 49 were available with crews. It is a sobering reflection that neither productive capacity nor man-power organization in Britain after two years of war were capable of doing better than two tanks per week. Matters did improve, but slowly. At Cambrai, fourteen months after the tank début, only 476 were available. At Amiens, nine months after Cambrai, 534 went into action together, and this was the largest number on any single occasion during that War. In other words, Haig never disposed of more than just over half the number he asked for only four days after their first appearance. If there is blame to be distributed over the story of British tanks during the First World War, it would certainly seem to lie more appropriately at other doors than Haig's. Nevertheless, Haig's own attitude found little support among other senior officers. Robertson, for example, writing to Haig on August 29th, had referred to the tanks as 'rather a desperate innovation'. Swinton has recorded how 'For eleven years I was puzzled as to why no Tanks had been employed in Mesopotamia, where they might on certain occasions have been valuable. I then discovered that General Maude, who was commanding the British forces in that theatre, did not ask for any because he heard from General Rawlinson, in December 1916, that they were no good.' A Tank Corps officer, writing of 1917, said: 'The Fifth Army Staff hated the very sound, as well as smell, of a Tank.' In September, 1918, Foch told Colonel Repington that: 'The infantry needed guns, tanks and aeroplanes, but these did not win battles and were only accessories. It was the infantry that won battles, and when men were short . . . such things as tanks and bombing squadrons should be provided on a moderate scale. It was an idea of amateurs that tanks and aeroplanes could win a war.' Perhaps Haig was an 'amateur' in this respect. The penultimate word on that subject must be the reminder that the much-vaunted German High Command *never* believed in tanks, and not more than a dozen German-built tanks were ever seen in action during the whole War.

In fairness, however, to those who did not have Haig's enthusiastic imagination concerning this new weapon, it must be added that, in 1916, there was plenty of room for doubt. It has already been noted that only 18 out of 49 tanks in France took an effective part in the action of September 15th. Mechanical troubles and steering difficulties were a constant curse of the early tanks. But even under optimum conditions, the Mark I Tank, 7 ft. 4½ in. high, 32 ft. 6 in. long (with tail), carrying a crew of 8, with its 6-cylinder 105 h.p. Daimler engine, maximum speed 3·7 m.p.h., was a very chancy instrument. On the battlefield, its effective speed was reduced to half a mile per hour. The infantry, delighted with them at first, soon began to have doubts. The East Surrey officer at Flers, quoted earlier, told this author: 'I personally don't believe anybody was frightened of them, nor indeed interested in them – they were too thin on the ground. It would have been different if they had been field kitchens.'

This may be a somewhat exaggerated opinion, but disillusionment certainly set in when it was seen how tanks attracted fire from enemy artillery and machine guns, to the detriment of men who were hoping to be sheltered by them. Such aggressive fighters as the Australians would have nothing to do with tanks if they could help it until after the brilliant action of Le Hamel in July, 1918. Before that, their slogan was: 'Na-poo Tanks.' For all of these reasons, as well as sheer prejudice, the tanks found many powerful enemies at many courts; among these was G.H.Q. itself, where a strong anti-tank lobby existed, whose machinations nearly broke the hearts of many fine tank officers. But for the unceasing work and influence of the first commander of the Royal Tank Corps, Major-General Sir Hugh Elles, K.C.M.G., K.C.V.O., C.B., D.S.O., and of the Commander-in-Chief himself, the Corps might easily have sunk away during the dark days of 1917. Instead, at a time when scepticism was at its height, Haig set in hand the plans which gave the tanks their first great opportunity of transforming modern war. For that reason, coupled with his unceasing support for the Arm, if he clearly cannot be described as a 'father' of the tank, he should be remembered as its 'god-father', who fulfilled the duty of watching over the infant during its first struggles with the harsh world outside the nursery.

*   *   *   *

The last big action of the Battle of the Somme was the capture of Beaumont Hamel on November 13th; five days later the Battle was officially closed down, though the soldiers in the line are not to be blamed if they were unaware of this decision. Beaumont Hamel had been a first objective on the first day of the Battle; together with Thiepval (captured on September 27th) on the opposite side of the narrow Ancre valley, this elaborately fortified locality formed the right-hand pivot of the whole German defence line on the Somme. If it had fallen on July 1st, the course of the Battle would have been very different; but the attack on that day, by the 29th Division of VIII Corps, was one of the most mismanaged and ill-starred of all on that dismal occasion. The 29th Division had over 5,000 casualties. The trench from which the

1/Newfoundland Regiment set out to storm the German line, and the trench which they were attacking, only some 500 yards away, still exist to remind us of the 710 officers and men of that battalion alone who fell at Beaumont Hamel on July 1st, 1916. It is an indication of the transformation that had taken place in British methods that when the village was captured by the 51st Division in November, that division considered its losses heavy at 2,200 in four days of bitter fighting.

The conditions under which the final phases of the Battle of the Somme were fought out defy description and imagination. This was particularly the case in the Ancre sector, as Canada should know. 'Here,' says the Official History, departing from its habitual restraint, 'in a wilderness of mud, holding water-logged trenches or shell-hole posts, accessible only by night, the infantry abode in conditions which might be likened to those of earth-worms, rather than of human kind. Our vocabulary is not adapted to describe such an existence, because it is outside experience for which words are normally required. Mud, for the men in the line, was no mere inorganic nuisance and obstacle. It took on an aggressive, wolf-like guise, and like a wolf could pull down and swallow the lonely wanderer in the darkness. When it was at its worst no more was feasible than to hold the line and to ensure that the troops in it were fed and regularly relieved.' On the map, the capture of Beaumont Hamel seemed to open up glittering prospects; General Gough and the two Corps Commanders chiefly concerned were eager to exploit their success, though Haig doubted the wisdom of this.[1] In the event, however, it was the ground and the weather which decided the issue, not the map. It was simply not possible to advance another yard. And so, under the leaden, snow-filled skies of winter in Picardy, the most terrible experience in the British Army's history came slowly to an end.

It is perhaps not strange after all, in the light of the curiosities of the British temperament, which translates defeats like Dunkirk into victories, and delights in making heroes of its enemies, like Napoleon or Rommel, that the victory won by Haig's army on the Somme in 1916 should have been persistently treated as an unmitigated disaster. For the truth is that this battle *was* a victory; and at the same time, of course, it *was* a disaster. It was above all a human disaster, because in the four and a half months of its duration the three largest Powers of Western Europe sustained losses amounting to about a million and a quarter men; from this frightful forfeit dates the decline of the West. To the British it was especially tragic because of the character of the men of Kitchener's Armies who gave their lives so lavishly, the loss of a generation of natural leaders whose absence is still being felt nearly half a

1. Official History, 1916, Vol. II, p. 511; and see p. 553 for Joffre's views.

century later. Indeed, the battle may stand as a lasting indictment of the sel-fishness which lies at the bottom of the famous 'voluntary principle', and the cowardice of politicians who did not dare to impose the concept of equal sacrifice upon the nation. Also, of course, and finally, it was a disaster because modern war is just that.

Nevertheless, within the terms of reference of the 1914–1918 War, the Battle of the Somme was an unquestionable Allied victory, mainly a British one, because it laid the essential foundation for the final defeat of the Germans in the field. In a way, the horrors of July 1st are as responsible for the ultimate success as any other factor; for what happened on that day shaped the whole course of the fight. When the Battle ended the British Army was still several miles short of the town of Bapaume which had been an objective for the *first day*. The losses and setbacks of the day had played a great part in finally disposing of the idea of positional warfare, with geographical prizes, and had forced the recognition that the true objective must, until it was broken, be the German Army itself. No measurement of gains on the map has any relevance to the true nature of the Somme victory, unless those gains are related to the cost to the enemy of taking that ground from him. The big stride forward made by the French on the first day, for example, proved in the long run to hold no more advantages than the slow progress of the British. It was only at the end of the Battle, when the German High Command reluctantly recognized that its Army could not stand such another ordeal, when, in fact, the Germans accepted defeat, that gains of ground acquired any significance. And then Bapaume fell quickly to the Allies, with much else besides, as the Germans withdrew to the Hindenburg Line. That withdrawal was ordered on February 4th, 1917, at the urgent desire of the Field Commanders, in particular Crown Prince Rupprecht of Bavaria. But the construction of the Line itself was begun in September, 1916, at the period when Haig's Army was making the best possible use of its second wind.

Ludendorff leaves no doubt as to why this was done; writing of new year prospects, he says: '[German] G.H.Q. had also to bear in mind that the enemy's great superiority in men and material would be even more painfully felt in 1917 than in 1916. They had to face the danger that "Somme fighting" would soon break out at various points on our fronts, and that even our troops would not be able to withstand such attacks indefinitely, *especially if the enemy gave us no time for rest*[1] and for the accumulation of material. . . . If the war lasted our defeat seemed inevitable. . . . The Field-Marshal [Hindenburg] and I were fully at one in this anxious view of the situation. Our conclusion was no sudden one, but had gradually grown upon us since we took over our

---

1. Author's italics.

posts at the end of August, 1916. Accordingly, the construction had been begun as early as September of powerful rear positions in the West. . . . Whether we should retire on them, and how the positions would be used, was not of course decided in September, 1916; the important thing then was to get them built.'

It was a settled German principle not to retire if this could possibly be helped; the decision to do so at the beginning of February, 1917, was dictated by one consideration only – the imperative need to avoid another Somme. There lies the victory.

The reason for it has been obscured by the rhetoric of great political figures and the sleight-of-hand of critics; yet it is clear enough. The stark truth is that the German Army lost at least as many, and probably more men on the Somme than the British and French together. Since Germany was the main prop of the Central Alliance, while Britain and France still counted on Russia and Italy as partners, this loss was even more serious to Germany than it was to them. It is to Sir Winston Churchill's statement in *The World Crisis* (backed by an impressive array of statistical tables) that 'in all the British offensives the British casualties were never less than 3 to 2, and often nearly double the corresponding German losses', supported by Lloyd George's assertion that on the Somme 'our losses were twice as great as those we inflicted', that much of the misconception is due. It is odd that two such astute politicians should have fallen into the trap of believing propaganda; yet inasmuch as their estimates of German casualties have any reality, these are based on complete acceptance of *contemporary* German figures put out at a time when the German Command was adopting deliberate subterfuges to conceal its losses. Students will find close and detailed analysis, based on post-war examination of German records, in the British Official History, showing the German losses on the Somme to have been as high as 680,000, compared with British and French losses of 623,907.[1] These are both maximum figures, arrived at in 1938 by Sir James Edmonds, after a careful re-examination of his own earlier estimates in the light of new information in the German Official Account of the War. This Account (Vol. XI) states frankly that the losses of 1916, '*without the wounded whose recovery was to be expected within a reasonable time*[2] amounted to a round figure of 1,400,000, of whom 800,000 were between July and October.' As the 'lightly wounded' averaged 30 per cent of the whole, this German evidence shows that Germany's losses during the year totalled 1,820,000; no army, no nation could stand up to that. Prince Rupprecht said: 'What still remained of the old first-class peace-trained German infantry had been expended on the battlefield.' Hindenburg said, in January,

1. Official History, 1916, Vol. II, p. xvi.
2. Author's italics.

1917: 'We must save the men from a second Somme battle.' Captain von Hentig of the General Staff of the *Guard Reserve Division*, wrote:

'The Somme was the muddy grave of the German field Army, and of the faith in the infallibility of the German leadership. . . .'

The Somme was Britain's first experience of the real cost of continental war on the grand scale; the shock was brutal. It is this fact which accounts, more than anything else, for the torrent of emotion which has gushed forth in Britain ever since the Battle, for the singular emotive force of its very name. In the days of the old Regular Army, fighting its 'little wars', casualties often equalled or exceeded those of the Somme in proportion, but the safe citizens of Britain were barely moved. Ticonderoga, Bunker Hill, Albuera ('eighteen hundred unwounded men, the remanant of six thousand unconquerable British soldiers, stood triumphant on the fatal hill!'[1]), Badajoz, Waterloo, all showed casualty rates which are comparable to those of the Somme. But it was not until a whole expeditionary force had been allowed to die of sheer mismanagement in the Crimea that the conscience of the British public was stirred on behalf of its soldiers. At Waterloo one British regiment was described as 'lying dead in square'.[2] Wellington's words to his Staff, in the middle of the long afternoon, 'Hard pounding, gentlemen. We shall see who can pound the longest', might have done for Haig at any time during the Battle of the Somme. The difference between the techniques and scales of 1815 and 1916 is that it took two years to do, in the twentieth century, what one day sufficed for in the nineteenth.

But there is a truer analogy with the Battle of the Somme than Waterloo, striking though that resemblance is. This is to be found in General Grant's campaign in Virginia in 1864, one of the most penetrating accounts of which may be found in General J. F. C. Fuller's book, *The Generalship of Ulysses S. Grant*.[3] Fuller explains the principles on which Grant operated with a quotation from one of the latter's ex-Staff Officers: 'This was the primal idea, the cardinal principle with which he began his campaigns as general-in-Chief – to employ all the force of all the armies continually and concurrently, so that

1. Napier.
2. Losses of 30 per cent (approximately the overall Somme average on July 1st, 1916) were common; 342 out of 860 in the 3rd Battalion, 1st Foot Guards; 177 out of 556 in the 28th Foot; 228 out of 635 in the 30th Foot; 280 out of 498 in the 73rd Foot; 246 out of 571 in the 1st Dragoon Guards, etc., etc. Two of the greatest captains of history, Wellington and Napoleon, disposing, between them, of forces just slightly fewer than Haig's assaulting infantry on July 1st, sustained approximately 45,000 casualties in half a day. The proportions of the carnage on July 18th, 1815, and July 1st, 1916, are very nearly identical.
3. John Murray, 1929.

there should be no recuperation on the part of the rebels, no rest from attack, no opportunity to reinforce first one and then another point with the same troops, at different seasons; no possibility of profiting by the advantage of interior lines; no chance of furlough troops, to re-organize armies, to re-create supplies; no respite of any sort, anywhere, until absolute submission ended the war.' 'In the circumstances,' comments General Fuller, 'not only do I consider that Grant was right to act as he did, but that he showed remarkable courage in shouldering the whole onus of the war, and in fixing the responsibility of defeating Lee, or being defeated by him, on his own shoulders.'

The similarity between Grant's ideas and Haig's will not escape present readers. Haig's Diary entry of January 14th, 1916, his letter to Kitchener on January 19th (see p. 184 for both), and his fixed opinion that 'We cannot hope to win until we have defeated the German Army' are all exactly in tune with Grant's concepts. Grant's objective was Lee's Army; Haig's objective was the German Army. Grant had the advantage of being in full command of a homogeneous force; Haig had the disadvantage of commanding only the smaller part of an Allied force. This made a severe difference to the working out of his plans, but not to his principles.

In execution both Grant and Haig bitterly experienced the wide gap between correct principle and successful application. Grant's campaign in Virginia, like Haig's on the Somme, opened with a bloody, daunting, tactically indecisive encounter. This was the Battle of the Wilderness, characterized by clumsy Federal tactics and high losses. General Fuller wrote: 'By the evening of May 6 both sides were fought to a standstill. . . . Most generals would have rested after such a battle, would have refitted their army in order to make certain of the next contest, and few would blame them for doing so; but such disturbing influences, which govern the determination of lesser men, were impotent against Grant. . . . The hour of this decision was in Sherman's judgment the supreme moment in Grant's life: "undismayed, with a full comprehension of the importance of the work in which he was engaged, feeling as keen a sympathy for his dead and wounded as anyone, and without stopping to count his numbers, he gave his orders calmly, specifically, and absolutely – Forward to Spottsylvania." ' Haig's decision on July 2nd, 1916, is a loud, clear echo of Grant's: 'The enemy had undoubtedly been severely shaken. . . . Our correct course, therefore, is to press him hard with the least possible delay. . . .'

Spottsylvania was another grim experience, an evil memory in the history of the United States; it took Grant just under a year to bring Lee's army to book. On May 11th, 1864, according to General Fuller, he wrote to Lincoln: ' "We have now ended the sixth day of very heavy fighting. The result to this time is much in our favour. But our losses have been heavy, as well as those of the enemy . . . I . . . propose to fight it out on this line if it takes all summer." The effect of this letter . . . "was instantaneous. It is hardly too much to say that from that moment dated Grant's real ascendancy over the people he represented." ' Haig, also, was determined to 'fight it out on this line if it takes all summer'. His enemy was able to hold out twice as long as Grant's, but it never occurred to him to doubt what the achievement of his Army in 1916 had been.

Reporting to Sir William Robertson on November 21st, he wrote: 'We must expect a very severe struggle and our utmost efforts will be required, but the results of the SOMME battle fully justify confidence in our ability to master the enemy's power of resistance. It is true that the amount of ground gained is not great. That is nothing. The strength of the defences overcome and the effect on the defenders are the real tests. Time after time in the last five months the Allies have driven the enemy, with heavy loss, from the strongest fortifications that his ingenuity could conceive and his unwearying labour could construct. Time and again his counter-attacks have been utterly defeated. If the memory of these experiences should fade during the winter a few successes by us at the beginning of next year's campaign will bring it back. The full value of these results will become evident in the future. . . .'

We have seen how closely the German leaders accorded with this reasoning.

When the German Army retired from the battlefield of the Somme in March, 1917, and Haig was at last able to go into long-coveted Bapaume, he stepped out of his car at two points on the Pozières ridge 'in order to gaze at that great expanse of battlefield captured step by step last year, beginning on 1st July. This great ridge must forever stand as a monument to the pluck, determination and skill of Britain's Imperial Army. Representatives from all parts of our Empire took a share in winning this victory over the flower of the German Army.'

Without a word of self-congratulation, indeed, without a mention of himself anywhere, he wrote, on March 31st: 'No one can visit the Somme Battlefield without being impressed with the magnitude of the effort made by the British Army. For five long months this battle continued. Not one battle, but a series of great battles, were methodically waged by numerous divisions in succession, so that credit for pluck and resolution has been earned by men from every part of the Empire. And credit must be paid, not only to the private soldier in the ranks, but also to those splendid young officers who commanded platoons, companies and battalions. Although new to this terrible "game of war" they were able, time and again, to form up their commands in the darkness of the night, and in spite of shell holes, wire and other obstacles, lead them forward in the grey of morning to the attack of these tremendous positions. To many it meant certain death, and all must have known that before they started. Surely it was the knowledge of the great stake at issue, the existence of England as a free nation, that nerved them for such heroic deeds. I have not the time to put down all the thoughts which rush into my mind when I think of all those fine fellows, who either have given their lives for their country, or have been maimed in its service. Later on I hope we may have a Prime Minister and a Government who will do them justice.'

Can anyone read that passage without sensing the vibration of the man's sympathetic imagination? Can anyone, having read it, really believe that he was insensitive? Can anyone, pondering the last sentence, doubt that he was prescient?

*   *   *   *

Note on Casualties.

Nothing has given rise to more disputation than the question of relative casualty figures in the Great War; the possibility of ever reaching a final conclusion about them is remote, in view of the large-scale destruction of documents by enemy action during the Second World War, both in London and Berlin.

In an argument about the Passchendaele figures in *The Journal* of the Royal United Service Institution in November, 1959, Captain Liddell Hart roundly accused the British Official History of 'suppression and distortion'. Captain Liddell Hart very kindly offered me access to his files, stating that if I had seen them I 'would hardly have been misled by the Official History' in the way that, according to him, I had been. Thanks to his hospitality, and with his assistance, I later examined the files which he considered to have a bearing upon this matter. I have to state that I found nothing in them which could stand as evidence in any serious, impartial historical examination. They threw much light on the curiosities of human nature, particularly the human nature of the Official Historian, Sir James Edmonds. Some of Edmonds's private letters in my own possession, couched in an exactly opposite sense to that of his conversations with Captain Liddell Hart at different times, indicate that he took a peculiar pleasure in being 'all things to all men'. But this has nothing to do with the carefully explained arguments of the Official History itself. Few works have ever received such watchful scrutiny, both before and after publication; the draft for 1916 (Vol. ii), containing Edmonds's conclusions on the Somme casualties, was seen before publication by over fifteen hundred combatant officers who served in the Somme offensive, as well as by the Canadian, Australian, French and German Official Historians, all of whom were free to comment upon it; their 'constructive criticism' is acknowledged by Edmonds. For these reasons, I am still persuaded that the Official History is the most reliable source for facts, though readers will note that I do not always follow Sir James Edmonds in his more general assertions.

A numerically different statement about Somme losses (though in substance agreeing with Edmonds) may be found in a most interesting essay by Sir Charles Oman, published in *The Nineteenth Century and After* in May, 1927. This was in answer to the figures given by Sir Winston Churchill in *The World Crisis*. Sir Charles Oman's views are of great significance, not simply because of his prestige as a military historian, but because, during the War, it was his task to investigate German casualty lists. He was, as he says, 'immersed in statistics from morn till eve during two years'; he refrains from drawing conclusions, and confines himself to the figures which, he says, 'are lamentable enough – but at least let us get them correct'. He places the German losses on the Somme at 560,000 – 'And what were the corresponding figures on the side of the British and French? Almost exactly the same, so far as I can make out, as those of their adversaries.' Sir James Edmonds's account appeared eleven years after this essay, and takes it fully into consideration.

9

The Year of Passchendaele – I

NINETEEN-SEVENTEEN was the black year of the war; it was also a decisive turning-point of the twentieth century, a year loaded with dire events. During 1917, the Russian Empire collapsed and the Bolsheviks seized power; the United States of America threw off Isolationism, and entered the European War; Great Britain faced the imminent threat of defeat by starvation, the consequence of unrestricted submarine warfare; the French Army mutinied; Italy sustained the disaster of Caporetto; the development of the heavy bomber placed civilian populations permanently in the line of battle; the long shadows of these transactions have lain across all the succeeding years. At the very heart of the matter lies the tragedy that, in 1917, the Western Allies threw away the slender, but distinct, advantages which they had won in the preceding year; they gave their enemies a breathing-space from which they were not slow to profit, while the defection of Russia created a new weakness which American intervention was powerless to compensate for more than another twelve months. At the root of this failure lies an internal dissension which now became a decisive factor in the War: the conflict of opinion between the military and civil leadership of France and Britain which not only debilitated the efforts of both countries, but also went far towards poisoning the relations between them. This conflict came into the open in December, 1916, when Lloyd George replaced Asquith as Prime Minister of Great Britain, and when General Nivelle replaced Joffre as Commander-in-Chief of the French Army.

Lloyd George's tenure as Secretary of State for War, from July to December, 1916, was not the most distinguished section of his career. Some disagreeable omens of future rupture between the Minister and the leading soldiers had been seen, but on the whole relations had not been bad. It was an unfamiliar field for Lloyd George, and while his temperament would always save him from being daunted by this, his intelligence was sufficient to make him a little careful; besides, the Army was already committed, when he took over, to large-scale actions with which he could hardly interfere, whatever his private views. In any case, these views were by no means as set as they later became; the misfortune is that, during his six months at the War Office, instead of coming closer to the ideas of his responsible advisers, he moved sharply away from them. The fault was not all on one side; they must bear the responsibility for failing to persuade him in the least degree. During the Second World War there were disagreements just as sharp between Sir Winston Churchill and his Chiefs of Staff, and we know from Lord Alanbrooke's diary how strained matters sometimes became – but never to the point of open breach.

Evidence of Lloyd George's equivocal posture came to Haig in September, 1916; on the 10th of that month the War Minister had paid a visit to the French Army, and on the following day to G.H.Q. Beyond noting Lloyd George's unpunctuality ('1½ hours late at lunch with Gen. Foch . . .') – and the manner in which he turned his trip into 'a huge "joy-ride"'! Breakfasts with Newspaper men, and posings for the Cinema Shows, pleased him more than anything else. No doubt with the ulterior object of catching votes' – Haig found little to complain of. His own impression of the man was unchanged; 'You will gather', he wrote to Lady Haig, 'that I have no great opinion of L.G. *as a man or leader.*' On the other hand he admitted, in the same letter, 'I have got on with [L.G.] very well indeed, and he is anxious to help in every way he can.' It was, then, a distinct shock when, six days later, Foch, on a visit to Haig's headquarters, told him that Lloyd George had questioned the French commander closely about the capacity of his British Allies. After enquiries about tactics and artillery, 'L.G. also asked his opinion as to the ability of the British Generals. Foch said "L.G. was sufficiently patriotic not to criticise the British Commander-in-Chief" but he did not speak with confidence of the other British Generals as a whole. Foch's reply was that he had no means of forming an opinion.' Haig was astounded. 'Unless I had been told of this conversation personally by Gen. Foch, I would not have believed that a British Minister could have been so ungentlemanly as to go to a foreigner and put such questions regarding his own subordinates.'

In our own advanced civilization, the word 'ungentlemanly' stands out as an anachronism; in Haig's day it had a more practical significance – it summed up, among other things, an entire mode of conducting business. It was this quality which, for example, made the whole functioning of the Stock Exchange possible without recourse to written pledges; business could be (and, amazingly, still is) handled on the principle that 'my word is my bond'. Trust and confidence are precise instruments in the conduct of affairs. Lloyd George achieved much, and deserves credit for it, by cutting through useless red tape; when he undermined trust, he became dangerous.

It may be imagined with what feelings, after this conversation with Foch,[1] Haig received the following letter from Lloyd George, dated September 21st:

'My Dear General,

'I found a considerable accumulation of work on my return from France or I should have written to you before to say how much I enjoyed my visit to your command and how agreeable were the impressions I carried away as regards both the preparations for what was then the new offensive to come and the spirit of the commanders and troops. I am more than glad to feel that all the thought and work, which go to make the success of an attack under modern conditions, have given you and your staff just cause for satisfaction.

'I can say, on behalf of my colleagues in the Cabinet as well as for myself, that the heartening news of the last few days has confirmed our anticipation and hopes that the tide had now definitely turned in our favour.

'I congratulate you most warmly on the skill with which your plans were laid, and on the imperturbable bravery of your troops. Such a combination augurs well for further successes, though I realise the difficulties which have to be faced and overcome.

'The story of the tanks has interested me greatly, and has quite captured the attention of the public.

'With best wishes, yours sincerely,

D. Lloyd George.

'P.S. I hope you will let me come over soon to visit the scenes of your fresh triumphs.'

A few days later (September 26th) Haig received further indications of Lloyd George's support in a telegram which read:
'My warmest congratulations on your conspicuous success reported in this afternoon's bulletin. The German communiqué is the best evidence of the pressure you are exercising on the enemy. My best wishes.'

Haig was prepared to give the Minister the benefit of every possible doubt about his main intentions, and responded with an invitation to him to visit the Army again. Replying to this on November 10th, Lloyd George wrote:

---

1. Foch's action in reporting Lloyd George's conversation to Haig has drawn some adverse comment. It is hard to see why. Unquestionably, the normal solidarity between the soldiers of both nations was reinforced in 1916 by the consciousness of being under special fire from the politicians. In addition, while Foch was not greatly pleased with his relations with Haig at this time, he was conscious of certain debts to the latter, who had tried to comfort him in troubles of his own. He withheld from Haig the full truth of Lloyd George's questions, but told it to his friend Wilson: 'Foch said that Lloyd George was *très monté* against Haig and he did not think Haig's seat was very secure.'

'. . . it is so important that soldiers and politicians should work together in this war. It is only by the most complete understanding and co-operation between the civil and military elements that we can hope to win. Sir William agrees and if it is convenient to you we shall pay a joint visit at an early date.

'The weather has been very unfortunate but you seem in spite of it to have made good progress.'

These unexceptionable statements drew from Haig the comment: 'I hope he will practise what he preaches! I invited him to stay in order to check some idle tales which have been going about regarding his last visit, and to show that at least those at the H.Q. of the Army in France have no feelings of ill-will towards him.'

Events now began to move swiftly. Haig's next meeting with Lloyd George took place only a few days after receiving this letter, at Paris, where the statesmen of the Allied Powers gathered to ratify the decisions reached by the military leaders at the Chantilly Conference of November 15th. Asquith and Lloyd George were the British representatives, both, according to Haig, 'in very good form'. No sooner, however, had the two Ministers returned to London, than they were plunged into the political crisis which ended in Asquith's resignation. This is not the place to re-examine the details of that crisis; the feverish atmosphere of the Whitehall corridors and of the London dinner-parties during that period has been well described in Lord Beaver-brook's book, *Men and Power*. If it all seems strangely remote from realities on the fighting fronts; if one forms the impression that beating the enemy in London was scarcely related to the job of actually fighting him in the field, this is not entirely without truth. It was, in fact, one of the reasons for Asquith's failure: despite his very great talents, his personality was not formed for the task of bestriding modern war. At least under his successor the whole nation began to learn that the war was a matter of personal import.

Lloyd George became Prime Minister on December 9th, 1916. One of his first acts was to reshape radically the machinery for the highest direction of the War, by the creation of a small, permanent War Cabinet. This at first consisted of only five men, Lloyd George himself, Mr. Bonar Law, Lords Milner and Curzon, and Mr. Arthur Henderson. Later it expanded to seven, and at all times reserved the right of consulting whatever Ministers or Service Chiefs were particularly concerned with the business of the day. It was rare for the deliberations not to involve numbers of Departmental Ministers and Civil Servants; but these attended only to expound their own causes. That done, they left; the decisions were those of the War Cabinet, whose members, says Lord Hankey, 'were to devote all their time and energy to the central direction of the British war effort, on which the whole energies of the nation were to be concentrated'. This was an enormous step forward. 'Gone', says Lord Hankey, 'were the scrambles of Ministers to get their pet subjects discussed at chaotic Cabinet meetings. Gone were the endless rambling discussions with no one to give a decision. Gone was the exasperating waste of time while the affairs of a department were discussed by people who knew little of the matter and had received no Memoranda on the subject. Gone were the humiliating and dangerous doubts of what the decision was, or whether there had been a decision at all. Although it was not realised at the time, the old Cabinet system had crashed – never, let us hope, to be resurrected. From now onward the Cabinet was destined to work to an Agenda paper. The discussions were to be prepared for by documents emanating from the responsible Ministers and circulated beforehand, and a reasonably rapid decision was ensured by the existence of a nucleus of unbiased men, unhampered by departmental prejudices, whose sole standpoint was that of winning the war. Moreover, the decisions were recorded and circulated the same day to all concerned by an organized secretariat.'

It is a matter for wonder that it had taken two and a half years for the British nation, headed by one of the most formidable assemblages of political intellect in its history, to arrive at this fundamental (and now very obvious) reorganization of its machinery of government. Unfortunately, there remained one deeply significant field in which no progress was made – rather the reverse; Lloyd George's streamlined War Cabinet was clearly a vastly improved instrument for taking decisions and implementing them, but to decide the broad direction which these decisions would follow, the large strategy of the War, something else was necessary; a steady, continuous stream of authoritative technical advice on which the decisions themselves would be based. This could only come from the Government's responsible Service advisers; if they were thought not to be competent in this regard, the Government had the duty, as much as the right, to dismiss them; but so long as they were there – the First Sea Lord and the C.I.G.S. – theirs must be the final say in all strategic matters. Otherwise the fine new War Cabinet would be a ship with a bold captain, but no rudder. Asquith understood this, as did Churchill despite much recrimination, during the Second World War; Lloyd George never understood it.

Beneath all Lloyd George's congratulatory words to Haig while the Battle of the Somme was in progress, beneath his outwardly cordial relations with Robertson, beneath his 'good form' in Paris, and the agreement which he and Asquith had signified there to the plans proposed by the soldiers for the campaign of 1917, lay a growing distrust and contempt for the military leaders both of France and Britain. A strong hint of this broke through in a conversation with Repington over lunch at the Carlton Hotel on October

25th: 'He burst out once, and said that we were all asked to keep silent and bow the knee to this military Moloch, but that he was responsible, and as he would have to take the blame, he meant to have his own way. So the antagonism is even deeper than R.[1] suspected, and I am not best pleased with the situation.' Repington's fears would have been intensified if he had been able to overhear a conversation between Lloyd George and Hankey just a week later: 'Lloyd George considered that the Somme offensive had been a bloody and disastrous failure; he was not willing to remain in office, if it was to be repeated next year; he said that Thomas, Bissolati, and others thought the same; they would all resign simultaneously and tell their respective fellow-countrymen that the war was being run on wrong lines, and that they had better make peace rather than repeat the experience of 1916. . . .'

It is unfortunate that when, only fifteen days later, at the Inter-Allied Conference in Paris, an ideal opportunity was presented to Lloyd George of expressing this very forcible dissent from the strategy which had been agreed, he did not take it. Possibly his mind was already filled with the internal politics which were then coming to a head. Certainly his apparent acceptance of the plans of the responsible Allied leaders led to grave misunderstandings. Haig and Robertson can hardly be blamed for taking the Prime Minister at his word, yet all the time his ideas were moving away from theirs to a startling degree. By February, 1917, his conclusions were hardening. Repington, lunching this time at 10 Downing Street, on February 9th, was 'thoroughly alarmed by the P.M.'s attitude. He seemed to me to be influenced by sentiment and prejudice, rather than by a reasoned view of the military necessities of the case, and although he had been the head and front of the demand for men under the Asquith leadership, he now seemed to me to be adopting an attitude which threatened danger for the success of our arms. He said that he was "not prepared to accept the position of a butcher's boy driving cattle to the slaughter, and that he would not do it". In making this sort of statement he assumes a kind of rage, looks savage and glares at one fiercely. I suppose that his colleagues and toadies quail under this assumption of ferocity. I said that he must place himself in the position of the soldiers who had a definite military problem before them, and must know, not only how many men they could have now, but also how many during the rest of the year. All organisation, strategy, and even tactics, I told him, hinged upon this decision.' It proved to be a decision to which, until the very end of the War, neither Lloyd George nor the War Cabinet could screw themselves.

*   *   *   *

1. Robertson.

The policy decided upon at Chantilly on November 15th, 1916, by the military leaders, and ratified by the representatives of Governments the following day, might be summed up very briefly as 'the mixture as before'. Joffre saw no reason to depart from his belief that the best way to make the growing superiority of the Allies effective was to apply it simultaneously. Nor did he feel inclined to change his mind about the identity of the main enemy. The swift overthrow of Roumania in the late summer by German armies assembled and deployed on interior lines provided an indication of what might be expected from adventures in the Balkans *if the main German forces were not tied down*. On the assumption that simultaneous Allied attacks on all existing fronts would achieve this end, Joffre desired to add an onslaught on Bulgaria to the early renewal of the offensives which were about to be broken off for the winter. He was uneasy about this breaking off, and won agreement to maintain pressure on the enemy even during the winter itself, if climatic conditions permitted. Haig stated that he could be ready to launch a large attack by February 1st, if the occasion arose, but added that he would much prefer to wait until May, when his armies would be able to make their maximum effort. Joffre accepted this; but the fear in his mind was that the Germans might again forestall the Allies by some *coup*, as they had done at Verdun. His fears, like his whole policy, were irrelevant; Joffre's days were numbered.

The fall of Joffre was the first clear sign that that which Haig had long feared was now a fact. For two and a half years France had borne the brunt of the struggle against the main forces of Germany. Throughout 1914 and 1915 the French Army had carried on the fighting on the Western Front virtually single-handed; casualties had been enormous: 200,000 in August, 1914, nearly 800,000 by the end of the year; 90,000 in Champagne in the spring of 1915, 100,000 in Artois, 190,000 in the double offensive of the autumn; over 300,000 at Verdun, 195,000 on the Somme. The apparent results were meagre; Germany still held her conquests firmly; her Army and her system of Alliances remained intact; the Roumanian campaign showed that her offensive capacity was far from exhausted. Both the people and the Army of France were now immensely weary and terribly depressed. A French Secret Service report on the morale of the soldiers in January, 1917, stated: 'The man in the ranks is no longer aware of why he is fighting. He is completely ignorant of anything happening outside his own sector. He has lost both faith and enthusiasm. He carries out his duties mechanically. He may become the victim of the greatest discouragement, display the worst weakness.'[1]

Haig had expected this; it had been the haunting fear of his whole period of command, a prime motive of his policy. Joffre was aware of it –

1. Spears: *Prelude to Victory*, p. 102.

hence his insistence on combined action by all the Allies during the coming year. But the effects of war-weariness had gone further than Joffre's solutions could reach. He himself, once the symbol of France's implacable resistance to the enemy, had now become for many the symbol of the slaughter of her sons.

For some time before the Chantilly Conference Haig had known that Joffre's position was becoming shaky. Lord Esher wrote to him from Paris, on November 1st: 'It is now the fashion here to glorify Nivelles [sic] at the expense of Joffre. . . .' The French political crisis developed apace, and on December 13th, in order to save itself, the Briand Ministry removed Joffre from direct control of the French Armies, appointing him 'technical adviser' to the Government, with an office in Paris and undefined duties. As Lord Esher had foreseen, he was replaced in command of the French forces on the Western Front by General Nivelle; but Nivelle did not inherit Joffre's control over French Armies in other theatres of war. Among those who also lost their commands at the same time as Joffre was Foch, who was not improperly identified with the fanatically offensive tactics which had cost the French so many casualties in the battles of 1915. Foch's conduct of the Somme fighting had shown that he was learning much in the hard school of experience, but by the end of 1916 his fellow-countrymen had lost patience. Foch, too, became an 'adviser', despite his passionate protest: 'I want to kill Boches. I want to kill Boches.' But not even the relegation of two of France's most out-standing soldiers of the War could appease the critical spirit that was now abroad.

Joffre quickly understood that his new post and title were merely nominal. On December 21st he learned that: 'The plan of operations of the French Armies on the Western theatre for 1917 had been entirely changed by General Nivelle without my having been in any way consulted.' His protests to the Government were ignored. He reflected: 'Under these conditions it might well be asked what role I was supposed to play.' By December 26th, having received no clear or satisfactory answer to this question, Joffre's mind was made up. He handed his resignation to M. Briand in person; the latter read it, and handed it back to him, 'merely saying, "You are right". In this brief exclamation there was a note of something like relief.' Doubtless, Joffre adds, Briand 'felt that my resignation was a rather pitiable ending to a political agitation which he had been incapable of dominating'. This was not quite the end; Joffre's next call was at the Elysée, where President Poincaré immediately informed him of his elevation to the rank of Marshal of France, 'adding that he felt a pride in being called upon to re-establish this dignity, the last recipient of which dated from before the war of 1870'. But the hard truth was, as the British Ambassador, Lord Bertie, wrote to Haig, that Joffre was 'being put on the shelf for Ornamental China and not for use'.

On the following day Haig himself was also promoted. The King wrote to him in his own hand:

'My dear Haig,

'It gives me great pleasure and satisfaction to tell you that I have decided to appoint you a Field-Marshal in my Army. By your conspicuous services you have fully merited this great position. I know this will be welcomed by the whole Army in France, whose confidence you have won.

'I hope you will look upon it as a New Year's gift from myself and the country.

'Believe me,

Very sincerely yours,

George R.I.'

A few days later, when he heard the news, Lord Haldane wrote:

'My Dear Field-Marshal,

'This is just a line requiring no answer, to congratulate you on this last distinction – the acquisition of the highest rank in the British Army.

'You are almost the only military leader we possess with the power of thinking, which the enemy possesses in a highly developed form. The necessity of a highly trained mind, and of the intellectual equipment which it carries, is at last recognized among our people. In things other than military they have, alas, most things still to learn, but in the science and art of war a trying experience has dictated the necessity of a gift such as yours won by the hard toil of the spirit.

'If I had had my way, you would have taken the place at the head of a real Great Headquarters Staff in London on the 4th August, 1914. But with Kitchener, who knew nothing of these things, this was impossible. What we needed then was by taking thought to penetrate the obscurity of the future and survey the conceivable theatres of war as one whole.

'But it took Moltke with sixty years following on his work, to teach the Germans this, and after all, they have not made the most of the lesson.

'Anyhow, here you are in the highest rank and with great success attained already, and as a layman who cares much for science in a war like this, I feel that I must send you this line of warm congratulation,

Yours very sincerely, Haldane.'

Haig's baton, unlike Joffre's, was a reward, not a consolation. But Haig's tribulations, also unlike Joffre's, lay ahead, in his dealings both with Britain's new Prime Minister, full of his secret fears and doubts, and with Joffre's successor, General Nivelle, fresh from a new triumph at Verdun (where, on

December 15th, the French had captured over 11,000 prisoners in a brilliantly-executed counter-attack), and full of his wonderful new Plan for final victory.

*   *   *   *

General Robert Nivelle was sixty-one years old. A colonel in 1914, he commanded his Artillery Regiment with such distinction that by March, 1915, he had risen to the rank of Corps Commander. In October, 1916, he was given command of the French 2nd Army at Verdun, and the two glittering successes won by that Army in October and December were placed to his credit. Both of them were 'limited' attacks; that is to say, they were launched on a narrow sector, with overwhelming artillery support, carefully prepared, and were broken off when their strictly defined objectives were reached. Both of these attacks had a profound effect on French politicians, depressed and daunted by the seeming impossibility of shaking the Germans in their positions. M. Briand, the Prime Minister, in particular, was impressed by the fact that, when he had queried one of these operations with General Nivelle, the latter 'had described exactly how he could conduct the operation, and had stated that he would send telegrams to him at such and such an hour from such and such points, which he had captured. Eventually, M. Briand sanctioned the attack, and General Nivelle carried it out absolutely as he had forecast.'[1] It certainly looked as though Nivelle had found at last the long-missing elixir of victory. He himself had no doubts of this; when he took his leave of the 2nd Army in December, he told them: 'The experiment has been conclusive. Our method has been tried out. I can assure you that victory is certain. The enemy will learn this to his cost.'[2]

Joffre's successor brought with him a new method, a new Plan. It was, above all, a plan for *quick* victory (Nivelle promised that if he did not succeed in breaking through he would stop the battle after forty-eight hours), contrasting brightly with the long-drawn-out fighting which was all that Joffre could offer. The French Government was delighted with it; when it came to persuading the British, the fact that, unlike almost every other French general, Nivelle could not only speak English, but speak it perfectly, through having an English mother, constituted an asset which was not lightly to be set aside. In political circles, and at the dinner parties which he attended in London, this polite, charming, handsome and so-easily-intelligible man won an immediate success; British professional soldiers, with two and a half years of practical experience of Gallic curiosities, were less easily influenced.

Nevertheless, politeness and charm have their advantages. Haig's first meeting with Nivelle was on December 20th, and his impressions were com-

1. Lloyd George: *War Memoirs.*
2. Spears: *Prelude to Victory*, p. 32.

pletely favourable; he wrote in his Diary: 'We had a good talk for nearly two hours. He was, I thought, a most straightforward and soldierly man. . . . As regards operations, Nivelle stated that he is unable to accept the plans which had been worked out for the French Armies under Joffre's directions. He is confident of breaking through the enemy's Front now that the enemy's morale is weakened, but the blow must be struck by surprise and go through in 24 hours. This necessity for surprise after all is our own conclusion. Our objective on the Somme was the relief of Verdun, and to wear out the enemy's forces with a view to striking the decisive blow later, when the enemy's reserves are used up. Altogether I was pleased with my first meeting with Nivelle. He is . . . alert in mind, and has had much practical experience in this war. . . . He is to write me his views.' Nivelle wasted no time in setting out his detailed intentions on paper; the very next day he wrote to Haig, who received the letter on December 23rd. This letter contained the very essence of the Nivelle Plan. Its first section outlined the 'Object to be attained':

'The offensive of the Franco-British Armies in 1917 must have as its object the destruction of the principal mass of the enemy forces on the Western Front. This result can only be obtained by a decisive battle, delivered by a numerically superior force against all the available forces of the enemy.

'It is necessary therefore:
     To pin down as large a part as possible of the enemy forces.
     To break through the enemy's front in such a manner that the break-through can be immediately exploited.
     To defeat all the forces which the enemy can bring against us.
     To exploit by every possible means the results of the decisive battle.'

Nivelle then turned to the question of 'Means':
'To realize this programme, it is indispensable to have at our disposal, apart from the forces destined at the outset to hold the enemy and break through his front, a mass of manoeuvre powerful enough to beat down all available hostile forces (*pour battre à coup sur toutes les disponibilités adverses*). . . .'

Nivelle estimated that this mass of manoeuvre should consist of twenty-seven divisions, formed in three Armies, all belonging to one nation, and therefore necessarily French. He went on to outline the '*Physionomie Générale*' of the operations as he saw it:

'The enemy forces will be held in the sector ARRAS - BAPAUME and in that between the OISE and the SOMME by attacks delivered respectively by the Armies under your orders and by the French forces.

'During this time, a vehement attack (*une attaque brusquée*) carried out on another part of the French Front will produce the break-through (*la rupture*).

This will be immediately followed by the rapid enlargement of the breach and by the concentration beyond it of the Armies of manoeuvre intended for the decisive battle.

'This battle, whose results will make themselves felt along the whole length of our front, will include an exploitation on a large scale, in which the British and French Armies will participate with all their available means.'

There arose the question of how the vital Mass of Manoeuvre was to be procured:

'To allow me to do this, it is essential that the British Armies should relieve a considerable number of French troops now holding the front between the SOMME and the OISE . . . I estimate that this front could easily be held by seven or eight divisions.

'This relief ought to be carried out without delay . . . I ask you therefore to see that it is carried out by January 15th at latest.'

Nivelle next discussed the British role in greater detail; it was, he said:
'(1) To allow me to form without delay the mass of manoeuvre which is indispensable to the decisive battle.
(2) To undertake on your contemplated front of attack a sufficiently broad and powerful offensive to absorb an important part of the available German forces.
(3) To participate in the general exploitation which will follow the decisive battle. . . .'

Nivelle then passed to what he evidently considered were minor points; among them he accepted that the extension of the British front would 'to a certain extent make it unnecessary for your Armies to pursue during the winter the offensive operations which they were to have undertaken in conformity with the decisions taken at the Conference of Chantilly on November 15th last'. Another point which he touched on in his concluding remarks was this:

'Finally, the plan of operations which I have explained to you does not exc ude the possibility, *if the need arises*,[1] of an operation for the conquest of Ostend and Zeebrugge, as this could not take place before the summer. . . .

'If our great offensive succeeds, it is certain that the Belgian coast will fall into our hands as a consequence of the retreat of the German Armies, without having to be directly attacked. If, on the other hand, our attack fails, it will always be possible to carry out the projected Flanders operations when the fine weather comes (*à la belle saison*).'

1. Author's italics.

In his final paragraph, Nivelle once again urged the speedy relief of part of the French front by the British, in order to enable him to build up his resources; it was, he said 'a question of capital importance which I want to settle without delay'.

There can be no doubt that this letter came as a surprise to Haig, opening up fields of speculation which had evidently not been examined in his cordial discussion with Nivelle three days before. This was something very different from the 'follow up' to the Somme which Nivelle had then seemed to be propounding. Haig discussed the letter with his Staff, and finally 'told Davidson to tell [Nivelle] that I am anxious to help him carry out his plans to the best of my ability. At present, however, I have (owing to sickness in the Australians and indifferent drafts for the Bantams Division) only about 50 divisions instead of 56, and so it is impossible to take over the full extent of the line desired . . . I must . . . keep adequate troops to attack with 36 divisions at least on the front from Arras to the Somme. In the event of the enemy's line not being pierced as hoped for by Gen. Nivelle, I shall expect the latter to relieve sufficient troops on my front to set free the necessary number of divisions for an attack north of the Lys'. Two points emerge from this entry: first, Haig was concerned because what Nivelle was asking for would cause a grave strain to his Army; secondly, it implied a complete abandonment of all existing British plans.

One of the commonest errors made in writing or speaking about the First World War (and, indeed, sometimes also the Second) is the treatment of campaigns or battles, like Passchendaele or Cambrai or Dieppe, as though they were isolated episodes which had been suddenly conceived by the Commanders and Staffs concerned. No great operation of modern war can be suddenly conceived and executed. This was particularly true of the battles of the First World War, and that which is generally known as 'Passchendaele', but more correctly called the Third Battle of Ypres, or the Flanders Offensive, is a notable instance. Nivelle's references to Ostend and Zeebrugge in his letter of December 21st to Haig, and Haig's reference to 'an attack north of the Lys' in his Diary entry of the 23rd, show that the intention of the British High Command to launch an offensive in Flanders in 1917 was already clearly formulated. The first origins of this offensive may, indeed, be traced back to Winston Churchill's proposal in October, 1914;[1] one of Haig's first steps on taking over the Command-in-Chief was to cause the project to be studied again, in January, 1916; all through that year the idea of an amphibious operation on the Belgian coast with large-scale naval co-operation was in his mind; not until June did he reluctantly abandon the thought of a

1. See p. 128.

northern offensive, under the pressure of preparations for the Somme. Evidently, there was some magnetic attraction about Flanders for both British Commanders-in-Chief and their Staffs; it behoves us to understand clearly what that attraction was.

If one studies the long, bulging line of the German front in France and Flanders, one sees at once that it divides into three sections; its outstanding feature is the huge central salient, the tip of which was the position assaulted by the British Army on the Somme; on either side of this long, sweeping curve there are two shorter, straighter lengths. Connecting, like hinges, the straighter parts with the salient, lie the two important rail centres of Metz and Roulers. Between these, across the base of the great salient, are the Ardennes, where lateral communications scarcely existed; if either Roulers or Metz should be retaken by the Allies, or brought under the domination of their artillery, the whole position of the German Armies in the Salient would be enormously complicated; in the case of Roulers, there was also the consideration of the vulnerability of the German right wing, cramped into the narrow corridor of Western Flanders; and both Metz and Roulers lay close to the Allied lines – close enough, on a map, to provide the most tempting strategic objectives of the whole Western Front. There was no other geographical target on the front of the British Armies to compare with Roulers, to match the possibilities which would be opened up by its capture. As the crow flies, the distance from Ypres to Roulers is approximately twelve miles.

This proximity is the prime reason why British strategy was drawn continuously northward throughout the War; but there were others. Chief among these was the question of the Channel ports. This took on two aspects: a defensive aspect, contained in the implied German threat to Dunkirk and Calais; a defensive aspect of a quite different kind in the German occupation of Ostend and Zeebrugge, and the damaging effect of their submarine base at the latter point. As has already been said,[1] German submarine activity became an increasing factor in the War all through 1916. A foretaste of what might be in store came in April, when 141,193 tons of British Merchant Shipping were sunk; during the next four months there was somewhat of a lull, and August losses were 'only' 43,354 tons; then, suddenly, there was a steep rise, to 104,572 tons in September, 176,248 tons in October, 168,809 tons in November, and a peak of 182,292 tons in December. The Admiralty held out little hope of being able to change this situation by naval action alone. Alarm in Government circles, and among those who knew what was happening, became acute; in January, 1917, Colonel Repington made his

---

1. See p. 189.

bitterest comment of the whole War: '. . . in my view it was at present a question whether our armies could win the war before our navies lost it.' Two months earlier, on November 21st, 1916, Mr. Asquith handed to Robertson an unsigned paper which said: 'There is no operation of war to which the War Committee would attach greater importance than the successful occupation, or at least the deprivation to the enemy, of Ostend, and especially Zeebrugge.'

Robertson accepted this paper, with or without signature, as an Instruction; fully aware, as he was, of the perilous situation at sea, and obliged as he was to accept the Admiralty's view (mistaken as it turned out) that the Zeebrugge U-boats were largely responsible for the heavy shipping losses, he had no alternative. On December 1st he told Joffre of the British Government's anxiety, and it was accepted that the main British effort for the coming year (which Haig wished to launch in May) should be made in the north, with the object of clearing the Belgian coast. Meanwhile, on the Somme front, the agreement with Joffre was, as we have seen, that pressure should be maintained as far as weather conditions allowed. Now, under Nivelle's new dispensation, both these agreed programmes were scrapped, and a new element was added – the request that the British should take over more of the line. Haig was in a dilemma. On the one hand, there was his set policy of conforming to French wishes and giving them full support in their operations, a policy strengthened by his excellent impression of Nivelle and his initial belief that this general would reveal a grip and thrust which had been noticeably lacking in Joffre's latter days; on the other hand, his Border caution and his personal experience of the War's disconcerting character, the disappointment which had attended so many high hopes, warned him that Nivelle's great blow might fail as so many had done before, in which case it was his first duty to consult British interests, now clearly defined. Whatever happened, it was clear that the British Army would be involved in heavy offensive fighting; if Nivelle's Plan succeeded there would be one long, sustained battle. (Nivelle's letters and Directives had little to say about the third phase of the action, after the break-through; this was referred to glibly as 'exploitation', which conjures up delectable images, but as every informed commander knew, against such stubborn defensive fighters as the Germans had shown themselves to be, this 'exploitation' was as likely as not to take on the aspect of a hard, grinding struggle. And this, indeed, proved to be the case, even in the very last days of the War, in November, 1918.) If the Plan failed, or only partially succeeded, then Haig's forces would have to undertake two offensives – one to help Nivelle, and then another to clear the submarine bases. And now Nivelle wanted him to take over more line as well. It was a tall order; one thing was immediately clear to Haig – he could not do it all unless he was reinforced. It was a somewhat dampening response which he sent off to Nivelle on December 25th:

'. . . I agree in principle with your proposals and am desirous of doing all that I can to help you on the lines you suggest. The extent to which I can help, however, depends on the number of divisions sent to me within the next two or three months from Salonika and elsewhere, and at present I have no definite information on this point. . . .'

Haig's reference to 'Salonika and elsewhere', and his making the early extension of the British line conditional on his being reinforced from those theatres, was based on the assumption that it was now a set policy of the Government to reduce such commitments. Neither he nor Robertson had grasped the extent of Lloyd George's determination to seek a decision elsewhere than in the West. Robertson had an inkling of it; in a letter to Haig of December 12th he said: 'Though he is off Salonika he is *on* Egypt, and wants to get to Jerusalem! For this he is hankering after 2 Divns. from France for the winter. He is also after lending some of your big guns to Italy for the winter.' But Robertson was not seriously disturbed: 'I have done my best with him, and in company with you I've no doubt we can keep him straight.' Robertson was too sanguine; Repington, to whom he recounted his discussions with Lloyd George, was nearer the mark. Sardonically (he was becoming very sour by now) Repington noted on December 30th: 'Robertson also says that L.G. wants a victory quickly, a victory while you wait. He does not care where. Somewhere where opinion will be impressed, like Damascus. R. has told him that Damascus may come in time, when rail and pipe lines are laid, and meantime what about Beersheba? L.G. didn't fancy that Beersheba would catch on, but Jerusalem might! This is War Cabinet strategy at the close of 1916, and if we can win on it we can win on anything.'

He added: 'The point is that all our best soldiers agree, and yet the politicians will not accept their opinion.' The misunderstanding, the failure to communicate or convince, and its consequences, were both profound. Nothing less than a fully-operating Joint Chiefs of Staff machinery under a Prime Minister who was also Minister of Defence, on the World War II model, could have solved this problem; in 1917 this did not exist even in men's minds; the body politic had not developed that far. On the contrary, as Spears wrote: 'The old coat of democracy, never intended for wear at Armageddon, was showing white at the seams.'

The Rome Conference, January 5th–7th, 1917, afforded to Lloyd George an opportunity of expounding his strategic ideas; he was not slow to take the chance, and argued them with all his habitual eloquence. His volatile temperament had undergone another shift: the scheme which he now advocated had nothing to do with Damascus, nor Jerusalem; he proposed a combined offensive by France, Italy and Britain on the Italian Front, in order to crush Austria. At the core of his plea, he has told us, were these two arguments: 'I laid great stress on the fact that the Austrians were the weakest enemy, and I suggested that we ought to strike at the weakest and not at the strongest point in the enemy front. Germany, I pointed out, was formidable so long as she could command an unbroken Austria, but if Austria were beaten Germany would be beaten too.'

Lloyd George's plan surprised his military advisers. Robertson, who was present, was amazed. He commented: 'Who actually drew up the document containing the plan, or whether it was the work of the Prime Minister himself, I am unable to say. The British General Staff had previously heard nothing about it, and none of the other Entente staffs had any knowledge of it. The incident was not a good omen for the future, since it was not only another proof of Mr. Lloyd George's indifference to military opinion on military matters, but it disclosed the intention to make use of his position in the Allied councils to secure approval to military plans of his own conception, and to which his own General Staff were unlikely to agree. It was also calculated to lower the General Staff in the eyes of the High Commands of other countries, and that at a time when British interests required that British control of the war should be increased.'

Much to Lloyd George's disappointment, and rather to his surprise, his plan, with all its attractions, was rejected both by the French and the Italians. Trying to explain this in his *War Memoirs*, he attributed the unpalatable fact to two causes: what he called 'the bondage of professional etiquette', and Franco-Italian jealousy. This analysis tells us more about its author than about the true reasons for the non-acceptance of his ideas. It was not because Cadorna[1] was 'ganging up' with his fellow soldiers against the politicians 'even though it involved the throwing away of the most promising chance afforded to him to win a great triumph for his country'; it was not because of national rivalry that Lloyd George's plan was rejected. It was because the French, fresh from the removal of Joffre and the adoption of Nivelle's plan, had no intention of summarily tossing it aside. There *would* be a great offensive on the Western Front; inevitably the British would take a large part in it; whatever promises might be made in Rome in January, once this offensive was launched, Britain and France would have their hands full; there was nothing but danger for Italy in embarking on a large adventure which she might easily find herself having to wind up alone. On the other hand, if Nivelle succeeded, he would succeed for Italy too. Cadorna was only being sensible, and Lloyd George might have saved himself much chagrin if he had

---

1. General Cadorna was Chief of the Italian General Staff.

cared to debate his plan seriously with his advisers before putting it forward. It would then have emerged that, whatever the intrinsic merits of his scheme, it was unreal because all three nations were already committed to other policies, and whatever the British might do, more logical Europeans would never reverse such agreements except on the advice of their General Staffs.

And now was seen an astonishing transformation. Lloyd George's first knowledge of the Nivelle Plan was on Christmas Eve, but at that stage his mind was filled with his own newly-forming ideas. Near Paris, on his way back from the Rome Conference, he met Nivelle himself, and invited that officer to London a week later to place his proposals before the War Cabinet. So successfully did Nivelle plead his case in London, despite the misgivings of Robertson and the War Office, that Lloyd George became completely converted. It was, in the end, not to Salonika, not to the Middle East, not even to his brain-child, the attack on Austria, that he lent his official favour; it was to a knock-out blow on the Western Front. His conversion was so complete that on January 17th, the day after the conference with Nivelle, he directed Robertson to send to Haig a 'special instruction' signifying the British War Cabinet's approval of Nivelle's Plan. It went even further; it emphasized the importance which the Cabinet attached 'to the agreement being carried out "both in the letter and in the spirit", and to the British armies taking their share of "the operation at the date laid down, or even before that date, with the forces available at the moment, if the weather and other conditions make operations possible and advisable. . . . On no account must the French have to wait for us owing to our arrangements not being complete." '1

It is not difficult to detect in the sharp wording of this 'special instruction' promptings from Nivelle himself, designed to overcome the hesitations which Haig had expressed to him. It was a dangerous stratagem, to invoke political interference with an Allied commander so early in the day; it was a stratagem which could only have worked because Lloyd George was prepared to lend an ear to it. His new-found enthusiasm for a Western offensive, expressed in such terms, might prove as unhealthy as his previous vacillations. Nor was it certain that these had really ended; beneath all his zeal on behalf of Nivelle, in the recesses of his mind the attachment to other solutions remained. The General Staff was again asked to set in hand preparations for an offensive in Italy *after* the Nivelle attack (although the whole point of this attack was that it should prove to be 'decisive'); Robertson wrote: 'To this I was obliged to demur. During the six weeks that had elapsed since the new Government came into office three different plans of campaign had been under

---

1. Robertson: *Soldiers and Statesmen*, ii, p. 199.

consideration – the Chantilly, Mr. Lloyd George's, and Nivelle's – and it was imperative that undivided attention should now be given to the one into which it had been decided that full efforts should be put. We could not as a matter of fact properly consider future operations in Italy without consulting French G.H.Q. and there we were already suspected of having no confidence in Nivelle's plan. Suspicion would naturally be increased if further doubts were cast upon its success by suggesting the examination of a project which might have to follow it. There was, in addition, the Flanders offensive to be remembered, *regarding which the instructions of the Government still held good,*[1] and while two plans of so far-reaching a nature were in being no useful study of a third one could be made. A General Staff paper elaborating these arguments was laid before the War Cabinet, and for the moment the subject was allowed to drop.'

*   *   *   *

Haig's perplexities were no less severe than Robertson's: what the latter suffered in bringing the Prime Minister to a steady conclusion, the former was experiencing in penetrating the precise intentions of his French colleague. There was, in every one of Nivelle's communications at this period, a grandiosity which might disguise their lack of precision to an amateur, but only underlined it to a professional soldier of experience. On January 2nd Nivelle wrote again to Haig, setting out his conception of the phases of the forthcoming battle, and showing that the passage of time and the awareness of difficulties had in no way diminished his optimism. His definition of the break-through, for example, included the capture of the whole of the enemy's artillery on the front attacked (*'la conquête du premier coup, de ses premières positions et de toute l'artillerie établie devant le front attaqué'*). But in an ominous phrase, out of tune with the generality of his statements, he also said that the battle would be a long one – *'cette bataille aura une durée prolongée'* – which was what Haig had always recognized, but contradicted the whole essence of the Plan. This drew from Haig one of his most carefully thought-out documents, a recapitulation of intentions without which it is not possible to understand his conduct of the War in 1917. He replied to Nivelle on January 6th:

'I will deal first with the plan of operations, on which the solution of all minor problems depends. It is essential that there should be no room for misunderstanding between us on this question.

'In your letter of January 2nd, you divide the operations into three phases.

1. Author's italics.

'In the first phase, you propose that strong attacks shall be made by our respective armies with the object, not only of drawing in and using up the enemy's reserves, but of gaining such tactical successes as will open the way for decisive action on the fronts of attack, either immediately or – later on – as a result of success obtained by you in the second phase. During this first phase adequate reserves are to be held ready either to exploit success immediately, or to continue to use up the enemy's reserves, according to the development of the situation.

'I have already agreed to launch such an attack as you describe, *but not to an indefinite continuation*[1] of the battle to use up the enemy's reserves. Such continuation *might result in a prolonged struggle like that on the Somme* this [*sic*] year, and would be contrary to our agreement that we must seek a *definite and rapid decision*.

'In the second phase, you propose that my offensive shall be continued while you seek a decision on another front. This I have also agreed to on the definite understanding that your decisive attack will be launched *within a short period – about eight to fourteen days* – after the commencement of the first phase; and, further, that the second phase also *will be of very short duration*. You will remember that you estimated a period of 24 to 48 hours as sufficient to enable you to decide whether your decisive attack had succeeded or should be abandoned.

'The third phase, as described in your letter of January 2nd, will consist in the exploitation by the French and British Armies of the successes previously gained. This is, of course, on the assumption that the previous successes have been of such magnitude as will make it reasonably certain that by following them up at once we can gain a complete victory and, *at least, force the enemy to abandon the Belgian coast*. On this assumption, I agree also to the third phase on the general lines described in your letter.

'But I must make it quite clear that my concurrence in your plan *is absolutely limited by the considerations I have explained above*, on which we have already agreed in our conversations on the subject. *It is essential that the Belgian coast shall be cleared this summer*. I hope and believe that we shall be able to effect much more than that, and within limitations of time, I will co-operate to the utmost of my power in the larger plans which you have proposed.

'But it must be distinctly understood between us that if I am not satisfied that this larger plan, as events develop, promises the degree of success necessary *to clear the Belgian coast* then I not only cannot continue the battle but I will look to you *to fulfil the undertaking* you have given me verbally to

1. All italics in this quotation are the Author's.

relieve on the defensive front the troops I require for my northern offensive. Thus, there is, in fact, *a fourth phase of the battle to be provided for in our plans.* The need to carry it out may not, and, I hope, will not arise. *But the clearance of the Belgian coast is of such importance to the British Government* that it must be fully provided for *before I can agree to your proposals.*'

Nothing could have been franker than this letter. Two points emerge from it with perfect clarity: first, Haig's participation in Nivelle's offensive was absolutely conditional on its decisive character, and on the understanding that it would be broken off quickly if this character was not fulfilled. Haig (and Robertson) knew full well that breaking off a large-scale action is easier said than done, but the assurance that it *would* be done was built into Nivelle's entire reasoning, and it was necessary to hold him to it – or give him the chance to state equally frankly that it could not be done. Four successive and most emphatic references to the Flanders offensive made it clear beyond doubt where the main British effort must be made, if Nivelle's attack did not achieve the decision for which he hoped. Only for the sake of final victory could Haig promise unlimited support to Nivelle; only Nivelle and his immediate Staff deeply believed that final victory was assured by the Plan. That was the contradiction at the root of the strategic dilemma of the British Command in 1917.

Nivelle's reply to Haig's formidable letter was despatched on January 11th, and reached Haig in London, where he was taking a short and business-laden leave. Nivelle was evidently shaken by Haig's Scottish precision, which forced him, in turn, to be more precise than anyone else had so far invited him to be. It now became clear that the whole vast question-mark of the Nivelle Plan concerned the third phase – the exploitation of the anticipated victory. Pushed to the wall, what Nivelle said to Haig was this:

'. . . one cannot prescribe the duration [of this phase]. . . .

'In fact, one cannot be too literal about particular phases, because quite obviously it could not enter your mind that, once engaged in a joint battle by our two armies, you could, on your own appreciation of the situation, abandon the battle and leave me alone at grips with the enemy (*seul aux prises avec l'ennemi*).

'If we embark on this battle, it is with the avowed intention (*la volonté formelle*) of following through to the end, and engaging all our forces in it. It would be disastrous to deliver battle under other conditions.'

As regards the Flanders offensive, should it be necessary (and once again Nivelle's wording shows how remote he considered this possibility to be), he reassured Haig that 'you will find me ready to give you all possible help in creating effectives'. Obviously, he added, it was impossible, at this stage, to go into detail on this subject; he ended by repeating that the earlier the joint offensive was launched, the better would be its chances of success.

This was not a reassuring communication. Haig had indeed succeeded in drawing some of Nivelle's obscurities into the open, but they looked no better out there. Haig commented in his Diary: 'We are agreed on nearly every point. The 3rd phase will not be started unless the 2nd is successful. The difficulty seems to me to be able to come to a decision that the 1st and 2nd phases have been sufficiently successful to justify starting the 3rd phase. Both the British and French are affected by that decision, as it will mean the abandonment of the northern operations if the 3rd phase is started. In other words, we fix all our faith on these operations being so successful that the Belgian Coast will be cleared indirectly.' There was, in fact, a persisting gap between the intentions of the two Allied commanders which could only be properly cleared up by the informed arbitration of their Governments. The opportunity for this was presented by Nivelle's visit to London two days after Haig had received his letter; we have seen how that visit coincided with a particular stage in the mental processes of Mr. Lloyd George. It will be appreciated that this was not a stage which lent itself to the cool and objective assessment of a tricky, but vital point of military reasoning. This was one of many occasions when the inarticulateness of Haig and Robertson worked to their country's disadvantage – just as Nivelle's eloquence did in the case of his own. It would seem that a degree of verbal felicity, something akin, perhaps, to the level exposition of a trained barrister in a complex case of Company Law, is a necessary part of the equipment of a general. Lacking that gift, it is a great pity that Haig did not show Lloyd George a copy of his letter to Nivelle of January 6th; there was no mistaking the reasoning of that – and yet . . . Robertson was scarcely less lucid on paper, and he was at this period pouring out papers for the information of the War Cabinet. They seem to have made little impression.

The Conference in London on January 15th and 16th was, in truth, a disaster. The overture to it, a morning meeting between Lloyd George, Haig and Robertson, was ominous: '. . . the P.M. proceeded to compare the successes obtained by the French during the past summer with what the British had achieved. His general conclusions were that the French Army was better all round, and was able to gain success at less cost of life. That much of our loss on the Somme was wasted, and that the country would not stand any more of that sort of thing. That to win, we must attack a soft front, and we could not find that on the Western Front. . . .' When Nivelle arrived in the afternoon, with the French Ambassador and four Staff officers, to submit the

French case, there was no agreed British position. It was an ineffective session, the main point at issue being the British relief of the French front; Haig insisted that, in order to carry this out, he must have four or five more divisions: 'These must either be sent from England, or I must reduce the strength of my attack. It must also be taken into consideration that the training of my troops will suffer, a very serious consideration. Success depends very largely on the efficient training of the troops who are detailed to attack.'

This was a problem which was often overlooked by the Government in such negotiations; it was complicated by the shortage of Labour forces in the British Army. Haig had noted in his Diary, on this subject, a week earlier: 'No difficulty about the relief of their fighting troops; the trouble is their rearward services; old men repairing roads, light railways, quarrying and breaking stone, etc. . . . we have not got the same class of old men . . . and would have to use fighting troops for the purpose . . .' – at the expense of rest and training, needless to say. But this was scarcely a matter for the War Cabinet in conclave with the French C.-in-C. The meeting broke up without a decision, and the War Cabinet then continued the debate alone 'without any soldier present'.

The result of these private deliberations was presented to Haig and Robertson at 11 a.m. the following morning. The War Cabinet had decided that the relief of the French must take place; Haig states the reasons they gave:

'(1) We had refused to send more divisions to Salonika, though strongly pressed by the French Government.
(2) We were fighting in France and the C.-in-C. of the French Army had elaborated a plan which we must do our utmost to make successful.
(3) The French Army was the largest force.

We must also agree to the date which the French wished. Their country was invaded, and they wished to clear the enemy out as soon as possible. Lastly, by attacking early the British would be able, if the attack by the French failed, to launch another attack later in the year at some point further north.'

With this much already decided, there was really nothing more to discuss with General Nivelle. Nevertheless, when he appeared at 11.30 he was able to impress the British Ministers once again with a discourse on French defensive methods. Not even Haig's dry intervention 'to tell the Committee that in one sector four British divisions had recently relieved five and a half French divisions' could spoil the excellent effect that Nivelle produced. He left the Conference well pleased with himself, as he might indeed be, for he had now secured the formal assent of the British Government to the Plan which had already been adopted by his own. This assent, as we have seen, was emphasized by the 'special instruction' which the War Cabinet sent to Haig the following day, with its stress on the need for speed. As Duff Cooper remarked: 'The fact was that Nivelle had proved the first and last person capable of persuading Lloyd George that Victory could be won on the western front. Lloyd George, believing for the nonce that the thing could be done, demanded that it should be done quickly.' The only concession made to the British soldiers was that reinforcements should be sent to Haig, and that with them he would complete the relief of the French by March 1st, instead of February 15th. When the conference broke up at last, 'The Prime Minister personally thanked me for the ready way in which I had done my best to help the Government out of a great difficulty with the French Government. It was past one o'clock.' But kind words could not dispel Haig's inner misgivings; he commented: 'I must say that these conclusions were hastily considered by the War Committee.' He had not heard the last of them yet.

*   *   *   *

From this point onwards, events gathered a momentum of their own, defeating all the efforts of generals and statesmen to control them. In Russia the rumblings of Revolution were beginning to be heard, bringing comfort to the Germans. At sea, the full application of unrestricted submarine warfare began to produce results which brought the direst alarm to the British Government – but also inexorably drew America into the War. This campaign mounted to a terrible peak in April, when 849,000 tons of Allied and neutral shipping (423 ships) were lost, of which 526,000 tons were British. The stubborn resistance of the Admiralty to the Convoy system was only overcome by the personal intervention of Mr. Lloyd George; not until August was there any tangible sign that the system was working effectively; in that month there was a sharp decline in shipping losses, and the continuance of this trend throughout the rest of the year showed that the U-boats had, indeed, been mastered by this and other methods. In France, two developments threatened grave injury to Nivelle's projected offensive.

Whatever his misgivings, Haig had left the London conference determined to give Nivelle his full and loyal support. On January 18th it was reported to him by Davidson that the Chief of Staff, Kiggell, 'did not seem altogether satisfied with the results of the Conference. I told D. to let him know my view, namely, that we must do our utmost to help the French to make their effort a success. If they succeed, we also benefit. If they fail, we will be helped in our turn, and we then have a right to expect their full support to enable us to launch our decisive attack, in the same way as we are now helping them.' Material factors, however, now began to make themselves felt. As far back as November 16th, there had been signs that all was

not well with the British lines of communication; on that day Geddes made
to Haig a 'very gloomy report regarding the state of the French railways.
Practically they seem to be breaking down because they are unable to keep
up their stocks of wagons, locomotives, etc.' Under the double strain of
accelerated British offensive preparations and an exceptionally severe winter,
not even the expert skill of Geddes had availed to remedy the situation. On
January 26th Haig noted: 'The railway situation has suddenly become worse.
This morning . . . a telegram was handed to me stating that from noon today
only food supplies, ammunition and material for the railways could be
carried – all other traffic must be stopped.'

The next day, remembering, no doubt, the jealousies and disgruntlement
which he had had to overcome at G.H.Q., Haig permitted himself one of his
rare moments of self-congratulation: 'The critical state of the Nord system
had been foreseen by me in September last . . . I tremble to think what our
position would now have been, had I not grappled then with the whole
question and brought in the best railway men from England and created a
new Department, viz. "Transportation", under a "Director-General" to deal
with it.' Nevertheless, he had to admit, on the day after, that: 'We are
certainly passing through a very serious crisis.' By February 2nd matters had
reached such a pass that Haig decided to write to Nivelle 'and tell him that
unless the means for importing our requirements are provided, we cannot
possibly be ready to attack at the time he wishes'.

At this juncture, the question ceased to be one concerning only the British
lines of communication; it affected the whole strategy agreed upon in
London. Nivelle, conscious of the hesitations of the British generals, and
insufficiently acquainted with Haig, was disposed to treat the railway problem as an excuse for procrastination. On February 13th Haig was forced
to report to Robertson that the situation was not improving, and that recent
communications from the French had been highly unsatisfactory. Robertson,
in turn, was obliged to pass on this report to the Government. It so happened
that he could scarcely have done so at a worse time, for Lloyd George was, at
this moment, furiously incensed against Haig. The reason for this was
relatively trivial, but it was a triviality of a kind which assumes a large aspect
in war. What had happened was this: at the end of January, a group of
foreign journalists had appeared at G.H.Q., and on February 1st Haig
'received' those representing the French Press, who had come to give an
account of the doings of the British Army to their people – a long overdue
gesture, in view of the widespread ignorance in France about Britain's contribution to the War. The technique of the Press Conference was, of course,
in its infancy in those days; it was understood by certain politicians, and
Lloyd George himself was a skilful practitioner of it; but soldiers did not,

generally speaking, understand it, nor the precautions which have to be taken
if privileges are not to be abused. Their sole concern was, at that time, with
military Security; it is indicative of the lack of understanding that both
Censorship and Public Relations came under Intelligence – a totally different
function – that is to say, under Charteris.

Since no military information was given away, the French journalists
were permitted to publish their reports of the meeting with Haig, which
they did according to their several styles. The publication of their stories was
noted by the British Press, which, in turn, 'wrote up' what Haig had said to
the Frenchmen. Charteris did not see the letter asking permission to publish
the British articles, nor was it passed to Haig. This lapse at G.H.Q. was
disastrous, for the manner in which Haig's 'interview' was presented was
entirely misleading. Remarks intended as amiable platitudes – 'confidence in
victory', and so forth – were treated as specific prophecies of early success:
'This year will be decisive . . . we shall see the event after which Germany
will appear as beaten in the military sense. It is possible that the year of
decision will also be the year of peace . . .' etc., etc.[1] Haig was not prophesying;
it was not his custom to do so; but this was dangerous stuff in 1917, in a
world that was wearying of war. Repington noted: 'Haig is reported to have
given some bombastic assurances to the French journalists that we shall break
the German lines this year and defeat the enemy. R. was very vexed about it,
and I have not heard one good word for it. My own impression that Haig
will disown a good deal of the supposed interview which appears in different
forms in different French papers. I hope so.' The next day, February 16th, he
wrote: 'Everybody much down on the Haig interview.'

Haig's first knowledge of what had taken place was on February 15th,
when he read *The Times*; it irritated him profoundly, though he could not
foresee how the ripples would spread. He wrote: 'As a matter of fact, I gave
no "interviews", but from time to time I have received eminent French
journalists who have visited our front. On these occasions I merely talked
platitudes and stated my confidence in a victorious termination of the war.
By some mistake a summary of one of these talks has slipped past the Censor.
I am much annoyed, as I hold that it is quite wrong for the Commander-in-
Chief's views to be published in the press at all. The Government at home
should give out all such reports.' But the fat was now in the fire. Three days
later Haig received a telegram from the Secretary of State for War, Lord
Derby, telling him that a question was to be asked in the House of Commons,
and asking what the Government should reply. The ludicrous aspect of the
whole thing, from Haig's point of view, was that every report from Paris

1. *The Times* account of Havas Agency report.

seemed to show that, garbled or not, the so-called interview had done much good in fortifying French opinion and the Alliance. But this did not satisfy London. On February 20th, after Mr. Bonar Law had made a somewhat half-hearted explanation in the House of Commons, Derby wrote to Haig:

'I am not one of those who think that your interview gives any military information to the enemy, but undoubtedly it has done this, it has created an atmosphere of expectation of complete victory which will cause a great feeling of despondency if the offensive does not produce, and produce immediately, the highest results. Luckily, the offensive is not immediate, and therefore I think the effect of the interview will wear off, and that the storm will abate as quickly as it arose. But there is no doubt it has been a storm, and a very disagreeable one.

'This leads me to what is really the object of this letter, namely, as to the course you should pursue with Charteris. You will get an official letter on the subject, but I cannot help saying that I think Charteris' action in passing the interview for publication without first submitting it to you is entirely un-justifiable. He has let you down very badly, and let you down in a respect which you in France can hardly realize at the present moment. He has destroyed in this country all confidence in his judgment, and everything which passes through his hands as having been approved by him will be subject of suspicion.'

In the War Cabinet, Lloyd George and Lord Curzon were the most vociferous against Haig; Lord Northcliffe, whom they summoned to discuss the incident with them, said: 'The general attitude of both of them was that of birds with ruffled plumage. . . .' Haig had this knowledge in mind when he composed his reply to Derby on February 22nd. In this, without accepting that any personal blame lay upon Charteris, he agreed that Propaganda and Censorship should be separated from Intelligence – "The difficulty is to find the right man *with experience* for Propaganda and censorship.' He then turned to the larger question: 'As regards the reputed "interview", *please note* (and tell your friends of the Cabinet) that I do not admit that what appeared in the papers was anything like what I said to the various Frenchmen who came to see me. And (privately) I think (from a cursory glance at papers of Wedy. just recd.) that Mr. B. Law might have made this clearer to the Ho. of Commons! But doubtless he knows his own business best. What however interests me most is to ascertain for whose advantage it has been to mis-represent what appeared in the French papers! If L.G. has a man in his eye who will run this great Army better than I am doing, let him appoint him without more ado. You will find that I am sufficient of a patriot to withdraw as a man, and I trust gracefully !'

Writing to his wife on the same day, he elaborated this thought: 'I am doing my best and have a clear conscience. If they have someone else who can command this great Army better than I am doing, I shall be glad to hand over to him, and will be *so happy* to come back to my darling wife and play golf and bring up the children. It has not yet come to this. I merely mention it, so that you can see how independent in spirit I feel, and that whatever I do is what I feel and judge to be best for the country.' Two days later Derby wrote: 'Don't be the least worried. The incident is closed. You have the complete confidence of the Army, the Nation – and for what it is worth, that of Yours ever, D.'

The incident, however, was not closed. Its effect upon Lloyd George remained. It was on the 22nd that Robertson informed Haig than an Anglo-French meeting would be held at Calais to discuss future plans in the light of the railway breakdown. The two Prime Ministers would both attend, with Robertson, Haig, Nivelle and General Lyautey, the French Minister of War. Robertson added that the object would be to arrive at 'a definite agreement' between 'the representatives of the two Governments'; 'the governing factor connected with the operations is that of railways'. Haig accordingly suggested that Geddes should also attend; it was odd that his name should not have been mentioned. But the whole conference was odd, because Haig had already met Nivelle, and, as so often happened when personal contact was established, had reached agreement with him not only on the subject of railways ('He at once sent a stiff wire to the French Government recommending that the Nord Railway Co. be placed on a sound footing'), but also on the co-ordination of the offensive: 'he agreed with me that *no attack should start until all our requirements had been provided* . . . I was much pleased with the results of our meeting as I had feared that Nivelle wished to attack in any case whether the British are ready or not.' There did not seem to be outstanding business calling for the attention of two busy Prime Ministers. The Conference was fixed, nevertheless, for February 26th.

It was on February 25th that the second event on the Western front to the prejudice of Nivelle's offensive began to appear. Haig wrote in his Diary: 'Important developments have been taking place on the 5th Army front. The enemy has fallen back on a front of 18,000 yards and has abandoned the villages of Warlancourt, Pys, Irles, Miraumont and Serre. Our advanced guards met with little opposition. The question to decide is whether the enemy has begun a big movement in retreat, or whether he has merely evacuated the ground referred to above for local reasons. . . . In favour of the first conclusion is the information gained from a prisoner of the 5th Foot

Guards that "the Germans intend to withdraw to the Hindenburg Line".... On the whole, such a withdrawal at the present time seems to have greater disadvantages than advantages for the enemy.... After dinner I discussed the situation with General Kiggell after getting information from Butler and Charteris. I agreed that Gough must push forward advanced guards to probe the enemy's front. The Third and Fourth Armies are to be instructed to be active in reconnoitring.'

Haig was too optimistic; he was not yet aware of the extent of the withdrawal which the Germans contemplated. We have seen what their motives were: to avoid another Somme. Their timing was brilliant; if their withdrawal was a confession of one defeat, it certainly went far towards saving them from another.

*   *   *   *

Lloyd George's desire for yet another inter-Allied conference was not inspired by anxiety about the Transport problem, although this served as an excuse for convening it. Lloyd George's aims were altogether more ambitious. On the day that the London Press carried its reports of Haig's unfortunate 'interview' with the French journalists, Lloyd George interrupted a conversation between Hankey and Commandant Bertier de Sauvigny, the French Liaison Officer at the War Office. He remained with them for two hours; he had much to say. He began by telling Bertier what an impression General Nivelle had made on the British War Cabinet; then, according to Bertier's report:[1]

' "For my part," he said to me, "I have complete confidence in him, and the deepest conviction that he is the only man who is capable of bringing the operations to a successful conclusion this year. But, for this to be possible, it is necessary in the last resort that he should be able to make use of all the forces on the French front, ours as well as the French Armies." Mr. Lloyd George is making every effort to bring his colleagues round to this point of view, but does not count on being successful, *unless Nivelle and the French Government take up a strong line on the subject*.[2] "There is no doubt that the prestige which Field-Marshal Haig enjoys with the public and the British Army will make it impossible to subordinate him purely and simply to the French Command, but if the War Cabinet realizes that this measure is indispensable they will not hesitate to give Field-Marshal Haig secret instructions to this effect, and, if need be, *to replace him*[3] if he will not give the support of all his forces when this may be required, with complete understanding and

1. Spears: *Prelude to Victory*, Appendix IX.
2. Author's italics.
3. Author's italics.

compliance. It is essential that the two War Cabinets should be in agreement on this principle. A conference should be held as soon as possible, for although the date by which the British Armies will be ready has been retarded by a fortnight owing to the congestion of the French railways, it is nevertheless so near that we must take a decision as soon as possible. I should like, therefore, to fix this interview for February 28th." '

The more one reflects upon this moment in British history, the more astounding it seems to be. It is difficult to refrain from using emotive words like 'plot' and 'conspiracy'. Coldly stated, we have the situation that the British Prime Minister, scarcely two months in office, in the presence of the Secretary of the War Cabinet, was discussing with a foreign officer how the greatest Army that Britain had ever possessed (her first Citizen Army, and including large Dominion contingents) could be placed under the command of another foreign officer, also recently appointed, and with little experience of high rank or responsibility. That is the bald essence of the matter. Lloyd George's motives were complex, personal, and not all dishonourable; but he had embarked upon an underhand course, and the methods by which he sought to gain his ends were necessarily devious. Naturally, he could not proceed without some semblance of authority from the War Cabinet as a whole. How was this to be obtained? Clearly, it was most unlikely to be obtained if Sir William Robertson was consulted. The War Cabinet met on Saturday, February 24th; according to Robertson: 'The Secretary of the War Cabinet, acting presumably on the Prime Minister's instructions, had telephoned to me to say that unless I had any special question to bring forward I need not attend the Cabinet meeting that day – a very unusual occurrence. Having none, I did not attend, and had no reason to suppose that any question connected with the coming conference would be considered.'

There now remained Lord Derby, a conscientious, if not brilliant Secretary of State, who considered that it was his duty to support, rather than harass the soldiers under him. Other members of the War Cabinet, too, might find the proposed transactions a little strong for their stomachs, if presented to them neat. It was not possible, however, to be too selective; and so Lloyd George had resort to subterfuge. According to Derby, this is what happened at the War Cabinet meeting: 'Mr. Lloyd George told us at the War Cabinet that, although an agreement had been arrived at at the Conference in London, there was nothing to which both our own representatives and those of the French had put their hand in a formal signature,[1] and it was very advisable, in view of possible recriminations afterwards to get those signatures. I therefore was under the impression that this was the sole object of the Conference so far

1. In fact, an agreement had been formally signed by Haig, Robertson and Nivelle.

as the fresh offensive was concerned, but that the matter of transportation was also going to be discussed.'[1]

The Calais Conference, then, was a deception. The War Cabinet was not informed of its true purpose. Both the C.I.G.S. and the British Commander-in-Chief were to be taken by surprise. As General Spears grimly commented: 'The method employed makes one think of latter-day American gangsters. They were to be "taken for a ride" to Calais, and there "put on the spot".' Appropriately to this intention, the deception was kept up to the end. The Prime Minister's party did not reach Calais until 1.15 p.m., and naturally the first item on the agenda was lunch. Haig sat next to Lloyd George, and suggested to him that they might have a quarter of an hour together (with Geddes also present) before the conference began. Lloyd George agreed to this, but as soon as lunch was over he 'hurried off to see M. Briand, in order, he said, to settle the programmes of the meeting. He was closeted with Briand for over half-an-hour, and then sent word to say that we would go to the Conference straight away, and without any preliminary talk with me and Geddes.'[2] What Lloyd George and Briand said to each other we do not know; in the light of what later transpired, Haig had no doubt that 'at the meeting with Briand, the procedure which was followed at the Conference was decided upon'. Certainly what followed was extremely odd.

The Conference proper started at 3.30 p.m., and, after a few introductory words from Lloyd George and Briand, passed straight to the question of transport. Thereupon it became, inevitably, somewhat technical, as discussion proceeded between Geddes and the French experts, M. Claveille (Minister of Transport) and General Raguenau. This was evidently not to Lloyd George's taste, and after a time he 'broke in and said that he thought it would be better if the railway specialists withdrew and settled their differences together, whilst the more important question of "Plans" was dealt with at once. For me this was quite a new and unexpected development. But doubtless this had all been planned by L.G. with Briand beforehand. The conference on transportation thus broke up after sitting for barely an hour'. The railway experts accordingly withdrew, and tea was taken. It was about 5.30 when the second part of the Conference resumed. Lloyd George at once called upon Nivelle to speak.

Nivelle acknowledged the fact that Haig had 'helped him in every way' and the 'accord' which existed between them. He then explained his Plan once more – familiar enough ground to everyone present. Again, Lloyd George displayed symptoms of impatience and dissatisfaction, and when Nivelle finished and asked if there were any questions, he 'said "that is not all – I want to hear everything" and to Briand he said, "Tell him to keep nothing back"

1. Derby to Haig, March 3rd, 1917.
2. Haig Diary: Duff Cooper gives the full entry; Blake's version is edited.

and so forth "as to his disagreements with Marshal Haig". This was quite a surprise to me, and apparently to Nivelle to some extent, for he said there was only the one point on which questions had arisen between us, namely regarding my arrangements for the attack near Arras – and he then explained how he had suggested to me not to extend my left so far north as the Vimy ridge, but to have a wider front of attack on the south side of the Scarpe. He stated he did not know exactly why I had not fallen in with his suggestion.'

Nivelle, remarks Spears, 'had not taken his cue'. The next phase of the discussion became technical again, with Haig explaining his reasons for including the Vimy ridge among his objectives (partly to cover the left flank of his advance, and partly because the ridge was 'a very important position for us to hold from a defensive view'), and for not extending further south ('. . . our advance would be held up immediately by the Hindenburg line. In fact, we attacked in a pocket.'). His explanation convinced at least one listener – the French Minister of War, General Lyautey. Encouraged by his approval, Haig went on to add that all this was a matter of tactics, and that while he would do his 'utmost to comply with the strategical requirements of Nivelle's plan . . . in the matter of tactics I alone could decide.' Once again Lloyd George intervened; he 'at once said, "he did not understand about strategy and tactics, he would like it clearly stated what the respective responsibilities were". It was then about 6.45 p.m. He therefore asked the French to draw up their proposals for a *system of command* before dinner, so that he, Robertson and I could discuss it after dinner, and a subsequent conference with the French Govt. would then be held tomorrow morning to decide finally. This was agreed to'.

For the second time that day, Lloyd George found absence a useful resource; he and Hankey took a walk in Calais; he did not appear at dinner, pleading 'illness'. Haig sat between Lyautey and Nivelle, and they all had 'quite a cheery talk'. Cheer, however, was rapidly dispelled once the meal was over. 'After dinner I went to Robertson's room and found him most excited over a typed paper which L.G. had given him containing the French proposals.' This is an understatement. Robertson had received the French proposals just as he was finishing his own dinner in company with his assistant, General Maurice. Spears writes: 'As a stimulus to good digestion they were a failure. Wully's face went the colour of mahogany, his eyes became perfectly round, his eyebrows slanted outwards like a forest of bayonets held at the charge – in fact he showed every sign of having a fit. "Get 'Aig", he bellowed. . . .'

Their joint inspection of the French document did little to reduce these apoplectic symptoms. The French proposals, which we now know had been drawn up several days before,[1] were, to say the least, 'cool'. They arrogated

1. Spears: p. 148.

to the French Commander-in-Chief full authority over the British forces in the West in everything which concerned operations, '... *et notamment:*

> *Le plan et l'exécution des actions offensives et défensives;*
> *Le groupement des forces en armées et groupes d'armées;*
> *Les limites entre ces grandes unités;*
> *La répartition des moyens matériels et ressources de toute nature entre les Armées.'*

A British Chief of Staff was to be appointed to French Headquarters, with a Quartermaster-General and staff under him; this Chief of Staff would be the vehicle through which Nivelle's orders to the British Army would be transmitted, and he would have direct access to the War Cabinet. The only matters specifically left to the direction of the British Commander-in-Chief were those affecting Personnel and Discipline; in other words, he would become a glorified Adjutant-General. In addition: '*Au cas où le Commandant-en-Chef Français disparaîtrait, ses attributions passeraient au nouveau Commandant-en-Chef Français à moins de décision nouvelle des deux Comités de Guerre.'*

The reaction of Haig and Robertson to this paper was similar only in one respect: both agreed that it was unworkable and deplorable. Beyond that, their temperaments and situations shaped their responses differently. Because they shared so many opinions about the conduct of the War, there has always been a tendency in historical writing to 'bracket' them, as though they felt and acted as one. This was not the case. Their personal relations were not particularly close; Haig, on the whole, respected Robertson; Robertson admired Haig. But Haig, preoccupied with the running of his great command, and unfamiliar with the feverish atmosphere of Whitehall during these dark days, failed to understand or fully sympathize with Robertson's problems. On January 6th, for example, we find Northcliffe telling Haig that he was not impressed with the C.I.G.S.: 'He said, "You call him Wully. I think Woolly would suit him better because he is not firm enough." There seems some truth in this opinion because the British Forces are not yet being concentrated at the decisive front, i.e., in France.' As far back as August, 1916, Lord Esher had found it necessary to write to Haig: 'If the combination of you and Robertson were to fail, no other is possible. . . . In any case, this old man alone stands between you and vacillating political counsels. . . . No C.-in-C. can withstand the stab in the back, which he is bound to get from people at home, unless he has someone to interpose a shield. This, I believe (until it is conclusively proved to the contrary), Robertson will do. Then, on the other hand, I am certain that any soldier situated as he is, in the mephitic atmosphere of the W.O., requires inspiration and breaths of fresh air from the C.-in-C. in the field. . . .' There is an element of pathos in the attempts of Robertson to extract this 'inspiration' and these 'breaths of fresh air' from Haig. Now, faced

by one of the most startling crises of his career, he must have found Haig's
attitude puzzling and irritating.

Together, the two soldiers went to see the Prime Minister. He, says Haig,
'now told us that the "War Cabinet had decided last week that since this was
likely to be the last effort of the French and they had the larger numbers engaged, in fact it was their battle", the British Army would be placed under
the French Commander-in-Chief's orders. He then asked my views. I said that
in my opinion it would be madness to place the British forces under the
French, and that I did not believe our troops would fight under French leadership. . . . He agreed that the French demands were excessive, but insisted
on Robertson and myself considering "a scheme for giving effect to the
War Cabinet's decision". I went with Robertson to his room. He seemed
thoroughly upset with the attitude of our Prime Minister. Colonel Hankey
. . . further added to our dissatisfaction by saying that "L.G. had not received
full authority from the War Cabinet" for acting as he was doing. General
Kiggell took part in our discussion and we agreed that we would rather be
tried by court-martial than betray the Army by agreeing to its being placed
under the French. Robertson agreed that we must resign rather than be partners in this transaction. And so we went to bed, thoroughly disgusted with
our Government and the politicians.'

Haig went to bed. Robertson did not. There is a quality of detachment
about Haig's narrative which strikes one even today. It gives no indication
that Robertson had argued furiously with Lloyd George against the French
paper, that tempers had risen high, that harsh words had been exchanged.
Nor does it suggest that a long night's work lay before Robertson and Maurice.
Haig, in fact, left the whole handling of the matter to the soldiers from the
War Office. No doubt he felt that, since his personal position was at stake, he
could not act otherwise. It is possible to detect here an immobility, deliberately
cultivated, similar to that which he had displayed when the question of Sir
John French was in debate. This was undoubtedly 'correct'; but one sympa-
thizes with Robertson, who had to handle the business, in his perplexities.

The next day, a new and hitherto somewhat enigmatic character came
into the foreground: Hankey, who had certainly been aware of at least part
of Lloyd George's intention, who had already given him valuable aid, who
admired him very much, but who was also a much wiser and better informed
man. Although belonging to another Service (Royal Marines), Hankey understood the substance within the objections of the Army leaders to Nivelle's
proposals. We need not question too deeply Lloyd George's statement that
the French paper went further than he had intended – it could scarcely have
been more sweeping. Within the narrow margin between what Lloyd George
wanted and what the French proposed, Hankey saw a space for manoeuvre

The King with Haig and his Army commanders: *left to right*, Birdwood, Rawlinson, Plumer, H.M. the King, Haig, Horne, Byng. (*Imperial War Museum*)

Field-Marshal Sir John French in August 1915. (*Imperial War Museum*)

Lord Kitchener and Sir William
Robertson (*Radio Times Hulton
Picture Library*)

Sir Henry Wilson. (*Radio Times
Hulton Picture Library*)

Generals John and Sir Hubert Gough.
(*Radio Times Hulton Picture Library*)

Brigadier-General Charteris being
presented to Queen Mary at Blendec-
ques in 1917. (*Imperial War Museum*)

Sir Herbert Lawrence

Sir Lancelot Kiggell. (*Mansell Collection*)

Sir John Monash with the Australian Prime Minister Mr Hughes and Lord
Burnham in September 1918. (*Imperial War Museum*)

King Albert of the Belgians with Sir
Hubert Gough, May 1917. (*Imperial
War Museum*)

Sir Edmund Allenby with Spanish
generals, March 1917. (*Imperial War
Museum*)

Lord Haldane. (*Radio Times Hulton
Picture Library*)

Mr Asquith. (*Radio Times Hulton
Picture Library*)

Lloyd George with (*left to right*) Thomas, Haig and Joffre, September 1916.
(*Imperial War Museum*)

Major Winston Churchill with General Fayolle in 1915. Captain Spears stands third from left. (*Imperial War Museum*)

Lord Curzon and Lord Milner. (*Radio Times Hulton Picture Library*)

Lord Derby. (*Radio Times Hulton Picture Library*)

Joffre, Haig and Foch at Beauquesne,
August 1916. (*Imperial War Museum*)

General Nivelle. (*Radio Times Hulton
Picture Library*)

Pétain at Metz in December 1918, when he was presented with the Baton
of a Marshal of France. Behind him, Joffre, Foch, Haig, Pershing, Gillain
(Belgium), Albricci (Italy), Haller (Poland). (*Imperial War Museum*)

Lord Balfour with Haig in the grounds of the Trianon Palace, July 1918.
(*Imperial War Museum*)

Briand and Joffre in Paris, 1916. (*Radio Times Hulton Picture Library*)

Clemenceau with Haig at Doullens Station, April 1918. (*Imperial War Museum*)

Prince Rupprecht (*left*) and the Kaiser, 1917. (*Imperial War Museum*)

The Kaiser with von Below, 1917. (*Imperial War Museum*)

Von Falkenhayn. (*Mansell Collection*)

Ludendorff. (*Radio Times Hulton Picture Library*)

General Pershing (*right*) and General Currie at Canadian Corps H.Q., April 1918. (*Imperial War Museum*)

Somme mud: taking ammunition along the Lesboeufs Road outside Flers,
November 1916. (*Imperial War Museum*)

German prisoners, Amiens, August 1918. (*Imperial War Museum*)

Tuesday 20 July.

Fine day - slight fall in glass -
Situation normal..

At 10.30 a.m. I attended some experiments
carried out at a disused Coal pit ab.t 2 mile
S. W. of Sillery under the arrangements of the
[O.C Indian Cav. Corps. The object of the experiment
was to test a bomb howitzer invented by a
man called Stokes - (a maker of ploughs
& harrows). The idea and the whole apparatus
is very simple.. An ordinary piece of
metal piping about 3 ft long is the howitzer.
The shell contains 56 lb. of high explosive -
in the base of the shell is a metal chamber
perforated with holes: into this is fitted
an ordinary 12 bore shot-gun cartridge
containing 120 grs of ballistite (instead of the
usual small charge).

To fire the gun, it is merely necessary to drop the
shell into the muzzle of the gun; the shell

and compromise. Robertson and Maurice were not likely to perceive this, since their attitude was governed by the strongest objection on principle as well as on practical grounds to the whole matter. Nor did Haig give them much help. Before breakfast, he drew up a short note for the C.I.G.S. and gave it to Robertson, 'requesting him to put it before L.G. and that I would not go to see him unless sent for'. In this note Haig said:

'In my opinion, there are only two alternatives, viz.,

1. To leave matters as they are now.

or

2. To place the British Army in France entirely under the French Commander-in-Chief.

'The decision to adopt the second of these proposals must involve the disappearance of the British Commander-in-Chief, and G.H.Q. What further changes would be necessary must depend on the French Commander-in-Chief and the French Government under whom he acts.

'So drastic a change in our system at a moment when active operations on a large scale have already commenced seems to me to be fraught with the gravest danger.'

With this Robertson had to be content, when he resumed his wrangle with the Prime Minister.

His mood was not improved by an interview with Nivelle, who professed complete surprise at the turn the Conference had taken. Prompted, no doubt, by what Roberston said, Nivelle (with Lyautey) then saw Haig, and both spoke to him of the ' "insult offered to me and the British Army by the paper which Briand had produced." They assured me that they had not seen the document until quite recently. Indeed, as regards Lyautey, he had not seen or heard of it until he entered the train at Paris to come to Calais. . . .' Lyautey was a man of rectitude; his word is evidence enough that the French had come prepared. Nivelle was not telling the full truth; but on his side, it seems likely that he was being truthful when he told Robertson that he 'never imagined that a proposal of this kind, communicated to him a fortnight before the conference took place by an officer attached to my staff, would be put forward by the Prime Minister not only without consulting me, but entirely without my knowledge'. Robertson's interview later with Lloyd George was as stormy as the preceding one. Nothing he could say, however, could shift Lloyd George from his determination to place the British Army under the French. A complete impasse, involving the break-up of the Conference, and an open clash between the Prime Minister and the C.I.G.S., was avoided by the address of Hankey, who produced a new draft proposal which included two important modifications of the French scheme: first, the subordination of the British Army was only to be for a limited period – the duration of the Nivelle offensive; secondly, Haig was given the right of appeal to the British Government, should he consider that the safety of the British Army was imperilled by the orders which he received from Nivelle. This formula was the only positive result of the whole transaction, because it was later embodied in the agreement by which Foch became Allied Generalissimo, in 1918. Such a proviso was, in fact, an essential element in the Unity of Command, when that command was exercised by a foreign officer fighting on his own soil and lacking an integrated Staff. And with this Robertson had to be content:

'The Prime Minister asked me if the final draft compelled Haig to obey Nivelle's order like a French commander. I said "Yes" and he replied that was what the Cabinet wished. During the day the agreement was signed by the delegates of both countries, including Haig and myself.'

But for Hankey, it is hard to see how a crisis of the most serious nature could have been avoided. On the other hand, compromise had its dangers too; it depends very much on the spirit in which it is applied, and that in turn depends considerably on the frame of mind engendered by the foregoing negotiations. It will be appreciated that this could scarcely be a happy one; as Repington commented, when he learned what had taken place: 'A bad business, and sure to breed endless mischief.' Haig's immediate comment was: 'It is too sad at this critical time to have to fight with one's Allies and the Home Government, in addition to the enemy in the Field.'

On this note the Calais Conference ended. Robertson lost no time in setting out the full story for the benefit of the War Cabinet. Haig, for the only time on his own initiative, addressed the King. He related all that had happened at Calais, and tried to interpret the final agreement as simply a formal expression of his own policy (as instructed by Kitchener) of 'closest co-operation of French and British as a united Army'. Indeed, his argument against formal Unity of Command was always that, under Joffre, it had existed in practice, and, given the same relationship based on trust, no special arrangement was necessary. Haig now wrote: 'I think, as the actual document stands, no difficulty should occur in carrying on just as I have been doing, *provided* there is not something behind it.' This was, indeed, the crux of the problem, and it could only be revealed by Nivelle and Lloyd George. Haig concluded:

'Your Majesty will observe that in my dealings with Mr. Lloyd George over this question, I have never suggested that I would like to resign my command,[1] but on the contrary, I have done my utmost to meet the views of the

---

1. Though such a step had been in his mind.

Government, as any change of Command at this time might be a disadvantage to the Army in the Field. It is possible, however, that the present War Cabinet may think otherwise, and deem it best to replace me by someone else more in their confidence. If this is so, I recommend that the change be made as soon as possible, because of the proximity of the date fixed for the commencement of offensive operations. At this great crisis in our History, my sole object is to serve my King and Country wherever I can be of most use, and with full confidence I leave myself in Your Majesty's hands to decide what is best for me to do at this juncture.'

The King was greatly disturbed; Lord Stamfordham, replying for him, wrote: 'The King begs you to dismiss from your mind any idea of resignation. Such a course would be in His Majesty's opinion disastrous to his Army and to the hopes of success in the coming supreme struggle. You have the absolute confidence of that Army from the highest to the lowest ranks: a confidence which is shared in full by the King. Such a step would never have His Majesty's consent, nor does he believe that it is entertained for a moment by his Government.

'The King is sorry to think that in the few weeks which yet remain for the completion of your arrangements for the attack your mind should be occupied and disturbed by a matter which everyone naturally presumed would have been settled as a primary factor in the initiation of this important and far-reaching undertaking.

'In conclusion I am to say from His Majesty you are not to worry: you may be certain that he will do his utmost to protect your interests, and he begs you to work on the most amicable and open terms with General Nivelle, and he feels all will come right.'

The King's optimism was ill-founded. On the very day that the Calais agreement was signed, Nivelle sent a letter to Haig which revealed clearly what his interpretation of their respective roles was. Its tone was peremptory; it was, said Haig, 'a type of letter which no gentleman could have drafted, and it also is one which certainly no C. in C. of this great British Army should receive without protest'. Robertson did his best to soothe Haig's feelings, but this was not easy. Not the least objectionable of Nivelle's demands was the immediate appointment of Sir Henry Wilson to be Chief of the British Mission at G.Q.G., and therefore the agent through whom Haig would receive Nivelle's orders. There were those at G.H.Q. who found it easy to believe that the hand of Henry Wilson was visible in all the Calais proceedings; this was not true. But it was not easy for Robertson to persuade Haig to accept him. Robertson himself was full of misgivings; on March 3rd, he wrote to Haig: 'We ought not to have *signed* the document. Still we did, and the

only thing is to get it quite clear . . . I think you may have great difficulties in
carrying out the hybrid arrangement. I trusted to Nivelle to play the game.
It all depends upon him and I hardly dare trust him.' Nivelle, on his side, was
convinced that Haig was trying to obstruct the conclusions reached at Calais.
To the extent that Haig was interpreting them in the manner which he described to the King, this was correct. By March 7th, matters had come to a
head, and Briand complained to the British Government, requesting that
Haig should be ordered without delay to conform to the decisions of the
Conference and to Nivelle's instructions. This time, however, Briand had
misjudged the climate of British opinion.

Now that they were fully informed, and had had an opportunity of understanding the issues that were at stake, the War Cabinet found the Calais solution increasingly distasteful. 'The exception,' says Robertson, 'was the Prime
Minister, to whose initiative the curtailment of Haig's powers had been
mainly due, and who now suspected him of seeking to regain them by the
creation of difficulties where none existed. Undoubtedly Haig's aim was to
secure a degree of control proportionate to his responsibilities, but it was not
the fact that he deliberately raised difficulties in order that the agreement
might break down. They were real and fundamental, and were bound to present themselves whatever the action of Haig might be.' This was indeed true;
the War itself was attending to that. For a brief space longer, Nivelle remained
sublimely aloof to the consequences of the manoeuvres which the Germans
were now conducting openly under his nose; for a few more days his preoccupation was that full 'command' of the British Army which had come so
dazzlingly close at Calais. Noting the receipt of another 'Instruction' from
Nivelle on March 7th, Haig remarked: 'It is difficult to receive these communications with patience. He, however, has gone beyond the letter and also
the spirit of the Calais Agreement. I suppose in time, if I give him enough
rope, he will hang himself! Meantime the process is annoying for me, and a
waste of time which ought to be devoted to thinking out plans for beating
the enemy, instead of replies to Nivelle.' The next day Robertson told him
the result of Briand's *démarche*: there was to be another conference of the
French and British leaders, in London. 'This time we must be careful to sign
nothing to which we do not agree', wrote Robertson. 'We must also try to
regain control over our Armies.'

The London Conference on March 12th, went a long way to redress the
damage that had been done at Calais. Lord Hankey attributes this happy result to the 'dexterity and resource' of Lloyd George; this is undoubtedly true
in a limited sense, but avoids the point that solidly united British opinion (even
Bonar Law disliked the Calais Agreement) had persuaded the Prime Minister
to change his tune. Two very significant modifications of the existing position

were arrived at – with surprisingly little difficulty, once the French perceived that the British side was not, this time, divided: first, it was agreed that Nivelle should not communicate directly with London, but should do so only through Haig; secondly, it was clearly stated that 'All the British troops stationed in France remain in all circumstances under the orders of their own chiefs and of the British Commander-in-Chief.' A second section dealt with the functions of the British Mission at G.Q.G., of which Wilson was to be the Head; it was agreed that all instructions or communications transmitted by him to Haig, must, except in some remarkable emergency, bear Nivelle's signature. Wilson's responsibilities to Haig were as clearly stated as his duties to Nivelle. And with this saner compromise, all parties had to be content. Haig signed the new agreement, adding this note:

'I agree with the above on the understanding that, while I am fully determined to carry out the Calais agreement in spirit and letter, the British Army and its Commander-in-Chief will be regarded by General Nivelle as allies and not as subordinates, except during the particular operations which he explained at the Calais Conference.

'Further, while I also accept the agreement respecting the functions of the British Mission at French Head-quarters, it should be understood that these functions may be subject to modifications as experience shows to be necessary.'

Haig was not the only one with reservations; the next day he noted: 'At 6 p.m. I received Sir Henry Wilson and Gen. Kiggell. . . . The former put forward very straightforwardly his reasons against going to French G.H.Q. as the head of the British Mission. Briefly, he felt sure that whatever he did he would be credited with intriguing against the C. in C. I told him that he would have my complete confidence in military matters, and that, looking to the future and the possibility that Nivelle's plans might not meet with a full measure of success, it seemed most desirable to have a senior British Officer and one who is trusted by the French at Nivelle's H.Q. So we decided that he should go to Beauvais.' Haig's decision to trust Wilson, despite a deep antipathy towards him, was not misplaced. Few periods in Wilson's career reflect so much credit on him as the one that followed; those Frenchmen who expected to find him a willing tool were disappointed; he remained at all times loyal to British interests and to the British Commander-in-Chief.

And so ended what Lloyd George and his supporters are disposed to describe as his first essay at the Unity of Command which he believed to be essential for winning the War – and, they would add, time proved him to be right, although there was all the difference in the world between making the British Army a contingent in the French Army, and subordinating both

C.-in-C.s to a Generalissimo. Others may see in the Calais affair something different: an expedient by which Lloyd George was seeking to by-pass and relegate two military leaders whose policies he detested, whom he found personally antipathetic, but whom he dared not dismiss.

Lord Hankey says that as late as the morning before the London Conference assembled, Lloyd George was still considering getting rid of Haig, and consulting Hankey on this subject: '. . . I made him a long speech . . . weighing all the pros and cons and winding up strongly in favour of Haig. He didn't like it, as he wanted me to report the other way, and argued and contested my points hotly, as he paced up and down the long Cabinet room.' One thing is certain: a cloud of mistrust was created at Calais which was never dispelled during the whole of the remainder of the War. Not only were new difficulties added to those (sufficiently formidable) which already existed in the relations of French and British Headquarters, but a special brand of poison was injected into the relations between the British Government and its leading soldiers. Neither Haig nor Robertson could ever bring themselves to trust Lloyd George again; he, for his part, endured an agony of frustration at their continued existence which led him inexorably to yet more devices. Much of the shrill hysteria which characterizes so large a part of his *War Memoirs* may be attributed to this. All in all, the Calais Conference may be regarded as a self-inflicted Allied defeat, a wretched and untimely aid to the enemy, one of the major tragedies of the War. Its full import would shortly be revealed.

*   *   *   *

The German retreat to the Hindenburg Line was conducted with great skill. It began, as we have seen, on the front of the British Fifth Army, then steadily extended a little way to the north, to the Third Army Front, and a long way to the south, along the fronts of the British Fourth Army, the French Northern Army Group (Franchet d'Esperey) and Reserve Army Group (Micheler), which was designed to be the spearhead of Nivelle's attack. The Germans fell back very deliberately, covered by stubborn rearguards which made good use of their machine guns. They left a zone of utter destruction behind them – a 'scorched earth', in which everything that could be of use to the advancing Allies was smashed and laid waste. Even the fruit trees in the orchards were cut down. Roads and buildings were mined; there were booby-traps everywhere. The weather was foul, the ground sodden. 'Pursuit' by the Allied Armies, no matter how vehemently ordered by their higher commanders, was hardly more than a pious hope; often the Allied advance guards were completely out of touch with the retiring enemy. The Cavalry, the only weapon of exploitation that they possessed, was seen to be almost completely ineffective in these circumstances. It has to be stated that the arm was not well handled; the French, in particular, held their horsemen in heavy masses, and these masses remained generally fixed in immobility by the prevailing conditions. But cavalry and infantry alike, after years of trench warfare, had lost the habit and art of movement. Broad horizons and empty country bewildered and frightened them; long dependence on massive artillery support created another inhibition, and further delays occurred as the guns struggled forward along the mined and miry roads. When every tribute is paid to German skill, there remains a degree of Allied ineptitude to account for the missing of what might have been a great opportunity of inflicting damage.

Nowhere was this ineptitude more vividly revealed than at G.Q.G. Perhaps the most astonishing element in the whole Nivelle story is the staggering self-confidence which he displayed in his early days of command. If the Germans timed their withdrawal well, it was certainly no problem for them to do so. Nivelle had made no attempt whatever to keep his intentions secret. As early as December 28th, 1916, Robertson wrote to Haig: '[Nivelle] very stupidly sent to the French Government his whole plan which he had previously given to you. This was sent to our Foreign Office and was hectographed off in the usual manner and I suppose there are now dozens of copies about London to say nothing about Paris. I know of about 10 copies that have been distributed about London. I myself did not in the end send it even to the War Cabinet. It would be well if you could get Nivelle to adopt a different procedure.'

Haig, however, now had other matters to attend to, and in any case the damage was done. The great attack was a subject of common gossip in the offices and salons of both capitals. The assurance which permitted this freedom of speech extended to the contemplation of the new situation created by the German withdrawal. As soon as Franchet d'Esperey became aware of what the Germans were about, he urged upon G.Q.G. that his Army Group should immediately launch a general attack. G.Q.G. steadily refused to take any notice of the changing position, or to alter its own plans. 'To admit that the enemy was about to retire and evacuate the salient it had been intended to pinch out', says Spears, 'was to admit failure, that Joffre had been right and Nivelle wrong'. For three weeks Nivelle held out against d'Esperey's urgings; when that dynamic general was at last permitted to go after the enemy, it was too late.

We have seen that Haig's first reaction to the news of the German retirement was one of unjustified optimism. It did not take him long to arrive at a more sober conclusion. The day after the Calais Conference ended, Charteris brought him more evidence of the scope of the German movement. This was on February 28th; from this point onwards, the divergence between Haig's interpretation of events and Nivelle's became acute; this was, indeed, the cause of the misunderstandings between them which led to the London meeting.

Haig wrote, after hearing Charteris's news: 'I discussed the situation with General Kiggell. He agrees with me that indications are mounting that the enemy is preparing for a big decisive stroke, either against the Western Front or against Russia . . . I decide to send my views on this matter . . . to the C.I.G.S. for submission to the War Cabinet. The latter have handed over the Army to the French for "Nivelle's battle", so it is necessary to open their eyes to possible dangers. The advisability of launching N.'s battle at all grows daily less, and so the Calais agreement may not perhaps be of any use to them.'

Haig's growing concern, during this perplexing period before German intentions became clear, was with the very safety of his Army. On March 2nd, he and Kiggell thrashed the whole question out together, and composed a considered statement for the War Cabinet. First, they discussed German motives: '[The enemy] cannot afford to stand as he did last year on the Somme and suffer destruction. He has therefore organized the area in rear of the threatened front to enable his troops to slip away. . . . His new line, called the "Hindenburg Line" is 60 kilometres shorter than his present one, so that he will economize 12 divisions (about) once he has reached his new line. This latter is said to be immensely strong, and has been constructed at the enemy's leisure. . . . His objects seem to be: To disorganize our offensive by causing our attacks to be made in the air, and so to cause us loss of time; to wear out our troops by causing us at each stage to renew our preparations for attack; to delay us (these preparations take much time to organize for each successive advance); to affect the moral of the Allies by disappointment at seeing the enemy able to escape at each successive stage, in spite of the greatest efforts made to prevent this. But the enemy means to gain victory and will spare no effort and stick at nothing. We must expect a gigantic hostile attack somewhere.'

Only in the last part of this assessment was Haig at fault, and this was a mistake of over-caution. We know now that the German High Command was *not*, in fact, planning a large land offensive. Their motive was defensive: 'The general situation', says Ludendorff, 'made it necessary for us to postpone the struggle in the West as long as possible, in order to allow the submarine campaign time to produce decisive results. Tactical reasons and a shortage of ammunition provided additional reasons for delay. At the same time it was necessary to shorten our front in order to secure a more favourable grouping of our forces and create larger reserves.' As ill-informed as the Allies as to the true state of Russia, Ludendorff, so far from planning an attack in the East, actually feared a heavy onslaught on the Austrians. Haig was not to know this. 'The Germans', he wrote, in his official letter, 'are whole-hearted believers in the principle that an offensive on the greatest possible scale, driven home with the utmost rapidity, violence, and determination, is the only method of forcing a quick decision.'

Haig might, in these words, have been prophetically describing the great German attack of 1918; what he did not possess was the knowledge that in 1917 they were depending wholly on the submarine. Correspondingly, he became extremely anxious about the direction of a possible German attack. He considered the Russian front, but was inclined to dismiss it 'unless the internal state of Russia is judged to be such that a considerable German tactical success would lead her to immediate collapse'. What no one knew was that this collapse would be brought about *even without* a German attack. Failing the Russian front, Haig's eyes were drawn to his own most sensitive area, the northern part of his line around Ypres, where it ran close to the sea and where 'the capture of our communications with England would mean the end of the war both for England and France'.

He ended: 'The prospects of a decisive tactical success for the Germans, on the Western front, would undoubtedly be greatest if their attack were launched at a moment when the reserves of the French and British Armies had already been committed to an offensive on some other portion of the front – always provided the allied attack could be held in check until the German attack had gained a decision. . . .

'Are we justified in relying on the proposed allied attack this spring turning him from his purpose, whatever that may be, before he has carried it through to success or failure?

'In my opinion the information so far available does not justify a final decision now on this point. . . .

'. . . on the present indications, I consider that the safety of the British Armies might be gravely endangered if I were to commit my forces beyond recall to any enterprise which would deprive me of the power to meet developments which appear to be possible, and perhaps even probable.

'For these reasons I consider that until the enemy's intentions become clearer sufficient reserves must be retained in my own hands, and especially in the Second Army area, to meet whatever action it is reasonably possible for the enemy to take. . . .'

Nivelle's reaction to this dispassionate reasoning was entirely predictable; it followed the pattern of his responses to Franchet d'Esperey. Haig told him on March 4th, what was in his mind, and Nivelle lost no time in replying. He refused to accept that the German withdrawal was likely to extend further than the front of the British Fifth Army. He asserted that the Hindenburg Line could now be taken in flank by both the British and French main attacks, and continued in words whose flavour can only be fully rendered by the original French:

'*Sous ce rapport, le mouvement de repli allemand serait donc, même s'il se généralisait, tout à notre avantage; et je base sur cette constatation une première décision qui est de n'apporter aucune modification fundamentale au plan générale d'opérations qui est arrêté; et en particulier, de maintenir la date fixée pour le déclenchement de nos attaques...*'

From this decision not to make any concession to the change in the situation caused by the German manoeuvre Nivelle refused to be shaken, either by the pleas of his friends or by the further actions of his enemies. But from this time forward the tone of his utterances was to be dictated more and more by desperation, and less and less by the assurance which had originally inspired them. Nivelle's own hour of tribulation was at hand.

On the day that the London Conference assembled to bring harmony into the strained relations of the French and British High Commands, Revolution broke out in Petrograd. The consequences of this were not foreseen – how could they be? At the time, there was a disposition in all the Western democracies to greet the event with approval; the Tsar's autocracy had always been an embarrassment to the high ideals with which the *Entente* sought to identify itself. It was even hoped that under a more democratic régime Russia might prosecute the War with renewed vigour. On the other hand, tremors of trepidation were also bound to be felt; even if Russia should gain new strength in the future, a present weakness was inevitable. The strain on Britain and France was bound to be increased: a new perplexity was born. At this juncture, when the need for authority and decision in Allied counsels was at its greatest, the Briand Ministry fell. On March 18th, the seventy-five-year-old lawyer Ribot formed a new Government, in which the Minister of War was Painlevé, a distinguished mathematician who himself became Prime Minister later in the year. Painlevé did not believe in Nivelle.

The full story of Nivelle's fall from grace cannot be told here.[1] What is interesting is to see that the French politicians, faced with a crisis in the conduct of the War, were no more adept at dealing with it than their British counterparts. Painlevé was no sooner in office than he became aware of a deluge of criticism of Nivelle's Plan both from within the French Army itself, and in political quarters. Two potent names in particular were associated with this: Freycinet, the elder statesman who had been a colleague of Gambetta in the organizing of the Armies of National Resistance during the War of 1870–71,

---

1. The best English account is by Spears, in *Prelude to Victory*.

and who had subsequently been Minister of War several times; and Messimy, also an ex-Minister of War, a Member of the Chamber of Deputies, and now also a Divisional Commander at the front. Besides these powerful voices, there was that of General Micheler, Commander of the Reserve Army Group; from the Headquarters of this clever but unstable officer there poured a stream of critical opinion which filled the new Minister and all who heard it with alarm. It was also known that General Pétain, Commander of the Centre Group, was extremely doubtful of the whole operation, though neither he nor his Staff were as vocal as Micheler and his subordinates. Painlevé was entirely at a loss as to how to act, as Lloyd George had been, though in justice to the Frenchman it has to be admitted that his problem was much more difficult, since he was faced with a clash of opinion at the highest levels of the Army itself. His solution was, nevertheless, no happier than Lloyd George's: he held a series of private interviews with the Army Group Commanders, at which Nivelle was not present, and without his consent. One by one, Micheler, Pétain and Franchet d'Esperey expressed their doubts to the Minister; all three were convinced that the German withdrawal, and clear signs of German preparations to meet the attack where they had not withdrawn, now made the full implementation of Nivelle's scheme most unlikely, while the attempt to carry off the big prize, in their opinion, was damaging to the prospects of valuable, smaller successes. Painlevé then confronted Nivelle with this evidence. But Nivelle was able to rally the last shreds of his assurance, and brushed aside the doubts of his subordinates. Painlevé permitted himself to be re-convinced. This was on April 3rd; the following day, the British bombardment opened on the Arras front, where their great diversion was all set to begin Nivelle's battle. On the 5th Painlevé received a formidable Memorandum from Messimy, urging that for the safety of the Army and the nation, the whole operation should be postponed and reshaped. In deep agitation, the Minister called yet another conference to decide what should be done; this took place within three days of the opening of the British attack, within ten days of the French one.

The conference took place at Compiègne (where G.Q.G. now dwelt) on the day that the United States of America declared war on Germany, April 6th. Leading the political side were the President of the Republic, Poincaré, the Prime Minister, Ribot, and Painlevé; on the military side were Nivelle, de Castelnau, Micheler, Pétain and Franchet d'Esperey. If anything, the proceedings were even more deplorable than those of the Calais Conference. Micheler, the fount of 'sedition', revealed his lack of character in a series of equivocal utterances which left the Ministers at a loss; the other Group Commanders, Pétain particularly, expressed professional doubts with precision but diffidence, which was only natural in the circumstances. Nivelle was furious, and offered his resignation. This was hastily refused, and the conference broke up in the most inconclusive manner, its sole decision being to take no decision, to leave matters as they were, to permit the offensive to go on. The whole business, says Spears, 'stands as a monument to the inefficiency of democracy at war, to the helplessness of Ministers facing technicians, and their total inability to decide between different professional opinions'.

For British students, there was yet another moral; Spears adds: 'The seed planted at Calais bore fruit at Compiègne. The British forces were under the orders of the French Commander-in-Chief, but the French C.-in-C. was under the control of the French Cabinet, who, in an emergency such as occurred, did not hesitate to use their powers without reference to the British Government. It was now quite evident that our Cabinet had abdicated its powers in favour not of a French general but of the French Government.'

The sole beneficial result of the weakening of Nivelle's position *vis-à-vis* his own Government was the improvement which it brought about in his relations with Haig: adversity proved to be a better bond than any signed agreement. On March 20th, a distinct amendment in the tone of communication between the two generals was perceptible, when Wilson told Haig: 'If the enemy goes on retiring [Nivelle] wants you to tell him what you think it all means, and what you think we ought to do in the future. . . . N. wants to know about your MESSINES scheme so as to see if he can fit in operations of his own if the retirement of the Boches knocks out the original scheme of great offensive.' This presented Haig with a cue he was not slow to take up. His own increasing conviction was that the only method to counteract the effects of repeated German withdrawals was to attack them in some region where they could not withdraw without serious danger to their communications: 'I am therefore in favour of at once going on with our preparations for attacking near Ypres. This may not suit the French!' The next day (March 21st) he addressed a long letter to Nivelle, explaining what was in his mind. If the Germans held to their present line 'it will still be my task to break through it towards Cambrai'. If the enemy continued to retire, however, the northern attack ought to be substituted for this; it would require some 35–40 divisions, and two months to prepare. On the other hand, it could be broken into phases, and the first of these (Messines) could take place in five or six weeks.

'The objective of the attack would be to reach the general line Courtrai–Roulers–Thourout as quickly as possible, opening the Dixmude defile to the Belgians, and forcing the enemy to evacuate Ostend.

'I should then continue to operate north-eastward and eastward, first to clear the Belgian coast and then to force the enemy to evacuate Belgium.

'A simultaneous attack along the coast from Nieuport would of course be highly advisable in combination with the operation described. Our Navy would also assist in any way possible, and I am sure that, under the assumed conditions, I should have all the help and co-operation that your Armies could give.

'In ordinary weather the ground would be quite fit for operations by the time my preparations could be complete, and indeed in fine weather it would be quite passable before that – probably by the end of this month.

'It is still quite possible that the enemy may anticipate any attack on my Second Army front by taking the offensive in that area himself. . . .'

In this letter one sees the clear outline of the Third Battle of Ypres as Haig would have wished it to be fought. There would be an early start (about the end of May), when, given normal weather, conditions would be at least reasonable. There would be subsidiary operations along the coast to assist the main attack. (Haig was being carefully reticent about his real intentions here, in view of Nivelle's proved lack of discretion; what he really had in mind was an amphibious assault, landing infantry and tanks from the sea.) There would be full French support. At the root of all the failures of 1917 lies the sad fact that, out of a plethora of plans, the British Army tried them all in bits. Nivelle still clung tenaciously to the remains of his own Plan; the Germans were clinging no less tenaciously to the positions they were now in, so that the Arras attack would have to go in; and Plumer reassured Haig that there was no sign of any German offensive preparation in the Ypres sector. When Nivelle came to visit Haig on the 23rd, he was decidedly in a mood of making amends; his habitual charm had full play, and he did nothing to challenge the views which Haig had set out: 'He is in complete agreement with me regarding the general plan, namely to launch our attacks as arranged and, if the enemy does not await our attack, to follow him up, and at the same time to organize attacks as soon as possible elsewhere.'

No doubt Nivelle was satisfied to find that Haig, at least, was sticking to the original undertaking. A long-absent cordiality between the two commanders was now seen: 'Nivelle was most pleasant, and I think is a straightforward man. . . . On the whole I like Nivelle; but he seems rather under the influence of Colonel d'Alençon, who dislikes the British.' Haig was not bearing malice. He was correct in attributing much of the unpleasantness of previous relations to d'Alençon, Nivelle's confidential Staff Officer and 'eminence grise', whose evil influences extended much further than mere Anglophobia. When Painlevé visited Haig next day ('a pleasant bright little man. Said to be a great mathematician and an extreme socialist') and questioned Haig about Nivelle as Lloyd George had questioned Foch before, the good impression of Nivelle's last visit was still with Haig: 'I was careful to say that he struck me

as a capable general, and that I was, of course, ready to co-operate with whoever was chosen by the French Government to be their Commander-in-
Chief. I said my relations with Nivelle are and have always been excellent.
The Calais conference was a mistake, but it was not Nivelle's fault.' Haig, of
course, did not know the full truth; his instinct to help a fellow soldier in
distress was responsible for the decidedly exaggerated statement that his
relations with Nivelle had always been 'excellent' (he had described the latter
once to Lady Haig as 'playing the "cad" '). It is not the least of the ironies of
this whole episode that the Ally whom Nivelle had tried to trick proved
more loyal to him than his own subordinates and compatriots.

*　*　*　*

The momentum of the drama increased; the climax approached. On
April 9th, Easter Monday, in driving sleet and icy rain the British attack
went in on the Arras front. It was launched by Allenby's Third Army on the
right, and Horne's First Army on the left, where the Canadian Corps faced
the Vimy Ridge. The Battle of Arras contained some of the bitterest fighting
of the whole war and caused severe loss to the British Army; much of this,
it must be sadly recorded, was waste. The features of the battle, briefly, were
these: first and foremost, it was an Artillery battle; the concentration of guns
was the largest yet seen on the British front – 2,879 in the Third and First
Armies, with another 519 on the subsidiary front of the Fifth Army. Haig's
main criticism of Allenby's original plan centred around his doubts as to the
efficacy of a short bombardment. The Third Army had suggested a bombardment lasting only forty-eight hours; Haig objected to this, and told Allenby:

'. . . As a result of past experience, it may be said definitely that, in view of
the great and prolonged preparations required, the enemy cannot be surprised as to the general front of an attack on a large scale, but only to some
extent as to its exact limits and as to the moment of assault.

'It is also beyond question that wire must be adequately cut before an
assault is launched and that the assaulting infantry should be satisfied before
starting that it has been sufficiently cut. It is far from certain that a 48 hours'
bombardment will prove sufficient to cut it adequately. . . .'

This was, indeed the core of the tactical impasse which characterized so
many of the battles of the War: a long bombardment forfeited strategic
surprise, while a short one risked leaving the enemy's wire uncut. It was not
until tanks became available in numbers that the short bombardment came
into its own; at Arras, in April, 1917, owing to production difficulties and
priorities, only sixty tanks (Mark Is, many of them survivors of the Somme)

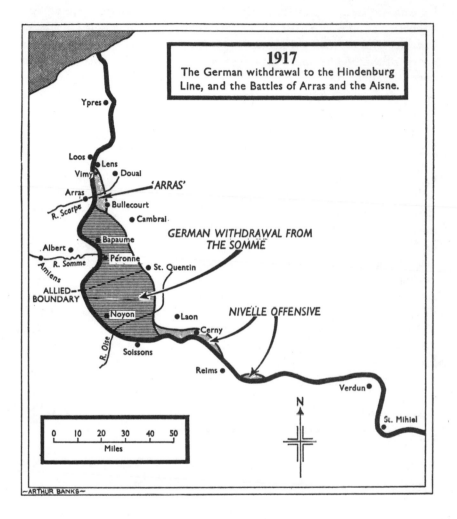

1917
The German withdrawal to the Hindenburg
Line, and the Battles of Arras and the Aisne.

Ypres

Loos • Lens
Vimy • Doual
Arras • 'ARRAS'
R. Scarpe • Bullecourt
• Cambrai

GERMAN WITHDRAWAL FROM
THE SOMME

• Bapaume
Albert •
R. Somme • Péronne
Amiens • St. Quentin
ALLIED
BOUNDARY

• Noyon • Laon
• Cerny
NIVELLE OFFENSIVE
R. Oise
Soissons
Reims •
Verdun •
St. Mihiel

N

0   10   20   30   40   50
Miles

~ARTHUR BANKS~

were present. Fully appreciating the need for surprise whenever possible, Haig pointed out to Allenby that a long bombardment, whatever its overall disadvantages might be, did offer opportunities for certain ruses (misleading variations of tempo in different sectors; stopping, so that the enemy manned his parapets, and then catching him with renewed fire, etc.). He added: 'Doubtless various such ruses, and others, are intended in the plan of attack, but there is no mention of them in the paper submitted. For these reasons the nature of the bombardment requires further consideration.' Allenby took these objections into account, and changed his plan; on April 2nd Haig recorded: 'The artillery arrangements of the Third Army are now quite satisfactory, and in accordance with [G.H.Q.] views on the subject.'

The second outstanding feature of the Battle of Arras was the remarkable success won on the first day – a happy contrast to the opening of the Somme. This was due to a number of causes, some of them local, others not. In the former category, the most striking feature was the skilful use of the network of cellars and galleries under the town of Arras. These were fitted with electricity and other necessary installations to house 25,000 troops, and tunnels were run from them into the front line itself, giving completely protected access to two divisions (and at the same time greatly helping to avoid congestion on normal lines of communication). Another local factor was the success of the tanks in assisting the capture of two formidable German defences: the Harp, and Telegraph Hill. But more significant than any of these were two more general considerations: the greater experience of British commanders, and the improved quality of the Army itself. The careful, meticulous planning which characterized the preparations of both the First and Third Armies, all carried out under the most difficult weather conditions, and, as we know, against the background of an acute transport crisis, is sufficient indication of the progress made by higher commanders and their Staffs. The Army, in the spring of 1917, had reached one of its peaks of the whole War – for the Citizen Army, which it now was, *the* peak. It may be said, truthfully enough, that it was still a long way short of the rare pitch of proficiency revealed by the first Expeditionary Force. It was, nevertheless, a decidedly different organism from that ardent but raw 'collection of divisions' which had gone into action on the Somme.

Despite the eternal grind of fatigue duties (especially in those areas taken over from the French), training had been going on vigorously all through the winter. Innovations (not all of them successful) based on battle experience were introduced and perfected: the self-contained platoon; the grouping of machine-gun battalions as part of the artillery barrage, etc. (Haig was a strong advocate of the grouping of automatic weapons, and even considered that the four Lewis guns which each infantry company now possessed 'might be handled more effectively if they were all grouped in one platoon under a commander'.) Familiarity with new weapons – flame-throwers, gas-canister-projectors, tanks when possible – was developed. New attack formations were practised. The artillery, especially, made great strides. On January 11th Haig noted: 'As regards artillery methods, we have nothing to learn [from the French]. Indeed, we were the first to adopt the time-table system which the French now use. On the other hand, the execution by the French gunners is better. This is not surprising seeing that their gunners have been trained for so much longer than our New Army men.'

It was, indeed, true that the vast expansion of the artillery arm had inevitably resulted in a lowering of technical standards. Fortunately, artillery casualties were rarely on the scale of those of the infantry; training could therefore be progressive, and veterans passed on their skill. Much improved munitions, including the invaluable '106' fuse, which exploded a shell on graze and thereby enormously eased the problem of wire-cutting, also helped the British Artillery to attain a new high level of proficiency which not only made a contribution to the battles of 1917, but in the following year played a major part in averting defeat. Behind the front, tremendous and ordered activity reigned. The rearward services were now mastering their jobs, although hampered by the continuing man-power shortage which brought any 'non-combatant unit' under repeated scrutiny. The system of Camps of Instruction and 'courses' for the study of every kind of military activity was in full swing, making further demands on man-power, but playing a vital part in the crammed training of new troops and officers.

In the air, the Royal Flying Corps was passing through a bleak period, during which the Germans were able to exploit one of the temporary advantages which the introduction of improved aircraft brought alternately to each side. Haig, whose interest in the Air Arm dated from his setback at the manoeuvres of 1912, had been aware of this situation for some time. As early as December 5th, 1916, after a discussion with Trenchard, 'I gave him a letter to the C.I.G.S. to again urge the necessity for placing orders without delay for a stronger type of engine.' Until this was provided, however, the Royal Flying Corps was at a grave disadvantage; all through January and February its losses were high. On February 16th, after another interview with Trenchard, Haig noted: 'Our pilots are having a hard time because the enemy have brought out a large number of new machines. But the spirit of our Flying men is excellent; the important thing in order to maintain moral is "to keep the breakfast table full". That is to fill up the casualties at once. Two days ago we had 16 officers casualties and yesterday 14.'

In March, as the date of the offensive approached, and the need to regain air supremacy became urgent, fighting increased in intensity, and the British situation did not improve. Haig recorded: 'The 17th March was a day of hard fighting. 30 pilots and observers were lost on that day and 6 machines were missing and 6 brought down. In the 10 days, 8th–18th, 79 pilots and observers have become casualties. . . . We have received 60 machines and engines from the French recently. This was very good of them.' Shortly afterwards the tide began to turn, and at the end of May Haig recorded: 'Trenchard . . . thinks enemy's losses are about 800 or more per month; ours were 420 for April.' This was still a serious rate of loss for an arm which had only been in existence for six years. The replacement problem, for the Flying Corps as well as for the Army as a whole, was harrowing; the scale of numbers employed was, of course, very different, but the expectation of life of the boy fliers, sent out with a minimum of training from England to face the enemy in inferior machines, was just as short as that of the young infantry subalterns in the line. It was not until the end of the year that the British regained real supremacy in the air.

The weakness of the British Army at this period, apart from the air struggle, was in its mobile element, and this weakness constitutes the third feature of the Arras fighting. The first day of the attack was a complete success; the Canadians captured almost the whole of the Vimy Ridge, while the Third and Fifth Armies moved rapidly on to their objectives further south. At Vimy the drama of the victory was most marked. 'Standing on the crest of the ridge', says Spears, '[the Canadians] gazed down on the level plain of Douai, the first Allied soldiers to do so since the far-off days of 1915, when for a few hours the French had held the northern extremity of the heights. It was an extraordinary sight, a glimpse of another world. Behind them lay an expanse of churned-up mud and desolation completely commanded from where they stood. . . . Below and beyond them on the German side lay a peaceful countryside with villages that appeared from a distance to be untouched by war. The men were wildly enthusiastic and their sense of victory was enhanced by finding battery after battery abandoned on the edge of the woods that fringed the eastern slopes of the ridge.'

These successes shocked the German Command; Ludendorff wrote: 'The battle of Arras on April 9th was a bad beginning for the decisive struggle of this year. . . . The consequences of a break-through of 12 to 15 kilometres wide and 6 or more kilometres deep are not easy to meet. In view of the heavy losses in men, guns and ammunition resulting from such a break-through, colossal efforts are needed to make good the damage.' So far, so good; the opening of the British contribution to Nivelle's offensive had exceeded what was expected of it (it will be remembered that Haig had had to argue energetically to include the Vimy Ridge among his objectives).

Ludendorff adds, however: 'The situation was extremely critical, and might have had far-reaching and serious consequences if the enemy had pushed further forward. But the British contented themselves with their great success and did not continue the attack, at least not on April 9th.'

It was not that the British 'contented themselves'; it was simply that the problems of movement were still beyond them. Everywhere along the line the attack 'stuck'. Neither commanders nor soldiers, after years of trench warfare, and particularly after the long, laborious, piecemeal struggle on the Somme, were able to make the instant adjustment to mobile warfare which such a break-through required. To be fair, it must be added that, in the pre-vailing conditions of the spring of 1917, they did not possess the weapons and resources which would have made the solution of their problem easier. The condition of the ground was, and remained, frightful; 1917 was undoubtedly the worst year of the whole War from the point of view of weather. The long bombardment had made this condition worse than ever; on April 12th, General Horne, commanding the First Army, told Haig that he 'thought he had used too many shells! It had broken up the soil so frightfully that all movement was now made most difficult'. At Vimy, none of the eight tanks which were allocated to the attack even reached their starting points. This was the defect of the artillery battle, this churning up of the landscape which rendered all movement well-nigh impossible, and made a mockery of mobility. The same thing was seen during the Second World War, after 'obliteration strikes' by heavy bombers; at Monte Cassino, at Caen and else-where, 'close support' proved more of a hindrance than a help. The only solution was the mass use of tanks, and only sixty tanks existed, despite Haig's pleas. Tanks would have shortened the bombardment; tanks would have speeded up the penetration. Failing tanks, resort was had to the only other available mobile arm – cavalry. The astonishing spectacle was seen of cavalry trying to charge in crater-fields; the result, as one might suppose, was high mounds of dead horses, much wasted gallantry, and no progress worth mentioning.

Nevertheless, when all allowance is made for material factors (and sooner or later these would have proved decisive) the fact remains that the British revealed a lack of 'push' after their initial victory. It was as though the scale of it had taken their breath away. Haig quickly became conscious that matters were going awry; on April 10th he 'urged on Allenby the importance of keeping the enemy on the move during the next 24 hours, before he can bring up his reserves. If the Third Army is held up on the west of Monchy le Preux I urged A. to push forward on the north of the Scarpe and then move S.E. in rear of Monchy, so as to turn the enemy's flank.' The next day Haig visited the Divisional Headquarters of the Third Army; General Haldane

(VI Corps) told him that: 'His difficulty was to get commanders of divisions to go forward and take control of the operations. They had been accustomed to sit behind trenches and command by the aid of the telegraph. Now their wires in the open soon got broken and they lost communication with their brigades who were advancing and fighting. He had seen all the divisional generals of his corps and he felt things were now moving better.'

Nevertheless, this state of mind persisted. The 10th and 11th of April were days of lost opportunity. On the 12th Haig realized that the great chance had gone: 'I pointed out that enemy had now been given time to put the Drocourt-Quéant line into a state of defence. . . . Our advance must therefore be more methodical . . . we must try and substitute shells as far as possible for infantry. . . .' The Battle of Arras now assumed the usual features of the War; it became a series of slow, often costly 'bites' at successive German positions, never fast enough to prevent the construction of more positions behind those taken. There were some good days – and some bad days; new evil reputations were added to the long list of those already established. For the Australians and for the Tank Corps, the name of Bulle-court was to be a sombre memory. The question that now arose was, how long was this 'methodical' struggle to continue? That would depend on Nivelle.

The weather on the Aisne in April, 1917, was no more friendly than along the British front further north. Preparations for the great French attack were hampered by the incessant rain and snow of a winter that extended across the whole span of spring. The very size of the operation – over 50 divisions, more than 5,000 guns – multiplied the difficulties. In addition, a powerful German spoiling attack on April 4th had disrupted a lengthy sector of the French front; not only that, but in the course of this attack the Germans captured a document which contained precise details of much of the French plan. Nothing was said about this misfortune at the Compiègne Conference two days later. What with one thing and another, it was scarcely surprising that in the final stages Nivelle found himself in the invidious position of having to ask Haig to accept successive postponements of the French assault – in marked contrast to his earlier exhortations to greater speed. Transmitting one of these requests to Haig on April 12th, Wilson remarked: 'I don't think there is any villainy in this change, which is far from suiting Nivelle's plans. . . .' The next day he added: '. . . these delays are the mischief but I really believe them to be unavoidable. . . . In a certain sense they are not all to the bad because they put Nivelle into a position – not quite of inferiority but – of apology to you which will be useful later on.' Haig was not vastly impressed by this consideration, and replied: 'The French Armies are making the main attack, so it behoves us to do all we possibly can to render their attacks successful . . . I trust . . . they will give us full credit for having done everything possible and in the most unselfish way, to make *their operations* a success!' This was, said Wilson, 'so truly a good comrade's letter that I showed it, as it stood, to Nivelle. He was very much touched.'

That was roughly the sum of comfort that Nivelle was able to enjoy during the last days of his hopes. From the front, ominous reports and misgivings flowed in from divisional and corps commanders, pointing out that in many places even the enemy's first positions had not been reduced by the French artillery, and expressing grave doubts about what they might find when they reached the second and third German lines. Behind him, he knew that the political leaders were filled with doubts, and that there were many who desired his head on a platter. As Robertson wrote to Haig on the 14th: '. . . poor Nivelle is going into action with a rope round his neck. . . . No more foolish or cruel thing can be done than to crab a man's plans once they have been decided upon and approved. In fact no plan should ever be crabbed. It should either be accepted or rejected, and if accepted criticism should be practically silent.'

An indisputable dictum: Robertson was uttering a blunt truth in his uncompromising way; but it was also an ideal which few governments, certainly in democracies, are likely to attain, and which was never in sight during the First World War. Robertson added in the same letter that, if the French attack should fail, it would be necessary to review the whole situation: 'In such a review three important points are – submarines; the Russian situation; and the necessity for getting back complete control of our own Armies.' Haig replied: 'I agree that the British Government should reassume full control over the British Expeditionary Force in France at the first favourable opportunity. But the question to settle is when the moment is favourable. I think it would create unnecessary friction and would therefore do more harm than good to the Allied cause to raise the question at the present time. All goes smoothly now. . . .'

Nivelle's attack went in on April 16th, through biting squalls of sleet and rain. 'Everywhere', says Spears, 'the story was the same. The attack gained ground at most points, then slowed down, unable to follow the barrage which, progressing at the rate of a hundred yards in three minutes, was in many cases soon out of sight. As soon as the infantry and the barrage became dissociated, German machine-guns were conjured as if by magic from the most unlikely places and opened fire, in many cases from both front and flanks, and sometimes from the rear as well, filling the air with a whistling sound as of scythes cutting hay. On the steep slopes of the Aisne, the troops, even unopposed, could only progress very slowly.' The French were now encountering for the first time the new system of 'defence in depth' which the

Germans under Ludendorff and Hindenburg substituted for the linear defence
which they had clung to with such loss on the Somme and at Verdun. A deep
area of their front was organized so that the advancing French found themselves in a succession of traps and ambushes; the deeper they penetrated, the
weaker they became; behind this zone lay the German counter-attack
divisions, waiting for their moment.

For the whole French Army, with its high-pitched hopes, April 16th
was tragic; within the large tragedy there were particular ones with their
own brand of horror. Among these we may note the fate of the Colonial
troops from Africa whom the French were now employing in increasing
numbers. The spectacle of the Senegalese attack, says Spears, was heartbreaking. 'We had been taught to believe theirs would be a headlong assault,
a wild savage onrush. Instead, paralysed with cold, their chocolate faces
tinged with grey, they reached the assault trenches with the utmost difficulty.
Most of them were too exhausted even to eat the rations they carried, and
their hands were too cold to fix bayonets. They advanced when ordered to
do so, carrying their rifles under their arms like umbrellas, finding what
protection they could for their frozen fingers in the folds of their cloaks.
They got quite a long way before the German machine guns mowed them
down.'

The attack was, in the context of what Nivelle had promised, a disaster;
only one of the three Armies initially launched made any worthwhile progress at all. German counter-attacks on the first day regained much of the
ground so hardly won by the French. Haig noted: 'French claim 10,000
prisoners, but the attitude of French officers attached to my Staff makes me
think they are not quite satisfied and that the much talked of victory has not
been gained by the French up to date. It is a pity that Nivelle was so very
optimistic as regards breaking the enemy's line.' The next day, very little
news was forthcoming from the French, and Haig remarked: 'This is always
a bad sign, and I fear that things are going badly with their offensive.' His
fears were justified. On the 18th the consequences of Nivelle's failure began
to make themselves felt. General Maurice visited G.H.Q., commissioned by
Lloyd George to discover Haig's views of the general situation. 'M. Albert
Thomas, who had just passed through London on his way to Russia, had told
L.G. that it was the intention of the French Government, if the offensive
operations near Soissons by the French did not develop successfully very
quickly, to stop them, and do nothing till 1918 when the Americans would
be able to help.'

This startling intelligence filled Haig with consternation. 'I must say
at once', he wrote in his Diary, 'that it would be the height of folly for the
French to stop now, just when the Germans had committed the serious fault

of retiring, meaning to avoid a battle, but had been forced to fight against their will. The enemy should be pressed everywhere without delay by all the Allies. If offensive operations are stopped in France, the enemy will be given time to recover from the blows he received on the Somme, at Verdun, Arras and now on the Aisne. He will also be able to transfer troops to other theatres which will call for counter measures on our part. This will mean increased demands on our shipping, and help the German in his submarine campaign. He would also have troops available for a threat against England.' The tone of this entry is unusually alarmist; the notion of a German invasion of England seems particularly far-fetched, in the light of what we now know.

It is hard to recapture the genuinely alarming nature of those times, but the effort has to be made. It was on this same day, for example, that Lord Derby wrote to Haig: '. . . the state of affairs now existing is really very bad indeed, and we have lost command of the sea.' The news from Russia was universally depressing; the question of her signing a separate peace had already arisen. Now the French had had a setback which, Haig knew only too well, could produce the most serious effect on morale. Even the entry of the United States into the War in April was at first a heavily disguised blessing, involving an immediate extra demand on Allied shipping and war production; if it also provided the French with an excuse for doing nothing at all, the gravest results might befall. Haig's correspondence during these critical weeks is full of the most gloomy reports and prognostications from all quarters; it was no satisfaction to him, despite what had passed between them, to learn from Wilson and Lord Esher that Nivelle was now in disgrace with the French Government, and likely to be dismissed very soon.

It is not strange, amid so many distressing perplexities, that Haig took a certain time to think his way through his problems. Three factors assumed priority in his mind, and had to be weighed against each other: first, he was currently engaged in a major offensive, in support of the French; secondly, there was the strong possibility that the French might, under the duress of disappointment, call off their own offensive (as Nivelle had, in any case promised to do, if it was not successful within forty-eight hours) and suspend future offensive operations indefinitely – the dismissal of Nivelle would be a token of this intention; thirdly, there was the apparently growing urgency of clearing the Belgian coast, to relieve the situation at sea. The equation between these forces was not yet clear in his mind when he met Nivelle on April 23rd; at the close of a long exposition, Haig 'requested him to assure me that the French Armies would continue to operate energetically, because what I feared was that, after the British Army had exhausted itself trying to make Nivelle's plan a success, the French Govt. might stop the operations. I would then not be able to give effect to the other plan, viz. that of directly capturing the Northern ports. Nivelle assured me that neither he nor his Government had any intention of stopping the offensive.' The apparent contradiction in Haig's reasoning can be accounted for. The proposition, at that stage, worked out like this: obviously, to continue at Arras must consume time and resources to the prejudice of the Flanders offensive which Nivelle's failure on the Aisne had now restored to the status of the main British effort of the year; on the other hand, if continuing at Arras could influence the French against the total suspension of offensive action which seemed to be implicit in the abandonment of Nivelle's plan, then Arras must go on, and its effect on the Flanders attack must be accepted. It was an ugly dilemma.

The march of events supplied its own solution, but it was not an attractive one. On the 28th, amid a welter of conflicting information from Paris, where the French Government was groping for answers to its own equally trying problems, one fact emerged – that Pétain's star was now in the ascendant, whatever Nivelle's present position might be. On that day Pétain became Chief of Staff of the French Army, a new appointment whose scope was far from clear. Some of the messages which Haig received from Paris suggested that it meant, in fact, the Command-in-Chief. And, as Haig noted, Pétain had 'described his tactics as "aggressive defensive" – "the basis is to avoid losses and to wait American reinforcements" '. Henry Wilson wrote: 'What is chiefly in my mind is this: that if Nivelle is removed and Pétain is put in his place the plan of operations agreed to by you and Nivelle will, as a matter of fact, be changed no matter how much Ribot and Painlevé may disclaim to the contrary, and if the plan *is* changed then all your arrangements for the future may be upset, or have to be modified. . . . My business therefore is to help, so far as I can, in making the French stick to their plan. . . .'

Haig discussed the case with Kiggell (at these moments one senses the lack of a strong character or opinion at his side; one feels that these talks were often almost monologues). It was clear that Pétain's promotion implied a reversal of the position taken by both Ribot and Painlevé when Haig had met them in Paris two days before; Haig's loyalty to his French colleague, under severe questioning by the French Ministers, had served only to delay Nivelle's fall, not to avert it. Now, he and Kiggell agreed, 'we must expect that the action of the French Armies will be limited to minor offensive objectives, in which no large losses are likely. There was thus no object in our pushing on to Cambrai. Such a position will cause a salient in our line, and will only be reached after considerable losses. It will not lead to decisive results. . . . We ought to aim

1.) At reaching a good defensive line. . . .

2.) At preparing several attacks to go in by surprise so as to hold the enemy and wear him out.

3.) At launching Ypres attack, for which troops should be economized.

'We must continue to press enemy in France in order to help the Italians and Russians by retaining enemy reserves here, and to induce the Italians and Russians to start attacking as soon as possible. . . .'

Summing up these conclusions in a note to Robertson the following day, Haig said: 'I think the time has now come for me taking up our "alternative plan" in earnest, and to this end we should ask the French to relieve some of our Divisions on our right, while we relieve their Divisions on the Belgian coast. But pressure on the German Army must not be relaxed in the meantime. This seems to me of first importance for the success of *our* plan. If I cannot come to an agreement with the French C. in C. (whoever he may be!) in this matter, it may be necessary to settle the question at the Conference.'

The Conference in question was held in Paris on May 4th; it provided both the sequel to what had happened at Calais in February, and the prelude to the vast battle which was to occupy nearly all that was left of 1917 – with the further crop of even more dire misunderstandings between soldiers and politicians that ensued from it. In the hot May sunshine (the brief summer of 1917 burst instantly upon the April snows; it was an extraordinary year) Mr. Lloyd George was scarcely recognizable. His earlier sullen anger was all gone; he was a man transformed. Haig had been warned by Esher of what to expect a fortnight before. After a lunch in the sun with Lloyd George on the balcony of the Crillon Hotel, Esher wrote: 'He has entirely changed his point of view as to the respective merits of the chiefs of the Allied army, their staffs, and powers of offence. It is almost comic to see how the balance has turned. For the moment I do not think *you* could do wrong. This instability of vision (if you can use such a phrase) is L.G.'s great weakness. With his tremendous vitality and indestructible spirit it is a source of danger. But luckily he never displays infirmity of purpose. He suffers from over-elasticity of mind which is a rare enough fault on the borderline between vice and virtue.'

When Haig met Lloyd George on the day before the Conference, he found that Esher had not been exaggerating: 'At 9.30 p.m. I saw the Prime Minister with Gen. Robertson. The former is afraid that the French Government is not going to act offensively! He is here, he says, to press whatever plan Robertson and I decide on. Rather a changed attitude for him to adopt since the Calais Conference.' When it came to Lloyd George's turn to speak at the Conference itself, Haig tells us that he 'made two excellent speeches in which he stated that he had no pretensions to be a strategist, that he left that to his

military advisers, that I, as C. in C. of the British Forces in France had full
power to attack where and when I thought best. He (Mr. L.G.) did not wish
to know the plan, or where or when any attack would take place. Briefly, he
wished the French Government to treat their Commanders on the same lines.
His speeches were quite excellent.'

It is easy to see now that they were a little *too* excellent. Lloyd George had
suffered some nasty shocks since Calais; he had gloomily witnessed a general
deterioration of the war situation; he had seen the French general under
whom he had placed the British Army fail, and fall into disgrace; he had seen
the British commander's efforts win a striking success; he was now faced
with a possible collapse of his principal Ally. His main concern was not to
mollify Haig or Robertson; he was concerned with bolstering up the French.
To achieve this, he adopted a pose; he was not being completely insincere in
this; no doubt he was genuinely pleased with what his country's Army had
done; but it was a dangerous frame of mind, containing a potential for mischief as large as his previous doubts. For the time being, however, the warmth
of the sunshine over Paris was matched by that which existed between the
British soldiers and their unpredictable Prime Minister. On May 5th Haig
wrote to his wife: 'I was very pleased with the way Lloyd George tackled the
military problem at the conference. . . . In fact, I have quite forgiven him his
misdeeds up to date in return for the very generous words he said yesterday
about the British forces in France, and the way in which he went for the
French Government and insisted on *vigorous action*. He did well.'

When Lloyd George spent a night at G.H.Q. on the 6th, Haig continued
in the same vein in his Diary: 'The P.M. was particularly pleased with his
visit to Paris because he felt that he had heartened up the French, and got
them to do what he wanted. He seemed quite converted in his views about
the British Army, was loud in its praises, and heartily congratulated me on
the success of my operations! If we had been "held up" like the French, he
does not know what would have happened! L.G. said that he was anxious to
help us in every way. I gave him notes of our requirements in guns, aeroplanes, etc., and he is to do his best to ensure what is needed being provided
forthwith.' Haig was much comforted. What he did not yet realize was that
there is little value in a wheel coming round full circle, if it is also in perpetual
motion. He believed that the stage was now cleared for his own great
offensive; he was to be cruelly disillusioned.

*   *   *   *

'Passchendaele' was the central act of 1917; only a few weeks remained
before it began. They were weeks of deep significance for the Alliance, but
above all for France. The war-weariness of the French people was now

becoming intense; a million dead in the field; the loss of the rich north-eastern provinces; the apparent hopelessness of the struggle; the example of Russia; finally, the bitter disappointment of Nivelle's failure; all these factors combined to bring matters to a head. Strikes broke out in all the major French industrial centres; anti-war agitation accompanied them. Worse was to follow. On May 3rd, while Haig was in Paris discussing future plans with Pétain and the French Ministers prior to the Conference, the 2nd Colonial Infantry Regiment refused to go into the line, shouting 'Down with the war!' There were other similar outbreaks; ten are officially recorded between April 29th and May 25th. It was possible to regard these as isolated pheno-mena, susceptible to local solutions; nevertheless, they were ominous. After May 25th, it was no longer possible to accept this interpretation; between that date and June 10th, no less than forty-five mutinies occurred, of varying degrees of seriousness. In some regiments, officers were assaulted; this was infrequent, and usually due to personal unpopularity. Formed bodies marched on Paris, some of them under the Red Flag. Many men simply dispersed. But the commonest form of indiscipline was the blunt declaration that the soldiers were prepared to hold their trenches, but would not take part in any more attacks. By the beginning of June, according to Painlevé, only two French divisions remained completely reliable on the central sector of the front, covering Paris.

Nivelle's already damaged reputation was finally destroyed by these events. On May 15th he was relieved of his command, and Pétain became Commander-in-Chief, while Foch returned from obscurity to take the not entirely congenial post of Chief of Staff. By a judicious mixture of firmness and concession, Pétain set about ending the actual mutinies. According to the French Official History, fifty-five soldiers were executed, forty-seven of them for acts of rebellion. Unrecorded local action probably makes the full figure somewhat larger; the disappearance of a considerable number of men who were deported to penal settlements created the impression at the time of much greater severity. But an army in the presence of the enemy cannot be terrorized into submission and order; it was Pétain's concessions, particularly in the matters of leave and food, which were most instrumental in quelling the mutiny – these, coupled with his own reputation as a careful general, who disliked grandiose offensive adventures. The men felt that they could trust Pétain with their lives. There was, in fact, a kind of unspoken compact between him and them: they would agree to obey; he would see to it that their obedience was not abused. It was, indeed, a primitive reassertion of that 'consent of the governed' which is the strength of democracy – but a luxury only rarely permitted to armies in the field, engaged in a life-and-death struggle. The full extent of the collapse of the Army's morale was well concealed; indeed, this concealment became a cardinal object of French policy both for the rest of the War (for obvious reasons) and after it. Nevertheless, the leaders of France, knowing what had happened, found themselves from this time onwards under special duress; French strategy, from May, 1917, was dominated by the fear of another mutiny, if the troops were pushed too far in their endurance. It was a very limiting consideration.

In this crisis, the French developed a talent for reticence and secrecy which was quite unexpected, and which might have served them well in other connections. Something had to be imparted to their Allies, on the eve of a major battle, but as little as possible. Most of Haig's information about what was happening came from British sources, from Spears or Esher. Recognizing its import he too said little about it. 'British Headquarters at home and in France,' Lloyd George complained, 'carefully kept to themselves the information conveyed to them, and it did not reach the ears of British Ministers for some time after the C. in C. and Sir W. Robertson had been acquainted with the facts.' Yet, as he also states, there was some point in this secrecy; *the Germans never found out until it was too late.* 'Had they done so,' says Lloyd George, 'they would certainly have taken steps to profit by the disaffection in the French lines in order to crumple up their most formidable military foe.' But the truth is that neither Haig nor anyone else at G.H.Q. learned the full extent of the damage until long afterwards. Lord Esher spoke to Charteris about a general decline in French morale on May 15th. Four days later, Charteris recorded: 'The news today is not good. The French are having very serious trouble in their own Army.' But on May 25th, just when this trouble was swelling to its most dangerous extent, he recorded: 'Things are better in the French Army....' Even so, he recognized the implications of what had already occurred: 'It means definitely that we cannot expect any great help from the French this year.' Unfortunately, Charteris did not carry this conviction to Haig.

The necessity for dissembling by the French leaders constitutes one of the many mischiefs of 1917. Whatever information he may have possessed, or not possessed, about the state of the French Army, Lloyd George had scarcely returned from his fortifying mission to Paris when he found himself once again assailed by doubts. The change in the French command seemed to him particularly ominous; did it mean that the Pétain school of thought would now prevail? If so, what would be the likely effect on the proposed British operations? These were valid questions; he would have been failing in his duty if he had not asked them. From the historian's point of view – and posterity's – it is important to know that the questions *were* asked – and answered.

On May 14th and on May 16th (the days immediately before and after

Pétain was appointed Commander-in-Chief) Haig received two telegrams from Robertson which indicated the confusion as well as the secrecy which surrounded French affairs; on the 16th Robertson said: 'War Cabinet ask me to impress upon you the necessity of seeing the general who is really responsible for deciding on combined operations with you. Previously you had proposed to see Nivelle and now that Pétain has replaced him Cabinet do not quite understand why you propose seeing Foch. Will you please say if you have reason to believe Foch is the supreme military authority in the matter? Cabinet think Pétain is more likely to be this authority as he is nominee of present government. Whoever you may see Cabinet ask me to emphasize the necessity of insisting upon full co-operation on the part of French armies and I think if you remain very firm you will ensure it while on the other hand any sign of intention on your part to embark on costly operations whether the French really do so or not may result in our fighting practically alone. To this or to a plan which contains the danger of it the Cabinet could not agree. Your difficulty is fully appreciated but Cabinet wish to make their view quite clear and also to afford you support in insisting upon the French fighting.'

Just in case anything might have been left unclear by this very forthright telegram, Robertson followed it instantly with a letter in which he underlined the main issue: 'The Cabinet are quite consistent in the desire to support our views as to the necessity for continuing real offensive action, but at the same time they are equally desirous of the French doing their share, because if they do not it is quite clear that you will have all the German divisions which can be scraped together on the top of you, and we shall find ourselves at the end of the year with depleted divisions and the French will not. This will not be good from many points of view. It is a very difficult matter for you to deal with, because of course you cannot guarantee that the French will do what they promise, but you can form a pretty good idea; and at any rate you should make your doubts known to the Cabinet if you have any.' In other words, there were two main questions: what the French would promise to do, and whether they would keep their promise. A lot depended on Haig's personal assessment of Pétain, now evidently the man in charge. Once again his first impression had been favourable, if not exactly gushing; at the Paris Conference, Haig had found Pétain 'most clear-headed and easy to discuss things with'. In answer to Haig's outline of his intentions, Pétain had replied that 'he was entirely agreed with my views and plans. . . . He was anxious to do his utmost to help me in every possible way.' At this stage, knowing practically nothing about the mutinies in the French Army, and very little about its new C.-in-C., Haig had no reason to disbelieve Pétain. Consequently, in his reply to Robertson, he said: 'I feel sure that, when the question of command has been finally settled, the French Armies will not fail to maintain the degree of offensive activity promised by the French Government at the recent Paris Conference.' To make doubly sure, he decided to raise the matter at his next meeting with Pétain; this took place at Amiens on May 18th.

There is no mistaking the purport of what happened at Amiens. Haig began by making sure that Pétain was, in fact, the successor of Nivelle and Joffre, the man with whom he would have to deal as commander in the field. With that point cleared up, he then, according to the Record of the conference, read out to Pétain the telegram which he had received from Robertson on the 14th (its tenor was the same as that of the 16th, but the wording was more diplomatic). He then, says the Record, 'stated that he wished to have an assurance from the French that their co-operation . . . would be whole-hearted'. In Haig's own words; 'I then asked him straight, "Did the French intend to play their full part as promised at the Paris Conference? Could I rely on his whole-hearted co-operation?" He was most outspoken and gave me full assurance that the French Army would fight and would support the British in every possible way.'

The official record of the meeting confirms this, and adds that Pétain went into details about four attacks planned by the French, one for mid-June, and another 'to coincide approximately with . . . the main British offensive from the Ypres salient, viz., about the end of July'. Haig accepted this assurance, no doubt with deep relief, and then expounded his own plans in detail, finally handing a copy of them to Pétain, with two maps. Pétain promised to submit his remarks as soon as possible. 'He again stated', says the Record, 'that he would do all he could to co-operate with the British operation in the North and that he regarded it as the main operation; and he added that he would do his utmost to attract as many hostile divisions as possible.' All this was entirely satisfactory, and Haig was correspondingly pleased; his earlier impressions of Pétain were confirmed: 'I found him businesslike, knowledgeable, and brief of speech. The latter is, I find, a rare quality in Frenchmen!'

Among those present at Amiens was Wilson. He had been in a state of rising agitation for some time past, for a number of reasons. His recently created post of Chief Liaison Officer had not worked out well; he felt now, that as the powers of Nivelle waned, he himself was regarded askance by the new men of the French Army as a 'Nivellite'; the effect of this sensation was increased by the fear that grew in him concerning what the Painlevé-Pétain combination might stand for; thirdly, he was afraid that Haig had no use for him. This was the easiest point to settle. He put it frankly to Haig on May 14th, and received an immediate answer:

'My dear Henry,
    'Don't be a B.F.! I expect to see you here tonight. I would have asked you

to come before but did not wish to bring you away from what seemed to me the most important work, viz., to get my requests for relief of troops etc. accepted by our Allies.

Yours,

D. H.'

Relations with Haig were restored as easily as that; with the French it was another matter. Wilson himself did not greatly help matters by 'telling Pétain some home truths' on May 11th. On the other hand, the more he heard of Pétain's policy, the less he liked it, and the more dangers he saw in it for the British Army. It was with some consternation, at Amiens, that he heard Pétain give such complete assurances to Haig, and saw Haig accept them readily. Only a week before, Pétain had told him that 'He is opposed to Haig's plans of attack'. Turning the matter over in his mind, Wilson felt certain that the seeds of a dreadful misunderstanding had been planted at Amiens. They had, indeed, and every credit is due to Wilson both for spotting the fact, and for the steps which he immediately took to deal with it. On May 20th, he addressed a remarkable letter to Haig:

'My General,[1]

'I had a long talk with Pétain this afternoon and as I raised some important points I want to give you my general impressions:—

'In order to impress on him the necessity for replying with great care and in great detail to the plan of operations and the maps which you gave him on the 18th at Amiens, I put the following case to him:—

'I said that the arrangements for the Messines affair and his simultaneous action have already been settled, but must be recorded in writing; but as regards your larger operation the French proposals for simultaneous action were much too vague and must be worked out in detail – length of fronts, objectives, number of divisions, *and* period, or length of time, over which fighting would be continued; for unless you were fully satisfied with the volume and duration of the French attacks we might, conceivably, find our-selves ... in a very uncomfortable and to me rather dangerous situation. ...

'I said that in our efforts to disengage Ostend and Zeebrugge if England got it into her head that the French had failed to help us at the critical moment

---

1. This Gallicism was Wilson's habitual mode of address to Haig; it was probably not intended deliberately to annoy, but could scarcely fail to irritate Haig, whose regard for French usages was not as high as Wilson's. In any case, Haig was not a General; he was a Field-Marshal. A small point? But is it wise to irritate a man with small points, when he is engaged in large affairs? Haig regarded the War as a serious matter, and Henry Wilson's merry quips did not amuse him; if he now treated a most serious issue too lightly, the reason might well be found in the distrust which Wilson's ordinary joking manner engendered.

of the campaign it was easy to see that a really bad feeling might be started which would be disastrous to the War.

'I painted the picture as vividly as my French would permit, so as to make Pétain put his *real* cards on the table. He listened very attentively and then asked me for my solution.

'I replied that in my opinion he must do one of two things:—

(a) Attack, perhaps with a less number of divisions but still, attack practically all the time we were engaged.

or

(b) Explain *now* that for certain reasons, which he must specify, he would confine himself to much smaller operations divided into much shorter periods of fighting.

'He replied somewhat as follows:—

1. Owing to his holding much too long a line . . . he could not attack with anything approaching the number of divisions you had at your disposal. . . .

2. He was opposed to any operations with such distant objectives as those which the Admiralty and our Cabinet were asking you to carry out – but he added that this was no business of his.

3. He would try and employ up to twenty-five divisions in operations during the summer.

4. [A matter of detail.]

5. His attacks . . . would be for strictly limited objectives, and when objectives were gained the whole movement would automatically cease.

6. He did not believe in another Somme.

'In short that my proposal at (a) was impossible whilst that at (b) was the course which he proposed to adopt, making each operation as big as he could but ceasing the fighting when the objective was gained.

'I told him that this being the case it was quite possible that the ill-feeling, which I feared, might really come into existence unless he stated his whole case and made clear beyond all possibility of doubt *exactly* what he was prepared to do and that he neither could nor would do anything more.

'He agreed and said he would submit those paragraphs to me before he signed the letter in order to see if I thought he had made them sufficiently clear.

'I liked Pétain today; he was clear and decided and when he saw what I was at he thanked me – I had spoken very openly – and told me he had not thought of that aspect but he now saw the necessity for a clear and unequivocal statement. He reminded me that you had asked him to express an opinion on your projects, but this he would never do, but he said to me that, with the amount of assistance he could give our Cabinet were setting you an impossible task.

'Oh dear, what a long letter and I am afraid rather confused but I have just tried to jot down, in sequence, the result of my conversation. I don't like to have it typed. I am so sorry for you!

Henry.'

The situation was extraordinary, and, looking back on it, harrowing. At this critical juncture, the whole execution of the British plan depended on the War Cabinet being assured that the French meant to fulfil their part of the bargain, as the British had done for Nivelle at Arras. The French C.-in-C. gave clear pledges that this was his intention; but the Chief British Liaison Officer now stated the contrary. Whom was Haig to believe? Scarcely had he received Wilson's letter, than he received Pétain's reply to the papers given him at Amiens. 'J'ai l'honneur', wrote Pétain (on May 23rd), 'de vous faire connaître que je suis d'accord avec vous pour l'exécution du plan d'opérations expose dans le projet que vous m'avez remis à Amiens. . . . Il demeure entendu que les armées françaises exécuteront, pour favoriser les attaques britanniques, deux offensives successives; l'une vers le 10 Juin . . . correspondant à l'attaque britannique sur Wytschaete -Messines; l'autre . . . au milieu de Juillet, pendant les opérations au nord d'Ypres. . . .'

To Haig, the meaning of this was quite clear: Pétain was standing by his agreement; the French would support the British attack. To Wilson (angry, because Pétain had not, after all, shown him the letter before sending it) it meant something quite different. 'Of course', he wrote in his Diary: 'this is quite hopeless. There is no sign of combined operations at all. No mention of the Boches being able to bring over divisions from Russia, no subordination of the French plan to ours, nothing but Haig's plan and Pétain's plan, which happen to come off in the same year.' Visiting Haig on the 26th, Wilson expressed these misgivings with some force. Haig remarked: 'He struck me as not quite friendly with Pétain. Wilson finds fault with P.'s letter to me. He would like to see Pétain acknowledge more fully that his position is subordinate to mine. I think it would be a serious mistake for me in any way to indicate to the French C. in C. that is he is "playing second fiddle". As a matter of fact, he knows it and has promised to support me in every possible way. Besides it was Nivelle's adoption of such an attitude towards me which caused so much friction between our respective Staffs. I told Wilson that the important thing for him is to find out how the orders given by Pétain to his Army Group Commanders are being interpreted – what attacks are being prepared? What do the troops intend to do? Are the attacks to be serious ones on a considerable scale and to last a long time or not?' Obviously, Haig found it difficult to believe what Wilson told him. This was one of those moments when human personality plays a tremendous part in war; if relations between Haig and Wilson had been closer, it might have been a different story, and much anguish might have been spared. It was a sad trick of fate that the man who, alone in the British Army at that time, had plumbed the nature and intentions of the new French commander, was the man who was most distrusted by the Army's chiefs. For Wilson it was the last and greatest frustration in a frustrating tour of duty; within a month it was over; the French, whom he admired so much, had informed him that they no longer desired his services in that post.

What is one to make of Pétain's behaviour? If Wilson is to be believed, if Pétain really did say that the objectives of the British attack (which depended on his co-operation) were 'no business of his', if he really considered that it was improper to discuss the pros and cons of a major Allied offensive with his British colleague, comment seems superfluous. This would, indeed, represent a total breakdown of true co-operation. In the light of what happened, moreover, Wilson seems to have been correct. It is hard to exonerate Pétain from the charge of deliberately misleading Haig – and through him, the British Government. Of course, at this stage, the French mutinies had not yet reached their most alarming pitch; it is possible that, but for what happened at the end of May, Pétain would, in fact, have given Haig much more help. On the other hand there is Wilson's repeated evidence that Pétain did not believe in the Flanders offensive at any time. It may be that a more complicated motive than Wilson perceived was at work here: that whether Pétain thought the British would succeed or not, he still wanted them to carry out their attack, in order to gain a breathing space for his own army, and that he was prepared to do just so much – but not a jot more – as would encourage them to do this. There is nothing in Pétain's subsequent career, before or after November, 1918, to suggest that any powerful sense of loyalty to his Allies acted as a prime force in him. One thing is quite clear: that in no speech or written communication did he do anything to deter Haig from his attempt to clear the Belgian coast. On the contrary, he reinforced the latter's belief in his support by offering, on May 27th, to place a French army under Haig's direct command to join in the offensive on the coastal sector, *in addition to the other promised diversions.*

When the first cold breath of disillusionment came, it was already too late, and, in any case, far from complete. On June 2nd, Haig recorded the first official intimation which he had received of disorders in the French Army: 'The "Major-General" of the French Army arrived about 6.30 p.m. and stayed to dinner. His name is General Debeney. He brought a letter from General Pétain saying that he had commissioned him to put the whole situation of the French Army before me and conceal nothing. The French Army is in a bad state of discipline. . . . This would prevent Pétain carrying out his promise to attack on June 10th! The attack would take place four weeks later. Then I discovered by questions that the attack promised already for the middle of July was the one that would be launched. . . .'

'Conceal nothing . . .'; a misleading phrase in a misleading speech; all that Haig learned from this communication was that the *first* of the French supporting attacks would in effect be abandoned. This was annoying news, but no more than that; there were, indeed, compensations for it: 'However, the Germans are now counter-attacking the French with considerable vigour in Champagne so I hope no reserves will be able to come to Flanders to oppose my attacks.' After all, as long as the Germans were occupied, it did not matter, in the short run, whether the French were attacking them, or vice versa; in the long run, only French attacks could *tie down* German divisions, but nothing was said to suggest that the later French diversions which had been promised at Amiens would not materialize. On the contrary, the remainder of the conversation with Debeney ('I thought him straightforward and businesslike') was taken up with the subject of the French contingent in Flanders. This was a pressing enough topic at the time, for this was already June 2nd; five days later, the long-prepared British attack on the Messines-Wytschaete Ridge was due to go in. And 'Messines' was the first stage of 'Third Ypres'.

It is all too easy, in books, to separate the various 'themes' which constitute any passage of human history. As it unfolds, however, these are much less clear, and have a disagreeable habit of running into each other. As we now switch our attention to what has gone down in history as 'Passchendaele', it will be well to remember that the following complications surrounded the opening of that great battle:

Fighting was still in progress on the Arras front, where over 150,000 British casualties were finally incurred in the cause of creating a diversion for Nivelle.

The French offensive along the Aisne, so far from being 'stopped' after forty-eight hours in the event of failure, had now brought in its train the usual succession of German counter-attacks, involving the French, too, in severe fighting.

A great part of the French Army was simultaneously in a state of mutiny.

Russia was now clearly not to be considered as an active support.

The Austrians were attacking the Italians with vigour.

The submarine menace remained acute.

The United States had not landed a single division in France.

The mood of the French people – and the British – was ugly and disturbed.

It must also be remembered that gigantic preparations were required for every large operation – those for Messines (for special reasons) had been going on for over a year. It was with no single preoccupation that Haig now entered this great undertaking, but amid a welter of confused events. Almost his only comfort was the quality of his Army; as Lloyd George said: 'The British Army was the one allied army in the field which could be absolutely relied on for any enterprise.'

10

The Year of Passchendaele – II

A T THE heart of the Flanders Campaign of 1917 there lay a strategic fault which Haig did not correct until it was too late, and which played a large part in vitiating all the operations in that theatre. The study of contemporary documents removes all possible doubt about Haig's motives in launching the campaign: first, foremost, and above all, his intention was to conform to what he understood to be the strong desire of the British Government and Admiralty to counter the submarine menace by clearing the Belgian coast. This, as we have seen,[1] fitted in well with his own assessment of strategic possibilities on the Western Front, and with his long-standing desire to add the influence of British sea-power to the Army's efforts. There were secondary motives, but they were a long way down the scale of importance; among them may be noticed the nature of the Ypres Salient itself. Shaped first by the accidents of First Ypres in 1914, severely dented by the Gas Attack of 1915, bulged first this way and then that by the crater fighting of 1916, overlooked on three sides, its only communications through the bottleneck of the shattered town, the Salient had remained a dreadful tactical liability to the British Army; the idea of breaking out of it was decidedly appealing. The opportunity to link this valuable tactical advantage to a major strategic enterprise was not lightly to be set aside; given certain conditions, the chance of achieving both ends simultaneously might have existed; but in the actual conditions of 1917, they militated against each other, creating a discordance which marred the whole battle. The coastal operations, conceived to include that amphibious element which had always held out such an appeal to Haig, conflicted with the break-out from Ypres towards Roulers which also promised so much. The two could only have been combined in the circumstances of an overwhelming British superiority, or of large-scale French efforts to divert the Germans; neither of these factors materialized. As a result,

1. See p. 249 *et seq.*

the attempt to proceed by both direct (northern) and indirect (north-eastern) routes led to the failure of both. But the issue – clear enough now – was never so clear at the time; we have noted Pétain's role in deluding Haig over one of the fundamental stipulations; we shall see how further complications one by one eroded all his prospects.

When it became clear, at the end of 1916, that Flanders would be the scene of a major British effort during the next year, Haig turned at once to the officer in charge of that sector, General Sir Herbert Plumer, commanding the Second Army. The foolish error of judging men by their appearance has rarely been more clearly exposed than in Plumer's case. To look at, he might have been the prototype of David Low's famous cartoon character, Colonel Blimp. Sir Philip Gibbs wrote of him: 'In appearance he was almost a caricature of an old-time British General, with his ruddy, pippin-cheeked face, with white hair and a fierce little white moustache, and blue, watery eyes, and a little pot-belly and short legs.' 'Daddy' Plumer, as he was known to some, 'Plum' to his associates, had been the custodian of the desolate Ypres sector since the spring of 1915, a thankless post, where the daily attrition of war on the Western Front was at its highest, but where, while great actions unfolded elsewhere, the chance of personal distinction was almost non-existent. In February, 1916, following the unfortunate occurrences of the crater battles of St. Eloi, Haig had seriously considered dismissing Plumer. 'Privately', he noted, 'I feel that Plumer is too kind to some of his subordinate commanders, who are, I fear, not fit for their appointments.' The sixty-year-old Second Army Commander was put on probation; Haig explained to Lady Haig: 'I thought it might be necessary to ask Gen. Plumer to go, but he is such a straightforward gentleman I shall try and keep him as long as I can.'

The word 'straightforward' recurs in Haig's writings, implying the highest praise (and a significant clue to Haig's own character); 'gentleman' was also of value; but it was not simply these qualities which caused him to refer to Plumer, just over a year later, as 'his most reliable Army Commander'. During that time, the Second Army had achieved a very special reputation. With Sir Charles Harington as his Chief of Staff, Plumer had created in it an atmosphere which was unique at the time. 'Trust, Training and Thoroughness' was his watchword; the whole Army was permeated by this inspiration. 'Plumer and Harington', wrote Charteris, 'are a wonderful combination, much the most popular, as a team, of any of the Army Commanders. They are the most even-tempered pair of warriors in the whole war or any other war. The troops love them. When a division is rattled for any reason, either because of very heavy casualties or because it thinks it has had unfair treatment, it is sent to the Second Army, and at once becomes as happy as sandboys. . . .' 'Nobody', he added, 'knows where Plumer ends and Harington begins.' This was incorrect; Harington knew. 'Plumer's personality', he wrote, 'so permeated the whole army that our task was made easy. . . . I say at once that he was the supreme head, he listened to all, and then made his decision which was final.' On January 25th, Haig instructed Plumer to begin preparations for the Flanders offensive, with General Rawlinson to supervise the coastal sector. It was a great pity, and a grave error, that he did not leave the offensive in Plumer's hands from first to last.

As was to be expected, in a situation which changed constantly as the year progressed, Haig's views of the campaign passed through a number of modifications. It is important to note that underlying them all was the quest for tactical surprises which would compensate for the impossibility of deceiving the enemy about the broad locality selected. This was at the root of his predilection for an amphibious attack near Ostend. When he talked to Rawlinson about the battle on February 10th, he recorded: 'I am of opinion that it is possible to make three simultaneous attacks. The attack on right by Plumer's Army; on left by Rawlinson's Army (as proposed by Plumer) and simultaneously an attack by surprise in centre with Tanks, *and without artillery preparation*,[1] to capture the high ground between Conservatory Hill and Broodseinde.'

This scheme promised well, provided it could be carried out early, and in full strength; the arrangement with Nivelle and the exigencies of the Battle of Arras put an end to such hopes. The weather, also, played its part; on March 22nd, Haig regretfully noted that 'the ground [at Ypres] is very wet for the most part and the digging of starting trenches at this season of the year is out of the question'. Meanwhile, despite the preoccupation of Arras, Haig's ideas were hardening upon a tactical consideration which was to prove of the greatest significance. Commenting to Nivelle, on April 1st, on a Belgian proposal that the northern attack should open with the British capture of the so-called Pilckem Ridge (nowhere more than 60 feet above sea-level), he wrote: 'This would not be a sound procedure and, moreover, an attack on the Pilckem Ridge would have very little prospect of success unless the high ground east and south-east of Ypres, *by which it is commanded and whence the approaches to it are overlooked*,[2] had first been secured.'

During the month, Haig made a major change in his Command structure: Gough, with his Fifth Army Headquarters, was appointed to command the northern sector of the offensive, in place of Rawlinson, who was now to be concerned solely with the amphibious project; Plumer's role became relatively secondary – organizing the diversionary opening of the operation at Messines. The consequences of this change were most serious; Gough never shared Haig's appreciation of the battlefield, especially of the vitally important central

1. Author's italics.
2. Author's italics.

area generally known as the 'Gheluvelt Plateau'. One can only suppose that
Gough's successes in the closing stages of the Battle of the Somme, coupled
with the remarkable *initial* success won by Allenby at Arras, had drawn Haig
to the conclusion that what he needed was a 'thrusting' general who could
exploit every opportunity that occurred. As regards the Second Army, he
noted in May that: 'On the whole, there is a fine spirit in the Corps I saw today, but I felt that the leaders have been on the defensive about Ypres so long
that the *real offensive spirit* has to be developed.' As between Rawlinson and
Gough, he simply preferred Gough. This was a great pity, if only because of
the delay involved in making a change at this late stage; Gough did not take
up his appointment until May 13th. Charteris had already remarked, a week
earlier: 'We go back to our original plan (northern offensive), but after a loss
of two months of most valuable time.' Time, in fact, was from now onwards
to be the factor of supreme importance.

It was on May 1st, in a paper[1] prepared for the War Cabinet as background
to the Paris Conference, that Haig laid down his views on the general situation and stated his intentions. Summing up in his Diary, he wrote:

'The guiding principles are those which have proved successful in war
from time immemorial, viz., that the first step must always be to wear down
the enemy's power of resistance and to continue to do so until he is so
weakened that he will be unable to withstand a decisive blow; then with all
one's forces to deliver the decisive blow and finally to reap the fruits of
victory.

'The enemy has already been weakened appreciably, but time is required
to wear down his great numbers of troops. The situation is not yet ripe for the
decisive blow. We must therefore continue to wear down the enemy until
his power of resistance has been further reduced. . . .

'I recommend that the pause which is forced upon us in vigorous offensive
operations be utilized to complete measures for clearing the coast this
summer.

'Success seems reasonably possible. It will give valuable results on land and
sea. If full measure of success is not gained, we shall be attacking the enemy on
a front where he cannot refuse to fight, and our purpose of wearing him down
will be given effect to. We shall be directly covering our own most important
communications, and even a partial success will considerably improve our
defensive positions in the Ypres salient. This is necessary in order to reduce
the heavy wastage which must occur there next winter as in the past, if our
troops hold the same positions.'

1. O.A.D. 428, 'The Present Situation and Future Plans'.

His conversations in Paris with the French leaders, civilian and military, as well as with Lloyd George; Lloyd George's own speeches at the Conference and subsequent friendly utterances – all conveyed to Haig the strong conviction that his plans had been accepted by his own government and by his Allies. The dismissal of Nivelle, as we have seen, gave rise to some qualms in London, but Haig's own relationship with the new French C.-in-C. remained entirely satisfactory. On the day that he met Pétain at Amiens, and gave him details of the proposed campaign, G.H.Q. circulated a Memorandum containing the first full exposition of the shape of the Third Battle of Ypres. Under six main headings, this Memorandum laid down: '1. The object of the operations is to gain possession of the Belgian coast. . . .' It divided the main operation into three parts: an attack on the Passchendaele-Staden Ridge, leading on to Roulers; in combination with this, an attack from Dixmude directed against the Forêt d'Houthoulst; subsequently, and depending on the success of these, the coastal and amphibious advances in the Nieuport-Ostend region. As a curtain-raiser to all this, to secure the right flank of the main attack from German observation and interference, the south-eastern flank of the Ypres Salient, from Messines to Zillebeke, would first be cleared. Diversions would be provided by British attacks at Arras (until July 1st) and subsequently by the French. Three out of the five elements outlined here never materialized; the attempt to include them all proved fatal. But there were signs of the times forthcoming, both from the enemy's side and from Haig's own army, which created deceptive reassurance.

There was no phase of the whole War that needed more careful probing and cool analysis than the year 1917, with its remarkable complex of events. At no period was the function of Intelligence more vital. It was now, under the stress of this special responsibility, that Haig's choice of Charteris to be at the head of the Intelligence Branch of his whole army proved to have been misjudged. This is not to say that Charteris was in every respect a bad Intelligence Officer; we have seen what his original 'brief' from Haig was; working for a Corps, or an Army, he carried it out satisfactorily. He had a good sense of method and organization. He was generally able to maintain a stream of authentic information on short-term issues – movement of German troops, tactical innovations, immediate intentions. He was far less qualified to assess broad issues, such as the moral condition of the German Army, or the interior state of Germany, in relation to actual field operations. Worse still, he was quite unable to impart to Haig the very real misgivings and qualifications with which he regarded much of the information that he gathered. All through the year there was a discrepancy, sometimes very substantial, between what Charteris thought privately, and what he proffered to Haig as a basis for the latter's plans. This, as we shall shortly see, had deplorable results. For the moment, as we regard Haig and his army poised on the brink of battle, it is important to note that optimistic opinions on Haig's part about his ability to inflict a heavy defeat on the Germans were by no means suddenly conceived. They were the result of a cumulative flow of evidence, much of it, indeed, correct.

Two solid facts must be borne in mind when one considers the problem of British Intelligence; first, that in December, 1916, the German Government had put forward Peace proposals; secondly, that in April, 1917, the Austrian Government undertook secret negotiations with a view to a separate peace with Russia. All other information concerning the Central Powers could thus legitimately be viewed against clear signs of weakening in their war-spirit. The question was, how grave was this weakening? It was a matter of degree; the answer involved subtleties which Charteris did not possess. The presentation of a true solution to Haig, who was additionally conscious of having inflicted a severe defeat on the enemy on the Somme, and who saw their retirement to the Hindenburg Line in its proper light, as a confession of defeat, was, needless to say, not without its difficulties. Charteris deserves some sympathy here. But while his own diary shows him to have been full of perplexity, Haig's diary shows that Intelligence reports provided a steady flow of comfort. On April 6th, Charteris drew to Haig's attention a circular issued by the German Food Controller which, said Haig, states 'that "Germany is faced with the prospects of famine" '. This was a developing theme: on April 12th, Charteris noted: 'The Duc de V. has just come back from Germany, where he has been a prisoner for two years, and reports a great lack of food and a great increase of Socialism. . . .' On the 20th he wrote: 'The reports of disaffection and food trouble in Germany culminated in that of the Berlin strike, which is too strong to be disregarded.' On the 23rd; 'A very interesting captured German document says, "since the 15th March the rations of the whole of the army have been reduced by one-third": This is the first direct indication that we have had that the shortage of food in Germany has forced the diminution of rations to the army.' All this seemed to point in an unmistakable direction. On the other hand, after Arras, Charteris admitted: 'The morale of the Germans is still rather puzzling. . . . On the whole, I think there is a lowering of their morale, but there were very marked exceptions, and one cannot draw any definite conclusions.' At the beginning of June he went further: 'The pleasure we have been taking in revolutionary tendencies in Germany, and in captured documents that enlarge on those tendencies, have had a rude shock. Our own country seems to be tainted with the same disease. . . .'

Besides the food question, there were other encouraging pointers to German conditions. Captured German orders showed that there was a serious shortage of certain metals, particularly copper. In conjunction with this news, on May 1st, further documents revealed a marked reduction of German Battalion strengths, which seemed to indicate a most significant breakdown in their manpower situation, despite the relief afforded by the collapse of Russia. At first Haig did not attach too great an importance to this factor – 'The enemy's fighting strength has not been broken', he wrote, 'and *it is essential to realize that it can only be broken by continued hard fighting. . . .'* Steadily, however, the idea grew in his mind that the German Army might be nearer to the point of collapse than he had so far supposed. On this issue the divergence between him and what Charteris privately thought was to become most marked. At a critical stage Charteris found himself bereft of his most valuable corrective support; he wrote on April 21st: 'Macdonough has been away from the War Office ill, which leaves a great gap so far as I am concerned, for his opinion is the only really valuable one with regard to Germany's intentions which I get to help me. He is always very sound, if cautious. French opinions are valueless: they think out what they would like to be happening and then manufacture evidence that it is happening.'

The same charge has been levelled at Charteris himself; in certain instances it can be upheld, but the general complaint against him is that he fed Haig's buoyant spirit with attractive tit-bits, and did not emphasize sufficiently the contrary elements. Thus, by June 2nd, we find Haig writing: 'Extracts from German correspondence which we have recently captured are the most encouraging I have yet read: hunger, want, sickness, riots, all spreading in the most terrible manner throughout the Fatherland.' On June 5th, the eve of the Battle of Messines, when doubt and despondency flourished in London and among many in France, Haig issued this paper[1] to his Army Commanders:

'After careful consideration of all available information I feel justified in stating that the power of endurance of the German people is being strained to such a degree as to make it possible that the breaking point may be reached this year. . . .

'If, during the next few weeks, failure to stop the steady, determined, never-wearying advance of our Armies is added to a realization of the failure of the submarine campaign the possibility of the collapse of Germany before next winter will become appreciably greater.

'In short, while it cannot be regarded as a certainty that final victory will be reached this year, the great efforts already made have undoubtedly brought it so near that it may be attained; and even one great and striking success, combined with general activity and steady progress on the whole front and a secure hold on all that has already been won, will have far-reaching results.

1. O.A. 799.

'Despite the distress in Germany and the short rations in the German Army we must still reckon on desperate efforts being made by the enemy to hold on in the hope of outlasting the determination of the Allies. But we have already overcome similar efforts on the SOMME, on the ANCRE, and at ARRAS. We are able to do so again. Every fresh success brings us nearer to the end of a long and desperate struggle: and we are now justified in believing that one more great victory, equal to those already gained, may turn the scale finally, and, at the least, will have even a greater effect than previous victories in Germany and on the World's opinion generally.

'This success will be gained, as it has been gained in the past, by the steady and unquenchable determination of all, co-operating with skill, to beat down all opposition to our advance, and to hold firmly what is won.

'I request that all ranks may be informed by their officers how far on the road to victory the splendid efforts already made have brought us and how hopeful a careful and unbiased examination of the evidence shows the present situation to be.'

It is easy enough, in the light of what *we* know, to mock at the optimism which led Haig to speak of Germany's breaking-point being reached, and a collapse 'before next winter'. The historical truth is that, within forty-eight hours, his Army had won a new victory so complete that it seemed to underline the force of every one of his hopeful predictions.

*   *   *   *

3.10 a.m. on Thursday, June 7th, 1917; for a brief half-hour the night had been so quiet, along the Messines-Wytschaete front, that nightingales could be heard singing in the woods. Then, before the horrified eyes of a German observer, 'nineteen gigantic roses with carmine petals, or . . . enormous mushrooms . . . rose up slowly and majestically out of the ground and then split into pieces with a mighty roar, sending up multicoloured columns of flame mixed with a mass of earth and splinters into the sky'. These mushroom explosions were the effects of nineteen huge mines, planted along the Messines Ridge, containing 957,000 pounds of explosive, all detonated together. Some of these mines had been begun in 1915; most of them were ready a year before the attack was made; during the intervening time the secret was kept from the enemy; the mines were maintained in the face of great difficulties, and against the set opinion of many that they could not retain their effectiveness. When they went off together, the shock was felt distinctly in London, on the spot it was like an earthquake. Before its reverberations could die away, they were caught up and redoubled in the fury of a barrage of 2,330 guns and howitzers. Behind this, 80,000 infantry of the Second Army rose from their lines to assault the ridge. Within three hours they had taken all their first objectives; after a pause for consolidation, they passed forward to the final objective, and within an hour this, too, was in their hands. Casualties amounted to one-fifth of those anticipated; in the attack and the subsequent fighting, spread over several days, they averaged just over 1,000 per division engaged – a total of 17,000; the Germans lost (including counter-attacks) 25,000 men, of whom 7,500 were prisoners, and 67 guns. During the afternoon of June 7th, Haig visited Plumer and congratulated him; as he said: 'The old man deserves the highest praise. . . .'

There could scarcely have been a more striking or encouraging prelude to the great offensive. Coming on top of Beaumont Hamel, and then Arras, Messines seemed to show conclusively that in spirit, in method, and in matériel, the British Army now possessed the power to storm the enemy's strongest positions, and inflict larger losses, while doing so, than it received. The Messines Ridge, won by the Germans in 1914, had remained ever since one of their principal ramparts on the Western Front. A captured German order showed the importance they attached to it: 'The unconditional retention of the independent strong points, Wytschaete and Messines, is of increased importance for the domination of the whole Wytschaete salient. These strong points must therefore not fall *even temporarily* into the enemy's hands. . . .' Now, strong points and salient alike had been wrested from them, as Vimy had been only two months earlier. Haig might well feel pleased – with Plumer, with his Army, and with himself. For the success was above all a triumph of method, and if Plumer was, without doubt, his most methodical and careful Army Commander, he himself had also by now evolved a system of direction which fitted the special functions of high command in this strange war.

Haig was only won over slowly from his reluctance to interfere with the man on the spot, either in preparing, or in carrying out battle plans. But throughout the Somme, and much more so in the later fighting, he was steadily drawn into matters of detail. We have seen how, in 1916, he began to adopt a 'Socratic' method of command; this was now highly developed, and was applied by him all through the Third Battle of Ypres, at Cambrai, and, indeed, to a greater or lesser degree, through the rest of the War. Messines proved an excellent example of its working. On May 20th, he drew up some notes for the Second Army's guidance in the forthcoming battle. Beginning with a few paragraphs of generalization on the subject of 'imposing our will on the enemy', Haig then passed to specific questions:

'*Questions for all Corps.*

'Have you got the enemy's batteries accurately located? Are changes of position occurring, and if so, in what manner? For example, is the enemy occupying alternative positions near vacated ones; is he re-occupying his old ones after a certain lapse of time, or do you see a general tendency to move his batteries back? Have you discovered any new positions in course of construction, and are they being camouflaged as they are made? . . . What information have you about the enemy's system of holding the line? Have your Intelligence and Artillery Reconnaissance Officers detailed information as to where he is placing his machine guns, etc.?

'How do you propose forming up the troops for the attack, and have you arranged to clear the danger zone of the enemy's barrage as soon after zero hour as possible?

'What is the strength of your mopping-up parties?

'. . . have you a detailed plan for stopping the bridges over the RIVER LYS or CANAL D'YPRES, as the case may be?

'Has the German constructed any new bridges over either of these?

'When did you have your portion of the Canal or River last photographed?

'Are your infantry trained to deal with low-flying hostile aeroplanes by Lewis Gun and rifle fire? This is most necessary as it is part of the German system now to seek for concentrations of troops at daybreak.

'Are you satisfied that the Inter-Corps and Inter-Division barrages are all co-ordinated and that, as far as possible, they meet with the views of Divisional Commanders?

'Have you arranged your barrage in depth from the moment of assault onwards?

'What is your plan for destroying the wire?

'Have you considered the number of heavy guns that it will be necessary for you to allocate to counter-battery work at zero?

'What use are you making of Smoke and Gas Shell?

'Have you in the case of all guns and howitzers followed the principle that they are to be placed as near the enemy as possible consistent with the tasks in hand?'

This was merely the general interrogation; Haig then passed to particular questions for each of the three Army Corps which were to take part in the assault. II Anzac Corps was asked:

'To what nature of bombardment do you propose to subject Messines, i.e., before the attack, and when the attack goes in?

'Have you an adequate Southern counter-battery group and are you satisfied that this group can not only protect your infantry advancing to the attack, but also protect your forward guns covering your infantry? You must remember that your infantry will suffer heavy losses if they have not a good and regular barrage to protect them when going in even if no hostile artillery fire is directed against them.

'What class of obstacle is the River DOUVE and how are you arranging to cross it?

'What are your arrangements for protecting your right flank when you move N.E.?'

He wanted to know from IX Corps:

'What class of obstacle is the STEENBECK?

'How do you propose to capture the village of WYTSCHAETE? L'ENFER WOOD?

'Are you satisfied that when your infantry reach their final objective, you will have enough guns well forward to deal effectively with the enemy?'

X Corps was asked:

'Are you satisfied with the counter-battery arrangements of the Corps on your left? It is vital to your success that these should be most thorough.

'Are the woods thick on your immediate front, and how do you propose to deal with them in the attack?'

The charge that Haig was careless about the lives of his soldiers, or that he was out of touch with the realities of war, cannot survive the inspection of this and many similar documents that bear his signature.

With officers like Plumer and Harington, this approach worked perfectly, because it fitted their own methods. Haig having very carefully gone into the problems of the operation, embodying the points made above, and others besides, in his Order to the Second Army of May 24th, Plumer took up the next stage of preparation. He was, says Harington, a great believer in the value of personal contact. 'He held Conferences at various Corps Head-quarters so as to save the Corps Commanders coming up to Cassel. He visited Divisional and Brigade Commanders daily and discovered their plans and got their ideas. We all did the same in order to help them and keep them in the whole picture and thus, when the orders were finally issued, every Commander felt that he had at any rate been consulted and had had his way [say?] and had talked personally to the Chief. He might not agree as to the pace of the barrage or the hour of attack, but anyhow he had been asked. All cheer-fully accepted the final decision and put their best into it. Similarly the Major-General, Royal Artillery, kept them informed of the intensive artillery support they were going to receive, the greatest concentration of the whole War. And in addition, a huge model of the Messines-Wytschaete Ridge was constructed. . . . It was about the size of two croquet lawns. On this all those taking part down to Platoon Commanders were able to study the ground. It was a wonderful study of human nature. He treated the whole Army as a family. He took them all into his confidence and trusted them. They trusted him and that Army went into the Battle of Messines in great heart knowing that their Chief had done everything possible for them.'

Small wonder that a distinguished Divisional Commander like Sir Tom Bridges could write of Plumer: 'I would sooner have had him behind me than any other Army Commander I had been with, for he was intrinsically sound and as loyal to his subordinates as he was to those above him.' And of Harington, even so critical an observer as Philip Gibbs said: 'For the first time, in his presence and over his maps, I saw that, after all, there was such a thing as the science of war, and that it was not always a fetish of elementary ideas raised to the nth degree of pomposity, as I had been led to believe by contact with other generals and staff officers.' Harington himself admits that 'there were instances in the War of the reverse of the picture' which he drew of Messines, 'when lower formations were not consulted but merely ordered into action with the result that they thought that neither the stages, nor the time of attack, nor the pace of the barrage was correct, and, therefore did not start in good heart. Simply the difference between the art of commanding by trust as against distrust.'

The foregoing account of Haig's methods, in the hands of competent, conscientious, scientific subordinates, may serve to correct some part of the widespread impression that the First World War was conducted only by 'muddling through' from one blunder to the next. By 1917, the professionalization of the Citizen Army had gone a long way, which was just as well, because in the twelve months that followed Messines, the Army would need every ounce of skill that it possessed to survive the ordeals with which it would be faced. If a great deal of what has been described now seems, after another World War, somewhat *vieux jeu*, or elementary, it must be remembered that for everything there has to be a first time, and that Haig and his subordinates were hammering out their modes of conduct in a situation which was entirely new and revolutionary. It is not surprising that Haig was so delighted with Plumer, although, Harington tells us, the latter was 'bewildered by the telegrams of congratulations which he received on every side'. To those who were now able to stand on the long-coveted Messines Ridge, and look down into the new German lines, the quality of the victory was evident; indeed, it was, if anything, slightly too brilliant, evoking tempting images of what might have been done if the operation had not been planned as a 'limited attack', if it had been pushed home with great force. These considerations were to have their effect upon the main battle, to which Haig's attention now turned. But before it could begin, there was one more man to reconvince, one who had not been impressed, even by the lustre of Messines: the Prime Minister.

*   *   *   *

On the day following the assault at Messines, June 8th, 1917, Lloyd George tells us that 'A committee of the Cabinet [was] appointed . . . to consider War Policy on all fronts – sea and land. It consisted of Lord Curzon, Lord Milner and General Smuts, with myself as Prime Minister in the Chair. Up to that date the Flanders project had never been submitted to the examination of the Government by the C.I.G.S. or the C. in C.' His account of the deliberations of this Committee, to which Mr. Bonar Law and Mr. Balfour were shortly added, forms a central part of his narrative of what he called 'The Campaign in the Mud'; that narrative, in turn, provides his most ferocious indictment of Haig and Robertson. Passchendaele, he wrote, was 'the battle which, with the Somme and Verdun, will always rank as the most gigantic, tenacious, grim, futile and bloody fights ever waged in the history of war'. He added: 'The tale of these battles constitutes a trilogy illustrating the unquenchable heroism that will never accept defeat and the inexhaustible vanity that will never admit a mistake. It is the story of the million who would rather die than own themselves cowards – even to themselves – and also of the two or three individuals who would rather the million perish than that they as leaders should own – even to themselves – that they were blunderers. Hence the immortal renown and the ghastly notoriety of the Verdun, Somme and Passchendaele battlefields; the fame won by sustained valour unrivalled in the annals of war; the notoriety attained by a stubborn and narrow egotism, unsurpassed amongst the records of disaster wrought by human complacency.' It is a necessary part of Lloyd George's presentation of this theme to suggest throughout that the War Cabinet (and he himself in particular) was in some way 'taken by surprise' in the mid-summer of 1917, when they 'discovered' that a great British offensive was imminent in Flanders. His entire account reads as though the offensive was undertaken hurriedly, without consideration, as though the preparations for it were hastily made, and as though Haig and Robertson were the only people who at any time truly believed in the affair. Such, indeed, is the angry pitch of his whole tale that the reader is compelled to search behind it for special reasons that would justify so much bitterness and emotion; they are not hard to find.

First, however, it is necessary to examine the extraordinary statement that preparations for a major enterprise, which had been begun before the end of 1916, were not known to the British War Cabinet until June, 1917, only a few weeks before the enterprise was due to be launched. If this were true, it would constitute the gravest criticism of Lloyd George's Government, the ultimate confession of its incompetence; if untrue, an entirely other light than his interpretation is thrown on the whole battle. In other words, if true Lloyd George was unfit to be Prime Minister; if untrue, the responsibility for Third Ypres is his. Of course, it is palpably incorrect that the Government could have been so ill-informed. The decisions of the Chantilly Conference of November, 1916, were on record; they had not been disavowed by the British Government. They had, certainly, been set aside for the duration of the Nivelle experiment, but when that ended in fiasco, it was made plain at the Paris Conference – at which Lloyd George was present – that a northern offensive, as laid down at Chantilly, with the express object of clearing the Belgian coast to relieve the submarine threat, was now the prior aim of the British High Command. Lloyd George's function at Paris had been to stimulate the French into active co-operation with the British plan. The whole meaning and tenor of the two telegrams which Robertson sent to Haig at the War Cabinet's instigation on May 14th and 16th was to make sure of this French support. As we have seen,[1] immediately after the Paris Conference, when Lloyd George visited Haig, the latter had given him 'notes of our requirements in guns, aeroplanes, etc., and he is to do his best to ensure what is needed being provided forthwith'. Is it to be supposed that Lloyd George never enquired what these things were needed for? Admittedly, after the astonishing indiscretion of Nivelle, both Haig and Robertson did their best, for simple reasons of military security, to limit the references to the Flanders attack; nevertheless, there was an unavoidable high minimum of such references. The words 'Ostend' and 'Zeebrugge' run like a refrain through the official papers of the entire half-year.

Not the least significant use of them was made by General Smuts[2], in a Memorandum on the Military Situation which he drew up for the Cabinet on April 29th. Smuts wrote: 'I feel the danger of a purely defensive policy so gravely that I would make the following suggestions in case the French carry out such a policy. . . . Our forces should then be concentrated towards the north, and part should go to the rear as a strategic reserve, *while the rest should endeavour to recover the northern coast of Belgium and drive the enemy from Zeebrugge and Ostend.*'[3] The truth of the matter is not that the War Cabinet first encountered this policy in mid-June, but that by then the Prime Minister's normal aversion to operations on the Western Front had returned; he had changed his mind again. The reasons for this are to be found not only in his personal distrust of Western Front methods and prospects – now greatly increased by the disappointment that followed Nivelle's failure – but

1. See p. 296.
2. Himself a member of the War Cabinet.
3. Author's italics.

also in the circumstances of the year, which underlined one of the most conspicuous failures of his Government.

If 'Ostend and Zeebrugge' provided the refrain of strategic thinking by G.H.Q. in France, the word 'Man-power' was equally the refrain of the War Office and the Government. As early as February 8th, the weekly Summary prepared by the General Staff for the War Cabinet had opened with these words: 'By far the most important feature to be noted in this week's summary is the breakdown of our own recruiting. In November last the War Office informed His Majesty's Government that unless steps were taken *at once* to provide more men for the Army it would be impossible after April next to keep it up to strength. Such measures as have been taken have proved to be quite inadequate, and the situation foreseen by the War Office has now arisen. . . .' On the following day, Haig sent for the Adjutant-General of the Expeditionary Force, 'and spoke to him regarding the serious state which will arise in April owing to the shortage of recruits from England. I told him to instruct his representatives with Armies to economize in men to the utmost extent possible.' All through the year this process of 'combing out' the B.E.F. continued; it could be no more than a palliative to the problem, and a dangerous one at that. Rear services have been an increasingly important factor in modern war; the temptation to cut them down reacted to the disadvantage of the fighting troops. Worse still, some fighting formations themselves were affected, particularly new ones, whose value was not appreciated by unimaginative Staff officers; both the Tank Corps and the Machine Gun Corps were sufferers in this respect.

Despite the urging of the War Office, no significant improvement in the situation appeared. By April the situation which the General Staff had predicted six months earlier had arisen. Haig noted on April 6th that, on current indications, his Army would be 136,000 below strength on July 1st, and 184,000 (the equivalent of fifteen divisions) on August 1st. There was worse to come. On May 26th Robertson wrote to him: 'Lord Derby and I had a long talk with the Prime Minister last night . . . and as an indication what the position is I may say that the Prime Minister told us that he was afraid *the time had now arrived when we must face the fact that we could not expect to get any large number of men in the future but only scraps.* He said this was because of the large demands for shipbuilding, food production, and *labour unrest*, and I am afraid that there is no getting away from the fact that there is great unrest in this country now as a result partly of the Russian revolution. There have been some bad strikes recently and there is still much discontent. An announcement even appeared in some of the newspapers yesterday with regard to the calling together of a committee of workmen and soldier delegates to consider the political situation. This shows the way the wind is apt to blow.'

This bad news provoked one of Haig's angriest and least considered outbursts. 'Your letter of May 26th', he replied, '. . . is very serious reading. I presume the General Staff will point out clearly to the Government what the effect of such a decision is likely to be. It would be well also to indicate what the results of our present operations might have reasonably been had our Divisions here been maintained at full strength. Briefly, the offensive in the Arras front could have been maintained at full pressure, at the same time as the attack in the north. And, in my opinion, the enemy would undoubtedly have been forced to withdraw to the line of the Meuse.

'As to what the effect of the curtailment of Drafts in the future may be (as foreshadowed in your letter), it is difficult to estimate until we know what is meant by "only scraps". There seems little doubt, however, that victory on the Western Front means victory everywhere and a lasting peace. And I have no further doubt that the British Army in France is capable of doing it, given adequate *drafts and guns.* . . .

'For the last two years most of us soldiers have realized that Great Britain must take the necessary steps to win the war by herself, because our French Allies had already shown that they lacked both the moral qualities and the means for gaining victory. It is thus sad to see the British Government failing at the XIIth hour.'

It is not necessary to pay too much attention to this letter; it was written in deep anger, and important parts of it run entirely counter to Haig's normal thinking. What is more to the point is to examine the position that gave rise to it. It should be remembered that, at this juncture, in its desperation, the recruiting branch of the War Office was preparing to fill the gaps in the Army's ranks with boys of $18\frac{1}{2}$, and with men between 41 and 50. Yet, according to Repington, who followed the man-power situation with close and penetrating attention throughout the War, there were $3\frac{1}{2}$ millions of men aged between 18 and 41 in civil life.[1] The reason for this was the system of 'certified (reserved) occupations' which was never so firmly gripped and rationalized during the First World War as during the Second. (Here, too, it may be added that there has to be a first time for everything.) On April 1st, Repington wrote: 'Every department is against the Army, and every new director or controller attempts to get men from the Army. A new Director of Timber Supplies is the latest bureaucrat created, and he went at once to ask for 25,000 men, though he admitted having six months' reserve timber in England. . . . The Board of Agriculture last September admitted that 100,000 A men in excess of needs of agriculture could be taken, but when the W.O. tried to get some of them, there was a howl, yet these were the Board's

1. See Repington: *The First World War*, pp. 505–507 and 568–570.

own calculations. Agriculture has 500,000 men of military age, Munitions 800,000,[1] the Admiralty a great many in supposed shipyards,[2] but many really doing other work; and then there are all the certified trades. Railways have behaved well, but every man with a cabbage-patch is now claiming exemption on agricultural grounds. . . . The country knows absolutely nothing of all these facts, and I cannot tell them.'

Nor was this all. At the end of March, using the War Office figures which were made available to him in confidence, Repington drew up a private table showing the distribution of the 4½ millions of men whom the British Army at that time had in uniform. It revealed that there were:

2,000,000 in France (actually 1,900,000)
1,710,000 in the United Kingdom
  234,000 at Salonika
  231,000 in Egypt (including 96,000 Indians)
   53,000 in East Africa (British, Indians and Africans)
  172,000 troops (British and Indian) ⎫
  118,000 camp followers   ⎬in Mesopotamia
                                  ⎭

The two figures which immediately attract the eye in this are, of course, those at the head of the table. It is remarkable to note that the B.E.F. only outnumbered the forces at home by some 200,000. Evidently the United Kingdom figure requires a further breakdown, and this Repington supplied:

'320,000 in hospital, including Dominion troops.
400,000 administrative troops.
130,000 Dominion troops, mainly drafts.
400,000 Home Defence troops.
400,000 troops for drafting.
 50,000 with other Government departments.'

Repington tells us that out of the Home Defence total (under Sir John French) only 100,000 were mobile troops; nevertheless, one cannot resist the feeling that this need was inflated. Of the 400,000 available for drafts, he adds, 'there are 230,000 infantry, but 180,000 of these on March 1st were either not trained or were young men of eighteen or nineteen. It is thought that by June some of the latter will have to be sent out. There were only 50,000 trained infantry drafts at home on March 1st. . . .' The contrast between the full figure for British drafts and that of the Dominion forces is particularly striking, when one recalls that there were 10 Dominion Divisions in the B.E.F., as opposed to 50 United Kingdom Divisions; the final figure,

1. Repington later (May 19th) reduced this figure to 528,000.
2. 85,000.

after analysis, compares even worse. And what is one to make of the 400,000 administrative troops, and the 50,000 with other Government departments? The War Office itself cannot escape a considerable measure of blame here; some 'combing out' on the lines which Haig had already instituted in the B.E.F. might have produced useful results.

Statistics make difficult reading, and there are more to come. They are essential if one is to understand the background against which Haig was working, and against which Lloyd George's ideas were developing. They are also essential if one is to understand the reasons for much of the suffering borne by the soldiers during 1917, and for the rest of the War. A part of this is expressed by Repington, who was a member of a Military Service Tribunal, in December, 1916: 'Sat on the Tribunal all the afternoon. Horrible process of sending fathers of families into the Army.' Not only fathers of families; it was now a question of young boys. Not only that; there were also the unfortunate men who returned to the front time after time, certified as having 'recovered' from wounds.[1] It was not uncommon to see men in fighting formations with three, four, five or even six wound stripes; such a thing should never have been seen. Even such heroes as General Carton de Wiart, who lost both an eye and a hand, and who became 'one of their most regular customers' at a certain London hospital, where 'they always gave me the same room ... even silk pyjamas with my name on were reserved for me ...'[2] should have been forcibly restrained. Leaving aside death and wounds, the strain imposed on fighting soldiers through the man-power shortage was, as we have seen, continuous and exhausting. And with this in mind, we may turn to our last statistical breakdown, the figure for the B.E.F. On June 4th the Adjutant-General at G.H.Q. reported to Haig that the Army's strength stood as follows:

'Total "effectives ..."'	70,506 officers	1,613,411 o.r.
Total "reinforcements"	1,828 ,,	63,456 ,,
Sick and at base	479 ,,	120,775 ,,

which, with Labour battalions and so forth, amounted to a total of 1,901,205. It was a huge force, in fine condition; but its effectiveness could only be maintained if it was kept up to strength.

From Lloyd George's point of view, all this took on a different meaning, and it is important to appreciate what this was. By 1917, he tells us, the Labour problem had become more than ever acute. 'Conscription, which had been adopted in the spring of 1916, was now in full operation. The

1. The author's father was one of these.
2. *Happy Odyssey*, the Memoirs of Lieutenant-General Sir Adrian Carton de Wiart, V.C., K.B.E., C.B., C.M.G., D.S.O. Jonathan Cape, 1950.

country was being rapidly denuded of its able-bodied manhood,[1] and to supply the insatiable demands of the Army, inroads had to be contemplated on those workers who had hitherto been privileged and exempt by virtue of the national importance of their occupations. Dilution . . . had to be correspondingly extended. Grievances multiplied in regard to wage rates. The growing shortage of food and the difficulty of ensuring a really equitable distribution of the limited supplies, was the most serious grievance of all. The growth of munition works led in some districts to housing shortages and congestion. The meagre supplies of beer and the lightening of its gravity caused much ill-feeling. "Swipes", as it was contemptuously called, was doubly unpopular. It was lacking in kick and quantity. . . . Whisky was very expensive and the districts which drew inspiration from that fountain complained of the drought. Then among the officials appointed by the Government to carry out its measures, not all were competent and tactful. . . . In short, there was an array of causes, great and small, which combined with the general upset of the old order and the griefs and anxieties of the War to breed a spirit of irritation and annoyance. In this condition the body corporate of the nation was assailed by a new infection. The coming of the Russian Revolution lit up the skies with a lurid flash of hope for all who were dissatisfied with the existing order of society. It certainly encouraged all the habitual malcontents in the ranks of labour to foment and organize discontent. Fishers in troubled waters, they did not create the unrest, but they took full advantage of it. Their activities sprang into special prominence in 1917, and seriously added to our difficulties.' The result of all this, he tells us, was 588 industrial disputes in 1917 (April and May saw some of the most serious of these) affecting 860,727 workers, and causing the loss of 5,966,000 working days. This was a scale that recalled the pre-war industrial crises; a gloomy preoccupation in the mind of one who had also to take major strategic decisions.

*   *   *   *

Lloyd George's new committee assembled to thrash out the question of the Flanders offensive on June 19th. For Robertson's guidance, Haig drew up, five days earlier, a statement on the 'Present Situation and Future Plans'.[2] He showed that pressure had been maintained on the enemy since the opening of the year's campaigning at Arras; that the first phase of the Flanders attack (Messines) had been completed successfully; that arrangements for direct French support in Flanders had been made; in addition, 'General Pétain is

1. Not only Repington and the War Office, but our Allies and enemies too might raise their eyebrows at this.
2. O.A.D. 478, June 12th.

also arranging for offensive operations on other portions of his front, on a sufficient scale to prevent withdrawal of German forces to oppose my advance; and, well prepared and supported by artillery, the operations intended by him should prove effective in wearing down the enemy opposed to him'. In short, he stated, the conditions which he had laid down in May for a successful attack had, with one exception, been fulfilled. That exception was the provision of drafts and guns to bring his army up to strength. Nevertheless, he added: 'With the drafts and guns already promised . . . I consider, on present indications, that it will be possible to carry through at least a portion of the operations intended, and my plans and preparations are being made to advance by stages so arranged that, while each stage will give a definite and useful result, it will be possible for me to discontinue the advance if and when it appears that the means at my disposal are insufficient to justify a further effort. . . . I am accordingly pushing on my preparations for the Northern operations but these cannot be complete for some time and the scope of my plans can and will be adjusted as may seem necessary to future developments in the situation.'

All this was sober and reasonable enough; the next part of the paper, however, containing Haig's assessment of the overall situation, is in a somewhat different vein. It requires to be quoted in full:[1]

'According to reports, the endurance of the German nation is being tested so severely that discontent there has already assumed formidable proportions. The German Government, helped by the long disciplinary training of the people, is still able to control this discontent; but every fresh defeat of the German armies, combined with a growing realization of the failure of the submarine campaign, increases the difficulty of doing so, and further defeats in the field may have unexpectedly great results, which may come with unexpected suddenness.

'The German army, too, shows unmistakable signs of deterioration in many ways and the cumulative effect of further defeats may at any time yield greater results in the field than we can absolutely rely on gaining.

'I attach notes on these points, as an Appendix to this paper.'

In this Appendix, Haig remarked that the collapse of Russia had not, so far, resulted in any large movement of German troops from the Eastern to the Western Front; he added that he did not expect, even if matters became worse in Russia, that more than 20 German divisions would be transferred, at the rate of 2 per week. The Bolshevik Revolution, it must be remembered, was still four months away in the future, and there were, in June, still hopes

1. Blake's version is much reduced by editing.

that Russia would continue to play an active part in the War. Haig then turned to the German army which, he said, now had only 35 fresh divisions left, while 105 divisions 'have probably lost an average of not less than 40% of their infantry'. This led him to one of his most controversial statements: 'Germany is within 4 to 6 months of a date at which she will be unable to maintain the strength of her units in the field.'

He referred to the effects of economic warfare, and to the evidence of declining morale, concluding:

'From all these definite facts, it is a fair indication that, given a continuance of circumstances as they stand at present and given a continuation of the effort of the Allies, then Germany may well be forced to conclude a peace on our terms before the end of the year.' It is important to note Haig's provisos, which were clearly written into his paper, whatever verbal misunderstandings may have arisen later. But even with the provisos, as we shall see, Robertson for one was extremely startled at Haig's conclusion.

Let us return to Haig's main document:

'From a careful study of the conditions, I feel justified in stating that con-tinued pressure with as little delay as possible certainly promises at least very valuable results; whereas relaxation of pressure now would strengthen belief that the allies are becoming totally exhausted, and that Germany can outlast them. Waning hope in Germany would be revived, and time would be gained to replenish food, ammunition, and other requirements. In fact many of the advantages already gained by us would be lost, and this would certainly be realized by, and would have a depressing effect on, our armies in the field who have made such great efforts to gain them.'

He was concerned not only with his own armies, but with his Allies.

'At the present crisis of the war French hope must have something to feed on. The hope of American assistance is not sufficient for this purpose. It is still too far distant and the French are living a good deal on the hope of further British successes. They can and will assist in these by keeping the enemy on their front fully employed, wearing him down, and preventing him from withdrawing divisions to oppose us. But they feel unable at present to do more than this, and it is useless to expect it of them – although any considerable British successes, and signs of a breakdown in the German power of resistance, would probably have an electrifying effect.

'That the British armies in France are capable of gaining considerable further successes this year I am confident, as are all ranks under my command; – it is only the extent of the success that is possible that is in doubt, and that depends mainly on three factors, viz:

Firstly, on whether the War Cabinet decides to concentrate our resources on the effort.

Secondly, on the degree of help given by Russia.

Thirdly, on the extent to which the German resolution and power of endurance stand the great strain they are undergoing.

'The first of these factors lies within the power of the War Cabinet. The second to some extent, and the third to a very great extent, depend on their decision.

'It is my considered opinion, based not on mere optimism but on a thorough study of the situation, guided by experience which I may claim to be considerable, that if our resources are concentrated in France to the fullest possible extent the British armies are capable and can be relied on to effect great results this summer – results which will make final victory more assured and which may even bring it within reach this year.

'On the other hand I am equally convinced that to fail in concentrating our resources in the Western theatre, or to divert them from it, would be most dangerous. It might lead to the collapse of France. It would certainly encourage Germany. And it would discourage our own officers and men very considerably. The desired military results, possible in France, are not possible elsewhere.

'I am aware that my motives in stating this may be misunderstood, but I trust that in the interests of the Empire, at what is undoubtedly a critical period of the War, whatever value the War Cabinet may attach to my opinion may not be discounted by any doubt of such a kind. I have reason to believe that the Commanders-in-Chief of British Forces in other theatres of war are entirely in agreement with the view that the Western front always has been and will remain the decisive one.

'The correct strategy to pursue, in accordance with the teaching of every great exponent of the art of war, is clear under such conditions.

'In my opinion the only serious doubt as to possibilities in France lies in the action to be expected of Russia, but even that doubt is an argument in favour of doing our utmost in France with as little delay as possible.

'Russia is still holding large German forces and every week gained makes it more impossible for the enemy to transfer divisions to the West in time, if we act promptly.

'There is still room for hope of increased Russian assistance, and successes in the West will surely increase the prospects of it.

'A passive attitude in the West, or mere minor successes, would not encourage the Russians; and delay under such conditions may make matters worse in Russia instead of better.

'In conclusion, I desire to make it clear that, whatever force may be placed at my disposal, my undertakings will be limited to what it is reasonably possible to succeed in.

'Given sufficient force, provided no great transfer of German troops is made, in time, from East to West, it is probable that the Belgian coast could be cleared this summer, and the defeats on the German troops entailed in doing so might quite possibly lead to their collapse.

'Without sufficient force I shall not attempt to clear the coast and my efforts will be restricted to gaining such victories as are within reach, thereby improving my positions for the winter and opening up possibilities for further operations hereafter if and when the necessary means are provided.

'A definition of the term "sufficient force" must depend on developments in the general situation; but provided that does not grow less satisfactory than at present I estimate that even the full programme may not prove beyond reach with the number of divisions now at my disposal, if brought up and maintained at establishment of men and guns. An increase in the forces available would, of course, give still greater prospects of complete success.

D. Haig.'

This paper is the fullest and most far-reaching statement of Haig's hopes and intentions. It is of vital importance for that reason, and also because it shows the complexity of the threads of his thoughts at the time. It has been said, for example, that '. . . there is little doubt now that his real motive was a strange belief that he could defeat the German army single-handed in Flanders'.[1] This paper disposes entirely of that theory; in it, and in *every* appreciation which he made at this juncture, he shows that he was still depending upon the underlying principle of the Chantilly agreement: inter-Allied support. We have to note the fact – not without amazement – that he was even still counting on a measure of Russian co-operation. It has also been said that his motive was 'to save France'; we must then note that, while the possibility of a French collapse was certainly in his mind (as it had been ever since 1915), one of the basic conditions of his whole plan was the tying down *and wearing down* of substantial German forces by the French. We perceive, too, that while he had large, distant objectives in mind, he also, *from the very first*, had lesser ones, and was prepared to settle for these if necessary. We see that he was aware, even before the attack began, that his motives might be misconstrued, and conscious that his analysis might be dismissed as over-optimistic; guided by these reflections, he had reviewed the situation carefully again, and had come to the same conclusions. There was nothing hasty, nor unconsidered in this judgment.

It was, nevertheless, wrong, and one of the first people to perceive this

1. Liddell Hart.

was Robertson. Evidently considerably astonished at the scope of the prospects which Haig held out (and conscious of the difficulties in the way of fulfilling the conditions which he had laid down), Robertson at once sent him a telegram saying: 'Your appreciation . . . arrives very opportunely and I entirely agree with your views and will support them to the utmost of my power. But I cannot possibly agree with some of the statements in the appendix. For example, extent of depletion of enemy reserves and deduction given in final paragraph. I hope, therefore, you will agree appendix not being circulated to War Cabinet. . . . It would be very regrettable at this juncture if different estimates of enemy resources were presented to the War Cabinet as it would tend to destroy value of your sound appreciation. You will have opportunity during discussion here to give such information regarding enemy's reserves as you deem necessary.' Haig agreed to the deletion of the appendix to his paper, but there is no doubt that he remained firmly wedded to the propositions contained in it. This was the fundamental cause of the bitterness which later came to inspire every version of the events that followed. He was, in fact, 'doing a Nivelle' – arousing expectations which, if they should not be fulfilled, would cloud every positive aspect of the campaign. It is surprising that, with his naturally cautious temperament, he did not recognize this risk.

Robertson, on the other hand, saw it only too well. He followed his telegram with a letter on the same day, June 13th, which opened with these ominous words: 'There is trouble in the land just now. . . .' There was indeed. Harrassed by his internal difficulties, Lloyd George was now less than ever disposed to add to them by taking the firm measures which alone could enable Haig's conditions to be fulfilled. Rather than face the tremendous demands of major operations on the Western Front, he had once more begun that restless search for expedients which was always the chief characteristic of his military policy. 'To forewarn you of what is in the air', wrote Robertson to Haig, 'so that you may be ready for them next week, the L.G. idea is to settle the war from Italy, and today the railway people have been asked for figures regarding the rapid transfer of 12 Divisions and 300 heavy guns to Italy! They will never go while I am C.I.G.S. but all that will come later. What I do wish to impress on you is this: Don't argue that you can finish the war this year, or that the German is already beaten. Argue that your plan is the best plan – as it is – that no other plan would even be *safe* let alone decisive, and then leave them to reject your advice and mine. They dare not do that. Further, on this occasion they will be up against the French.' And to this, Robertson added in a postscript: 'We have got to remember, as we do, that the Government carry the chief responsibility, and that in a war of this kind many things besides the actual Army must be considered. Having remembered this, however, we are entitled to see that unsound military plans are not adopted – or all other plans may come to nought.'

Lloyd George did not reciprocate Robertson's understanding; the Prime Minister was now once more in the full flood of what General J. F. C. Fuller has called the 'Strategy of Evasion'; he could never bring himself to understand that: 'The main bases and the main theatre of war were fixed by geography and logistics, and no juggling with fronts could alter this. . . . All these peripheral endeavours to discover a penetrable front were a waste of effort and in the expenditure of man-power – the vital factor in mass-warfare – costly in the extreme. The stalemate laughed each to scorn.'[1] The irony was that Lloyd George's attempts to 'by-pass' the man-power problem ended by making it much worse.

Once again, Haig sat down to review his arguments. Once more, he set his pen to a long and detailed account of his intentions, this time for the War Cabinet itself. Rarely can any battle have been the subject of so much heart-searching, before it began, as the Third Battle of Ypres. Prompted by Robertson's warnings, Haig's new paper[2] dealt in greater detail with the advantages to be gained from an advance in Belgium: 'A very limited advance will enable our guns to make OSTEND useless to the German navy, and will, at the same time, render DUNKIRK – one of our most important ports – immune from long-range hostile gun fire . . . an advance sufficient to bring the ROULERS-THOUROUT Railway within effective range of our guns would restrict [the enemy's] railway communications with the coast to those passing through GHENT and BRUGES. A short further advance, bringing us within effective heavy-gun range of BRUGES, would most probably induce the evacuation of ZEEBRUGGE and the whole coast line. The consequences of extending our front to the Dutch frontier would be so considerable that they might prove decisive.'

Haig proceeded to develop this theme to some distance, and then added: 'Comparing this operation with anything that we might do in other theatres its advantages are overwhelming.

'It directly and seriously threatens our main enemy, on whom the whole Coalition against us depends.

'It is within the easiest possible reach of our base by sea and rail and can be developed infinitely more rapidly, and maintained infinitely more easily, than any other operation open to us.

'It admits of the closest possible combination of our naval and military strength.

'It covers all the points which we dare not uncover, and therefore admits

1. J. F. C. Fuller: *The Conduct of War 1789–1961*, Eyre & Spottiswoode, 1961.
2. O.A.D. 502, June 17th.

of the utmost concentration of force; whereas, for the same reason, any force employed in any other theatre of war can never be more than a detachment, with all the disadvantages of detachments. . . .

'In no part of any theatre of war would so limited an advance promise such far-reaching results on Germany, and through Germany, on her allies and on neutrals.'

Haig concluded: 'In my opinion the time and place to choose are now beyond dispute. We have gone a long way already towards success. Victory may be nearer than is generally realized if we act correctly now. But we may fall seriously short of it if at this juncture we fail to follow the correct principles.' To this he appended a special paper, comparing the prospects in Belgium with those in Italy. The arguments against Italy, he said, were 'overwhelmingly stronger than those in favour of it'. The core of his case was expressed in this paragraph: 'It is at best very uncertain that we could defeat Austria. If the Germans elected to send divisions round to meet us on the Italian frontier their railway facilities are better than ours in the proportion of 5 to 2; and as it is Germany's interest to uphold Austria just as much as it is ours to overcome Austria it is practically certain that she would endeavour to do so, either by attacking the French violently, or by transferring divisions to the Italian front.'

And on this small mountain of paper Haig rested his case until the meeting of Lloyd George's committee on June 19th.

The day was auspicious only in one respect: it was Haig's birthday. 'It is new for me to receive so many congratulations as I did today', he remarked. 'Usually my birthday has passed almost unnoticed and often forgotten, even by myself.' The War Cabinet committee assembled at 11 a.m., and it soon became clear that congratulations were not on the agenda of that body. 'The members of the War Cabinet', wrote Haig, 'asked me numerous questions, all tending to show that each of them was more pessimistic than the other. The Prime Minister seemed to believe the decisive moment of the war would be 1918. Until then we ought to husband our forces and do little or nothing, except support Italy with guns and gunners. . . . I strongly asserted that Germany was nearer her end than they seemed to think, that *now* was the favourable moment for pressing her and that everything possible should be done to take advantage of it by concentrating on the Western Front *all* available resources. I stated that Germany was within six months of the total exhaustion of her available manpower, *if the fighting continues at its present intensity*. To do this more guns and men are necessary.' There can be no doubt that Haig used unusual force and warmth in putting forward his views on this occasion.

'When Sir Douglas Haig explained his projects to the civilians', writes Lloyd George, 'he spread on a table or desk a large map and made a dramatic use of both his hands to demonstrate how he proposed to sweep up the enemy – first the right hand brushing along the surface irresistibly, and then came the left, his outer finger ultimately touching the German frontier with the nail across. . . . It is not surprising that some of us were so captivated by the splendour of the landscape opened out to our vision that their critical faculties were overwhelmed. Mr. Bonar Law, Lord Milner and I remained sceptical.'

Lloyd George never forgave that finger-nail. Even Charteris, who had supplied the information on which this was based, whistled when he heard what Haig had said: 'D.H. gave the definite opinion that if the fighting was kept up at its present intensity for six months Germany would be at the end of her available man-power. This is going rather farther than the paper I wrote for D.H. on the 11th of June. . . .'

The meeting on the 19th was short – Lloyd George had to attend his daughter's wedding. The next day, Haig read his paper comparing the advantages of attacking in Belgium with those of operations against Austria. 'Much talk and many questions.' He was asked about the strength of the German artillery; about casualties and their likely effect on the man-power situation; above all, about the degree to which French support could be counted on. As regards the questions concerning his own army, he founded his case in reply on the successes won at Vimy and Messines; as regards the conduct of his Allies, he depended on Pétain's repeated assurances. The argument swayed to and fro without coming nearer to a decision. And then, says Haig, 'A most serious and startling situation was disclosed. . . . At today's Conference Admiral Jellicoe, as First Sea Lord, stated that owing to the great shortage of shipping due to German submarines, it would be impossible to continue the war in 1918. This was a bombshell for the Cabinet and all present. A full enquiry is to be made as to the real facts on which this opinion of the Naval Authorities is based. No one present shared Jellicoe's view, and all seemed satisfied that the food reserves in Great Britain are adequate. Jellicoe's words were, "There is no good discussing plans for next Spring – we cannot go on".'

To say that this was a 'bomb-shell' was to put it mildly. 'This startling and reckless declaration I challenged indignantly,' wrote Lloyd George, 'but the First Sea Lord adhered to it.' This was, in fact, the turning-point of the Conference. Discussion continued for several more days, during which Lloyd George forcefully presented his case in a lengthy and well-argued Memorandum in which he said: 'I earnestly entreat our military advisers as well as the Cabinet to think again before they finally commit the British Army to an attack, the failure of which may very well weary the Allied nations into accepting any plausible peace that may be offered them by an equally weary foe.' He pressed his own belief in attacking Austria with all his habitual eloquence.

Haig responded to this with yet another paper, in which he stated: '. . . in view of the deliberate opinion expressed by the Prime Minister that he has "grave misgivings of the advice" which he had received from his Military Advisers, I have again most carefully reviewed the opinions which I have expressed in the various documents submitted by me since the 1st May last for the information of the War Cabinet. This further investigation of the problem has confirmed me as strongly as ever in those opinions.' Again he referred to the state of the German army, which, he said, 'has already lost much of that *moral* force without which physical power, even in its most terrible form is but an idle show'. Robertson added that, for his part: 'He had shown, and he understood the War Cabinet agreed, that we must continue to be aggressive somewhere on our front, and we ought, of course, to do this in the most promising direction. The plan provided for this and would enable us to derive a real advantage till the enemy showed signs of weakening, while at the same time it permitted of our easing off if the situation so demands. Doubtful situations, such as the present one, had always arisen in war, and great mistakes had been made by endeavouring to find a fresh way round as soon as the strain began to be felt. We should be on our guard against this mistake.'[1]

All this, one feels, had now become academic, after Jellicoe's intervention. The Admiral continued to insist that the Navy would be in grave difficulty unless the Belgian coast was cleared. The committee was in a cleft stick; Lloyd George, Bonar Law and Milner remained unrepentantly opposed to the offensive; Smuts, Balfour and Curzon supported the Army leaders. The Prime Minister did not exercise a casting vote; on the contrary, he says, 'It was . . . decided that I should once more sum up the misgivings which most [sic] of us felt *and leave the responsibility to Sir William Robertson and Sir Douglas Haig*,[2] on the understanding that if the progress they made with the operation did not realize the expectations they had formed, it should be called off and effective help be rendered to the Italians to press their offensive.' In fact, Haig came away with no sense that his plans had been properly endorsed by the Government; he noted that there was to be yet another conference with the French Government in two weeks' time to go into the whole matter again. Meanwhile, however, 'I am to go on with my preparations'. It was a distinctly tame ending to what had shown every sign of being a ferocious and critical debate. The reason for this was, once again, Jellicoe. The alarm which Haig

1. Lloyd George's summary.
2. Author's italics.

and Lloyd George shared over Jellicoe's views drew them together, despite their own strategic disagreements. Sir Eric Geddes, now a member of the Board of Admiralty, painted to Haig a gloomy picture of the state of affairs there: 'The First Lord (Carson) has recently married, is very tired, and leaves everything to a number of incompetent sailors! Jellicoe, [Geddes] says, is feeble to a degree and vacillating. Only one Admiral (Halsey) is fit for his post. There is no *fixed policy*. . . .' On the day after the discussions on Army policy had ended, Haig and Geddes breakfasted with Lloyd George to talk about naval matters. It was at this meeting that Haig urged that Geddes should replace Carson, and that a sweeping reconstitution of the Board of Admiralty should take place – a conversation which, Lloyd George tells us, 'finally decided me'. It is one more curiosity of those strange and complex times that Lloyd George should attach such weight to Haig's recommendations on naval affairs, and so little to his views on the work of his own Service.

It is also a curiosity that, apart from the decidedly equivocal proceedings of the Cabinet committee, no formal Government approval of the vast undertaking on which Haig was embarking was given until less than a week before it began. On July 10th Robertson told Haig that Painlevé 'assures me . . . that the French Army will be able to assist us by attacking on its own front, and that the French Government intends that it should do so'. President Poincaré, visiting G.H.Q. on the same day, had been 'profuse in his good wishes for the success of our future offensive'. This disposed of the last query about the French. Yet no word came from the British Government. Five days later, the preliminary bombardment opened, strictly speaking, without Government consent. Five days later still, Robertson wrote to Haig: 'When you left, Cabinet had not definitely approved your plans. Up to the present no official approval of your plans has been given. I dare say that tomorrow or the next day I shall be told that your plans are approved.' This, Haig commented, was 'somewhat startling. . . . The fact is that the Cabinet does not really understand what preparations for an attack really mean for the forces and Commanders in the field'. That night the King's Messenger brought Robertson's news that the Cabinet had, at last, given its approval, but so hedged with references to possible failure that Haig could not feel that he had their confidence.

The next day Robertson himself came over to see Haig: 'I urged him to be firmer and play the man; and, if need be, resign, should Lloyd George persist in ordering troops to Italy against the advice of the General Staff. I also spoke strongly on the absurdity of the Government giving its approval now to operations after a stiff artillery fight had been going on for three weeks. I handed him my reply to his official letter informing me of this approval. In it I requested to be told whether I had the full support of the Government or not.' On July 25th, six days before the battle began, Haig at last received his reply; Robertson telegraphed: 'War Cabinet authorizes me to inform you that having approved your plans being executed you may depend on their whole-hearted support and that if and when they decide again to reconsider the situation they will obtain your views before arriving at any decision as to cessation of operations.'

Grudgingly, belatedly, but necessarily, the Government acknowledged its responsibility for 'Passchendaele'. Writing to Lord Derby on the eve of battle in a rare mood of bitterness, Haig remarked: 'How different to the whole-hearted, almost unthinking support given by our Government to the Frenchman (Nivelle) last January.'

The contrast was, indeed, striking; yet there was one resemblance between Haig and Nivelle now: each of them, in Robertson's grim phrase, went into action 'with a rope around his neck'.

*   *   *   *

The preliminary bombardment for 'Third Ypres' opened on July 15th; the infantry went over the top at 3.50 a.m. on July 31st – sunrise, but there was no sun. Already, long before the great attack was launched, unpropitious omens were discernible at the front, quite apart from the doubts and hesitations of the Government. On June 21st Charteris wrote: 'The longest day of the year, and we have not yet even begun the really big effort. . . . We fight alone here, the only army active. We shall do well, of that there is no reasonable doubt. Have we time to accomplish?' This question went to the heart of the matter. Fifty-three days – nearly eight weeks – separated the assault at Messines, the first part of the Flanders offensive, from the Battle of Pilckem Ridge, the opening of the second part. A great deal of the misfortune and the misery that followed is attributable to this protracted delay. That it was unwelcome to Haig is evident from the many references to the need for prompt action in his papers and orders. Yet he must be held responsible for it to a large extent. His first detailed statement of his intentions to his Army Commanders on May 7th envisaged a delay of some six weeks between 'Messines' and the main attack; this was already much too long an interval. It will be recalled that in 1916 Haig argued strenuously with Joffre that preparatory attacks should not be separated from the main effort by more than about a fortnight. The same considerations applied to Messines. Indeed, the possibility of immediately exploiting that victory was foreseen in the orders given to Plumer; it was realized that by edging forward the northern wing of the Second Army, valuable ground and observation might be gained in what Haig always recognized as the key sector of the big offensive – the Gheluvelt 'plateau' immediately east of Ypres. Plumer was prepared to carry out this further step, in his own way, but Gough preferred to make the operation quite distinct from Messines, and part of the Fifth Army's general assault. Immeasurable ill flowed from this option.

The decision to entrust the main role in the Flanders battle to the Fifth Army under General Gough must be regarded as Haig's gravest and most fatal error. Sir Hubert Gough was the youngest of his Army Commanders; at forty-seven, he was probably one of the youngest men in any army to hold such a position – an example of that continuous desire on Haig's part to bring young men forward which we have noted earlier. Because Gough was a cavalryman, and it became the fashion to jeer at 'cavalry generals'; because it was Gough's Army which suffered the great disaster of March, 1918, which led to his dismissal, much unfair criticism has been uttered about this officer, who is still, at the moment of writing, alive – the last survivor of the High Command of the First World War. Two criticisms of his conduct in 1917 can legitimately be made: first, he did not grasp the strategic fundamental of the Ypres battle, either before it began, or while it was in progress; secondly, he permitted himself to be badly served by his Staff, with consequent unfortunate tactical results, to say nothing of the loss and suffering imposed on the soldiers under him. The first of these two criticisms will emerge in the ensuing narrative. The second may be dealt with now. General Gough himself told this author, in 1958, that he attributed much of the reproach subsequently levelled against him and his Army to the unfortunate manner of his Chief of Staff, Major-General Neil Malcolm. Inasmuch as a Staff takes a large part of its 'tone' from the chief Staff Officer, this would appear to be true; General Malcolm was a military intellectual, with a share of the impatience and arrogance that often go with this quality, both in the Army and in civil life. The Universities can afford many examples. That stern critic of inadequate commanders, Sir Philip Gibbs, tells us that: 'General Gough . . . was extremely courteous, of most amiable character, with a high sense of duty. But in Flanders, if not personally responsible for many tragic happenings, he was badly served by some of his subordinates; and battalion officers, and divisional staffs, raged against the whole of the Fifth Army organization, or lack of organization, with an extreme passion of speech.

' "You must be glad to leave Flanders", I said to a group of officers trekking towards the Cambrai Salient.

'One of them answered violently:

' "God be thanked we are leaving the Fifth Army area!" '

It can only be a matter of sadness to all 'Goughie's' many admirers that he should have allowed such sentiments to become associated with him.

Gough himself has told us, in his book *The Fifth Army*, what the effect of the transfer of control to his Army was. As Messines opened, he held a conference with his new Corps Commanders. (It must be noted here that the transfer of an Army did not mean the physical movement of the formations, or even the subordinate headquarters comprising it; it referred only to the Army Staff itself. Consequently it is rubbish to make any comparison between the fighting qualities of one *Army* and another. But the Staffs can be compared.) At this conference, Gough tells us: 'The details of the operations which lay before us were considered, *and a slight change in the plan was made*;[1] it was proposed to pivot on the left with the French, while the right flank advanced along the Passchendaele Ridge. This would eventually bring our general direction *northwards*[2] to clear the Houthoulst Forest, and Roulers would cease to be an objective of the Fifth Army.' He adds: 'The original plan had been for me to capture the high ground on my right, as a preliminary operation ... however, I told the Commander-in-Chief that I would prefer to make this attack part and parcel of the major operations, as a partial attack, even if successful, would only throw the troops employed into a very pronounced salient, and expose them to the concentrated fury of all the German artillery, and to this change the Commander-in-Chief agreed.'

It is extremely difficult to understand why Haig did agree to this change in the plan. It was anything but 'slight' – it was fundamental; moreover, it ran counter to all Haig's own ideas; he realized this, when it was too late. We can only conclude that this was another example, and this time a disastrous one, of his principle of allowing the utmost freedom of action to the man actually entrusted with operations.

Gough's argument for not immediately seizing the high ground (nowhere higher than 64 metres) in the centre of the battlefield was quite unsound, as he realized after the battle had begun. The problem facing the Fifth Army was a matter of timing; it is clear that the danger of pushing troops into an exposed salient was real enough, but the answer was to follow the attack towards Gheluvelt *at once* with progressive expansions of the front on either side of it, to occupy and spread the enemy's artillery. This neither Gough nor his Staff ever fully understood, though Haig made the matter perfectly clear when he discussed the Fifth Army plan with Gough on June 28th: 'I urged the importance of the right flank. It is in my opinion vitally important to occupy and hold the ridge west of Gheluvelt in order to cover our right flank and then push along it to Broodseinde. The main battle will be fought on or for this ridge so we must make our plans accordingly. The main difficulty

1. Author's italics.
2. Author's italics.

seems to be at the beginning of the attack, in advancing from a comparatively small salient to the attack of a wider area. I impressed on Gough the vital importance of the ridge in question, *and that the advance north should be limited until our right flank has really been secured on this ridge.*'[1]

Still apprehensive the next day, Haig visited Lieut.-General Sir Claud Jacob, commanding II Corps opposite Gheluvelt ridge, and again 'I emphasized the importance of securing the Gheluvelt ridge to cover the right flank'. During the four weeks that followed, however, there is no sign that any significant change was made in the Fifth Army's plan. We can only attribute this either to plain misunderstanding, or to stubbornness on the part of the Fifth Army Staff. Haig himself, however, should have taken steps to make sure that his intentions were being implemented.

Thus, before any action was even commenced, we see that the army was driven off its true axis of advance. To Haig, Roulers had always been the key to the German positions in Flanders; Gough, commanding the main attacking Army, had abandoned Roulers as an objective. It is only possible to account for this by reference to the Admiralty's obsession with the submarine bases at Ostend and Zeebrugge. What Gough was planning was nothing less than a frontal attack on those bases, supported by an operation towards their lines of communication; what Haig had originally envisaged was the severing of the lines of communication, and *only then* a frontal attack,[2] supported by an amphibious operation. The difference was essential. But it was not only this dangerous change of emphasis which bedevilled the offensive. If the initial programme itself can be castigated as too leisurely, subsequent delays greatly enhanced this fault. July was a month of continuous frustration. On the 1st, General Malcolm came to Haig to report that the French on the left of the Fifth Army were not yet ready, and he suggested that the attack should therefore be delayed. Haig noted: 'I am averse to postponing, so I told Malcolm to make out a plan for holding back the left of the Fifth Army, while the right takes the Gheluvelt ridge.' On the 7th, Gough again asked for a delay of five days, on account of artillery losses. Haig told him: 'Every day is of consequence.' Nevertheless, on the 12th, Haig had to agree to a three-day postponement of the battle. On the 21st, General Anthoine, commanding the 1st French Army on Haig's left, pointed out that, owing to weather conditions, the French bombardment could only be rated at one day's value, instead of the ostensible seven days that it had lasted; he wanted further delay. On the 25th, Gough told Haig that he was ready to attack on the 28th, but thought it better to wait two or three days more for the French to complete

1. Author's italics.
2. On the Western Front every attack was frontal, there being no flanks; but flanks could be made by changing the direction of an advance.

their preparations. Haig agreed. Gough attributes the loss of six days to the French, and this loss, he says, 'turned out to be fatal to our hopes'.

Certainly the direct assistance of a French Army was, at this stage, more trouble than it was worth. It was away on the French front itself that Haig really wanted support, but the French Government, as we have seen,[1] had made it a set policy to interpose French troops between the British and the sea. General Anthoine was not to be blamed for the delays of his Army; they stemmed from the collapse of French morale earlier in the year. His artillery was complete as regards guns by July 1st – but a third of his gunners were on leave, in accordance with the promises Pétain had had to make to restore morale. When Haig exclaimed, on the 23rd: 'What a nuisance these French are!' this was in no sense a reflection on Anthoine, with whom his relations were excellent from the first. Indeed, he came to hold Anthoine in higher regard than almost any other French general with whom he was associated, and this esteem was reciprocated to such an extent that Anthoine's Anglophilia made him suspect to his compatriots. But there are other grounds than these for exonerating Anthoine and his Army from blame for the troubles that now ensued; it was not the six days' delay which General Gough attributed to the French that caused the damage at 'Third Ypres'. It was the long weeks after Messines during which the alerted enemy was given time to recuperate and prepare, while the short summer slipped past. Nor can this be blamed entirely on Haig, although his command changes did worsen the situation. The truth is that it was not 'Passchendaele' itself that was beyond the power of the British Army; it was 'Passchendaele' plus Arras. Arras was fought and continued for the sake of Nivelle; and the man who had put the British Army at Nivelle's disposal was, after all, Lloyd George.

Gough had significantly changed the plan; Gough and Anthoine together had insisted on equally significant delays. There were other omens, also, which indicated what kind of a task it was that lay ahead. As the Fifth Army deployed its batteries on the level Flanders plain to the north of Ypres, the Germans reacted violently. When Haig spoke to Robertson on the 22nd of an artillery fight that had been in progress for three weeks, this was a fact. Gough had spoken to him as early as the 7th about the loss of 27 guns out of 36 on the XIV Corps front, and heavy losses continued. All along the line, the massed British batteries were subjected to a furious counter-bombardment. On the 19th a distinguished battalion commander,[2] training his men for the battle, noted in his diary: 'Until yesterday most of those addressing us, with a comprehensive sweep of the pointer across the map, have declared that by "Zero hour" all the German trenches will be obliterated by our shells

1. See p. 128.
2. Brigadier-General J. L. Jack, D.S.O., then commanding 2/West Yorks, 8th Division.

– a tale we have heard before. The last lecturer, however, on the artillery role, ominously omitted to provide this comforting assurance. Our Air offensive has already commenced. Now the Battle Bombardments have opened at Ypres; it is whispered that they have drawn a considerable reply from the enemy. . . .'

On July 28th, when he was taking his battalion up to the line, the same officer recorded: 'We proceed through the entrenched field artillery positions, the pieces of the battery nearest us all out of action, lying with broken wheels and shields or overturned by the successive bombardments that sweep the extensive lines of guns from end to end, and necessitate large replacements after dark.' Yet on the 25th Lieut.-General Sir Noel Birch, Chief Artillery Adviser at G.H.Q., had reported to Haig that he was 'confident the upper hand over the German artillery had been gained'. The Official Historian dryly records that this optimism was not justified. The German artillery remained a factor to reckon with most seriously. The British 1st Division, holding a small sector among the sand-dunes at Nieuport, pending the amphibious attack, knew this only too well. On July 10th two unfortunate battalions were practically annihilated in an exposed bridgehead; survivors stated that between 70 and 80 per cent of their strength had become casualties under the German artillery fire. This also was an omen.

It is impossible to avoid the sense, during the final days before the attack went in, of a dangerous divergence of opinion between the front and rear of the Army. The physical difficulties of mounting a large offensive from the wet, devastated and well-nigh shelterless Ypres Salient were enormous; danger and fatigue – above all, fatigue – told upon the spirits of the troops and regimental officers. The wonder is that their cheerfulness kept up as well as it did. Brigade and Divisional Commanders in their turn were acutely aware of many difficulties. Further back a different atmosphere reigned – or if not, it was affected for the benefit of the Commander-in-Chief. General Jacob (II Corps) expressed himself on the 17th as 'most confident'; Haig commented: 'When officers live in such close touch with their men, look after their wants, and know what is going on, there can be little doubt as to the result of any operation.' The next day General Birch sent in a satisfactory artillery report: '. . . hostile fire is said to have slackened as the result of our bombardments. . . .' On the 20th, Haig was with II Corps again – his attention still correctly concentrated on the vital Gheluvelt sector – and 'spent an hour going through their schemes in detail. Every detail had been carefully worked out, every possibility it seemed to me had been foreseen and provided for. Every commander said he was satisfied that his plan was complete, and that it would succeed. All this gave me immense satisfaction and a great feeling of confidence.' Visiting XIX Corps (Lieut.-General H. E. Watts) on the same day, he found 'the same thoroughness and the same confidence in victory'. The next day he went to XVIII Corps (Lieut.-General Sir Ivor Maxse) and XIV Corps (Lieut.-General the Earl of Cavan). At the end of the day he told Gough 'how thoroughly satisfied I was with all the preparations made by his subordinate commanders, and the confidence which I noticed existed among all ranks'. He added that the artillery battle, which had been troubling Gough, was in a fair way to being won. On the 27th Birch again confirmed this view, while Gough reported that Fifth Army patrols were actually occupying the German front line: 'We have never before found the enemy abandoning ground in this way before our attack', wrote Haig. 'The situation looks most satisfactory.' The following day, Charteris 'reported situation satisfactory for our attack'; Trenchard reported most severe air fighting: 'Our aviators "drove the enemy out of the air" said T. to me.' On the 30th 'General Anthoine . . . was in excellent spirits and quite confident . . . all his divisional generals feel confident of reaching the final objective tomorrow'. A final flying visit to the Corps Headquarters of the Fifth Army confirmed this impression. The last sentence of Haig's Diary entry on the eve of battle reads: 'Report received this afternoon states that of 136 Tanks to be moved up to positions E. of Canal and Ypres, 133 are in position and all is well.'

There were few dissentient voices speaking aloud. One of the few was Lieut.-General Sir John Du Cane, who gloomily told Haig on the 26th that his XV Corps had already suffered 10,000 casualties since taking over the Nieuport sector from the French. At Tank Corps Headquarters there were long faces, and forebodings which conflicted sharply with the favourable statement quoted by Haig. The 'Swamp Map' was growing bluer and bluer – 'blue', says General Fuller, who was then Chief Staff Officer at Tank H.Q., 'was the colour used to denote the bogs created by the destruction of the drainage dykes. By July 31 from the Polygone de Zonnebeke through St. Julien and northwards past Langemarck the Steenbeck had become a wide moat of liquid mud.' The 'Swamp Map' was sent daily to G.H.Q. 'until H.Q. Tank Corps were instructed to discontinue sending them'.[1] There is no evidence that Haig ever saw one of those 'Swamp Maps'; had he done so, he might have felt differently about some of the reports he was receiving. On the other hand, G.H.Q.'s own liaison officers were reporting steadily on conditions from personal observation. Whatever became of their statements, the hard fact remains that the full import of ground conditions did not sink in, either at Fifth Army Headquarters, or at G.H.Q.

There, Charteris was again writing privately in a distinctly different tone

1. Letter in *The Spectator*, January 10th, 1958. See also his autobiography.

from that of his reports to Haig: 'Before this reaches you we shall have attacked again, the most important attack and, indeed, the only one that now matters for this year's fighting on this theatre. It is impossible to forecast the result. The only thing that is certain, is the most unfortunate of all things, a big casualty list. All the preparations are, I think, as good and as well advanced as those of our other two big attacks this year, and if we get as much success in this as in the others, great things will happen. My one fear is the weather. We have had most carefully prepared statistics of previous years – there are records of eighty years to refer to – and I do not think that we can hope for more than a fortnight, or at best, three weeks of really fine weather. There has been a good deal of pretty hot discussion, almost controversy, as regards the time of attack.

'We cannot hope for a surprise; our preparations must have been seen, and even if not, our bombardment must have warned the Germans, and no doubt they are already moving up troops towards our battle area. I had urged D.H. to attack on these grounds some days ago in spite of the fact that our preparations were not fully completed; it was a choice of evils. The Army Commanders wanted more time; the last conference was definitely heated. The Army Commanders pressed for delay; D.H. wanted the attack to go on at once, and in the end he accepted the Army Commanders' view. He could, indeed, do nothing else, for they have to carry out the job. I came away with D.H. from the conference when it was all settled, and reminded him of Napoleon's reply to his marshals, "Ask me for anything but time.' D.H. was very moody, but once a decision is made he will not give it another thought. With reasonable luck it will make little difference, but we have so often been let in by the weather that I am very anxious.'

This anxiety was well justified; it would have been better to express it more loudly and more often.

* * * *

More bitter controversy has surrounded the Flanders campaign of 1917 than any other of that War, with the possible exception of Gallipoli. To understand why this should be so, it is first necessary to isolate and identify the elements in its motivation and preparation – which, it is hoped, the fore-going pages will have done. It is also necessary to identify the stages of the campaign itself, and the different modes in which it was fought, under varying conditions. What follows can only be a bald account of a very terrifying and searing human experience, but it will have that aim. The three and a half months of fighting which followed the British assault on

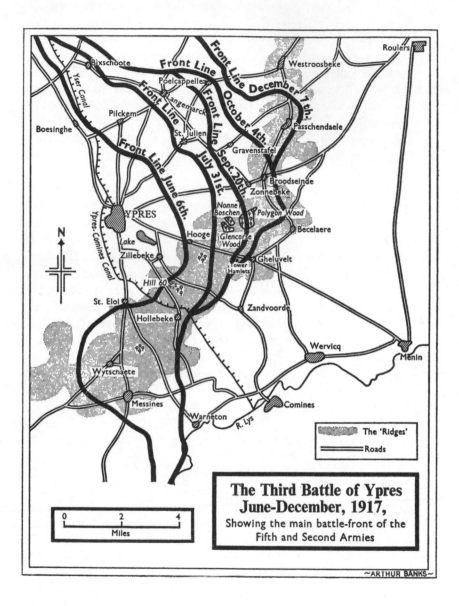

The Third Battle of Ypres
June-December, 1917,
Showing the main battle-front of the
Fifth and Second Armies

~ARTHUR BANKS~

July 31st deserve deeper discernment than can be gained by lumping them together under the grim and misleading title of 'Passchendaele'.

The British Official History lists nine separate battles which together constitute 'Third Ypres'; these do not include the heavy diversionary operation at Lens in mid-August which involved the Canadian Corps in violent action, nor do they include the supporting operations of the French. General Ludendorff divides the main Flanders battle into five stages. From our own more distant stand-point, it is probably most helpful to divide it into three. The first of these comprises the battles of Pilckem Ridge (July 31st), Gheluvelt Plateau (August 10th) and Langemarck (August 16th), all fought under the general direction of the Fifth Army. There follows a long pause in the main action, though, as we shall see, a continuing series of highly controversial minor actions were conducted under dreadful conditions, in pursuance of certain shibboleths – 'rectifying' the front line; 'gaining jumping-off positions'; 'keeping up the offensive spirit', and so forth. The next stage is marked by a series of unmistakable victories, in reasonable weather, under the control of the Second Army. These are known as the battles of the Menin Road Ridge (September 20th), Polygon Wood (September 26th) and Broodseinde (October 4th). The final stage, still under the Second Army, consists of the attempt to exploit these victories under the sharply deteriorating weather conditions of autumn, and the struggle for a 'winter line' on a battlefield which had become well-nigh indescribable – a vast wasteland of water-filled craters, laced by strips and stretches of evil, treacherous mud. These battles are called Poelcappelle (October 9th), Passchendaele I (October 12th) and Passchendaele II (October 26th). The village of Passchendaele (an almost unrecognizable landmark practically surrounded by water) was captured by the Canadians by brilliant organization and method on November 6th; six days later the Third Battle of Ypres was officially closed down.

The opening of the whole thing, Pilckem Ridge, set the tone of much that was to follow; it was a not inconsiderable success, with glimpses of tempting vistas beyond, curtained off immediately by sheets of driving rain. This was the last grand-scale set-piece assault of the British Army in that War, the last resort to massive and open preparation which the 'artillery battle' had to be. Fourteen British divisions and two French, backed by over 2,000 guns and howitzers, rose to advance together on July 31st on a wide front of some 30 kilometres. On the right, five divisions of the Second Army, without much difficulty and without heavy loss, made the small gains required of them to protect the flank of the main attack. On the left, four divisions of the Fifth Army (XVIII and XIV Corps), with the French, also made good progress without suffering unduly. But in the centre, the vital sector, where five divisions of II and XIX Corps attacked the Gheluvelt plateau, gains were small, losses were high, and worse still, the enemy was able to retaliate from this area against the more successful portions of the attack. It was here that the German tactics of counter-attacking with fresh divisions specially ear-marked for this duty were most vigorously and most successfully employed all through the afternoon, turning the British 'attack' into a desperate defence, much hampered by the prevailing uncertainty about where units really were. It was here that massed German artillery came to life and revealed the short-comings of the British bombardment, the error of the optimistic statements made to Haig by his Artillery Adviser. Low cloud, mist and, later, heavy rain, made it all the harder to deal with these problems. Charteris wrote:

'The chief peculiarity of the fighting on the 31st was, of course, that owing to the weather we could make practically no use of our aircraft. . . . To show what this means, it is enough to say that during the Messines battle in June we received two hundred of what we call "N.F." [Now Firing] calls. These are calls sent down by the aeroplanes of fresh targets not previously identified, and which are then taken up by our artillery under direction from the air; on the 31st of July we did not receive a single call of this nature, owing to bad visibility.'

Haig had never supposed that there would be anything easy about this great, and possibly decisive, battle which he was launching. In his final Instructions to his Army Commanders on July 5th, when he laid down the first objective of the Fifth Army as the capture of the Passchendaele – Staden ridge, he had written: 'To drive the enemy off that Ridge from STIRLING CASTLE in the south to DIXMUDE in the north is likely to entail very hard fighting lasting perhaps for weeks; but as a result of this we may hope that our subsequent progress will be more rapid.' The first reports that began to flow into his Advanced Headquarters, in railway coaches near Ypres, at 7 a.m. were all encouraging. At 11 a.m. he noted with satisfaction the com-parative success on the left flank: 'XIV Corps on green line and in touch with the French on their left, who are on green line and up to red line on their left. The latter's losses are small and moral is high. *This is of vital importance for the Allied cause at the present time.*'[1]

During the afternoon of this patchwork day he visited Gough, and learned about the difficulties being encountered in the centre of the attack, the right of the Fifth Army: 'Fighting on our right had been most severe. This I had expected. Our Divisions had made good progress and were on top of the ridge which the Menin road crosses, but had not advanced sufficiently eastwards to have observation into the valleys beyond.' Nevertheless, it had been, he considered, 'a fine day's work. Gough thinks he has taken over

1. Author's italics.

5,000 prisoners and 60 guns or more. The ground is thick with dead Germans, killed mostly by our artillery. I sent Alan Fletcher and Colonel Ryan[1] round the Casualty Clearing Stations. They report many slight cases, mostly shell fire. Wounded are very cheery indeed. Some 6,000 wounded had been treated in ten hours up to 6 p.m.' At the end of the day, his estimate of total casualties was 15,000; this figure would seem to have been too low, but not far from the truth; it was in striking contrast to the 57,000 of the first day of the Somme.

Charteris's information that afternoon was that the enemy's front divisions had all suffered severely; as regards the vital matter of their reserves, according to Charteris, only three divisions were immediately available, while '3 to 5 divisions may appear in 3-5 days after our main attack (i.e. on 3rd Aug.). 10 divisions can be made available after the 7th August.' The need for speed was evident; at the same time, the entire experience of the War taught the futility of rushing such matters. Guided by these conflicting considerations, Haig framed his further instructions to Gough: 'I told Gough to continue to carry out the original plan; to consolidate ground gained, and to improve his position as he may deem necessary, for facilitating the next advance; the next advance will be made as soon as possible, *but only after adequate bombardment and after dominating the hostile artillery.*' Already, on the first day of battle, Haig was having to temper the views of the Fifth Army Commander; the hope of a quick break-through, with immediate exploitation, which was the foundation of Gough's plan, had faded. As the Official History pertinently remarks, it was this hope (stimulated by Vimy and Messines) which had led to the abandonment of the original G.H.Q. concept of the battle: a series of successive deliberate 'bites' at the German position. During the days that followed, Haig moved back steadily to this idea; if it had been carried out on the first day, much of the loss and confusion that occurred when over-strained troops were subjected to counter-attack, out of reach of their own supports, and without artillery backing, would have been avoided.

There was never a time during the whole War when a truly 'all-out' attack could have succeeded, because there was never a time when the weapon which alone could make it possible was sufficiently developed – a really mobile tank, capable of going long distances. Much, however, could be done, as was later to be shown, by a judicious mixture of determination and restraint. It was the importance of the latter ingredient which led one of the most scientific commanders of the War, General Sir John Monash, to write: 'The battle plan having been ... crystallized, no subsequent alterations were permissible, under any circumstances, no matter how tempting.' This

1. A.D.C. and G.H.Q. Medical Officer respectively.

apparent inflexibility resulted, paradoxically, in more, not less flexibility. The
reason for this, as Monash said, was that: 'This fixity of plan engendered a
confidence throughout the whole command which facilitated the work of
every commander and staff officer.' Given the communications hazards of
those days, this was of supreme importance. In particular, in the heat and
confusion of action, it meant that the artillery knew what the infantry were
about and, generally speaking, where they were; the infantry thus knew that
they could count on artillery support. What marred July 31st, 1917, more
than anything else was the example it afforded of the opposite of this.

At the end of the day, Haig noted: 'Heavy rain fell this afternoon and
aeroplane observation was impossible. The going also became very bad and
the ground was much cut up. This has hampered our further progress and
robbed us of much of our advantage due to our great success.' The rain
continued. The next day was 'terrible'; 'The ground', wrote Haig, 'is like a
bog in this low-lying country'. On the 4th Charteris wrote: 'All my fears
about the weather have been realized. It has killed this attack. Every day's
delay tells against us. We lose, hour by hour, the advantage of attack. The
Germans can reorganize and reinforce. We can do nothing but wait. Even if
the weather were to clear now, it will take days for the ground to harden, if
indeed it ever can, before the winter frost. It is very difficult to keep from
saying, "I told you so". But I am glad that I fought as hard as I did against
that delay of three days in our attack. I went up to the front line this morning.
Every brook is swollen and the ground is a quagmire. If it were not that all
the records of previous years had given us fair warning, it would seem as if
Providence had declared against us. It is terribly disappointing for us at
G.H.Q., but it is much worse for the men. Yet through it all they are cheerful,
amazingly so.'

In after years, Charteris was to speak of the weather breaking in Flanders
in August 'with the regularity of the Indian monsoon'.[1] Despite the fact
that he added that 1917 provided 'the wettest August recorded for thirty
years', much was made of this statement by those who wished to damn Haig
and the whole campaign. Yet, according to the then Commandant of the
Meteorological Section, Mr. G. Gold, who was brought from civil life to
run this important branch of G.H.Q., this reference to a 'monsoon' is 'so
contrary to recorded facts that, to a meteorologist, it seems too ridiculous to
need formal refutation'.[2] Mr. Gold has also stated that: 'The rainfall directly
affecting the first month of the offensive was more than double the average;
it was over five times the amount for the same period in 1915 and in 1916.' He
quotes 157 mm. of rain at Vlamertinghe in 1917, as against 29 mm. in 1916,

1. Charteris: *Field Marshal Earl Haig*, p. 272.
2. Letter in *The Spectator*, January 17th, 1958.

and 30 mm. at St. Omer in 1915 (there being no rain-gauge at Vlamertinghe in that year). To G.H.Q., all this spelt a shocking disappointment.

Three operational questions now assumed priority in Haig's mind. The first was the need for the French to give him more help. On August 1st he sent a message to Pétain to the effect that: '. . . now is the critical moment of the war, and the French must attack as strongly as possible and as soon as possible, so as to co-operate with the British in dealing the enemy as strong a blow as possible.' This was the first of a series of pleas by Haig to Pétain, urging him to fulfil his promises. Haig's second problem concerned the strategy of his own armies. On this same day he visited the Corps H.Q.s of the Fifth Army; he found General Jacob 'quite confident of being able to capture and hold the [Gheluvelt] ridge in his next attempt'. At XIX Corps, however, General Watts told Haig how he had been 'obliged to retire owing to artillery fire from the main ridge on the east. This confirms my view that progress cannot be made by an advance towards the Forêt d'Houthoulst until the main Broodseinde – Staden ridge is taken.' It now became a question, once again, of trying to get this idea over to Gough, and making him reshape his plan. The next day Gough and Malcolm were at Haig's Headquarters: 'I showed him on my relief map the importance of the Broodseinde-Passchendaele Ridge, and gave it as my opinion that his main effort must be devoted to capturing that. Not until it was in his possession could he hope to advance his centre. He quite agreed.' The trouble was that Gough's whole Army was laid out for a different purpose. He might agree with Haig, but nothing less than a major redeployment could give effect to that agreement. It is marvellous that no note of impatience crept into Haig's diary, even now, after so many attempts to make the Fifth Army conform to his views.

The third question was one of tactics. Gough was a 'thruster', who wanted to get on with the battle, weather or no weather. Haig 'told him to have patience, and not to put in his infantry attack until after two or three days of fine weather, to enable our guns to get the upper hand and to dry out the ground'. Gough was intending to attack again on August 4th, but in the face of the downpour, and this clear instruction from Haig, he abandoned that attempt.

This pause gave time for G.H.Q. to circulate a tactical appraisal, based on the experience of July 31st, which analysed the German counter-attack method and indicated how it might be overcome. 'A primary consideration with us', ran this Memorandum, 'in fixing the depth to which to push an attack is the factor of artillery preparation and the final artillery barrage to cover the troops in their final objective. Do we take sufficiently into consideration the physical capacity of the infantry? . . . In short, in the earlier stages of the offensive our furthest objective must be not only within the power of our artillery, but within the power of our infantry (having regard to the state of the ground existing at the time of the attack, and to the discipline and training of the divisions), so that we may gain the great advantage of beating off the enemy's counter-attacks.' There was reason to suppose, the paper added, that some units which had gallantly pushed farthest on July 31st 'were too weak and too exhausted to maintain the positions won. If they were too exhausted, this points to the green line[1] having been beyond their physical powers. If they were too weak in numbers, it points to a need to reconsider our dispositions. . . .' The answer, concluded G.H.Q., lay in making shorter bounds, and in holding back larger numbers of men for the difficult later stages when the enemy counter-attacked, instead of using large masses for the relatively simpler task of capturing the enemy's front. Attention was also drawn to the importance of mopping-up – always a difficult problem, throughout the war, but particularly bad in the broken country east of Ypres where there were wide areas of shell-torn woods. The value of machine gun barrages, especially for breaking up counter-attacks, was stressed: 'We are at present well ahead of the enemy in the use of massed machine guns in this manner, and it is important to develop it to the utmost. All Corps and Divisional Commanders should satisfy themselves that the methods now taught at our machine gun schools, and successfully practised in battle on many recent occasions, are fully understood and applied in their commands.'

This was merely a polite way of saying that many commanders needed to find out what those methods were, and stick to them. There was much jealousy and silly scorn at subordinate headquarters for scientific methods worked out in the Army's 'Schools'. Haig had no time for such attitudes. A few days later he was at the main Machine Gun School near Etaples, with three Army Commanders, many Corps Commanders and Staff Officers. They saw a demonstration of 'box barrages' and other devices. 'The officer in charge . . .' wrote Haig, 'is Major Barrie, the amateur golfer. Before the war he knew nothing of military matters! Now he is most proficient and has everything under his command in excellent order.' It took a long time to make some of the old Regulars understand what men like Barrie were about.

It was uphill work for Haig at this period to make his subordinate commanders comprehend that, although he certainly wanted the attack to go forward, the last thing he desired was for them to smash their commands up in the attempt to achieve this. Because the popular image of 'Third Ypres' is one of endless hopeless endeavours by gallant soldiers at the behest of an

1. The third of the day's objectives.

obstinate and unrealistic Commander-in-Chief, it may be as well to show at once how Haig approached this problem. On August 17th, after the failure at Langemarck, Gough told Haig that he 'was not pleased with the action of the Irish divisions of the XIX Corps (36th and 16th Divisions)'. This view was confirmed by General Watts. Haig's immediate comment was:

'I gather that the attacking troops had a long march up the evening before the battle through Ypres to the front line and then had to fight from zero (4.45 a.m.) till nightfall. Consequently the men could have had no sleep, and must have been dead tired.'

Reflecting later, he added: 'The cause of the failure to advance . . . is due, I think, to commanders being in too great a hurry! Three more days should have been allowed in which (if fine and observation good) the artillery would have dominated the enemy's artillery and destroyed his concrete defences. After Gough has got at the facts more fully, I have arranged to talk the matter over with him.' But Gough was himself an offender. On September 7th Haig 'discussed with Kiggell the wisdom of making small attacks on farms and isolated strong points, such as Gough has been doing on the Fifth Arm front. In my opinion, unless we have dominated the enemy's artillery completely, our troops cannot retain a small area captured, because of the hostile artillery fire which can and will assuredly be concentrated on it; and also because our own guns have so destroyed the defences, before our troops attack them, that little is left to consolidate. These small operations are also very wasteful in ammunition. I decided therefore to stop Gough from going on with these little attacks'.

Two days later, he told Gough of this decision, but that officer 'said that the 42nd Division (Mitford) and 61st Division (McKenzie) were shortly leaving the front, and that for the sake of training and morale they ought not to go without having taken the two points which they recently attacked with one or two companies, but failed to hold after they had taken them. I agreed, *provided the troops themselves felt equal to the task*.[1] Gough is to see the commanders concerned'. What followed is most instructive. The next day: 'Gough told me that the 42nd and 61st Divisions are very anxious to take the strong points . . . before they go out of the line. . . .' But Kiggell had also been doing some investigating on his own account, and 'reported that he is afraid that some of Gough's subordinates do not always tell Gough their true opinion as regards their ability to carry out an operation. I therefore decide to go tomorrow and see the G.O.C. V Corps (General Fanshawe) with reference to the small attacks prepared for the 13th'. When Haig visited V Corps next day, 'Fanshawe thought the 61st Division had been in the line so

1. Author's italics.

long (over 3 weeks) that the troops were not fresh enough to undertake the attack . . . with good prospects of success. Similarly the 42nd Division was not sufficiently trained. He was inclined to cancel the proposed small attacks. . . .' Shortly after this Major-General C. J. Mackenzie [*sic*], commanding the 61st Division, arrived, 'so I was able to have a few words with him. He thought his division had not suffered unduly considering the terrific shell fire experienced each day. He was anxious to take Hill 35 before going out of the line, and felt confident that his men could take it. I said that it was primarily for him and the corps commanders to decide whether these small enterprises should be undertaken or not'. This closed the interview; Haig retired in some bafflement, but not before he had noted that McKenzie's Chief of Staff was 'looking ill and nervous – hardly fit for our present fighting'. The situation now was that the Divisional and Army Commanders wanted to fight, while the Corps and supreme Commanders had doubts – amply shared, one may suppose, by the units concerned. Haig went on to have lunch at Fifth Army Headquarters – 'All very cheery.' After lunch, however, his doubts overcame him; he took Gough aside and 'questioned whether it was advisable to make more attacks on a small scale before the main operation is launched, and said that the first question to be decided was "were these attacks necessary for the success of the main attack?" If not, then they should not be made. If a division has failed, the best thing to do is to withdraw it for training before it is asked to attack again. G. is to see the corps and divisional commanders this afternoon and will then report'. No doubt fortified by Haig's visit, Lieut.-General Fanshawe was now able to stress his point of view. The next day: 'Report from Fifth Army. General Gough has decided to give up the minor operations which he proposed to make. . . .' Once again, Haig's personal intervention had stopped a useless action and saved many lives. But it should not be necessary for the Commander-in-Chief of a great force of over sixty divisions to supervise the engagements of companies and platoons.

All this anticipates our narrative. On August 10th, II Corps made its second large attempt to capture the Gheluvelt plateau. Haig wrote at the end of the day: 'The attack was most satisfactory. . . .' This was scarcely the case; the Official Historian refers to the fighting as 'Failure at Gheluvelt'. The reason he gives for failure is 'the undiminished strength of the German artillery concentration on and behind' the plateau. The Fifth Army, he tells us, continued to spread its counter-battery fire over the whole Army frontage 'in preparation for the renewed general offensive'. 'As a result, the German artillery concentration opposite II Corps remained unmastered.' The German forward zone, 800 yards deep, was duly overrun by the attackers, but then came no less than six counter-attacks which regained most of the ground that

had been lost by the enemy. A feature of the defence which was now beginning to make itself felt most seriously was the 'pill-box' – the reinforced-
concrete machine gun post with walls four feet thick which the Germans
were now using in large numbers all over the Flanders front. A fair number
of them are still there, dotted among the open fields and copses, or in-
corporated in the farms. It is salutary to look at those fields through the slits
in these structures, and see them, with the eye of imagination, as the German
machine gunners saw them. The technique for attacking pill-boxes was well
established and understood – to mask them by concentrated fire and smoke,
and work round behind them. 'However', as Captain Falls has said, 'even
with good tactics, the human body is lucky to prevail over ferro-concrete,
and many brilliant attacks failed, with nothing to show but a few corpses
sprawled about the strong points.' In some cases, many corpses.

The rain continued unabated, and the next attack had to be delayed until
August 16th. This was Langemarck; this time the whole front of the Fifth
Army was involved, as well as the French on the left. Charteris sums up the
day: 'We attacked at dawn. I was up with the Corps H.Q. We did fairly well
on the left, but failed elsewhere.' Haig described the result as 'only moderate'.
Once again, pill-boxes, artillery and, above all, successive counter-attacks,
had proved too hard a nut to crack. Sporadic fighting continued for over a
week, with mixed, but on the whole disappointing results. On the 19th the
Tank Corps, with the sympathetic co-operation of Lieut.-General Sir Ivor
Maxse of XVIII Corps, won almost its only success of the whole campaign,
at St. Julien. Haig noted: '. . . advances made with 11 Tanks on one mile of
front. All objectives taken, 12 infantry casualties, and 14 men of Tanks hit.
Without Tanks we would have lost 600!' This was a timely feat, for in the
context of the man-power shortage the enemies of the Tank Arm were hot
in pursuit of it; St. Julien, as one tank historian says, probably saved the tanks
and made Cambrai possible.

There was little else of consolation. The battle had stuck. On the 22nd
Gough and Jacob 'stated that they were well pleased with the progress on our
right flank'. But Haig now saw clearly that a radical change of method was
necessary. On the 25th II Corps was handed back to the Second Army; on
the 28th, after another attempt to get forward on a three-Corps front which,
says the Official History, 'resulted in considerable further casualties and very
little gain of ground', Haig decided to transfer the main role in further
operations from Gough to Plumer.

So far the great offensive had produced almost undiluted disappointment.
Two rays of comfort from the battle-front, however, helped to sustain Haig
at this time: at Lens, between August 15th and 23rd, the Canadians had won
a distinct success, after bitter fig hting. At Verdun, Pétain belatedly fulfilled on

August 20th the first of his promised attacks, and this was a clear victory; penetrating to a depth of three kilometres on a front of eighteen kilometres, the French inflicted many casualties and took 6,000 prisoners, as well as important ground. 'This defeat should have a great effect on the enemy', Haig remarked, 'because they thought the French Army had become a negligible quantity.' He was right; Ludendorff drew the conclusion that: 'The French Army was once more capable of the offensive.' Neither he nor Haig knew that Pétain had no notion of exploiting this psychological *coup*.

Haig was comforted also by what he heard from Charteris about the Germans; on the 20th the latter told him: 'Already 29 enemy divisions have been exhausted in the battle in Flanders, and 4 divisions opposite Lens – a total of 33 divisions since the beginning of August.' These are the most dangerous of military statistics; they confuse two quite separate categories: the fact of the physical removal of units from a battle, and the supposition that they are therefore 'exhausted', 'used-up', or whatever the current jargon may be. Charteris was all too good at this sort of thing; on the 27th he 'reported that the state of the enemy's reserves is today the most favourable for us since the war began! Apparently he has only 4 "fresh" divisions available . . . i.e. divisions which have not been hammered during the last 3 months.' The divergence between what Charteris was telling Haig and what the Intelligence Branch at the War Office believed was increasing, adding to Robertson's difficulties in dealing with a Prime Minister who, as early as August 9th, had, according to Robertson's Deputy, 'said openly before the whole Conference of the Allied representatives that he had no confidence in the General Staff or their plans and that he had known all along that this latest offensive was doomed to failure, and a good deal more in the same strain. . . .' Certainly nothing had happened yet that could alter Lloyd George's views, or mitigate his doubts. More than ever he wanted to see the main theatre of operations transferred to Italy; less than ever was he disposed to grapple with the now acute man-power problem on the Western Front. 'The P.M. sent me a friendly message . . .' Haig noted on August 16th. 'I told Robertson to thank the P.M. for his message, but what I want is tangible support! men, guns, aeroplanes!' On the 22nd he told Robertson: 'You must force the Govt. to give me the means to keep going. . . . The one black spot in the whole picture of the war is our P.M.'s desire to gain ground in secondary theatres as if he did not believe in our ability to beat the Germans themselves and wished to gain something with which to bargain at a Peace Conference.'

Haig undoubtedly felt deeply offended at Lloyd George's scepticism; it seemed to him to be an insult to Britain's great Citizen Army and its leaders. That apart, he was certain that the British effort was striking a massive blow at the main enemy. If, under Charteris's prompting, he was being too optimistic, it is nevertheless to be noted that German accounts substantially support this view. Before we leave this equivocal stage of the Flanders battle, let us see how it appeared to the enemy commander, General Ludendorff. 'From July 31st till well into October was a period of tremendous anxiety', he tells us. July 31st, 'besides a loss of from two to four kilometres of ground along the whole front . . . caused us very considerable losses in prisoners and stores, and a heavy expenditure of reserves. In August fighting broke out on many parts of the Western Front. In Flanders the Entente attacked again. . . . The 10th August was a success for us, but on the 16th we sustained another great blow'. This was Langemarck, which we have described above as a British failure; similarly with the (to us) abortive efforts later in the month.

Ludendorff goes on: 'The 22nd was another day of heavy fighting. The 25th August concluded the second phase of the Flanders battle. It had cost us heavily. . . . The costly August battles in Flanders and at Verdun imposed a heavy strain on the Western troops. In spite of all the concrete protection they seemed more or less powerless under the enormous weight of the enemy's artillery. *At some points they no longer displayed the firmness which I, in common with the local commanders, had hoped for.*[1] The enemy managed to adapt himself to our method of employing counter attacks . . . I myself was being put to a terrible strain. The state of affairs in the West appeared to prevent the execution of our plans elsewhere. Our wastage had been so high as to cause grave misgivings, and had exceeded all expectation. . . .'

Out of 22 British divisions so far engaged (one of them twice), 14 had had to be withdrawn to refit. Casualties, according to the Official History, for the whole month were 3,424 officers and 64,586 other ranks – not very many more than for the *first day* of the Somme. The Official Historian adds, however: 'The casualties alone do not give the full picture of the situation; for, apart from actual losses, the discomfort of the living conditions in the forward areas and the strain of fighting with indifferent success had over-wrought and discouraged all ranks more than any other operation fought by British troops in the War, so that, although the health of the troops did not suffer, discontent was general. . . . The memory of this August fighting . . . has remained the image and symbol of the whole battle, overshadowing the subsequent successful actions of the campaign and preventing the true estimation of them, even in some cases stopping any knowledge of them from reaching the public ear.'

At least we learn from Ludendorff that the view did not look any better from the other side of the hill.

*   *   *   *

1. Author's italics.

During the second phase of the Flanders offensive the contradictions which had always been inherent in it were brought into stark relief. This phase witnessed, on the fighting front, a complete reversal of the pattern to date, a series of definite and most hopeful victories; but behind the front, in Government circles, increasing pessimism about Flanders, an increasing desire to place the weight of the Allied effort elsewhere. This desire was stimulated by the apparent success of the Italian offensive on the Isonzo – the eleventh battle of that name, launched on August 19th. Fifty-two divisions and 5,000 guns were assembled for this attack; its opening stages, as so often happened, were bright with promise; by the end of the month, the Italians claimed 27,000 Austrian prisoners and an advance of some six miles across the rocky Carso plateau. On August 26th Lloyd George wrote to Robertson: 'Do you not think that a new situation has arisen there which requires immediate action on the part of the Allies to support the Italian attack, make up their deficiencies and enable them to convert the Austrian retreat into a rout? It would indeed be a severe reflection upon us all if later on it were discovered that we missed a great chance of achieving a signal and far-reaching military success for the Allied cause through lack of readiness to take advantage of an opening made for us by the Italian army.' Six days later, Haig received on his breakfast table a telegram from Robertson which said: 'General Foch arrives London September 3rd on behalf of French War Cabinet to press British War Cabinet to agree to his sending 100 heavy guns from French First Army to Italy at once; if, as I suppose, this will affect your plans, it is very desirable that you should come over and see War Cabinet.' Haig departed at once for London.

The proposition with which he was now faced was not entirely a novelty. On that same day, General Anthoine had transmitted to him a request from Pétain that guns should be transferred from the French 1st Army to Champagne, where Pétain was expecting a powerful gas attack. He appeared to think that the departure of 100 French guns to Italy would weaken his front seriously in the face of this attack, unless the loss was compensated. The argument seems somewhat far-fetched, in view of the strength of the French artillery in 1917, and the current inactivity of their main Army. Haig, however, 'said that since Pétain had supported me so generously I felt most anxious to give him all that he asked for as soon as possible, and rely upon him to return the guns in good time for our next operation.' The following day (September 4th) Haig attended a War Cabinet meeting; the final decision was left in his hands. 'After explaining that it was the wish of the Cabinet that the guns should be sent, if I could possibly spare them, Lloyd George spoke to me alone, and said that it was very desirable to help the Italians at this juncture because the French were trying to supplant us in their affections!

We must not give the French the power of saying that *they wanted* to send
100 guns, but the British would not let them go. I said that I would review
the whole gun situation on the battlefront, and if we could possibly liberate
50 guns, it would be done. He said he was very grateful.'

On September 7th Haig told Pétain and Foch that he was 'prepared to
liberate 100 guns (about) from French First Army provided General Pétain
could replace them in time for the attack as planned . . . General Pétain at
once agreed that he could meet my request. . . . This ended the discussion on
the question of the guns in the most friendly way.' An important by-product
of this meeting was an improvement in Haig's relations with Foch, which
had previously been somewhat strained. Foch, Haig remarked, 'seemed on
arrival at Amiens to have all his "hackles" up but my few friendly words
quickly calmed him, and we all were on the best of terms. His experiences in
London should have done him good. He had gone there behind the back of
Pétain and myself to get the British War Cabinet to sanction 100 French guns
being withdrawn from *my* command. The War Cabinet then handed the
question to me to arrange with Pétain. This we have done satisfactorily for
all. I found Pétain today straightforward and clear in his views, and most
businesslike. And, as he said himself today, "The Marshal and I never argue
and haggle over such matters".' The incident seemed to be completely closed
three days later, when Haig received a telegram from Lloyd George: 'My
colleagues and I are much gratified at the manner in which you have met
them in regard to Italy. Please accept our best thanks for the promptitude
with which you have carried out our wishes in a matter which was of great
importance to interallied policy.' If Haig expected some reciprocity in his
future dealings with the Prime Minister, however, he was to be disagreeably
disappointed. Italy became a 'running sore' for the remainder of the year's
campaigning.

As this work has repeatedly attempted to demonstrate, none of the issues
of the War can be regarded in isolation. This question of the guns is an
excellent example of that fact. Among the considerations in Haig's mind
when he made the generous gesture which has just been described were the
following: in a Memorandum to Robertson on September 3rd, he pointed
out that the conditions which had forced him to make a pause in his offensive
'demand increased artillery support, not a diminution of it; and so important
is this that I have decided to forego useful operations elsewhere on my front,[1]
and to develop to the very utmost my artillery fire on the main battle front.'
In the same paper he injected a note of potential gloom which was not only
in marked contrast to his general optimism, but also affords an important clue
to those final stages of the campaign which have been so much criticized:

1. This refers to a projected second attack on Lens.

'Apart from the great offensive results to be obtained by success it is necessary for my advance to push on for defensive reasons. The positions now reached would be so far from satisfactory for defence during the winter that the advisability of withdrawing my line behind the STEENBEEK, *and abandoning some of the ground won will come into consideration if our advance is unable to make considerable further progress.*[1] Such abandonment of ground would be very unsatisfactory to the men who have won it by immense efforts, as well as to public opinion.'

A further consideration stemmed from the character and methods of the Army Commander to whom the brunt of the next attack had been entrusted.

If Gough and his subordinates had been 'in too great a hurry', this was not a fault that could ever be laid at Plumer's door. He began by telling Haig that he would require an interval of three weeks before launching the next stage of the attack. This was agreed. A firm believer in artillery, Plumer asked for 1,339 guns and howitzers, and actually deployed on his offensive front no less than 1,295, of which 575 were heavy and medium pieces. This was the densest British artillery concentration of the War. The key sector of offensive frontage was reduced to 4,000 yards, with 4 divisions in the attack – compared with July 31st, double the force in half the space. The density of artillery was 1 piece to every 5·2 yards of front, compared with 1 piece per 9 yards at Vimy, 1 per 7 yards at Messines, and 1 per 6 yards on July 31st. The rolling barrage itself, apart from counter-battery groups, was 1,000 yards deep, in five belts, including one of 240 massed machine guns. The depth of advance was to be limited to 1,500 yards; a halt would then be made while the whole huge mass of artillery was moved forward again, and then the 'dose' was to be repeated at six-day intervals. Four such operations, it was calculated, would win the whole of the Passchendaele-Staden ridge. All preparations were made with the Second Army's characteristic thoroughness and forethought. There was only one thing that was wrong with this plan: instead of following the Messines victory after an interval of 21 days, it was to occur after an interval of 105 days. 'Ask me for anything but time. . . .'

The Battle of the Menin Road Ridge was launched on September 20th. Two days before, Haig visited Second Army Headquarters, and subjected Plumer's staff and subordinate commanders to his now habitual searching questions. We have seen how exhaustive they could be; this occasion was no exception. Here are some of the general questions which Haig put (there is no space for the detailed queries):

'1. Are the results of your counter-battery work and preliminary bombardment so far satisfactory? Can you reach all the enemy's batteries? . . .

1. Author's italics.

3. How are you dealing with organized shell-holes during this preparatory period?

4. Are you satisfied that your infantry when halted on intermediate objectives will be able to recognize the rear limit of the Protective Barrage?

5. What special means have you taken to deal with the enemy's machine guns at the various stages of the attack?

6. . . .

How do you propose to deal with organized shell-hole defences and concrete structures that may withstand the effects of bombardment and barrage? Are you satisfied that your communications are in working order all through and will not break down? . . .'

The Second Army had considered these matters. 'In every case', Haig wrote, 'I found the officers full of confidence as to the result of the forthcoming attack. Every detail had been gone into most thoroughly, and their troops most carefully trained. . . . Altogether I felt it most exhilarating to go round such a very knowledgeable and confident body of leaders.' As regards their Chief, 'The old man was full of good spirits and most confident'. The next day, visiting the Fifth Army, which was to make supporting attacks, Haig again put a series of questions; here, the answers did not always please him so much. 'I am inclined to think that the Fifth Army Staff work is not so satisfactory as last year.'

'In a well-planned battle', wrote General Monash, '. . . nothing happens, nothing can happen, except the regular progress of the advance according to the plan arranged. . . . It is for this reason that no stirring accounts exist of the more intimate details of such great set-pieces as Messines, Vimy, Hamel and many others. They will never be written, for there is no material on which to base them. The story of what did take place on the day of the battle would be a mere paraphrase of the battle orders prescribing all that was to take place.' The Battle of the Menin Road Ridge was such an occasion. Zero hour was at 5.40 a.m. By midday, except on the extreme right flank, at an abominable locality known as Tower Hamlets, both the Second and Fifth Armies were in occupation of all their objectives, consolidating and awaiting the German counter-attacks. General Birdwood, commanding I Anzac Corps in the very heart of the Second Army assault, describes the day in these words: 'Our own artillery barrage was magnificent – quite the best the Australians had ever seen. Creeping forward exactly according to plan, the barrage won the ground, while the infantry followed behind and occupied all the important points with a minimum of resistance. . . . Three lines of objectives had been laid down, and the third of these was reached by

10.15 a.m., our men being in great heart. At 3.15 came the expected German counter-attacks, but so effective was our artillery fire that by 7 o'clock the attack had been killed.' The influence of weather may be judged from the fact that, in the late September sunshine, the Air arm was able to send down 394 messages, of which about a third produced immediate artillery action, as compared with *none* on July 31st. The effect on the enemy was unmistakable.

Ludendorff wrote: 'Another terrific assault was made on our lines on the 20th September.... The enemy's onslaught on the 20th was successful, which proved the superiority of the attack over the defence. Its strength did not consist in the tanks; we found them inconvenient, but put them out of action all the same. The power of the attack lay in the artillery, and in the fact that ours did not do enough damage to the hostile infantry as they were assembling, and above all, at the actual time of the assault.' The Menin Road Ridge was a clear victory, a triumph for Plumer and the Second Army.

Haig was naturally much encouraged by the result of this battle. On the 22nd he wrote: 'There is no doubt that the enemy commanders are meeting with increased difficulties in getting their men to attack.' The next day he found himself in the unusual position of urging the now disillusioned Gough to press his next attack further, telling him, '... we shall be able to accomplish things *after* the next offensive which we could not dare even to attempt now.' The next phase of Plumer's preparations continued in fine, dry weather. Nevertheless, there were signs and symptoms which were less encouraging: reluctantly, on the 23rd, Haig had to abandon all thought of his cherished amphibious operation;[1] impatiently, on the 25th, he learned that Pétain had postponed the date of the next French supporting attack, which was to have gone in either on that day or the next. News from Russia was universally bad. The French were again asking for the British to think of taking over some of their line. A heavy German spoiling attack, also on the 25th, seemed to threaten Plumer's preparations for his own new blow. It was an anxious day, the burden of which was scarcely lightened by a visit from Lloyd George accompanied by Hankey, both in a gloomy frame of mind. Lloyd George

1. Among the special preparations for this were landing craft, and tanks fitted with their own ramps for climbing the sea-wall at Ostend. Haig had watched a demonstration of this device on July 16th. His diary entry contains a sketch of the profile of the sea-wall, and the comment:

'A gun and limber, heavy motor tractor, a couple of motor lorries were in turn all pulled up the wall without much trouble, and in a short space of time (5 minutes each). I saw the tanks ascend the wall twice – wonderful performance to look at and done without any effort!'

His interest in the technical side of war was never eclipsed by his weighty preoccupations as Commander-in-Chief.

was particularly despondent at the news that the Italians, in the face of tremendous physical difficulties on the Carso, and stiffening Austrian resistance, had stopped their offensive. It had cost them 165,000 casualties in about one month. General Anthoine's prediction to Haig that the 100 guns diverted to Italy 'would be lost to both theatres' had been lamentably fulfilled. It was no consolation that, as Robertson wrote, Cadorna's decision had made the War Cabinet 'awfully sick with him, and I think also with themselves'. But Lloyd George's chief worry was the situation in Russia, and he wanted Haig's advice as to what should be done if Russia dropped out of the war. Haig had no doubts: 'My opinion without having gone into details is that we should go on striking as hard as possible with the object of clearing the Belgian coast. We should be prepared to make and win the campaign.' This was the last thing Lloyd George wanted to hear; his mind was already working on quite different expedients.

Plumer's second 'step-by-step' blow was struck on September 26th – the Battle of Polygon Wood. It was launched on a narrower total front than the Menin Road battle – 8,500 yards; the artillery concentration, however, was just as dense; the system was unchanged. The German spoiling attack on the previous day had so far failed in its purpose that even zero hour was not altered. Nevertheless, on the front of the unfortunate division concerned (33rd) there was some inevitable confusion. Here, and on the flanks, the attack did not have the clockwork character of the first blow. The Australians of I Anzac Corps, however, fresh divisions specially brought in, were able to gain their objectives and beat off counter-attacks with the same dash and ease as on the 20th. Birdwood writes: 'At 5.50 a.m. on the 26th our barrage came down; it was perfect, breaking out with a single crash, and raising a dense wall of dust.'

Behind this wall of dust and smoke, the Australian infantry swept over the German positions to a depth of 1,200 yards, inflicting heavy losses. Prince Rupprecht, commanding the Germans in Flanders, stated: 'It is to be hoped that another attack will not follow too quickly, as we have not sufficient reserves behind the front.' Ludendorff tells us: '. . . the 26th proved a day of heavy fighting, accompanied by every circumstance that could cause us loss. We might be able to stand the loss of ground, but the reduction of our fighting strength was again all the heavier.' The Germans found themselves forced to reconsider very carefully their defensive methods. Charteris noted: 'The general situation as regards the battle is strangely like the Somme. Now, as then, we had worn down the German resistance to very near breaking-point; then, as now, the weather went against us. It is a race with time, and a fight with the weather. One thing is certain, no other army but ours could fight on as we are fighting. D.H. is asking for the last ounce from it and getting a wonderful response.' This was on September 27th; there were still six weeks to go.

The success of Plumer's methods had now been proved repeatedly. The only reservation about them was that the deliberation on which they were founded took no account of the lateness of the season, the imminence of what Henry Wilson called 'the time of the mud'. Fortified by the stream of optimistic reports with which he was being supplied by Charteris, Haig now drew the attention of his two Army Commanders to the wider possibilities that had been revived by Plumer's successes. At a meeting with the latter and Gough on September 28th he 'urged the necessity for preparing to exploit our success after the attack following that of 4th October. I am of opinion that the enemy is tottering, and that a good vigorous blow might lead to decisive results. If we could destroy, or interrupt for 48 hours, the railway at Roulers there would probably be a débâcle, because the enemy would then have to rely on only one railway line for the supply of his troops between Ghent and the sea. In order to exploit our success with good results, there must be *fresh* troops available, also Tanks and cavalry. Army commanders are to work out details. . . .' Four days later, at another conference, 'I pointed out how favourable the situation was and how necessary it was to have all necessary means for exploiting any success gained *on the* 10th,[1] should the situation admit, e.g., if the enemy counter-attacks and is defeated, then reserve Brigades must follow after the enemy and take the Passchendaele ridge at once. . . . Both Gough and Plumer quite acquiesced in my views, and arranged wholeheartedly to give effect to them when the time came. At first they adhered to the idea of continuing our attacks for limited objectives. Charteris emphasized the deterioration of German Divisions in numbers, morale and all-round efficiency. . . .'

Haig's optimism about the operations of his own army, now in the full flood of success, was tempered by two less agreeable factors. He was becoming increasingly irritated by Pétain's inactivity. On the 27th, he had asked Anthoine to press Pétain to mount his next attack quickly; on the 29th, Colonel de Bellaigue, Chief of the French Mission at G.H.Q., told him that this could not take place before the 10th or 15th of October. The strain of the year could not fail to have its effect even on Haig's marble calm; this news provoked one of the angriest outbursts in his Diary: 'What a wretched lot the majority of the French are! Here is an attack which was promised for the *middle of September* not ready to go in till the 15th October. I doubt if it will go in then! If the "intention to attack" existed the attack would have been ready to time. Gemeau[2] tells me that the morale of the French troops is now

1. Author's italics.
2. Commandant Gemeau, French Liaison Officer.

excellent; what is wrong is the "material".... History will doubtless conclude that the French are not playing the game !'

Their game, of course, was a complicated one. Pétain was being less than frank at this stage. However, when Haig met him on October 6th, relations seem not to have been too severely impaired: 'General Pétain . . . came to see me at 4 p.m. He said he was heart-broken (*navré*) at the delay in putting in his attack on the Aisne. He could not override the decision of the Generals on the spot, and sending the guns to Italy had further delayed things. . . . He was . . . anxious to support my offensive to the fullest extent possible and had told General Anthoine that he was free to make use of his reserves, and that he would send him more troops to replace them.' With this Haig had to be content. It meant that the heaviest blow struck by the British Army during the whole campaign was robbed of that French support on which Haig had always counted. What the effects might have been otherwise, it is impossible to calculate.[1]

On October 3rd, the eve of the British attack, there was more bad news: 'A great bombshell arrived in the shape of a letter from C.I.G.S. stating that the British Government had "approved in principle" of the British Army in France taking over more line from the French, and details are to be arranged by General Pétain and myself. This was settled at a Conference at Boulogne on September 25th at which I was not present. Nor did either L. George or Robertson tell me of this decision at our interview. All the P.M. said was that "Painlevé was anxious that the British should take over more line". And

---

1. Haig's view of the state of the French Army at this stage was significant, and this entry is particularly important for the light which it throws on that question. It should be read in conjunction with a further passage from a letter to Robertson on October 8th:

'Though the French cannot be expected to admit it officially, we know that the state of their armies and of the reserve manpower behind the armies is such that neither the French Government nor the military authorities will venture to call on their troops for any further great and sustained offensive effort, at any rate before it becomes evident that the enemy's strength has been definitely and finally broken. Though they are staunch in defence and will carry out useful local offensives against limited objectives, the French Armies would not respond to a call for more than that, and the authorities are well aware of it.'

It is difficult to reconcile this evidence, and the general tenor of his comments at the time, with the letter which he wrote to Charteris in March, 1927, referring to Churchill's comments on the Flanders campaign, in which he said: 'It is impossible for Winston to know how the possibility of the French Army breaking up in 1917 *compelled me to go on attacking*. It was impossible to change sooner from the Ypres front to Cambrai without Pétain coming to press me not to leave the Germans alone for a week, on account of the *awful* state of the French troops! You even did not know the facts, as Pétain told them to me in confidence.'

This letter has provided the main basis of the argument that 'Passchendaele was fought to save the French'. In the general sense, that the growing exhaustion of France

Robertson rode the high horse and said that it was high time for the British now to call the tune, and not play second fiddle to the French, etc., etc., and all this when shortly before he must have quietly acquiesced at the Conference in Painlevé's demands! R. comes badly out of this, in my opinion, especially as *it was definitely stated (with the War Cabinet's approval) that no discussion re operations on the Western front would be held with the French without my being present.*' This entry marks the beginning of a perceptible decline of confidence and co-operation between Haig and Robertson, whose full effects were seen in the small measure of support which Haig gave to Robertson when the latter's troubles came to a head early in 1918, and led to his resignation from the post of C.I.G.S. Haig was now aware that Robertson's enthusiasm for the Flanders offensive did not match his own. On September 27th Robertson had written: 'I confess I stick to it more because I see nothing better, and because my instinct prompts me to stick to it, than to [*sic*] any convincing argument by which I can support it.' An increasing source of difference between them was the conflicting estimate of Germany's condition between G.H.Q. Intelligence (Charteris) and War Office Intelligence (Macdonogh).

Matters had not yet come to a break, however. On October 9th Robertson told Haig: '. . . you must let me do my job in my own way. I have never yet given in on important matters and never shall. In any case, whatever happens, you and I must stand solid together.' He added gloomily: 'He (Lloyd George) is out for my blood very much these days . . . I am sick of this d—d life.' The next day he became even sicker. The now desperate Prime Minister, turning

made it, in Haig's view, imperative for the British to assume the main burden of fighting, that argument is valid; in the particular sense, Haig's own day-to-day comments do not bear it out. It may be urged that he refrained from mentioning Pétain's pleas, even in his Diary, on grounds of secrecy. Against this are the stubborn facts that:

(1) the Diary *does* contain references to the state of the French Army which would have been highly dangerous if made public, and

(2) it contains later entries, such as those quoted, in an opposite sense.

There is the further fact that Haig's methodical mind caused him to record every important meeting which he attended, and among these, of course, meetings with the French C.-in-C. Four such meetings with Pétain are recorded during the course of the battle:

September 7th, to discuss guns for Italy;

October 8th, to discuss *French* attacks;

October 18th, to discuss the extension of the British front – with the understood corollary that this would put an end to *British* attacks;

November 1st, to discuss the question of a Supreme Allied Command.

It would appear that, as commonly happens, the lapse of ten years had created a confusion in Haig's mind, that he was mixing up Flanders with Arras, Pétain with Nivelle, and his own continuous anxiety about his Allies with both. On the other hand, in other respects his mind was perfectly clear and lucid at that time. The letter is a puzzle, as contrary to Haig's character as to the facts recorded in his Diary.

daily more strongly against his official military advisers, but shrinking from
the act of removing either or both of them, had recourse to yet another ill-
judged expedient: he summoned Sir John French (C.-in-C. Home Forces)
and Sir Henry Wilson (currently unemployed) to a meeting of the War
Cabinet and asked them to submit papers giving their advice on the conduct
of the War. 'The fact is', wrote Robertson to Haig, 'it is a *very* weak-kneed,
craven-hearted cabinet, and L.G. . . . is allowed to run riot. We shall see what
we see.' Haig noted: '*R. thinks he should resign.*' Whatever their immediate
differences, this was a shocking thought to Haig at this stage: 'I wrote him a
note and said that he ought not to resign until his advice has been rejected.
In any case he must send in a protest showing with reasons why the Government ought not to call in outside advisers, now that the General Staff has
been organized and is in existence for the main purpose of advising the
Government and giving a *reasoned* opinion on strategical problems.' For the
time being, Lloyd George's new manoeuvre drew Haig and Robertson
together again, and pushed their differences into the background.

It was against this confused and depressing picture that Plumer's third
attack was launched: the Battle of Broodseinde, on October 4th. It followed
the same pattern as the previous two. Although the overall frontage was
wider than on September 26th (14,000 yards), and involved 12 divisions, the
main front of penetration, opposite Broodseinde and Passchendaele, was still
a narrow one, 5,000 yards shared between I and II Anzac Corps. Once again,
there was the same great stress on artillery. This arm was now beginning to
feel the strain of the heavy work that had been laid upon it during the whole
campaign; the Second Army's losses in 18-pounders alone during September
(through wear and tear as well as enemy action) were 350; its Artillery casualties between October 4th and 8th reached the high level of 10 per cent of
those of the Infantry. It may be said that Broodseinde marked the high-water
line of the Royal Artillery's contribution; henceforward deteriorating ground
conditions and increasing fatigue reduced its effectiveness. On October 4th,
however, it played its part superbly. It was assisted in this, on the main front,
by one of those accidents of war which can never be counted on, but which
can transform events.

German tactics, under the mauling which the British attacks inflicted, had
undergone a change; from the immediate counter-attacks which had lamentably failed at the Menin Road and Polygon Wood battles, they had now
switched to more deliberate efforts at a longer interval after the British
advance. Such an attack had, by coincidence, been prepared for this very day,
with a zero hour almost identical with the British. The first effect of this was
alarming: the German barrage fell upon the Anzac troops while they were
forming for their assault. A captain in the first line of the 2nd Australian

Division told the author: 'We thought at the time that the casualties were very heavy, and we thought of course that we had been seen getting on to the tape.' Casualties were heavy indeed, but they did not prevent the I and II Anzac Corps from rising up and advancing when the British barrage came down dead on 6 a.m. The Germans were less fortunate. Their attacking battalions were caught in the British barrage, and then immediately set upon by the infantry. They were, says General Birdwood, 'swept away in many individual combats by my Australians. There could be no doubt as to the completeness and importance of our success.' General Monash, commanding the 3rd Australian Division, wrote after the battle: 'Great happenings are possible in the near future. . . . Our success was complete and unqualified. Over 1,050 prisoners and much material and guns. Well over 1,000 dead enemy counted and many hundreds buried out of reach.[1] We got absolutely astride of the main ridge.' The 2nd Division captain quoted above, halted with his men on the first objective, told the author that casualties and men coming back from the further objectives 'told us that they had actually seen the German gun teams hitching up their guns and limbers and galloping away, and that there before them were green fields and pastures, things of course we had never seen before in the Ypres sector'. To right and left of the Anzacs the successes won were less marked, but none the less valuable to the result. Ludendorff wrote: 'The battle of the 4th October was extraordinarily severe, and again we only came through it with enormous losses.' The German Official monograph on the campaign speaks of this as 'a black day'. The Australian Official Historian says: 'An overwhelming blow had been struck and both sides knew it.'

'Let the student', the Australian Official Account goes on, 'looking at the prospect as it appeared at noon on 4th October, ask himself: "In view of three step-by-step blows, all successful, what will be the result of three more in the next fortnight?" ' This was, indeed, the question. At a conference with Plumer and Gough on the afternoon of the battle, Haig urged that the next stage should be launched two days earlier than originally planned. Charteris, he tells us, gave it as his opinion again that the Germans had 'few more available reserves'. But Charteris himself wrote: 'We are far enough on now to stop for the winter, and there is much to be said for that. Unless we get fine weather for all this month, there is no chance of clearing the coast. With fine weather we may still do it. If we could be sure that the Germans would attack us here, it would be far better to stand fast. But they would probably be now only too glad to remain quiet here and try elsewhere. *Anyhow, there are reasons far more vital than our own interests here that give us no option.*[2] But it

1. Figures in all cases refer only to 3rd Australian Division.
2. Author's italics.

is a tremendous responsibility for D.H. Most of those at the conference, though willing to go on, would welcome a stop.'

The 'vital reasons' are a puzzle. One thing is certain: there is no evidence other than his own words to link them with the condition of the French Army. On October 7th Repington was talking to Pétain, who told him that the morale of the French Army at the front was now completely restored, though he feared the effects of political propaganda and scandals on the civil side. Pétain added that he 'had the greatest respect for Haig and admired his tenacity and the great achievements of our Armies, but could not think that our attack in Flanders was good strategy'. It would seem that Charteris's 'vital reasons' must have subconsciously stemmed from some quite different consideration – perhaps not unconnected with his own activities and prognostications. We have a clue to this in a further comment of his, dated October 8th:

'Documents taken on the 4th show that the Germans are very hard pressed to hold their ground . . . but unless we have a very great success tomorrow it is the end for this year so far as Flanders is concerned, and next year the Germans will have their troops from Russia. With a great success tomorrow, and good weather for a few more weeks, we may still clear the coast *and win the war before Christmas*.[1] It is not impossible but it is pouring again today.'

*   *   *   *

The final phase of the campaign bore throughout the characteristics which have generally been associated with the whole of it. The rain which set in on the afternoon of Broodseinde continued almost without interruption for the remainder of the month; such dry intervals as occurred could make no impact on a battlefield where drainage had been completely destroyed, where shell-holes (full of water) were practically contiguous over wide areas, where roads and tracks had vanished out of sight in what one Engineer officer called 'a porridge of mud'. It was a month of dire misery and absolute frustration. Looking at it from the other side, Ludendorff wrote: 'It was no longer life at all. It was mere unspeakable suffering.' His troops were defending; at least they did not have nightmare problems of movement. The British Official History remarks: 'That the attacks ordered were so gallantly made in such conditions stands to the immortal credit of the battalions concerned.' But why were the attacks ordered?

As usual, there is no single, simple answer to this question. Haig's reasons for going on with the offensive were complex. The outstanding reason, valid

1. Author's italics.

for the first part of this last phase, was clearly that he had just won three considerable victories and wanted to exploit them. He knew that the Germans had sustained a heavy blow (the extent of it was undoubtedly exaggerated by Charteris, but Ludendorff and other German writers have confirmed the cost to them). He appreciated that no other Allied army was in a position to fight the enemy hard, and feared what might be the results if all initiative was handed back to the Germans. He had never doubted that this would be a long battle; as far back as August 21st he had told his Army Commanders: 'It is essential that we should be in a position to *continue the battle well into November.*'[1]

Haig feared also the likely effects of Russia's collapse, and the large increase of German strength that would accrue from it before long. If there was a chance, even the slenderest chance, of hammering Germany to her knees before the end of the year, and before her Eastern armies were liberated, he felt that this chance had to be taken, whatever the cost. Finally, he knew too that Pétain was now at last going to play a part in the campaign again, and after all the pressure which he had put on the French commander to attack, he could scarcely now inform him that the British were giving up the game. All this was in his mind on October 9th, the dismal day of the Battle of Poelcappelle.

Summing up the small rewards that were gained on this day of excruciating struggle, and surveying the conditions under which they were won, Haig called it 'a great success'. Charteris was (privately) more realistic; he wrote: 'I was out all yesterday at the attack. It was the saddest day of this year. We did fairly well but only fairly well. It was not the enemy but mud that prevented us from doing better. But there is now no chance of complete success this year. We *must* still fight on for a few more weeks,[2] but there is no purpose in it now, so far as Flanders is concerned. I don't think I ever had great hope of a big success yesterday, but until noon there was, at least, still a chance ... when one knows that the great purpose one has been working for has escaped, somehow one sees and thinks of nothing but the awfulness of it all. Yesterday afternoon was unutterably damnable. I got back very late and could not work, and could not rest. D.H. sent for me about 10, to discuss things. He has to bear the brunt of it all. He was still trying to find some grounds for hope that we might still win through here this year, but there is none.' How then, we may ask, did it come about that, at the end of this same day, Haig was writing: '... the enemy is now much weakened in moral and lacks the desire to fight.' Who told him that? It could only have been

1. Haig's italics. He was urging the need to be economical with man-power.
2. In a footnote here Charteris added later: 'The French were still appealing for the protection provided by our attacks.' He gives no evidence for this.

Charteris himself, who, according to an officer who served under him,[1] 'considered that it was his duty to keep up Douglas Haig's morale'. It was a poor service.

Three days after the undoubted setback at Poelcappelle, the first direct attack on Passchendaele was launched under equally appalling conditions. This was the last flash of Anzac fire in this arduous campaign in which those fine soldiers had taken such a notable part for so long. The Australians, Gough told Haig, were determined to put their flag on the ruins of Passchendaele. It simply could not be done. As an example of prevailing conditions, General Monash tells us: 'The average "carry" from the front line was over 4,000 yards, through a heavy morass, and each stretcher took sixteen bearers, in four relays of four men each – instead of two men as normally.' Repington, visiting the Second Army, found some of the light railways 'bodily embedded in the mud up to the top of the little locomotives; the whole railway has subsided into the morass. . . .' The gunners, above all, had a heartbreaking time; not only was there the fantastic problem of feeding the guns with shells across the crater-swamps, where mules were known to vanish under the clinging mud with all their loads; the guns themselves could not find hard ground to fire from. Barrages were, in consequence, feeble and wild, no protection to the infantry after the first round, the first recoil into the soft earth. The Air Force could give no help whatever. Under these circumstances, as Monash said, 'the display of gallantry and self-devotion of the troops was altogether beyond praise'. But there was next to nothing to show for it; Passchendaele would have to be taken by inches. Yet Haig was not alone in his conviction that the thing should and could be done. On October 14th Repington found such a cool and sober officer as Plumer 'heart and soul for the Flanders offensive. I asked him whether he was thinking of his present tactical objectives, or whether he had in his mind the strategy of next year and its possibilities. He said that he had both, and had fully considered the future possibilities'.

As the middle of the month came and went, the prospects of exploiting the September victories vanished with it. As late as the 15th Kiggell told Repington that 'the Huns are weakening and may give way at any moment'. But this was a dream that was disappearing fast, and now it was other considerations that came more sharply into play. Among these was the swamp itself. General Harington, who studied the line daily with anxious care as Plumer's Chief of Staff, and returned to study it again after the War, standing in the cemeteries where so many of the men whose battle orders he had signed lay buried, wrote: 'I still ask the critics to state where our advanced

1. General Sir James Marshall-Cornwall, K.C.B., C.B.E., D.S.O., M.C., in conversation with the author in 1960.

troops could have spent the winter of 1917. In theory anywhere. In practice nowhere. We find these convenient lines in War Games but not in War.' The Passchendaele ridge was needed now, not as a springboard for attacking Roulers, but simply because it was higher ground above the universal bog.

Towards this obnoxious yet desirable goal the Army struggled on. There was an attack on October 22nd; the gains were lost later that day. On this day the Petrograd Soviet denounced the Karensky Government; the Bolshevik leader Trotsky demanded immediate peace; the second stage of the Russian Revolution was at hand. On the following day Pétain put in his attack on the Aisne, and won another of his brilliant 'small' victories, 8,000 prisoners and 70 guns taken on a six-mile front. But on the next day, October 24th, the Austro-German forces broke into the Italian line at Caporetto, taking 10,000 prisoners, and beginning one of the most spectacular routs of the War. On the 26th, in knee-deep mud, again on the 28th ('The 7th Division were really engulfed in mud in some places...' wrote Haig), and on the 30th, the British forces inched up towards Passchendaele. On November 6th the Canadian Corps, relatively fresh, captured the shattered village by a triumph of what might be called aquatic engineering, and by sheer courage. Charteris wrote: 'We have now got to where, with good weather, we should have been in early September, and with two months in front of us to carry on the operation and clear the coast. Now, from the purely local point of view, it is rather a barren victory, and if the home people decide on a defensive next year, it will be almost lives and labour thrown away.'

Six days after the capture of Passchendaele, Haig ordered operations in Flanders to be brought to an end. The Germans were in no condition to challenge this decision. The great offensive was over. What was the result? Measured on the ground, it was trifling: at the point of deepest penetration, just over 10,000 yards. At the end of three and a half months, the Army had not even completely reached the first of the objectives laid down. Measured against the intention to capture the German submarine bases on the Belgian coast, it was a failure. For a time, encouraged by Charteris, Haig believed that the Germans would make a voluntary withdrawal in Flanders as they had done after the Somme. The steady build-up of their divisions from Russia dispelled this dream. Measured against the desire to inflict a decisive defeat on the German Army, the offensive was also a failure. Was it entirely barren? Was it 'senseless'? Such definitions cannot be upheld.

It is extremely difficult, at a distance, to arrive at exact comparisons between the nature of one operation and another. Some survivors of both battles have firmly stated that the Somme was a far worse experience than Flanders. Others take a different view. It has to be borne in mind that the Army of 1917 was a different organism from that of 1916; better trained, more proficient, it was nevertheless more disillusioned; it lacked the buoyant enthusiasm of the first generation of Kitchener's volunteers. The moral effect of this inexorable struggle in that hideous arena was consequently more marked; Sir Philip Gibbs has said: 'For the first time the British Army lost its spirit of optimism.' The Ypres area itself, 'with its slimy canals, beeks, sloughs, bogs and inundations; its shelled duckboard tracks, its isolated outposts, its incessant shelling and incessant rain, its mists and fogs, its corpses and its pestilential, miasmic odours',[1] engendered a vast depression of the human spirit which was more significant than the actual casualties sustained.

The casualties have given rise to endless controversy which there is no way of definitely settling. The Official History (published in 1948) gives corrected British casualties as 244,897. This total has been disputed, and it has been said that the Official Historian ' "cooked" the figures'.[2] To those who are disposed to believe this, it can only be suggested that they read the appropriate volume of the Official History with great care, and study the remarkable documentation with which British casualties are presented. If Sir James Edmonds was really 'cooking' the figures, he set about it in an astonishingly open and above-board way. Personally, this author after very long and sincere consideration, does not find the Official total surprising or suspicious. It amounts to approximately 60 per cent of that reached during the fighting on the Somme, and this would seem to be right, for a number of reasons. First, the battle lasted a substantially shorter time: 105 days, as against 141 days. Secondly, unlike the Somme, ground and weather conditions forced long intervals between the actual attacks; one of these gaps, as we have seen, lasted over three weeks. Thirdly, in general, fewer troops were engaged; battalion strengths were lower (on June 28th Haig noted that his infantry was 99,000 below establishment) and many of the attacks were conducted with a relatively small number of divisions. Fourthly, as stated above, the infantry were better trained, their tactics more flexible than in 1916. Fifthly, they enjoyed far stronger artillery protection (whenever this failed, the effect was immediately felt). Sixthly, the nature of the battlefield, and the prevailing conditions, were such that the *sense* of loss was bound to be greater than its actuality. Visibility, in the cratered fighting area, was extremely limited, and communication (even within a unit) most difficult. It was possible to see one's comrades vanish – apparently lost – and to lose all contact with them perhaps for days. We have seen that at times it took sixteen men to carry one stretcher case. Let nobody suppose that they all belonged to the R.A.M.C. Sixteen men on a stretcher could 'wipe out' a platoon. Runners and messengers could take as much as seventy-two hours to reach the rear and return (if they were

1. From *The Story of the 29th Division*.
2. Captain Liddell Hart, in *The Spectator*, December 6th, 1957.

fortunate enough to survive). The breakdown of transport in the battle zone involved many fighting troops in fatigues and carrying parties which again reduced the strength of units and gave them a decimated look. There was, in fact, every circumstance to swell this appearance, coupled with an evident failure, for most of the time, to get on, which made it more poignant. One of the advantages, after all, of advancing even a little way, is that you do not have to contemplate yesterday's corpses. Many of the British dead at Ypres were still unburied when the Germans attacked in April, 1918.

What of the German losses? The British Official History states frankly: 'They must be conjectured.' Not everyone will follow Sir James Edmonds in his estimate that they totalled 400,000. It seems a high figure. But that they at least equalled those of the Allies, and probably considerably exceeded them, seems a safe assumption. Here again, reality can only be approached by dismissing the general image of the battle. Because it was, strategically, a British offensive, that image is one of endless British attacks, coming to grief in the mud around the pill-boxes. In fact, as on the Somme, every British advance, no matter how slight, was followed by German counter-attacks, sometimes as many as seven in a day. Indeed, it is likely that, incident by incident, the Germans did even more attacking during the Flanders battle than the British. Not only did they hold the policy of counter-attacking immediately, but, as we have seen, in the later stages they went further and mounted independent assaults of their own, such as those on September 25th and the ill-fated effort on the day of Broodseinde. Against the very much more powerful British artillery of 1917, many of these onsets met the fate meted out to the British in the early part of the Somme battle when the Germans had so many factors in their favour. German accounts, certainly, do not suggest that their losses were anything but most severe; the Chief of Staff of their *IV Army* called Flanders 'the greatest martyrdom of the War'. In fact, if Flanders had not inflicted the decisive defeat on the enemy that Haig had aimed at, there can be no doubt whatever that it carried forward very substantially that wearing-out of the German Army without which he never supposed that victory could be won.

It is illuminating, at this stage, to turn once again to the enemy Commander's view. Ludendorff expressed no doubts about the effects of the Flanders battle, and was particularly precise about that very last phase of it which has provoked so much controversy in Britain. 'October came', he wrote, 'and with it one of the hardest months of the war. The world at large – which began in my immediate neighbourhood – saw only Tarnopol, Czernovitz, Riga, and later Osel, Udine, the Tagliamento and the Piave.[1] It

1. These were the victories of the Central Powers in 1917 which suggest what more might have happened, but for the British offensive.

did not see my anxiety, nor my deep sympathy with the sufferings of our troops in the West. My mind was in the East and Italy, my heart was on the Western Front . . . the wastage in the big actions of the Fourth Battle of Flanders was extraordinarily high. In the West we began to be short of troops. The two divisions that had been held in readiness in the East and were already on the way to Italy, were diverted to Flanders. . . . These days were the culminating point of the crisis. The fifth act of the great drama in Flanders opened on the 22nd October. Enormous masses of ammunition, such as the human mind had never imagined before the war, were hurled upon the bodies of men who passed a miserable existence scattered about in mud-filled shell-holes. . . . And through this world of mud the attackers dragged themselves, slowly, but steadily, and in dense masses. Caught in the advanced zone by our hail of fire they often collapsed, and the lonely man in the shell-hole breathed again. Then the mass came on again. Rifle and machine-gun jammed with mud. Man fought against man, and only too often the mass was successful. What the German soldier experienced, achieved, and suffered in the Flanders Battle will be his everlasting monument of bronze, erected by himself in the enemy's land. . . . And yet it has to be admitted that certain units no longer triumphed over the demoralizing effect of the defensive battle as they had done formerly.' From this it is to be inferred that, when German morale did at last collapse, some nine months later, this was the end of a process which had been begun in Flanders.

This was not generally apparent at the time, in the aura of disappointment that surrounded the decline of the year. Yet it was perceptible to some. Haig, certainly, was far from accepting that the balance sheet was unfavourable. In his Despatch he wrote: 'What was actually accomplished under such adverse conditions is the most conclusive proof that, given a normally fine August, the capture of the whole ridge, within the space of a few weeks, was well within the power of the men who achieved so much.' He added: '. . . the ultimate destruction of the enemy's field forces has been brought appreciably nearer'. Looking beyond the German field forces, while the battle was still in progress, Hankey summarized in a conversation with Lloyd George on October 15th the reasons for going on with it. This summary stands as a diagnosis of what the campaign was ultimately about, and what it achieved.

The record of Hankey's views, which he dictated immediately after the conversation, says: 'He pointed out that we were not fighting Germany with one weapon only. We were attacking with the military weapon, the blockade weapon, the weapon of morale, and by attacking the allies of Germany. The military operations in Flanders reacted upon every one of these weapons. Haig's operations must be measured not only by the military objects which they achieved, but by their general effect on Germany. They strengthened the effect of the blockade by draining the manpower of Germany, increasing the strain on her manufacturing resources, and thereby reducing the amount available for the civil population, and by the strain on railway communications. The Flanders operations reacted on the morale of the German people by reducing their faith in their military commanders, by the loss of relatives, and by engendering a feeling of hopelessness. Finally, these operations reacted on Germany's allies by showing that the story of Germany's invincibility was a mere fiction. Hence it appeared to him that there was every reason for continuing these operations, viewing it not solely from a military aspect, which was not properly his concern, but from a wider point of view.'

Needless to say, Lloyd George was unconvinced; he had already reached the conclusion that the War would not be won until 1919. All that Hankey said was true; but much had yet to be endured in the proving of it.

*   *   *   *

The outcome of Lloyd George's latest device for by-passing his responsible advisers was once again disappointment. Neither Sir John French nor Sir Henry Wilson was truly in a position, once squarely faced with the problem, to offer authoritative alternatives to the strategy of the General Staff. Wilson, however, took the opportunity to argue again for an idea which had been growing steadily in his mind: an inter-Allied organization which would at last bring a degree of practical unity to the direction of the War effort. When Haig read the papers submitted to the War Cabinet by the two generals, he remarked of French's: 'It is a poor production and is evidently the outcome of a jealous and disappointed mind. H. Wilson came to no conclusion but advises an "Inter-Allied Council" being formed with (presumably) himself as head of the British Staff section.' This was on October 31st; Haig was not far wrong; it was on that very day that the War Cabinet decided to work on Wilson's recommendation. It had made an immediate impression on Lloyd George; he saw in it what seemed to be, at last, a foolproof system for limiting the powers of the British generals whose policy he detested so much. On October 17th Wilson wrote in his Diary: 'It became very clear to me tonight that Lloyd George means to get Robertson out, and means to curb the powers of the C.-in-C. in the field. This is what I have been advising for $2\frac{1}{2}$ years, and this is what the whole of my paper is directed at – not to getting Robertson out, but to forming a Superior Direction over all C.G.S.s and C.-in-C.s. Lloyd George said tonight that the French were favourably inclined, and this agrees with what Painlevé told me last week.'

The matter was settled with remarkable briskness at the Allied Conference at Rapallo in November. At the fifth session of that Conference, on November 7th, a Supreme War Council was set up, to consist of representatives of each of the signatory Powers (France, Italy, U.S.A., Britain), meeting at least once a month, and assisted by a permanent body of 'Military Representatives' who would act as technical advisers. Lloyd George explained the purpose of the scheme to the House of Commons on November 14th; it was 'to set up a central body charged with the duty of continuously surveying the field of operations as a whole, and, by the light of information derived from all fronts and from all Governments and Staffs, of co-ordinating the plans prepared by the different General Staffs, and, if necessary, of making proposals of their own for the better conduct of the war'. As envisaged at Rapallo, these were the limits of the responsibilities of the new body; it would have no executive functions. This was an anomaly which could scarcely be expected to continue; to be genuinely effective, the Supreme War Council would have, sooner or later, to be fitted with 'teeth'. But was this ever possible? If one grants, as one should, that this was an important experiment in the progress towards that real Allied unity which was not seen until the Second World War, one must also admit that in the circumstances of 1917 (or, indeed of the whole of the First War) such a degree of practical, organizational unity was never capable of being achieved. It was Pétain who, with his habitual shrewdness, put his finger at once on the weakness of the proposed system, in a conversation with Haig on November 1st.

Unity of Command, Pétain told Haig, 'was possible amongst Allies only when one Army was really the dominant one as in the case of the Central Powers. Our case was different. The British and French Armies were now in his views on an equality. Therefore, he and I must exercise command, and if we disagree, our Governments alone can settle the point in dispute'. Unpalatable as it may be, Pétain's analysis was correct. What made a Joint Chiefs of Staff apparatus possible, and with it the Supreme Commander system applied in World War II, was, quite simply, American preponderance, which ensured that, in the last resort, decision would be arrived at. This was much assisted by the fact that, despite different usages, the British and the Americans actually speak the same language, which permitted a degree of integration which is not normally possible. The post-war struggles of N.A.T.O. to acquire something similar point to the difficulties that may be encountered, even in peace-time; while a moment's reflection confirms that, without American preponderance again, N.A.T.O. could be nothing but a farce. Among the four Allies concerned in 1917 no such preponderance existed, or if it did, it would not be admitted. Consequently, action would always be confined to what was agreed, and could never rest on what was ordered. Foch himself, when he became Generalissimo in 1918, accepted that. Even Eisenhower, in 1944, was not tempted to go far beyond this limit. Haig was acutely aware of it. Fortified by his conversation with Pétain, he told Lloyd George on November 4th, when the latter was on the way to Rapallo, 'that the proposal had been considered for three years and each time had been rejected as unworkable. I gave several reasons why I thought it could not work, and that it would add to our difficulties having such a body. The P.M. then said that the two Governments had decided to form it; so I said, there is no need saying any more then!' According to Repington, 'some very crisp remarks on each side' followed this exchange. Nevertheless, walking up the Champs Elysées later with Lloyd George, Haig found him 'quite a pleasant little man when one had him alone'. 'But I should think most unreliable', he added.

Once the matter was settled, Haig, as usual, was inclined to make no further bones about it; he had more urgent things to attend to. He did not like it; he did not think it would work. But, as he wrote to Robertson on November 12th: 'The object of ensuring common plans and co-ordination in executing them is of course admirable, and I think that as the Government has apparently decided on this Scheme all we can do is to try to work it until and unless we find that it is not possible to do so.' The main weakness of the scheme, he said, was this: 'In the past three years we have seen so much of the influence of the conflicting interests of States and of the failure of some Governments to realize that in the conduct of the war the common good is the highest interest and should over-ride all others, that I fear if agreement is reached at all on important questions of strategy it will be reached only by compromise – and the danger of action in war based on compromise is evident. Moreover, Governments may not confirm the plans agreed on by this War Council, or they may not all act loyally on their agreements.'

The particular problem, Haig foresaw, would arise out of the functioning of the military side of the Council. Inevitably there would be complications, with possibly dangerous consequences, of the roles of the C.I.G.S. and of the Commander-in-Chief. 'As regards your own position', he told Robertson, 'that of our own War Cabinet, the relations between you and it, between it and the Supreme War Council, and between the latter (and the military representatives on it) and yourself, it is evident that very careful organization will be required if utter confusion is not to be the result. But that is not a matter for me to offer opinions on. . . . If it were still possible however to prevent this Supreme War Council from coming into existence, I think it would be greatly to the interest of Great Britain to do so.'

Haig was not prepared to go as far as Charteris in commenting on the fairly evident ulterior motive of Lloyd George in championing the new organization. Charteris, on the same day, wrote: 'It is utter rubbish so far as fighting is concerned. It will mean delay in any attack on the Germans and will break down at once if the Germans attack us.[1] But it also means that the Cabinet is going to oust D.H. or Robertson, or both.' That this was, indeed, at the root of the matter, soon became evident. In his letter to Robertson, Haig had pointed out that 'Prime Ministers and Governments change somewhat frequently in some of the Allied countries. . . .' Less than a week after the Rapallo Conference, Painlevé's Ministry fell, and he was replaced by Clemenceau, who fortunately remained in power until the end of the War. It was, then, a new French Prime Minister who decided who should be the French Military Representative on the Supreme War Council. The British nomination was Wilson, a clear indication of Lloyd George's lack of confidence in the British General Staff. Clemenceau's attitude was different. 'It appears . . .' lamented Wilson on November 27th, 'that Clemenceau wants to change the whole Superior Council, and put Foch on as C.G.S. and put Pétain on. This would mean Robertson and Haig, and we should be where we have been all along . . . Lloyd George is angry, and says that he will have a row with Clemenceau tomorrow.' Having a row with Clemenceau was apt to be an unprofitable experience. When the matter was finally settled, the French selection was General Weygand, Foch's Chief Staff Officer and *alter ego*. General Callwell, Wilson's biographer, sums up the fruits of this tortuous exercise: 'Owing to his very close relations of long standing with Foch, Weygand would for all practical purposes, be simply a mouthpiece of the French C.G.S. The French "Technical Adviser" . . . would naturally be disposed to give the Allied Ministers forming the Council the same advice as Foch was giving the French Government. Lloyd George's and Sir Henry's conception of the Technical Adviser, *at the outset*,[2] was that of a military expert who would be wholly independent of his War Office . . . and would be prepared to express views entirely different from those entertained, as the case might be, by Foch or Robertson, *the officers who were responsible*[3] to their respective Governments and to their respective countries. But Cadorna[4] was the Italian C.G.S.; and in due course General Bliss, the U.S. Chief of Staff, was appointed the American Representative on the Council. Wilson's position was, in fact, going to be the exceptional one, not Weygand's.'

In other words, Lloyd George's achievement had been, once again, to place his country at a grave disadvantage in the formulation of the policies of the Alliance. The fact that, in doing so, he also added severely to the already considerable burdens laid upon the British Chief of General Staff and Com-

1. Prophetic insight, but not astonishing.
2. Author's italics.
3. Author's italics.
4. Italian Representative. In fact, he was the ex-C.G.S., but it amounted to the same.

mander-in-Chief, is relatively a secondary matter, but not unimportant to them in the difficult times that lay ahead.

* * * *

On the Western Front, the worst year of the War snuffed out after a blaze of light as treacherous as any that had gone before. It had never been Haig's intention to limit his efforts to Flanders; to obtain the fullest results from the efforts made there he had planned to make other thrusts which would help to confuse the enemy and divert his strength. One such attack had taken place at Lens in August; a second blow in that region had been considered, but the project was abandoned in order to conserve artillery. A third scheme, however, was prepared, and flourished through association with proposals put forward by the Tank Corps, when it was realized that the Flanders battlefield would not permit the full employment of that Arm. On September 16th, while Plumer was still preparing his intervention at Ypres, Haig noted: 'I discussed with Byng some operations which he proposed . . . and I told him I would give him all the help I could.' This may be regarded as the starting-point of the Battle of Cambrai, launched by the Third Army just over two months later.

To Tank Corps historians and to the champions of armour, Cambrai marks a most significant date, because this was the first true 'Tank battle' in history, the first time that the new Arm was used in sufficient numbers and under proper conditions to show what it could do: 476 tanks were engaged in the battle, Mark IVs, a very distinct improvement on the Mark I and the Mark II, though still a slow and cumbersome weapon with many defects which quickly became apparent. Tank design and tactics had, nevertheless, gone a long way since the début at Flers, fourteen months earlier; of the total stated above, 378 were fighting tanks; 54 were supply tanks, or gun carriers, capable of transporting a 60-pdr.; 32 were wire-destroying tanks, fitted with grapnels; 2 were bridging tanks; 9 were equipped for wireless communication duties; 1 was for laying telephone cable. General Hugh Elles, the first commander of the Corps, led it into action in person, in his tank 'Hilda', flying the largest Tank Corps flag which could be procured. Despite its losses (179 tanks on the first day, November 20th) and despite what followed, the Tank Corps had every reason to be proud and delighted with what it achieved; after Cambrai there could be no further argument; the decisive weapon of land warfare in the mid-twentieth century had now definitely arrived. A new dimension of war was established. Haig's armies had at last discovered what the real answer to wire and machine guns was, and in the following year they put that answer to full use.

But they had to wait until the following year. Cambrai opened with a success more brilliant than any yet seen. On a front of six miles, in the space of four hours, two successive lines of the Hindenburg position were carried with trifling loss; over 100 guns and some 6,000 prisoners were taken. German resistance largely collapsed before the unheralded onset of the great mass of tanks. When the news reached England, losing nothing in the telling by the War Correspondents, great excitement was engendered; the church bells were rung for the victory. This celebration was premature. The dominant Bourlon ridge, overlooking the whole area of the British advance from its left flank, was never cleared. Haig found himself, against all his hopes, engaged in a stern, wearing struggle for this ridge, which lasted for seven days, and then had to be abandoned through the sheer shortage of troops. Three days later, on November 30th, the Germans counter-attacked, and inflicted (without benefit of tanks) as great a surprise as they themselves had sustained on the 20th. A large slice of the British gains of that day was wrested back; a portion of the original British front was also lost. After two days, Haig authorized a withdrawal from the remainder of the pronounced salient in which the Third Army now found itself. When this was carried out, almost the whole British achievement was nullified; casualties and captures on both sides were roughly equal. The stalemate of 1917 had been reasserted; it was a cruel disappointment.

The set-back at Cambrai represents the lowest ebb of Haig's career. It created difficulties for him which greatly complicated those which inevitably arrived with the return of Germany's division from the East and their offensive in the following March. It weakened his prestige and position at a time when he needed every support he could get. It laid him open to criticism and attacks more severe than any that he had yet experienced. Not all of these were unjustified; some of them were. At the root of all of them lies the question whether the Battle of Cambrai should have been fought at all. To this, the answer may be found in the remarkable success won on the first day. Haig's intention was to round off the year with a heavy blow at the enemy, and this he certainly achieved. But the small, vital degree of failure, *also on that day*, points to an unclarity of intention, an imprecision of execution, for which he must bear a part of the blame – though not the full blame which he so readily shouldered when the exasperated Government called for an enquiry. In the light of the several enquiries which were finally carried out into the handling of this battle, it would now seem clear that the Third Army had allowed itself to be so preoccupied with the first stage of the fight that it never properly considered what would come next. Every credit is due to General Byng and his staff for the remarkable degree of surprise which they achieved on November 20th; but what is the good of effecting a huge surprise, unless the purpose of it is clearly understood? The failure at Bourlon was crucial. The reason for it was to be found in the allocation of troops, for which the Army Commander was responsible. It was a case of Gheluvelt Plateau all over again. The Third Army's attack was too even; insufficient resources were allocated to make sure of the vital point. During the days that followed, Haig repeatedly urged on Byng the vital need to carry the ridge; but it was too late.

There were other failures. The tanks swept through the uncut wire, and over the wide trenches of the Hindenburg Line, dropping their great fascines into these trenches, clearing them for the jubilant infantry. But still the only arm of exploitation available was the cavalry, and once again the complete ineffectiveness of Horse soldiers on a modern battlefield was demonstrated. The British cavalry were no more capable of pursuing a defeated enemy at Cambrai than the French had been during the German retreat earlier in the year.[1] Their complete failure gave the Germans the opportunity they needed to rally and regroup. Nor was the infantry in any condition to assume the burden of exploitation in addition to what they had already done. Not all of them had enjoyed a walk-over. Most of them were tired. Many units were under strength. In addition it has to be stated that some commanders fell short of what was needed. There were those who still distrusted tanks, and did not sufficiently adapt their tactics to the requirements of what was, for the first time, the chief Arm in the battle. Among these, General Harper of the 51st Division must be mentioned. He deliberately set aside the drill for co-operation between infantry and tanks recommended by the Tank Corps, with inevitable unfortunate results for his men. Here again one senses a lack of 'grip' on the part of the Third Army Staff, whose task it was to see that Divisional commanders conformed to the needs of the situation and the plan. Other officers, also, seemed to be out of touch. Touring the Third Army front on the 22nd, Haig noted that the 51st Divisional H.Q. 'were very far back', and then, passing on to the 62nd Division under General Braithwaite, added: 'I thought B. should also have been closer up with his division.' This was the same phenomenon which had been observed at Arras: a fruit of long years of positional warfare which left officers and men bewildered by a war of movement.

As regards the German surprise on the 30th, the blame for this has to be divided between G.H.Q. and the Third Army; but the greater part must fall on the Third Army, which received clear warnings from Lieut.-General Sir T. D'O. Snow, commanding VII Corps in the most sensitive sector. As early as the 25th, General Snow had told his Divisional commanders to be ready for a German attack, but he made little impression either on Third Army or

1. Cavalry were effective in 1918, however, against Germans who were demoralized.

on his left-hand neighbour, III Corps. On the 28th his Chief Staff Officer telephoned Third Army H.Q. and reported unusual enemy activity. Major-General Vaughan, Chief of Staff of Third Army, made this record of their conversation: 'Discussed question and agreed that an attack from north and south was a good and likely operation from enemy point of view. VII Corps are in touch with III Corps about it and are on the alert. Told VII Corps we would arrange to keep Guards handy to help if required. Cavalry could also move up if wanted. . . .'

The casual tone of this reply to General Snow is suggestive. The Official History states: 'This reassurance, if it could be regarded as such, was not followed by action. The Third Army issued no warning order, ordered no movement of reserves, took no steps to ensure that troops in the rear areas should be readily available.' When Byng himself reported later on the reverse that had been sustained, he asserted that his Army had been ready for the German attack, and attributed the misfortunes of the day to the lack of training of the troops and junior officers, as well as to a certain lack of staunchness among the machine gunners. Haig accepted this statement officially, but characteristically tempered the criticism of the troops; that he was not personally satisfied with it is revealed by the fact that he ordered a second enquiry into the episode, independently of that demanded by the Government. Within weeks of the completion of this enquiry, Byng's Army was again involved in desperate defensive fighting. The marked – indeed, decisive – success which it then won may fairly be linked with the close investigation of its methods instituted by Haig only such a short time before. Two years of offensive strategy had diverted the British Army's attention from defensive problems; if the recognition of the potentialities of tanks was one part of Cambrai's 'silver lining', the achievement of the Third Army in March, 1918, was certainly another.

But underlying every question about Cambrai is the fact of the weakness and the weariness of the troops involved. Against the arguments for launching the battle, said Haig in his Despatch, 'I had to weigh the fact that my own troops had been engaged for many months in heavy fighting, and that though their efforts had been uniformly successful, the conditions of the struggle had greatly taxed their strength. Only part of the losses in my divisions had been replaced, and many recently arrived drafts, still far from being fully trained, were included in ranks of the Armies. Under these conditions it was a serious matter to make a further heavy call on my troops at the end of such a strenuous year'. It certainly was a serious matter; it is on this very issue, linked with his decision to press the attack on Bourlon when the first forty-eight hours of fighting had failed to produce the result he anticipated, that the gravamen of the criticism of Haig himself must rest. He accepted from the first that everything depended on the result of the initial onset. He simply did not possess the reserves for a long battle. Not only had Flanders exhausted and depleted his Army, but the Italian débâcle had now caused five divisions to be drawn from it for that theatre. With them, much to his own disgust, went Plumer and his Staff; 'Was ever an Army commander and his staff sent off to another theatre of war in the middle of a battle?' asked Haig in despair. As it turned out, although no doubt their presence helped to encourage the Italians, these British forces found little employment in Italy; under a new commander, General Diaz, the Italians halted the Austro-German offensive mainly by their own efforts. Once again, the attempt to commute troops between two fronts had resulted in their being lost to both. But the point here is whether, knowing of this weakness in his Army, Haig was justified in launching and pressing the Cambrai attack. The answer, unfortunately, has once more to be sought in the role of Charteris. Summarizing the lessons of the battle, the Official History states that Haig 'under-estimated the power and the tenacity of his adversary'. This would seem to be entirely true, and can only be attributed to the manner in which Charteris carried out his duties.

On the night before the battle, Charteris wrote: 'I am confident we shall get complete surprise with all its advantages, and we shall have 48 hours before the Germans can reinforce. But within 64 hours they can have as many troops as we have. It is a tremendous responsibility for D.H. and for the first time in the War "I" has been for holding back and "O"[1] has been all for going on.' Haig wrote on the same night: 'Charteris reported . . . that the enemy is in absolute ignorance of our preparations for tomorrow's attack. No aeroplane activity; no artillery fire; no wireless; no listening telephone work. All seems favourable.' The contrast in tone is significant; similarly on the 25th Charteris wrote: 'Things have not gone well. Our troops are tired, and the Germans are getting up large reinforcements; we have none available.' But two days later Haig was writing: 'Charteris reported no change in the enemy on Cambrai battlefront since yesterday. His troops are very thin on this front except at Bourlon. In fact, the situation is most favourable for us, but unfortunately I have not got the necessary number of troops to exploit our success.'

Again we see a marked difference; but there is worse to come. General Marshall-Cornwall, then an officer in the Intelligence Branch, told this author that he 'became aware before the battle that the Germans were moving three divisions to the area, showing that they had wind of it. He identified these divisions, and told John Charteris, who refused to take action or inform Douglas Haig. Marshall-Cornwall was so worried that he went to Davidson

1. Operations Branch of G.H.Q.

and told him, and D. told him not to leave G.H.Q., as he felt like doing, but to report such instances to him (D.)'.[1] There is no doubt that when Haig made the fatal decision to press the attack on Bourlon after November 21st, while he was certainly influenced by such considerations as the great difficulty of holding the ground won without complete possession of the ridge, and by the desire to divert German attention from the Italian front, the main factor in his mind was the belief that the Germans were weak and that success was within easy reach. It was this that caused him to allow the battle to take a course which was not only quite contrary to his original intention, but also nearly produced a disaster.

At the height of the fighting during the German counter-attack, on December 3rd, Haig wrote to Lady Haig: '. . . whatever happens, the responsibility is mine. However, with that HELP which has never failed me yet, I hope we may get through this critical time'. Despite all the setbacks, all the disappointments of this wretched year, of which Cambrai was the hardest knock, he never lost his inner poise, fortified by his religious belief. It was, above all, the sense of lack of support behind him that distressed him most. On December 9th he wrote to Robertson: 'I gather that the P.M. is dissatisfied. If that means I have lost his confidence, then in the interests of the cause let him replace me at once. But if he still wishes me to remain, then all carping criticism should cease, and I should be both supported and trusted.'

It was a vain wish; Lloyd George was reaching the end of his tether. Haig added: 'Whatever happens, however, you must remain as C.I.G.S. as it would be the height of folly to make any change at this crisis in the head of the General Staff. We must be prepared in wartime for ups and downs, and should do our best to go on an even keel.' This thought, too, was a long way from any possible reality. On the last day of the year, Repington wrote: 'The end of a dramatic year. The crumbling of Russia, the Italian defeats, the U-boat successes, and the slow advent of the Americans have all been serious for us, and if the war goes on we shall have a hard time. . . . The real point of danger is the War Cabinet, which is without the courage to face the music of facts.'

Charteris who, whatever his failings, could sometimes see a long way, wrote on December 25th: 'The fourth Christmas at war, and though the outlook is so black, yet still I think it will be the last War Christmas. How different each Christmas has been . . . 1917, the year wrecked by the Calais Conference and still with these great battles won, with all the cards in our hands and our only real anxiety lest they should be wrongly played. We cannot fail to win. Each year inevitably shows success more certain, but for the next few months the prospect is the most gloomy since 1914.' And this, certainly, was no exaggeration.

1. Author's note of conversation.

11

The Year of Victory – I

NINETEEN-EIGHTEEN was Haig's year, the year of his vindication, in which he was seen to be a chief architect of Allied
victory. Its opening, however, found him at the nadir of his fortunes, facing direct and indirect attacks upon his personal position from his
Government, and a massive increase in enemy strength in the field, gravely
threatening his army. The indirect attacks were the first to take effect. As far
back as November 1st, 1917, Charteris had written: 'The Cabinet are in full
cry against D.H. and against our strategy.' Twelve days later he was more
specific: 'At home, L.G. has opened his attack upon the Army generally and
on D.H. and Robertson in particular. I am told he will go for individuals on
the Staff here, as the easiest way of hitting D.H. I discussed this with D.H.
tonight and again offered my resignation, if he thinks it would strengthen his
own position. He will not have it. He says, which is quite true, that when
Joffre let his Staff be altered from Paris he only precipitated his own downfall.'

This attitude on Haig's part, a mixture of habitual loyalty to subordinates,
special affection for Charteris, and apprehension at what might be portended,
could not survive the setback at Cambrai. On December 7th Lord Derby,
who, as we have seen, had long felt personal misgivings about Charteris,
wrote in a letter to Haig: '. . . The War Cabinet are constantly saying that the
statements and views you have put forward at different times regarding the
moral and numerical weakening of the enemy are not borne out by the opposition your troops encounter, *and so it appears to me and the General Staff here.*[1]
And so you can imagine, the events of the 30th and subsequent days have not
reduced the feeling that you had not been as well advised by your Intelligence
Staff as you ought to be. It is felt that not only is too much made of indications of the enemy's weakness, but that indications and information regarding
his remaining strength are not fully and fairly represented to you. On the

1. Author's italics.

whole the Cabinet think that it is essential you should have a more reliable
D.M.I. and have so informed me. Naturally I am very averse from interfering
with the selection of the principal officers for your Headquarters Staff, but I
feel that the Cabinet would not be properly meeting their responsibilities if
they overlooked the necessity for making a change. You will agree that it is
very necessary the War Cabinet should have the fullest confidence in the
opinions and judgments of officers of your Staff, and this they will not have
so long as Charteris remains D.M.I.'

Haig was now in a quandary. Charteris again offered to resign ('He had
much rather do anything than be a source of trouble to me'), but Haig refused
to hear of this. On the other hand, from various sources of whom the most
significant was Kiggell, Haig had learned to what an extent Charteris had lost
the confidence of many in the Army itself. In October, Repington had noted
that 'Plumer is rather sarcastic about Charteris' optimism'. Rawlinson was
another who had little time for him. John Masefield (who had been visiting
the B.E.F.), asked by Esher what he thought of Charteris, replied: ' "It would
be lèse majesté to say" which is rather funny. I wonder what the principal
boy said or did?' And now Kiggell told Haig that 'although he did his work
well at H.Qrs. he was much disliked in Corps and Armies. I told K. to see
Charteris, and that if what he (K.) said was based on good evidence, we ought
to give Charteris another appointment, but that there was no question of
moving C. because of supposed inefficiency in his work. No one had done or
could do the intelligence work better than C. but I realized fully C's faults
towards his equals and his own subordinates. At the same time in C's professional interests, it was a mistake for him to specialize in Intelligence work'.

Meanwhile, until Kiggell reported, Haig had no intention of submitting,
even to Derby's forthright suggestions. He replied to the latter on the 10th:
'I regret that the War Cabinet consider the views put forward by me have
not been borne out by events. However that may be, I cannot agree that
Charteris should be made "whipping-boy" for the charge of undue optimism
brought against myself. His duty is to collect, collate and place before me all
evidence obtainable in regard to the enemy. He has unusually high qualifications for that duty and I am quite satisfied with the manner in which he has
performed it since I have been in command. The responsibility for the judgment formed on the evidence obtained and for the views put forward to the
War Cabinet rests on me and not on him; and if the War Cabinet are not
satisfied with the views put forward by me it is I, and not Charteris, who must
answer for those views. . . .'

Derby was not to be persuaded; and now Robertson chimed in: 'I have
seen the letter you sent to Derby. . . . It is a matter for your consideration
whether you really are doing the best for the general cause by retaining an

officer in who so many people have no confidence.' Kiggell's report bore out
Robertson's doubts; on December 11th Haig noted: 'General Lawrence . . .
arrived and stayed the night. I have arranged for him to take over charge of
the Intelligence Branch in place of Charteris. The latter has made himself so
unpopular with the authorities at the W.O. and with the War Committee, as
well as with the Army and Corps commanders here that in order to avoid
friction and to maintain confidence in our Intelligence I am obliged to change
him. I am sorry to lose him.' To Lady Haig, who had always disliked
Charteris, he wrote, a few days later: 'It is over a year since Derby and the
War Office have set their faces against poor Charteris, and although he has
done his work admirably and his Intelligence Branch is in excellent order, I
feel that it would be wrong of me to keep an officer at this time who seems
really to have upset so many people and to have put those who ought to work
in friendliness with him against him.'

So Charteris departed from the Intelligence Branch, and Lawrence came
in his place. The whole transaction worked out oddly. This was the same
Herbert Lawrence who had handed in his papers when Haig received the
Colonelcy of the 17th Lancers instead of himself after the South African
War. He had done good work at Gallipoli, and had commended himself to
Haig as a sound Divisional commander in France during 1917. But there was
little to draw the two men together, and apparently much to keep them apart.
Lawrence was Haig's contemporary, and yet, as a result of the earlier setback
to his career, he was now only a Major-General, while Haig was a Field-
Marshal. But no difficulty of any kind arose between them. Indeed, scarcely
had Lawrence arrived at G.H.Q. when he received yet another promotion
in office, to Chief of Staff. He was only D.M.I. for a matter of weeks, during
which, however, he found occasion to speak enthusiastically to Haig 'of the
efficient state and good organization of the Intelligence Branch, and gave it as
his opinion that Charteris had produced a fine piece of work'. There is no
reason to doubt this; the machine which Charteris created was good enough;
what was wrong was the way in which he handled it. Charteris himself stayed
on at G.H.Q. until his health broke down at the very end of the War. He continued to give Haig the benefit of his opinions, and at this stage, it may be
noted, many of them were eminently sound.

The story of Charteris's removal has been thought worth telling in some
detail, because it formed the starting point of a pattern. Haig's fears that he
might suffer the same treatment as Joffre were not far wrong; what happened
to Charteris was the thin end of the wedge. Writing to Haig on December
17th, Lord Esher said: 'Personally, to be quite frank, I regret that you had to
give up Charteris. I should myself never have kept him so long, but then he
suited you, and was faithful. What I venture humbly to think a mistake is the

admission, to the unscrupulous men who want to shelter themselves behind somebody, that you were at fault in retaining this officer's services.... Robertson, in my humble opinion, has taken the wrong line in this business. . . . However, solidarity among soldiers is a visionary thing. Never have we been able to achieve it, since I first took an interest in the Army, so far back as the old Wolseley days. . . . Robertson is having the wind knocked out of him. . . . These fellows will beat him black and blue, until he has not a breath in his body.'

This letter is pure Esher, full of sound sense and silky malice. Robertson was indeed in trouble; his turn was soon to come, but it was not yet. In the meantime, the Government was looking for more scalps. One of them was Gough, as Derby warned Haig on December 23rd.[1] Haig had already transferred the Fifth Army back to the right flank, away from Ypres where its renown had suffered so seriously. On December 14th he told Gough that General Neil Malcolm was to be transferred to a Division. He also 'mentioned to Gough how many Divisions had hoped that they would not be sent to the Fifth Army to fight. This feeling I put down to his Staff. I had not told him before because it might have had an effect on his self-confidence during the battle. It was, of course, a surprise to Gough to learn this, but from the facts which I gave him, he realized that there were cases bearing out what I told him'. For the time being Gough was saved, but doubts about him in London did not diminish.

The attack now returned to G.H.Q. itself. General Kiggell was the first target, and Haig noted that questions were being asked about the state of his health on December 20th. There can be no doubt that the strain of 1917, coupled with private worries, had told upon Kiggell. Many people will be familiar with the story of how he burst into tears at the sight of the Passchendaele battlefield, exclaiming: 'Good God! Did we really send men to fight in that?' Since Kiggell had every means of knowing what conditions were like throughout the battle, this emotional outburst is a clear proof that his nerves had suffered badly. Haig, probably partly through being too close to him, was not convinced that Kiggell was at the end of his tether, though aware that things were not altogether as they should be. He wrote: 'Personally I think Kiggell is much better than he was two years ago . . . I spoke to him. He goes on leave tomorrow and returns 28th December. We agreed together that if either he feels that he is not up to the work, or, having regard to the very serious situation now developing, viz. great increase of German divisions on the Western Front, I think he is not fit for the work, I will ask him to go home. But at the present he seems better than he has been for some time, and

1. This is a date that needs to be remembered in all discussion of blame attaching to Gough for events in March 1918.

I am very loth to part with Kigg's help and sound advice.' Haig comforted himself with the thought that, in any case, Butler could take over and preserve continuity. When he met Derby in London on January 1st, 1918, he was soon disillusioned. It was a gloomy conversation, beginning with Derby's account of how the latest attack on Robertson had only been staved off by his own threat to resign if either Robertson or Haig were moved. 'Derby then spoke to me about Kiggell's state of health. In view of the hard times to be faced by the Army in France he considered that I was unwise to retain "a tired man". I said that I had Butler on the spot to replace K. if the latter was unfit to do his work. D. at once said that neither he nor the Cabinet would approve of Butler becoming C.G.S. in France. I gathered from what Derby said that Butler was not liked by any of the "Authorities" at home.'

And so, within a very short space of time, Haig lost both his Chief of Staff and his Deputy Chief of Staff. He put up a fight for the interests of both of them. For Kiggell he did his best to procure the Jersey Command: He wrote this tribute to Kiggell in a letter to Derby on January 26th: 'He certainly deserves well of his country, and I hope that with a rest he may still be able to play a part. He has a fine brain, very sound and practical as a soldier, very farseeing and absolutely honest and straightforward – qualities most difficult to find even among soldiers.' Two days later, when he said good-bye to Kiggell, the latter's future was still not settled, to Haig's distress. 'He seemed to me glad to have a rest, and said that he "would do his best to get fit again". . . . Kiggell has stood by me in many anxious days, and I am sorry to see him go, with such critical times before us here in France.' These sentiments do Haig credit, but it has to be recorded that, from a military point of view, the departure both of Charteris and of Kiggell was a benefit to the Army. When Lawrence took over from the latter, and General Cox succeeded as D.M.I., both of these important aspects of Staff work were gripped as they had not been before. Above all, in Lawrence, Haig found a 'right arm' that he had always lacked, and this was essentially not a war that individuals could tackle alone. In Butler's case, Haig was able to soften the blow by giving him an Army Corps; it proved to be a doubtful kindness in the days of terrible stress that lay ahead. Other Staff changes that should be noticed in this 'purge' were the Quartermaster-General, the Engineer-in-Chief and the Director-General of Medical Services. It was a thorough sweep. Was it just in time to avert calamity? Or was the absence of familiar faces and personalities a handicap to Haig in the crisis that was now so close upon him? The true answer is probably mixed; on balance the new team would appear to have been better. The result, certainly, did them all credit.

Changes in the composition of G.H.Q., however, did not complete the measures which the Government felt constrained to take. On January 19th

Haig learned from Robertson that General Smuts, accompanied by Hankey, would visit him at G.H.Q. in the course of a tour of the Army which they were making. 'I think', wrote Robertson, 'the proposal emanated from the P.M. from what I can hear. He was remarking that he did not know many of the various Generals at the front, and therefore he suggested that it would be a good thing for Smuts to go round and see as many as he could and so be able to tell him his opinion about them.' Accepting this, Haig welcomed his visitors two days later, remarking: 'Both seem to be anxious to help and are friendly.'

It must have been a very trying and embarrassing occasion both for Smuts and for Hankey, for Lloyd George has been quite frank about what their real mission was: it was to find a replacement for Haig. 'It is easy now to say: "You ought to have sacked him"' wrote Lloyd George in his *War Memoirs*, '. . . Who could be put in his place? It is a sad reflection that not one amongst the visible military leaders would have been any better. There were amongst them plenty of good soldiers who knew their profession and possessed intelligence up to a point. But Haig was all that and probably better within those limits than any others within sight. . . . Had we removed Haig, we might have set up in his place a man who had not his mastery of the profession, and with no other greater gifts to make up for that deficiency. When I was considering the problem I sent General Smuts and Sir Maurice Hankey around the front to report to the War Cabinet on affairs generally, and I confidentially asked them to look and see for themselves whether amongst the Generals they met, there was one whom they considered might with advantage attain and fill the first place. They came back with a very disappointing report. . . .'

In this strange admission of disappointment at learning that the Army was in the best possible hands, Lloyd George unwittingly pays to Haig one of the most remarkable tributes of any that he ever received; for nobody could have wanted to be rid of him more than Lloyd George. For the record, it may be added that among those who were considered at the time as possible replacements for Haig were Plumer, Allenby and Lord Cavan. Charteris's nomination, he tells us, would have been Lord Trenchard, a most interesting idea. Haig himself might well have endorsed it.

The confidential mission had reported in Haig's favour; there remained the question of Robertson. The process of 'beating him black and blue' was by now going on apace. It came to a head at the beginning of February, over a question of strategic direction of the War which will require to be discussed elsewhere. Here we need only note that the process of sweeping changes in the higher command of the Army reached its climax in what was, virtually, the dismissal of Robertson in February, and his replacement by Sir Henry

Wilson. For the Army, on the threshold of its greatest ordeal, this last change was a most serious and dangerous matter.

* * * *

The British Army in France was now at one of its lowest ebbs of the War. The prophecy made by the General Staff in November, 1916, and repeated with such emphasis to the War Cabinet in February, 1917,[1] was fulfilled; the Government's inability to solve the man-power problem had produced its predictable result – a weakening of the Army in the field which was rendered all the more serious by the accession of German strength from Russia, and the threat of a great new offensive in the West. The full effect of this weakening was seen at the end of January, 1918: at that date, 5 divisions were still in Italy, under General Plumer, reducing the B.E.F. to 47 British divisions, 10 Dominion divisions, and 2 Portuguese; this diminished Army had taken over more than 28 miles of front from the French, as agreed at Boulogne on September 25th, 1917; the infantry alone were 100,000 men below strength;[2] a radical reorganization of the Army's structure, designed not so much to overcome the man-power shortage as to disguise it, was in progress. In addition, the Cabinet had bluntly informed the War Office that it saw no prospect of raising anything like the numbers estimated to be needed for the 1918 campaign. As early as November, 1917, Haig had predicted a shortage of 250,000 infantry by the end of March, and 460,000 by the end of October; the Army Council now added that this figure might be expected to rise to 530,000 men by the end of the year. Charteris gloomily summed up the situation on January 26th: 'So . . . we are confronted with:

1. A longer front to hold.
2. Reduced establishment to hold it.
3. No hope of reinforcements.
4. A German attack in greater strength than anything we have yet experienced.

Not a cheerful prospect.'

Controversy, of one kind or another, has surrounded every aspect of the deterioration of the British Army's condition in early 1918. The detachment to Italy has been attacked and defended; on the one hand, the need to give psychological support to the Italians was urged, with suggestions of the advantages that might have accrued from helping their earlier offensives; on the other hand, the almost complete idleness of the British and French contingents in Italy, and the large preponderance of Allied strength in that theatre to no purpose, were held to reveal the falseness of its promise. The extension of the

1. See p. 321.
2. Smuts's memo to War Cabinet, January, 1918.

British front reawakened all the disputes which had surrounded this topic from the very beginning of the War. On the French side, simple comparisons of the lengths of front held by each Allied Army were constantly being adduced as proofs of inequality of effort; at the end of 1917 the French were holding 350 miles with 108 divisions (972 battalions) while the British were 'holding' less than 100 miles with 62 divisions (744 battalions). On the British side, it was pointed out that the British were not, in fact, 'holding' at all, but attacking continuously from the beginning of April, 1917, until the end of November; that almost half the German divisions in France were massed on their front, despite its shortness; and that, while considerable stretches of the French front could remain passive (less than one-seventh of the French Army occupied the 150 miles from St. Mihiel to the Swiss frontier), any rupture of the British line was always liable to have the most damaging results. By the middle of February, 1918, the picture had changed and was rapidly clarifying; the extended British front (126 miles) was held by 59 divisions, facing 81 German divisions, while 99 French and one American division faced 71 German divisions along 324 miles of front. A further 25 German divisions in central reserve brought their total to 177; its steady increase during the following weeks brought no alteration in these proportions, nothing to ease Haig's anxieties.

But neither the question of the Italian detachment nor that of the extension of the front aroused the bitterness of feeling, the irate charges and countercharges, nor the ill results of the controversy over the actual strength of the British Army – a matter which, one might suppose, would be the easiest to settle. The reason for this is, without doubt, the attitude taken up by Lloyd George. Having come to the decision not to reinforce the Army in France, in case it might be launched into another of those offensives which he so much hated, and having seen this decision place the Army in the gravest peril of the whole War, Lloyd George, both at the time, in 1918, and later, when he wrote his *War Memoirs*, bent his unusual dialectical skill to the work of obscuring the facts.

In April of that year Lloyd George told the House of Commons: 'Notwithstanding the heavy casualties in 1917 the Army in France was considerably stronger on the 1st January 1918, than on the 1st January, 1917.' This statement was challenged in the Press by General Sir Frederick Maurice; a Parliamentary debate took place with considerable prospect of the Government being overthrown. But Lloyd George, enjoying one of his most spectacular triumphs, turned the tables upon the Opposition by the revelation that the statement had been based on figures supplied by General Maurice's own department of the War Office. The attack on the Government fizzled out; General Maurice's career in the Army was at an end. It was not until

Lord Beaverbrook's book, *Men and Power*, appeared in 1954, that we learned that corrected figures had been supplied by Maurice, and were in Lloyd George's possession at the time of the debate. It is certain that the true facts were not as told to the House of Commons. We also know that, at that period, verbal victories over British generals were agreeable to the Prime Minister, perhaps in default of the victories over the Germans which his policy had made so difficult. General Maurice was one of the unluckiest of his victims. Haig's first comment on the affair was characteristic; Maurice's action, he noted, was 'a grave mistake. No one can be both a soldier and a politician at the same time. We soldiers have to do our duty and keep silent, trusting to Ministers to protect us.' A few days later, when he heard how the debate had gone, he was less censorious: 'Poor Maurice!' he wrote to Lady Haig. 'How terrible to see the House of Commons so easily taken in by a clap-trap speech by Lloyd George.' As Haig well knew, the situation which Maurice had tried to bring to light had very nearly made him, too, a victim.

At the core of the dispute between Lloyd George and Maurice (or, more significantly, between the Government and the General Staff) lay one of those misunderstandings which, in a more wholesome context, might be dismissed as laughable, but here indicate only the bitter rejection of the opposing point of view – even when supported by statistics – which was such a marked characteristic of relations between the 'brasshats' and the 'frocks' in the last years of the War. The truth is not difficult to grasp. The *total numbers* of the Army in France had, indeed, increased between January, 1917 and January, 1918; counting heads – or mouths to feed – the difference was:

January 8th, 1917	1,646,600
January 5th, 1918	1,949,100

It was this comparison which gave the Prime Minister his cheap victory over the British Generals. What was contained in General Maurice's second paper, the information which alone could give these bare totals meaning, is the fact that this increase was entirely due to the long-overdue expansion of the non-fighting element of the B.E.F., in particular the Labour units whose absence had so hampered the Army in earlier years, and which were still inadequate for the work they had to do. However, by bringing in Italian Labour companies, Chinese coolies, and Natives from South Africa, as well as by using German prisoners of war wherever this was permissible, an increase of 399,450 had been effected in the 'Lines of Communication' strength; unfortunately, this was accompanied by a simultaneous fall of 78,500 in the strength of the fighting troops, and this was entirely due to recruiting failures in the United Kingdom. Meanwhile, in subsidiary theatres of war, Britain was maintaining 35,695 officers and 852,620 men (including Indians and other coloured contingents), while at home there were 74,403 officers and 1,486,459 other ranks, of whom 607,403 (excluding Dominion forces) were available for general service. As an observer remarked, there were 'a lot of troops in Norfolk'.

The only remedy for this most serious situation which the War Cabinet could suggest was a major reorganization of the Army itself. Both France and Germany had, as the War continued, changed their divisional establishments to conform with the special nature of the conflict; it was, above all, an artillery war, requiring an unusual proportion of guns to infantry. The French and Germans both possessed more guns than Britain was able to maintain in the field, and were accordingly able to increase the number of their divisions by reducing the infantry component in each. There was much to be said for the 'handier', more compact formation which resulted. The British War Office considered a similar reorganization in November, 1917; Haig, however, was against it. In a letter to the War Office, dated November 24th, he wrote: 'I am strongly opposed to any drastic alteration or reduction in the composition or organization of a division, as it would undoubtedly create considerable dislocation throughout the army both tactically and administratively. Moreover, any reduction in the present establishment would be extravagant in so far as staffs are concerned, and the question of finding commanders and staffs is becoming increasingly difficult. I am convinced that the retention of our existing organization combined with the maintenance of units up to establishment will prove the truest form of economy in regard to man-power.' Two considerations need to be held in mind to understand Haig's position: first, the French and German reorganization was carried out to procure an *increase* in the numbers of their divisions, while the British intention was formulated against the background of a *decrease* in actual fighting strength; secondly, France and Germany had possessed mass armies from the beginning, so that this reorganization involved only one change for them, while for Britain, whose mass army had had to be created out of nothing by a prodigious feat of organization, this innovation meant a double burden.

Nevertheless, despite Haig's opposition, on the recommendation of a Cabinet sub-committee which did not contain a single soldier, reorganization was ordered in January. Each brigade was to be reduced from four battalions to three, and the division accordingly from twelve battalions to nine, while its Pioneer battalion was reduced from four to three companies. Ignoring the small matter of the Artillery, Machine Gunners, Engineers, Signals, Transport and other supporting units which would have to be provided, the Cabinet Committee suggested that a surplus of battalions would remain, after gaps in the ranks had been filled, from which new divisions could be built. This, of course, was rubbish; the surplus was minute, and was swallowed up immediately the battle began, as reinforcements. Meanwhile 141 battalions were disbanded in the B.E.F.; the only discretion left to the Commander-in-Chief in the matter was that he was offered a list of 145 out of which to make a choice.

Since the British, even in their more radical moments, are apt to be a conservative race, and as the Army is distinctly a conservative institution, it was decreed that no 'Regular' or 'First-line Territorial' battalion should be disbanded. The change was thus not simply a matter of each division losing three battalions; the proportions varied; some lost as many as six, and gained three from elsewhere. The amount of movement involved was considerable. In the event, the reorganization was not completed until late February in the First, Third and Fifth Armies, while the Fourth Army, the largest, did not finish it until March 4th – just seventeen days before the Germans attacked. It will be realized that for the still essentially amateur British commanders and staffs there was very little time to learn the appropriate tactics of the new formations. Defences designed for wholly different groupings had to be re-fashioned (if possible). It all added up to one more complication, one more difficulty. Yet another, but a more fortunate one as it turned out, was that the Dominion contingents declined to harass themselves in this way, so that ten divisions in the Army retained their old composition. It meant that they could not be interchanged with British divisions as before, but it also meant that Haig did have ten strong units left in his otherwise depleted and threatened force. As we shall see, he made good use of them.

* * * *

'The Army had come victoriously through 1917; but it had become apparent that the holding of the Western Front purely by a defensive could no longer be counted on. . . . The enormous material resources of the enemy had given his attack a considerable preponderance over our defence, and this condition would have become more apparent as our best men became casualties, our infantry approximated more nearly in character to a militia, and discipline declined. . . . Against the weight of the enemy's material the troops no longer displayed their old stubbornness; they thought with horror of fresh defensive battles and longed for a war of movement. . . . The interests of the Army were best served by the offensive; in defence it was bound gradually to succumb to the ever increasing hostile superiority in men and material. This feeling was shared by everybody. In the West the Army *pined for the offensive*,[1] and after Russia's collapse expected it with the most intense relief.' Thus Ludendorff; this remarkable passage provides us not only with the motivation of the German General Staff in 1918, but also with a valuable footnote to the

1. Author's italics.

story of the British effort in 1917. It also shows how events fulfilled Haig's dictum of March, 1917, that 'The Germans are whole-hearted believers in the principle that an offensive on the greatest possible scale, driven home with the utmost rapidity, violence and determination, is the only method of forcing a quick decision.'[1]

The débâcle at Cambrai was the writing on the wall for the British Army. Haig's reaction to any threat of attack was to meet it by an attack of his own; what he desired to do in 1918 was to continue his offensive in Flanders, both to reap the rewards of which he had been cheated by the dreadful weather of the previous year, and to deny the enemy the initiative which the collapse of Russia had restored to them in the West. After Cambrai it was evident that such action was out of the question. On December 6th the much-maligned British Intelligence (still under Charteris) summed up Germany's prospects:

'In the early spring (not later than the beginning of March) she should seek to deliver such a blow on the Western Front as would force a decisive battle which she could fight to a finish before the American forces could take an active part, i.e., before mid-summer.

'For such a battle it is essential that Germany should choose a battlefield where the Allies are defending some objective of vital importance to them. By this means alone can Germany ensure that the Allies do not escape the blow by short retreats and delaying actions. Numerous objectives of this nature are offered on the Western Front, e.g., VERDUN, NANCY, CHALONS, REIMS, AMIENS, BETHUNE, HAZEBROUCK and DUNKIRK.'

It is worth noting that in this paper, its first serious study of German offensive potential, the British Intelligence at G.H.Q. had correctly named the month in which the Germans would attack, and all three of the localities where they would do so. On the eve of the attack itself neither G.Q.G. nor the Military Representatives of the Supreme War Council at Versailles were able to do as much. But the conclusions to be drawn from the Intelligence summary were inescapable.

It was seven months since Haig had held a meeting of all his Army Commanders, seven months during which such routines had been in suspense while the Army maintained its series of great attacks beginning with Messines. On the day after receiving Charteris's statement, Haig resumed the routine, but the future operations which he now had to discuss were of a very different kind: 'The general situation on the Russian and Italian fronts combined with the paucity of reinforcements which we are likely to receive, will in all probability necessitate the adopting of a defensive attitude for the next

1. See p. 279.

few months. We must be prepared to meet a strong and sustained hostile offensive. It is therefore of the first importance that Army Commanders should give their immediate and personal attention to the organization of their Army zones for defensive purposes, and to the training of their troops in defensive tactics. . . .'

He went on at once to discuss the requirement of these tactics: 'Depth in defensive organization is of the first importance. . . . The economy of troops in the front line system is most important in order that as many men as possible may be available in reserve. The front line should generally be held as an outpost line covering the main line of resistance a few hundred yards in rear. . . .' He added a note of warning on what he saw would be a persistent difficulty: 'As regards the actual construction of defences, it is recognized that the limiting factor will always be the labour available; it is therefore of the utmost importance that this labour should be used as economically as possible and to the best advantage. . . .'

This much already clear, on the following day his Intelligence Branch supplied him with an extremely accurate forecast of the German accession of strength available for 1918 (890,000 men), and four days after that, on receipt of the information from the French that large German concentrations had been detected in the Mézières area, he reached the right answer to the problem of where the main German blow would fall: '*I pointed out that a concentration in the area* he [French Liaison Officer] mentioned *threatened Amiens and might foreshadow an advance* in force *S.W. of St. Quentin* much more than an attack on Chalons. I suggested that he should find out the state of the defences of Amiens.' The extension of the British front brought Amiens into the area of responsibility of the British Army; Haig then found out to his cost what the state of the defences of Amiens was. Meanwhile, long before anyone else, he and his Staff correctly judged the time and place of the German offensive; there remained the delicate matter of meeting it.

At this stage, once again, Haig's inability to communicate, especially with politicians, proved to be a serious disadvantage, aggravated by Lloyd George's mood of wilful misunderstanding in his pursuit of dialectical victories. The War Cabinet assembled on January 7th, with Haig present: 'All were most friendly to me. . . . As regards the enemy's action, I stated that I thought that the coming four months would be *the critical period* of the war. Also that it seemed to me possible that the enemy would attack both the French and ourselves, and that he would hold Reserves in hand ready to exploit wherever he might have gained a success. . . . In my opinion, the best defence would be to continue our offensive in Flanders, because we would then retain the initiative and attract the German Reserves against us. It is doubtful whether the French Army can now withstand for long, a resolute and continued offensive on the

part of the enemy.' Nothing could have been more unfortunate than this
harking back to the idea of renewing the Flanders attack. The whole notion
was such anathema to Lloyd George that it obliterated in his mind the accurate
predictions of the coming year's events with which Haig had preceded it.

A new train of thought started in the Prime Minister's agile brain, which
he followed up when they met again at lunch two days later. 'We had a very
cheery party', wrote Haig. 'Conversation turned on the length of the war and
some betting took place. Derby bet the P.M. 100 cigars to 100 cigarettes that
war would be over by next New Year. L.G. disagreed. I said I thought the
war would be over because of the *internal* state of Germany. Reports indicate
that she could not continue after the coming autum . . . I also emphasized the
critical nature of the coming four months on the Western Front if Germany
did not make peace. Germany having only one million men as Reserves for
this year's fighting, I doubted whether they would risk them in an attempt to
"break through". If the Germans did attack it would be a gambler's throw.
All seemed to depend on the struggle now going on in Germany between the
Military and Civil parties. If the Military party won, they would certainly
attack and try and deliver a knock-out blow against the Western Front. We
must be prepared for this. The Prime Minister by cunning argument tried to
get me to commit myself to an opinion that there would be "no German
offensive", that the "German Army was done", but I refused to agree with
his suggestions.'

Unfortunately, this refusal was not fully conveyed. Inarticulate people
frequently do not realize how far-reaching their communication failure is, a
fact which makes it even more dangerous. Over a fortnight later, Charteris
noted: 'L.G. tried to get D.H. to commit himself to the opinion that the
German Army was down and out, and that therefore there would be no
German offensive, in spite of the fact that all the Intelligence reports show
conclusively that the Germans are staging an attack. D.H. refused to commit
himself, but the Cabinet seem to have made up their minds that there will be
no attack. . . . Bonar Law tackled D.H. on the same point later. . . . The whole
inner meaning of this is the *man-power* problem. We are far below establishment. The Government either cannot or will not bring us up to strength, and
is trying to unload its responsibility on to G.H.Q.' This analysis would seem
to be correct. Some sympathy may be spared for Lloyd George and other
Ministers, as they listened to Haig trying to give expression to the somewhat
complicated reasoning at the root of his belief that an attack was not necessarily
Germany's best move, but that she was likely to carry one out all the same.

We have seen from what Ludendorff said that though Haig's view of the
condition of Germany seemed to be in contradiction of his view of German
policy, it was nevertheless not far wrong. At the bottom of it all was the

thought expressed clearly enough by G.H.Q. Intelligence: 'If Germany attacks and fails she will be ruined'.[1] Ludendorff might believe that he would not fail; Haig's trust in his Army inspired him with certainty that the enemy would nevertheless be defeated – and thus ruined. Lloyd George's stubborn refusal to see sense in the submission either of Haig himself or of the General Staff remains unforgiveable. It will not do to excuse it as an attempt to save lives by withholding men from generals who would only have wasted them in attacks. The truth is that it was part of the subterfuge by which he tried to conceal his greatest failure – the mobilization of the nation. Summarizing Lloyd George's contribution to the deliberations of the Supreme War Council in February, Repington wrote: 'L.G. went on to threaten a Social Revolution if the country were asked for more men, and made the most of the argument.' Making every allowance, the unavoidable conclusion is that Lloyd George did not really trust the British people. The victims of this distrust were, in the end, not so much the generals whom he loathed, as the soldiers with whom he professed to sympathize.

For the soldiers and the generals of the British Army alike, the problem of the hour now assumed a dreadful simplicity: it was a question of filling a quart measure with a pint of fluid. At every stage, in every context, the sheer shortage of men asserted itself as a ruling factor. It amounted to this: linear defence had now been exposed as ineffective against modern offensive methods; defence in depth was therefore a necessity; but defence in depth depends upon the ability to launch counter-attacks, which in turn depends upon the existence of substantial reserves. For his whole front Haig had only eight divisions in G.H.Q. Reserve, and ten more, unevenly distributed, in reserve under Armies and Corps. Thus the Fifth Army, with over forty miles of front to hold, had only one of its divisions out of the line when it was attacked, and this a division which had been withdrawn for recuperation from heavy Gas casualties, rather than for active operations; its neighbour, the Third Army, by contrast, was able to retain four divisions behind twenty-eight miles of front. The only alternative to powerful counter-attacks was an elaborate defensive system, with all manner of obstacles, fieldworks and en-trenchments spread over a wide area. The creation of such a system depended on the availability of Labour. Despite the huge growth of the Labour forces in the B.E.F., this did not exist. Once again we must remark the misleading nature of statistical totals, unless they are broken down carefully; thus, at the New Year, there were 302,904 men on the 'ration strength' of the Labour force, 134,610 white, 98,574 coloured, and 69,720 prisoners of war. But of these, through sickness, leave and rest requirements, only 209,118 were at

1. G.H.Q. Intelligence Branch, January 7th, 1918.

work - a third of the total out of the reckoning at once. Of the remainder, 91,097 were on the main Lines of Communication. (It must be remembered that prisoners could not be used in the fighting zone, and the advisability of using coloured contingents in it was very questionable.) This further reduction left 118,021 in the Army areas; only 1,714 of these were actually at work on defences at the turn of the year; by the time of the German attack, this figure had swelled to some 27,000 – still very low. What were the others doing?

The answer is simple: out of the total with the Armies (i.e., where the battle would be fought), over 32,000 were working on roads, nearly 15,000 on railways, over 20,000 in workshops and stores, 26,000 on hutting and camps, while the rest were distributed among such other activities as quarrying, ammunition dumps, salvage, hospitals, burials, sanitation, laundries, agriculture, port construction and working, depots and other duties. In that static, extraordinary war, the Army had acquired, besides its combatant function, many of the attributes of a vast and complex social organism. The services provided by all these people were of great value, in many cases essential (communications, for example, particularly across the devastated area of the old Somme battlefield behind the Fifth Army front); the question remains whether, in what was recognized as an outstanding emergency, more of them could not have been temporarily switched to defence work. In their absence, once again, the fighting troops had to do much for themselves, at the expense of rest and training – the latter more necessary than ever in view of their unfamiliarity with defensive tactics and their own new organization.

Haig's approach to his problem was shaped by three considerations: first, the mounting evidence of his Intelligence Branch, plus his own reasoning, convinced him that the main German blow would fall on the British front; secondly, he recognized that his front would be broken (on February 15th he reminded Gough 'that whenever we had attacked we had always been able to break the enemy's front, and to advance well into the German system of defence. We must expect the Germans to do the same if they attacked in force. So his "Reserve Lines" must have his attention'); thirdly, the battle would, in the last resort, only be won by counter-attack, and this could only take place if the French closely co-operated by providing reserves. (By the same token, if the blow *should* fall on his Allies, Haig would support them in the same way.) He and Pétain were fully agreed on this; the cordiality between them at this stage was very marked, better, in fact than Haig's relations even with Joffre had been. On December 17th, after a visit to Pétain, Haig 'was much struck with the different bearing and attitude of the present Officers at G.Q.G. The present ones seem much more simple, more natural and practical than their predecessors, and are more frank in their dealings with the British. In fact, the relations between G.Q.G. and G.H.Q. are better than I have known them.' A few weeks later, when Wilson warned Haig that he suspected Pétain of 'not playing straight', Haig commented 'I can't believe this', and attributed Wilson's attitude to his disagreements with Pétain in the previous year. But, as we shall see, Wilson was right and Haig was wrong.

Endless disputation has surrounded Haig's dispositions for meeting the German onslaught. The bitterest accusations have been levelled by Lloyd George, as one might expect, in view of his responsibility for the chronic weakness of the Army in face of the enemy. Haig's strategy was guided by two main considerations: one was this numerical weakness, the other geography. The British Official History has made the geographical point perfectly clear:

'North of the Scarpe, where the front line lay only just over 50 miles from the Channel coast, there was no room for any "elastic defence", nor for a series of delaying actions; time could be gained only by hard fighting and stubborn resistance. South of the Scarpe there was some space for manoeuvre; *provided the French stood fast*[1] and the important railway centre at Amiens remained securely guarded, the Fifth Army and the right of the Third Army might be permitted to give ground, if this became necessary, without un-covering any vital point. It was obvious too that in the southern area, *French assistance might reasonably be expected to be forthcoming without delay, and in any case French reinforcements could be brought to the British right wing near the Oise in far less time than would have been required to transport them to the left wing in Flanders,*[2] right across an existing system of communications. All therefore pointed to keeping the centre and left strong at the expense of the Fifth Army front recently taken over.'

It was in accordance with this analysis that Haig distributed his forces; from left to right, on the eve of attack, they were spread out as follows:

	Divisions	Miles of Front
Second Army	14	23
First Army	16	33
Third Army	16	28
Fifth Army	14	42

To redress the imbalance in some small degree, Haig sent to the Fifth Army area the whole of his Cavalry, three divisions, representing a rifle strength equal to that of one division of infantry, but of course much more mobile and potentially useful in the moving battle which he anticipated in this sector. It

1. Author's italics.
2. Author's italics.

must be remembered that he had *no intention* of holding this ground; his eyes were fixed elsewhere. On February 23rd he visited the First Army and went up the Vimy Ridge; he noted: 'I look upon this part of our front as the backbone and centre of our defensive system and [it] must be held firmly at all costs.'

It was a sombre reflection that 'At this very spot on 9th April last, we advanced 5 miles on the first day! We must give the enemy credit for being able, if he does attack, of doing the same'. No matter how ungrammatically expressed, this was Haig's ruling thought; the Germans *would* break through; the northern sector was where this could not be permitted. Only the arrival of the French could swing the main course of the battle; until then even his G.H.Q. Reserve could be no more than a local palliative which, until the enemy revealed his hand exactly, Haig divided equally between his four Armies, two divisions behind each front.

Denigrators of the Duke of Wellington have tried to make a case out against him on the grounds that he was only enabled to win the Battle of Waterloo by the timely arrival of Blücher. This ignores the fact that the Duke only fought the Battle of Waterloo on the understanding that Blücher would take part in it. Similarly, Haig's conduct in 1918 has been criticized because he was forced to lean so heavily on French support to repel the German attack. The truth is that his dispositions were made (like Wellington's) on the assumption that support would be forthcoming. The real question is whether that assumption was justified – and, of course, hindsight enables us to answer that question with an instant negative. But it is important to understand what the real reason for this mistake was: as in 1917, there was a wide gap between Pétain's words and his deeds. It must be remembered that the reason advanced by Pétain for his urgent demands that the British should extend their front at the end of 1917 had been the need to form a Reserve of not less than 40 divisions; this he had done, so that his Army now had 62 divisions in line, and 40 behind them. Haig's had 45 in line and 13 behind them.[1] It was this disproportion which dictated his dependence on the French *under any circumstances*. The circumstances which Haig preferred were those of a 'gentleman's agreement' between the two Commanders-in-Chief, without whose co-operation all action would be blighted anyway; there were, nevertheless, alternatives to this, and since, in the end, it was one of the alternatives that prevailed, we need to examine them.

The Supreme War Council, created in November, 1917, had directed its Military Representatives to make a study of the general situation, and present concrete recommendations. After two months of cogitation, they presented

1. The French figure omits Corps Reserves; five divisions have to be deducted from British Reserves accordingly, for comparison. See p. 398.

their conclusions at the end of January. We need not concern ourselves with more than two of their propositions: the first, an overall scheme for 1918, is important because it provides us with a background against which to view the second. The Military Representatives concluded that no decision was likely in the West in 1918, nor was one to be envisaged in the Balkans; their recommendation for the year was a knock-out blow against Turkey. The comment of the British Official History is that 'Their Note . . . showed no real grasp of the situation'. Nevertheless, the second proposal which interests us, contained in Note 14, had in it more than a germ of sense: it recommended the formation of a General Allied Reserve for the Western and Italian Fronts. This proposition was discussed, and a resolution drafted by Lloyd George was passed agreeing to the creation of such a Reserve. An Executive Committee of the Supreme War Council would decide the strength, composition and location of this Reserve; this Committee would also decide its transportation and concentration arrangements; it would determine when and where the Reserve should be used; it would then hand over to the relevant Commander-in-Chief the appropriate number of troops. The Committee had the right to visit any theatre of war. It was to consist of the permanent Military Representatives of Britain, America and Italy, with General Foch for France; Foch was to be President. As may be imagined, when the news of this arrangement was announced, reactions were varied and sharp. Repington called it a form of lunacy, adding: 'This is the gammon that is going on before the great German offensive.'

It was more than 'gammon'. The decision to form a General Allied Reserve under the Supreme War Council afforded to Lloyd George his last opportunity to rid himself of the British military leaders whom he so greatly disliked; he was not slow to take it. Both Haig and Robertson attended the meeting of the Supreme War Council; both reacted against it, in different ways, and in different degrees. Haig diagnosed the significance of the resolution immediately: 'To some extent it makes Foch a "Generalissimo".' This was correct, for a moment's reflection shows that whoever controlled the Reserves controlled the Armies. But Haig's qualification – 'to some extent' – is also significant; it was not simply Foch, but his Committee which was to assume the authority of a Supreme Commander. The specific right was reserved to each member of the Committee, 'in case of irreconcilable differences of opinion on a point of importance', 'of appeal to the Supreme War Council' itself. It was not, then, a straightforward military command in the accepted sense that General Foch was to wield. Robertson's comment is that he 'would have preferred any system of command to that of the Executive Committee, for nothing could have been less suitable as an organ of command'. His anger was visible to those present, and when the meeting was over he 'remained

sitting alone in his place, motionless, his head resting in his hand, glaring silent-
ly in front of him'. It had been a bad session for him; the previous day he had
openly dissociated himself from the Supreme Council's strategy, to the fury of
Lloyd George, who had given it the backing of the British Government. Now
there was this; Robertson, in his turn, was also reaching the end of his tether.

Haig was less perturbed. On the one hand, he saw distinct long-term
advantages in greater unity between the Western and Italian fronts, if that
could be achieved. On the other hand, as he wrote to Lady Haig on February
5th: '. . . although it was decided to form an Inter-Allied Reserve, before the
Committee can handle it they must form it. Now I cannot part with any of
my troops – so if they want a Reserve it must be found from French and
British troops in Italy – the five divisions I sent there are really the Reserves
of the British forces in France – or bring troops from Salonika or elsewhere.'

In other words, if the resolution resulted in a strengthening of the Western
Front, he was not disposed to fret too much about details at this stage; they
would, in any case, sort themselves out quickly enough in a crisis. But one
difficulty he did see, and drew the Supreme War Council's attention to it at
the meeting when the resolution was passed: '. . . I asked the following
question, "by what channel am I to receive orders from this new body?" This
was rather a poser, because this resolution to appoint an International Committee involves a change in Constitutional procedure. Finally, L.G. said
"Orders would be issued by the members of the body nominated by the
Supreme Council." I asked that the exact position might be made clear to me
in writing.' No doubt Haig was remembering the Nivelle affair. His objection
to the status of the new committee was repeated with emphasis by the Army
Council, as soon as it learned what had been decided. That body told the
Government: 'Constitutionally the Army Council are responsible for the
safety and welfare of the British Army. The powers conferred on the
Executive Committee, however, will enable it to disregard the Army Council,
in that it is allowed to interpose directly between the Council and Commander-in-Chief.' The existence of the Committee, added the Army Council,
would 'place Commanders-in-Chief in an impossible position'.

Two quite separate issues had, in fact, been exposed; as the dispute developed, Robertson was to become the chief protagonist in one conflict, Haig
in the other. Robertson's quarrel was on a matter of principle: the admissibility
or otherwise of delegating to such a body as the Executive Committee at
Versailles either the responsibility for the British Army's safety, or the decisive
voice in strategy implied in the terms of Lloyd George's resolution. Haig's
opposition took the form of a simple refusal on grounds of safety to spare any
troops for the proposed General Reserve, an attitude which was endorsed by

Pétain. Perhaps because this practical issue – the sheer shortage of men in his Army – seemed to him to be vastly more important than theoretical questions; partly, too, because he felt that Robertson himself was to a certain extent responsible for the shortage; but certainly also because of the steady decline of his confidence in Robertson ever since the Boulogne conference in September, 1917, Haig gave no support to the latter in the final struggle which broke out between him and the Prime Minister as soon as they returned to London.

Lloyd George was now determined to be rid of Robertson; the problem was, how to obtain this end without a political storm. If his *War Memoirs* are to be believed, his imagination was at this stage fevered with visions of a military cabal, waiting to take over the country and rule it by Prussian methods. This made him more careful than he might otherwise have been. Robertson was offered a choice between remaining as C.I.G.S. with powers reduced to what they were before he went to the War Office – before, in fact, he made his 'bargain' with Kitchener – or exchanging places with Henry Wilson at Versailles, and becoming a Deputy C.I.G.S. and Member of the Army Council. Since it was evident that he would scarcely consider the first alternative, the question was whether he would accept the second. Much pressure was put upon him to do so. Haig who had been sent for from France, to test his reactions to what was proposed, was among those who urged acceptance on Robertson – '. . . this was no time for anyone to question where his services were to be given. It was his *duty* to go to Versailles or anywhere else if the Government wished it'.

This conversation took place on February 11th; on the same day Haig saw the King and 'urged H.M. to insist on R. going to Versailles'. Haig was doing Robertson an injustice; his private belief was that 'in the back of [Robertson's] mind he resents Henry Wilson replacing him in London, and means to embarrass the Government to the utmost of his power'. Such a course would be bound to earn Haig's disapproval; but it is indicative of how far apart the two men were that Haig should suppose that Robertson entertained such an idea. Four days later, at Lloyd George's instigation, Mr. Balfour interviewed the intransigent Wully, who, he reported, 'observed, repeatedly and with great insistence, that the fact of his having been offered whichever of the two posts he preferred had, in his view, nothing to do with the question. If his objection had merely been that the powers now given to the Council at Versailles, and therefore to the British Member of it, overshadowed the position of the C.I.G.S., it might have conceivably been worth while to transfer his activities from London to Versailles. But this was not his point of view at all. He objected to the new system, and he equally objected to it whether he was expected to take a share in working it as C.I.G.S. or to take a share in working it as Military Member of the Supreme War Council. *An objectionable object in the middle of the table (to use his own metaphor) was equally objectionable from whichever end of the table you looked at it.*'[1] No argument that Balfour could adduce made the slightest impression on Robertson; it was a wrong system, and he would have no part of it. At the end of the interview he told Balfour that he 'was very anxious that the scheme should be so modified that the Military Member at Versailles should be the subordinate and representative of the C.I.G.S. *In that case he would be quite ready either to retain the position of Chief of the Staff or go to Versailles.*'[2]

Once again Haig's views were sought. On February 15th he learned that Robertson had definitely decided to resign, and that the Government wished to consult him again. The following day he met all his Army Commanders: General Cox informed the meeting '*that we must be prepared to meet a very severe attack at any moment now*'.[3] A discussion of tactics followed, ending on an optimistic note: 'All felt confident on being able to hold their front.' But it was with sombre preoccupations that Haig now travelled to London, where he immediately heard from Derby that Robertson was out, and that Henry Wilson was to be C.I.G.S. in his place. He commented privately: 'How petty all this squabbling in high places is compared with the great problem of beating Germany, and the present anxiety of Commanders in France.'

Two busy days followed. Haig's first visitor was Robertson, saying 'he goes on half-pay tomorrow'. Haig assured him that 'I had never approved of the proposals now put forward by the Foch Committee for creating and commanding the General Reserve, nor, indeed, of the Versailles Military Organization itself'. We do not know whether Robertson was comforted by this statement or not. Nevertheless, it was the truth, which Haig lost no time in repeating to Lloyd George later that morning: 'I made it quite clear to the P.M. that I had never approved of any of the arrangements now under discussion. When asked, I had stated my reasons for disagreeing, but once the Cabinet had given its decision, I had loyally done my best to make the system run. I had only one object in view, viz., to beat the Germans. L.G. said that was so and warmly thanked me.'

Lloyd George took this opportunity of raising another matter, telling Haig of the peace feelers which were being put out by Austria, and of the suggestion that he should meet an Austrian plenipotentiary in Geneva. 'He asked me what I thought of the suggestion. I said he ought certainly to meet him and to leave no stone unturned in order to arrive at a settlement with Austria and detach her from Germany.' Two more interviews followed:

1. Author's italics.
2. Author's italics.
3. Haig's italics.

the first was with Henry Wilson, eager to settle the question of who should succeed him at Versailles: 'After talking over the matter I decided that Henry Rawlinson would be the best man': this was agreed. Finally, there was Derby: 'He looked tired and harassed. He did not know whether to resign or stay on as S. of S. for War. I told him that in the interests of the Army there should be no change, and that he should remain on. He said he would accept my advice.'

The next day was just as active. Haig's first assignment was with Bonar Law, who wanted to know how to answer certain questions which were likely to be asked in the House. 'He spoke very freely and I told him that difficulties might arise between me and Versailles if I were ordered to earmark certain Divisions as "General Reserve". This could not be done without upsetting plans for the defence of my front, and I would rather be relieved of my command than do it. Mr. Law said that the P.M. has asked him to read a statement of the position of affairs. . . . The document stated that I "thought it a workable scheme". I said that was not my opinion because I thought it a bad scheme and unsound since it set up *two* authorities who would give me orders, i.e. dual control. "He must not say that I thought the scheme workable but that I will do my best to work under it." He said that he quite saw my point and would make that clear if asked.' After Bonar Law there was Derby again, still worried about whether to resign or not, but Haig was satisfied to record that his urge to do so seemed to be diminished. A chance encounter with Lord French passed off amicably: 'I asked him to come to France when things are quieter.' The last meeting of the day was with Rawlinson, just over from France. Haig told him of his new appointment: 'He accepted it and assured me that he was only anxious to serve where I thought he could be of most use. He was also prepared to decline the appointment if I thought that it was in the interest of the Service that he should do so.' That thought was not in Haig's mind.

The next day, February 19th, Haig returned to France. Looking back over the crowded incidents of the past forty-eight hours, he recorded: 'I think I can fairly claim, as the result of my visit to London, that a generally saner view is now taken of the so-called military crisis, and the risk of a quarrel between "civilian and soldier" (which last Saturday seemed imminent) has been avoided.' To a large extent that was true; an open breach had certainly been averted, and with it the strong likelihood of a most damaging political crisis. Nevertheless, bitter feelings had been stirred, suspicions had been aroused, and a contentious element nourished which long outlasted the War itself; Haig's own reputation suffered severely from this; it is thus particularly interesting to see what his motives were. The detachment, the absence of anger or indignation with which he records this experience, is so striking as to be almost unnatural; but its purpose was plain – to damp down the fires, to keep the peace at home and concentrate warlike endeavour against the enemy in the field.

This, indeed, was a laudable objective, but, like so many in the War, not achieved without its casualty rate. In *The Times* on the 20th, Haig read Lloyd George's speech setting out the reasons for Robertson's departure: 'The Prime Minister of course makes out an excellent case for himself, which the bulk of the House (not understanding military matters) thoroughly endorses. Indeed, Sir William comes out of the controversy as a "mulish, irreconcilable individual". This must, I think, always be the result of controversies between statesmen and soldiers in which the issue is not simple, and when the former tell the story. Sir William would have done better to have resigned when the Government rejected his advice regarding the Western Front, and decided on sending an expedition to Syria to fight the Turks. Opposition statesmen shed crocodile tears over Robertson's departure, but human nature being what it is, the latter is well-nigh forgotten already.'

So Robertson departs from the centre of the stage. This was a change which worked out less to Haig's disadvantage than he had the right to expect, yet his reactions to it were throughout lukewarm. Charteris for one commented on the small support which Haig gave to one who had, whatever his faults, been Haig's most loyal ally: 'I think he should have backed up Robertson: it might have helped, and could not have made matters worse.' It is hard not to conclude that, besides his desire to lower the political temperature, Haig had decided that Robertson was, in any case, a weak vessel. On February 5th he wrote to Lady Haig: 'I, like you, am sorry for Robertson, but then it seems to me (and I can write it to you privately) that he had not resolutely adhered to the policy of "concentration on the Western Front". – He has *said* that this is his policy but has allowed all kinds of resources to be diverted to distant theatres at the bidding of his political masters. So I think he ought to have made a firmer stand before.' The evident pique with which this old complaint is uttered shows how far relations between the two men had declined. Haig was being unfair to Robertson – and to himself. The fact is that he fully agreed with Robertson's case; he knew what was at stake; he had little time for Wilson; he feared Lloyd George's intentions deeply. (He went so far, on February 11th, as to tell the King that 'Lloyd George had a strong desire, in my opinion, to disintegrate the army'.) Yet he gave Robertson no real backing. It was a sad business. But for the steady erosion of confidence between the two men – uncompensated by personal attachment – one feels that Haig would have mustered his strength for this throw; in any case, one feels that he *should* have done so. And one must sympathize with Robertson's remark to Repington a few weeks later that 'he had found that he had more friends than he knew, but fewer on whom he could count than he expected'.

*   *   *   *

Only four weeks separated these transactions from the great German attack. When it came, it burst upon the British Army with a violence not before equalled, and attention has generally focused upon this characteristic. Just as important was the matter of duration; there were, in fact, *two* onslaughts. The most dangerous crisis of all, the occasion which produced Haig's famous 'Backs to the Wall' order, arose during the second of these, not the first; in April, not in March; at Ypres not at Amiens. Analysis fails if it does not take both attacks into account together – indeed, one should really go further: the whole opening campaign of 1918 was overshadowed, not only by the two offensives which took place against the British, but by the strong probability of a third, *even after* the powerful diversionary efforts against the French. Haig's mind, certainly, was concerned throughout with what might happen in the later stages of the battle, with the dangers that would arise when his reserves were exhausted, if the Germans were still able to threaten his vulnerable northern sector. It was a fear that did not leave him until well into July. Criticism of his handling of the early stages of the fighting, the dramatic episode which has gone down into history as the 'March Offensive', is wide of the mark if it does not recognize the influence of these misgivings.

Conscious of the enemy's growing strength, in marked contrast with the weakness of his own army, Haig's anxieties multiplied. The day after he returned to France General Cox reported that 179 German divisions had been identified on the Western Front; the figure steadily increased: 182 by March 3rd, 185 a week later, 187 on March 18th, 190 on March 22nd, 196 on April 6th, rising to 203 by April 14th, and a peak of 208 in the middle of May. By March 2nd G.H.Q. Intelligence had correctly forecast that the attack would fall on the Third and Fifth Armies, and three days later warned that it might take place 'in the near future'. There was not much that Haig could do about it. His plans had been drawn up according to an equation of men and space: where there was space, there were fewer men; where there was less space, there were more men. Work was proceeding everywhere, with visible and encouraging results; barbed wire was in short supply, but nevertheless 20,000 tons of it, equivalent to 1,000 miles of entanglements, were erected in one month. Complex defensive systems sprouted where none had existed before. The problem was to duplicate them in 'back lines', which alone could be depended on to stop the enemy; and this was a matter of Labour. On the eve of the offensive the Fifth Army was only able to muster 8,830 labourers at a time on defences – a pathetically small number for a front of 40 miles. It was to the

Fifth Army's front and its commander that Haig's attention was increasingly drawn.

Once again, it would appear, a grave misunderstanding had arisen between G.H.Q. and Fifth Army Headquarters. Haig did not realize the extent of it until the battle developed, although he felt certain forebodings long before that. At the beginning of February, in reply to representations from Gough about the weakness of his front, G.H.Q. had carefully defined the Fifth Army's role. From the beginning, large withdrawals in this area were antici- pated. In a Memorandum of February 4th, G.H.Q. went so far as to state that 'it is for consideration whether our main resistance in the Fifth Army area should not be made behind the line of the River Somme', a suggestion which spelt a deliberate retirement to almost half the distance later enforced by the Germans. The idea was rejected on balance, mainly because of the extreme difficulty of carrying out such an operation at short notice (it will be recalled that Ludendorff's decision to go back in this sector in 1916 was taken some four months before the actual move). Nevertheless, the notion of a *fighting withdrawal* to the Somme remained prominent. In the instructions issued to the Fifth Army on February 9th it was clearly stated that the Forward, and even the Battle Zones of the Army were not to be fought for with large-scale counter-attacks: 'It may well be desirable to fall back to the rearward defences of Péronne and the Somme. . . .' These two names now took on much the same significance as the Gheluvelt Plateau at Ypres. Gough's main mission was bluntly stated: '. . . your policy should be to secure and protect at all costs the important centre of Péronne and the River Somme to the south of that place.'

Whatever happened, Gough was told, Péronne must be held; a fully organized bridgehead must be constructed: 'The organization and preparations for the defence of the Péronne bridgehead will be completed in detail as soon as possible. . . .' This was a priority. In addition, when the demands of the bridge- head had been met, a defensive zone along the banks of the Somme was to be prepared. A glance at a map reveals that these were very considerable projects; to Gough with his 8,000 labourers and thinly stationed infantry, they had an unreal sound. As the Official History remarks, they 'seemed to him merely a counsel of perfection'. One sympathizes with him in his dilemma; but the upshot was that while G.H.Q. was expecting him to fight his battle according to a stated pattern, the dispositions forced upon him by his sheer lack of num- bers and facilities imposed a quite different shape.

While this potential hazard was developing, a new, yet familiar, note intruded upon Haig's deliberations. On March 5th Derby wrote to him again, saying: 'It looks now as if an attack might come within a very short time on your front, and on that part of the front of which Gough is in command.

You know my feelings with regard to that particular officer. While personally I naturally have no knowledge of his fighting capacity, still, it has been borne upon me from all sides, civil and military, that he does not have the confidence of the troops he commands, and that is a very serious feeling to exist with regard to a Commander at such a critical time as the present. I believe the Prime Minister has also spoken to you on the subject. . . . I know that on you must be the responsibility, and you must be the person to decide on his re-tention or not, but if by any chance you yourself have any doubts on the subject, I hope by this indefinite offer . . . to give you a loophole which would make your task easier if you desired to make a change. . . . You and I are such old friends, that I know I can write perfectly frankly to you. . . . I know your extraordinary loyalty to your subordinates, and recognizing that, I beg you to believe that if you change any commander, however, well he has served you, for one whom you think is perhaps less tired, I will do my best to see that the man you send home is not left on the rocks.'

Two days after the despatch of this letter Haig made a personal inspection of the Fifth Army Front; circumstantial evidence suggests that he was prompted to do this by what Derby had written, but in fact this was simply the last stage of a tour of Army sectors, interrupted by a visit to Pétain on the 6th. What he found did not encourage him. His first call was on General Butler, his ex-Deputy Chief of Staff, now commanding III Corps, holding the extreme right of the British line along the River Oise. 'As the result of my visit to the III Corps area', Haig noted, 'I think it has a very wide front to defend with three divisions, but for a considerable portion of that front there are river and marsh obstacles, which are said to be impassable at the present time.' Here again one meets one of those peculiar failures of communication which haunted relations between the Fifth Army and G.H.Q. – but the more inexplicable this time, since Butler was an ex-G.H.Q. man, and one who had always been very close to Haig. The truth is that Gough, correctly interpreting the significance of the arrival of General Oskar von Hutier to command the *XVIII Army* opposite him, had told his Corps Commanders as far back as February 3rd that 'in view of the fact that the battle of Riga was opened by the enemy (von Hutier) forcing the passage of the Duna, that section of the line guarded by the Oise should not be considered as immune from attack'.

And yet the overriding impression left upon Haig, confirmed over a month later, was that of Gough's letter to G.H.Q. of February 1st, in which he stated: 'Of my 40 mile front, owing to the difficult country South of the River Oise and the course of that river itself, the Southern 12 miles are not likely to be the scene of a serious hostile attack. . . .' There was a contradiction here which had evidently not been resolved, and which affected Gough's whole front, since his ability to concentrate reserves would depend entirely upon the frontage attacked.

Haig came away from his visit to Butler's III Corps feeling distinctly uneasy; he wrote: 'On the whole I don't like the position and . . . as a result of my visit I ordered the 50th Division to move south to reinforce Fifth Army area from Fourth Army.[1] I have no more troops available to send him, without uncovering *vital* points elsewhere.' It was not only Butler's situation that worried him. The XVIII Corps front, under Lieut.-General Sir Ivor Maxse, was as well organized as any, yet Haig noted that while 'Every detail had been thought out . . . I thought that they were taking it too much for granted that enemy would do what they had planned that he should do. . . .' This is the most dangerous mistake in war; as von Moltke the Elder once told his generals at an exercise: 'You will usually find that the enemy has three courses open to him, and of these he will adopt the fourth.' Despite what he had seen, and his own apprehensions, Haig was far from wishing to move Gough – a dangerous step in any case, on the eve of a great battle. He understood Gough's problem: 'The French handed over to him a wide front with no defences, and Gough has not enough labour for the work.' At the same time, he remarked, 'Reserve lines call for more attention.'

At the root of everything lay the question of Man-power – whether for the purpose of building defences, or of forming a strategic Reserve. The latter question had reached a state of complete impasse. Wilson recorded on February 25th: 'A talk with Haig about his ear-marking some divisions for the Versailles Reserve. He flatly refuses, says he won't be responsible for his line, and rather than do it he would resign. He is quite prepared to agree to any divisions we have in Italy being treated as General Reserve, but no others. All this is difficult.'

It was a ticklish problem indeed; and Haig was quick to notice that Wilson's difficulties were not all of the same hue: 'Now that he has become C.I.G.S. in London, he did not appear so anxious to make the Versailles Staff under Rawlinson very strong. Indeed, differences between these two have already begun to show themselves on the matter of the organization of Versailles. . . .' Before he had even taken up the reins of his new office, Wilson had begun to perceive defects in his own brain-child, the Supreme War Council, and had written: '. . . Milner and I agreed that he should put in someone junior to me, and let me have a directing voice in Versailles if I was C.I.G.S. The whole thing is rather muddlesome.' Muddlesome it certainly was, at that time, with Robertson standing out for this very principle, and in the process of being removed for doing so! And now there was the added complication that

1. 'Fourth' until March 13th, when Plumer returned from Italy, thereafter 'Second' again.

Rawlinson himself, a practical soldier above all, was backing Haig. Rawlinson wrote in his diary on February 25th: 'H.W.'s point is that if Haig contributes eight divisions to the General Reserve he will get more help from the French than he would in any other way, if the Boche attacks him. Haig's answer is that if he sends any division away he cannot be responsible for the safety of his front, and of his army, as owing to the shortage of men, he has barely sufficient troops now to meet the attack which the Germans are preparing to make on him. If he hands over his divisions to the Executive Board they, at Versailles, will not get the information as quickly as he will, they will be in doubt as to where the main German attack is coming,[1] and will hold on to the reserve until they know. Meantime, the British line may be broken. So he refuses to budge from his position of not giving up any more divisions than the two from Italy. H.W. was rather nonplussed, for D.H's arguments are unanswerable. He is the only man who can say how many divisions he needs to hold his front, and he naturally does not place any reliance on a committee acting promptly.'

This was one of those delicate junctures in affairs which can only be worked out satisfactorily by trust and understanding; unfortunately, these had both been grievously undermined by recent political events. The two men with whom Haig had now to work did not have his confidence; he wrote to Lady Haig on this same day: 'Sir H. Wilson and Rawlinson . . . are both humbugs, and it is difficult to decide exactly what is at the bottom of the mind of each of them. . . . But we'll see – Meantime, both profess great friendship for me.' He was doing them an injustice; they really were trying to help him; the moral is that suspicions, once engendered, do endless damage before they are stilled.

Fresh from his tour of the Fifth Army, Haig repaired again to London, where the Supreme War Council met on March 14th. He had an interview with Derby the day before, at which 'Before I consented to talk about anything I placed before him the serious situation as regards drafts. By June our shortage will amount to 100,000.' There was little comfort for him on this issue. Haig, however, felt bound to come back to it when he met Lloyd George and Bonar Law before the Supreme War Council meeting the next day: 'I pointed out that the deficiency of men would make the situation critical by June. If the enemy attacked, our position would be worse. In the month 7th April to 7th May last year the Germans ran through 47 divisions and they actually had 42 in reserve when our attacks began. We must expect *at least* to suffer similar losses.'

Lloyd George's response to such unpalatable truths was once again to

1. Quite correct: Versailles did indeed misjudge the location of the German attack.

attempt a dialectical victory: 'They did their best to get me to say that the Germans would not attack. The Prime Minister remarked that I had "given my opinion that the Germans would only attack against small portions of our front". I said that "I had never said that. The question put to me was if I were a German general and confronted by the present situation, *would I attack?"* I now said that the German Army and its leaders seem drunk with their success in Russia and the middle east, so that it is impossible to foretell what they may not attempt. In any case, we must be prepared to meet *a very strong attack indeed on a 50-mile front, and for this, drafts are urgently required.* We then spoke about the question of forming a General Reserve. Lloyd George did his best to frighten me into agreeing to earmark certain divisions. He spoke of all the other general Commanders-in-Chief having agreed and I alone stood out. He then tried to flatter and wheedle me. I was equally firm. I said amongst other things that this was a military question of which I was the best judge. I only had eight divisions under my hand; the position of these *may* vary from day to day, and only the Commander-in-Chief in close touch with the situation could handle them. Versailles was too distant and not in touch with the actual military situation. Finally Lloyd George agreed that it was too late to touch my divisions now, in view of the apparent imminence of a large attack.'

The Supreme War Council sat down to a formal meeting at 11.30 a.m. Haig records: 'The question of the General Reserve was the first point dealt with – Lloyd George opened the discussion and put my case very well. He finally proposed that, although neither I nor Pétain could contribute towards the General Reserve at once, the intention to form a Reserve should still be maintained, and that as the American troops arrived and set free British and French units, the decision should be given effect to. Colonel Hankey drafted a very skilful decision on these lines which was unanimously adopted at the afternoon sitting.' And so, in the characteristic manner of committees, a 'compromise solution' was reached. It was a warning of what the Executive Board might have attempted. On the other hand, the resolution embodied the only possible sense – that a Reserve was an excellent thing to have, *as soon as there were enough fresh troops to provide it.* And there the matter had to rest.

No one was happy, Wilson least of all. He wrote: 'Douglas Haig . . . says he can't and he won't give any divisions to the General Reserve. He explained that he had not enough for G.H.Q. Reserve, so the thing was impossible, and he said that, if I wanted a General Reserve, I must make some more divisions and I must get more man-power. I could not get him to see the problem in any other light. I impressed on him the fact that by refusing to contribute to the General Reserve he was killing that body, and he would have to live on

Pétain's charity, and he would find that very cold charity. But I was quite unable to persuade him. . . . At this juncture I am clear that, if we have to choose between a General Reserve and Haig, we must choose Haig, wrong as I believe him to be.'

On the day after this meeting of the Supreme War Council a bright beam of personal satisfaction shone through Haig's accumulated perplexities: a son was born to him. On the following day he returned to France, and there, on March 19th, he received Mr. Churchill, the new, energetic Minister of Munitions. They discussed Munitions policy, and then 'He asked my views on making peace. I stated that from the point of view of British interests alone, if the enemy will give the terms Lloyd George recently laid down, we ought to accept them at once. . . .' It was ironical, to say the least, that such a conversation should arise on this day; after dinner, Haig recorded, 'Lawrence brought me the reports on the examination of certain prisoners showing that *the enemy's intention is to attack about March 20th or 21st*'. The final test was immediately at hand – for Haig, for Pétain, and for the whole war organization of the Allies.

*   *   *   *

No full account of the great series of German offensives which took place in the first part of 1918 can be attempted here. Their story – and particularly that of the first of them, which burst upon the British front on March 21st – is one of the great dramas of the War. The stunning violence of the German bombardment by nearly 6,000 guns; the huge weight of the infantry attack, 62 divisions, of which 50 were identified in battle by British Intelligence on the *first day*; the fog, which lent eerie mystery to the enemy's movements, and nullified much of the British defensive system; the total annihilation of forward units; the breakdown of communications; the new German tactics of infiltration by 'Storm Troops'; all these elements, added to the thousand-and-one harrowing details of defeat in the field and sudden retreat, have lent tones of awe and wonderment to narratives of the 'March Offensive'. Blame has been freely distributed on the British side: on Haig, for not making Gough's Army stronger; on Gough, for not handling it better; on subordinate commanders, for losing their grip on the battle; on the soldiers, for giving way. Some measure of this blame is undoubtedly rightly applied; we have seen that Haig and Gough were not properly understanding each other, and much mischief certainly flowed from this; lower commanders were as unfamiliar with the problems of rapid movement to the rear as they had shown themselves to be with those of rapid advance at Cambrai; the Army itself was utterly untrained and unprepared for this sort of fighting. But the fog on March 21st was cruel luck; the achievements of units which did not have to contend with it, particularly on the Third Army Front, show that neither the British defences nor the troops who manned them were without merit. And later in the year, when the fog changed sides, there could be no doubting the vast assistance which attackers can derive from it. Those tart critics who have treated the fog as an alibi for the British Army should have paused to reflect upon the large effort spent by all combatants on perfecting artificial fogs; with more modern equipment, these became a standard part of the armoury of World War II. The truth is that, in the face of this overwhelming handicap, General Gough and his Army put up a superb fight; they suffered an unmistakable tactical defeat, but in doing so won a strategic victory which may in all seriousness be regarded as the turning point of the War.

The more deeply one looks into the story of the German offensives, the clearer it becomes that the main weight of blame - if that is what we are seeking - lies on the German side. The extreme skill with which so many details of their great enterprise were worked out, coupled with its dramatic successes in the early days, has obscured for many the strategic and tactical blunders which it contained. Above all, its ultimate failure was directly attributable to that vein of opportunism which is a chief characteristic of German strategy - a characteristic seen at its most vivid under Hitler. But Hitler inherited this weakness, and Ludendorff was one of the most striking examples of it. He even went so far as to say, at one stage of the battle, when Prince Rupprecht enquired what the strategic objective was: 'I forbid myself to use the word *strategy*. We chop a hole. The rest follows. We did it that way in Russia.'

This was in accordance with the German General Staff doctrines that 'strategy is made up of expedients', and that 'strategic victory follows tactical success'. Both of these sayings embody notable truths, but as doctrines could be pernicious. It was not an accident that Haig, with his single-minded devotion to tested strategic principles, ended the War as a main architect of victory, while Ludendorff, despite great brilliance, saw his expedients collapse in defeat. At critical moments, not only in this first battle, but throughout the offensive campaign, this lack of a single, overriding strategic purpose betrayed him; finally he was mocked by the circumstance that the 'one more push' which Haig has been so much criticized for seeking - his legendary 'obstinacy' - could, on several occasions, have brought success; but Ludendorff had given up; he had turned his attention elsewhere, in pursuit of the illusion of tactical gains.

And in tactics, too, his much-vaunted methods contained the seeds of destruction. Infiltration, certainly, was an excellent technique; all armies were feeling their way towards it, and the Germans deserve credit for being well ahead in working out the details of its application. But the resort to special formations, to the 'Storm Troops', was a desperate and retrograde step. It was, in fact, another expedient, and one that could only be justified by victory; in defeat, it was found that the slaughter of the best soldiers, concentrated in these formations, left the army as a whole weakened and a prey to demoralization. Time and again in history – the Second World War affords numerous illustrations – commanders have been tempted to cream off their armies into special units. During the eighteenth century the habit of removing from battalions their Light and Grenadier companies for special enterprises nearly wrecked the British Army; the growth of Napoleon's Imperial Guard was in proportion to the general decline of quality of his armies, and contributed to it. The idea, is at bottom, a gamble; if it does not come off, the player's plight is very much worse than before. So it was with Ludendorff; he missed his strategic prizes, and his tactical triumphs were obtained at the cost of the vital force of his army.

Nevertheless, the immediate impact of the German blow was tremendous, particularly against Gough's Fifth Army. German objectives were unlimited, but they set themselves, as a minimum target, the British gun line; all too often they succeeded in reaching it; the Fifth Army alone lost 380 guns during the first day. The only reassuring factor, at the end of that day, was the relative failure of the German attacks upon the Third Army. Here the defenders were stronger, visibility was better, the Royal Flying Corps was able to make a most valuable contribution to the battle, and German tactics (especially in the case of General von Below's *XVII Army*) were distinctly clumsier than in the southern sector. General Byng's Army suffered heavily, and was forced to make withdrawals; the retention of the Flesquières Salient as a 'false front' proved to be a costly error, for which G.H.Q. must bear at least half the blame; yet this Army had no sense of defeat, but rather was conscious of having held the enemy off and inflicted terrible losses on him. It was to the south that the great damage was done, and by its very nature accurate reporting of it was impossible. Haig was, as we have seen, in any case contemplating the certainty of large retirements on this front. In the absence of detailed information he found no cause for uncommon alarm; he concluded his diary entry for March 21st with these words:

'Having regard to the great strength of the attack (over 30 extra divisions having reinforced those holding the original German front line for the battle) and the determined manner in which the attack was everywhere pressed, I consider that the result of the day is highly creditable to the British troops; I therefore sent a message of congratulation to the Third and Fifth Armies for communication to all ranks.'

Congratulation was premature, but there was still some time to go before this fact became apparent at G.H.Q. Haig's entry for March 22nd begins: 'All reports show that our men are in great spirits. All speak of the wonderful targets they had to fire at yesterday. Enemy came on in great masses.' This description might serve for some of the happier portions of the Third Army defence, but it was by no means an accurate reflection of the day's fighting as a whole. By 8 p.m. on the second day a new note was creeping in: 'Gough telephoned "Parties of all arms of the enemy are through our Reserve Line." I concurred on his falling back and defending the line of the Somme and to hold the Péronne Bridgehead in accordance with his orders. I at once sent to tell General Pétain and asked his support to enable us to hold the line of the Somme and Péronne Bridgehead. I expect a big attack to develop towards Arras.'

In this passage are clearly revealed the three elements which guided Haig's attitude to the first stages of the battle: first, he thought of the Somme line and the Péronne 'bridgehead' as concrete realities, whereas despite Gough's vigorous last-minute efforts, these were largely imaginary; secondly, he depended absolutely on Pétain for the reinforcement of the southern front, in accordance with their agreement – but Pétain was by now convinced that this attack was a feint, and that the main blow would shortly fall on his own army in Champagne; thirdly, Haig's attention never wandered from his northern front, and in this he was entirely correct, although the German attack, when it came, was made not at Arras but even further to the north.

It was on the third day of the offensive, March 23rd, that Haig began to grasp the reality of what had happened. At 9.30 that morning he went to call on Byng, and found him 'on the whole . . . quite satisfied with the situation of his army'. He then travelled on to Gough's Headquarters in the little red-brick commune of Villers Bretonneux – a name shortly to become famous. Unpleasant news awaited him: 'I was surprised to learn that his troops are *now behind* the Somme. . . . Men very tired after two days' fighting and long march back. On the first day they had to wear gas masks all day which is very fatiguing, but I cannot make out why the Fifth Army has gone so far back without making some kind of a stand.' Here the fatal lack of understanding between G.H.Q. and the Fifth Army emerges clearly. Haig's own words, on March 8th, after his visit to the Fifth Army, 'Reserve Lines call for more attention', point to the root of the confusion. The Reserve Lines barely existed – in some cases they consisted only of markings on the ground. Thus, when the Battle Zone was lost, there was nothing for the Fifth Army to fall back upon – except the cratered wilderness of the old Somme battlefields and the overgrown systems of 1916, pointing in all directions except the right ones. Partly because of this absence of rear support, neither Gough nor his subordinate commanders had bent themselves to the problems of a fighting retreat. As the Official History comments: 'To British troops, whose instinct is to fight it out where they stand, there came no thought of "elastic yielding".... No warning seems to have been given to any brigade or battalion commanders, and therefore none to the lower ranks, that in certain circumstances there might be an ordered retreat; divisional routes had been reconnoitred for this, but information of such nature was certainly withheld from Regimental officers.'

The result was a series of largely disconnected, costly, though magnificent defensive actions in the forward areas; these certainly slowed up the German advance, and took a heavy toll of it; but they could not stop it, and as each section was overwhelmed, irretrievable loss mounted up in the Fifth Army. A deadly by-product of this kind of fighting was that, where there were no uncaptured survivors, there was no precise information. This was an enormous handicap to the artillery, whose first tidings of German progress were often the appearance of the enemy in the battery positions themselves. But it must be added here, in fairness to the Army Commander, and more especially to his subordinates, that a fighting retreat is the most difficult operation in war, and that the psychological difficulty is not the least. A Commander-in-Chief may contemplate a retreat (as Haig did), and an Army Commander may ostensibly accept the idea. But at every subsequent stage down the hierarchy there will be inevitable resistance, as far as the front line where the enemy's pressure is immediately felt. For every intermediate commander, on whom the responsibility of authorization must fall, the fear of acting too hastily, of being thought 'windy', of letting down neighbouring formations, of being rebuked or removed by superiors less in touch with the situation and jealous of their own 'fighting reputations', must weigh heavily. An echo of this frame of mind was heard in 1944, when Field-Marshal Montgomery found himself at loggerheads with the American commanders under him, trying to stem the German offensive in the Ardennes; Montgomery urged an elastic defence in which judicious withdrawal would play its rightful part; the Americans demurred: 'Faith and pride made them reluctant to execute any "voluntary withdrawals"; to do so was "un-American". Every yard the Germans were allowed to gain was a reflection on American honour.'[1] The influence of such concepts must not be underrated; the workings of military honour and professional susceptibility can only be overruled by the most direct orders from the very top. In 1918 Haig believed that his orders had been sufficiently direct – to fight on the line of the Somme; but shortage of time and shortage of men had rendered this impossible; Gough had not made that fact plain.

1. Chester Wilmot: *The Struggle for Europe*, Collins, 1952, p. 596.

Aware now that the battle was going against him in an alarming manner, Haig bent himself to the high-level action which he alone could provide, and which was his only means of influencing the situation. He transferred himself to an Advanced Headquarters at Dury, and there, during the afternoon of the 23rd, he was visited by Pétain. 'He has arranged to put two Armies under General Fayolle on my right to operate in the Somme Valley and keep our two Armies in touch with one another. P. seems most anxious to do all he can to support me and agrees that the only principle which should guide us in our movements is to keep the two Armies in touch. In reply to my request to concentrate a large French force (20 divisions) about Amiens, P. said he was most anxious to do all he can to support me, but he expected the enemy is about to attack him in Champagne. Still he will do his utmost to keep the two Armies in touch. If this is lost and the enemy comes in between us, then probably the British will be rounded up and driven into the sea! This must be prevented even at the cost of drawing back the North flank on the sea coast.'

The very repetitiveness of this entry tells a story. One can almost hear Pétain's repeated assurances of support; one can feel Haig's growing uncertainty. The reference to the British being 'rounded up' strikes an ominous note. If Haig's first reactions to the German stroke had been slow, in the absence of information, his proposal about Amiens shows that he was now thinking very correctly ahead, for the extreme tip of the German advance was scarcely a quarter of the way to that town at this stage. But Pétain's view of the future was extraordinary; as subsequent events showed, he was *already, on the third day*, envisaging the possibility of the British and French Armies becoming separated. Admittedly, he was agreeing that this must not happen, but his apprehensions constituted the most significant victory gained by the Germans so far.

Something had clearly to be done, and done at once, about the Somme front. Despite his misgivings, Haig arranged with Plumer to thin down the Second Army's defences, releasing divisions for the battle in the south. He noted: 'It is most satisfactory to have a Commander of Plumer's temperament at a time of crisis like the present.' He was not to know that on this very day the fundamental weakness of Ludendorff's plans had been exposed. Faced with a success beyond all their expectations, the Germans were bewildered and uncertain about how to handle it. The basic opportunism of their thinking made itself felt; there was a change of plan at Supreme Headquarters, described by General von Kuhl in these words: 'Hitherto the main feature had been the attack of the *II* and *XVII Armies* against the British. To the *XVIII Army* fell only the protection of the attack from the French. Now the French and British were to be separated and both attacked simultaneously. This meant shifting the whole attack a good way to the left.' The British

Official History comments: 'He might have added that there were not only three directions but three objects: to separate the French and British, to drive the British into the sea, and to defeat the French. These manifold objectives in reality required more troops than Ludendorff had at his disposal.' It was an astonishing step to alter the axis of the German advance and re-define its object at such an early stage, particularly in view of the stubborn defence of the British Third Army. It indicated a complete misreading of the actual situation. This proved fatal, as one might suppose. But before it could make itself felt a new, profound crisis befell the Allies, already foreshadowed, and displacing every other consideration from Haig's mind.

March 24th was the critical day. At the front, as the day wore on, it emerged out of all the confusion of contradictory reports, that the momentum of the German advance was, if anything, increasing. French intervention had not had the expected result. Some of the leading French divisions arrived on the battlefield without their artillery; some were without their ammunition columns; all their commanders faced grim problems of adjustment to the fluid conditions of the fight. Anglo-French co-operation was never at its best when carried out in close proximity; March, 1918, proved to be no exception to this rule. Projected joint counter-attacks failed to materialize; the Somme line was definitely lost; on the Third Army front the Germans entered Bapaume. Haig's problems were acute. He sent Lawrence to the southern sector, to meet Gough and General Fayolle, under whose orders the Fifth Army now came. He himself concentrated on the Third Army area; he told Byng 'to *hold on with his left at all costs to the right of the First Army near Arras. . . .*' For the more distant future, his intention was 'to concentrate all reserves I can by thinning my line in the north. With these reserves I hope to strike a vigorous blow southwards if the enemy penetrates to the region of Amiens'. This plan, naturally, would depend on a strong defence being maintained in front of Amiens itself. Meanwhile Intelligence about the enemy was disquieting: '62 divisions have already been identified in the battle – of these 48 are fresh from reserve. Enemy has still 25 in reserve. At least 12 of these are on the front of our Third and Fifth Armies.'

The most significant meeting of the day took place late that evening. At 11 p.m. Pétain arrived again at Haig's Advanced Headquarters, accompanied by General Clive, Head of the British Mission at G.Q.G.; Lawrence was also present. Haig wrote: 'Pétain struck me as very much upset, almost unbalanced and most anxious. I explained my plans as above, and asked him to concentrate as large a force as possible about Amiens astride the Somme to co-operate on my right. He said he expected every moment to be attacked in Champagne, and he did not believe that the main German blow had yet been delivered. He said he would give Fayolle all his available troops. He also told me that he had seen the latter today at Montdidier, where the French reserves are now collecting, and had directed him (Fayolle) in the event of the German advance being pressed still further, to fall back south-westwards to Beauvais in order to cover Paris. It was at once clear to me that the effect of this order must be to separate the French from the British right flank, and so allow the enemy to penetrate between the two armies. I at once asked Pétain if he meant to abandon my right flank. He nodded assent, and added, "It is the only thing possible, if the enemy compel the Allies to fall back still further." From my talk with Pétain I gathered that he had recently attended a Cabinet meeting in Paris and that his orders from his Government are "*to cover Paris at all costs*". On the other hand to keep in touch with the British Army is no longer the basic principle of French strategy. In my opinion, our Army's existence in France depends on keeping the British and French Armies united. So I hurried back to my headquarters at Beaurepaire Château to report the serious change in *French strategy* to the C.I.G.S. and Secretary of State for War, and ask them to come to France.'

It was 3 o'clock on the morning of the 25th when Haig returned to G.H.Q. and Lawrence immediately telegraphed to Wilson. His message went further than merely asking the latter to come over at once with Derby; Haig was now quite clear as to what the purpose of this visit must be. It was 'to arrange that General Foch or some other determined general, who would fight, should be given supreme control of the operations in France. I knew Foch's strategical ideas were in conformity with the orders given me by Lord Kitchener when I became Commander-in-Chief, and that he was a man of great courage and decision as shown during the fighting at Ypres in October and November 1914'.[1]

Haig, in effect, was now asking for a Generalissimo, and Foch was the man he wanted. Pétain's 'charity', as Wilson had prophesied, had turned out to be 'cold' indeed; the vital issue was to have him overruled, and this could only be done by a Supreme Commander. Other minds were working in the same direction, though with less clarity than Haig's, since they were not so immediately in touch with the crisis. During the afternoon of the 24th, Wilson records: 'Foch telephoned asking me what I thought of the situation, and we are of one mind that someone must catch hold, or we shall be beaten. I said I would come over and see him. . . . There is no mistaking the gravity of the situation, nor the entirely inadequate measures taken by Haig and Pétain in their mutual plans for assistance.' When Haig's telegram arrived, Wilson decided to leave for France at once. It so happened that Lloyd George had already sent Lord Milner to France (that same day) with full powers to

1. Haig Diary, March 25th.

handle the situation for the British Government in conjunction with the French. Thus, on the 25th, while the line of battle swayed back still further, bringing defeat apparently more close, the *personae* were rapidly assembling for the one dramatic act which could avert a terrible catastrophe for the Allies.

In the transactions of the next thirty-six hours, involving a number of men, each one of whom was undergoing his own particular stresses, viewing a desperate situation from the angle of his own trepidations and constructions, some confusion was inevitable, and it is not to be wondered at that conflicting reports of what actually happened should exist. Wilson, for example, tells us that he went straight to an interview with Haig and Lawrence on the 25th, and there 'After much talk I told Haig that in my opinion we must get greater unity of action, and I suggested that Foch should co-ordinate the action of both C.-in-C.s. In the end Douglas Haig agreed. I could not help reminding him it was he (Douglas Haig) with Clemenceau's assistance, who killed my plan of a General Reserve. . . .' Wilson continued with such 'I told you so' conversation, which Haig must have found very irritating. His own description of the meeting is short: 'I gave [Wilson] my views on the situation in the presence of my C.G.S., General Lawrence. Briefly, everything depends on whether the French can and will support us *at once* with 20 Divisions of good quality, north of the Somme. A far-reaching decision must be taken at once by the French P.M. so that the *whole* of the French Divisions may be so disposed as to be able to take turns in supporting the British front as we are *now confronting the weight* of the German Army single-handed.'

Haig's mind was clearer now than Wilson's; the latter, despite what he wrote in his diary, was far from clear. Later that day he even canvassed the notion of Clemenceau taking general command of the Allied armies. Foch, to whom he broached this idea, was not attracted by it. The truth is that Henry Wilson's views on a number of subjects were changing. He no longer held the unrestricted admiration for Foch which had once possessed him; also he still preferred the thought of an inter-Allied organization to that of a single personal command – in which he was ahead of his time, but it was not a helpful preference at this juncture.

It was not until March 26th that all the distinguished personages involved in this critical episode could be brought together, in the little town of Doullens, mid-way between Amiens and Arras. Three conferences took place there in quick succession that morning. The first was at 11 a.m., when Haig met his Army Commanders, Horne, Plumer and Byng. Gough was not present; officially, this can be explained by the fact he was now under General Fayolle; he was also, of course, very occupied with the affairs of his Army. Nevertheless, as a practical matter, his absence seems strange. Haig set out the object of the fighting: to hold on to Amiens, and at the same time prevent a break between the First and Third Armies. The Third Army front was where his attention was now fixed: all available reserves, he announced, were being sent to that area. Byng was able to strike an encouraging note: 'In the south near the Somme the enemy is very tired and there is no real fighting taking place there. Friend and foe are, it seems, dead beat and seem to stagger up against each other.' This was true; the battle was already noticeably slowing down. The next meeting was at 11.40, when Milner and Wilson joined the Army Commanders' Conference. Milner wished to understand what was in Haig's mind before entering into discussions with the French. Clemenceau had expressed the fear that Haig was preparing to fall back on the Channel Ports; Wilson's mind was engaged upon too many things at once to offer any clarity. But Haig cleared up Milner's problems at once: he explained that his whole object was to have a fighting French general in supreme command, with the specific object of holding Amiens. He finally disposed of the Versailles Executive Board, or any similar arrangement, with the words: 'I can deal with a man, but not with a committee.'

The main conference began at 12 noon. The British representatives were Milner, Wilson, Haig, Lawrence and Major-General A. A. Montgomery; the latter represented Rawlinson, the British Military Member at Versailles, and took notes of what occurred. On the French side there were Poincaré, Clemenceau, Pétain, Foch and his Chief of Staff, Weygand. Haig, it has been remarked, looked tired and anxious as he entered the meeting – as well he might; he had had very little sleep during the last forty-eight hours, and he was conscious that the whole issue of the War might depend upon what immediately followed. He was the first to speak, explaining the situation which had developed during the last five days, and that his whole object now was to hold on north of the Somme. A reference to the Fifth Army, now under French orders, drew from Pétain the interjection that this Army was 'broken', that it no longer existed; this, in turn, drew a sharp retort from Wilson.

It was then Pétain's turn to speak; he agreed that Amiens should be held, but dwelt upon the difficulty of moving up French divisions in time, and refused to make any guarantees. At this, Foch broke in to say: 'We must fight in front of Amiens, we must fight where we are now. As we have not been able to stop the Germans on the Somme, we must not now retire a single inch.' Haig promptly took up this cue, saying: 'If General Foch will consent to give me his advice, I will gladly follow it.' Clemenceau and Milner then retired into a corner; Clemenceau called to Pétain; Milner consulted briefly with Haig again. Then Clemenceau drafted and proposed a formal agreement, entrusting to Foch 'the co-ordination of the action of the British and French Armies in front of Amiens'. Haig would not have this; he tells us:

'This proposal seemed to me quite worthless, as Foch would be in a subordinate position to Pétain and myself. In my opinion it was essential to success that Foch should *co-ordinate the action of all the allied armies on the western front.* Both Governments agreed to this.'

And with this the significant business of the conference ended. Poincaré remarked: '*Je crois, messieurs, que nous avons bien travaillé pour la victoire.*' Wilson commented afterwards: 'Douglas Haig is ten years younger tonight than he was yesterday afternoon.' Haig had reason for satisfaction: the desperate, but solitary remedy which he had perceived at Dury on the night of the 24th was now a fact, and even though the achievement still only existed on paper, there was now at least a very strong chance of averting otherwise certain catastrophe.

Haig's role in the appointment of Foch was crucial, and as it represented a startling deviation from his previously held opinions, it requires further comment. In considering Doullens, and all that followed, one point has to be held firmly in mind: that Haig's action was dictated by the imperative need to overrule Pétain,[1] and make the defence of Amiens an absolute priority for the only army able to do it – the French. It was an empirical solution. There were many who supported the idea of a Supreme Commander on principle, and naturally they have seen the Doullens decision as a vindication of that principle. For the French, of course, it was by no means disagreeable to have one of their own countrymen exalted to this high position, although, for Clemenceau, no great admirer of Foch, this pleasure was distinctly tempered. He remarked tartly to Foch: 'Well, you've got the job you so much wanted.' Foch retorted: 'A fine gift; you give me a lost battle and tell me to win it.' But leaving aside personalities and private theories, the essence of Doullens is this: all but *one* of the personages there were preoccupied with the overwhelming question of how to avoid defeat. The odd man out was Pétain. It was his attitude which forced the decision to take the shape it did. Haig has recorded that at the conference 'Pétain had a terrible look. He had the appearance of a commander who has lost his nerve'. We learn from a totally different source, Poincaré, of a most revealing incident just before the conference began. Clemenceau drew Poincaré aside, and said to him: '*Pétain est agaçant à force de pessimisme. Imaginez-vous qu'il me dit une chose que je ne voudrais confier à aucun autre qu'à vous. C'est cette phrase: "Les Allemands battront les Anglais en rase campagne; après quoi ils nous battront aussi." Un général devrait-il parler et même penser ainsi?*'

For the frightened men – it is no dishonour to them to use this adjective; the circumstances warranted fright – the glimpse, the very aura, of a deeper

1. Herein lies the profound difference from the 'Nivelle solution' proposed at Calais in 1917.

fear, of an *acceptance* of the possibility of defeat in the field, was the sharpest possible spur to agreement without pausing to consider technical difficulties or theoretical advantages. Clemenceau, as we now know, was right. Pétain, a brilliant practitioner of battle, high among the best on either side, was nevertheless unsuited to great command by this defect of temperament normally concealed by level-headed realism. Usually calm, precise, terse, un-flamboyant, he appealed to Haig as much as any French commander; but at bottom there was this terrible difference between them. Pétain was a pessi-mist. It was seen in 1918, and its full meaning became apparent in 1940. The difference between those years was that in 1918 Pétain *was* the odd man out at the level of decision, and Foch was at hand, while in 1940 Pétain was supported by a phalanx, and there was no Foch in France. It thus became the role of a junior 'two-star' officer, Charles de Gaulle, to separate himself from the tide of affairs and rally the nation.

*   *   *   *

The decision was taken; it remained to win the battle. Beyond that, there was the question of winning the War. From this point onwards, the Allies would be setting about that task under a totally different form of command from any adopted previously; because the end-product was victory, won in just under eight months, many people have been tempted to ascribe, either to Foch personally, or to the new system itself, virtues which neither possessed. Foch himself had certainly changed during the course of the War; disappoint-ment had taken its toll of him. But the Foch of March to November, 1918, was still at heart the Foch of earlier years: full of courage (that was why he was there); dedicated to the offensive; cryptic and enigmatic in speech; given to large gestures; often imprecise in his appreciations. All these facets of his nature made themselves felt as the year wore on. Pétain, a sardonic and often accurate observer, placed his finger on yet another truth when he told Repington in September that Foch 'now has a position of great authority, though it largely depends *on his being successful*'.[1] General Monash, another acute observer, wrote: 'It has come to be an article of faith that the whole of the successive stages of the great closing offensive of the war had been the subject of most careful timing, and of minute organization on the part of the Allied High Command, and of our own G.H.Q. Much eulogistic writing has been devoted to an attempted analysis of the comprehensive and far-reaching plans which resulted in the delivery of blow upon blow, in a prescribed order of time and for the achievement of definite strategical and tactical ends. All who played any part in these great events will know that it was nothing of the kind. . . .'

1. Author's italics.

And Foch himself, in a lucid passage, agrees with this: 'What later on was known by the term "unified command" gives a false idea of the powers exercised by the individual in question – that is, if it is meant that he commanded in the military sense of the word, as he would do, for example, in the French Army. His orders to Allied troops could not have the same characteristic of absolutism, for these troops were not his. . . . But by persuasion he could stimulate or restrain their Commanders-in-Chief, decide upon the policy to follow, and thus bring about those concerted actions which result in victory, even when the armies concerned are utterly dissimilar.'

Above all, in considering Foch's position, it is important for the modern student not to confuse it with the functioning of Supreme Commanders during the Second World War – Eisenhower, for example. The essence of Second World War studies is the emergence of remarkable Anglo-American joint Staff organizations: not only the joint Chiefs of Staff (in conclave with their numerous experts) from whom commanders like Eisenhower took their orders, but fully integrated Staffs such as S.H.A.E.F.,[1] which worked *to* Eisenhower. There were rubs, there were frictions; but at the root of everything was the invaluable principle of integration, made possible by the bond of a common language. And this integration was expressed in voluminous, careful Staff work, so that the Supreme Commander became, in effect, simply the authorizing agent of plans worked out for him, for operations conceived and directed at a higher level. This is not a denigration; these acts of authorization could involve dire responsibilities, searching tests of character, as when Eisenhower had to decide whether or not to launch the Normandy invasion in the face of the most disturbing weather reports. The method was, in any case, correct. It was utterly different from Foch's procedure.

His appointment was, we have shown, an expedient; his technique was an outdated reversion to the personal command of earlier centuries. It worked, during its short existence, because his main function was a moral one – to exercise a stimulus rather than to devise scientific plans. For the latter purpose he was quite unequipped, and made no attempt to equip himself; until the very end, he ran the War with a small personal staff of about twenty officers. The machinery of the Supreme War Council at Versailles was allowed to run down into disuse, neither directing Foch nor serving him, as it might have done. Against the whole evolving trend of modern war, Foch chose to work by personal inspiration and influence, that is to say, in a stratosphere far removed from the practical considerations of battle. As may be supposed, this often proved maddening for the commanders under him. Within a month, Haig was brought to such a pitch of irritation that he even advocated Foch being

1. Supreme Headquarters Allied Expeditionary Force.

made French Commander-in-Chief, as well as Generalissimo, just so that he should possess a proper Staff. This, of course, would have meant the complete reversal of the whole Doullens concept, and would have created the very situation which Haig himself had opposed in the case of Nivelle. That he should even have contemplated such a thing shows how faulty the new system was. But the truth is that in 1918, with polyglot armies, the best that could be worked out was a compromise; no one should suppose that it was anything more than that.

Difficulties, indeed, began to appear on the very first day of Foch's new command. On leaving Doullens, Foch had gone to the Fifth Army area, where he had met Gough. A most regrettable interview took place, during which Foch addressed brusque words to Gough, all the more unforgivable in that they seemed to question the personal courage of that brave officer. Haig, when he heard about it, commented that 'Foch had spoken most impertinently'. Supreme Commanders sometimes have a habit of doing that. In any case, it was not only Foch who was censuring the unfortunate Gough; Milner and Wilson both took the opportunity of speaking to Haig about him. He replied that 'whatever opinion at home might be, and no matter what Foch had said, I considered that he (Gough) had dealt with a most difficult situation very well. He had never lost his head, was always cheery and fought hard'. It was no good. The pressure against Gough which had been building up for so long could not now be withheld; Haig had to agree to let him go, and bring in Rawlinson from Versailles in his place. Haig offered to resign himself, but this Wilson would not have, remarking some days later to Lloyd George that the Government 'would not get anyone to fight a defensive battle better than Haig, and that the time to get rid of him was when the German attack was over'.

Meanwhile, the fighting continued, and along the Somme front, until Rawlinson arrived, it was still Gough and his battered Army who had to do much of it. Three days after Doullens, when Haig met Foch, the latter 'was full of apologies. He tells me that he is doing all he can to expedite the arrival of French Divisions, and until they come we can only do our best to hold on to our present positions'. This was an art which had been well learned by now, in both the Third and Fifth Armies. The pace of the German advance was becoming slower and slower. Indeed, on the day of Foch's appointment, Ludendorff was urged by his Staff to break off the Somme attack, and try again elsewhere. The failure of a heavy blow against the Third Army on the 28th drew him towards this decision; an even more marked failure on April 5th persuaded him that 'The enemy's resistance was beyond our powers. . . . O.H.L. was forced to take the extremely hard decision to abandon the attack on Amiens for good'. Gough and his Army had not fought in vain; it was a cruel fate that brought dismissal after so gallant a fight against such hopeless odds.

Despite minor troubles, Haig's first relations with the new Supreme Commander were good. On March 29th (the day when Foch had to apologize for the slow arrival of French troops) Haig nevertheless remarked: 'I think Foch has brought great energy to bear on the present situation. . . . He and I are quite in agreement as to the general plan of operations.' As critical hours passed, however, he became less satisfied. News of certain poor performances by the French on the following day forced him to take the matter up with Clemenceau, who was visiting Advanced G.H.Q. Clemenceau saw his point at once and 'gave orders for the French to support us energetically. . . . I sincerely hope that Clemenceau will get his order carried out! C. spoke most freely about Foch's position. He had no fears about me loyally doing my best to co-operate. It was Pétain and Foch who he feared would squabble. "Pétain", he said,"is a very nervous man and sometimes may not carry out all he has promised." Personally, I have found Pétain anxious to help and straight-forward, but in the present operations he has been slow to decide and slower still in acting. At times his nerve seems to have gone. . . .' Two days later this situation repeated itself, and once again Clemenceau had to intervene on Haig's behalf with Foch. It was a curious irony that the French Prime Minister should have been the best champion of the British Commander-in-Chief; to Clemenceau it quickly became apparent that the Doullens agreement was not all that it might have been. A second inter-Allied meeting was convened at Beauvais on April 3rd, at which Lloyd George and Wilson were present, with Clemenceau, Foch and Pétain. At Clemenceau's instigation, a new convention was signed, entrusting to Foch 'the strategical direction of military operations. The C. in C. of British, French and American Armies will have full control of the tactical action of their respective Armies. Each C. in C. will have the right of appeal to his Government, if in his opinion his Army is endangered by reason of any order received from General Foch'. This important modification also carries its reminder of the Nivelle affair. For Haig it implied a reversion to the principles on which he had then taken his stand: 'I . . . explained that this new arrangement did not in any way alter my attitude towards Foch, or C. in C. French Army. I had always in accordance with Lord Kitchener's orders to me regarded the latter as being responsible for indicating the general strategical policy, and, as far as possible, I tried to fall in with his strategical plan of operation.' No one realized quite how quickly the new formula would be tested.

Intimations of what might be in store were contained, however, in a report of heavy German concentrations opposite the British First Army, received by Haig on the eve of the Beauvais meeting. He at once diagnosed a probable attack between Arras and La Bassée, and ordered Byng (Third Army) 'to keep his reserves on his left rear, i.e., northern flank'. This was a significant reversal of previous orders to Byng, and implied an evident diminution of the British effort in the Somme sector, with correspondingly increased French responsibilities. At Beauvais, before the meeting broke up, Haig 'asked the Governments to state that it is their desire that a French offensive should be started *as soon as possible* in order to attract the enemy's Reserves, and so prevent him from continuing his pressure against the British. Foch and Pétain both stated their determination to start attacking "*as soon as possible*". But will they ever attack? I doubt whether the French Army, as a whole, is now fit for an offensive.' It was depressing to face the renewed hazards of battle with these doubts about his Allies, which had already played such a large part in his strategy in 1917, still active in his mind. Two days later they received further confirmation, this time from the Chief of the French Mission at G.H.Q., General de Laguiche, who deplored the slowness of his countrymen's preparations to attack, and told Haig that 'He considers the long time spent on trench warfare has given French commanders a false idea of what is wanted in the present situation. . . . Personally I believe that the French Army, from the highest to the lowest, is thoroughly tired of the war, and they don't mean to attack to help the British.' This was unjust, but a not unnatural conclusion to be drawn from his current negotiations with Foch.

On April 5th the last major German assault on the Somme ended in failure; the next day more evidence came in of preparations for a new attack in the north. Haig diagnosed that 'a surprise attack by three or four divisions against the Portuguese front is also to be expected. The First Army is quite alive to these possibilities and is prepared to meet them.' Nevertheless, he felt impelled to take the matter up in the strongest possible terms with Foch; he wrote to him that evening:

'All information points to the enemy's intention to continue his efforts to destroy the British Army. With this object in view he appears to be preparing a force of 25 to 35 Divisions to deliver a heavy blow on the Bethune-Arras front. . . . In view of this threatening situation, I submit that one of the three following courses should be given effect to without delay, viz. – either

1. A vigorous offensive in the next five or six days by the French armies on a considerable scale, in order to attract the enemy's reserves,

or

2. The French to relieve the British troops south of the Somme (a total of 4 divisions),

or

3. A group of 4 French divisions to be located in the neighbourhood of St. Pol as a reserve to the British Front.'

Lacking the reasoned advice of a trained Staff, Foch was unable to make a proper assessment of relative dangers. His attention was still fixed on the Amiens front, and the most he was prepared to offer to Haig, when they met the following day, was a counter-attack in that region, in conjunction with the British Fourth Army.[1] Haig commented: 'Personally, I do not believe that either Foch or Pétain has any intention of putting French divisions into the battle. As regards my requests for either taking over British front south of the Somme, or placing a French reserve near St. Pol, Foch said he was unable to do either; but he had ordered a reserve of four divisions and three cavalry divisions of the French army to be located south-west of Amiens (i.e. in a very safe place). This was, he said, the best that he could do at present. . . . I wired to the C.I.G.S. result of my meeting with Foch, and suggested that he (Wilson) should come out to discuss the situation, and try to get better arrangements from Foch.'

Cutting across these matters of high strategy, and adding greatly to Haig's anxieties, was his consciousness of criticism of his handling of the March battle, which had already cost his Army heavy loss. He wrote to Derby on April 6th: 'It is the duty of everyone to do his utmost in his own particular line to help the State to weather the storm. Personally, I have a clear conscience, and feel that I have done the best with the means at my disposal and am prepared to continue on here as long as the Government wish me to do so. But, *as I have more than once said to you and others of the Government, the moment they feel that they would prefer someone else to command in France, I am prepared to place my resignation in your hands.* The needs of the State and the wishes of the Committee[2] must take first place, and the interests of individuals must be ignored. So do not consider me.' This letter was discussed by the War Cabinet on the 8th, and Wilson records: 'Later on Lloyd George asked me if I did not think we ought to take Haig at his word; but I said that, failing some really outstanding personality, and we have none, I thought we ought to wait for Haig's report.'

Clear enough on this question, Wilson was less correct on the larger issue; he was aware of the grave threats which still hung over the British Army, and warned Foch of them in a telegram on the 7th. But, like Foch, he was still obsessed by the Amiens front, and discounted the possibility of a big attack on the northern flank of the British line. It requires some stature to ignore a serious present danger and give attention to one that has not yet materialized. At this stage only Haig was capable of doing this. The three men met on April 9th; it was an unsatisfactory encounter. Haig records: '*Foch declined to take over any part of the British line*, but is determined to place a

1. Really the Fifth Army, renamed Fourth when Rawlinson took over.
2. He meant the War Cabinet.

Reserve of four French Divisions with their heads on the Somme immediately west of Amiens. In case of necessity he proposed to march these N.E. to take a share in what he calls the *"bataille d'Arras"*. I pointed out the very great inconvenience caused by the insertion of these troops into the area of the Fourth Army. . . . Also it will be well-nigh impossible for these French Divisions to take part in the Arras battle until the British are forced a long way back from their present line. It is also a sad fact that there are very few French Divisions with good enough morale to face the Germans in a stand-up fight. . . . I found Foch most selfish and obstinate. I wonder if he is afraid to trust French Divisions in the battle front. . . . Henry Wilson did not help us at all in our negotiations with Foch. His sympathies almost seem to be with the French.' He was not being quite fair to Wilson, who also disliked Foch's proposal, and even advised Haig 'to register a note showing the disadvantages'.

All discussion, however, swiftly became academic. While the meeting was still in progress, news came in of the German onset astride the River Lys, between La Bassée and Ypres – further north than Haig himself had expected, and very far away indeed from the Amiens front on which Foch and Wilson were still fixing their minds. This attack was a small affair, compared with the great blow of March 21st, but it affected that very area where the British could not afford to give ground. The main threat, against the First Army, bursting through the weak defences of the Portuguese Corps (just about to be relieved), pointed straight at the vital rail centre of Hazebrouck, which was to the British what Roulers was to the Germans; the extension of the attack to the Second Army front also brought a threat to Dunkirk. The Germans enjoyed the advantage that both the First and Second Armies had been 'milked' for reinforcements for the battle in the south, and many of their divisions were exhausted units from the Somme, in the process of refitting. Thus a very much smaller deployment of German reserves was able to produce a very much larger danger, and the fighting by which this was averted was amongst the severest of the War.

Conducting the desperate battle, Generals Horne and Plumer, in admirable co-operation, bent their energies to holding off the Germans; Haig and Wilson, as the latter came to full appreciation of the peril, bent theirs to obtaining that support from the French, through Foch, which was the whole object of having a Generalissimo. Foch, clinging resolutely to two principles – that no large unit should be relieved while battle was in progress, and that counter-attack was the only final solution – resisted bitterly every attempt to win relief for the hard-hit British troops. In this he showed his habitual 'nerve' and resolution, but, as the War so often showed, these virtues in a general were often paid for by excessive suffering and bloodshed of the soldiers. By

April 14th, Haig was writing: 'the British Divisions are fast disappearing.'
Foch relented slowly, disputing every concession. His position, it must be
admitted was a difficult one. The pressures upon him were great: on the one
hand Haig, urgently demanding support in his mortal fight; on the other
hand Pétain, unwilling to risk any large part of his army, knowing its weakness, sceptical of the value of offensives; beside them both, looming larger in
importance as each week passed, General Pershing, dedicated to the creation
of a large, independent American Army which would deliver the final strokes
of the War, and firmly adverse to dribbling away his untrained formations
in the maelstrom of Allied disasters.

Turning our attention aside from the unfortunate soldiers, grappling with
the enemy in the field, it is the conflict of wills of the commanders that must
here concern us. On the second day of battle Haig wrote to Foch: 'The
enemy will without a doubt continue to strike against my troops until they
are exhausted. It is therefore vitally important, in order to enable us to continue the battle for a prolonged period, that the French Army should take
immediate steps to relieve *some part* of the British front, and take an active
share in the battle. As to what portion of our front should be taken over by
the French, I leave you to decide. . . .' Foch agreed to move up 'a large force
of French troops ready to take part in the battle'. But he refused to take over
any part of the British line, and it soon became apparent that his 'large force'
was no more than the three Cavalry and four Infantry Divisions already
promised. On the 11th, acutely conscious of the magnitude of the task which
he had to carry out – 'The most important thing is to keep connection with
the French. With this object in view I must be strong at and south of Arras.
I must also cover Calais and Boulogne' – Haig sent Davidson to Foch to urge
that the French should come to Flanders. 'General Foch', says the Record of
their interview, 'replied that the British forces must hold on where they stood
and that he could not guarantee any more reinforcements being sent north
beyond the divisions already ordered. He gave General Davidson a map
showing his views on the manner in which the enemy should be held in the
First and Second Army fronts.' Foch was always free with such advice; it did
not often add to his popularity.

It was on this day, April 11th, sensing the critical sway of the battle,
which was taking place as much in the hearts of his men as across the muddy
Flanders fields, that Haig issued an Order of the Day which has entered into
the British Army's heritage. Drafted in his own hand, with only three
corrections, it read as follows:

'To all Ranks of the British Forces in France.

'Three weeks ago today the Enemy began his terrific attacks against us on a 50-mile front. His objects are to separate us from the French, to take the Channel ports and destroy the British Army.

'In spite of throwing already 106 divisions into the battle and enduring the most reckless sacrifice of human life, he has as yet made little progress towards his goals.

'We owe this to the determined fighting and self-sacrifice of our troops. Words fail me to express the admiration which I feel for the splendid resistance offered by all ranks of our Army under the most trying circumstances.

'Many amongst us now are tired. To those I would say that victory will belong to the side which holds out longest. The French Army is moving rapidly and in great force to our support.

'There is no other course open to us but to fight it out! Every position must be held to the last man: there must be no retirement. With our backs to the wall, and believing in the justice of our cause, each one of us must fight on to the end. The safety of our homes and the freedom of mankind alike depend on the conduct of each one of us at this critical moment.

D. Haig. F.M.'

Many of those to whom this message was addressed never received it; they had already 'fought on to the end'. Some have doubted whether British soldiers, in any case, really care for exhortations in moments of danger. Others, at the time, had different doubts; Charteris, for example, wrote: 'I wish D.H. had *not* issued his order. It will immensely hearten the Germans when they hear of it, as they must. I do not think our own men needed it to make them fight it out. If the French are really hurrying to our assistance, they should be here in a few days, almost as soon as the order will reach the front-line troops. If they are not, it may have a really bad effect to raise hopes in the troops' minds.' But however legitimate some of these doubts may be – and a generation familiar with certain addresses to the Eighth Army during the Second World War will supply its own gloss – there seems little doubt that Haig's simple, feeling words did have a powerful effect. As an example of this, it may be useful to quote another Order of the Day, issued at a level where such things are less common, by a subaltern of the 1st Australian Division, shortly after Haig's message had reached the troops. It read:

'Special Orders to No. . . . Section:
1. This position will be held and the section will remain here until relieved.
2. The enemy cannot be allowed to interfere with this programme.
3. If the section cannot remain here alive it will remain here dead, but in any case it will remain here.

4. If any man through shell shock or other cause attempts to surrender
   he will remain here dead.
5. Should all guns be blown out, the section will use Mills grenades and
   other novelties.
6. Finally the position as stated will be held.'

This order was discovered on the bodies of the men of the section.

The battle raged on; Haig's arguments with Foch also continued unabated.
On April 14th he commented: 'Foch seems to me unmethodical and takes a
"short view" of the situation. For instance, he does not look ahead and make
a forecast of what may be required in a week in a certain area and arrange
accordingly. He only provides from day to day sufficient troops to keep the
railway accommodation filled up.' The next day Foch informed General du
Cane, his British Liaison Officer: '*La bataille de Hazebrouck est finie.*' This
statement has been acclaimed as a brilliant piece of intuitive penetration; it
would have been startling to the officers and men actually engaged in the
battle, if they had heard it. Possibly it embarrassed Foch himself, ten days
later, when, in one of the final convulsions, the French lost Mont Kemmel,
one of the bastions of the Flanders front. On hearing Foch's oracle, Haig
found it necessary 'to place on record my opinion that the arrangements made
by you are insufficient to meet the present military situation'. Two days later
Wilson chimed in with a note to Foch saying:

'. . . It seems to me essential that we face the facts as they really are and
that we look a little more into the future than we have been doing.

'Two courses are open to us if the enemy challenge us in battle along our
present line south and east of Ypres.

(a) We can accept battle on our line of today.
(b) We can shorten our line by withdrawing. . . .

'You favour (a).

'That being so, I think you must act in accordance with that decision and
bring up sufficient troops to defeat all the enemy's attacks. . . .'

He added in a note to Haig: 'I do so hope that Foch will focus the present
situation and see things as they *really* are.'

Slowly, despite these disagreements, the German offensive was brought
to a halt, as its predecessor had been on the Somme. There were many bleak
moments; the hard-won ground at Passchendaele was given up to shorten
the line; a retirement even to the Ypres Canal line, as proposed in the crisis
of the Second Battle of Ypres, was mooted; Mont Kemmel was lost on the
25th; on the 29th Plumer himself, one of the most stout-hearted warriors,

was frankly dismayed, and Haig had to comfort himself with the reflection that 'the situation is never so bad, nor so good, as first reports indicate'. This adage proved to be correct in its happier sense; on the following day German Headquarters took the decision to break off the offensive. On May 3rd Haig noted: 'The conclusions I drew from my talks with G.O.C.s divisions and others today are that our troops are in good heart and have the upper hand of the Germans. . . . Secondly, that the Germans do not seem likely to take the offensive westwards towards the line Hazebrouck-Aire at this moment, and that the enemy is having a wretched time in this salient.' The danger had passed.

True to form, on this very day, Foch was again proposing to Haig a British offensive. Haig informed him that preliminary preparations for such a move were already in hand, but that he felt that 'the present moment is not a suitable time'. He added dryly: 'I note with satisfaction that an offensive is about to be delivered by the French Army.' The British Army had survived; what was just as remarkable, so had the Entente, even though it was distinctly less 'cordiale'.

The cost had been dreadful. The casualty returns presented to Haig on May 6th for the period March 21st–April 30th were 9,704 officers and 230,089 other ranks. These figures were only slightly too high; the British Official History finally placed the total at 236,300. This loss, it must be remembered, was incurred in just 40 days of defensive fighting; those who blame First World War generals for being too 'offensive-minded' should contrast it with the total of 244,897 for the 105 days of the Passchendaele offensive. They should remember, too, that over 70,000 of these British casualties were prisoners – that is to say, irrecoverable. In addition, the French, although playing a much smaller part in the two battles, lost over 90,000 men, of whom some 15,000 were prisoners. German losses would appear to have been slightly higher than those of the Allies; as has been said, their tactics were often clumsy, their attacks pushed home with furious desperation, regardless of loss. One British Regimental History, for example, describing an attack on the Third Army on March 28th, says: 'The enemy, who was coming on in great numbers, *shoulder to shoulder*,[1] offered a splendid target to the rifles and Lewis guns.'[2] This was a common experience. But the Germans, of course, lost fewer prisoners.

The damage done to the British Army was most serious. In a table of 'Estimated Strength of Divisions', also recorded in Haig's diary on May 6th, we find that 15 divisions were credited with a strength of 900 or more other ranks per battalion, 19 with 800–900, 6 were below 800, and 10 were regarded

1. Author's italics.
2. War History of the 1/Queen's Westminster Rifles.

as 'exhausted', of which 5 were to be broken up. The only large unit which remained intact at the end of this bitter fight was the Canadian Corps.

Faced with the grim reality of catastrophe, the Government discovered that it did, after all, have troops available for France, and learned to its cost that this was where they had to be. Between the beginning of the year and March 21st, the following numbers were sent to France from the United Kingdom:

British Category 'A'	129,357
British Category 'B'	5,299
Total	134,636
Dominion	32,384
Labour Force	7,359
Grand Total	174,379

Between March 21st and August 31st, the following were sent:

British Category 'A'	418,990
British Category 'B'	49,925
Total	461,915
Dominion	73,190
Labour Force	8,005
Grand Total	544,005

In addition, 2 Divisions came from Italy and 2 from Palestine; 9 separate battalions came from Italy, 23 from Palestine, and 12 from Salonika; a total of approximately 100,000 men. As the Official History says: 'It is obvious that the British Armies in France could have been brought up to full establishment before March 21st without unduly weakening the forces elsewhere had the Government so willed.' Heavy fighting and heavy losses there would have been in any case; but on the Fifth Army front in particular sheer numerical weakness played a great part in the disaster that befell. Much suffering and much loss, to say nothing of the reputation of their luckless commander, might have been spared the Fifth Army, if Lloyd George and his Government had taken a different view of their responsibilities. This was what was in Haig's mind when he wrote, on April 3rd, after a meeting with Lloyd George: 'I gathered that L.G. expects to be attacked in the House of Commons for not tackling the manpower problem before, also for personally ordering Divisions to the east at a critical time against the advice of his Military Adviser, viz., the C.I.G.S. (Robertson). He is looking out for a scapegoat for the retreat of the Fifth Army. . . . He was much down upon Gough. I championed the latter's case. . . . I said I could not condemn an officer unheard, and that if L.G.

wishes him suspended he must send me an order to that effect. L.G. seems a "cur" and when I am with him I cannot resist a feeling of distrust of him and of his intentions.'

This instinctive distrust was well justified; at this very time Repington was writing: 'I . . . hear that Haig is doomed, and suppose that he will be the next scapegoat, on the pretext that he said he could hold on if attacked. But, after all, he is still holding on.' Just over a month later Haig wrote to his wife: 'As you know, I am ready to serve wherever the Government thinks fit to send me, and I don't want to stay here a day longer than the Government have confidence in me. At the same time, I think they will find it difficult to find a successor *at the moment*.' He was right; and therefore spared to reap his victory.

*   *   *   *

Fully aware that his tenure of command might be terminated at any moment; conscious of the weakness of his army; well knowing that Germany's strength was far from exhausted, and that yet another blow against the British was both possible and likely, it is the most remarkable tribute to Haig's stability of character and intellect that, no sooner had the German attacks on the Lys died away, than he began to consider the counterstrokes which, he knew, could encompass their ruin. When all was said and done, despite every dispute between them, what bound him and Foch together through many difficulties was this fact: that neither of them ever contemplated anything less than victory, nor did either ever cease to work for it with might and main. None of the arguments between the two men during the April fighting were permitted by Haig to influence his dealings with the Generalissimo.[1] On May 1st he recorded that: 'Foch and I were in complete agreement. I recognized the difficulty he was in to find Reserves at the *decisive* point, and said I would do my best to exchange tired British Divisions for fresh French ones which would be brought to the battle area as soon as possible. I said I would detail four Divisions to go to the French front. . . .' The following day, after yet another Allied conference at Abbeville, Haig noted with approval:

'We were all agreed that:
1. touch with the French and British Armies must be maintained;
2. that the Channel Ports must be covered.

If, however, circumstances required the C. in C. to decide between the two objects, then rather than allow the Armies to be separated, a retirement would be made toward the Somme. But Foch expressed himself as quite certain that this would not be necessary.'

1. Foch was appointed 'Commander-in-Chief of the Allied Armies in France' on April 14th.

The accord continued. There were still shocks in store: even before the Battle of Lys the ended, the Germans made one more quick thrust at Amiens, on April 24th, and succeeded in capturing Villers Bretonneux, on its little plateau from which they could see right across to the spire of Amiens cathedral. On the following day, however, the third anniversary of Anzac Day, the Australians retook the town, and the Germans abandoned their attempt. This day was also marked by the first Tank versus Tank battle in history – a small enough affair, but portentious, and a complete victory for the Royal Tank Corps. The question of German future intentions was now fundamental; 147 of their Divisions had been committed to battle out of the 208 present on the Western Front, but there were still 44 in reserve, the large majority of them being with Prince Rupprecht's Army Group, facing the British. There was every indication that their next blow, or at any rate, a very early blow, would fall on the British Front between Arras and Albert.

Despite this, and despite fresh fears that the French were seeking, through Foch, to carry out an '*Amalgame*' of the British and French Armies as some of their leaders had long desired, Haig stood by his promise to Foch, and allowed four of his divisions to go to what was regarded as a 'quiet' sector of the French front, along the Aisne. Henry Wilson, now thoroughly disillusioned with his Allies, viewed this decision with alarm; he wrote to Haig on May 16th: 'The French are shaping to take us over administratively as well as strategically. This will not do. . . . The Americans want to pool food. Someone else wants to pool oats. Someone else wants to pool tanks. Someone else wants to pool aeroplanes. Meanwhile our tired divisions commence a *roulement*, and little by little and bit by bit our glorious army will disappear. Our bases will be taken over followed by our Mercantile Marine followed by the Royal Navy. I write half in joke, whole in earnest. When one sees a danger it is not difficult to avoid it. But don't let us have any illusions.' Haig was not disturbed; he had bluntly told the French Liaison Officer, Gemeau, on April 19th, that 'it was desirable to tell Foch that any idea of a permanent "Amalgam" must be dismissed from his mind at once, because that would never work. . . . He assured me that I could implicitly depend on Foch's good faith'. Meanwhile Haig and Foch had more significant matters to discuss.

On the day that Wilson was penning his wry letter Haig received another visit from Foch. The latter was deeply concerned at the manpower shortage in the British Army; he had heard that there were '1,400,000 men wearing khaki in England', and, as a Frenchman, could not help contrasting this position with that of his own exhausted country. He was determined to have the matter taken up at the highest level, between the two Governments; Haig, naturally, was not averse to this.

The discussion on manpower concluded, Haig tells us: 'Foch also explained to me an offensive project which he wishes me to carry out if the enemy does not launch his big attack within the next few weeks. I agreed with his general plan, and said I would study my share of the undertaking, and let him know. But he must not write his plan nor allow the French commanders to talk about it. Success will depend mainly on secrecy. Foch stayed to lunch. He was most pleasant and anxious to be helpful.' This was a crucial conversation; it marked a definite turning point in the War, for, from this day onwards, Haig had a clear and precise offensive aim. Foch himself, the originator of it, under the stress of circumstances, changed his ideas; the end product was certainly not what he had envisaged – it was modified by the facts of war in much the same way as the original concept of the Battle of the Somme in 1916 had been modified in the event. But Haig never lost sight of the possibilities, and, amid all his other preoccupations, clung to the guiding thread which he and Foch had spun together. He wasted no time; on the following day, May 17th, he and Lawrence visited Rawlinson: 'I told R. to begin studying in conjunction with General Debeney[1] the question of an attack eastwards from Villers Bretonneux in combination with an attack from the French front south of Roye. I gave him details of the scheme.'

This was the beginning of the Battle of Amiens, the beginning of Germany's downfall.

Before this downfall was accomplished, however, there were new crises to be faced; they did not all work out to Haig's disadvantage, although they created new strains upon him and upon his army. On May 27th, in spite of clear warning both from the British and American General Headquarters, the French were caught completely by surprise by the German diversionary attack on the Aisne. The first object of this attack was to draw away French reserves from the British front, so that a *coup de grâce* could be delivered at the British Army. Bad Staff work by the French, and, equally important, bad tactics by the local Army Commander, General Duchesne, resulted in the Germans being able to make the longest advances carried out by any army in the West since the beginning of trench warfare. The heaviest stroke, by cruel luck, fell upon the British IX Corps, four weak divisions which were supposed to be resting after their exertions in the earlier battles. The main reason for the disaster was the flat refusal of Duchesne to apply the principles of defence in depth laid down by Pétain. There would seem to have been as grave a misunderstanding between G.Q.G. and 6th Army H.Q. as there had been between Haig and Gough in March, but with much less reason; Gough, at least, knew what was coming, and did his best; Duchesne knew nothing, and what he did was actively pernicious. The effect of the German opening

---

1. Commanding the First French Army, on Rawlinson's right.

success was prodigious: on the 29th they entered Soissons; on the 31st they reached the Marne. Ludendorff was dazzled by his own achievement; once again, his fatal opportunism took charge of his senses – he was tempted to try another throw. Foch, planning his own offensives, based on the French Army, was thrown into confusion, though he did not lose heart. Haig was glad of the temporary relief from threat to his own front; each day was valuable for the refitting of his army. There was relief also, though this did not affect him, from some of the sniping at home, now that it was seen that, even with the blessing of a Generalissimo, the French Army was no more immune from hammerings than the British.

As the German attacks against the French continued, with successes which, though never quite so spectacular as that of May 27th, remained disturbing, three conflicting needs tugged at Haig together. First, evidently, there was the question of supporting his Allies in their emergency, as he had desired them to support him. But, secondly, there was the factor of the presence of large German reserves opposite his own Army; 39 fresh divisions on May 29th, 35 on May 31st, 32 on June 3rd – a declining force, but still very formidable. Finally, there was his own offensive plan. The one hopeful feature of the situation for the Allies was the rapid growth of the American forces in France. On May 1st there were 7 American divisions (double strength) on the Western Front, of which 4 were fit for action; during the month 8 new (untrained) divisions arrived, over 200,000 men. The flow expanded, thanks to a great British shipping effort and the defeat of the submarine campaign, to 250,000 in June and the same in July. It was the fixed determination both of the United States Government and of the commander of the American Expeditionary Force, to unite these divisions in a great national army; this desire was perfectly intelligible, though in the over-heated atmosphere of 1918 it sometimes appeared obstructive to the hard-pressed Allies. Thus, on May 1st, Haig remarked that he thought 'Pershing was very obstinate, and stupid. He did not seem to realize the urgency of the situation. . . . He hankers after a *"great self-contained American Army"* but seeing that he has neither Commanders of Divisions, of Corps, nor of Armies, nor Staffs for same, it is ridiculous to think such an Army could function unaided in less than two years' time'.

Meanwhile, however, what the British forces could do to assist the Americans, they would; on May 7th Haig discussed the training of four American Divisions in the British sector with his Director of Training, General Bonham Carter: 'I impressed on Bonham Carter that our Officers are not to command, and order the Americans about, but must only *help* American Officers by their advice and experience to become both *leaders* in the field, as well as *instructors*. For the moment, *training as leaders* should take the first place.' He had no doubts about the potential fighting quality of the American soldiers; at a meeting of the Supreme War Council at Versailles on June 1st, 'The French suddenly asked Lloyd George ... to agree to send all American troops now with British to hold extended sectors in French area and relieve French Divisions for battle. I said that it would be very wrong to employ these new troops in the way proposed by the French, because, being on so wide a front, the companies would never get a chance of getting together and training. I hoped to quicken up the training of the Americans, and to render four Divisions fit for the line by the middle of June. ... In view of the doubtful condition of many French Divisions I thought it a waste of good troops to relieve the French Divisions by Americans.'

Three days later, Foch stepped up his demands. In addition to the Americans, he now asked for three British Divisions to be placed astride the Somme immediately, while Haig should prepare to transport *all* his reserves to threatened points if necessary. The reserves of the French forces on the British front had already gone, and Haig warned Plumer to prepare for the departure of their whole contingent. His reaction to Foch's request was one of apprehension: 'I replied that I am complying with his order at once, but I wished to make a formal protest against any troops leaving my Command until the Reserves of Prince Rupprecht's Armies had become involved in the Battle.' This protest was addressed to Foch, copies of the correspondence going to the War Office. In London these produced great anxiety. On June 7th Lord Milner[1] and Wilson went to Paris to thrash the matter out with Haig, Foch and Clemenceau. What followed was, in effect, the last serious argument about the working of the Supreme Commander system until the very eve of the Armistice. Haig's diary entry, an unusually full one, thus needs to be given in full:

'Lord Milner explained why the British P.M. had asked for this meeting; briefly, Foch had moved many reserves (French and American Divisions) from behind the British Front, and, in view of the large number of enemy reserves still available for action against the British, the Government had become genuinely anxious.

'I then read my memo stating I was in full accord with Foch as to the necessity for making all *preparations* for moving British troops to support the French in case of necessity. But I asked that I should be consulted before a definite order to move any Divisions from the British area were given. I had repeated to London the telegram which I had sent to Foch, in order to warn the British Government that the situation was quickly reaching a stage in

1. Milner had now replaced Derby as Secretary of State for War; 'his one idea seems to be as helpful as possible', commented Haig.

which circumstances might compel me to appeal to them (the British Cabinet) under the Beauvais Agreement. In my opinion, the order about to be issued by Foch imperilled the British Army in France. I hoped that everything that forethought could do would be done now and in the immediate future to prevent circumstances arising which would necessitate such an appeal. Foch stuck out for full powers as Generalissimo to order troops of any nationality wherever he thought fit and at shortest notice. Milner and Clemenceau agreed that he must have these powers, and the latter urged Foch and myself to meet more frequently. C. strongly forbade any orders being sent direct from French H.Q.[1] moving French or any units in my area, without passing through my hands first of all. This was with reference to the departure of certain French Divisions and guns from D.A.N.[2] which had been ordered direct, without even notifying General Plumer or G.H.Q. on the subject.

'The effect of the Beauvais Agreement is now becoming clear in practice. This effect I had realized from the beginning, namely, that the responsibility for the safety of the British Army in France could no longer rest with me because the "Generalissimo" can do what *he* thinks right with *my* troops. On the other hand, the British Government is only now beginning to understand what Foch's powers as Generalissimo amount to. This delegation of power to Foch is inevitable, but I intend to ask that the British Government should in a document modify my responsibility for the safety of the British Army under these altered conditions.

'The C.I.G.S. asked Foch if he still adhered to the same strategical policy as he had enunciated at Abbeville on May 2nd. F. replied that he did, namely, first to secure the connection of the British and French Armies, second, to cover both Paris and the Channel Ports. And in reply to F. I said I agreed with these principles.'

This episode in no way diminished the understanding between Foch and Haig; rather it cleared the air, as both of them returned to their own pre-occupations – Haig to keep a close eye on the growing evidence of a new German attack in preparation on the Arras front, and on Rupprecht's reserves, Foch to the series of great battles which were fought out on the French front during June and July. The first German blow was halted by June 2nd, but two days after the Paris meeting Ludendorff struck again. By June 11th this attack also had been brought to a halt, the Americans taking their first large part in battle at Belleau Wood. Inexperience cost them heavily; youth and enthusiasm, however, carried them forward. It was a good omen for the

1. He means Foch's H.Q.
2. *Détachment de l'Armèe du Nord*, the French group in Flanders.

future. A surprise attack by the French 10th Army, under the aggressive General Mangin, now re-emerging from semi-disgrace for his part in the Nivelle fiasco, was also an omen; it showed that there was life yet in the French Army, despite Haig's misgivings. The last phase of the great German offensives began on July 15th, and though Haig's forces had meanwhile been active, it will be as well to pass straight to this episode, to complete the story of his relations with Foch during the period of the French Army's tribulation.

This time the French were not taken by surprise; and this time local commanders did not flout the principles of defence in depth. The German assault was made in great strength, and was designed to be the final stroke at the French before turning to finish off the British Army. In some sectors it gained ground, but the main part of it fell upon air; the French, particularly Gouraud's Army, had prepared a trap for their enemies as effective as that into which they themselves had stumbled in April, 1917. The Germans were quickly stopped. Three days later the indefatigable Mangin flung his troops, supported by Americans, British and some 350 Renault tanks, upon the flank of the great German bulge towards Paris. Taken by surprise as the French had been in May, the Germans sustained a most serious defeat; they lost some 100,000 men, of whom 35,000 were prisoners, and 650 guns. This was the swing of the pendulum; the initiative seized by Mangin (against Pétain's convictions, but with Foch's blessing) remained in Allied hands. Ludendorff was actually in the process of discussing with Rupprecht the details of the offensive on the Lys which Haig had been expecting daily, when he learned of what had happened in Champagne. Rupprecht's attack was postponed; before it could materialize, Haig had launched his own offensive, and from that moment until the end there was no question of anything but defence for the Germans.

Baldly narrated like this, the sequence of events sounds simple, the action easy. It was no such thing. Robustly optimistic as he always was, Foch could no more exactly read the future than another man. While he awaited the last German blow he was acutely conscious of its dangers; as a precautionary measure he ordered four British divisions with a Corps Headquarters to move to Champagne. Haig was on leave in London when the order arrived; it was Lawrence who had to deal with this serious matter first. The manner in which he did so is indicative of his judgement. British G.H.Q. did not believe strongly in the likelihood of a German attack in Champagne; all the signs pointed to one against some part of the British line; Lawrence, therefore, while not disobeying the Generalissimo's order, tempered it, until Haig's return on July 14th. He sent one division off at once, with another to follow, holding back the other two for Haig's decision. It was no mean responsibility for a Chief of Staff to order away two divisions from the Army's slender reserves at such a time; Lawrence accepted it unhesitatingly. When Haig arrived, he approved Lawrence's action and then found that Foch was not only asking for the original four divisions, but for four more besides – 'And all this when there is nothing definite to show that the enemy means to attack in Champagne. Indeed, Prince Rupprecht still retains twenty-five divisions in reserve on the British front.'

Haig, as was now customary, arranged to meet Foch at once to discuss the matter. Before he could do so, however, at 12.35 a.m. on July 15th, he received a telephone message from Wilson: 'War Cabinet has discussed Foch's orders for moving British Reserves to east of France. They feel anxiety that Rupprecht has large reserves left and will attack the British front, and it is directed "that if you consider the British Army is endangered or if you think that General Foch *is not acting solely on military considerations*,[1] they (the War Cabinet) rely on the exercise of your judgment, under the Beauvais Agreement, as to the security of the British front after the removal of these troops. . . ." I note that the Government now tells me "to use my judgment" in obeying *orders* given me by "the Generalissimo of the Allied Armies". On June 7th at the Conference in Paris . . . I was directed to obey all his orders at once, and notify War Cabinet if I took exception to any of them. . . . This is a case of "heads you win and tails I lose". If things go well, the Government take credit to themselves and the Generalissimo; if badly, the Field-Marshal will be blamed!'

By the time Haig met Foch, the Germans had declared their hand; the French were being attacked on a front totalling some fifty-five miles. For once British Intelligence had been at fault – its attention fixed too closely on Rupprecht. This, of course, altered the whole position for Haig. He found Foch 'in the best of spirits. . . . I put my case strongly to Foch why I was averse to moving my reserves from my front until I knew that Rupprecht's reserves had been moved to the new battle front. I mentioned 88 additional heavy batteries had come against the British front . . . in June. Prisoners and deserters stated that an attack on the Lys salient was to be ready mounted by the 18th inst., while the front from La Bassée Canal to the Somme was ready to receive troops. . . . All these facts and many others pointed to the intention of the enemy to attack the British front at some time soon. Foch agreed with me but said his first object was to hold up the present attack at all costs as soon as possible. He only wanted my Divisions as a reserve in case of necessity, and they would be in a position *ready to return to me at once* in case the British front was threatened. Under these circumstances, I agreed to send the next two Divisions as arranged'.

1. Author's italics.

It was a grave responsibility for Haig to assume, not lightened by know-ledge of Lloyd George's latent hostility. Neither Haig nor Foch could forecast Mangin's great success only three days later; but for that victory, the Germans would indeed have struck on the Lys almost immediately. Haig would then certainly have been accused of jeopardizing his Army, and if there had been another disaster it is hard to believe that he would have survived it. The greatness of generals is seen at moments like this, as much as in actual battles. The weakness of politicians, also revealed, requires no commentary.

12

The Year of Victory – II

IN THE crisis of the Empire in March and April, when Gough's Army was reeling back in defeat, and Haig was searching for troops to bolster the crumbling front, loyalty impelled the Australian Government to give up, once again, its dream of a united Australian Army Corps; piecemeal, the five Australian divisions were drawn into the defensive battle; their presence was immediately felt. As the Somme sector simmered down, all through April, May and June, a flow of reports came in from there, striking a note of cheerful discord with the general gloom. On April 25th there was Villers Bretonneux; on May 9th, Haig noted that Monash's 3rd Division had 'During the last three days . . . advanced their front about a mile, and gained the observation over the slopes to the east. The ground gained was twice as much as they had taken at Messines last June, and they had done it with very small losses; some 15 killed and 80 wounded; and they had taken nearly 300 prisoners. . . .' On May 19th, at a cost of some 40 casualties, the Australians took over 400 prisoners. On June 11th they advanced 1,000 yards near Morlancourt, with 300 prisoners. By now they had their own Australian-born Corps commander, Monash, and were only awaiting the arrival of their 1st Division from Flanders to be united at last. In their own sardonic fashion, they described their tactic as 'peaceful penetration'; whatever the name for it, it had two most important effects: it kept the Somme front fluid, and it denied the Germans the moral ascendancy here to which their victories should have entitled them. Well might Haig remark, after an inspection in May: 'The Australian is a different individual now to when he first came, both in discipline and smartness. Altogether it was a most inspiring sight.' When a disturbance broke out at Etaples Base Camp, following the arrest of two Australians for gambling, Haig told the officer in charge to 'look leniently' on the matter, adding in his Diary: 'We must help the men to amuse themselves, and card playing is not really hurtful as long as the stakes

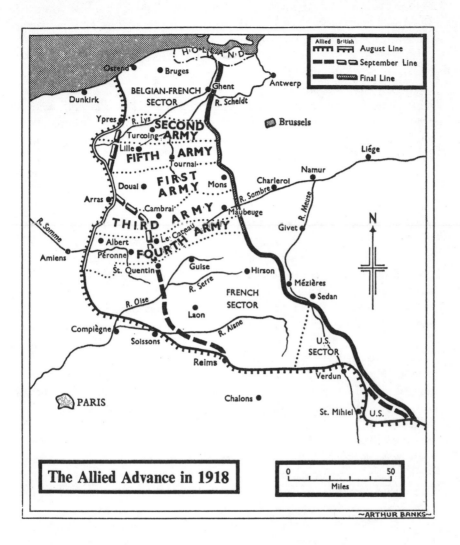

The Allied Advance in 1918

Allied / British:
- August Line
- September Line
- Final Line

HOLLAND

Ostend • Bruges
Dunkirk
Ghent
BELGIAN-FRENCH SECTOR
Antwerp
R. Scheldt
Ypres • R. Lys
Turcoing
SECOND ARMY
Lille
FIFTH ARMY
Brussels
Liége
Tournai
FIRST ARMY
Douai • Mons
Namur
Charleroi
R. Sambre
Arras • Cambrai
THIRD ARMY
Maubeuge
Givet
R. Meuse
Le Cateau
FOURTH ARMY
Albert
Péronne
R. Somme
Amiens
St. Quentin
Guise • Hirson
Mézières
R. Serre
Sedan
FRENCH SECTOR
R. Oise
Laon
Compiègne
Soissons
R. Aisne
U.S. SECTOR
Reims
Verdun
PARIS
Chalons •
St. Mihiel • U.S.

N

0   50
Miles

~ARTHUR BANKS~

are kept within limits. The men too are well able to take care of themselves in these matters.' The Germans could confirm that they were able to take care of themselves in other matters too; for the Australians were now veterans, the spearhead of the British Army in 1918.

All this Australian activity promised well for the great stroke which Haig had instructed Rawlinson to prepare. Towards the end of June, profiting by the enemy's preoccupation with the French, Rawlinson proposed a somewhat more ambitious operation – penetration of a less 'peaceful' kind – preparatory to the main blow. Haig approved of the Army Commander's plan 'to improve his front south of the Somme, and take advantage of the low moral of the German divisions now opposite the Australians. But I told C.G.S. to arrange for some American troops to take part; to have an adequate reserve of Tanks; and 1 cavalry division at hand in case enemy is caught unawares and some of his units bolt.' On these lines the project matured; the detailed planning was entrusted to General Monash, who Haig visited on July 1st: 'I spent about an hour with M. and went into every detail with him . . . M. is a most thorough and capable Commander who thinks out every detail of any operation and leaves nothing to chance. I was greatly impressed with his arrangements.'

Lieutenant-General Sir John Monash was a phenomenon: a Jew, a civil engineer by profession, a 'Saturday-afternoon soldier', he brought to the profession of arms an efficiency that was only rarely matched by Regulars. War, above all, was serious to him. One of his Staff officers has told this author: 'He treated war as a business. I don't believe he thought about anything during the War except winning the War.' He lacked the affability that long regimental experience confers on the good Regular officer in his relations with other ranks; he lacked the sociability that Mess life stimulates; he was not a 'front-line' soldier. He made up for this in brain-power, organization, and relentlessness of purpose. In that war, of which the martyred infantryman has become the symbol, Monash's views on the role of infantry contain the core of his thinking, the deepest reason for his success, and for the total confidence that his men placed in him. 'I had formed the theory', he wrote, 'that the true role of the infantry was not to expend itself upon heroic physical effort, not to wither away under merciless machine-gun fire, nor to impale itself on hostile bayonets, nor to tear itself to pieces in hostile entanglements . . . but on the contrary, to advance under the maximum possible protection of the maximum possible array of mechanical resources, in the form of guns, machine-guns, tanks, mortars, and aeroplanes; to advance with as little impediment as possible; to be relieved as far as possible of the obligation to *fight* their way forward; to march resolutely, regardless of the din and tumult of battle, to the appointed goal, and there to hold and defend the territory gained; and to gather, in the form of prisoners, guns and stores, the fruits of victory'.

The first indication of what this unusual theory could mean in practice was shortly seen; the action took place around the village of Le Hamel, near Villers Bretonneux, on July 4th – Independence Day – just a fortnight before the French counter-stroke at Villers Cotterets. In essence, it was a 'tidying-up operation', designed to clear the enemy out of an awkward salient and to win further observation to the east while denying a valuable view into the British back areas to the Germans. The troops concerned were some ten battalions of the 4th Australian Division, with sixty of the new Mark V tanks and four supply tanks. Eight companies of American infantry from the 131st and 132nd Regiments of the 33rd U.S. (National Guard) Division were also to make their first offensive appearance on the British front. There was strong artillery support but *no preliminary* preparation by the guns. This was not a complete novelty but still enough of a rarity; there were, however, other innovations even more important. The Tanks were carefully trained beforehand in co-operation with the Australian infantry, who, ever since Bullecourt, had been sceptical of their value. Now each infantry company learned to know its supporting tanks individually. Monash believed that the tanks could go forward beside the infantry immediately behind the barrage. There were many who doubted, pointing out the risk of the lofty tank-frames being hit by their own artillery. But the thing was tried and proved entirely successful. The four carrier tanks took forward loads equal to those of a bearer party 1,250 strong. Aircraft distributed 100,000 rounds of ammunition to the machine-gunners as they occupied their new positions – the first use of an air-lift of supplies on a field of battle. Surprise was cultivated throughout.

More important than all this, however, was the significance that Monash attached to his battle-plan. 'A perfected modern battle plan', he wrote, 'is like nothing so much as a score for an orchestral composition, where the various arms and units are the instruments, and the tasks they perform are their respective musical phrases. Every individual unit must make its entry precisely at the proper moment, and play its phrase in the general harmony.' This was no figure of speech; Monash meant exactly what he said. He now introduced the command system that was to become standard in the Australian Corps for the rest of the War, and an accepted 'drill' in World War II: 'Although complete written orders were invariably prepared and issued . . . very great importance was attached to the holding of conferences, at which were assembled every one of the senior commanders and heads of departments concerned in the impending operation. At these I personally explained every detail of the plan, and assured myself that all present applied an identical interpretation . . . the battle plan having been thus crystallized, no subsequent alterations were permissible, under any circumstances, no matter how tempting.'[1]

We have seen what importance he attached to this last point. On this occasion his conviction was not long in being put to the test. General Pershing had been uneasy all along about the American participation in the action; he had soon reduced it from eight to four companies. Each platoon of these four companies, however, had a special function in Monash's plan. It may be imagined with what dismay, at the last moment, he learned that Pershing wanted to pull the Americans out altogether. 'I well knew that . . . the withdrawal of those Americans would result in untold confusion . . . so I resolved to take a firm stand and press my views as strongly as I dared; for even a corps commander must use circumspection when presuming to argue with an Army commander.' Circumspect or not, Monash in effect told Rawlinson: 'No Americans, no battle.' Rawlinson agreed to leave the Americans in, and Haig readily assented when the case was put to him, taking on himself the responsibility of answering for them to Pershing. Monash comments: 'It appeared to me at the time that great issues had hung for an hour or so upon the chance of my being able to carry my point.'

What followed was a portent. 'No battle within my previous experience,' wrote Monash, 'passed off so smoothly, so exactly to timetable, or was so free from any kind of hitch. It was all over in 93 minutes.' The Australians lost 51 officers and 724 other ranks, the Americans 6 officers and 128 enlisted men, the Tanks had 3 machines damaged and 13 men wounded; 41 German officers, 1,431 other ranks, 2 field guns, 26 trench mortars and 171 machine guns were captured, besides their other losses. It was a clear sign; above all it vindicated and established this method of making war, whose novelty may seem questionable to later generations, but which, in 1918, was a revolution. Monash's plan was published as a Staff brochure by G.H.Q., and his method was adopted for the whole Fourth Army in the larger attack that was soon to come. It was on this that Haig's mind was now fixed. He was delighted with the results of Le Hamel, but determined that nothing should prejudice the main event. Rawlinson, he records, on July 5th 'wished me to approve of him making another attack south of the Somme to advance his line still further. I did not approve of his proposal, because it would result (if successful) in extending our line at a time when reserves are very small.'

For the rest of the month, the great question for Haig was the equation between the potential threat of Rupprecht's reserves, especially in the Lys area, and his own desire to resume the offensive which, Le Hamel had demonstrated, might have sensational results. On July 16th, the second day

1. See p. 347.

of the last German attack upon the French, when he had already agreed to
'lend' his reserves to Foch, he ordered Byng and Horne to prepare offensive
schemes; reporting this to Rawlinson later that day, Haig told him that 'The
preparations for these attacks, I hoped, would distract the attention of the
enemy from the *main operation* on my front, which would be carried out by
his (the Fourth) Army'. On this day, too, he added the last touch to the basic
preparations for Rawlinson's stroke: 'As soon as my XXII Corps[1] . . . is
returned to me, and Rupprecht's reserves (now 20–23 divisions) have become
engaged, I intend to send the four Canadian divisions to Rawlinson. . . .'
Eyeing Rupprecht all the time, Haig pushed forward his own plans. From his
diary one feels the rebirth of his confidence in victory at about this time; he
and Wilson agreed 'that our present position is much more satisfactory than
it was in March before the first great German attack'. Haig sensed now what
his Intelligence Department had predicted in January – the ruin that would
surely follow the failure of Ludendorff's huge gamble. On July 20th he
permitted himself the first game of golf that he had played in France since the
very beginning of the War; on the links at Le Touquet, during the next few
days, he recouped his energy after the stresses of the spring, for the stern bout
that lay ahead.

By the 22nd, with the encouragement of Mangin's splendid enterprise,
Haig noted: 'The general indication is that *an attack will be made*,[2] but in view
of the Crown Prince being in command on the Marne, I do not think the
Military Authorities in Germany can allow him to fail. So I expect that
reserves will be sent to him from Rupprecht's Army.' The next day his
thinking advanced a further stage: 'As we are fairly well prepared to meet an
attack by Rupprecht upon my Second Army, it is most likely that the attack
won't be delivered. So I am prepared to take the offensive and have approved
of an operation taking place on Rawlinson's front, and steps have been taken
to make preparation very secretly in order to be ready, should the battle now
being fought out on the Marne cause the situation to turn in our favour.'
Visiting Foch on the day after this, Haig informed him of what was afoot:
'We agreed to proceed with the operations east of Amiens as soon as possible.
Rawlinson and Debeney are meeting today, if necessary, to co-ordinate their
plans.'

From this moment the preliminaries of the second decisive battle of
the War gathered their own momentum; on the 27th there was information
at last of troop-train movements southwards from Rupprecht's area, and
these continued;[3] on the 28th Foch placed Debeney's 1st French Army

1. Sent to the French area.
2. In Flanders.
3. It was no large transfer, but enough for Haig.

directly under Haig's orders; at the same time he asked for operations to be 'hurried on'; on the 29th there was welcome news of reductions in German battalion strengths, indicating the severe losses sustained in their unsuccessful offensives; on that day, Haig met all his Army Commanders. There were two meetings, Rawlinson being absent from the first, fully occupied with his own affairs. At this meeting, Haig 'explained the policy and future plans of the Generalissimo. He intends to keep the initiative, and feels that we Allies have "turned the corner".' He drew attention to the need for tactical unity in the Army – the lack of which had done so much to mar Cambrai. He added: 'Army commanders must do their utmost to get troops out of the influence of trench methods. We are all agreed on the need for the training of battalion commanders, who in their turn must train their company and platoon commanders. This is really a platoon commander's war.' That after-noon Rawlinson told him that all was in order to advance the date of the attack two days, as Haig had asked; 'All his arrangements were being pushed forward satisfactorily'. There remained Debeney; on the 30th Haig wrote 'to tell him that I would not call at his Hqrs. until operations had started, in order not to excite suspicion by appearing there'. In any case Rawlinson and Debeney were acting in close unison. There were now clear indications that the Germans had given up all immediate thought of an attack in Flanders, which lifted a weight from Haig's mind; on August 3rd, Foch told him that he believed that 'the Germans are breaking up'.

By August 5th, preparations were practically complete. Haig had studied Rawlinson's plan, and pointed out certain weaknesses in it at a conference with him, Debeney and Kavanagh, commanding the Cavalry Corps: 'I thought that the Fourth Army orders aimed too much at getting a *final* objective on the old Amiens defence line, and stopping counter-attacks on it. This is not far enough, in my opinion, if we succeed at the start in surprising the enemy. So I told Rawlinson (it had already been in my orders) to arrange to *advance as rapidly as possible* and capture the old Amiens line of defence . . . and to put it into a state of defence; *but not to delay*; at once reserves must be pushed on to capture the line Chaulnes-Roye. The general direction of the advance is to be on Ham . . . I said that the cavalry must keep in touch with the battle and *be prepared to pass through anywhere between the river Somme and the Roye-Amiens road*. Also that a cavalry brigade with a battery R.H.A. and some whippet tanks are to be placed under General Monash's orders . . . for pursuit and to reap the fruits if we succeed. . . .' So for the second time we find Haig urging Rawlinson to greater boldness before a great battle on the Somme; in the conditions of 1916 Rawlinson's more deliberate methods were apter; now it was Haig's turn to be right. The difference was that, whereas in 1916 the Germans were holding a carefully prepared defensive position, in

1918 they were aligned along a fluid offensive front; also, the Allies now possessed weapons which did not exist in 1918, while the British Army had become adept in the art of war by bitter experience.

Superficially, Rawlinson appeared to be much weaker than he had been in 1916; he disposed of only three Army Corps (15 divisions) and the Cavalry Corps. His artillery amounted to 2,070 guns and howitzers, one field piece to every 29 yards of front, one heavy to every 59 yards. At the peak of the Passchendaele fighting the density of artillery had been as much as one piece per 5.2 yards. But it was not on artillery, nor on infantry masses, that either Haig or Rawlinson depended to win this battle; it was the weapon of surprise – the tank. The Fourth Army had under command no less than 534 tanks (compared with 476 at Cambrai), consisting of 342 of the new and excellent Mark Vs, 72 light, faster whippets, and 120 supply tanks. Just under 800 air- craft completed the formidable mechanical array at Rawlinson's disposal.

Important as this material strength was, it was completely overshadowed by the devotion to surprise which permeated every part of the Fourth Army plan. There had been huge material endeavours before and they had often come to nothing; surprise had been much neglected, despite all Haig's efforts, yet it had always produced results. Now it was to be everything. The Fourth Army Staff were meticulous over details: secrecy was dinned into all ranks; deception was practised in every possible way. Tremendous care was taken with the registration of new batteries; all forward movement of troops or vehicles after August 1st was done by night; aeroplanes flew over the whole area to report on anything that looked suspicious. But the prodigies of secret preparation were the introduction into the area of two large formations, the presence of either of which would, if perceived, have given the game away completely – the Cavalry Corps and the Canadian Corps. With the Cavalry, coming out of reserve, the problem was entirely one of conceal- ment – difficult enough, with their long horse-lines and large forage dumps, in the empty uplands of the Somme; with the Canadians, already identified by the enemy on the front of the First Army, deception on the grand scale was required.

The performance that followed is reminiscent of the preliminaries of Alamein and the D-Day ruses. It was worked out by the Staff of the Fourth Army, and it is not difficult to detect the hand of their wily commander. At Rawlinson's request, two Canadian battalions, with two casualty clearing- stations and the wireless section, were transferred from First Army to Second Army and put into the line opposite Kemmel Hill. This was an excellent feint, for the Canadians had not so far been engaged in any of the heavy fighting of the year; what was more likely than for the Germans to believe that this first-rate unit would be used to retake the key position of the northern front? The Canadians were soon identified there and this evidence, in conjunction with greatly increased air and wireless activity in the First and Second Army zones, completely deceived the enemy. It was almost a week before they realized they they had 'lost' the Canadians, and by then the battle was about to open. General Currie, their commander, told Haig that 'it had been a hustle to be ready in time', but the Canadians were great 'hustlers', and, as Haig noted, they were 'very keen to do something'. To cover their arrival in the Fourth Army area, 100,000 strong, a further ruse was adopted, again double-edged. It was decided to keep the Canadians out of the line until the very eve of the attack, in order not to risk identification. The sector they were to occupy ran some 7,000 yards south of Villers Bretonneux, in the area of the French 1st Army. This portion of the front was now taken over by the Australians (who by now had almost proprietary rights to the whole Somme battlefield) – a manoeuvre which suggested the exact opposite of what was intended. It could only have been construed by the Germans as a freeing of French troops for offensive action, and an anticipation of quiescence by the Australians. Not that these aggressive soldiers were ever particularly quiescent. In order for them to take over this new sector and hold it up to the last moment, their own left flank near Morlancourt was relieved on July 30th by the British III Corps. On their last night at Morlancourt the Australians carried out one more act of 'peaceful penetration' – a raid which netted 3 officers, 135 other ranks, 36 machine guns and 2 trench mortars. The Australians came away well pleased with themselves, but they had stirred up much mischief.

As though to demonstrate once more the chanciness of war, even with the most careful planning, the most original thinking, the completest attention to surprise, August 6th brought an ugly shock. It was on this day that Haig settled that the big attack should go in on the 8th, but it was on this day, too, that the Germans reacted to the Australian frolic of a week before. They fell upon III Corps with a powerful assault division of Württembergers, specially brought in for the purpose. The 58th and 18th Divisions were caught in the middle of a relief and driven back 800 yards with a loss of 200 prisoners and many other casualties. Most British line divisions were by now neither morally nor materially the equal of the Dominion divisions. Both the 58th and the 18th had been severely handled in the great retreat; their battalions were weak, and contained many young soldiers. There was no lack of bravery, but skill and spirit were often wanting among these conscripts. This truth was to be vividly demonstrated by force of contrast during the next few days. Meanwhile, the weakest element of the Fourth Army – III Corps – was faced with the hardest task. Haig noted: 'General Butler has now been told that, so far as his corps is concerned, the battle has begun, and he must carry out his orders as best he can, so as to cover the left of the Australian Corps when they advance on the 8th.' In other words, instead of resting on the eve of battle, III Corps had to spend its energy on recovering lost ground and then pass straight into the main offensive.

The real question, however, was whether this German blow had been truly a local counter-manoeuvre, or whether it indicated a larger awareness of what was coming. The anxious Staffs concluded with relief that this was not the case, though Haig realized that 'we must expect hard fighting on that sector of the front'. Zero hour was fixed for the British at 4.20 a.m. on the 8th – just before first light; for the French, forty-five minutes later, since they would not have the benefit of tanks, and required a short preparatory barrage. Haig moved his Advanced Headquarters into a special train, for mobility in the campaign which he now envisaged. 'I have 9 officers living in my train. The General Staff occupy a second one accommodating 8 more. Thus the whole is very long, half a mile about! and all say they are very comfortable.' This equivalent of Field-Marshal Montgomery's famous caravan was to be his abode for almost the whole remainder of the War. If he felt anxious, on the eve of battle, he also felt a new confidence; to the King, who visited him on August 7th, he 'expressed the belief that the British front would be much further forward before winter arrived'. As he went to bed he noted: 'Evening reports state all is normal.' The Germans, indeed, were unsuspecting. They were digesting Ludendorff's latest Order of the Day, dated August 4th, and opening with these words: 'I am under the impression that, in many quarters, the possibility of an enemy offensive is viewed with a certain degree of apprehension. There is nothing to justify this apprehension provided our troops are vigilant and do their duty ... we should wish for nothing better than to see the enemy launch an offensive, which can but hasten the disintegration of his forces. ... ' Shortly afterwards he drew up a more anxious paper, dwelling on the necessity for defence in depth to guard against surprise, but by the time it arrived the soldiers it was meant to instruct were mostly on their way to the Fourth Army's prisoner-of-war cages.

August 8th, like March 21st, opened with dense mist in the Somme valley. On some parts of the front the maximum visibility was no more than ten feet. When the mist cleared a day of brilliant sunshine followed. At last the weather, which had so fatally betrayed the British Army a year before, had changed sides. The rolling barrage came down with crackling precision, and the long lines of tanks and infantry swept forward through the misty half-light, Canadians on the right, Australians in the centre, III Corps on the left. Not until the mist cleared could they actually see the effect they were producing, but they began to have the 'feel' of it straight away. Except on one sector, there were no checks, no untoward halts. The forward movement, necessarily slow in the mist, continued steadily; the supports, coming up behind, never collided with the front divisions, but passed through them dead on time and without a hitch. By seven o'clock the Australians were all on their first objective; by half-past ten on their second; by eleven o'clock the Canadians were up alongside. As the mist cleared and the sun burst through at about this time, a remarkable sight was seen in the wide spaces of the centre of the field: '. . . the whole Santerre plateau seen from the air was dotted with parties of infantry, field artillery, and tanks moving forward. Staff officers were galloping about, many riding horses in battle for the first time. . . . Indeed, at this stage there was more noise of movement than of firing, as the heavy batteries . . . were no longer in action; for the infantry had gone so far that it was no longer possible for them to shoot. . . . No enemy guns seemed to be firing and no co-ordinated defence was apparent. . . .'[1] By 1.30 p.m. the main fighting was over. The Australians had occupied all their objectives, except on their extreme flanks, where their neighbours were behind them; the Canadians had advanced almost eight miles.

It had been a sensational day, but not devoid of hazards. By common consent the tanks had done marvels. Against German infantry and machine guns they had proved irresistible, and countless infantry lives had been saved by their action. The German artillery, on the other hand, had not suffered the loss of morale that the year's high casualties had brought about in the infantry. They stuck to their guns, often shooting the tanks at point-blank range. Ten tanks of the 1st Battalion attacked Le Quesnel in the Canadian sector; nine were set on fire by direct hits from field guns at 70 yards. A line of twelve tanks, topping the crest of a rise that marked their starting line with the 5th Australian Division, had six knocked out immediately by field guns at a range of half a mile, another immediately afterwards, and three more shortly after that. Collaboration between the whippets and the cavalry, of which much had been expected, proved an illusion. Wherever German machine guns remained undestroyed, the cavalry were held up; once again, some of its most effective interventions of the day were done dismounted, a sad disappointment to many. On the other hand, the whippets themselves were most successful, outflanking batteries, supporting patrols, mopping up, and many of them experiencing adventures similar to, though it would scarcely be possible to equal, those of the legendary tank 'Musical Box'. The armoured cars of the 17th Battalion, once the long, straight Roman road which bisects the battlefield was cleared, plunged into the German back areas, shooting up infantry and transport, and capturing a Corps staff.

In the centre victory was complete. The Canadians captured 114 officers,

1. Official History.

4,919 other ranks, 161 guns, and uncounted hundreds of machine guns and mortars; their losses were about 3,500. The Australians captured 183 officers, 7,742 other ranks, 173 guns, and hundreds of smaller trophies. Their losses were under 3,000. Only on the flanks was there any setback. III Corps had spent a bad night against an alert enemy. Gas-shelling had inflicted many casualties; surprise was out of the question; the Germans were as strong as the attackers; the ground, steep and well-wooded, was much more difficult than the smooth terrain of the centre. The main objective of the Corps was the Chipilly spur, thrusting its high promontory into a wide southward bend of the Somme, overlooking and constricting the left of the Australian advance. III Corps was not able to progress beyond its first objective here, with the result that the Australians were caught in enfilade by machine guns and field artillery sited on the spur. They suffered their most serious casualties and only failure at this point. When every allowance is made for the special conditions which applied to the III Corps front, there remains a contrast between the performance of the British divisions and that of the Dominion troops so marked that a further explanation has to be sought. The Official Historian makes this comment: '. . . there was not only a shortage of experienced officers and non-commissioned officers, but the ranks of the infantry units had been filled up with young recruits from home. These convalescent divisions had not entered with great enthusiasm on the hard task of preparing a field of battle . . . the willing co-operation usually exhibited before an attack was absent.' After four years of war, the British Army was showing signs of war-weariness which did not so much affect the soldiers of the younger nations who had spent less time on the Western Front.

Nor was this feeling confined to the British. In the French sector, where the going was very much easier, the absence of 'push' was even more marked. General Debeney's instructions to his Army had been vehement in the French manner: '. . . the attacks will be conducted with but one preoccupation, to achieve the greatest rapidity in a succession of forward bounds. . . . Alignment is not to be sought; it is forbidden to wait for neighbouring divisions . . . the attacks will be pushed on and continued until night; from the very first day the troops must go "très loin".' This programme did not materialize. Starting three-quarters of an hour after the Canadians, whose advance naturally eased their progress on the left, the French moved so deliberately that when the Canadian line halted, it was five hours before the French came up abreast of them. Haig found Debeney during the afternoon 'almost in tears because three battalions of his Colonial infantry had bolted before a German machine gun'. This was less than kind, but it is clear that the French 1st Army was not performing well. The French had shown great fire in their own counter-attack in July under Mangin. They were to show it again and again before the War ended. But Debeney was no Mangin, and the French Army of 1918 was not of the same calibre as the fine troops who had been squandered in 1915 and 1916.

Whatever deficiencies may have appeared in the French ranks and in the line divisions of the British Army, they were nothing to those exposed among the Germans. The German official Monograph on the battle sums up the day from their point of view: 'As the sun set on the 8th August on the battlefield the greatest defeat which the German Army had suffered since the beginning of the war was an accomplished fact. The position divisions between the Avre and the Somme which had been struck by the enemy attack were nearly completely annihilated. The troops in the front line north of the Somme had also suffered seriously, as also the reserve divisions thrown into the battle during the course of the day. The total loss of the formations employed in the *II Army* area is estimated at 650 to 700 officers and 26,000 to 27,000 other ranks. More than two-thirds of the total loss had surrendered as prisoners.' Ludendorff wrote: 'August 8th was the black day of the German Army in the history of the war. This was the worst experience I had to go through . . . our losses had reached such proportions that the Supreme Command was faced with the necessity of having to disband a series of divisions . . . 8th August made things clear for both army commands, both for the German and for that of the enemy.' Well might Haig write in his diary: '. . . the situation had developed more favourably for us than I, optimist though I am, had dared to hope.' This was the beginning of his vindication, a moment from which he never looked back.

The attack continued on the following day, but the initial impetus could not be maintained. Only 145 tanks were fit for action; German reserves were arriving on the scene; many of the British troops were tired after their great exertions; the only notable gain of the day was the capture of the Chipilly spur by the 131st U.S. Regiment, attached to III Corps. Monash records his disappointment at the semi-defensive orders given to his Corps: 'I should have welcomed an order to push on . . . in open warfare formation . . . the order stood, however. . . .' There can be little doubt that both on this day and the next the British Fourth Army found it difficult to make the adjustment to the new conditions of open warfare and movement created by their own success on the 8th. Rawlinson, not unnaturally, feared another Cambrai, and felt it necessary to prepare some defensive positions against the possibility of a counter-attack. As for the French, the combined exhortations of Foch, Haig and Debeney could not reinstil in their divisions the offensive spirit which so many failures had undermined. On August 10th Foch threw in the French 3rd Army on the right of the 1st; this intervention helped to pull that wing of the battle forward, but in general the advance that day was small.

German resistance was stiffening and, worse still, the Allies were now approaching the old battlefields of 1916 with their maze of trenches, their jungles of rusty wire, and their concrete fortifications. The ground was wholly unsuitable even for heavy tanks, let alone whippets and cavalry. A change of plan was evidently required.

In effect, it was Haig who now took charge of the operations, imposing his own plan, as he had clung to the idea of this battle ever since May. On August 10th 'General Foch came to see me at 11 a.m. He wishes the advance to continue to the line Noyon-Ham-Péronne, and to try to get the bridge-heads on the Somme. I pointed out the difficulty of the undertaking unless the enemy is quite demoralized, and we can cross the Somme on his heels . . . we must expect German reserves to arrive very soon in order to check our advance. My plan to advance my left on Bapaume and on Monchy-le-Preux will then become necessary. In Foch's opinion the fact of the French 1st Army's and now the 3rd French Army's getting on without meeting with serious opposition shows the enemy is demoralized. I agree that some German divisions are demoralized, but not all yet!' Haig ordered Byng to prepare to advance on Bapaume, thus opening the battle outward to the north, as Foch had already done in the south. A visit to the front assured him that this was the right course to take: 'I came away more determined than ever to press our offensive from our Third and First Army fronts.' The next day he noted: 'Morning reports show enemy's opposition is stiffening on the battle front.' He changed his orders to Byng into a precise instruction 'to break the enemy's front, in order to outflank the enemy's present battle front'. When Foch came to see him that night, 'After a talk, he approved (in view of the increased opposition) of my reducing my front of attack. . . . He asked me to attack with my Third Army. I told him that three weeks ago I had discussed with Byng the possibility of the Third Army co-operating and today I had seen Byng and given him definite orders to advance as soon as possible on Bapaume.' Foch was still not entirely satisfied; he hated to give up a fight while there was any promise left in it; from the lofty eminence of his position he was less able to judge what the extent of that promise was. He continued to urge that the Fourth Army and 1st French Army should press their advance pending the opening of Byng's attack. But the Army Com-manders themselves had little relish for this action; on the 13th Debeney asked Haig for a postponement of further operations, and a little later Haig heard that Rawlinson 'considered that the attack would be very costly. I sent word to say that if he had any views to express to come and see me in the morning'.

Rawlinson indeed had views, and he expressed them with some force; according to the Official Historian, he went so far as to ask Haig: 'Who commands the British Army, you or Foch?' Whatever may be the truth of this, it is a fact that he showed Haig revealing photographs of the enemy's defences, and reported to him that General Currie was decidedly averse to attempting to capture them: 'I accordingly ordered the date of this attack to be postponed, but preparations to be continued with vigour combined with wire-cutting[1] and counter-battery work.' He then wrote and told Foch what he had decided. The response was immediate, by telegram; Foch 'saw no necessity for delay Fourth Army and 1st French Army attack . . . which should be carried out as soon as possible'. Haig replied that nothing had happened to cause him to change his opinion: 'I therefore much regret that I cannot alter my orders to the two armies in question. I hope to be with you at Sarcus today at 3 p.m.'

The meeting of the two commanders that afternoon, as usual, produced agreement, though not without some vigorous interchanges. Foch questioned Haig sharply; he 'wanted to know what orders I had issued for attack? when I proposed to attack? where? and with what troops?' One senses Foch's dynamic, aggressive energy pulsing through this interrogation. Haig, for his part, was equally forthright: 'I spoke to Foch quite straightly and let him understand that *I was responsible to my Government and fellow citizens for the handling of the British forces.* F.'s attitude at once changed and he said all he wanted was early information of my intentions so that he might co-ordinate the operations of the other Armies, and that he now thought I was quite correct in my decision not to attack the enemy in his prepared position. But notwithstanding what he now said, Foch and all his Staff had been most insistent for the last five days that I should press on along the South bank and capture the Somme bridges above Péronne, regardless of German opposition, and British losses.' Foch has very frankly acknowledged Haig's influence on him: 'I definitely came around to the opinion of Field-Marshal Sir Douglas Haig. . . .' While the matter was in balance, however, Haig might have echoed Monash's earlier words: 'It appeared to me at the time that great issues had hung . . . upon the chance of my being able to carry my point.'

It would have been a disaster now to blunt the edge of the Allied counter-stroke against the still powerful Somme defences. Already, though Haig and Foch were not to know the full story for some time, terrible damage had been done to the Germans; already a fateful decision had been taken. German morale, so staunch through so many trials, was now unmistakably breaking up. The German 38th Division, entering the battle from reserve, met 'drunken Bavarians who shouted to the 94th Regiment: "What do you war-prolongers want? If the enemy were only on the Rhine – the war would then be over!"'

1. By artillery.

Other retreating troops shouted to the 263rd Reserve Regiment: 'We thought
that we had set the thing going, now you asses are corking up the hole again.'
Ludendorff, at a meeting of the High Command with the Kaiser on August
11th, reported 'that the warlike spirit of some of the divisions left a good deal
to be desired . . . when the Kaiser and Crown Prince suggested that too much
had been asked of the troops, Ludendorff replied that the collapse of the
II Army on the 8th August could not be accounted for by the divisions being
over-tired. He offered his resignation, but it was not accepted.'[1] It was at this
same meeting that the Kaiser uttered the words: 'I see that we must strike a
balance. We have nearly reached the limit of our powers of resistance. The
war must be ended.'

*   *   *   *

Haig shared the Kaiser's view. After Amiens he had but one preoccupation
– to end the War in the shortest possible time. The Third Army's main
attack[2] opened on August 21st; on that day Haig received a visit from
Churchill, who wanted to discuss Munitions policy with him: 'He is most
anxious to help us in every way. . . . His schemes are all timed for "completion
in *next June*!" I told him we ought to do our utmost to get a decision this
autumn. We are engaged in a "wearing out battle" and are outlasting and
beating the enemy. If we allow the enemy a period of quiet, he will recover,
and the "wearing out" process must be recommenced. In reply I was told
that the General Staff in London calculate that the decisive period of the war
cannot arrive until next July.' This was a proposition which Haig simply
refused to entertain. He was already aware of the War Office view, which
had been imparted to him in a 33-page Memorandum from Wilson in July.
In the margin of his copy he had scribbled: 'Words! Words! Words! lots of
words and little else. Theoretical rubbish! Whoever drafted this stuff could
never win any campaign.' Drawing the attention of the Official Historian to
this document in 1927, he wrote: '. . . you will, I think, thank God, that the
G.S. in London in 1918 had no influence over our military decisions at
G.H.Q. in France.' It was not 1919 that he cared about; it was the present.

Byng's attack did not begin with any such dramatic flourish as that of
August 8th, but its progress was immediate and indicative. On the 22nd,
recognizing the signs, Haig told his Army Commanders:

'Risks which a month ago would have been criminal to incur, ought now
to be incurred as a duty.

'It is no longer necessary to advance in regular lines and step by step. On
the contrary, each division should be given a distant objective which must be

1. Official History, 1918, Vol. IV.
2. Known as the Battle of Albert, or Bapaume.

reached independently of its neighbour, and even if one's flank is thereby exposed for the time being.

'Reinforcements must be directed on the points where our troops are gaining ground, not where they are checked. . . .'[1]

In a late-summer heat-wave reminiscent of that of 1914, the Third Army, supported by the Fourth, pressed forward. On August 26th Haig extended his front again, drawing in part of the First Army on Byng's left. On the 29th the magnificent New Zealand Division entered Bapaume, concluding an historical phase of the fighting, although, on the ground, the steady advance of the Allies did not cease for a moment. The British Army's operations between August 21st and September 1st had gathered in 34,000 prisoners and 270 guns, mainly due, Haig later stated, 'to the excellence of the staff arrangements of all formations, and to the most able conduct . . . of the Third Army by its Commander, General Byng'. Foch wrote to him:

'My dear Field Marshal,

'Your affairs are going on very well; I can only applaud the resolute manner in which you follow them up, without giving the enemy a respite and always extending the breadth of your operations. It is this increasing breadth of the offensive – an offensive fed from behind and strongly pushed forward on to carefully selected objectives, without bothering about the alignment nor about keeping too closely in touch – which will produce the greatest results with the smallest casualties, as you have perfectly understood. No need to tell you that General Pétain's Armies will carry on ceaselessly in the same style.'

This month of victory was the crucial month of the War; the British Army's achievements had never been so striking. Yet, despite its much-improved tactics, its formidable armoury, and the general collapse of German morale – except among selected units (machine gunners in particular) – the price paid was heavy: between August 7th and August 29th, the Adjutant-General reported Infantry and Cavalry casualties amounting to 3,495 officers and 79,302 other ranks. To those who, at a distance, were less in touch with the 'feel' of the battle, less aware of the forward momentum, the mien of success, these figures could hardly be viewed without apprehension. Nor was this decreased by the knowledge that Haig's Armies were now approaching the most redoubtable of all German positions, the ill-famed Hindenburg Line. It was towards the storming of this great system – 7,000–10,000 yards deep, and containing every defensive device that German ingenuity could

1. O.A.D. 911.

provide – that Haig's thoughts were now concentrated. He believed that it should be possible to exploit the advances already made in such a way as to take these defences from the rear. Nevertheless, it was apparent that a stern test still lay before his troops.

A test for Haig himself, also: on September 1st, as his preparations for this enterprise went forward, he received a telegram marked 'Personal' from Wilson. It was brought to him by General Davidson, who was aware of its contents, and had already shown it to Lawrence. It read: 'Just a word of warning in regard to incurring heavy losses in attacks on Hindenburg Line as opposed to losses when driving the enemy back to that line. I do not mean to say that you have incurred such losses, but I know the War Cabinet would become anxious if we receive heavy punishment in attacking the Hindenburg Line, without success.' Signed 'Wilson'. Davidson remained standing while Haig digested this; having read it, the Commander-in-Chief quietly put it aside, and asked Davidson what the devil he was waiting for. He expressed his private feelings, however, in his diary: 'It is impossible for a C.I.G.S. to send a telegram of this nature to a C. in C. in the Field as a 'personal' one. The Cabinet are ready to meddle and interfere in my plans in an underhand way, but do not dare openly to say that they mean to take responsibility for any failure though ready to take credit for every success! The object of this telegram is, no doubt, to save the Prime Minister . . . in case of any failure. So I read it to mean that I can attack the Hindenburg Line if I think it right to do so. The C.I.G.S. and the Cabinet already know that my arrangements are being made to that end. If my attack is successful, I will remain on as C. in C. If we fail, or our losses are excessive, I can hope for no mercy! I wrote to Henry Wilson in reply. What a wretched lot of weaklings we have in high places at the present time!' To Wilson himself he wrote:

'My dear Henry,

'With reference to your wire re casualties in attacking the Hindenburg Line – what a wretched lot! and how well they mean to support me! What confidence! Please call their attention to my action two weeks ago when the French pressed me to attack the strong lines of defence east of Roye-Chaulnes front. I wrote you at the time and instead of attacking south of the Somme I started Byng's attack. I assure you I watch the drafts most carefully.'

Wilson was clearly somewhat ashamed of himself, on receiving this, for he told Haig that his wire 'was only intended to convey a sort of distant warning and nothing more! All so easy to explain in talking, all so difficult to explain in writing'. But whichever way one looked at it, it was a poor diet for a Commander about to enter upon the most taxing and potentially decisive stroke of the War.

What might be done by boldness was revealed, once again, by the irrepressible Australians on August 31st. Their 2nd Division startled even Rawlinson by its sudden seizure of Mont St. Quentin, the bastion of the Somme sector. Delighted though he was, Haig did not permit himself to be carried away by this incident; his main attention was on the battle further north, where, on September 2nd, the Canadians (now with First Army) broke through the Drocourt-Quéant 'switch' line. This action, says the Official Historian, 'had immediate effect; O.H.L. recognized defeat. About mid-day they issued orders for retirement behind the Sensée and the Canal du Nord and, farther south, to the Hindenburg Position, beginning that very night. . . . Thus . . . the whole great salient won in March 1918 was to be abandoned'. Haig wrote: '. . . the end cannot now be far off, I think. Today's battle has truly been a great and glorious success.' The next three weeks were taken up with the steady advance of his three offensive Armies, First, Third and Fourth, through the outlying defences towards the main Hindenburg Line; all the British forces were weary, and many divisions much weakened – a battalion was lucky to go into action with more than 400 men in its ranks; German rear-guards continued to fight stubbornly, although their morale was now sinking steadily – troop trains were seen bearing the inscription 'Slaughter cattle for Wilhelm & Sons'; yet there was no flight, but an organized retirement which differed from that of 1917 only in that it did not take the Allies by surprise, and never shook them off.

The truth is that, at this critical stage, errors were being made by both the German and Allied Supreme Commands. Given the condition of the German Army, it now seems clear that Ludendorff should have accepted the advice which he was given on September 6th to admit the probability of being turned out of the Hindenburg Line and prepare immediately for a large retreat to the line Antwerp-Meuse; but this he would not hear of. At the same time, it must be said that Marshal Foch's[1] strategy reveals little but vigorous opportunism. As he expressed it to Haig on August 22nd, it was 'a simple straightforward advance by all troops on the western front and to keep the enemy on the move'. In the slogan that Foch himself coined, this was announced as '*Tout le monde à la bataille*'. But what it meant in effect, as the British Official Historian points out, was that 'Strategically the main offensive was made at the wrong place, because the Army that was most fighting-fit happened to be holding that front'. In other words, because the British Army, summoning up all its resolution and a marvellous courage, was *able* to constitute itself the pacemaker of the counter-stroke, once again the decisive battle would take the form of a frontal assault on the most

1. Foch was created *Maréchal de France* on August 6th.

powerful position which remained in German hands. This is not to be hyper-critical of Foch; given the general state of the French Army (despite numerous magnificent rallies by individual formations), and given Pétain's overall frame of mind, in addition to the continuing unpreparedness of the bulk of the Americans, it is hard to see what else he could have done. If he had not taken advantage of Haig's attacks, the great likelihood is that there would have been no advance at all, and no victory in 1918. Nevertheless, the criticism stands that, so long as the Allies attacked, Foch was not greatly concerned about how or where. He was definitely mistaken in pressing the British Fourth Army to continue its advance at Amiens; and at the end of August we find Haig stepping right outside the sphere of his own operations, and urging on Foch the need to strike the Hindenburg Line not only frontally, but against its flanks.

Haig's intention was to set the Belgians in motion, together with Plumer's Second Army, first against the northern part of the Ypres Salient, and then swinging round against Roulers, the objective of his great offensive in 1917; this, he reckoned, would materially assist in dislocating the Germans on his left. On the right, however, it was the French and Americans who would have to help him. The American Army had long been assembling on the St. Mihiel sector, east of Verdun, where it planned, in conjunction with the French, to wipe out the sharp-nosed German salient in front of Metz. The fixed determination of General Pershing to draw his Army together, and commit it to an enterprise of its own, had already had disagreeable reper-cussions on Haig's operations. On August 12th, in the midst of victory, Pershing had told him that he proposed to withdraw the five American divisions with the British. There were outspoken exchanges between the two commanders, which, fortunately, did not permanently affect their relations. In the event, three divisions went, the other two remaining to be a substantial support to the British Army in its future battles. On August 25th, as the last of the departing Americans entrained, Haig wrote: 'What will History say regarding the action of the Americans leaving the British zone of operations when *the decisive battle* of the war is at its height, and the decision still in doubt!'

Two days later, however, he was even more concerned with what the Americans would be doing when they reached their destination. As originally planned, the St. Mihiel attack was aimed in the general direction of Metz, that is, eccentrically, *away* from the axes of advance of the British and central French forces. Haig pointed out the disadvantages of this to Foch: 'I urged him to put the Americans into the battle *at once* in order to enable an im-portant advance to be made without delay, *concentrically*, viz., against Cambrai, against St. Quentin, and against Mézières from the South.' Foch saw the force of this suggestion, but it was too late to give it the effect that Haig desired; Pershing flatly refused to allow his Army to be used except as an entity; equally, he clung to his long-awaited attack on the St. Mihiel salient. It was a singular example of the deficiencies of Foch's title when it came to *ordering* action by any Army other than his own nationals. The most that he could obtain was a diminution of the American effort at St. Mihiel, which robbed that endeavour of part of its prize, and a promise that the Americans would reassemble afterwards on the Argonne, for the stroke towards Mézières. This meant for the Americans a weakening of both their efforts, and much difficulty and loss on an unfamiliar battlefield. One sees Pershing's point; one appreciates Foch's dilemma; the fact remains that it would have been helpful if he had exercised his powers as Generalissimo *before* Pershing's deployment was so far completed, instead of waiting for Haig's prompting.

Despite these contretemps, the situation at the beginning of September had a most hopeful look. On the 4th, Foch told Haig that he believed 'the German is nearing the end'. This was precisely Haig's own thought, but he was conscious that it was not widely shared in England. He wrote to Wilson on the 7th: 'I propose coming over on Monday for a couple of days, as I am anxious to have a talk with you and the Secretary of State. The situation has changed so rapidly and, as I look at it, seems so different from what it was when you home authorities made your plans for the provision of men, aeroplanes, tanks, etc. that it seems most desirable to review your figures in the light of the existing state of affairs. . . .' The next day he told Churchill (as ardent a visitor to the zone of operations in that war as in the next) that: 'I considered that *the Allies should aim at getting a decision as soon as possible*. This month or next, not next spring or summer as the Cabinet proposed.' This was, indeed, a vision which none but he had so far perceived. It guided all his thoughts, not only at his meetings in London, but in settling the immediate operations of his Armies. Rawlinson, for example, after the remarkable successes of the Fourth Army, now had 'the bit between his teeth'. On the 6th he was asking Haig for more reserves, in order to press his advance, but Haig was instructing him 'to rest as many of his troops as possible so as to be ready for our next battle'. And two days later he added: '. . . *my objective is to strike a blow as soon as possible in co-operation with the other Allies*. If I were to reinforce him now, my reserves would become used up before the time for combined action had come.'

It was at his meeting with Milner on September 10th that Haig declared himself for the benefit of the War Cabinet: 'I had specially asked for this interview, and I stated that the object of my visit was to explain how greatly the situation in the field had changed to the advantage of the Allies. I considered it to be of first importance that the Cabinet should realize how all our plans and methods are at once affected by this change.

'Within the last four weeks we had captured 77,000 prisoners and nearly 800 guns! There has never been such a victory in the annals of Britain, and its effects are not yet apparent. The German prisoners now taken will not obey their officers or N.C.O.s. . . . The discipline of the German Army is quickly going, and the German Officer is not what he was. *It seems to me to be the beginning of the end*. From these and other facts I draw the conclusion that the enemy's troops will not await our attacks in even the strongest positions.

'Briefly, in my opinion, the character of the war has changed. What is wanted now at once is to provide the means to exploit our recent great successes to the full. Reserves in England should be regarded as Reserves for the French front, and all yeomanry, cyclists and other troops now kept for civil defence should be sent to France *at once*.

'If we act with energy now, a decision can be obtained in the *very near future*. . . .

'Lord Milner fully agreed and said he would do his best to help.'

How far Haig's thinking was ahead of that of even the most pugnacious and reasonably informed members of the Government may be judged from the Memorandum which he received on the following day from Churchill, setting out the perspective of the War against which the latter was framing his Munitions policy. Among other curiosities, it contained this sentence: 'We should be content to play a very subordinate role in France, and generally in the Allied Councils, during 1919, and count on having solid forces and conserved resources available for the decisive struggles of 1920, or held in hand for the peace situation if our Allies break down meanwhile.' That Memorandum is dated September 5th, 1918. Haig noted in the margin against the sentence quoted: 'What rubbish! Who will last till 1920 – only America??' He found all this style of talk profoundly irritating; he knew that he was wielding England's last Army; and he knew that it could win.

*   *   *   *

The storming of the Hindenburg Line was the last great exploit of the British Army in the War; it led directly to the collapse of the Central Powers. Haig's responsibility for this decisive feat was, as we have seen, firmly planted by Wilson's extraordinary telegram of September 1st, and his own response to it. The distinguishing and hopeful feature of the enterprise was that, at last (and this also was partly due to Haig), it would be joined to simultaneous, related efforts by the other Allied Armies: the Belgians in Flanders, the French and the Americans in the Argonne. Foch was the directing force; the planning was largely evolved by him and Haig together, in their frequent discussions. Haig had no illusions as to the difficulties and dangers of the task that faced him. In his Despatch dated December 21st, 1918, he wrote:

'The results to be obtained from these different attacks depended in a peculiarly large degree upon the British attack in the centre. It was here that the enemy's defences were most highly organized. If these were broken, the threat directed at his vital systems of lateral communication would of necessity react upon his defence elsewhere.

'On the other hand, the long period of sustained offensive action through which the British Armies had already passed had made large demands both upon the troops themselves and upon my available reserves. Throughout our attacks from the 8th August onwards, our losses in proportion to the results achieved and the numbers of prisoners taken had been consistently and remarkably small. In the aggregate, however, they were considerable, and in the face of them an attack upon so formidably organized a position as that which now confronted us could not be lightly undertaken. Moreover, the political effects of an unsuccessful attack upon a position so well known as the Hindenburg Line would be large, and would go far to revive the declining morale not only of the German Army but of the German people.

'These different considerations were present in my mind. The probable results of a costly failure, or, indeed, of anything short of a decided success, in any attempt upon the main defences of the Hindenburg Line were obvious; but I was convinced that the British attack was the essential part of the general scheme, and that the moment was favourable.

'Accordingly, I decided to proceed with the attack. . . .'

Haig's strength of purpose was not matched in the political circles behind him. On September 21st, after the successful completion of the last of the British preparatory advances, Lord Milner told him 'that if the British Army is used up now there will be no men for next year. He was quite satisfied that I should do what I deemed best in the matter of attacking or not. I pointed out that the situation was most satisfactory and that in order to take advantage of it every available man should be put into the battle at once. In my opinion, it is possible to get a decision this year, but if we do not, every blow that we deliver now will make the task next year much easier.' Milner was only half-convinced, though content to leave the ultimate responsibility to Haig; two days later he told Wilson that 'He thinks Haig ridiculously optimistic and is afraid that he may embark on another Passchendaele'.

The factors which had stultified the Passchendaele campaign now no longer operated. The 'wearing-out battles' had done their work; the Germans were losing heart; the Allies were co-operating; these were profound differences. On the day that he spoke to Milner, Haig also conferred with his Army Commanders; each of them stated his views:

'Plumer considered that the enemy was unaware of his and the Belgian preparations. The enemy is preparing to go back to the Passchendaele ridge, and to shorten his line southwards also.

'Birdwood[1] also thought that the enemy was preparing to go back on his front as far south as Lens.

'Horne agreed also to this. As regards the rest of our First Army front, he was of opinion that the enemy would not move back until attacked.

'As regards our Third and Fourth Army fronts, I think that the enemy must hold on at all costs to the Cambrai-St. Quentin front *until* his troops on the Champagne and Laon fronts have been withdrawn, otherwise their retreat will be cut off. . . .

'After talking over the situation, I decided that the order of attack is to be as follows:

American/French attack	Z day
First Army ⎫ Third Army (left) ⎭	Z + 2
Byng attacks Canal[2] and crosses	Z + 4
Rawlinson attacks Canal and crosses	Z + 4

All were quite pleased with my arrangements. Before my intervention Byng and Rawlinson were each inclined to try and get the better of each other.'

Two days later the dates were settled with Foch, who also agreed on measures of direct French support for the British. Haig noted: 'Foch is admirable at making the French generals do what he wants.' Haig had already discussed his plans with King Albert of Belgium, under whose orders the British Second Army was to act. On the 24th he 'spent a long morning seeing the heads of Branches'. On the 25th he visited the Third Army, and found the Corps Commanders confident. On the 26th the French-American attack was launched in the Argonne; Byng and Rawlinson 'both assured me that everything was satisfactorily arranged and that they were fully confident of success in the forthcoming attack; but Byng insisted that the fighting is sure to be hard. . . .' Calling in on the Australians, Haig found Monash in the midst of a Corps Conference: 'Monash begged me to go in and see them all, even at the risk of delaying matters. So I went into the room and shook the senior officers by the hand and said a few words of encouragement. I told

1. Commanding the re-formed Fifth Army.
2. The Scheldt, or St. Quentin Canal.

them that the biggest battle of the war had started this morning, "the enemy would be attacked by 100 divisions in the next 3 days. . . ." All seemed very much heartened by my brief address.'

And now the battle opened. British participation was pulled forward one day, beginning on the 27th with the assault of the First and Third Armies. General Byng's prediction that the Germans would fight hard was borne out: there was still spirit in the German Army, even enough, in places to allow them to make damaging counter-attacks; but these soldiers no longer had the stamina of 1916 and 1917; failure quickly discouraged them. In two days Horne and Byng made a breach in the enemy's defences twelve miles wide and six miles deep. On the 28th, against smaller forces and less staunch resistance, the Belgians and the Second Army also made considerable progress, passing 'far beyond the farthest limits of the 1917 battles'.[1] On the 29th the main British attack, by the Fourth Army and the right of the Third, went in. It was on this day that the most remarkable success of all was achieved, by the veteran 46th North Midland (Territorial) Division,[2] which crossed the difficult obstacle of the St. Quentin Canal at Bellenglise, bursting through the German defences, and capturing 4,000 prisoners and 70 guns at a cost of some 800 casualties. The only blight upon these triumphs was the misfortune of the American 27th and 30th Divisions which, through over-eagerness, advanced too far, failed to 'mop up', and were taken in the rear by parties of Germans with machine guns, emerging from the dug-outs and tunnels which abounded in this elaborate defensive system. The Americans were under command of the Australian Corps, and it fell to those troops to make good the damage done through inexperience and too much enthusiasm. This apart, Haig had every reason to be elated; the gloomy forebodings of the authorities in London were set at naught; misgivings even nearer to hand had been refuted: '. . . an Army Commander (gather it was Byng) stated in August . . . that we would never get beyond the Hindenburg Line! Now we are through that line!'

Summing up the effects of this mighty blow in his Despatch, Haig wrote: 'The effect of the victory upon the subsequent course of the campaign was decisive. . . . In the fighting of these days, in which thirty British and two American infantry divisions and one British cavalry division were engaged against thirty-nine German divisions, over 36,000 prisoners and 380 guns had been captured. Great as were the material losses the enemy suffered, the effect of so overwhelming a defeat upon a moral already deteriorated was of even larger importance.' Indeed, its meaning extended outside Germany. It was on

1. Haig Despatch.
2. Sherwood Foresters, North and South Staffs., Lincolns and Leicesters; from the very heart of England.

September 30th that Bulgaria accepted the Allied Armistice terms, the first visible break in the ranks of the Central Powers. The previous day, Ludendorff had told a Council of War at Spa that 'the situation of the Army demands an immediate armistice in order to save a catastrophe'. He added: '. . . our situation admits of no delay, not an hour is to be lost.' On October 2nd a representative of the Supreme Command told the Reichstag: 'the war is lost'. Hindenburg handed to the new German Chancellor, Prince Max of Baden, a Note stating: 'O.H.L. maintains the demand made on Sunday the 29th of September of this year for the immediate issue of the peace offer to our enemies. . . . The situation . . . is becoming more acute every day. . . . In these circumstances, the proper course is to break off the struggle in order to spare the German people and their Allies useless sacrifices. Every day's delay costs the lives of thousands of our brave soldiers.' With much pain, the Government agreed; a request to President Wilson for an Armistice was drawn up on October 4th, and forwarded to Washington next day. On the 6th Haig was visiting Foch, and found him studying the text of the German Note in a newspaper. Foch pointed to the paper; he said: 'Here you have the immediate result of the British piercing the Hindenburg Line. The enemy has asked for an armistice.' It was a generous acknowledgement.

*   *   *   *

'A battle lost is a battle one thinks one has lost.'[1] The decisive victory of the Allies on the Western Front at the end of September, 1918, was won in the mind and heart of Ludendorff. On the battlefield, despite the achievements of the British Army, the issue of the struggle was less clear than his image of it. In the Argonne, the inexperience of the American Staffs produced a supply breakdown (intensified by their chronic Transport shortage) which in a matter of days brought their advance to a halt and reduced their forward units to a state almost of starvation. Without American impetus to pull them forward, the French were disinclined to make large or costly efforts. The Belgian advance was methodical, unmarked by any quality of dash. On the British front, too, there was a perceptible slowing up: the initial attack carried the line forward to within three miles of Cambrai; it took nearly a fortnight to complete the capture of the town. From the recesses of his martial spirit the German soldier summoned up reserves of courage and determination exceeding that of his leaders. All through October, while statesmen were discussing the Armistice preliminaries, heavy fighting continued; British casualties during the month amounted to 5,438 officers and 115,608 other ranks. The German Army sacrificed itself heroically in the vain hope of reversing the inexorable march of fate, or at least of imposing such

1. Joseph de Maistre.

delays as would enable negotiators to strike a better bargain. What it could no longer do was to lend any further support to wilting allies; the long attrition which the Army had endured in battle had brought it to the last spasm of its amazing energy; the attrition of the economic war against the home population was now also producing its effect. For all its fine resistance, now that its leaders were mentally defeated, the German Army might well have given up the struggle at any stage of the October battles; the political conditions for this, however, proved to be unexpectedly elusive. At the heart of the long delays we may find the malignant influence of a concept which was to have equally sombre effects in 1945: 'unconditional surrender'.

The battle, ferocious as it continued to be, now occupied less and less of Haig's attention. Byng and Rawlinson told him on October 1st that they considered 'the enemy has suffered very much, and that it is merely a question of our continuing our pressure to ensure his completely breaking. They agreed that no further orders from me were necessary, and both would be able to carry on without difficulty.'[1] This they did, in conjunction with their colleagues, the other Army Commanders, a steady frontal push by all five Armies – all that was possible in the face of the failure of Britain's Allies to produce large effects at the hinges of the German line. It was slow work; the British Army was by now very tired:[2] the ground over which it was advancing was seamed with the difficulties and obstacles produced by four years of war and enemy occupation; above all, no suitable arm or weapon of exploitation existed. This was a severely limiting factor, which went far to reduce the value of the Allied victories at this stage. Haig was fully conscious of it; he had urged Wilson to collect mobile troops for the pursuit, and on September 24th wrote again to ask for 'Yeomanry, cyclists, motor machine-guns, motor lorries, etc. In fact anything to add to our mobility. The resources of the French and of ourselves here are being strained to the utmost for the coming effort. Anything you can spare should be sent to us *at once.*'

1. This does not mean that Haig did not continue to exercise careful daily command: but the change in the texture of his Diary from about the middle of July, 1918, is most striking. The entries themselves contain more of general observation, as though at last he found time to look around him; the associated papers become fewer, and generally shorter. Victory supplies its own commentary; it is the difficult times leading up to it that supply the great debates.

2. The Australians fought their last action on October 5th. They were then withdrawn to rest, having been in action since March 27th. In that time they had captured 29,144 prisoners and 338 guns. Between August 8th and October 5th they engaged 39 separate divisions; they liberated 116 named localities; their casualties were 21,243 of all ranks. Of these, just under 5,000 were killed. There was hardly a day on which they were not attacking. As these figures indicate, the fighting of the First World War was not *always* a hopeless blood-bath.

There was little that the C.I.G.S. could do; even the ordinary supply of the Army was endangered at this juncture by a railway strike, let alone the despatch of new formations.[1] In any case, the inadequacy of horsed soldiers had already been fully demonstrated – hence Haig's reference to cyclists and motorized troops. Nor was this the only expedient which occurred to him; on October 7th he was talking to Major-General Salmond, commanding the Royal Air Force: 'In reply to my question as to whether he was ready to support the Cavalry Corps with large numbers of low-flying machines, in the event of the enemy breaking . . . he replied that all were quite ready to act, and he could concentrate 300 machines practically at once.' Yet the truth remains that neither cavalry nor the relatively primitive aeroplanes of 1918 contained the answer to Haig's problem; it lay in the next war, in the Air-supported Armoured Divisions of 1939–1945.

October 10th was a day of particular note. Two days earlier the Third and Fourth Armies had struck another concerted blow, driving the Germans out of their last remaining defensive positions behind the St. Quentin Canal. This event extracted from Mr. Lloyd George the first whisper of congratulation from the British Government to their victorious Army or its Commander since the great advance had begun. The wording of the message was calculated to counteract any pleasure that it might have given: 'I have just heard from Marshal Foch of the brilliant victory won by the First, Third and Fourth Armies, and I wish to express to yourself, Generals Horne, Byng and Rawlinson, and all the officers and men under your command my sincerest congratulations on the great and significant success which the British armies, with their American brothers-in-arms, have gained during the past two days. . . .'

Lloyd George's reference to the 'past two days' (changed for the benefit of the Press to 'few days') was nothing less than an insult; did the Prime Minister know nothing of what had happened in August and September? Had he not heard of Amiens or the Hindenburg Line? The mention of the Americans was also unnecessary in a message to the British Army; why not add the French and Belgians and have done with it? But, above all, there was the disagreeable suggestion that the exploits of the Army were only deserving of notice if Foch said so. The inner truth about this pose is that Lloyd George was finding in Foch a convenient alibi to cover his own errors and also his obstruction of Haig, who was now being disconcertingly proved right about too many things. Lloyd George was already feeling his way towards the position expressed in an unusually fatuous sentence of his *War Memoirs*, to the effect that Haig 'did well in the concluding stages of the 1918 campaign –

1. '. . . I have full confidence in the good sense of our railwaymen at home. Some means will be found to keep up our supply of ammunition . . .' Haig remarked.

under Foch's supreme direction'. We have seen how ridiculously wide of the mark this patronizing judgement was. Haig himself was little troubled at Lloyd George's gesture. He made no reference to it in his Diary, but contrasted it in a letter to Lady Haig with all the other congratulations which he had received: 'The Prime Minister's shows the least understanding of the great efforts made by the *whole* of the British Army.'

October 10th, however, contained more significant matters than Lloyd George's telegram. On that day Foch showed Haig 'a paper which he had handed to the Allied Conference in Paris on the subject of an Armistice. He said that his opinion had not been asked, but he had nevertheless given his Prime Minister his paper. He had now heard that the Conference agreed with what he had written and were very pleased to have his paper. His main points were:

1. Evacuation of Belgium, France and Alsace-Lorraine.
2. Hand over to the Allies to administer all the country up to the Rhine with three bridgeheads on the river. The size of each of the latter to be 30 kilos. from the crossing drawn in a semi-circle.
3. Germans to leave all material behind, huts, supplies, etc., etc., railway trains, railways in order.
4. Enemy to clear out in 15 days from signing of agreement.

I remarked that the only difference between his (Foch's) conditions and a "general unconditional surrender" is that the German Army is allowed to march back with its rifles, and officers with their swords. He is evidently of opinion that the enemy is so desirous of peace that he will agree to any terms of this nature which we impose.'

Haig had thought about Peace often enough before, but this conversation drew his attention to its problems with immediacy; during the next few days we find him moving towards the attitude from which, once adopted, he never departed. It consisted partly in a calm view of present circumstances, and partly in a farseeing view of the future. As regards the former, he had no doubts that the enemy was beaten; that very evening he told Lawrence, who was tending to a somewhat gloomy opinion, even fearing a German counter-attack, that '*the enemy has not the means, nor has the German High Command the will power*, to launch an attack strong enough to affect even our front line troops. We have got the enemy down, in fact, he is a beaten Army, and my plan is to go on hitting him as hard as we possibly can, till he begs for mercy.' On the other hand, there was evidence enough of German doggedness, and ability to protract their last-ditch stand. Lawrence had his revenge on the 12th, when news came in of a check to the Third Army, due to 'the enemy suddenly strengthening his rear guard and taking the offensive.' Haig was unperturbed – 'this must always be expected in operations of this nature', he commented – but he began to see now a potential conflict between making the enemy 'beg for mercy' and actually ending the War. The next day he wrote to Wilson:

'My dear Henry,

'Re this question of an armistice asked for by the enemy, kindly let me know how far Foch, as Generalissimo, has power to involve the British Army. If I do not concur in such terms as he may wish to impose, what am I to do? The question may not arise, but it is desirable that I should know what the British Government wish me to do.

Yours,
D. Haig.'

Wilson, also, was thinking about the Armistice; this letter crossed a long telegram from him to Haig, in which he sought to clarify some of the confusion which had arisen in the Press and elsewhere. For this the Germans were responsible, for there can be no doubt that their approach to President Wilson personally, on the basis of his Fourteen Points, was a calculated attempt to divide the councils of the Allies. Henry Wilson now warned Haig that the Fourteen Points were 'in no sense the definition of an armistice', and that operations must continue until actual Armistice terms had been laid down and accepted. This Haig already realized, and had warned the Army accordingly, knowing how potentially demoralizing to weary men may be the belief that the end is in sight. A second telegram from Wilson answered his question: 'It is quite clear that Foch cannot have power to dictate terms of an armistice as such terms must include Austria and other theatres as well as the naval situation.' Yet what now took place, with the modification of British Naval representation only, was the acceptance of Foch's ideas; French desires to be avenged and requited for all that they had suffered merged with President's Wilson's aversion to military autocracies and the universal distrust which the Kaiser's autocracy had by now inspired; Haig's voice, urging moderation, cried in the wilderness, and exposed him to yet more misunderstanding of his motives.

He explained these motives at his meeting with the War Cabinet on October 19th. First he saw Wilson at the War Office: 'He gave his views on conditions of armistice. He considers that "The Germans should be ordered to lay down their arms and retire to the east bank of the Rhine." I gave my opinion that our attack on the 17th inst. met with considerable opposition, and that the enemy was not ready for unconditional surrender. In that case, there would be no armistice, and the war would continue for at least another year!' This was what Haig was concerned above all to avoid; he had now come round, after further talks with Lawrence, to the definite conclusion that 'it is in the interests of Great Britain to end the war this year'; and to this he clung, unmoved by any revengeful sentiment or anger. At the War Cabinet meeting which immediately followed his discussion with Wilson, Lloyd George 'asked my views on the terms which we should offer the enemy if he asked for an armistice. I replied that they must greatly depend on the answers we give to two questions:

1. Is Germany now so beaten that she will accept whatever terms the Allies may offer? i.e., unconditional surrender.
2. If he refuses to agree to our terms, can the Allies continue to press the enemy sufficiently vigorously during the coming winter months, to cause him to withdraw so quickly that he cannot destroy the railways, roads, etc?

The answer to both is in the negative. The German Army is capable of retiring to its own frontier, and holding that line if there should be any attempt to touch the *honour* of the German people, and make them fight with the courage of despair.

'The situation of the Allied Armies is as follows:

FRENCH ARMY: worn out and has not been really fighting latterly. It has been freely said that the "war is over" and "we don't wish to lose our lives now that peace is sight."

AMERICAN ARMY: is not yet organized: it is ill-equipped, half-trained, with insufficient supply services. Experienced officers and N.C.O.s are lacking.

BRITISH ARMY: was never more efficient than it is today, but it has fought hard, and it lacks reinforcements. With diminishing effectives, morale is bound to suffer.[1]

The French and American Armies are not capable of making a serious offensive *now*. The British alone might bring the enemy to his knees. But why expend more British lives – and for what?

'In the coming winter, the enemy will have some months for recuperation and absorption of 1920 class, untouched as yet. He will be in a position to destroy all his communication before he falls back. This will mean serious delay to our advance if war goes on to next year.

'The Prime Minister seemed in agreement with me . . . I was asked what the attitude of the Army would be if we stuck out for stiff terms, which the enemy then refuses, and war goes on. I reminded the P.M. of the situation a

1. Two days later Haig was warned by the Adjutant-General that the B.E.F. would have to be reduced to thirty-six divisions in 1919.

year ago when there were frequent demands for information as to what we were fighting for. . . . The British Army had done most of the fighting latterly, and everyone wants to have done with the war, *provided* we get what we want. I therefore advise that we only ask in the armistice for what we intend to hold, and that we set our faces against the French entering Germany to pay off old scores. In my opinion, under the supposed conditions, the British Army would not fight keenly for what is really not its own affair.

'Mr. Balfour spoke about deserting the Poles and the people of Eastern Europe, but the P.M. gave the opinion that we cannot expect the British to go on sacrificing their lives for the Poles.

'Admiral Wemyss, First Sea Lord, then came in and the views of the Navy for an armistice were stated. They seemed most exacting and incapable of enforcement except by a land force.'[1]

In the discussion which followed, it seemed to Wilson that 'Lloyd George and Milner rather agreed with Haig'. This was still his impression (and certainly Haig's) two days later, when the War Cabinet continued its deliberations in the light of a Turkish peace overture. With or without Lloyd George's support, Haig repeated these views to Foch on the 24th, but he made no impression in that quarter: 'Foch said that he insisted on having bridgeheads across the Rhine, and on occupying all German territory on the left bank as a guarantee to ensure that the enemy carries out the terms of peace which will be imposed upon her. He tried to make out that the enemy on the eastern side of the Rhine, opposed by the three allied bridgeheads, is in a less favourable position for battle than if he were astride the river holding the German frontier of 1870. Of course the contrary is the case; indeed the unfavourable frontier was the main reason why Moltke urged the annexation of Metz and district in 1871. On the whole, Foch's reasons were political not military, and Lawrence and I were both struck by the very unpractical way in which he and Weygand regarded the present military situation. He would not ask himself, "What does the military situation of the Allies admit of their demanding?" "What terms can we really enforce?" '

1. Students may care to compare Haig's account (given in full in Blake's *Private Papers of Douglas Haig*, pp. 332–334) with the record quoted by Lloyd George in Chap. LXXXV of his *War Memoirs*. There are certain interesting discrepancies, not to mention a great difference in tone. Above all, not only the words but the idea behind the query 'But why expend more British lives – and for what?' are missing from the official record. This was partly Haig's fault. He tells us: 'When I had finished my remarks, Hankey (the Secretary of the War Cabinet) came in and I had to repeat most of what I had said for him to note down.' No doubt the argument lost something in the second telling which it did not regain until Haig was privately communing with his Diary again that night.

The next day, there was a conference at Foch's headquarters: 'He asked me to give my opinion first of all. I gave practically the same as I had given to the War Cabinet in London last Saturday. Pétain followed and urged the same terms as Foch, viz. the left bank of the Rhine with bridgeheads. Pershing, although two days previously he had acquiesced in my views, now said ditto to Foch. The latter then asked me if I had any further remarks to make. I said that I had no reason to change my opinions. I felt that the enemy might not accept the terms which Foch proposed because of military necessity only – and it would be very costly and take a long time (perhaps two years) to enforce them, *unless the internal state of Germany compels* the enemy to accept them. We don't know very much about the internal state of Germany[1] – and so to try to impose such terms seems to me really a gamble which may come off or it may not. It struck me too that the insistence of the two French Generals on the left bank of the Rhine means that they now aim at getting hold of the Palatinate as well as of Alsace-Lorraine! Pétain spoke of taking a huge indemnity from Germany, so large that she will never be able to pay it. Meantime, French troops will hold the left bank of the Rhine as a pledge!'

Everything depended, as Haig perceived, on the condition of Germany. The quality of German resistance in the field did not encourage him to believe that the Fatherland was yet on the point of collapse; he underestimated the force of the movements taking place there. But more than that, he distrusted those movements themselves, and wished to avoid bringing Germany to a position where she would have to surrender unconditionally, recognizing the dangers of the duress under which she would do so. It was not that he agreed wholeheartedly with the view which Esher had expressed to him in July, 1917: 'For us and for France and for America, "peace with the Hohenzollern" is the best peace we can have.' Haig was undoubtedly a royalist, but there is not the slightest indication that he felt any particular sympathy towards the Hohenzollern dynasty, as opposed to some other form of government in Germany. What he did accept, however, was that the convulsions which might unseat the Hohenzollerns would not, in the end, profit the Allies. (The fate of the Romanoffs was providing daily evidence of this.) Haig felt in his bones that it was bad policy to press for a punishing peace, at the risk of the social collapse which alone would enable it to be enforced, and at the further risk that the Germans would not accept it in their hearts.

He told his wife, on October 26th, the day after the meeting with Foch: '... it is most important that our Statesmen should think over the situation carefully and not attempt to so humiliate Germany as to produce a desire for revenge in years to come.' He wrote again on November 1st, as the signs of

1. Shades of Charteris! Haig had travelled far since the hey-day of the 'principal boy'.

German collapse multiplied (Turkey accepted the Allied armistice terms on October 30th; Austria was on the point of doing so), and as the Allied politicians visibly hardened their hearts: 'I am afraid the Allied Statesmen mean to exact humiliating terms from Germany. I think this is a mistake, because it is merely laying up trouble for the future, and may encourage the wish for revenge in the future. Also, I doubt if Germany is sufficiently low yet to accept such terms. However we shall see. Personally I feel that there are many good officers in Germany like myself for instance who would in a similar situation rather die than accept such conditions.' The logic which began with accepting that Great Britain would benefit most by an early peace had led him to the prescient understanding that the whole world would be the loser by a peace which trampled Germany in the dust, without actually destroying her Army. It was this very thing that produced the legend of 'the stab in the back', and all that followed from it.

Six days after Haig had thus expressed himself, and three days after the British Army's last big attack, German plenipotentiaries crossed the line of battle to receive the Allied Armistice terms from Foch. Ludendorff had already gone – dismissed on October 26th. The Kaiser himself was about to go; he abdicated on November 9th and fled to Holland the next day. After him, there was a general tumbling of German Kings, Princes and Arch-Dukes. The Imperial Navy had mutinied; revolution stalked the streets. Allied policy remained frozen in the face of all these signs; it continued to be framed in harsh terms of 'guarantees'; it took no cognizance of the complete fall of the military autocracy from which the exaction of such 'guarantees' had seemed an appropriate concept. As Lloyd George wrote (fifteen years later): 'Beyond question, it was a disaster that we had to lay Germany prostrate before we could reach a peace settlement.' He might have added that, having laid Germany prostrate, it was also disastrous to continue to act as though she was still in full possession of her aggressive powers. Haig, who had been one of the few to foresee the long war against Germany, was not only one of the first to perceive the possibility of ending it, but also one of a very small number who understood the conditions in which it required to be ended. On November 27th he wrote in his Diary: 'The French are anxious to be very strict. . . . We must not forget that it is to our interest to return to Peace methods at once, to have Germany a prosperous, not an impoverished country. Furthermore, we ought *not* to make Germany our enemy for many years to come.' As Major-General Fuller has remarked:[1] 'Whatever his defects in the field may have been, Haig realized, unlike so many of his contemporaries, that peace is the true aim of war. For this he deserves our unstinted approbation.' It was a deep misfortune that Haig's views, despite

1. Letter in *R.U.S.I. Journal*, February, 1962.

his victories, were now habitually disregarded by the British Government, already much concerned with the slogans appropriate to winning the forthcoming General Election.

*　　*　　*　　*

The end came at 11 a.m. on November 11th, 1918. Haig's record of the day is terse and unemotional; he explained to his Army Commanders the procedure to be adopted for the advance to the German frontier; he then 'pointed out the importance of looking after the troops during the period following the cessation of hostilities – very often the best soldiers are the most difficult to deal with in periods of quiet! I suggested a number of ways in which men can be kept occupied. It is as much the duty of all Officers to keep their men amused, as it is to train them for war. Staff Officers must attend to this. If funds are wanted, G.H.Q. should be informed and I'll arrange for money to be found'. This was an unconscious pointer to what Haig's future preoccupations were going to be. After the Army Commanders' conference, they all went off together, and were 'taken on the Cinema'. Then it was back to the round of any other day of the War. There was no exultation, not even any reference to the special part which his Army had played in bringing this Armistice into existence. Yet that part was unmistakable; since July 18th, when Mangin had struck back at Soissons, beginning the series of large-scale Allied counter-attacks, the British Army had taken 188,700 prisoners and 2,840 guns; the three other Allies on the Western Front, France, America, and Belgium, had taken between them 196,700 prisoners and 3,775 guns. For this achievement, since the beginning of August, the British had paid a price of over 350,000 casualties. From first to last, the Western Front had cost them a loss of some $2\frac{1}{2}$ millions of men, killed, wounded and prisoners.

Haig expressed no view, either of the achievement or of the cost, in his Diary that day; he reserved this for his Final Despatch, which he completed on March 21st, 1919. It is a document which has been greatly neglected, but repays study. In it he firmly attributes the duration of the War to Britain's unpreparedness 'at any rate for a war of such magnitude'; no doubt he was remembering the scaling down of his and Haldane's original Territorial Force proposals. This unpreparedness, he continued, compelled hurried im-provisation, 'and improvisation is never economical and seldom satisfactory'. It meant that 'our Armies were unable to intervene, either at the outset of the war or until nearly two years had elapsed, in sufficient strength adequately to assist our Allies'. Further, 'just as at no time were we as an Empire able to put our own full strength into the field, so at no time were the Allies as a whole able completely to develop and obtain the full effect from their greatly superior man-power'. On the contrary, it was the enemy who 'was able to gain a notable initial advantage by establishing himself in Belgium and northern France. . . .' The breakdown of secondary fronts (Russia and Italy in particular), the polyglot nature of the Alliance, all these factors, he pointed out, contributed to make the War longer. Finally, there was the phenomenon of the continuous battle-front: 'So long as the opposing forces are at the outset approximately equal in numbers and morale and there are no flanks to turn, a long struggle for supremacy is inevitable.' The longer the struggle, the greater, of course, the loss; but moreover, 'There can be no question that to our general unpreparedness must be attributed the loss of many thousands of brave men whose sacrifice we deeply deplore, while we regard their splendid gallantry and self-devotion with unstinted admiration and gratitude.'

None but the last of these were sentiments or precepts which were likely to become popular in the aftermath of the holocaust. Nor did Haig's general conclusions, unblinking and uncompromising, greatly commend themselves to a generation shuddering at the catastrophe whose after-effects were emerging day by day. Above all, Haig's words were devoid of comfort for those who sought to put forward the theory that there had been, all along, an easier road to victory. His conclusions were framed in 'the conviction that neither the course of the war itself nor the military lessons to be drawn therefrom can properly be comprehended, unless the long succession of battles commenced on the Somme in 1916 and ended in November of last year on the Sambre are viewed as forming part of one great and continuous engagement'.

He went on:

'To direct attention to any single phase of that stupendous and incessant struggle and seek in it the explanation of our success, to the exclusion or neglect of other phases possibly less striking in their immediate or obvious consequences, is in my opinion to risk the formation of unsound doctrine regarding the character and requirements of modern war.

'If the operations of the past $4\frac{1}{2}$ years are regarded as a single continuous campaign, there can be recognized in them the same general features and the same necessary stages which between forces of approximately equal strength have marked all the conclusive battles of history. . . .

'. . . In a battle joined and decided in the course of a few days or hours, there is no risk that the lay observer will seek to distinguish the culminating operations by which victory is seized and exploited from the preceding stages by which it has been made possible and determined. If the whole operations of the present war are regarded in correct perspective, the victories of the summer and autumn of 1918 will be seen to be as directly dependent upon the two years of stubborn fighting that preceded them.'

This, then, was Haig's own theory of the War; this was why he kept the Battle of the Somme going until the winter snows arrived, and planned to continue it the following year; this was why he kept on in Flanders right into November, and wished to press on again there next spring; this was why it never occurred to him to make any kind of apology for his strategy either at the time, or during the remainder of his life. As he repeated elsewhere in the same Despatch: 'It is in the great battles of 1916 and 1917 that we have to seek for the secret of our victory in 1918.' Nothing ever shifted him from this opinion. It followed directly from his saying in March, 1915: 'We cannot hope to win until we have defeated the German Army.' Neither in Haig's war against Germany nor in the next did any alternative elixir of victory appear.

Epilogue

'EARLY IN 1919,' wrote Sir Winston Churchill, 'Lord Haig walked ashore at Dover after the total defeat of Germany and disappeared into private life.' This is not the exact truth, but sufficiently close to it; he remained Commander-in-Chief of the Expeditionary Force until April, 1919, when he became C.-in-C. Home Forces; this post was abolished at the end of January, 1920. Thereafter, as Churchill says: "Titles, grants, honours of every kind, all the symbols of public gratitude were showered upon him; but he was given no work. He did not join the counsels of the nation; he was not invited to reorganize its army; he was not consulted upon the Treaties; no sphere of public activity was opened to him.' This strange state of affairs can only be explained by reference to the personal factor; Lloyd George, overwhelmingly victorious in his 'coupon election', pursued his antagonism without charity; indeed, with the persistence of a tribal feud, he continued it beyond the grave. Haig made no protest at his treatment; when attacks upon him began to appear in print, and to become fashionable, he made no answer; he wrote no books or newspaper articles; practical as ever, he had found new work to do.

In this military study there is no space to put down the full story of the hard, taxing, but freely-given labour by which Haig made himself the Founder of the British Legion. Yet the fact that this work occupied the rest of his days, from the very moment when his public duties ceased until the day of his death (probably much hastened by this toil), constitutes an important gloss upon the frame of mind in which he had commanded his Army. The fact that he had begun to move towards acceptance of this post-war duty some two years before the War ended is also significant; it provides the true answer to the charge that he was ever callous or insensible to the sufferings of his men. It was on February 20th, 1917, with the Somme a fresh memory, and the prospect of equally punishing battles immediately ahead, that he addressed a letter to the Secretary of State for War in which he pressed for adequate pensions, medical benefits and organized work schemes for disabled officers. 'I strongly urge', he said, 'that there should be no delay in dealing with this matter, which, if allowed to continue, will constitute a scandal of the greatest magnitude.' This was the starting-point of his labours for all ex-Servicemen. On April 13th, 1917, just after the opening of the Battle of Arras, he wrote to Lady Haig: 'As you know, I don't go out of my way to make myself popular, either by doing showy things or by being slack in the matter of discipline – I never hesitate to find fault, but I have myself a tremendous affection for those fine fellows who are ready to give their lives for the Old Country at any moment. I feel quite sad at times when I see them march past me, knowing as I do how many must pay the full penalty before we can have peace. It is satisfactory to hear that a much larger percentage than usual are slight bullet wounds during this last battle.' On July 9th, in the month when 'Passchendaele' was launched, he was writing again to Lord Derby about the question of Employment Bureaux for disabled officers: '. . . I think it most desirable that delay in putting the machinery to work should be avoided as far as possible.'

In this, as in so much else, Haig's wisdom was larger than that of his political masters. The Demobilization Scheme which he drew up for the War Office in October, 1917, was ignored by them. When Winston Churchill became Secretary of State for War in 1920, his main task was that of returning the Citizen Army to civil life; he found 'that Sir Douglas Haig forecasted accurately the state of indiscipline and disorganization which would arise in the Army if pivotalism, i.e. favouritism, were to rule in regard to the discharge of men. . . . It is surprising that the Commander-in-Chief's prescient warnings were utterly ignored, and the Army left to be irritated and almost convulsed by a complicated artificial system open at every point to suspicion of jobbery and humbug.' The scandal over Demobilization was but the precursor of the much greater scandal of the neglect of the ex-Servicemen during the days of economic depression which followed. It was to this problem that Haig now addressed himself, on the three principles of 'unity, comradeship and peace'.

The first achievement, which only his reputation among the ex-soldiers could have accomplished, was to bring together the various ex-Service organizations; there were four of them in existence, with inevitably conflicting interests and policies. In June, 1921, these were welded together in the British Legion. Next, there was comradeship. 'Really', Haig wrote in March, 1922, 'there *ought* to be no question of "rank" in the Legion–we are all "comrades". That however is not possible and we must legislate to ensure that the "other ranks" are adequately represented.' This was the foundation of the Legion's democracy. Finally, peace; many ex-servicemen's associations in other lands have become political instruments, lobbies and pressure groups, concerned with battles almost as ferocious as those of the wars in which their members fought. The British Legion is a splendid exception; this also is thanks to Haig. He never lost sight of the main function, nor of how it should be carried out. 'As charitable organizations develop and their machinery becomes more systematized', he wrote in 1923, 'so do they act "according to regulation" and lose sympathy with the unfortunate who need help. So we must guard against this and I think occasionally change the subordinates who interview the needy ones, replacing them by others who have more recently felt the pinch of poverty and can appreciate more the value of a kindly word.'

Having brought the British Legion into being, Haig then conceived a wider vision; the unity of all such associations in the British Empire Service League. To South Africa and to Canada he brought his message of unity and comradeship with persuasive effect; he planned to carry it also to Australia and New Zealand. But the labour which he had already done was by now too much; on Sunday, January 29th, 1928, he died suddenly, at the age of sixty-seven. The last business he transacted in his life concerned the British Legion. The news of his death shocked a nation which had been disposed to forget him. Sir Winston Churchill writes: 'Then occurred manifestations of sorrow and regard which rose from the very heart of the people and throughout the Empire. Then everybody saw how admirable had been his demeanour since the Peace. There was a majesty about it which proved an exceptional greatness of character. It showed a man capable of resisting unusual strains, internal and external, even when prolonged over years; it showed a man cast in a classic mould.'

Note on Frontispiece

Sir William Orpen, K.B.E., R.A., went to France as a War Artist in April, 1917. He met Haig on May 11th. At lunch, before he began his portrait, 'The C.-in-C. was very kind, and brought me into his room afterwards, and asked me if everything was going all right with me. I told him I had a few troubles and was not very popular with certain people. He said: "If you get any more letters that annoy you, send them to me and I'll answer them." '

Haig himself tells us a little more about Orpen's 'troubles': 'Major Orpen, the artist, came to lunch. I told him that every facility would be given him to study the life and surroundings of our troops in the field, so that he can really paint pictures of lasting value. The War Office already wanted to see the results of his labours in return for the pay which he is now receiving! As if he were a sausage machine into which so much meat is put and the handle is turned and out come the sausages! And Art is a fickle mistress!'

'Never once, in all the time I was in France', says Orpen, 'did I hear a "Tommy" say one word against 'Aig. . . . When I started painting him he said, "Why waste your time painting me? Go and paint the men. They're the fellows who are saving the world, and they're getting killed every day." '

Orpen was also able to extract one of Haig's rare jokes. On his second visit to G.H.Q. there was a tremendous explosion nearby. 'The explosions went on, and out came the Chief. He walked straight up to me, laid his hand on my shoulder and said: "That's the worst of having a fellow like you here, Major. I thought the Huns would spot it", and having had his joke, went back to his work. He was a great man.'

Index

E